Not For Tourists Guide to
LONDON

T0047312

Not For Tourists, Inc

Skyhorse Publishing

designed by:
Not For Tourists, Inc
NFT_{TM}—Not For Tourists_{TM} Guide to London

Printed in China
Print ISBN: 978-1-5107-7744-6
Ebook ISBN: 978-1-5107-7745-3
ISSN# 2162-7215
Copyright © 2023 by Not For Tourists, Inc.
16th Edition

Every effort has been made to ensure that the information in this book is as up-to-date as possible at press time. However, many details are liable to change—as we have learned.
Not For Tourists cannot accept responsibility for any consequences arising from the use of this book.

Not For Tourists does not solicit individuals, organizations, or businesses for listings inclusion in our guides, nor do we accept payment for inclusion into the editorial portion of our book; the advertising sections, however, are exempt from this policy.

www.skyhorsepublishing.com

10 9 8 7 6 5 4 3 2 1

Maps 1–24 · **Central London**

Table of Contents

Dear NFT User,

Here it is, a guide to the most delicious, intoxicating, awe-inspiring, groovy destinations in the city. The best places for quaffing, boogying, spending, and caffeinating ourselves silly in one of the best cities in the world. Or just spots that we like—those that become part of our everyday as Londoners and which we've chosen to share with you.

Map 1 · **Marylebone (West)**

N

Road A501

Chapel Street

Edgware Road A501

Walmer Street

Edgware Road

Cabbell Street

Old Marylebone Road A501

Transept Street

Harcourt Street

Stalbaer Pl

Walmer Place

Enford Street

Wyndham Circus M
Wyndham Mews

Salisbury Pl

Bickenhall Street

Porter St

Junct Mews

Homer Street

Homer Row

Watsons M

Crawford Place

Cato Street

Molyneux Street

Bryanston Place

York Street

Crawford Street

Crawford
Mews

York Street

Upper Montagu Street

Gloucester Place A41

Durweston Street

Knox Street
Thornton Place

Spring
MS

Montagu Mansions

Clay Street

Sherlock

Kenrick
Place

Baker Street A41

Broadstairs Place

Essex Gardens A4209

Edgware Road A5

Norfolk Crescent
Quadrangle
Triangle
Cambridge Sq

Brendon Street

Shroudland Street

Beverston
Mews
Wyndham M

Wyndham Street

Montagu Place

Wyndham Mews West

Montagu Row
Montagu MS N

Dorset Street

Carlton St

Rodmarton

Blandford

Kendall St
Norfolk Cres
Oxford
Square

Norfolk Cres
Burwood Pl

◄31

Harrowby Street

Castlereagh St

Nutford Place

Brown Street

Seymour Place

Bryanston Mews West

Bryanston Square

Bryanston Square

Bryanston Mews W

Montagu Square

Montagu Square

Montagu Square

Gloucester Place Mews

Gloucester Place A41

MARYLEBONE

Blandford

George Street A41

◄2►

Titchborne Row
Park Cres

Porchester Place

Kendal Place

West
Portsea Pl

Portsea Place

Portsea Sq

Archery Close

Edgware Road A5

Shourcliffe Street

Seymour Place

Seymour Place

Clenston Mews
Wythburn Pl

George Street

Montagu
Mansions
Montagu
Brunswick MS

Montagu Street

Portman
Close

Portman Close

Carlton St

George Street A41

Robert Adam
Baker Street A41

Baker's Mews
Baker's Mews

Fitzhardinge

Connaught Street

St Georges

Albion Cl
Albion St
Halls
Aston M

George's Fields

Frederick
Cl

Hampden
Gurnby
Street

Upper Berkeley Street

Great
Cumberland
Place

New Quebec St

Quebec MS

Berkeley Mews

Portman Square A41

Portman Square

Portman Square A41

Portman
Square
A41

Fitzhardinge

Seymour Mews

Seymour
M

Connaught Close

Albion Close

Stanhope Close

Connaught Place

Seymour   Street

Bryanston   Street

Great Cumberland Place

Quebec Street

Bryanston
Street

A5204

Portman Square

Portman Mews
South

Granville

Orchard Street

Edwards M

Bayswater Road A402

Marble Arch A402

Marble
Arch

Great Cumberland Place

Tyburn Way

Marble Arch

Oxford Street A40

The (North Carriage Drive) Ring

Cumberland Gate A40

Speakers
Corner

North Row

Dunraver Street

Green   Street

Red Pl

North Row

North Audley Street

Balderton Street

Providence Court

B

**Hyde
Park**

PAGE
342

Park Lane

Park Lane A4202

Woods Mews

Lees   PL

Upper   Brook   Street

Park Street

Grosvenor

Ge

Brook Gate

Culross Street

Blackburne's M

A4202

Grosvenor Gate

Upper Grosvenor Street

Grosvenor St

◄9▼

Grosvenor
Square

Grosvenor

0.25 mile   0.25 km

Marylebone (West)

Map 1

Where the mullah meets the hookah, a stroll down Edgware Road is soundtracked by gurgling shisha pipes and bangin' Arabic pop music. To the east, ostentatiously bejewelled madams patrol Montague Square. They'd turn their noses up at a shawarma at **Maroush Express**. Good, more for the rest of us.

Cinemas
• **Everyman Baker Street** • 96 Baker St

Coffee
• **Borough Barista** • 60 Seymour St
• **Caffe Nero** • Edgware Road Station, Cabbell St
• **Daisy Green** • 20 Seymour St
• **Pret A Manger** • 556 Oxford St
• **Starbucks** • 26 Edgware Rd

O Landmarks
• **Marble Arch** • Oxford St & Park Ln
• **Speakers' Corner** • Cumberland Gate & Park Ln

Nightlife
• **Arizona Lounge** • 134 Marylebone Road
• **Duke of York** • 45 Harrowby St

Post Offices
• **Baker St** • 111 Baker St
• **Edgware Rd** • 354 Edgware Rd

Restaurants
• **Daisy Green** • 20 Seymour St
• **Locanda Locatelli** • 8 Seymour St
• **Maroush Express** • 56 Edgware Rd
• **Twist** • 42 Crawford St

Shopping
• **Primark** • 400 Oxford St
• **Spymaster** • 11 Howard St
• **Totally Swedish** • 32 Crawford St

Supermarkets
• **Sainsbury's** • 116 Baker St

Map 2 · **Marylebone (East)**

Boating Lake

Inwell PI
Chapel

1 **2**

Glentworth
Chape

Melcombe P

Baker Street A41
Allsop Place

Outer Circle

Outer Circle

PAGE
348

York Terrace West
York Gate
York Terrace East
York Terrace
Place

Marylebone Road A501

Park Square
Gardens

Park Square East

Palo Alto

York St

Brunswick

Ulster PI

Park Sq W

◄76

Marylebone Road A501

Marylebone Road A501

Crescent Gardens

Bickenhall St
Bickenhall Street

Porter St
Romney

Baker
Street

Loxborough Street

Nottingham Place

Oldbury Place

Marylebone High Street

Devonshire Place M
Devonshire Place

Park Crescent A4201

Park

3►

Great Portland
Street

York Street A41

Sherlock M
David M

Chiltern

Kenrick PI

Nottingham
Street

Paddington Street

B520

Devonshire Mews West
Devonshire Row Mews

Devonshire M

Bridford M

Portland Place A4201

Great Portland Street B506

Spring St

Clay Street

Montagu

Durweston St

Baker Street A41

Paddington Street
Gardens

Ashland PI
Grotto
Pas

Garbutt
Buildings

Beaumont Street

Devonshire
MS

Devonshire Mews South

Devonshire St

Weymouth
MS

Weymouth

Hallam

Hallam
Mews
North

Boswell

Dorset Street

Broadstone Place

B524

Beaumont
Mews

Clarke's PI

Wimpole St

Bosworth

Blandford Street

Kendall PI

Cramer St

Moxon
Street

De Walden
Street

S Woodstock
Street

Wheatley St
Browning
Street

Westmoreland
Street

Upper Wimpole
Mews

Wimpole Mews

Weymouth
Street

New Cavendish
Street

Mansfield
Mews
North

Mansfield
Street

Cavendish
MS
Duchess
MS

Gildea St

Langham Street

George Street

Portman Close

Manchester Mews

Hertford
House

Aybrook

St Vincent
St

Cross Keys
St

Jacob's Well M

Bulstrode
Street

Marylebone High Street

Bulstrode St

Harley St

Queen Anne Street

Mansfield
St
Duchess

New Cavendish
Street

Ali Souls M

Langham Mews

Robert Adam St
Manchester

Manchester
Square

Spanish
PI

Hinde St

Bentinck M

Bentinck Street

Welbeck

Wimpole Street

Queen Anne
St
Portland
PI

Chandos St

Chandos
PI

Riding House

Little Titchfield St

Portman Square

Fitzardinge St

Duke's MS

Hinde M
Hinde Street

Marylebone Lane

Thayer Street

Welbeck Street

Wigmore
St

A5204 Cavendish Place **A5204**

A5204 Cavendish Place **A5204**

Portman Square

Seymour

Seymour
St

Wigmore Street **A5204**

Square

Cavendish

Cavendish
Square **A5204**

Little Portland
Street

Margaret Street

Orchard Street A41

Edwards Mews

Duke St

Gray's Yd
Picton PI

Aldburgh
MS

St Christopher's
Place

Cavendish
Square

Great Portland
Street

Regent Street

B

Granville

◄1

Barrett St

James Street

Barrett St

Marylebone Lane

Henrietta Place **B406**

Henrietta Place

Holles Street

Great Castle Street

Portman Mews South

Oxford Street A40

Oxford Street A40

Chapel
PI

Chapel St

Old Cavendish St

Oxford Street A40

Oxford Circus

North Row

Lumley St

Weighhouse Street

Marylebone Lane

Bond Street

Blenheim St
Dering
St

Tenterden St

Little Argyll

Regent Street

Barlow Place

Brown Hart
Gardens

Brown Hart
Gardens

Duke's PI
St Anselm's
Place

Gilbert Street

Binney St

Davies Mews

New Bond Street

Haunch of
Venison Yd

Woodstock St

Market P

Providence
Court

George Yard

Grosvenor Square

Three
Kings Yard

Brook Street

Avery Row

Square Hanover Street

Princes Street

Oxford
Circus

Lees

Lees
PI

Grosvenor Square

T

9▼

Brook's Mews

● Jimi Hendrix
Memorial
Blue Plaque

Maddox St

10►

svenor Street

Grosvenor
Hill

Bourdon St

Bruton

Lumley

Little Marlbo

Lowndes

| 0.25 mile | 0.25 km |

Marylebone (East)

Map 2

Granted, the plush boutiques and old moneyisms of Marylebone are far removed from most Londoners' lives, but that's not to say you can't go window shopping, and with **VV Rouleaux** nearby, you could even craft your own outfit. Don't forget to stop in at **Claridge's** to tell Gordon Ramsay to f*** off, then sedate yourself in the beautiful book haven that is **Daunt**.

Coffee

- **Back on Track Coffee** • 3 Wimpole St
- **Caffe Nero** • 273 Regent St
- **Costa** • 69 Wigmore St
- **Paul Rothe & Sons** • 35 Marylebone Ln
- **Pret A Manger** • 31 Cavendish
- **Pret A Manger** • 18 Hanover St
- **Starbucks** • 22 Princes St
- **Starbucks** • 14 James St

O Landmarks

- **General Sikorski Statue** • Portland Place
- **Hertford House** • Manchester Sq
- **Jimi Hendrix Memorial Blue Plaque** • 23 Brook St
- **St. Christopher's Place** • 23 Barrett St

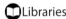

Libraries

- **Royal College of Nursing Library** • 20 Cavendish Sq

Nightlife

- **Claridge's Bar** • 55 Brook St
- **Inn 1888** • 21 Devonshire St
- **The Phoenix** • 37 Cavendish Sq
- **Purl** • 50-54 Blandford St

Post Offices

- **Marylebone** • 24 Thayer St

Restaurants

- **Chiltern Firehouse** • 1 Chiltern St
- **Comptoir Libanais** • 65 Wigmore St
- **Diwan** • 31 Thayer St
- **Fischer's** • 50 Marylebone High St
- **The Golden Hind** • 73 Marylebone Ln
- **Goodman Mayfair** • 24-26 Maddox St
- **Hush Brasserie** • 8 Lancashire Ct
- **Patty & Bun** • 54 James St
- **Pollen Street Social** • 8 Pollen St
- **Royal China** • 24-26 Baker St
- **Royal China Club** • 40-42 Baker St
- **Trishna** • 15 Blandford St
- **Zoilo** • 9 Duke St

Shopping

- **Browns** • 39 Brook St
- **Daunt Books** • 83 Marylebone High St
- **Divertimenti** • 227-229 Brompton Road
- **Fenwick** • 63 New Bond St
- **French Sole** • 61 Marylebone Ln
- **Gray's Antique Market** • 58 Davies St
- **John Lewis** • 300 Oxford St
- **La Fromagerie** • 2 Moxon St
- **Niketown** • 236 Oxford St
- **Paul Smith** • 38 Marylebone High St
- **Postcard Teas** • 8 Dering St
- **Selfridges & Co.** • 400 Oxford St
- **VV Rouleaux** • 102 Marylebone Ln
- **Zara** • 333 Oxford St

Supermarkets

- **Marks & Spencer** • Bond St Station
- **Waitrose** • 98 Marylebone High St

Map 3 · Fitzrovia

Fitzrovia

There's a whole recent trend for upmarket Fiztrovians to roam east in return for trendsetting East Enders giving their neighbourhood a bit of cool cred—they're all swapping galleries and premises and god knows what else in some kind of grown-up-exchange programme. Fitzrovia has its own history of cool though; you might be lucky enough to see a star or two at the BBC on Great Portland.

Map 3

Cinemas

- **Odeon Tottenham Court** • 30 Tottenham Ct Rd

Coffee

- **The Attendant** • 27A Foley St
- **Black Sheep Coffee** • 5 Goodge St
- **Kaffeine** • 66 Great Titchfield St
- **Lantana** • 13 Charlotte Pl
- **Pret A Manger** • 298 Regent St

Landmarks

- **BT Tower** • 60 Cleveland St
- **Charlotte Street** • Charlotte St
- **Middlesex Hospital** •
  Mortimer St & Cleveland St
- **Pollock's Toy Museum** • 1 Scala St
- **Sinner Winner Man** • 216 Oxford St
- **Tottenham Court Road** •
  Tottenham Ct Rd

Libraries

- **RIBA British Architectural Library** •
  66 Portland Pl

Nightlife

- **100 Club** • 100 Oxford St
- **The Albany** • 240 Great Portland St
- **Bourne & Hollingsworth** •
  28 Rathbone Pl
- **Bradley's Spanish Bar** • 42 Hanway St
- **Bricklayers Arms** • 31 Gresse St
- **Charlotte Street Hotel** • 15 Charlotte St
- **The Cock** • 27 Great Portland St
- **The Fitzroy Tavern** • 16 Charlotte St
- **The Holy Tavern** • 55 Britton St
- **London Cocktail Club** • 61 Goodge St
- **Market Place** • 11 Market Pl
- **The Remedy** • 124 Cleveland St
- **Rising Sun** • 46 Tottenham Ct Rd
- **The Roxy** • 3 Rathbone Pl
- **Shochu Lounge** • 37 Charlotte St
- **The Social** • 5 Little Portland St
- **Yorkshire Grey** • 46 Langham St

Post Offices

- **Great Portland St** • 173 Great Portland St

Restaurants

- **Archipelago** • 53 Cleveland St
- **Barrica** • 62 Goodge St
- **Berners Tavern** • 10 Berners St
- **Brazilian Gourmet** • 70 Cleveland St
- **Govinda's** • 9 Soho St

Iberica etc.

- **Iberica** • 195 Great Portland St
- **ICCo** • 46 Goodge St
- **Kin Cafe** • 22 Foley St
- **Koba** • 11 Rathbone St
- **Market Place** • 11 Market Pl
- **Naroon** • 60 Great Titchfield St
- **Portland** • 113 Great Portland St
- **Ragam** • 57 Cleveland St
- **The Riding House Cafe** •
  43 Great Titchfield St
- **Roka** • 37 Charlotte St
- **Salt Yard** • 54 Goodge St
- **Thai Metro** • 38 Charlotte St
- **Yalla Yalla** • 12 Winsley St

Shopping

- **The Aquatic Design Centre** •
  26 Zennor Trade Park
- **Braviccimo** • 78 Margaret St
- **Computer Exchange** • 32 Rathbone Pl
- **Chess & Bridge** • 44 Baker St
- **Fan New Trimmings** • 47 Berwick St
- **Harmony** • 100 Oxford St
- **Hobgoblin Music** • 24 Rathbone Pl
- **Mango** • 229 Oxford St
- **Scandinavian Kitchen** •
  61 Great Titchfield St
- **Urban Outfitters** • 200 Oxford St

Supermarkets

- **Marks & Spencer** • 55 Tottenham Ct Rd
- **Sainsbury's** • 17 Tottenham Ct Rd
- **Tesco** • 10 Goodge St

Map 4 • Bloomsbury (West)

Bloomsbury (West)

Map 4

Bloomsbury didn't incite and excite Britain's most prolific set of literature writers for no good reason. These streets ooze the kind of romanticised idea of London that had Virginia Woolf and E.M Forster zoned in as inspiration. Clever people have lived here in Bloomsbury and cleverer people still visit. **The British Museum**'s Age of Illumination collection highlights the world's learners.

Cinemas

- **Horse Hospital** • 30 Colonnade
- **Odeon Tottenham Court** • 30 Tottenham Ct Rd

Coffee

- **Black Sheep Coffee** • 5 Goodge St
- **Costa** • 104 New Oxford St
- **London Review Cake Shop** • 14 Bury Pl
- **Pret A Manger** • 40 Bernard St
- **Pret A Manger** • 64 New Oxford St
- **Ruskins Cafe** • 41 Museum St
- **Starbucks** • 112 New Oxford
- **Store Street Espresso** • 40 Store St

Emergency Rooms

- **University College Hospital** • 235 Euston Rd

O Landmarks

- **Bloomsbury Square Garden**
- **British Museum** • Great Russell St
- **Centre Point** • 101 New Oxford St
- **Kingsway Tram Tunnel** • Theobald's Rd & Southampton Row
- **Senate House** • Malet St & Torrington Sq
- **SOAS** • Thornhaugh St
- **Student Central** • Malet St
- **Tavistock Square** • Tavistock Sq
- **University College London** • Gower St

Libraries

- **Anthropology Library** • Great Russell St
- **Birkbeck College Library** • Malet St
- **German Historical Institute Library London** • 17 Bloomsbury Sq
- **Institute of Advanced Legal Studies Library** • 17 Russell Sq
- **University of London, Senate House Library** • Malet St

Nightlife

- **All Star Lanes** • Victoria House, Bloomsbury Pl
- **Bloomsbury Bowling Lanes** • Bedford Way
- **Marquis Cornwallis** • 31 Marchmont St
- **The Old Crown Public House** • 33 New Oxford St
- **The Plough** • 27 Museum St
- **The Princess Louise** • 208 High Holborn

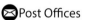Post Offices

- **Marchmont St** • 33 Marchmont St

Restaurants

- **Alara** • 58 Marchmont St
- **Bi Won** • 24 Coptic St
- **Savoir Faire** • 42 New Oxford St

Shopping

- **Blade Rubber Stamps** • 12 Bury Pl
- **British Museum shop** • Great Russell St
- **Gosh!** • 1 Berwick St
- **James Smith & Sons** • 53 New Oxford St
- **London Review Bookshop** • 14 Bury Pl

Supermarkets

- **Waitrose** • Brunswick Sq

Map 5 • Bloomsbury (East)

1
2

Caledonia St
Keystone Cres
Omega Pl
York Way
Collier Street
Northdown St
Killick St
Cumming St
Joseph Grimaldi Park

King's Cross St. Pancras

Pentonville Road A501

Pentonville

Euston Road A501
Euston Road A501

King's Cross Road

78

79

Penton Rise

Penton Rise A201

Midland Rd

Bidborough Street

Judd Street B504

Belgrove St

Birkenhead St

Argyle Square Gardens

St. Chad's Place

St. Chad's St

Field Street

Leeke Street

Weston Rise

Holford Gardens

Ossulston Street

A

Hastings Street

Thanet Street

Sandwich Street

Tonbridge St

Speed Pl

Whidborne St

Tankerton St

Loxham St

Argyle Street

Britannia Street

Wicklow Street

King's Cross Road A201

Vernon Sq

Vernon Rise

Holford Sq

Percy Circus

Cartwright Gardens

Cartwright Gardens

Leigh Street

Cromer Street

Swinton Street A201

Swinton

Great Percy St

Percy Circus

Pakenham St

Great Percy St

Cumberland Gdns

Great

ST. PANCRAS

Compton Pl

Kenton Street

Marchmont Street

Handel Street

Tavistock Place

Wakefield MS

Regent Square Park & Garden

Sidmouth Street

Harrison Street

Frederick Street

Ampton Place

Sage Way

Ampton Street

Wells Sq

Wharton Street

Percy Yd

Percy Circus

Granville Street

Gwynne

Granville

Lloyd Baker St

Tavistock Place

Wakefield Street

St. George's Gardens

Heathcote Street

Fleet Sq

Seddon St

Cubitt Street

Hardwidge M

Cubitt Street

Wren Street

Calthorpe Street B502

Gough St

Farringdon Road A201

Margery St

Attneave St

Bartley St

Yardley St

Wilmington Sq

Easton Street

Wakefield Street

Handel Street

Herbrand Street

Brunswick Square

Brunswick Square Gardens

Mecklenburg Street

Mecklenburg Square Gardens

St. Andrew's Gardens

Langton Clo

4

6

Bernard Street B502

Russell Square

Brunswick Sq

Grenville St

Guilford Street B502

Coram's Fields

Guilford Street B502

Guilford Place

Ormond M

Millman Mews

Long Yard

Doughty Street

Brownlow St

Coley St

Gough St

Phoenix Place

Roseberry

Rosebery Avenue A401

Roseberry Avenue

B

Queen Square Place

Cosmo Pl

Queen Square

Powis Place

Ormond Street

Ormond Yd

Great Ormond Street

Barton St

Great James Street

Rugby St

Kirk St

John's Mews

Northington St

John St

Millman Street

The Dickens House Museum

Roger Street

North M

Elm Street

Mount Pleasant

Pooled Bridge

Mount Pleasant

Warner St

Baker's Row

Southampton Row A200

Bloomsbury Sq

Old Gloucester Street

Gage Street

Boswell Street

New North Street

Ormond Close

Dombey Street

Harpur Street

Emerald Street

Richbell Place

Cockpit Yd

Great James St

Sandland St

Hulsworthy Street

Boyseld

Warner St

Vine Hill

Eyre Street Hill

Bath Ct

Herbal Hill

Ray St

Crawford Pass

Topham Street

Bakers Row

Clerkenwell Close

Theobald's Road

Clerkenwell Road A5201

14

15

Bloomsbury Way

Bloomsbury Way A40

Red Lion Square

Princeton St

Red Lion St

Lamb's Conduit St

Bedford Row

Jockey's Fields

Raymond Buildings

Gray's Inn Field

Verulam St

Portpool Lane

Portpool La

Leather Lane

Hatton Wall

Hatton Garden

Leopards Ct

0.25 mile

0.25 km

Bloomsbury (East)

Map 5

Agog with students, this tract of Bloomsbury is a bustling cultural playground. The brilliant **Curzon Cinema** resides in the belly of the **Brunswick Centre**, a Brutalist masterpiece with some posh shops thrown in for good measure. For contrast, stroll over to Lamb's Conduit Street and enjoy some boutique shopping.

Cinemas

• **Curzon Cinema** • 1 Brunswick Sq

Coffee

• **The Espresso Room** • 31-35 Great Ormond St
• **Knockbox Coffee** • 29 Lambs Conduit St
• **Pret A Manger** • 15 Theobald's Rd
• **Store Street Espresso** • 54 Tavistock Place

O Landmarks

• **Charles Dickens Museum** • 48 Doughty St
• **Gray's Inn Field** • Theobald's Rd
• **Doughty Street** • Doughty St & Guilford St

Libraries

• **Holborn Library** • 32 Theobald's Rd
• **Royal National Institute of the Blind Research Library** • 105 Judd St
• **Pancras Square Library** • 5 Pancras Rd

Nightlife

• **The Blue Lion** • 133 Grays Inn Rd
• **Calthorpe Arms** • 252 Gray's Inn Rd
• **The Clerk & Well** • 156 Clerkenwell Rd
• **The Lamb** • 94 Lamb's Conduit St
• **The Perseverance** • 63 Lamb's Conduit St
• **Pimp Shuei** • 59 Mount Pleasant
• **The Water Rats** • 328 Grays Inn Rd

Post Offices

• **Mount Pleasant** • Farringdon Rd & Rosebery Ave

Restaurants

• **Banh Mi Bay** • 4-6 Theobalds Rd
• **Ciao Bella** • 86 Lamb's Conduit St
• **Fryer's Delight** • 19 Theobalds Rd
• **Honey & Co** • 54 Lamb's Conduit St
• **Itadaki Zen** • 139 King's Cross Rd
• **The Lady Ottoline** • 11 Northington St
• **Mary Ward Centre** • 42 Queen Sq
• **Paolina Thai Snack Bar** • 181 King's Cross Rd
• **You Me Sushi** • 180 Grays Inn Rd

Shopping

• **The Brunswick** • Hunter St
• **Folk** • 53 Lamb's Conduit St
• **Gay's the Word** • 66 Marchmont St
• **International Magic** • 89 Clerkenwell Rd
• **Magma** • 117 Clerkenwell Rd

Map 6

A village in the city provides a perfect contrast of a pretty green square separated by only a row of shops from the rest of the corporate world. Potter off the main square for back-alley Belgium beers at **The Dovetail**.

Coffee

• **The Ethiopian Coffee Company** • 61 Amwell St

Libraries

• **Finsbury Library** • 245 St John St
• **Marx Memorial Library** • 37 Clerkenwell Green

O Landmarks

• **City University London** • Northampton Sq
• **The House of Detention** • St James's Walk

Nightlife

• **1920** • 19 Great Sutton St
• **Bandstand Busking** • Northampton Sq
• **The Betsey Trotwood** • 56 Farringdon Rd
• **Café Kick** • 43 Exmouth Market
• **The Dovetail** • 9 Jerusalem Passage
• **The Harlequin** • 27 Arlington Wy
• **Old Red Lion** • 418 St. John St
• **The Slaughtered Lamb** • 34 Great Sutton St
• **The Three Kings** • 7 Clerkenwell Close
• **Wilmington Arms** • 69 Rosebery Ave

Restaurants

• **Caravan** • 11 Exmouth Market
• **Dans Le Noir** • 69 St John St
• **The Eagle** • 159 Farringdon Rd
• **Morito** • 32 Exmouth Market
• **Moro** • 34 Exmouth Market
• **Pham Sushi** • 159 Whitecross St
• **SandwichMan** • 23 Easton St
• **Sushi Tetsu** • 12 Jerusalem Passage

Shopping

• **EC One Jewellery** • 41 Exmouth Market
• **The Family Business Tattoo Shop** • 58 Exmouth Market
• **Gypsy Blood Tattoo** • 332b Goswell Rd
• **Metro Imaging** • 32 Great Sutton St
• **Timorous Beasties** • 46 Amwell St
• **The Wyvern Bindery** • 187 Hoxton St

Supermarkets

• **Tesco Express** • 1 Brewnhouse Yard
• **Waitrose** • Aylesbury St & St. John St

Map 7 • **Barbican / City Road (South)**

N

1 2

Goswell Road A1

Nelson Street
Oak Cres
Coombs St
Bath Cres
Combs St
Nelson Terr
Graham St

Wakley Street

Sidney Gro
Ashland Pl
Owen Row

Wynyatt St
Hill Street

City Road A501

Garden Row

New Charles St

83

Moreland Street

King Square
Kings Square Garden

Central Street

Central Street

Southampton Sq
Ashby St
Sebastian St

Percival Street B

6

Compton Street

Dallington Street
Berry St
Northburgh St

Brewhouse Yard

Great Sutton St
Sutton Lane

Clerkenwell Road A5201

St. John's Sq
Briset St
Albion Pl
Eagle Court

St John Street B501

Smoke house Yd

The Green

Glasshouse Yd

Charterhouse Buildgs

Charterhouse St B500
Charterhouse Ms

15

Barbican

Church of St Bartholomew the Great

Cloth Fair

Long Lane

West Smithfield

Cock Lane

Hosier Lane

Snow Hill

London Wall A1211

Nelson Street

City Road A501

Micawber Street
Windsor Terrace
Thoresby Street

Shepherdess Walk B144

City Road A501

Lever Street B502

Lever Street B502

Radnor Street

St. Luke's Garden

Mitchell Street

Old Street A5201

Garrett Street
Nag's Head Ct
Baltic
Golden Lane

Fortune Street
Fortune Street Garden

Fann St

Beech Street B100

Barbican Centre

BARBICAN

PAGE 324

St Giles's

Wallside
Monkwell

London Wall A1211

Underwood Row
Nile Street

Wenlock
Shepherdess Pl

City Road

Britannia Walk

Provost Street A1200

Sturt St

Peerless Street
Baldwin Street
Cranwood St

Old Street Old St

84

Featherstone Street

ST. LUKE'S

Bunhill Row B144

Bunhill Fields Burial Grounds

8

Bunhill Fields

Chiswell Street

Finsbury Sq

Moorgate

16

0.25 mile   0.25 km

Ugly as the brutalist Barbican might be, its surrounds have happily morphed into one of those areas that thrives on its appalling looks and survives on a generation of media peeps. Where the cool crowds flow, top notch hang-outs will follow. Old Street, or Silicon Roundabout, was designed for those who mainline coffee for survival while **Bunhill Fields** provides necessary respite.

Map 7

Cinemas
• **Barbican Centre Cinema** • Silk St & Whitecross St

Coffee
• **Costa** • 68 Goswell Rd
• **FWD:Coffee** • 161 Whitecross St
• **Notes Coffee Roasters** • 1 Ropemaker St
• **Pitch 42** • Whitecross St Market
• **Popular Cafe** • 85 Lever St
• **Pret A Manger** • 9 Goswell Rd
• **Pret A Manger** • Ropemaker St
• **Shoreditch Grind** • 213 Old St

O Landmarks
• **Barbican Centre** • Silk St
• **Bunhill Fields Burial Ground** • 38 City Rd
• **Church of St Bartholomew the Great** • Kinghorn St
• **LSO St Luke's** • 161 Old St
• **St. Giles** • Fore St

Libraries
• **Barbican Library** • Silk St
• **Wandsworth Town Library** • 11 Garratt Ln

Nightlife
• **The Gibson** • 44 Old St
• **Nightjar** • 129 City Rd
• **The Two Brewers** • 121 Whitecross St

Post Offices
• **Old Street** • 185 Old St

Restaurants
• **Carnevale** • 135 Whitecross St
• **Nusa Kitchen** • 10 Old St
• **Original Bagel and Sandwich** • 22 Goswell Rd

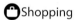
Shopping
• **Evans & Witt** • 58 Long Lane
• **Red Dot Cameras** • 86 Goswell Rd
• **Whitecross Market** • Whitecross St

Supermarkets
• **Waitrose** • Whitecross St

Map 8 • Liverpool Street / Broadgate

Liverpool Street / Broadgate

Map 8

A grimy maw that spews trendos onto Bishopsgate, Liverpool Street is the gateway to the nowness of Brick Lane and Shoreditch. Its arse-end lets out suits and money into the borders of the City.

Coffee

• **AMT** • Liverpool St & Broadgate Circle
• **Costa** • 1 Ropemaker St
• **Starbucks** • Liverpool St Station

O Landmarks

• **Fulcrum** • Broadgate

Libraries

• **Bishopsgate Library** • 230 Bishopsgate

Nightlife

• **The Book Club** • 100 Leonard St
• **Callooh Callay** • 65 Rivington St
• **Lounge Bohemia** • 1 Great Eastern St
• **Q Shoreditch** • 55 Tabernacle St
• **Red Lion** • 1 Eldon St
• **Worship Street Whistling Shop** • 63 Worship St
• **XOYO** • 32 Cowper St

Restaurants

• **Duck and Waffle** • 110 Bishopgate
• **Gaucho Broadgate** • 5 Finsbury Ave
• **Hoxton Grill** • 81 Great Eastern St
• **Lantana** • 55 City Road
• **The Princess of Shoreditch** • 76 Paul St

Supermarkets

• **Tesco** • 158 Bishopsgate

Map 9 • **Mayfair / Green Park**

MAYFAIR

Hyde Park
PAGE 342

Green Park
PAGE 354

Brook Gate AA202

Culross Street

Grosvenor Square

Three Kings Yard

Brook's Mews

Davies Street B406

Maddox

Grosvenor Gate

Upper Grosvenor St

Grosvenor Square

Grosvenor Street

Broadbent Street

Grosvenor Hill

Bloomfield Pl

Conduit Street B4

Park Lane AA202

Reeves Mews

Adams Row

Mount Row

Bourdon Street

Berkeley Square

Bruton Street

Bruton Lane

Grafton Street

Coach & Horses Yard

Clifford Street

Cork Street

New Bond Street

Old Bond Street

Burlington

Mount Street

Balfour Place

S Audley

Aldford Street

Mt Street Gardens

Mount Street Garden

Farm Street

Berkeley Square Gardens

Hay Hill

Albemarle Street

Rex Pl

Balfour Mews

South Street

South Audley Street

Chapel Hill Street

Hay's Mews

50 Berkeley Sq

Hay Hill

Stafford St

Hyde Park
PAGE 342

Deanery Street

Tilney

Stanhope Ga

Chesterfield Gardens

Waverton Street

Charles Street

Queen Street

Clarges Mews

Berkeley Street

Down St

Old Bond Street

Piccadilly A4

Dover Yard

Chesterfield Street

Curzon Gate

Pitt's Head MS

Market Mews

Shepherd Street

Hertford Street

Half Moon Street

Clarges Street

Bolton Street

Stratton Street

Mayfair Pl

Dover St

Green Park

Piccadilly A4

Bennet St

Arlington Street

St James's Street

Park Place

Ryder St

Achilles Way

Park Lane

Brick Street

Brick Street

Yarmouth Place

Piccadilly A4

Blue Ball Yd

Little St. James's St.

Hamilton Place

Grantham Pl

Down Street MS

Down St Station

Wilder House

Catherine Wheel Yard

Cleveland Row

Apsley House

Hamilton Mews

Hard Rock Cafe

Green Park
PAGE 354

Ambassadors

Stable Yd Road

Stable Yard

Apsley Way

Constitution Hill

The Mall

Fri

Hyde Park Corner

Knightsbridge A4

Hyde Park Corner

Grosvenor Crescent B310

Grosvenor Place A302

Duke of Wellington Place

Buckingham Palace Gardens

Memorial Gardens

St. James's Park

Halkin Street

Chapel Street

Chester Street

Little Chester M

Wilton St

Buckingham Palace

Belgrave Mews S

Ground

Chester

Belgrave Square

Upper Belgrave Street

Wilton Cr

Wilton Row

Grosvenor Place A302

Spur Road

Hobart Place

Eaton Square

Eaton Mews

Eaton Place

Lower Grosvenor Place A3214

Buckingham A3214

Buckingham Gate

Buckingham Gate

Birdcage Walk

Stafford Place

Palace Place

Palace Street

Castle Lane

Petty France

St James's Park

0.25 mile

0.25 km

Mayfair / Green Park

Map 9

A taste of Old Money is a decent enough reason to visit Mayfair; splashing out on High Tea at **The Ritz** is pretty much an investment in one's cultural education. The upside to might-rich neighbourhoods? Art galleries. Ones that give away wine. All the time. Pop down Cork Street on an eve to quaff all the free champagne at a private view then go off somewhere far more interesting.

Cinemas

• **Curzon Mayfair** • 38 Curzon St

Coffee

• **Caffe Nero** • 50 Curzon St
• **Costa** • 9 Eldon St
• **Starbucks** • 52 Berkeley St
• **SOHO Coffee Co.** • 10 Grosvenor St

O Landmarks

• **50 Berkeley Square** • 50 Berkeley Sq
• **Apsley House** • 149 Piccadilly
• **Buckingham Palace** • The Mall
• **Down Street Station** • Down St & Piccadilly
• **Hard Rock Cafe** • Piccadilly & Old Park Ln

Libraries

• **Mayfair Library** • 25 South Audley St
• **Royal Society of Chemistry Library and Information Centre** • Piccadilly

Nightlife

• **1707 Wine Bar** • 181 Piccadilly
• **bbar** • 43 Buckingham Palace Rd
• **Chesterfield Arms** • 50 Hertford St
• **Mahiki** • 1 Dover St

Post Offices

• **Mayfair** • 32 Grosvenor St

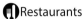Restaurants

• **Alain Ducasse at The Dorchester** • 53 Park Ln
• **Burger & Lobster** • 29 Clarges St
• **Corrigan's** • 28 Upper Grosvenor St
• **The Drawing Room at Brown's** • Albemarle St
• **El Pirata of Mayfair** • 5 Down St
• **Galvin at Windows** • Park Ln, 28th Floor
• **Gymkhana** • 42 Albemarle St
• **Kitty Fisher's** • 10 Shepherd Market
• **L'Autre** • 5 Shepherd St
• **Nobu** • 19 Old Park Ln
• **The Ritz** • 150 Piccadilly
• **Theo Randall** • 1 Hamilton Pl

Shopping

• **Dover Street Market** • 18 Haymarket
• **Green Valley** • Berkeley St
• **Stella McCartney** • 23 Old Bond St

Supermarkets

• **Marks & Spencer** • 78 Piccadilly
• **Sainsbury's** • 38 Stratton St

Map 10 · Piccadilly / Soho (West)

Oxford Street A40
Holles
John Princes
Great
Castle St
Great Portland
Marylebone Pass

Blenheim
Street
Dering Street

Oxford St A40

Market Place

Eastcastle Street

Winsley St

Wells Street

Haunch of Venison Yd

Brook Street

Tenterden Street

Princes Street

Hanover Sq

Swallow St

Oxford Circus

Oxford Street A40

Noel

A

New Bond Street

Hanover Street

Little Argyll Street

Argyll Street

Hills Place

Ramillies   Place

3

Poland Street

D'Arblay St

Avery Row

B406

Maddox Street

2

St George Street

Masons Arms Ms

Mill St

Pollen St

Ramillies St

Great Marlborough Street

Portland Ms
Livonia Street

Bloomfield Pl
Bruton Place

Conduit   Street

B406

9

Regent Street A4201

Kingly Court

Kingly Street

Foubert's Pl

Lowndes Ct
Marlborough Ct

Newburgh St

Marshall Street

Dufour's Pl

Broadwick Street

Berwick Street

Barlow Place

Coach & Horses Yard

Boyle St

New Burlington Place

Great Pulteney Street

Lexington Street

Ingestre Place

Hopkins Street

11

Peter St

New Burlington Street

Beak Street

Warwick   Street

Upr John St

Golden Square Gardens

Bridle Lane

Clifford Street

Old Burlington Street

Savile Row

Heddon   Street

Regent Place

Upr James St
Lwr

Lwr John St

James St

Cork St Mews

Cork Street

New Bond Street

B

Burlington Gardens

Vigo Street

Regent   Street

Brewer St

Sherwood St

Denman Street

Smith's Court

Great Windmill Street

Archer Street

Grafton St
Hill

Albemarle Street

Stafford Street

Old Bond Street

Sackville Street

Swallow Street

Air Street

Glasshouse Street

A4201

Statue of Eros

Shaftesbury

Royal Academy

Burlington Arcade & Piccadilly

Albany Cvd

Vine St

Carnaby St

Piccadilly Circus

Haymarket

Dover Street

Piccadilly   A4

23

Duke

Piccadilly   A4

Arlington Street

St. James

Jermyn Street

St Alban

Coventry

Bennet Street

Ryder

Ormond

Apple Tree Yard

St. James's St

Ryder Yd

Carlton

0.25 mile   0.25 km

Piccadilly / Soho (West)

Map 10

Forget visions of Austin Powers "yeah baby" grooviness, Carnaby Street is a slick study in consumerism with all major streetwear labels present, but the grand dame of department stores, **Liberty**, retains top marks for a unique shopping experience. **Polpo** restaurant is a winner in the small plates game.

Coffee

- **Costa** • 11 Argyll St
- **Pret A Manger** • 298 Regent St
- **Pret A Manger** • 27 Great Marlborough
- **Rapha Cycle Club** • 85 Brewer St

O Landmarks

- **Burlington Arcade** • Piccadilly
- **Carnaby Street** • Carnaby St
- **Kingly Court** • Kingly St & Foubert's Pl
- **Statue of Eros** • Piccadilly Circus

Nightlife

- **5th View** • 203 Piccadilly
- **Ain't Nothing But The Blues Bar** • 20 Kingly St
- **Beyond Retro** • 19 Argyll St
- **The Blind Pig** • 58 Poland St
- **Courthouse Bar** • 19 Great Marlborough St
- **The John Snow** • 39 Broadwick St
- **Lucky Voice** • 52 Poland St
- **The Red Lion** • 14 Kingly St
- **The Windmill** • 6 Mill St

Restaurants

- **Bao** • 53 Lexington St
- **Bob Bob Ricard** • 1 Upper James St
- **Bodean's BBQ** • 10 Poland St
- **Brasserie Zedel** • 20 Sherwood St
- **Cecconi's** • 5 Burlington Gardens
- **Dehesa** • 25 Ganton St
- **Dishoom** • 22 Kingly St
- **Kulu Kulu** • 76 Brewer St
- **Mildred's** • 45 Lexington St

- **The Photographers' Gallery** • 16 Ramillies St
- **Ping Pong** • 45 Great Marlborough St
- **Polpo** • 41 Beak St
- **San Carlo Cicchetti** • 215 Piccadilly
- **Sartoria** • 20 Saville Row
- **Sketch** • 9 Conduit St
- **Social Eating House** • 58 Poland St
- **Taro** • 61 Brewer St
- **Yauatcha** • 15 Broadwick St
- **Yoshino** • 3 Piccadilly Pl

Shopping

- **Anthropologie** • 158 Regent St
- **Apple Store** • 235 Regent Street
- **Beyond Retro** • 19 Argyll St
- **Burlington Arcade** • 51 Piccadilly
- **Cos** • 222 Regent St
- **Fortnum & Mason** • 181 Piccadilly
- **Hamley's** • 188 Regent St
- **Hatchards Bookshop** • 187 Piccadilly
- **Lazy Oaf** • 2 Ganton St
- **Liberty** • 214 Regent St
- **Lillywhites** • 24 Lower Regent St
- **Muji** • 41 Carnaby St
- **Phonica** • 51 Poland St
- **Richard James** • 29 Savile Row
- **Rigby & Peller** • 22 Conduit St
- **Whole Foods Market** • 20 Glasshouse St

This is still the heart of the red light district, but it's no longer such a sordid affair. Berwick Street is still loved for its record shops and market.

Cinemas

- **Apollo Theatre** • Shaftesbury Ave
- **Curzon Soho** • 99 Shaftesbury Ave
- **Prince Charles Cinema** • 7 Leicester Pl

Coffee

- **Flat White** • 17 Berwick St
- **Kaffeine** • 66 Great Titchfield St
- **Starbucks** • 60 Wardour St
- **Toi & Moi Cafe** • 38 Berwick St

Landmarks

- **Berwick Street Market** • Berwick St & Rupert St
- **John Snow Water Pump** • Broadwick St
- **Waxy O'Connor's** • 14 Rupert St

Nightlife

- **The Blue Posts** • 22 Berwick St
- **The Blue Posts** • 28 Rupert St
- **The Comedy Store** • 1 Oxendon St
- **De Hems** • 11 Macclesfield St
- **Experimental Cocktail Club** • 13 Gerrard St
- **Freedom** • 66 Wardour St
- **The French House** • 49 Dean St
- **The Lyric** • 37 Great Windmill St
- **Village** • 81 Wardour St
- **The Yard Bar** • 57 Rupert St

Restaurants

- **Balans** • 60 Old Compton St
- **Bar Bruno** • 101 Wardour St
- **Blanchette** • 9 D'Arblay St
- **Bocca di Lupo** • 12 Archer St
- **Bone Daddies** • 31 Peter St
- **Brewdog Soho** • 21 Poland St
- **Busaba Eathai** • 110 Wardour St
- **Copita** • 27 D'Arblay St
- **Ember Yard** • 60 Berwick St
- **Gelupo** • 7 Archer St
- **Jazz Club** • 10 Dean St
- **Maoz** • 43 Old Compton St
- **Mildred's** • 45 Lexington St
- **The Palomar** • 34 Rupert St
- **Randall & Aubin** • 16 Brewer St
- **Snog** • 9 Brewer St
- **Soho Joe** • 34 D'Arblay St
- **St Moritz** • 161 Wardour St
- **Tamarind Kitchen** • 167 Wardour St
- **Tokyo Diner** • 2 Newport Pl
- **Won Kei** • 41 Wardour St

Shopping

- **Algerian Coffee Store** • 52 Old Compton St
- **Cass Art Soho** • 49 Brewer St
- **Gerry's** • 74 Old Compton St
- **I. Camisa & Son** • 61 Old Compton St
- **Reckless Records** • 30 Berwick St
- **Sister Ray** • 75 Berwick St
- **Sounds of the Universe** • 7 Broadwick St

Map 12 · **Soho (East)**

N

1

2

Street

A40

Soho Street

A40

Bainbridge Street

Streatham Street

Bloomsbury

Tottenham Court Road

New

Oxford

Street

A40

3

Falconberg Mews

Falconberg Court

Earnshaw Street

Bucknall Street

Dyott Street

Street

4

Soho Square

Sutton Row

FA Headquarters

Soho Square Garden

St. Giles High

Ender

Carlisle Street

Goslett Yard

Soho Square

Denmark Street

Street

A40

Dean St

Chapone Pl

Frith Street

Orange Yard

Manette Street

Denmark Street

Ellcroft St

New Compton St

A

Royalty Mews

Bateman Street

Greek St

Charing Cross Rd

Stacey St

St Giles Pas

B404

Neal Street

Neal's Yd

heard Street

Old Compton Street

Phoenix St

The Phoenix Garden

Giles Street

A401

Monmouth St

Old

Compton St

Moor Street

Shaftesbury Ave

13

Bourchier

Macclesfield Street

Romilly Street

Street

A401

Earlham Street

Earlham Street

Shelton Street

Old Brewer Yard

11

Avenue

West Street

Ching Ct

haftesbury

Horse & Dolphin Yd

Gerrard Place

Litchfield Street

Tower Ct

Tower St

Mercer Street

Langley Street

Dansey Place

Gerrard Street

Newport Pl

A400

Slingsby Place

CHINATOWN

Lisle Street

Little Newport St

Great Newport St

Long

Acre

B402

Leicester St

Charing

Cross

Road

Leicester Square

Greek Yard

B404

Rose St

Garrick Street

King Street

24

Leicester Square Garden

0.1 mile

0.1 km

While **The Three Greyhounds** (opposite Soho House) might be one of the cheapest pubs in central London, **Jazz After Dark** on Greek Street certainly isn't, but it does have an undeniably attractive ambiance. Blend in with the winos at Soho Square with a shop-bought bottle while **G-A-Y** showcases the more colourful side of Soho.

Cinemas

• **Vue West End Cinema** • 3 Cranbourn St

Coffee

• **Caffe Nero** • 32 Cranbourn St
• **Caffe Nero** • 43 Frith St
• **Maison Bertaux** • 28 Greek St

Landmarks

• **Denmark Street** • Denmark St
• **FA Headquarters** • 25 Soho Sq
• **Old Compton Street** • Old Compton St
• **The Phoenix Garden** • 21 Stacey St
• **Soho Square** • Soho Sq

Nightlife

• **Bar Termini** • 7 Old Compton St
• **Cafe Boheme** • 13 Old Compton St
• **Comptons** • 53 Old Compton St
• **G-A-Y Bar** • 30 Old Compton St
• **G-A-Y Late** • 5 Goslett Yard
• **Garlic & Shots** • 14 Frith St
• **Jazz After Dark** • 9 Greek St
• **Karaoke Box** • 18 Frith St
• **Milroy's** • 3 Greek St
• **The Montagu Pyke** • 105 Charing Cross Rd
• **Ronnie Scott's** • 47 Frith St
• **Salsa!** • 96 Charing Cross Rd
• **The Royal George** • 133 Charing Cross Rd
• **The Three Greyhounds** • 25 Greek St
• **The Toucan** • 19 Carlisle St

Restaurants

• **10 Greek Street** • 10 Greek St
• **Baozi Inn** • 24 Romilly St
• **Bar Italia** • 22 Frith St
• **Barshu** • 28 Frith St
• **Bi Bim Bap** • 11 Greek St
• **Ceviche** • 17 Frith St
• **Garlic & Shots** • 14 Frith St
• **Haozhan** • 8 Gerrard St
• **Imperial China** • 25 Lisle St
• **The Ivy** • 1 West St
• **Koya** • 49 Frith St
• **The Bodega Negra Cafe** • 16 Moor St
• **La Porchetta Pollo Bar** • 20 Old Compton St
• **Le Beaujolais** • 25 Litchfield St
• **Maison Bertaux** • 28 Greek St
• **Sartori** • 15 Great Newport St
   The Three Greyhounds • 25 Greek Street

Shopping

• **Fopp** • 1 Earlham St
• **Forbidden Planet** • 179 Shaftesbury Ave
• **Foyles** • 107 Charing Cross Rd
• **Hank's Guitar Shop** • 27 Denmark St
• **Wunjo Guitars** • 5 Denmark St

Map 13 · **Covent Garden**

N

1
2

Bedford Sq

ford Sq

Bloomsbury Way A4200
Drake St
Drake St

4

Bedford Avenue
Bloomsbury Square Gardens

A4200
A400

Great Russell Street
Gilbert Place
Bloomsbury Square

Fisher St

Little Russell St
Galen Pl
Vernon Place
Catton Street

Bury Pl

Bainbridge Street
Streatham St
Willoughby Place
Coptic Street
Stedham Place
Museum Street
Bloomsbury Way A40
Southampton Pl
Barter Street

A
New Oxford Street A40
New Oxford Street

Earnshaw Street
Dyott Street
Bloomsbury St A400
Museum Street
Holborn
Gate St

Bucknall Street
High Holborn
A40
Newton Street

reet A40
St Giles High St
Smart's Place
Stukeley Street
14

Filtercroft St
St Giles High St
Grape St
Macklin Street

Denbeigh Street
New Compton St
Endell St
Parker Ms
Great Queen Street B402
Remnant Street

Shaftesbury Avenue
A401
Shorts Gardens
Betterton Street
Parker Street
Kingsway A4200

Neal St
B401
Drury Lane
Wild Ct

Monmouth Street B404
Neal's Yd
Nottingham Ct
Dryden Street
Wild Street
Keeley Street

Earlham Street
Seven Dials
Shelton Street
Arne St
B402

B
Ching Ct
Old Brewers Yd
Langley Street
Kemble Street

Litchfield Street
Tower St
West Street
Mercer Street
Long Acre
Russell Street
Kean Street

Slingsby Place
Neal Street
Covent Garden
Bow Street B401

Great Newport
B402
Floral Street
Royal Opera House
Wellington St B401
Tavistock Street
Aldwych A4

Street
12
Rose St
Catherine Street

Cranbourn St
Garrick Street
King Street
24
London Transport Museum
Strand A4

Leicester Square
Greek Yd
London Transport Museum
Lancaste

St Martin's Ln B404
Upr St Martin's Ln B404
STRAND
Burleigh St

Henrietta Street
Southampton Street
Exeter Street

Bedfordbury
Bedford Ct
Maiden Lane
Savoy Row

Place
0.25 mile
0.25 km

Covent Garden

Map 13

Covent Garden is a shopper's delight, especially on Endell Street and Neal Street. However, such activity will not offer a respite from the Piazza and its hordes of spatially unaware folk. Stop for fish and chips at **Rock & Sole Plaice**. Come the evening, sip cocktails at **Freud** or convene with the ghost of Bernard Shaw at the **Lamb & Flag**.

Coffee

- **Bagariat** • 24 Rose St
- **Bagel Factory** • 18 Endell St
- **The Black Penny** • 34 Great Queen St
- **Caffe Nero** • 30 Monmouth St
- **Caffe Nero** • 83 Long Acre
- **Pret A Manger** • 65 Long Acre
- **Starbucks** • 10 Russell St
- **WatchHouse** • 7 Upper St Martin's Ln

O Landmarks

- **Oasis Sports Centre** • 32 Endell St
- **Seven Dials** • Upper St Martin's Ln & Earlham St

Nightlife

- **Compagnie Des Vins Surnaturels** • 8-10 Neal's Yard
- **The Cross Keys** • 31 Endell St
- **Freud** • 198 Shaftesbury Ave
- **Lamb & Flag** • 33 Rose St
- **The Poetry Cafe** • 22 Betterton St

Post Offices

- **High Holborn** • 181 High Holborn

Restaurants

- **Battersea Pie** • Covent Garden Piazza
- **Café Mode** • 57 Endell St
- **Flat Iron** • 17 Henrietta St
- **Flesh & Buns** • 41 Earlham St
- **Lanzhou Noodle Bar** • 33 Cranbourne St
- **Lima Floral** • 14 Garrick St
- **Mon Plaisir** • 21 Monmouth St
- **Punjab** • 80 Neal St
- **Rock & Sole Plaice** • 47 Endell St
- **Sarastro** • 126 Drury Ln
- **Souk Medina** • 27 Litchfield St

Shopping

- **The Astrology Shop** • 78 Neal St
- **Ben's Cookies** • 13 The Piazza
- **Blackout II** • 51 Endell St
- **Coco de Mer** • 23 Monmouth St
- **Libidex at Liberation** • 49 Shelton St
- **London Graphic Centre** • 16 Shelton St
- **Lululemon** • 125 Long Acre
- **Neal's Yard Dairy** • 17 Shorts Gardens
- **Poetry Cafe** • 22 Betterton St
- **Pop Boutique** • 30 Short's Gardens
- **Rokit** • 42 Shelton St
- **Rossopomodoro** • 50 Monmouth St
- **Stanfords** • 7 Mercer Walk
- **Tabio** • 51 Neal St
- **Urban Outfitters** • 42 Earlham St

Supermarkets

- **Sainsbury's** • 129 Kingsway

Map 14 • **Holborn / Temple**

Queen Square
Gardens
Russell
Square
Gardens

Southampton Row A4200

Queen Square Place
Powis Place
Great Ormond Street
Ormond
Yard
St. John's Street
Old Gloucester Street
Long Yard
Roger Street
Elm Street
Rugby Street
North M
King's Mews
Mount Pleasant
Warner Street
Baker's Row
Farringdon Road A201

Clerkenwell Road

1

2

5

Bedford Place
Southampton Place
Cosmo Pl
Bloomsbury Sq Gardens
Bloomsbury Square

Great Russell St
Bury Place
Museum St
New North St
North Court
Dombey St
Richbell Place
St-James's Pl
James
St.
Emerald St

Theobald's Road A401

Raymond Buildings
Bedford Row
Jockey's Fields

Gray's Inn Gardens
Gray's Inn Rd

Verulam St
Portpool Lane
Portpool Lane
Hatton Wall
Leather Lane
Baldwin's Gardens
Leopold's
St Cross Street
St. Cross
Greville
Hatton Garden

Hatton Garden

A

Bloomsbury Way A40
Vernon Place
Red Lion Square
Princeton Street
Bedford Row
Sandland St
High
Square South
Dorrington St
Beauchamp St
Brooke St

Bloomsbury Way

Galen Pl

Barter St

Fisher Street
Catton Street
Eagle Street
Brownlow St

Holborn A40
High Holborn A40
⊖ Holborn
Whetstone Park
Lincoln's Inn Fields
Newman's Row Park & Garden
Stone Bldgs
Southampton Buildings

Chancery Lane
⊖ Chancery
Lane
✉

✉ Holborn

13

Remnant St
Gate St
High Holborn
Kingsway
Wild Court
Keeley Street
Sardinia St
Portsmouth
Sir John Soane's Museum
Lincoln's Inn Fields (Fickets Fields)

HOLBORN

Serle Street
New Square
Bishop's Ct
Cursitor St
Southampton Bldgs
Furnival St
Norwich St
Printers Inn Ct
Barnard's Inn
Fetter Lane
Bream's Bldgs
New Fetter Lane A4
Bartlett Ct

Holborn
Andrew

15

Great Queen Street B402
Wild Street
Kean Street
Kemble St
Sardinia St
The Old Curiosity Shop
Inn Fields
Portugal St
Carey Street
Chancery Lane B400
Rolls Bldgs
Rolls Passage

Bow Street B402
Bull Inn Ct

St Clement's Lane
Clare Market
London School of Economics

Royal Courts of Justice

Fleet Street
Fetter Lane
Norwich St
Cursitor St
Gough Sq
Pemberton Row
Site of Sweeney Todd's Barber Shop

Aldwych A4
Aldwych A4
Aldwych A4
Strand A4
Strand A4
Strand A4
Strand A4
PAGE 368
BBC Bush House
Melbourne Pl
Houghton St

Wellington Street B401
Tavistock St
Exeter St
Burleigh St
Strand
Southampton St
Wellington Street
Somerset House
Aldwych Tube Station
King's College
Lancaster Place A301
Savoy Place
Savoy Pl
Savoy Row
Strand A4
Surrey St
Arundel St
Milford Ln
Maltravers St
Temple Pl
Essex St
Devereux Ct
Little Essex St
Fountain Court
Middle Temple Ln
Brick Ct
Elm Ct
Pump Ct
Crown Office Row
Fleet Street
Bouverie St
Pleydell Ct
Bouverie St
Serjeants Inn
Whitefriars St
Carmelite St
Tudor St
Temple Lane
Kings Bench Walk
Tallis St

B

PAGE 366
⊖ Temple
Victoria
Middle Temple Gardens
Inner Temple Gardens
Embankment

Victoria Embankment A3211

Victoria Embankment, New Bridge St
Victoria Embankment, New Bridge St
Victoria Embankment, Blackfriars Bridge

24

River Thames

| 0.25 mile | | 0.25 km |

An essential cog in London's machine, this area is resplendent with curios (**Old Curiosity Shop**, **Sweeney Todd's**), public squares full of depressed lawyers and legions of serious-looking people being integrated into The System. The ghosts of London's past hover around Temple and the Strand, where you'll also find **Aldwych Film** for brunch and a flick.

Cinemas

• **Aldwych Film** • 1 Aldwych

Coffee

• **Caffe Nero** • 333 High Holborn
• **Fleet Street Press** • 3 Fleet St
• **Pret A Manger** • 8B Leather Ln
• **Pret A Manger** • 240 High Holborn
• **Prufrock Coffee** • 23-25 Leather Ln
• **Starbucks** • 10 Kingsway
• **Starbucks** • 99 Kingsway
• **Triple Two Coffee** • 14 Leather Ln

O Landmarks

• **Aldwych Tube Station** • Strand & Surrey St
• **BBC Bush House** • Aldwych & Kingsway
• **Hatton Garden** • Hatton Garden
• **Inner Temple Garden** • Inner Temple
• **King's College London** • Strand
• **Lincoln's Inn Fields** • Newman's Row
• **London School of Economics and Political Science** • Houghton St
• **The Old Curiosity Shop** • 13 Portsmouth St
• **Royal Courts of Justice** • Strand
• **Sir John Soane's Museum** • 13 Lincoln's Inn Fields
• **Sweeney Todd's Barber Shop** • 186 Fleet St
• **Somerset House** • Somerset House Trust, The Strand

Libraries

• **British Library of Political and Economic Science** • 10 Portugal St

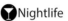

Nightlife

• **Bar Polski** • 6 Little Turnstile
• **Bounce** • 121 Holborn
• **Cittie of Yorke** • 22 High Holborn
• **The Craft Beer Co.** • 82 Leather Ln
• **The Enterprise** • 38 Red Lion St
• **The Seven Stars** • 53 Carey St

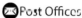

Post Offices

• **Aldwych** • 95 Aldwych
• **Grays Inn** • 24 Grays Inn Rd

Restaurants

• **Asadal** • 227 High Holborn
• **Indigo** • 1 Aldwych
• **Radio Rooftop Bar** • 336 Strand

Shopping

• **Konditor & Cook** • 46 Grays Inn Rd

Supermarkets

• **Sainsbury's** • 129 Kingsway
• **Sainsbury's** • 60 Fetter Ln

Map 15 · **Blackfriars / Farringdon** Ⓝ

Bath St
St. John St
Church Gardens
Aylesbury St
Great Sutton St
B501
Clerkenwell Road A5201
Charterhouse
Goswell Road A1

Ray Street
RaySt Bridge
Ray St Br
Vine St Br
St. John's
Albe Wy
Fann Rd

Summers Street
Bath Court

Clerkenwell Road A5201
Broad Yd
Turk's Head Yd
Smoke house Yard

The Green

6

Fann St

St. John's Place
St. John's Square
Briton Street
Briset St
Charterhouse Sq

Portpool
Hatton Wall

Bit
Kirby St

Saffron Hill
Saffron St
Tunmill St

Albion Pl
Benjamin St
Eagle Court

St. John's Gardens

Charterhouse Ms

Carthusian St

Aldersgate Street A1
Beech B100

Cross St
St Cross
Hatton Garden B521

Farringdon

Cowcross Street

Greenhill's Rents

Charterhouse
Charterhouse St
Lindsey St

Long Lane
Middle St
Barth. cl
Half Moon

Barbican

Cripplegate

Chancery Lane
Beauchamp St
Dorringtons

Greville St
Bleeding Heart Yard
Shoe Lane

Charterhouse Street

East Poultry Avenue
West Poultry Avenue
Smithfield

Cloth Fair
Bartholomew Cl
Barth. pl

Brooks Mkt
Ely Place
Ely Pl

Little Britain

7

London

Holborn A40

West Smithfield
Snow Hill

Hosier Lane
Cock Lane
Snow Hill Ct

Little Britain

St. Bartholomew's Hospital

Montague Street
Aldersgate Street A1

Printers Inn Ct
Furnival Street

St. Andrew Shoe Lane
Plumtree Ct

Holborn Viaduct A40

Gilspur St

Little Britain

Postman's Park

Angel Street

Carey St

Norwich Street
Bream's Buildings

Fetter Lane A4
New Fetter Lane A4
Barnett's

New Davies Ct
Tur. La
Newcastle Clo

Green Arbour Ct
Bishop's Ct

Old Bailey

Newgate Street A40
King Edward Street

Christchurch Greyfriars Gardens

Foster Lane

Cheapside

Plough Place

Stone St
Bear All

St. Georges Ct

Warwick Sq
Warwick Lane

Paternoster Square

St. Paul's

Rolls Bldgs

Gough Sq
Little New Street
Pem.

St. Bride St A201
Poppins Ct

Old Fleet La
Old Seacoal La
Limeburner La

Amen Corner

St. Paul's Cathedral

16

New Change

14

Daily Express Building

Fleet Street
Ludgate Circus

New Bridge Street A201
Bridge Lane

Ludgate Hill
Pilgrim St
Old Bailey

Amen Ct

St. Paul's Chyd
Ave Maria

Churchyard
Carter Lane

St. Paul's Chyd

Festival Gardens

Fleet Street
Playdell
Whitefriars Street
Bouverie Street

Salisbury Ct
Dorset Buildings
Dorset Place

Black F. playhouse Yd

Carter Lane
Ap. St
Pilgrim St
St. Andrew's Hill

St. Paul's
Sermon Ln
Knightrider St

Carter Lane
Godliman St
Distaff

Serjeants Inn
Hood Court
Pump Ct

Whitefriars St
Hutton St
Bride Ct

Watergate

Addle Hill

Serman Ln

Inner Temple
Hare Ct
Elm Ct
Crown Office Row

Tudor Street
Tallis St
Carmelite St

John Carpenter St

Queen Victoria Street

Castle
Bennet's Hill
Castle Baynard Street

Queen Victoria Street

Middle Temple

Victoria Embankment

Temple

Blackfriars

New Bridge St
Puddle Dock

Baynard Street
Upper Thames St

Lambeth Hill

Middle Temple Gardens

Victoria Embankment
Victoria Embankment A3211

White Lion

Millennium Bridge

Upper Th

High Timber

0.25 mile   0.25 km

Blackfriars / Farringdon

Map 15

The choices for eating out and drinking in this quarter are myriad, but we recommend getting your chops around a side of cow: **Smith's** is a solid option. Get a feel for sixteenth-century London with a potter around the old Livery Halls, then make like a Dickensian Oliver in the gated Charterhouse Square.

Coffee

- **Alchemy Coffee** • 8 Ludgate Broadway
- **Caffe Nero** • 30 Newgate St
- **Caffe Nero** • 118 Newgate St
- **Costa** • 13 New Bridge St
- **Costa** • 46 Cowcross St
- **Pret A Manger** • 101 Turnmill St
- **Pret A Manger** • 5 St John's Sq
- **Pret A Manger** • 10 Pasternoster Sq
- **Pret A Manger** • 101 New Bridge St
- **Pret A Manger** • 143 Fleet St
- **Starbucks** • 1 Paternoster Sq
- **Starbucks** • 3 Fleet Pl
- **Starbucks** • 30 New Bridge St
- **The Wren** • 114 Queen Victoria St

O Landmarks

- **Daily Express Building** • 121 Fleet St
- **Millennium Bridge** • Millennium Bridge
- **Old Bailey** • Old Bailey
- **Postman's Park** • Little Britain

Libraries

- **Shoe Lane Library** • Little New St

Nightlife

- **Fabric** • 77 Charterhouse St
- **Fox and Anchor** • 115 Charterhouse St
- **The Happenstance** • 10 Paternoster Sq
- **The Hat and Tun** • 3 Hatton Wall
- **Ye Old Mitre** • 1 Ely Pl
- **Ye Olde Cheshire Cheese** • 145 Fleet St
- **Ye Olde London** • 42 Ludgate Hill

Post Offices

- **Farringdon Road** • 39 Farringdon Rd

Restaurants

- **Bleeding Heart** • Bleeding Heart Yard
- **Le Cafe du Marche** • 22 Charterhouse Sq
- **Smiths of Smithfield** • 67 Charterhouse St
- **St. John** • 26 St John St
- **Tinseltown** • 44 St John St
- **Vivat Bacchus** • 47 Farringdon St
- **Ye Olde Cheshire Cheese** • 145 Fleet Street

Supermarkets

- **Sainsbury's** • 23 Farringdon Rd

37

Map 16 · **Square Mile (West)**

Map 16

Square Mile (West)

Aah, the City, that faceless square mile at which we direct such disgust and vehemence for the state we're in. Despite meltdowns and protests, the world continues to turn, stocks are traded, and bonuses return. This place has always been empty at the weekends so you can enjoy the caryatids and Doric columns in peace. And of course take in the duomo at San Paulo (so much more romantic sounding, don't you think?)

Coffee

• **Costa** • 99 Gresham St
• **Pret A Manger** • 30 Gresham St
• **Starbucks** • 143 Cheapside

O Landmarks

• **The Guildhall** • Gresham St
• **St Mary le Bow Church** • Cheapside
• **St Paul's Cathedral** • St Paul's Church Yard
• **Temple of Mithras** • Queen Victoria St

Post Offices

• **Southwark** • 136 Southwark Bridge Rd

Libraries

• **City Business Library** • Aldermanbury Sq
• **Guildhall Library** • Aldermanbury

Nightlife

• **The Samuel Pepys** • Stew Ln
• **Three Cranes** • 28 Garlick Hill
• **Ye Olde Watling** • 29 Watling St

Restaurants

• **Coq d'Argent** • 1 Poultry
• **Sweetings** • 39 Queen Victoria St

Shopping

• **Church's** • 90 Cheapside
• **Space NK Apothecary** • 145 Cheapside

Supermarkets

• **Marks & Spencer** • Cannon St Station

Map 17 · Square Mile (East)

Square Mile (East)

London's most Jekyll-and-Hyde-like hood. **The Counting House** is for after-work beers, while the possibility of shopping at the Royal Exchange is laughable, but who says you have to buy? By night, well, just don't go there.

Map 17

 ## Coffee

- **Pret A Manger** • 43 King William St
- **Starbucks** • 48 Gracechurch St

 ## Landmarks

- **Bank of England** • Threadneedle St
- **London Stone** • 111 Cannon St
- **The Royal Exchange** • Cornhill
- **Threadneedle Street** • Threadneedle St

Nightlife

- **The Counting House** • 50 Cornhill

Post Offices

- **Moorgate** • 45 London Wall

 ## Restaurants

- **Burger and Lobster** • 52 Threadneedle St
- **Coya Angel Court** • 31 Throgmorton St
- **Gaucho City** • 1 Bell Inn Yard
- **Hispania** • 72 Lombard St
- **The Mercer** • 34 Threadneedle St
- **Nusa Kitchen** • 2 Adams Ct
- **Simpson's Tavern** • 38 Ball Court Alley, Cornhill

Shopping

- **Bremont** • 12 The Royal Exchange

 ## Supermarkets

- **Marks & Spencer** • Cannon St Station
- **Sainsbury's** • 10 Lombard St

Map 18 • **Tower Hill / Aldgate**

N

1 **2**

91

Liverpool
Street
Station

PAGE
411

A

8 Tower 42
(Natwest Tower)

Jewish
Soup
Kitchen

Aldgate
East

London Wall Wormwood St A1211

Houndsditch A1211

Camomile
Street Bevis
Marks

St Botolph Street

Aldgate

Aldgate High St

The Gherkin

Dukes Place A1211

95

17 Leadenhall
Market

Goodmans Yard

The Lloyds
Building

London
Wall

Tower
Gateway

Pudding Ln

Tower
Hill

The
Monument

Byward Street A3211

Royal Raven
Lodgings

Lower Thames Street A3211
Lower Thames Street

Tower of
London Park

Tower of
London

Thames Clipper

0.25 mile   0.25 km

River Thames

Tower Hill / Aldgate

Map 18

Though on the fringe of the financial cesspit, Aldgate is brilliant to walk and gawp around in. Go siege the **London Wall** alongside the tourists. Alternatively go become one yourself at **Pudding Lane**.

 Coffee

- **Caffe Nero** • 22 London St
- **Curators Coffee** • 9 Cullum St
- **Starbucks** • 48 Gracechurch St
- **Starbucks** • 48 Minories
- **Trade Coffee** • 47 Commercial St

O Landmarks

- **The Gherkin** • 30 St Mary Axe
- **Jewish Soup Kitchen** • Brune St & Tenter Ground
- **The Lloyd's Building** • 1 Lime St
- **Leadenhall Market** • Gracechurch St
- **London Wall** • Cooper's Row & Trinity Sq
- **The Monument** • Monument St
- **Pudding Lane** • Pudding Ln
- **St Dunstan-in-the-East** • St Dunstan's Hill
- **The Ravens** • Tower Hill
- **Thames Clippers** • Tower Pier
- **Tower 42** • 25 Old Broad St
- **Tower of London** • Tower Hill

 Libraries

- **Artizan Street** • 1 Artizan St
- **The Women's Library** • 10 Portugal St

 Nightlife

- **Kenza** • 10 Devonshire Sq
- **The Minories** • 64 Minories
- **Revolution** • 140 Leadenhall St

 Post Offices

- **The City of London BO** • 12 Eastcheap

 Restaurants

- **Gunpowder** • 11 White's Row

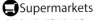 **Shopping**

- **Petticoat Lane Market** • 119 Middlesex St

Supermarkets

- **Sainsbury's** • 45 Fenchurch St

Map 19 · **Belgravia**

N

1

Hyde Park

PAGE 342

South Carriage Drive

Hyde Park

37

Knightsbridge

Knightsbridge A4

Knightsbridge A4

Hyde Park Corner

Duplex Ride
Studio Pl

Seville
Street

William St

Wilton Row

Wilton Place

Hyde Park Corner

Knightsbridge A4

2

Park Lane

Park Lane

Piccadilly A4

Old Barrack Yard

Grosvenor Crescent

Apsley Way

CONSTITUTION HILL

Duke of Wellington

Grosvenor Place B310

9

Buckingham
Palace Gardens

A

Kinnerton Street

Wilton Crescent

Motcomb Street

Belgrave Mews W

West Halkin St

Halkin St

Belgrave
Square

Wilton Cres

Halkin
Street

Chapel Street

Montrose Place

Headfort Place

Groom Pl

Chester Street

Wilton St

Grosvenor Place B302

B

Chesham
Pl

Chesham Clo

Lyall
Mews

Lyall Street

Place Street

Lowndes Close

Belgrave Place Street B310

Eaton Mews

Eaton
Square

Belgrave Mews S.

Eaton Square

Eaton Mews N

Eaton
Square

Eaton Place B310

Eaton
Square

Chester Square

Hobart Place

Grosvenor Gardens

Lower Grosvenor Place B302

Eccleston Mews

Eaton Mews S.

Eaton Square

Ebury Mews

Chester
Square

Ebury Mews

Eccleston Street

Buckingham Palace Rd

46

Sloane
Square

Sloane
Square

Cadogan
Gate

Ellis Street

Wilbraham Pl

Sloane Terrace

Eaton Gate A3217

Cliveden
Place

Minera Mews

Eccleston Street

Ebury Mews E.

Victoria
Station

PAGE 415

Caroline
Terrace

Chester Row

Chester Row

Ebury Street

Ebury Street

Eccleston Bridge

Elizabeth Street

Terrace

Holbein Mews

Graham
Terrace

BELGRAVIA

Ebury
Square

Semley Place

Buckingham Palace Road A3214

Eccleston Bridge

Belgrave Road A3214

2

Pimlico Road A3214

20

Bloomfield Ter

| 0.25 mile | 0.25 km |

Belgravia

Map 19

Ugg and Range Rover fetishists are in a constant state of climax around here. It sure is pretty when the sun isn't being blocked by expensively coiffured bouffants, but one suspects the plummy accents and tasteless richness would dent anyone's enthusiasm for chic dog clothes (**Mungo & Maud**) or curry (**Amaya**).

Coffee

• **Tomtom Coffee House** • 114 Ebury St

Libraries

• **Instituto Cervantes** • 15 Devereux Ct
• **Victoria Library** • 160 Buckingham Palace Rd
• **Westminster Music Library** • 35 St Martin's St

Nightlife

• **The Blue Bar** • The Berkeley Hotel • Wilton Pl
• **Nag's Head** • 53 Kinnerton St
• **The Plumber's Arms** • 14 Lower Belgrave St

Restaurants

• **Amaya** • Motcomb St
• **Boisdale** • 15 Eccleston St
• **Colbert** • 50 Sloane Sq
• **Noura** • 12 William St
• **The Pantechnicon** • 19 Motcomb St
• **The Thomas Cubitt** • 44 Elizabeth St

Shopping

• **Daylesford Organic Farmshop and Cafe** • 44 Pimlico Rd
• **Mungo & Maud** • 79 Elizabeth St
• **Peter Jones** •Sloan Sq

Supermarkets

• **Waitrose** • 27 Motcomb St

45

Victoria / Pimlico (West)

Since the Tower of London closed for business, prisoners have been routinely tortured at weekends in Victoria Station. Surrounding the transit hubs is a dignified 'hood Churchill and Mozart called home. Do a late-night tramp photoshoot on the steps of the magnificent houses of Lupus Street (with a camera from **Grays**) before heading to **The Cask & Glass** for a knees-up with your new pals.

Coffee

- **Caffe Nero** • 31 Warwick Wy
- **Costa** • 3 Cardinal Walk
- **Costa** • 115 Buckingham Palace Rd
- **Pret A Manger** • 173 Victoria St
- **Pret A Manger** • Unit 36B • Victoria Station
- **Pret A Manger** • 92 Buckingham Palace Rd
- **Starbucks** • Buckingham Palace Rd & Lower Belgrave St

Post Offices

- **Vauxhall Bridge Road** • 167 Vauxhall Bridge Rd

Landmarks

- **Little Ben** • Victoria St & Vauxhall Bridge Rd
- **Westminster Cathedral** • 42 Francis St

Nightlife

- **The Cask & Glass** • 39 Palace St
- **The Warwick** • 25 Warwick Wy
- **Windsor Castle** • 23 Francis St

Restaurants

- **Grumbles** • 35 Churton St
- **The Phoenix** • 14 Palace St
- **Pimlico Fresh** • 86 Wilton Rd

Shopping

- **Capital Carboot Sale** • Lupus St
- **Grays of Westminster** • 40 Churton St
- **Rippon Cheese Stores** • 26 Upper Tachbrook St

Supermarkets

- **Marks & Spencer** • Victoria Mainline Station

47

Map 21 · **Pimlico (East)**

N

Howick Place

Artillery Row

Greycoat Pl.

1

Artillery Row

Greycoat Street

Chadwick Street

Peter Street

Great

Elizabeth Court

Monck Street

2

A326 Marsham Street

North Street

Mayfair Street

Peter Street

Dean Street

Victoria Tower Gardens

Thirleby Road

Howick Place

Francis St

Greencoat Row

Rochester Street

Rochester Row

Medway Street

Newburn St

Perkin's Rents

Dean Trench St

Smith Square

Dean Stanley St

Coburg Close

Emery Hill Street

Greencoat Place

Willow Place

Chapter Street

Horseferry Road

B323

Horseferry Road

B323

Horseferry Road

Romney Street

Dean Bradley St

Thorney Street

Lambe

A3212

Millbank

Rochester Row

B321

Rochester Street

Greycoat Street

Vincent Square

Maunsel Street

Rutherford Street

Regency Street

22

Vincent Square

Westminster School Playing Fields

Fynes Street

Page Street

St. John's Gardens

Ryle Street

Page Street

Westminster Gardens

Millbank Tower

Millbank

A3212

A Vincent Square

Vincent Street

Vincent Street

Vincent Street

Marsham Street

Herrick Street

Bul. St

Vauxhall Bridge Road A202

Vincent Square

Hide Place

Chapter Street

Regency Street

Montaigne Close

Montaigne Close

Mont. Cl

Bloomburg St

Stanford St

Osbert

Douglas Street

Erasmus Street

Herrick St

Tate Britain

Ossd St

A3213

120

Chatworth Way

Charlwood Place

Charlwood St

Thorndike Street

Garden Terrace

Tachbrook Street

A202

Bessborough Gardens

Causton Street

Cureton Street

Ponsonby Place

John Islip Street

Herrick

Atterbury Street B326

PAGE 476

Chelsea College of Art & Design

Millbank

A3212

Riverside Gardens

B Moreton Place

Moreton Ter Ms

More. Ter MS

Moreton Terrace

Moreton St

St. George's Drive

Rampayne Street

Drum Gate

Ponsonby Terrace

Pimlico

Bessborough St

Balniel Pl

Bessborough Place

Lindsay Square

Balniel St

Linds St

Bessborough Gardens

A202 Vauxhall Bridge

Bridgefoot

Clarendon St

Belgrave Road A3213

Lupus Street

Lupus Street

St. George's Square

Aylesford St

St. George's Square Garden

Aylesford Street

Balvaird Place

Grosvenor Road

Chichester Street

St. George's Square

St. George's Sq Mews

River Thames

Claverton Street

Grosvenor Road A3212

Pimlico Gardens

Grosvenor Road A3212

Grosvenor Road

A302 Wandsworth Road

Parry Street

| 0.25 mile | 0.25 km |

Map 21

Hugging the curve of the Thames, this princely patch of Pimlico combines the stately Tate with imposing embankment architecture and ancient houses. Check out the old-money splendour of Vincent Street before grabbing lunch at the **Regency**, a true gem of a caf. Much fun can be had by pretending you actually live around here, so in this spirit head to the **Morpeth** as your local.

O Landmarks

• **Millbank Tower** • 21 Millbank

Libraries

• **Pimlico Library** • Lupus St
• **Royal Horticultural Society Library** • 80 Vincent Sq

Nightlife

• **Morpeth Arms** • 58 Millbank

Restaurants

• **Goya** • 34 Lupus St
• **The Regency Cafe** • 17 Regency St
• **The Vincent Rooms** • 76 Vincent Sq

Map 22 · **Westminster**

Westminster

Map 22

The long shadow of government falls over these parts, beautiful as they are. Protesters and wannabe Guy Fawkeses head to Parliament Square, where they can harangue whichever bunch of jokers are ensconced in the Houses of Parliament. Get away from tourists at the tiny **St. Stephen's Tavern**, or grab a classy cocktail at **The Cinnamon Club**. If you must shop, head to Victoria Street.

 Coffee

- **Cafe Fresco** • 11 Tothill St
- **Iris & June** • 1 Howick Pl
- **Pret A Manger** • 49 Tothill St
- **Starbucks** • 27 Victoria St

O Landmarks

- **Big Ben** • Bridge St
- **Field of Remembrance** • Victoria St
- **New Scotland Yard Sign** • 8 Broadway
- **St. John's Smith Square** • Smith Sq
- **UK Parliament** • Victoria St & Abingdon St
- **Westminster Tube Station** • Westminster Bridge Rd

 Nightlife

- **The Albert** • 52 Victoria St
- **The Cinnamon Club** • 30 Great Smith St
- **The Feathers** • 18 Broadway
- **The Speaker** • 46 Great Peter St
- **Two Chairmen** • 39 Dartmouth St
- **St. Stephen's Tavern** • 10 Bridge St

Map 23 · **St. James's**

St. James's Park

St. James's Park Lake

ST. JAMES'S

The Green Park

Marlborough House Gdns

The Mall

Green Park

Piccadilly Circus

Leicester Square

TKTS

Economist Plaza

St. James's Square

Giro the Nazi Dog

Waterloo Gardens

Memorial Gardens

Birdcage Walk

Birdcage Walk

St. James's Park

10 **11** **9** **24** **22**

0.25 mile   0.25 km

St. James's

Dignified, decadent, exclusive, Pall Mall and St. James's Street are where the aristobrats come out to play. With stuffy gentlemen's clubs, bespoke tailors, and the stale scent of a cigar-fuelled colonialist past pervading, you'll want to sweeten up with a macaroon at **Laduree**.

Cinemas

- **Empire Cinemas Haymarket** • 63 Haymarket
- **ICA Cinema** • The Mall & Horse Guards Rd
- **Odeon Leicester Square** • 24 Leicester Sq
- **Odeon Panton Street** • 11 Panton St
- **Vue Cinema Piccadilly** • 19 Lower Regent St

Coffee

- **Borough Barista** • 15 Charles II St
- **ICA Cafe** • The Mall
- **Pret A Manger** • 8 King St

O Landmarks

- **Economist Plaza** • 25 St. James's St
- **Giro the Nazi Dog** • 9 Carlton House Terrace
- **King George VI & Queen Elizabeth Memorial**
- **Leicester Square** • Leicester Sq
- **TKTS** • Leicester Sq

Libraries

- **London Library** • 14 St James's Sq
- **Westminster Reference Library** • 35 St Martin's St

Nightlife

- **Dukes Hotel** • 35 St James's St
- **Institute of Contemporary Arts** • The Mall

Restaurants

- **Cafe Concerto Green Park** • 61 Piccadilly
- **Laduree** • 71 Burlington Arcade

Shopping

- **Partridges Deli** • 2 Duke of York St

Map 23

Map 24 • **Trafalgar Square / The Strand**

Ⓝ

1

2

Longacre A401

Charing Cross Road

Litchfield Street

Earlham Street

Shelton Street

Monmouth St

Tower Street

Great Newport St

Langley Street

Neal's Street

Betterton Street

Neal's Yard

B402

B401

Aldwych

Piccadilly Circus

Great Windmill Street

WestSt

Gerrard Place

Dolphin Yard

Gerrard Street

Little Newport St

Lisle Street

Leicester Place

Whitcomb Street

Wardour Street

Newport Court

Newport Place

Bear St

Charing Cross Road

Cranbourn Street

Leicester Square

Leicester Square

Ⓐ

Irving Street

Whitcomb St

Orange Street

St. Martin's Street

Pall Mall East

Cockspur Court

Cockspur Street

Warwick Ho St

House Terrace

A4

Suffolk Place

Suffolk St

Spring Gardens

The Mall

Horse Guards Rd

St. James's Park

Ⓑ

Ⓒ

Slingsby Pl

Upper St. Martin's Lane

B404

Long Acre

Floral Street

King Street

Rose Street

Garrick Street

New Row

Bedfordbury

St. Martin's Lane B404

Charing Cross Rd A400

St. Martin's Place

William IV Street

Adelaide St

Chandos Place

Agar St

Bedford Court

Bedford Street

Jane Austen Residence

The Actors' Church

Henrietta Street

Maiden Lane

Southampton St

Chandos Place

Duncannon St

St. Martin-in-the-Fields

Eleanor Cross

National Gallery & National Portrait Gallery

PAGE **478**

Trafalgar Square

Trafalgar Square A4

Northumberland Ave

Corner House Street

Craven Street

Hungerford Lane

Villiers Street

Charing Cross Station

PAGE **410**

Embankment

Adam Street

Durham Ho St

York Bldgs

John Adam Street

Lower Robert St

Robert St

Adelphi Terrace

York Buildings

Strand

Strand

Buckingham St

Strand

Strand

Tavistock Street

Wellington Street B401

Exeter Street

Burleigh St

Savoy Street

Savoy Way

Savoy Row

Savoy Place

Savoy Buildings

Savoy Hill

Ivybridge La

Savoy Steps

Carting Lane

Right-hand Drive Street

Sewer Lamp

Cleopatra's Needle

Victoria Embankment Gardens

Montreal Pl

Lancaster Place A301

Waterloo

Strand

Wellington Street B401

12

13

14 ▶

River Thames

Ⓑ

Top Secret Tunnels

Craig's Ct

Great Scotland Yard

Whitehall Place

Scotland Pl

The Banqueting House

Northumberland Avenue

Whitehall A3212

Whitehall Court

Whitehall Gdns

Horse Guards Avenue

Victoria Embankment Gardens

Victoria Embankment

Embankment Place

Horse Guards Parade

Whitehall Gdns

Victoria Embankment Gardens

10 Downing St

Downing Street

Parliament Street A3212

Richmond Terrace

Derby Gate

King Charles Street

Westminster

A3211

Jubilee Gardens

23 ◀

St. James's Park

22 ▼

| 0.25 mile | 0.25 km |

Trafalgar Square / The Strand

Map 24

The hawkers came and removed the flying rats and lo! the Square was clean and visible. This ain't Mary Poppins—don't feed the birds, you dirty tourists. Eat at **Wahaca**, one of London's few good Mexicans, then walk it off on **Waterloo Bridge** and watch the sun set over the Thames. Aah. That's why you love London.

Coffee

- **Caffe Nero** • 10 Bedford St
- **Caffe Nero** • 36 St Martin's Ln
- **Coffee Island** • 5 Upper St Martin's Ln
- **Costa** • 17 Embankment Pl
- **Notes** • 31 St Martin's Ln
- **Pret A Manger** • 7 St Martin's Ln
- **Starbucks** • 1 Villiers St

O Landmarks

- **10 Downing Street** • 10 Downing St
- **The Actors' Church** • 29 Bedford St
- **Banqueting House** • Whitehall
- **Cleopatra's Needle** • Embankment
- **Eleanor Cross** • Strand
- **Jane Austen Residence** • 10 Henrietta St
- **Right-Hand Drive Street** • Savoy Ct
- **Sewer Lamp** • Carting Ln & Strand
- **St Martin-in-the-Fields** • Trafalgar Sq
- **Top Secret Tunnels** • 6 Craig's Ct
- **Trafalgar Square** • Trafalgar Sq

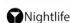Libraries

- **Charing Cross Library** • 4 Charing Cross Rd
- **Royal United Services Institute Library** • Whitehall

Nightlife

- **The Chandos** • 29 St Martins Ln
- **The Coal Hole** • 91 Strand

- **Covent Garden Comedy Club** • The Arches
- **Gordon's Wine Bar** • 47 Villiers St
- **The Harp** • 47 Chandos Pl
- **Haxells Restaurant & Bar** • 372 Strand
- **Heaven** • The Arches
- **Maple Leaf** • 41 Maiden Ln
- **Punch & Judy** • The Covent Garden Piazza
- **Retro Bar** • 2 George Ct
- **The Sherlock Holmes** • 10 Northumberland St
- **Zoo Bar & Club** • 13 Bear St

Restaurants

- **Benito's Hat** • 19 New Row
- **Cafe in the Crypt** • Trafalgar Sq
- **J Sheekey** • 28 St Martin's Ct
- **Portrait Restaurant & Bar** • St Martin's Pl
- **Rules** • 35 Maiden Ln
- **Thai Pot** • 1 Bedfordbury
- **Wahaca** • 66 Chandos Pl

Shopping

- **London Camera Exchange** • 98 Strand
- **Rohan** • 11 Mercer St
- **Stanley Gibbons** • 399 Strand

Supermarkets

- **Marks & Spencer** • Charing Cross Station

KENSAL RISE

WEST KILBURN

KENSAL GREEN

Kensal Green

KENSAL TOWN

25

EALING

Wormwood Scrubs

NORTH KENSINGTON

Westway

Westbourne Pk

Elgin Cres

WHITE CITY

NOTTING HILL

28

ACTON

EAST ACTON

Wood Ln

SHEPHERD'S BUSH

Holland Park Ave.

HOLLAND PARK

HOLLAND

Acton Park

Uxbridge Rd

32

33

Holland Rd

Wendell Park

Shepherds Bush Green

Shepherds Bush Rd

TURNHAM GREEN

Goldhawk Rd

Dalling Rd

40

34

Bath Rd

Ravenscourt Park

Hammersmith Rd

WEST KENSINGTON

Chiswick Common

39

King St

41

Talgarth Rd

CHISWICK

Great West Rd

HAMMERSMITH

38

42

BARONS COURT

Hogarth Ln

CASTELNAU

Lillie Rd

Dawes Rd

Chiswick Cemetery

Fulham Palace Rd

Fulham Cemetery

47

University of Westminster Station

Thames River

FULHAM

48

Duke's Meadow

BARNES

Putney Park

Fulham Palace Gardens

MORTLAKE

The "new Notting Hill" label weighs heavily on the Kensals. They look east for inspiration, ignoring the Harlesden yardies at their backs. **Trellick Tower** is perfect for real—"I mean it, I'll jump"—attention-seekers.

Coffee

• **Lisboa Cafe** • 57 Golborne Rd
• **Neev & May** • 155 Ladbroke Grove

O Landmarks

• **Trellick Tower** • 5 Golborne Rd

Libraries

• **Kensal Library** • 20 Golborne Rd
• **Queen's Park Library** • 666 Harrow Rd

Post Offices

• **Maida Hill** • 377 Harrow Rd
• **Portobello Road** • 325 Portobello Rd

Restaurants

• **Lowry and Baker** • 339 Portobello Rd
• **Made in Brasil** • 12 Inverness St
• **Thai Rice** • 303 Portobello Rd

Shopping

• **Honest Jon's** • 278 Portobello Rd
• **Rellik** • 8 Golborne Rd

Supermarkets

• **Iceland** • 512 Harrow Rd
• **Miah's Oriental Foods** • 369 Harrow Rd

Map 26 · **Maida Hill**

Maida Hill

Not as posh as Maida Vale or as cool as Ladbroke Grove, Maida Hill is slightly grubby to the south, not helped by the distinctly unlovely Harrow Road. Things get more upmarket heading north, but the beating heart of the hill can be found Saturdays around Harrow Road's new market. On one of those rare sunny London days get down to the **Union Tavern** and grab a canal side table.

Post Offices
• **Kilburn Park** • 29 Malvern Rd

Nightlife
• **Union Tavern** • 45 Woodfield Rd

Restaurants
• **Mosob** • 339 Harrow Rd
• **Tsiakkos & Charcoal** • 5 Marylands Rd

Map 27 · **Maida Vale**

1

2

Fordingley Road

Saltram Crescent

Malvern Crescent

Malvern M

Malvern Road

Malvern Close

Hampton

Stafford Close

Stuart Rd

Chip Gdns

Cambridge Road

Nelson Cl

Cambridge Road

Kilburn Park Road B414

Kilburn Park Road

Perry Tree Green

Randolph Gardens

Andover Place

Greville

Carlton Vale

Carlton Hill Side

Carlton

Road B414

Lanhill Road

Kilburn Park Road B414

MAIDA VALE

Paddington Recreation Ground

St Georges RC School

Griffin

Oakington Road

Byron Ct Byron M

A

Essendine Primary School

Essendine Road

Widley Road

Wymering Road

Morshead Road

City of Westminster College

Grantully Road

Randolph Avenue

Lanark Road

Maida Vale A5

◄**26**

Elgin Mn

Elgin Avenue

Maida Vale ⊖

Elgin Ms

68►

Rowington Cl

Thorngate Rd

Sevington St

St Peter's Pl

Shirland Road B413

Delaware Road

Castellain Rd

Paddington Sports Club

Lauderdale Road

Biddulph Road

Ashworth Road

Randolph Avenue

Lanark Road

Vale Close

Maylands Road

Surrendale Place

Sutherland Avenue

Downfield Cl

Aldsworth Clo

Braden St

Clearwell Drive

Warwick Avenue

Elnathan Mews

Pindock M

Castellain Rd

Sutherland Avenue

Lanark M

Sutherland Av

St Josephs RC Primary School

Lanark Road

Maida Vale A5

B

Square

Senior Street

Barnwood Cl

Formosa Street

Bristol Gardens

Warwick Avenue

Bris Cl M

Formosa St

Warwick Avenue

Warrington Crescent

Randolph Crescent

Randolph Avenue

Lanark Place

76►

Bourne Terr

Lord Hills Road

Desb Cl

Delamere Terrace

Chichester Road

Blomfield Villas

Bourne Terr

Clifton Villas

Blomfield Road

Clifton Gardens B413

Warwick Avenue ⊖

Randolph Avenue

Clifton Road

Clifton Place

Clifton Road

St. John's Wood

Westbourne Green

30▼

Harrow Road A404 Westway A40

Royal

Warwick Place

Warwick Avenue

Clarendon Gardens

Randolph Mews

Blomfield Road

Randolph Road

Eliz Cl Brown Cl Robert Cl

Clar Ter

31▼

Clifton

Aberdeen Pl

Fishe

Court

Norwich Ter

Aberdeen Pl

0.25 mile	0.25 km

You don't come to Maida Vale for the nightlife, end of story. Though pretty, canal-side walks are a different matter. Away from 'Little Venice' are endless rows of identical-looking Edwardian mansion blocks on peaceful, tree-lined avenues. It's clean, peaceful, and nice (translation: quite dull). Locals frequent the cafés and eateries around the Maida Vale tube station and on Clifton Road.

Coffee

• **Starbucks** • 168 Randolf Ave

Libraries

• **Maida Vale Library** • Sutherland Ave

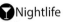

Nightlife

• **The Bridge House** • 13 Westbourne Terrace Rd
• **The Elgin** • 255 Elgin Ave
• **Prince Alfred** • 5A Formosa St
• **The Warwick Castle** • 6 Warwick Pl
• **The Waterway** • 54 Formosa St

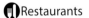

Restaurants

• **Banana Tree** • 166 Randolph Ave
• **Le Cochonnet** • 1 Lauderadale Rd

Look at that Westway and tell us you can't hear the opening chords of "London Calling." Maybe Rudie didn't fail but he moved up and moved out. This is the quiet, leafy Notting Hill of gated gardens away from the Hugh Grant-hungry tourists scouring Portobello Road. Head to Clarendon Cross or Portland Road for food and stuff. Grab a bite at **Julie's** or wander down to Holland Park Avenue for organic treats at **Jeroboams Deli**.

Coffee

• **Starbucks** • 76 Holland Park Ave

Nightlife

• **Julie's Restaurant & Champagne Bar** • 135 Portland Rd

Shopping

• **The Cross** • 141 Portland Rd
• **Daunt Books** • 112 Holland Park Ave
• **Jeroboams** • 96 Holland Park Ave

Map 29 · **Notting Hill Gate**

1

2

Bonchurch Rd. B450

St Michaels Gdns

Orchard Close

Morgan Rd.

Chesterton Rd.

Woodfield Rd.

Ranville Rd.

Elkstone Rd.

Woodfield Place

Bevington Rd.

Harrow Road A404

Chippenham Mews

Oxford Gardens

Cambridge Gardens

Malvern Close

Westway

Tavistock Crescent

Elmfield Way

Alfred Road

26

Norfolk Rd.

Tavistock Gardens

Tavistock Road

Great Western Road A4207

Westway A40

25

McGregor Road

St Lukes Mews

Westbourne Park Road B412

Aldridge Road Villas

Westbourne Park Road A4207

A

Ladbroke Grove

Golden Cross Mews

Lancaster Road

Powis Terrace

Talbot Road

Dartmouth Close

WESTBOURNE GREEN

Westbourne Green Sports Complex

Chesterton Rd.

Railway Ms.

Lancaster Road

Alba Place

Portobello Road Market

St Stephens Mews

30

St Stephens Gardens

Park Road

Haydens Place

Elgin Mews

Convent Gardens

Powis Terrace

Courtnell Street

Moorhouse Rd.

Sutherland Place

Northumberland Place

Talbot Road A4207

Kildare Terrace

Durham Terrace

Westbourne Park Road

Portobello Road

Blenheim Crescent

Codrington Mews

Elgin Crescent B415

Talbot Road

Colville Houses

Colville Road

Colville Terrace

Colville Square

Colville Mews

Lonsdale Mews

Artesian Rd.

Chepstow Road A4207

Bristow Place

Hereford Mews

Newton Road

Monmouth Rd.

28

Elgin Crescent

Arundel Gardens

NOTTING HILL

Lonsdale Road

Vernon Yard

Westbourne Grove

Wellington Close

Hearn's Mews

Chepstow Road

Botts Mews

Hereford Road

Westbourne Grove A4206

Newton Rd.

Ladbroke Grove B450

Ladbroke Gardens

Longlands Court

Denbigh Terrace

Denbigh Close

Chepstow Villas

Pembridge Villas

Chepstow Place

Ledbury Mews

Ledbury Road

Chepstow Villas

Leinster Square

Princes Square

Ladbroke Grove B450

Stanley Gdns

Kensington Park Gardens

Kensington Park Road B415

Denbigh Terr.

Pembridge Crescent

Simon Close

Portobello Road

Chepstow Cres.

Pembridge Mews

Dawson Place

Pembridge Square

Princes Square

Princes Mews

B

Ladbroke Square Gardens

Ladbroke Square

Highbury Crescent

Bulmer Mews

Pembridge Square

Ossington Street

The Limes

Chepstow Place

Ossington Close

Palace Court

Moscow Road

Bay

Lansdowne Walk

Willby Rd.

Ladbroke Road

Ladbroke Walk

Ladbroke Terrace

Victoria Gardens

Bulmer Place

Notting Hill Gate

Pembridge Gardens

Pembridge Road A4206

Linden Gardens

The Mall

Dartmouth Place

Astoria Grove Ms.

St Petersburgh Place

Ossington Street

St Petersburgh Mews

Orme Court

Orme La.

Palace Court

Bayswater Road

Lansdowne Rise

St. John's Gardens

Aubrey Road

Campden Hill Square

Uxbridge Street

Hillgate Place

Jameson Street

Newcombe Street

Farmer Str.

West Mall

Campden Hill Road A4204

Kensington Church Street

Notting Hill Gate A402

Palace Gardens Terrace

Broadwalk Court

Holland Park

Holland Park Avenue A402

Campden Hill Square

Aubrey Walk

Kensington Place

Edge Street

Peel Street

Campden Street

Bedford Gardens

Strathmore Gardens

Kensington Gardens Square

Kensington Church Street

Ken. Ma.

Palace Gardens Terrace

Kensington Gardens

34

Holland Park Mews

Wycombe Sq.

Campden Hill Gate

KENSINGTON

35

PAGE 342

Notting Hill Gate

Map 29

It is hard to believe that until relatively recently this now home of the mega-rich was Kensington's rough bad-boy slum. Traces of the Gate's multicultural past are in the wrinkles of the old eccentrics in the **Uxbridge Arms**, the lively **Portobello Market**, and the buzz of the summer Carnival. To feel old and bitter, go scowl at skinny jeans-clad teenagers in the **Notting Hill Arts Club**. Browse the stacks at **Rough Trade Records** and sit back in leather sofa luxury with a Peroni for a flick at the historic **Electric Cinema**.

Cinemas

- **The Electric Cinema** • 191 Portobello Rd
- **Gate Picturehouse** • 87 Notting Hill Gate
- **Notting Hill Coronet** • 103 Notting Hill Gate

Coffee

- **Caffe Nero** • 113 Westbourne Grove
- **Caffe Nero** • 53 Notting Hill Gate
- **Coffee Plant** • 180 Portobello Rd
- **Pret A Manger** • 65 Notting Hill Gate
- **Starbucks** • 227 Portobello Rd
- **Starbucks** • 26 Pembridge Rd

Landmarks

- **Portobello Road Market** • 223 Portobello Rd

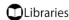Libraries

- **North Kensington Library** • 108 Ladbroke Grove
- **Notting Hill Gate Library** • 1 Pembridge Sq

Nightlife

- **Notting Hill Arts Club** • 21 Notting Hill Gate
- **Sun in Splendour** • 7 Portobello Rd
- **Trailer Happiness** • 177 Portobello Rd
- **Uxbridge Arms** • 13 Uxbridge St
- **Windsor Castle** • 114 Campden Hill Rd

Post Offices

- **Kensington Church St** • 190 Kensington Church St
- **Ladbroke Grove** • 116 Ladbroke Grove

Restaurants

- **Beach Blanket Babylon** • 45 Ledbury Rd
- **Cafe Diana** • 5 Wellington Terrace
- **The Ledbury** • 127 Ledbury Rd
- **Osteria Basilico** • 29 Kensington Park Rd
- **Ottolenghi** • 63 Ledbury Rd
- **The Shed** • 122 Palace Gardens Terr
- **Taqueria** • 141 Westbourne Grove

Shopping

- **The Grocer on Elgin** • 6 Elgin Crescent
- **The Hummingbird Bakery** • 133 Portobello Rd
- **Melt** • 59 Ledbury Rd
- **Music & Video Exchange** • 38 Notting Hill Gate
- **Notting Hill Farmers' Market** • Kensington Church St
- **Portobello Road Market** • Portobello Rd
- **R Garcia and Sons** • 248 Portobello Rd
- **Retro Man** • 28 Pembridge Rd
- **Retro Woman** • 20 Pembridge Rd
- **Rough Trade** • 130 Talbot Rd

London's unofficial 'Little Beirut' seems to attract both camera-clad tourists (who have strayed too far from Hyde Park) as well as Londoners (who look for food gems on Westbourne Grove). While the place is bustling, beware of the overpriced, and frankly sh***, tourist traps on Queensway. Alternatively, do it like the Victorians did and get a rub down at **Porchester Gate Spa**.

Coffee
• **Arno Coffee** • 77 Bishop's Bridge Rd
• **Pret A Manger** • 127 Queensway
• **Starbucks** • 49 Queensway

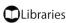
Libraries
• **Paddington Library** • Porchester Rd

Nightlife
• **All Star Lanes** • Bloomsbury Pl & Southampton Row
• **The Cow** • 89 Westbourne Park Rd

Post Offices
• **Queensway** • 118 Queensway

Restaurants
• **Al Waha** • 75 Westbourne Grove
• **The Cow** • 89 Westbourne Park Rd

Shopping
• **Planet Organic** • 42 Westbourne Grove
• **Porchester Gate Spa** • Queensway & Porchester Rd

Supermarkets
• **Sainsbury's** • 88 Westbourne Grove
• **Waitrose** • 38 Porchester Sq

Map 31 · Paddington

Map 31 · Paddington

Warwick Avenue

Blomfield Road

Maida Avenue

Warwick Crescent

Warwick Avenue

Westway A40
Harrow Road A404

Westway
Flyover

PADDINGTON

Bishops Bridge Road A4206

Harrow Road A404

Marylebone Flyover A4204

Paddington
Green

Church Street

Edgware Road A5

Broadley
Street
Gardens

Harrow Road Flyover A404

Harrow Road

Marylebone Road A40

Paddington
Station

Edgware
Road

Chapel Street

Old Marylebone Road A501

South Wharf Road

Praed Street

Paddington
Bear Statue

Praed Street

St. Michaels
Street

A4205

Sale Place

Sussex Gardens

A4209

The
Quadrangle

Sussex Gardens

Norfolk
Square

Gloucester
Square

Oxford
Square

Lancaster
Gate

Hyde Park Gardens

Hyde Park Sq.

Bayswater Road A402

Connaught Street

Kensington
Gardens

Bayswater Road A402

Tony Blair's
House

Marble Arch

Hyde
Park

0.25 mile   0.25 km

Paddington

Map 31

Paddington Bear may not seem so cuddly if he were one of today's commuters hanging around Paddington Station. This area can seem like zombie land, a mass of tired-looking, harassed faces grabbing food from one of the endless chain eateries. It's not all bad news though. Evening boredom can be banished by listening to famous war correspondents' exotic tales over a meal at the **Frontline Club**. For all other woes solve it with a swift half at **The Victoria**.

Cinemas

• **Frontline Club** • 13 Norfolk Pl

Coffee

• **Beany Green** • 6 Sheldon Square
• **Caffe Nero** • 14 Spring St
• **Caffe Nero** • Paddington Station
• **Costa** • 254 Edgware Rd
• **Markus Coffee Company** • 13 Connaught St
• **Pret A Manger** • 4 Sheldon Sq
• **Serpentine Bar & Kitchen** • Serpentine Rd

Emergency Rooms

• **St Mary's Hospital** • Praed St & Winsland St

O Landmarks

• **Paddington Bear Statue** • Paddington Station
• **Tony Blair's House** • Connaught Sq & Seymour St
• **Westway Flyover** • Westway

Nightlife

• **Frontline Club** • 13 • Norfolk Pl
• **The Victoria** • 10 Strathearn Pl

Post Offices

• **Edgware Rd** • 354 Edgware Rd
• **Paddington** • 4 Praed St

Restaurants

• **Bonne Bouche** •129 Praed St
• **Casa Malevo**• 23 Connaught St

Supermarkets

• **Sainsbury's** • Paddington Station
• **Sainsbury's** • 12 Sheldon Sq

Map 32 · Shepherd's Bush (West)

Don't be scared. This part of town won't bite ... much. Things may look a bit drab, and indeed you wouldn't want to spend your Friday nights in many of the pubs here, but on Uxbridge Road looks truly can be deceiving. While it's nothing special from the outside, **Esarn Kheaw** will blow your head off with authentic Thai green curry and leave you begging for more. Then swoon under the chandeliers to an off-the-radar act at restored dance hall **Bush Hall**.

Nightlife

• **Bush Hall** • 310 Uxbridge Rd
• **White Horse** • 31 Uxbridge Rd

Restaurants

• **Abu Zaad** • 29 Uxbridge Rd
• **Esarn Kheaw** • 314 Uxbridge Rd
• **Vine Leaves Taverna** • 71 Uxbridge Rd

Shopping

• **Damas Gate** • 81 Uxbridge Rd
• **Nut Case** • 352 Uxbridge Rd

Map 33 · Shepherd's Bush

SHEPHERD'S BUSH

BBC Television Centre

White City

Wood Lane

Wood Lane A219

Wood Lane A219

Macfarlane Road

Ariel Way

Ariel Way

Reuar Road

Silver Road

South Africa Road

White City Road

South Africa Road

Ring Road

White City Close

Hammersmith Park

Frithville Gardens

Stanlake Villas S

Stanlake Road

Loris Road

Tunis Road

Abdale Road

Swindon Street

Uxbridge Road A4020

Warbeck Road

Cornthorpe Road

Coningham Road

Lime Grove

Frithville Gardens

Market

Greenside Road

Pennard Road

Shepherds Bush Market

Bulwer Street

Aldine Place

Aldine Street

Caxton Road

Tadmor St

Sterne St

Bourbon

Lane

St Elmo Rd

Lena Gardens

Batoum Gardens

Osram

Qsram

Loris Rd

Barb

Mews

Devonport Road

Cathnor Road

Ellerslie Road

Ellerslie Road

Ariel Way

Whitchurch Road

Evesham Street

Oldal Street

St Anns Road

Mortimer Road

Frithville Gardens

West Cross Route A3220

West Cross Route A3220

West Cross Route A3220

West Cross Route A3220

West Cross Route A3220

Crescent

Queensdale

Nutfield Rd

Queensdale Road

Queensdale Cres

Swanscombe Road

St Anns Villas

St James's Gardens

St James's Gardens

Queensdale

Addison Ave

Royal Cres

Royal Crescent

Royal Crescent Gardens

Holland Park Avenue

Wilsham Street

Norland Rd

Sirdar Road

Avondale Park

Runcorn Pl

Hesketh Pl

Penzance Pl

Pottery Lane

Mary Pl

Portland Rd

Kenley St

Portland Rd

Camelford St

Darnley Ter

Barnley Ter

Boyne Ter

Clarendon Rd

Uxbridge Road A4020

Shepherd's Bush

Uxbridge Road A4020

Shepherds Bush Green

Holland Road

Shepherds Bush Green

Shepherds Bush Common

Shepherds Bush Green A402

Holland Road A402

Holland Rd A402

Upper Addison Gardens

Sinclair Gardens

Sinclair Road

Charecroft Way

Millers Way

Gayford Road

McFarlane Rd

Wells Road

Sulgrave Rd

Wilcox Gdns

Rockley Road

Sinclair Gdns

Woodstock Grove

Hopgood St

Sterne St

Gerald Rd

Grima Edils

Grima Edils

Holland Rd A402

Grafton

Melina Rd

Minford

Gardens

Westwick

Gardens

Ashley Road

Rylett Rd

Anley Road

Poplar Grove

Cromwell Grove

Melrose Terrace

Melrose Gardens

Astrop Ter

Astrop Ms

Beauclerc Road

Aldbourne Road

Stowe Road

Batoum Gardens

Trussley Road

Aynhoe Road

Havelock Cl

St Vs

Benbow Road

Cromwell Grove

Melrose Terrace

Shepherds Bush Road A219

Wingate Road

Cobbold Rd

Goldhawk Road A402

Goldhawk Road

Richford Street

Bamborough Gardens

Adie Road

Ellerslie Road

Lakeside Road

Waterworth Rd

Waterworth Road

Addison Gardens

Lower Addison Gardens

Bolingbroke Road

Blythe Road

Irving Road

Fielding Road

Milson Road

Redan Street

Springvale Ter

Blythe Mews

Sterndale Road

Sterndale Road

Dewhurst Road

Blythe Mews

Blythe Road

Masbro Road

Girdlers Road

Auriol Road

Fielding Road

Russell Gdns

Russell Gardens

Holland Rd

Elsham Road

Shepherds Bush Road A219

Batoum Gardens

Cromwell Grove

Melrose Gardens

Osman Road

Lena Gardens

Dalling Road

Overstone Rd

Iffley Road

Bassein Park Road

Scrubs Lane

Trussley Rd

Amor Road

Trussley Road

Hebron Road

Devonport Road

Erica St

Adie Rd

Applegarth Rd

Haarlem Rd

A

B

28

32

34

40

41

0.25 mile

0.25 km

Shepherd's Bush

Map 33

'The Bush' has had a bit of a face-lift over the past few years. Once the former grime hub of West London, it now sports one of Europe's biggest shopping centres, **Westfield**, and with it comes more traffic and more chain shops. Even the Beeb is on its way out. Fear not though, for **Shepherds Bush Market** still keeps the place decidedly unpretentious, while the **Empire** continues to attract the best up-and-coming bands. Experience some in-yer-face theatre at **Bush Theatre**.

Cinemas

• **Vue Shepherds Bush** •
Shepherds Bush Green & Rockley Rd

Coffee

• **King Coffee Shop** • 72 Uxbridge Rd
• **Starbucks** • 62 Uxbridge Rd

O Landmarks

• **BBC Television Centre** • 101 Wood Ln

Libraries

• **Shepherds Bush Library** • 6 Wood Ln

Nightlife

• **Bush Theatre** • 7 Uxbridge Rd
• **The Defectors Weld**• 170 Uxbridge Rd
• **O2 Shepherd's Bush Empire** • Shepherd's Bush Green

Post Offices

• **Shepherds Bush Road** • 146 Shepherd's Bush Rd

Restaurants

• **Busaba Eathai** • Westfield Shopping Centre
• **Hoja** • 39 Goldhawk Rd
• **Jasmine** • 16 Goldhawk Rd
• **Mr Falafel** • 15 Uxbridge Rd
• **Popeseye** • 108 Blythe Rd

Shopping

• **Westfield Centre** • Ariel Way

Supermarkets

• **Sainsbury's** • 164 Uxbridge Rd

Map 34 · West Kensington / Olympia

Kensington

Holland Park

Kyoto Garden

Kensington (Olympia)

Barons Court

West Kensington

EARLS COURT

Holland Park Avenue A402

Holland Road A3220

Kensington High Street A315

Warwick Road A3220

North End Road B317

W Cromwell Road A4

Hammersmith Road

Cromwell Road

0.25 mile

0.25 km

West Kensington / Olympia

West Ken is a Jekyll-and-Hyde kind of place. The calm, village atmosphere around Holland Park soon gives way to an 'in your face' cluster of kebab shops and grime once you go south of High Street Kensington. While the hordes head to Hyde Park, locals in the know make a beeline to the more intimate Holland Park with its peaceful **Kyoto Garden**, sublime in autumn. Olympia Exhibition Centre gets that middle class blood boiling—Erotica Show anyone? Near the tube, **Café Continente** is the place to go for an irresistible stack of blueberry pancakes.

 ## Coffee

• **Cafe Continente** • 62 N End Rd

 ## Landmarks

• **Kyoto Garden (Holland Park)** • 100 Holland Park Ave

 ## Libraries

• **Barons Court** • North End Crescent

Nightlife

• **The Cumberland Arms** • 29 N End Rd
• **Famous 3 Kings** • 171 North End Rd
• **Society Bar** • 380 Kensington High St

 ## Post Offices

• **Olympia** • 8 North End Rd

Map 35 · **Kensington**

N

KENSINGTON

Holland Park

Cricket Ground

Camden Hill Tennis Club

EARL'S COURT

Earl's Court

SOUTH KENSINGTON

Kensington Palace Gardens

Kensington Gardens

PAGE 342

High Street Kensington

29

34

36

42

43

Kensington Road

Kensington High Street A315

Kensington Church Street

Kensington High Street

Cromwell Road A4

Cromwell Road

Warwick Road A3220

Warwick Gardens

Pembroke Road

Earls Court Road A3220

Earls Court Road A3220

West Cromwell Road A4

Warwick Road

Palace Gardens Terrace

Vicarage Gate

A4204

A315

0.25 mile   0.25 km

Kensington

Map 35

Kensington is the London of Disney fantasy—Princesses tip-toeing around grand old homes and taking tea at 3 p.m. It's the kind of place where a gentile mews cottage will set you a back a cool mill, but if you live here you'll still have some change left over for an SUV and a box of organic veg. You're not going to score any cool points for hanging out here but there's nothing better than frisbee and a picnic (from **Whole Foods**, of course) in Hyde Park on those treasured London summer days. If you've got the cash to splash, High Street Ken has the goods but instead take a detour to **The Builders Arms** for a not-so-posh pint.

Coffee

- **Pret A Manger** • 149 Kensington High St
- **Starbucks** • 25 Kensington High St

Landmarks

- **Kensington Palace Gardens** • Kensington Palace Gardens

Libraries

- **Kensington Central Library** • Phillimore Walk

Nightlife

- **Builders Arms** • 1 Kensington Ct Pl
- **The Devonshire Arms** • 37 Marloes Rd
- **Yashin Sushi** • 1 Argyll Rd

Post Offices

- **Kensington High St** • 208 Kensington High St

Restaurants

- **Balans Soho Society** • 187 Kensington High St
- **Clarke's** • 124 Kensington Church St
- **Kitchon W8** • 11 Ahingdon Rd
- **Maggie Jones's** • 6 Old Court Pl

Shopping

- **Ben's Cookies** • 12 Kensington High St
- **Trailfinders** • 194 Kensington High St
- **Urban Outfitters** • 36 Kensington High St
- **Whole Foods Market** • 63 Kensington High St

Supermarkets

- **Sainsbury's** • 162 Earl's Ct Rd
- **Tesco** • 100 W Cromwell Rd
- **Waitrose** • 243 Kensington High St

79

Map 36 · **South Kensington / Gloucester Rd** (N)

1 **2**

The West Carriage Drive

Hyde Park

South Carriage Drive

Kensington Gardens
PAGE 342

Albert Memorial

A

gh Street A315

Kensington Road A315

Kensington Gore A315

Kensington Road

Kensington Road

Prince of Wales Terrace

Kensington Ct Rd

Canning Pl

Cambridge Pl

De Vera Gardens

Albert Place

Ken sington Ct Ms

Douro Place

Palace Gate B325

De Vere Gardens Place Ms

Hyde Park Gate

Res

Hyde Park Gate

Hyde Park Ms

Park Gate

Queen's Gate

Jay Ms

Jay Ms

Bremner Rd

Kensington Gore

Princes Gate

Princes Gate Court

Low. Gdns

Princes Gate

Monroe

Court

Royal Albert Hall

Prince Consort Road

37▶

Princes Gardens

Albans Grove

35

Cottesmore Gardens

Victoria Road

Launceston Place

Gloucester Road B325

Victoria Grove

Kensington Gate

Kensington Gate.

Queen's Gate Mews

Queen's Gate Terrace

Gore Street

Queen's Gate

Callendar Road

Ayrton Road

Wills Way

Imperial College Road

Unwin Road

Exhibition Road

Princes Gardens

Imperial

Princes Gardens

Eldon Road

Kynance Pl

Petersham Place

Elvaston Place

Imperial College
PAGE 365

Kingsley

Cornwall

Kynance Mews

Cornwall Gardens

Cornwall Gdns

Petersham Mews

Elvaston

Queen's Gate

Imperial

College Road

Frankland Road

Ostan

Cornwall Gardens

Cornwall MsS

SOUTH KENSINGTON

Emperor's Gate

Grenville Place

Southwell Gardens

Queen's Gate Place

Queen's Gate Place Mews

Museum Lane

The Science Museum
PAGE 474

Victoria & Albert Museum
PAGE 468

McLeod's Ms

Reece Mews

Queen's Gate Gdns

stone Mews

Queen's Gate

Natural History Museum
PAGE 472

Cromwell Road

B

Cromwell Road A4

Stanhope Gardens

Stanhope Mews East

Queensberry Place

Queensberry Ms

Thurloe Place

Cromwell Ms

Pelham

Thurloe Sq

Cromwell Road A4

Gloucester Road

Ashburn Gardens

Gaspar Ms

Gaspar Ms

Ashburn Pl

field Grns

Courtfield Gdns

Ashwood Ms

Gloucester Rd

Greville Mews

Gloucester Mews West

Ashburn Road

Stanhope Gardens

Stanhope Gardens

Manson Ms

Queensberry Way

Harrington Road

Reece Mews

Bute St

Reece Mews

South Kensington

43 ▼

Gloucester Park

Colbeck Mews

Courtfield Gardens

Harrington Gardens

Wetherby Pl

Rosary Gardens

44 ▼

Stanhope

Stanhope Ms W

Clareville Grove

Clareville St

Harrington Road

Manson Place

Queen's Gate

Harrington Road

Gloucester Rd

Harrington Road

Gle Pl

Reece Mews

Sumner Pl

Sumner Place Ms

45 ▼

Onslow

B304

Onslow Cres

Old Brompton Road A3218

Onslow Square

Onslow Gardens

Wetherby Gardens

Bina Gardens

Roland Gardens

Rosary Gdns

Selwood Terrace

Selwood Pl

ham Road

Neville Ter

Sumner Pl

0.25 mile   0.25 km

Once known as Albertopolis, this place started out as Prince Albert's playground of learning. These days the museums are the carrot that draws the tourists westwards from the buzzing centre. Free entry to museums mean more money for treats, and if it's treats you're after then fresh gelato at **Oddono's** won't fail to disappoint. If your idea of a good night out consists of more than a few quiet shandies then we suggest checking out another 'nabe.

Cinemas
• **Cine Lumiere** • 17 Queensberry Pl

Post Offices
• **Gloucester Road** • 118 Gloucester Rd

Coffee
• **Café Deco** • 62 Gloucester Rd
• **Pret A Manger** • 99 Gloucester Rd
• **Pret A Manger** • 15 Old Brompton Rd
• **Starbucks** • 17 Gloucester Rd
• **Starbucks** • 83 Gloucester Rd

Restaurants
• **Da Mario** • 15 Gloucester Rd
• **Jakob's** • 20 Gloucester Rd
• **The Kensington Creperie** • 2 Exhibition Rd
• **Oddono's** • 14 Bute St
• **Tombo** • 29 Thurloe Pl

O Landmarks
• **Albert Memorial** • Kensington Gardens
• **Imperial College** • South Kensington Campus
• **Royal Albert Hall** • Kensington Gore

Shopping
• **Maitre Choux** • 15 Harrington Rd
• **Partridges Deli** • 17 Gloucester Rd

Libraries
• **French Institute Library** • 17 Queensberry Pl
• **National Art Library** • Cromwell Rd
• **Natural History Museum** • Cromwell Rd

Supermarkets
• **Sainsbury's** • 158 Cromwell Rd
• **Waitrose** • 128 Gloucester Rd

Map 37 · **Knightsbridge**

Move on over Z-list celebrity, only the truly rich shop here! While you can't move on for fur or tourists, Knightsbridge is still a great place to shop. Window shop, that is. **Harrods** and **Harvey Nics** are the big boys here, and if you're after £40 soap you are in the right place. For the rest of us there's the **Victoria & Albert Museum**—free entry, brilliant cafe to escape the crowds, and multiple naked male sculptures to ogle.

 ## Coffee

• **Caffe Nero** • 124 Brompton Rd
• **Pret A Manger** • 132 Brompton Rd
• **Starbucks** • 44 Brompton Rd

 ## Landmarks

• **Holy Trinity Brompton** •
  Brompton Rd & Knightsbridge
• **Victoria & Albert Museum** • Cromwell Rd & Thurloe Pl

Libraries

• **Goethe-Institut Library** • 50 Princes Gate

 ## Post Offices

• **Knightsbridge** • 6 Raphael St

 ## Restaurants

• **Daquise** • 20 Thurloe Square
• **L'Eto Brompton** • 243 Brompton Rd
• **Ognisko** • 55 Prince's Gate
• **Zuma** • 5 Raphael St

 ## Shopping

• **Divertimenti** • 227 Brompton Rd
• **Harrods** • 87 Brompton Rd
• **Harvey Nichols** • 109 Knightsbridge
• **Rigby & Peller** • 2 Hans Rd

 ## Supermarkets

• **Sainsbury's** • 112 Brompton Rd

Map 38 · **Chiswick**

N

2

Hardwicke Road
Acton Green Common
Mills Row
Bridge Street
Alfred Rd
Belmont
Essex Place
Dolman Road
B409
South Parade
B409
Bath Road B409
Priory Gdns
Addison Grove
Gainsborough Rd
Wolstead Way
Prebend Gdns
Sta

Kirton Close
Belmont Grove
Balfour Grove
Arnott
Chiswick Com mon
ACTON GREEN
Chiswick Common
Chiswick High Road
Road

Turnham Green
Flanders Road
Roman Road
Lonsdale Road

Fishers End
Tishers End
Fishers Rd
Bolton Rd
Chiswick S Bldg
A315
Chiswick High Road **A315**
Thornton Avenue

A
Turnham
Turnham Grn
Ter Ms
Turnham Green Terrace
Mayfield Avenue
Thornton Avenue
Upham Park Road
Ennismore Avenue
Merton Avenue

Stamford Brook
A315

Hurlingham Place
Heathfield Ter
Barley Mow Passage
Bourne Place
Duke Road
Duke Road
Duke's Avenue
Lind; Pas
Gardens
Prince of Wales Terrace
Glebe St
Glebe Street
Devonshire
Devonshire Road
Elliott Rd
Wind
Ms Mews
Charlotte
Fromow's Cnr
Cranbrook Road
Verona Ct
✉
39▶
Chiswick High Road
Homefield Road
Airedale Avenue
Fielding Avenue
Middlesex Ct
A315

CHISWICK

Waverdon Avenue
Gardens
Duke Road
Binns Road
Reckitt Road
Quick Road
Dale Street
Glebe Street
Devonshire Road
Alexandra Road
Swanscombe Rd
Swanscombe Terrace
Brackley Terrace
St
In
Alkenden Road
Coombe Road
Wilton Avenue
Beverley Road
Airedale Avenue

Barrowgate Road
Park Cottages Rd
Park Road North
Fraser
Wood Street
Devonshire Street
Devonshire Road
Ashbourne Grove
Balfern Grove
Cornwall Grove
A316
Homefield Recreation Ground

Hogarth Lane **A4**
Park Road
White Swan Mews
Bennett Street
Eastbury Grove
Dorchester Grove **A316**
Great West Road **A4**
Netheravon

Great West Road
Chiswick Gro's
British Gro Sth
British Gro. Pas

Hogarth Lane **A4**
Sutherland Rd
Short Ms
Nicholas Ms
Paxton Road
Hogarth Roundabout · Flyover
Great West Road **A4**
Netheravon Road
Eyot Grn

Chiswick Sq

Chiswick Wf

Burlington Lane
Chiswick House Grounds
Church Street
Mawson
Fuller's Griffin Brewery
Chiswick Mall

Chiswick Eyot

River Thames

B

Corney Road Cemetery
Dartmouth
Corney Road
Station Road
Chiswick Ch Wf
Pages Yd
Boston Gdns

Alexandra Avenue
Grantham Road
Promenade Approach Road
Corney Reach
Bedford Ho Ms
Malthouse Drive
Cavendish Road
Latimer Place
Prompt
Thames Crest

Leg of Mutton Nature Reserve

Terry Grn
Verdun Road
Lonsdale Road
Howsman

Burlington Lane
A316
Edensor Road
Mdow Place
Alexandra Gardens
Market Drive
Promenade Approach Road
Edensor Gardens

Harrod's Sports Ground
B350
Barnes Bridge

A316 Alexandra Avenue

`|—————— 0.25 mile ——————|`   `|—————— 0.25 km ——————|`

Chiswick

Map 38

Lean, green and thankfully not so mean. Chiswick's tranquil, leafy, village feel is perhaps what draws families and well-heeled couples with its stacks of laid-back continental style pavement dining and quaint cafes on the High Road. Hit Devonshire Road for boutique shopping, and on sunny days it's all about ice-cream from **Foubert's** and an afternoon chilling out on Acton Green. **The Roebuck** serves up a top-notch Sunday roast but the **High Road Brasserie** still remains the place to be seen.

Coffee

• **Tamp Coffee** • 1 Devonshire Rd

Libraries

• **Chiswick Library** • Duke's Ave

O Landmarks

• **Fuller's Griffin Brewery** • Chiswick Lane South

Nightlife

• **George IV** • 185 Chiswick High Rd
• **The Packhorse & Talbot** • 145 Chiswick High Rd
• **The Roebuck** • 122 Chiswick High Rd

Restaurants

• **Chris's Fish Bar** • 19 Turnham Green Terrace
• **Faanoos** • 472 Chiswick Road
• **Foubert's** • 2 Turnham Green Terrace
• **Franco Manca** • 144 Chiswick High Rd
• **High Road Brasserie** • 162 Chiswick High Rd
• **La Trompette** • 5 Devonshire Rd
• **Kalamari** • 4 Chiswick High Rd
• **Zizzi** • 231 Chiswick High Rd

Shopping

• **The Cove Spa** • 300 Chiswick High Rd
• **Gail's Bread** • 282 Chiswick High Rd
• **Outsider Tart** • 83 Chiswick High Rd
• **Oxfam Books** • 90 Turnham Green Terrace
• **Wheelers Garden Centre** • Turnham Green Terrace

Stamford Brook

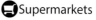

Wedged between Chiswick and Hammersmith, on the surface Stamford Brook may seem like not much more than a tube station and some rather nice, note 'expensive', houses. Brookites, however, know that it's all about that big blue below the A4—The Thames—for a lazy Sunday stroll or long Saturday brunches at **L'Amorosa**. Farther up King Street, **Tosa** serves up some authentic Japanese yakitori while thirsty Brookites head to **The Carpenter's Arms** for oysters and a Guinness in the garden.

 ## Coffee

• **Artisan Coffee** • 372 King St

Nightlife

• **The Raven** • 375 Goldhawk Rd

 ## Restaurants

• **The Carpenter's Arms** • 89 Black Lion Ln
• **L'Amorosa** • 278 King St
• **Saigon Saigon** • 313 King St
• **Tosa** • 332 Kings St

 ## Supermarkets

• **Sainsbury's** • 120 Chiswick High Rd
• **Tesco** • 327 King St

Shopping

• **Thai Smile** • 287 King St

Map 39

Far enough out on the tube to scare the tourists, this area is a haven for locals who want it all on their doorstep. International flavours colour the Goldhawk Road, Ravenscourt Park offers a calm little slice of green while pretty Thames walks must surely conclude with a visit to the city's most picturesque pub, **The Dove**. Furnival Gardens is the spot to watch the annual Oxbridge boat race.

Coffee
• **Caffe Nero** • 1 King St

Nightlife
• **The Dove** • 19 Upper Mall

Post Offices
• **King St** • 168 King St

Restaurants
• **Donde Carlos** • 143 Goldhawk Rd
• **Lowiczanka Polish Cultural Centre** • 238 King St
• **Mahdi** • 215 King St
• **Sagar** • 157 King St

Shopping
• **Bushwacker Wholefoods** • 132 King St
• **Patisserie Sainte-Anne** • 204 King St

Supermarkets
• **Iceland** • 111 King St
• **Tesco** • 327 King St

Map 41 · Hammersmith

Hammersmith

While the shops and pubs on offer along the main drag (King Street) are all pretty drab, Hammersmith has three great venues for the more culturally inclined. **The Apollo** hosts mainstream bands and big-name comedians; **The Lyric** is an affordable way to indulge in some modern theatre, and **The Riverside Studios** offer a satisfying selection of foreign and art house films. London's vegetarians flock to **The Gate**, with its seriously original and inventive menu.

 Cinemas

• **Riverside Studios** • Crisp Rd & Queen Caroline St

 Coffee

• **Starbucks** • 200 Hammersmith Rd

Emergency Rooms

• **Charing Cross Hospital** •
Fulham Palace Rd & St Dunstan's Rd

 Libraries

• **Hammersmith Library** • Shepherds Bush Rd

 Nightlife

• **Brook Green Hotel** • 170 Shepherd's Bush Rd
• **The Distillers** • 64 Fulham Palace Rd
• **Eventim Apollo** • 45 Queen Caroline St
• **The Hampshire Hog** • 227 King St
• **Lyric Hammersmith** • King St

 Post Offices

• **Hammersmith** • 168 King St

 Restaurants

• **The Gate** • 51 Queen Caroline St
• **Rangrez Indian Restaurant** • 32 Fulham Palace Rd

 Supermarkets

• **Tesco** • 180 Shepherd's Bush Rd

Map 41

Map 42 · Barons Court

Barons Court doesn't have a scene as such, but it is elegantly lovely. Ignore North End Road—a fried chicken blot among Edwardian mansions—and instead get lost in Lille Road's antique stores. **Curtains Up** offers intimate theatre in the pub vaults. If you need a change from polished chic, seek the **Colton Arms** for a jug-pint in its cottage style garden.

O Landmarks
• **Empress State Buidling** • Marchbank Rd

Y Nightlife
• **Colton Arms** • 187 Greyhound Rd
• **The Curtains Up** • 28 Comeragh Rd
• **The Fulham Mitre** • 81 Dawes Rd

Post Offices
• **Dawes Road** • 108 Dawes Rd
• **Olympia** • 8 North End Rd

Shopping
• **Curious Science** • 319 Lillie Rd

Supermarkets
• **Co-Op** • 88 N End Rd
• **Iceland** • 290 North End Rd

A lively mix of Aussies, Saffas, rich kids, and sweaty Chelsea fans occupy these neighbourhoods. Fulham Broadway is the focus of the action offering heaving bars and clubs. Earl's Court is slightly more sedate while West Brompton is positively sleepy in comparison. On Brompton Road '60s boho café **The Troubadour** is still a happening spot for live music and a coffee while **Vingt-Quatre** is a 24-hour institution serving fry-ups to clubbers in the early hours.

Cinemas

- **Cineworld Fulham Road** • 142 Fulham Rd
- **Vue Fulham** • Fulham Rd & Cedarne Rd

Coffee

- **Cafe du Coin** • 229 Earls Ct Rd
- **Caffe Nero** • 480 Fulham Rd
- **Caffe Nero** • 174 Fulham Rd
- **Chairs & Coffee** • 512 Fulham Rd
- **Pret A Manger** • Fulham Broadway Retail Centre
- **Starbucks** • 259 Old Brompton Rd
- **The Troubadour** • 263 Old Brompton Rd

O Landmarks

- **Stamford Bridge** • Fulham Rd & Moore Park Rd

Libraries

- **Brompton Library** • 210 Old Brompton Rd
- **Institute of Cancer Research Library** • 237 Fulham Rd

Nightlife

- **Chairs & Coffee** • 512 Fulham Rd
- **The Blackbird** • 209 Earl's Court Rd
- **The King's Head** • 17 Hogarth Rd

Post Offices

- **Earls Court** • 320 Earl's Court Rd

Restaurants

- **Bodean's** • 4 Broadway Chambers
- **Flora Indica** • 242 Old Brompton Rd
- **Harwood Arms** • Walham Grove
- **Vingt Quatre** • 325 Fulham Rd

Shopping

- **Fulham Broadway Centre** • Fulham Rd

Supermarkets

- **Sainsbury's** • Fulham Broadway
- **Tesco** • 459 Fulham Rd
- **Waitrose** • 402 North End Rd

Map 44 · **Chelsea**

Map 44

This area drips old money, 4x4s, and people who own rather large things, like, say, Devon. The only way to do Chelsea is to be seen doing it—and if you're paying all that money at least make it worthwhile. Engage in some (super) star-gazing at **The Bluebird Café**. For a more sedate affair hang out with the locals, property investors 'n all, at local Victorian boozer **The Drayton Arms**.

Emergency Rooms

• **Chelsea and Westminster Hospital** • 369 Fulham Rd

Nightlife

• **Brinkley's** • 47 Hollywood Rd
• **The Drayton Arms** • 153 Old Brompton Rd

Restaurants

• **The Bluebird** • 350 King's Rd
• **Haché** • 329 Fulham Rd

Shopping

• **Cambio de Tercio** • 163 Old Brompton Rd
• **Furniture Cave** • 533 Kings Rd
• **Richer Sounds** • 258 Fulham Rd

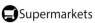
Supermarkets

• **Sainsbury's** • 295 Fulham Rd

Map 45 · **Chelsea (East)**

Chelsea (East)

Chelsea East is what Hollywood thinks all of London is like, full of dapper English chaps and potential princesses. King's Road buzzes as it did when it spawned the Swinging '60s, and foodies are spoiled around Cale Street. For a cheaper and sweeter taste of the area get to **The Hummingbird Bakery** for addictive oh-so-good cupcakes.

Cinemas

• **Everyman Chelsea** • 279 King's Rd

Coffee

• **Caffe Nero** • 66 Old Brompton Rd
• **Starbucks** • 123 King's Rd

Libraries

• **Chelsea Library** • King's Rd

Post Offices

• **Elm Park** • 66 Elm Park Rd

Nightlife

• **The Anglesea Arms** • 15 Selwood Terrace
• **Chelsea Potter** • 119 Kings Rd

Restaurants

• **Le Columbier** • 145 Dovehouse St
• **The Hummingbird Bakery** • 47 Old Brompton Rd
• **Made In Italy** • 249 King's Rd
• **My Old Dutch Pancake House** • 221 King's Rd

Shopping

• **Anthropologie** • 121 King's Rd
• **British Red Cross Chelsea** • 69 Old Church St
• **Nomad Books** • 781 Fulham Rd
• **Sweaty Betty** • 125 King's Rd

Supermarkets

• **Waitrose** • 196 King's Rd

Map 46 · **Sloane Square**

Thurloe Close
Alexander Place
South Terrace
Egerton
Crescent Place
Pelham Street
Road A308
Brompton Road A4
Pont Street B319
Chesham Place
Pavilion Street
Shafto Mews
Pavilion Road
Lennox Gardens Mews
Lennox Gardens
Ovington Gardens
Milner Street
First Street
Walton Street
Donne Place
Ovington Street
Halsey Street
Cadogan Square
Sloane Street A3216
Cadogan Lane
Cadogan Place
Chesham Street
Cadogan Gate
Moore Street
Ovington Square
Clabon Mews
Ellis Street

Richards Place
Denyer Street
Hasker Street
Draycott Avenue
Mossop Street
Rosemoor Street
Halsey Mews
Whitehead's Grove
Draycott Place
Bray Place
Coulson Street
Culford Gardens
Cadogan Gate
Draycott Terrace
Rawlings Street
Cadogan Terrace
Wilbraham Place
Sloane Terrace
Eaton Mews West
Eaton Gate A3216

A

Marlborough Street
Sydney Street
Britten Street
Whitehead's Grove
Cale Street
Astell Street
Danube Street
Godfrey Street
Jubilee Place
Elystan Place
Sprimont Place
Markham Street
Byward Street
Coulson Street
King's Road A3217
Simons Street
Sloane A3217/Cliveden Place
Square

Sloane
Square

Ellis Street
West Eaton Place
Eaton Terrace
Caroline Terrace
Chester Row

Saatchi
Gallery

Duke of York Square

SLOANE
SQUARE

B

Hemus Place
Danvers Street
Riley Street
Shawfield Street
Radnor Walk
Flood Street
Smith Terrace
Woodfall Street
Markham Square
Wellington Square
Royal Avenue
St. Leonard's Terrace
Ormonde Gate
Turks Row
Franklin's Row
Lower Sloane Street
Holbein Mews
Sloane Gardens
Bunhouse Row
Passmore Street
Whittaker Street
St. Michael's
Graham Terrace
Bloomfield Terrace
Pimlico Road
Dove Walk
Ranelagh Grove

Burton's
Court

Burton's
Court

Royal Hospital Road B302

Cheyne Walk
St Loo Avenue
Christchurch Street
Robinson Street
Redesdale Street
Tedworth Gardens
Tedworth Square
Ralston Street
Caversham Street
Chelsea Square
Ormonde Place
Durham Place
Bramerton Street
Paradise Walk
Tite Street
Dilke Street

East Road
West Road

Chelsea Bridge Road A3216
Ebury Bridge Road B11
Ebury Bridge
Grosvenor

Chelsea
Physic
Garden

Chelsea
Embankment Gardens

Chelsea Embankment A3212

Embankment Gardens

Royal Hospital

Ranelagh
Gardens

Chelsea Grounds

River
Thames

| 0.25 mile | 0.25 km |

You've got to love a place that spawns an adjective. If you've never met any 'Sloaney' types and are curious as to why the whole of London gets so riled about them, take a walk along the King's Road and observe. **Peter Jones** stands tall over the square and offers everything you didn't know you wanted. This rather beautiful 'nabe also hosts some bank-breaking eateries, such as **Claude Bosi's**, as well as its fare share of cultural fair—the **Saatchi Gallery** being the finest example.

Coffee

• **Pret A Manger** • 35 King's Rd
• **Starbucks** • 65 Sloane Ave
• **Starbucks** • 123a King's Rd
• **Tomtom Coffee House** • 114 Ebury St

O Landmarks

• **Saatchi Gallery** • Duke of York HQ, King's Rd

✉ Post Offices

• **Royal Hospital Chelsea** • East Rd

Restaurants

• **The Admiral Codrington** • 17 Mossop St
• **Claude Bosi's Oyster Bar** • 81 Fulham Rd
• **The Good Life Eatery** • 59 Sloane Ave
• **Restaurant Gordon Ramsay** • 68 Royal Hospital Rd

Shopping

• **Partridges** • 2 Duke of York Sq
• **Peter Jones** • Sloane Sq
• **Rigby & Peller** • 13 Kings Rd
• **Space NK Apothecary** • 307 King's Rd

🚌 Supermarkets

• **Sainsbury's** • 75 Sloane Ave

Map 47 · **Fulham (West)**

N

1   2

41

42▶

Metropolitan Open Land

Frazier Drive

Church Road
Ball Drive

Wide Centre

King Henry's Road
Colinth Road
Aspenlea Road
Greyhound Road
Gasden Ter
Ellerton Street
Bracket Mews
Kenmyl Road
Titmuss Road
Humbolt Road
Disbrowe Road
Brecon Road

Skenwith Road
Roseday Road
Nella Road
Averill Street
Delorme Street
Audit Close
Bayonne Road
Chaldon Road

Bowfell Road
Wingrave Road
Larnach Road
Lillie Road A3218
Crescent
Perham Road

A
Poley Road
Cillaine Road
Silverton Road
Crabtree Lane
Lillie Road Recreation Ground

Rannoch Road
Hannell Road
Strode Road
Munster Road
Dawe...

Adam Walk
Calbey
Nilton Street
Fulham Cemetery
Bronsart Road
Mablethorpe Road
Rowallan Road

Highspot Road
Woodgate Road
Lydia Street
FULHAM WEST
Allestree Road

Meadowbank Close
Queensmill Road
Kingwood Road
Wayfold Road

Milshot Close
Langthorne Street
Atalanta Street
Brancroft Street
Marne Square

Kenyon Street
Danehurst Str
Wardo Ave

Eternit Walk
Inglethorpe Street
Harbord Street
Childerley Street
Lambrook Terrace
Sotus Str
Ellerby Street
Warfold Cerne
Fulham

Eternit Walk

Craven Cottage Fulham Football Field
PAGE 379
Gresmill Street
Finlay Street
Ellerby Street
A219 Fulham Palace Road
Foothall Lane
Colimb Lane

Barn Elms School Sports Centre
Stevenage Road
Doneraile Street
Doncastle Street
Bishop's Park Avenue
Bishop's Park Road

River Thames

WWT The Wetland Centre

48▶

Bishop's Park

Fulham Palace Meadows Allotment Gardens

Putney Bridge

aders Gardens

Fulham

0.25 mile   0.25 km

This area is an estate agent's wet dream. Leafy, well heeled, on the river, and made for families. Catch the great English game at **Craven Cottage** before making the most of the riverside and grabbing a pint at **The Crabtree Tavern**. Now that you're tipsy, head to **The River Café** where you'll feel less pained shelling out for top-notch, dead-posh grub.

 ## Nightlife

• **The Crabtree Tavern** • Rainville Rd

 ## Restaurants

• **The River Café** • Thames Wharf, Rainville Rd

 ## Post Offices

• **Kenyon Street** • 58 Kenyon St

 ## Supermarkets

• **Sainsbury's** • 179 Fulham Palace Rd

Map 48 · **Fulham**

N

1 2

43

Little

Croston Road

William Cliff...

Estcourt Road

Ethel Road

Haldane Road

Heckfield Place

Barclay Road

Cassidy Road

Dawes Road A3219

Hannel Road

Bronsart Road

Rylston Road

Filmer Road

Salisbury Road

Girondel Road

Bunthowfield Road

Lancaster Court

Darlan Road

A304 Fulham Road

Shottendale Road

Einstein Road

Harbledown Road

FULHAM

Mablethorpe Road

Rosaville Road

Sherbrooke Road

Rostrevor Road

42

Parkville Road

Wheatsheaf Terrace

Ronalian Road

Alestree Road

Munster Road

Orbain Road

St. Olaf's Road

Verona Road

Bloom Park Road

Marville Road

Clonmel Road

Kelvedon Road

Kilmaine Road

Reporton Road

Pegoton Road

Winchendon Road

Linville Road

Parsons Green

Kingwood Road

Wyfold Road

Marrall Square

Danehurst Street

Ward's Avenue

Bishops Road

Vera Road

Rylston Road

Chesilton Road

Redgolds Road

Purser's Cross Road

St. Maur Road

Whittingstall Road

Fulham Road A304

St. Marks Road

Bramber Road

A

Chesilton Road

Sulivan Street

Lambrook Terrace

Gowan Avenue

Fulham Road A304

Mimosa Street

Lettice Street

Doria Road

47

Crookham Road

Dancer Road

49

Fulham Palace Road A219

Kimbell Gardens

Trinity Gardens

Colehill Lane

Horder Road

Burnfoot Avenue

Ringmer Avenue

Waldemar Avenue

Heckfield...

Durrell Road

The Arches

The Mertlan Place

Draycott Mews

B

Egerley Road

Colehill Gardens

Lisor Road

Oxberry Avenue

Dorncliffe Road

Fulham Park Road

Fulham Park Gardens

Landridge Road

Elysium...

New Kings Road A308

Cristowe Road

Elthiron Road

Perrymead Street

Wandsworth Bridge Road

Bettridge Road

Hurlingham Road

Bishop's Park Road

Bishop's Avenue

Moat Gardens

Fulham Road A304

The Drive

Delight Court

Burlington Road

Fulham High Street A219

Rigault Road

Buer Road

Elysium Street

Rostrevor Road

Grimston Road

Ewald Road

Colby Road

Foskett Road

Hurlingham Stadium Pitch

Concurry Road

Bishop's Park

Fulham Palace Meadows Allotment Gardens

Fulham Palace Gardens

Ranelagh Avenue

Napier Avenue

Hurlingham Club Gardens

Mendora Mews

Broomhouse Road

Edenhurst Avenue

Hurlingham Gardens

Putney Bridge Station

Ranelagh Gardens

Prior Bank Gardens

Steeple Close

Church Gate

Gonville Street

Willow Bank

Bridge Avenue

Putney Bridge

Bridge Approach

Putney Bridge Tube Pill Box

Hurlingham Club...

0.25 mile 0.25 km

Fulham

Map 48

This part of town is rather lovely and rather boring in equal measure. Expensive homes belonging to Chelsea FC players sit alongside the often overlooked romantic beauty of Fulham Palace. On the main drag of Fulham High Street is **Hurlingham Books** with its walls stacked high with texts on anything and everything. With not much else going on away from here we suggest contemplating life while staring out at the mighty Thames in Fulham Palace Gardens. When you're done then warm up in their elegant tearoom, **Fulham Palace Cafe**.

 Coffee

• **Local Hero** • 640 Fulham Rd
• **Tinto Coffee** • 411 Fulham Palace Rd

O Landmarks

• **Putney Bridge Tube Pill Box** • Putney Bridge Station

 Libraries

• **Fulham Library** • 598 Fulham Rd

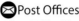 Post Offices

• **Fulham** • 851 Fulham Rd

 Restaurants

• **Fisher's Chips** • 19 Fulham High St
• **Fulham Palace Cafe** • Bishop's Ave
• **Royal China** • 805 Fulham Rd

Shopping

• **Hurlingham Books** • 91 Fulham High St

Map 49 · **Parson's Green**

Parson's Green

Map 49

You know you're in a classy neighbourhood when the kebab house (**Kebab Kid**) gets people travelling across London. This part of town ain't cheap and unless you're looking for a sedate Sunday lunch you'll most likely not find yourself here. If, however, you are looking for a chow down then **The White Horse** (known locally as the 'Sloany Pony') is the place to be, hands down. Otherwise head to charming **Duke On The Green** for a pint in style—they even show the footy!

Coffee

• **Caffe Nero** • 142 Wandsworth Bridge Rd
• **Starbucks** • 44 New Kings Rd

Restaurants

• **Kebab Kid** • 90 New Kings Rd
• **Koji** • 58 New King's Rd

Nightlife

• **Amuse Bouche** • 51 Parsons Green Ln
• **Duke on the Green** • 235 New Kings Rd
• **The White Horse** • 1 Parson's Green Ln

Supermarkets

• **Tesco** • 601 King's Rd

Map 30 · Sands End / Imperial Wharf

Time was, if you asked any Londoner where Sands End is you'd receive a blank look and a bemused 'you wot?' These days the area sees a lot more foot traffic thanks to a newish London Overground stop and the development of Imperial Wharf. Jazz seems to be a major draw to the area with the autumn Jazz Festival and the **606 Club** on Lots Road.

O Landmarks

• **Lots Road Power Station** • 27 Lots Rd

Nightlife

• **606 Club** • 90 Lots Rd

Restaurants

• **Sands End** • 135 Stephendale Rd
• **Yamal Alshem** • 5 The Blvd

Map 51 · **Highgate**

Map 51 · **Highgate**

Highgate Golf Course

Highgate Allotments

Highgate Wood

Storey Road

Yeatman Road

Gleaner Hill Road

North Hill Avenue

North Hill

Sheldon

Denewood Road

Avenue

Stormont Road

View Road

View Road

View Close

Willoughby

Church Road

Archway Road A1

Muswell Hill Road

Sunny

Parkview Mews

A

Bishopswood Road

Broadlands Road

Grange Road

B519

Kingsley

Talbot Road

Bishops Road

Pond

B550

Wood Lane

Hampstead Lane B519

HIGHGATE

Broadlands

Hillcrest

Southwood Lane

The Park

The Park

Hillside Gdns

Highgate

☒ ⊖

Highgate

52 ▶

Hampstead Heath

PAGE 338

◀ **58**

Hampstead Lane B519

Bishops Close

Grimshaw Close

Castle Yd B519

B550

Southwood Lane

Jacksons Lane

Southwood

Highgate Avenue

Shepherds

Shepherds Close

Archway Road A1

North Grove

North Road B519

Southwood Lane

Somerset Gdns

Kingsley Place

Lawn Road

Northwo

Fitzroy Park

The Grove

Fitzroy Park

High Trad Grove

The Grove

Cholmeley

Crescent

Cholmeley

Causton Road

Wembur Road

The Headon

West Hill

South Grove

Pond Square

Castle Ms

Bacon La

Townsend Yd

Highgate

Broadbent Close

Duke's Head Yd

Park lands

Park lands

B

West Hill

Wrhamburys Lane

Swains Lane

Highgate

Bisham Gardens

High Street

Cholmeley Park

Winchester Place

Winchester Rd

Hornsey Gardens

The Kiln Ln

Fitzroy Close

Highgate West Hill

Merton Lane

Holly Lodge Gdns

Grant

Highgate Cemetery

○

Highgate Cemetery

PAGE 340

Cromwell Avenue

Cromwell Place

Hornsey S

Hornsey

Hazellville Road

Hillway

DARTMOUTH PARK

Highgate Cemetery

Waterlow Park

Hornsey Lane

Highgate Hill B519

Cromwell Avenue

Fitzwarren

Oakeshott

Avenue

Makepeace

Swains Lane

59 ▼

Karl Marx's Grave

○

Highgate Cemetery

Waterlow Road

Holbrook Close

Despard Road

Gerdon Close

Langbourne

Avenue

St. Anne's Cl

| 0.25 mile | 0.25 km |

Highgate

Map 51

On the cusp of north London you'll find the little suburban gem that is Highgate. Hemmed in by parks, woods and a golf course, the area is an escapist paradise from the chaos of the city, and its well-heeled residents' plush fur is surprisingly—and pleasantly—soft to the touch.

Coffee

• **Caffe Nero** • 62 Highgate High St
• **Costa** • 66 Highgate High St

O Landmarks

• **Highgate Cemetery** • 1 Swain's Ln
• **Karl Marx's Grave** • Highgate Cemetry

🍸 Nightlife

• **The Angel Inn** • 37 Highgate High St
• **The Boogaloo** • 312 Archway Rd
• **The Flask** • 77 Highgate West Hill
• **Prince Of Wales** • 53 Highgate High St
• **The Woodman** • 414 Archway Rd
• **The Wrestlers** • 98 North Rd

Post Offices

• **Highgate Near Station** • 361 Archway Rd

🍴 Restaurants

• **The Bull** • 13 North Hill Ave
• **The Red Lion & Sun** • 25 North Rd

🛍 Shopping

• **Highgate Butchers** • 76 Highgate High St
• **Hops N Pops** • 389 Archway Rd
• **Mind** • 329 Archway Rd
• **Oxfam** • 47 Highgate High St

Map 52 · **Archway (North)**

Something unexpected is happening here. Designer boutiques keep popping up; fashion labels we've never even heard of—cafés so fashionably quirky they should really be in Shoreditch. But real change takes time and at night this becomes even more obvious.

O Landmarks

• **Parkland Walk Nature Reserve** • Parkland Walk
• **Suicide Bridge** • Hornsey Ln & Archway Rd

Restaurants

• **Bombay Rickshaw** • 172 Archway Rd

Shopping

• **Pax Guns** • 166 Archway Rd

Map 53 · **Crouch End**

CROUCH END

STROUD GREEN

Abandoned Warehouse

Coolhurst Lawn Tennis & Squash Rackets Club

Shepherd's Hill Allotments

Elthorne Park

0.25 mile

0.25 km

Crouch End

Map 53

Crouch End gets a bit of a bad rap. It's boring, people say. Just prams and middle-class media types. But, you know, it could be a lot worse. It's safe, with plenty of decent pubs (**The King's Head**), eateries (**Banners**) and a great record shop (**Flashback**). It might be low on the hipster scale, but for plain ol' good livin' it ticks all the boxes.

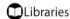 Landmarks
• **Abandoned Warehouse** •
Parkland Walk & Crouch End Hill

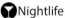 Libraries
• **Highgate Library** • 1 Shepherds Hill
• **Hornsey Library** • Haringey Park

Nightlife
• **The King's Head** • 2 Crouch End Hill
• **The Queens Pub & Dining Rooms** •
26 Broadway Parade
• **Stapleton Tavern** • 2 Crouch Hill

Post Offices
• **Crouch End** • 28 Topsfield Parade

Restaurants
• **Banners** • 21 Park Rd
• **Bistro Aix** • 54 Topsfield Parade
• **Jai Krishna** • 161 Stroud Green Rd
• **The King's Head** • 2 Crouch End Hill
• **Wow Simply Japanese** • 18 Crouch End Hill

Shopping
• **Flashback** • 26 Topsfield Parade
• **Haelen Centre** • 41 The Broadway
• **Organic Food** • 188 Stroud Green Rd
• **Soup Dragon** • 27 Topsfield Parade
• **Walter Purkis And Sons** • 17 The Broadway

Map 54 · **Hornsey**

N

1 **2**

Middle Lane
Middle Lane
Miles Walk
Lightfoot Road
Greig Close
Mulberry Close
Elmfield
Roseberry Gardens
Hermiston Avenue
Rokesly Avenue
Hillrid
Harold Road
Glebe Road
Ferrestone Road
Ribblesdale Road
Gisburn Road
Denmark Road

Wightman Road B138
Hampden Road

A
Tottenham Lane A103
Church Lane A103
Tottenham Lane

Tottenham Lane A103
Elmer
Montague Rd
Oakley Gardens
Rathcoole Avenue
Harvey Road
Cranford Way

Fairfield Gardens
Fairfield Road
Aubrey Road
Sloane Ms
Ferme Park Road
Nelson Road
Inderwick Road
Sports Pitch
Spencer Road
Rathcoole Gardens
Rathcoole Gardens
Cranford Way

HORNSEY VALE
HARRINGAY

Weston Park
Weston Park

Bourne Road
Drylands Road
Gladwell Road
Landrock Road
Inderwick Road
Uplands Road
Cranford Way
Cranford Way

◀53
55▶

Cecile Park
Wennersley Road
Mayfield Road
Denton Road

Elm Grove
Dashwood Road
Stationers Park
Chettle Court

Ridge Road
Highbank Way

B
Mount View Road
Mount View Road
Mount View Road

STROUD GREEN
Ferme Park Road
Granville Road
Oakfield Road
Harringay
Railway Approach

Ossian Road
Darren Close
Quernmore Road
Albany Road
Addington Road
Quernmore Road
Elmr Road
Hall Road
Burgoyne

The Grove
Ossian Mews
Stapleton Hall Road

62
▼

Crescent
Stapleton Hall Road
Lancaster Road
Oakfield Road
Dagmar Road
Connaught Road

Wightman Road B138

Lothair Road South
Lothair
Alroy Road
Endymion

0.25 mile	0.25 km

Hornsey

Unless you live in Hornsey, if you're in Hornsey, your bus has probably broken down. In this dystopian residential area you'll be lucky to find a tuft of grass let alone a shop. A modicum of life exist up at Tottenham Lane, but that's pretty much Crouch End. **Ridge Cafe** is worth a stop for a cup of coffee and you can watch sport at the unpretentious **McCafferty's**.

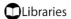
Libraries
• **Stroud Green Library** • Quermore Rd

Nightlife
• **McCafferty's Crouch End** • 128 Tottenham Ln

Restaurants
• **Ridge Cafe** • 97 Tottenham Ln
• **Sumak** • 141 Tottenham Ln

Shopping
• **Micycle N4** • 8 Ferme Park Rd

Map 54

Map 55 · Harringay

1   **2**

Hampden Road

Lausanne Road

Frobisher Road

Falkland Road

Wightman Road B138

Falkland

Fairfax Road

Effingham Road

Admiral Place

Beresford Road

◄54

A

Allison Road

HARRINGAY

Hewitt Road

Seymour Road

Warham Road

St Peters Mews

Salisbury Road

B152

Pemberton Road

Kimberley Gardens

Mattison Road

Chesterfield Road

Duckett Road

Wightman Road

Harringay

Railway App

◄62

B138

Cavendish Road

Duckett Ms

A105

Roseberry

Burgoyne Road

Rutland Gardens

Umfreville Rd

Railway Fields Nature Reserve

Green Lanes

Warwick Gardens

Afterbury Rd
Oxford Rds

Woollaston Rd

Railway Fields

B

Alroy Road

Lothair Road S

Cottingley Road

Dancred Road

Venetia Road

Sybil Mews

Lothair Road North

Doncaster Gdns

Grafton Gardens

Harringay Green Lanes

B138

B150

Endymion Road

Wiltshire Gdns

American Gardens

Urban Mews

Finsbury Park Avenue

Woodview Close

Vale Terrace

Surrey Gardens

Hermitage Road

Vale Gro

Endymion Road

Finsbury Park

PAGE 334

Green Lanes A105

Eade Road

Vale Road

Hermitage Road

Rowley Gardens

Linkway

Eade Road

63 ▼

Woodberry Grove

Manor House

0.25 mile   0.25 km

Seven Sisters Road   A503

Harringay

Map 55

Green Lanes was once an endless strip of restaurants which although good, meant that the only dinner option was Turkish. The last few years have seen so many new openings, it's becoming a bit (dare we say it?) hip. The spirit of the place remains resolutely the same though and Turkish grocer **Yasar Halim** stands proud in the middle of it all. Get ribs for dinner at **Autograf** and indulge in some vodka. Or if beer's more your thing, head to **Brouhaha**. Long-standing favourite, **The Salisbury**, is a failsafe choice for a good night and if you need your organic groceries, **Beans and Barley** will keep you happy.

Coffee

• **Beans and Barley** • 595 Green Lanes
• **N4 Eatery** • 351 Green Lanes

O Landmarks

• **Railway Fields Nature Reserve** • 381 Green Lanes

Nightlife

• **Brouhaha** • 501 Green Lanes
• **The Beaconsfield** • 359 Green Lanes
• **Jam In A Jar** • 599 Green Lanes
• **The Salisbury** • 1 Grand Parade, Green Lanes

Post Offices

• **Harringay** • 37 Grand Parade

Restaurants

• **Autograf** • 488 W Green Rd
• **Bun & Bar** • 553 Green Lanes
• **Devran** • 485 Green Lanes
• **Gökyüzü** • 26 Grand Parade
• **Hala** • 29 Grand Parade

Shopping

• **Beans and Barley** • 595 Green Lanes
• **Harringay Local Stores** • 581 Green Lanes
• **Yasar Halim** • 491 Green Lanes

Supermarkets

• **Sainsbury's** • 4 Williamson Rd

Map 56 · **Hampstead Village**

Templewood Road

West Heath

North End Way

Spaniards Road

Templewood Avenue

Sligo... Road

Grange

Redington Road

Firecrest Dr

Birchwood Drive

Redington Gardens

PAGE 338

Heath Drive

Heath Brow

Redington Gardens

Heath Drive

Whitestone Walk

Heysham Lane

East Heath Road

Hampstead Heath

A

Spedan Close

Whitestone Lane

Oak Hill Park

Branch Hill

Upper Terrace

Lower Terrace

Judges Wlk

Windmill Hill

Hampstead Heath

Kingswell Gardens

East Heath Road

Oak Hill Way

Terrace

Admiral's

Vale of Health

Oak Hill Park Ms

Tower

Kemplay's Walk

Upper Terrace

Hampstead Grove

Heath Street

Oak Hill

Hampstead Observatory

Frognal Rise

Windmill Hill

Holford Road

Frognal

Mount Vernon

Hampstead Grove

Wind mill Hill

The Mount Sq

The Mount

Hampstead Sq

Cannon Place

57

Church Row

Frognal

Holly Bush Hill

Holly Walk

Holly Mount

Elm Row

New End

Grove

Cannon Lane

Mount

Squire's

Well Road

Cannon Lane

Church Row

Holly

Bush Vale

Hampstead

A502 Heath Street

Hampstead

Streatley Place

New End Square

White Bear Place

Well Road

Frognal Way

Ellerdale Road

Oriel Court

Church Row

A502 Heath Street

Rosslyn Hill A502

GilSpur Yd

Back Lane

Boad's Ms

Flask Walk

Well Walk

Christchurch Hill

Well Walk

Gainsborough Gardens

TC (Private)

Perrin's Walk

Ellerdale Close

Perrins Lane

Bird in Hand Yd

Gardnor Rd

Flask Walk

B511

Prince Arthur Ms

Spencer Walk

B

Ellerdale Road

Fitzjohn's Avenue

Prince Arthur Road

Gayton Road

Gayton Road

Crescent

Willow Road

Heath Side

Ankwright Road

Netherhall Gardens

Martyr's Yd

Hampstead High Street

Willoughby Road

Denning Road

Christchurch Hill

Vale of Health

Fitzjohn's Avenue

Rosslyn Hill A502

Greenhill

Vane Close

Vine Close

Mulberry Close

Pilgrim's Place

Kemplay Road

Carlingford Road

Willow

B511

Lyndhurst Ter

Thurlow Road

Shepherds Walk

Pilgrim's Lane

Pilgrim's Lane

Keats Grove

Fitzjohn's Avenue

Road

Eldon Grove

Tower

67

Downshire Hill

Willow

Road

Keats Grove

Lyndhurst Road

0.25 mile		0.25 km

PN
(Hamp...)

Map 56

Sure, leafy Hampstead Village defines posh, but there is still some fun to be had. Head to Flask Walk for cute and eccentric local shops. The **Duke of Hamilton** is as good a pub you're likely to find anywhere.

Cinemas

• **Everyman Cinema Club** • 5 Hollybush Vale

Coffee

• **Caffe Nero** • 1 Hampstead High St
• **Ginger & White** • 4 Perrin's Ct

O Landmarks

• **Hampstead Observatory** •
  Lower Terrace & Hampstead Grove

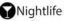Nightlife

• **The Duke of Hamilton** • 23 New End
• **The Flask** • 14 Flask Walk
• **The Freemasons Arms** • 32 Downshire Hill
• **Holly Bush** • 22 Holly Mount
• **The Horseshoe** • 28 Heath Rd

Restaurants

• **La Creperie De Hampstead** • 77 Hampstead High St
• **The Louis Patisserie** • 32 Heath St

Shopping

• **Happy Returns** • 36 Rosslyn Hill
• **Keith Fawkes** • 1 Flask Walk
• **Mystical Fairies** • 12 Flask Walk

Map 57 · **Hampstead Heath**

Vale of Health

1

2

Willow Road

Willow Road

Cannon Place

Hampstead Grove

Pilgrims Place

Kemplay Road

Pilgrim's Lane

Pilgrim's Lane

HAMPSTEAD

Downshire Hill

Hampstead Ponds

Rosslyn Hill A502

Church Row

Downshire Hill

Willow Road

Keats Grove

Hampstead Ponds

Parliament Hill

A

Gardens

Keats Grove

Heath Hurst Road

Park Walk

South Hill Park

South Hill Park

Parliament Hill

Hampstead Heath
PAGE
338

Keats' House

Mayon Mews

South End

South End Green

St. Crispins Close

Parliament Hill

The Old Orchard

Nassington Road

Tanza Road

Belsize Court

Belsize Lane

Lane

◀**56**

Pond Street B518

South End Close

Constantine Road B518

Constantine Road

Children's Playground & Paddling Pool

Rowland Hill

Byron Mews

Flag Cressy

Agincourt Road

Constantine Road

Mackeson Road

Lisburne Road

Parliament Hill Athletics Track

Orman Road

Street

Fleet Road B518

Fleet Road

Fleet Road B518

Roderick Road

Shirlock Road

Courthouse Road

Savernake Road

Adventure Playground

Aspern Grove

Aspern Grove

Wood Wlk

Lawn Road

Estelle Road

Bona Road

Haverstock Hill A502

Aspern Gro

Menlo Place

Aspern Gro

Tennis Court

Lawn Road

Garnett Road

Mansfield Road B518

Mansfield Road

Glenloch Road

Belsize Grove

Belsize Park

Downside Cres

Lawn Road Flats

Park Road

Dunboyne Rd

Kingsford Street

Rochford Street

Southampton Road B517

Lismore Circus

Elaine Grove

Oak Village

Oak Village

Grafton Road

Barrington Close

Kiln Place

B

Antrim Grove

Haverstock Hill A502

◀**67**

Upper Park Road

Tasker Road

Parkhill Walk

Lamble Street

Vicars Road

Grafton Road

◀**58**

Antrim Road

Mews

Fountain

Parkhill Road

Southampton Road

Quadrant Grove

Haverstock Road

Wellesley Road

Kiln Place

GOSP

Elizabeth Mews

Englands Lane

Steeles Mews North

Eton Gardens

BELSIZE PARK

Malden Road B517

Grafton Terrace

Wellington Road

Grafton Road

Dale Rd

Cress Road

OAK

Steeles Road

Steeles Mews South

Provost Road

Maitland Park Villas

Herbert St

Malden Road B517

Gilden Road

Ashdown Cres

Wellington Road

Grafton Road

Cliff Road

Menu Chase

GOSPEL OAK

Kentish Town City Farm

Steeles Road

Mansfield Park

St. Thomas's Gardens

Grafton Road

Queen's Crescent

▼**71**

72▶

Woodyard

Aspen Place

Arctic St

0.25 mile

0.25 km

Hampstead Heath

Map 57

Believed to be the inspiration for CS Lewis's Narnia, Hampstead Heath was absorbed into London proper during the Victorian era but still feels more like one of the Home Counties. With the exception of the blight on the landscape that is the **Royal Free Hospital**, the area is charming with boutique shops and restaurants on the South End Road, which cater to a refined and heavy-walleted crowd.

 Coffee

• **Starbucks** • 5 South End Rd

 Emergency Rooms

• **Royal Free Hospital** • Pond St & Fleet Rd

O **Landmarks**

• **John Keats House** • 10 Keats Grove
• **Lawn Road Flats** • Lawn Rd & Garnett Rd

 Libraries

• **Heath Library** • Keats Grove

 Nightlife

• **The Garden Gate** • 14 S End Rd
• **Roebuck** • 15 Pond St

 Restaurants

• **Mimo La Buffala** • 45 South End Rd
• **Paradise** • 49 South End Rd
• **Polly's** • 55 South End Rd
• **The Roebuck** • 15 Pond St

 Shopping

Daunt Books • 51 South End Rd
• **Giocobazzi's Delicatessen** • 150 Fleet Rd

Map 58 • Parliament Hill / Dartmouth Park

1

2

Pk

West

Holly Lodge Gdns

West Hill

Rd

Grove

Highgate West Hill

Highgate
Cemetery

HIGHGATE

Oakeshott

Hillway

Fitzroy Park

Millfield Place

Avenue

Makepeace

51▶

Millfield Lane

Langbourne

Avenue

Avenue

Highgate West

Swains Lane

Highgate
Cemetery

West Hill Court

Brookfield

Parliament Hill

St. Anne's
Close

Hillway

Bromwich Avenue

Chester

Raydon

Rd

Church Walk

Swains

Lane

St. Albans Road

St. Albans Road

Road

Bertram
Street
Winscombe
Street

Hampstead
Heath

**PAGE
338**

Highgate Road

Brookfield Park

Kingswear Road

Croft down

Bramble

Bramshill

Parliament
Hill Fields
Athletics Track

Croftdown

Road

**DARTMOUTH
PARK**

Dartmouth
Park Avenue

Dartmouth

Adventure
Playground

Woodsome

Road

Maiden

Dartmouth Park Hill

Savernake Road

Rona Road

Estelle Road

◀57

Lissenden

Grove

Grove Ter

Grove Terrace

Laurier Road

York Rise

Laurier Road

Cathcart

Gardens

Road

Dartmouth Park Road

Lissenden Gdns

Glenhurst Avenue

Dartmouth

Park

Road

Bellgate
Mews

Road

B

Mansfield Road

B518

Gordon House Road

B518

Chetwynd

Twisden Road

Spencer Rise

Wyndham Road

Elaine

Grove

Julia

Lamble

Street

Wesleyan
Place

Churchill Road

Park Hill

Junction

Barrington
Ct

Grafton Rd

Kiln
Place

Meru Cl

Highgate Road

**GOSPEL
OAK**

Ingestre

Road

59▶

Hemingway Close

Oak Village

Carrol Close

B518

Burghley Road

Fur

Little

Dale
Road
Cress

Kentish
Town City
Farm

72

Sanderson
Close

Lady Somerset Road

Road

Oakford Road

A400
East Rd

Bracknock Road A5200

Southcote Rd

Tufnell
Park

Weddington Road

Burghley

Carker

Evans

Barnby

Street

Highgate

Rd

Fortess Road

0.25 mile

0.25 km

An area you stumble upon by accident, on your way somewhere else, probably Hampstead Heath or Highgate Cemetery. Then you realize how nice it is. Maybe you should try the little restaurants? Soon you find yourself having pizza at **Al Parco** every week and trekking all across London just to find out what new ales they're serving at **The Southampton Arms**. You could live here. You really could.

Nightlife

- **The Southampton Arms** • 139 Highgate Rd

Restaurants

- **Al Parco** • 2 Highgate West Hill
- **Bistro Laz** • 1 Highgate West Hill
- **Kalendar** • 15 Swains Ln
- **Lalibela** • 137 Fortess Rd

Tufnell Park

Map 59

Surrounded by the rougher Archway, Kentish Town, and Holloway and immortalised by Simon Pegg in cult comedies *Spaced* and *Shaun of the Dead*, unassuming Tufnell Park has been quietly fashionable for years. Unwind with a book and a coffee at **Rustique**. **The Dome** hosts everything from the latest cutting-edge electronica to seasoned indie rock acts.

Emergency Rooms
• **Whittington Hospital** •
  Magdala Ave & Dartmouth Park Hill

Libraries
• **Highgate Library** • Chester Rd

Nightlife
• **Aces And Eights Saloon Bar** • 156 Fortess Rd
• **Boston Arms** • 178 Junction Rd
• **The Dome** • 178 Junction Rd
• **The Lord Palmerston** • 33 Dartmouth Park Hill
• **Siorai Bar** • 114 Junction Rd

Restaurants
• **Rustique Cafe** • 142 Fortess Rd
• **The Spice** • 161 Fortess Rd

Shopping
• **North London Adoption Centre** • 135 Junction Rd

Map 60 · **Archway**

N

1 **2**

Cromartie Road

Highgate Hill B519

Holbrook Close

Waterlow Road

Despard Road

Gordon Close

Salisbury Walk

Cheverton Road

Pilgrims Way

Harberton Road

Cardinals Way

Beaumont Rise

Sunnyside Road

Cromwell Road

Rise A103

Cressida Road

Parolles Road

Bickerton Road

Bredgar Road

Miranda Road

St Johns Way

Hillside Park

Elthorne Park

Duncombe Road

Partington Close

Westacott Close

Beachcroft Way

51

52

Whittington's Cat
Dick

Bank's Hitchhiking
Charles Manson

Toll House

Archway Mall

Junction Road A400

Archway Rd A1

Archway Mews

Fairbridge Road

Sussex Way

Old Forge Road

Marlborough Rd

Landseer Road

53

Calve Grove

Buxton Road

Mowatt Close

Courtauld Rd

Fairbridge Road

Jutland Close

Porter Square

Hornsey Road A103

A

St Johns Way

Grovedale Road

Giesbach Road

Elthorne Road

Ashbrook Road

Schofield Way

Routledge Ct

Zoffany Street

B

St Johns Villas

Junction Road A400

Windermere Road

Wittey Road

Brookside Road

St Johns Mews

Sandalls Road

Grim Tram Race

Holloway Road A400

St Johns Grove

Pemberton Gardens

Pemberton Terrace

Francis Place

Morney Road

59

**UPPER
HOLLOWAY**

Wedmore Gardens

Hampton Road

Marlborough Yd

Marlborough Road

Davenant Road

Fortnam Road

Pomoja Lane

Cornwallis Square

Cornwallis Square

Bavaria Road

Ringmer Gardens

Sussex Way

Kingsdown Road

Kingsdown Road

Whewell Road

Ramsay Road

Sussex Close

Mildord Road

Station Road

Station Road

Whittington Park

Rupert Road

Rupert Road

Beaumont Mews

Foxham Gardens

Foxham Gardens

Beversbrook Road

Wedmore Street

Alexander Road

Tollington

Ingleby Road

61

Tufnell Park Playing Fields

Campdale Road

Dalmeny Rd

Tytherton Road

Salterton Rd

Tavistock Terrace

Fairmead Road

Manor Gardens

Windsor Road

Mercers Road

Mercers Road

**TUFNELL
PARK**

St Georges Avenue

Archibald Road

Carleton Road

Carleton Road

Tufnell Park Road

Tufnell Park Road

Hercules Street

Hercules Place

Hertslet Road

Holloway Road A1

Sussex Way

Fairbridge Road

Seven Sisters Road A503

Mayton St

73

0.25 mile   0.25 km

Map 60

As grey and gritty as ever, Archway could really do with a fresh lick of paint. At night, there are enough old man boozers to keep you busy, but bear in mind, nicer places are only a short bus ride away.

Coffee

• **Cafe Metro** • 4 Junction Rd

O Landmarks

• **Dick Whittington's Cat** • 89 Highgate Hill

Libraries

• **Archway Library** • 23 Highgate Hill

Nightlife

• **Mother Red Cap** • 665 Holloway Rd

Restaurants

• **500 Restaurant** • 782 Holloway Rd
• **Il Mio Mosaic** • 24 Junction Rd
• **Nid Ting** • 533 Holloway Rd
• **St Johns Tavern** • 91 Junction Rd

Shopping

• **Second Chance** • 7 St John's Way

Supermarkets

• **Co-Op** • 11 Junction Rd
• **Sainsbury's** • 643 Holloway Rd

Holloway (North)

Map 61

The borough of Islington, in which North Holloway sits, is supposed to be either a byword for liberal middle-class cosiness or else grim inner-city deprivation, depending on who you talk to. This bit has neither, just lots of dull grey streets. Down on Holloway Road, **El Molino** is a great place for tapas.

Coffee
• **Caffe Nero** • 400 Holloway Rd

Cinemas
• **Odeon Holloway** • 419 Holloway Rd

Libraries
• **North Library** • Manor Gardens

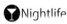## Nightlife
• **The Owl and Hitchhiker** • 471 Holloway Rd
• **The Swimmer** • 13 Eburne Rd

Restaurants
• **El Molino** • 379 Holloway Rd
• **The Landseer** • 37 Landseer Rd
• **North Nineteen** • 194 Sussex Wy

Shopping
• **Holloway Car Boot** •
  Opposite Odeon Holloway Cinema, Holloway Rd

Supermarkets
• **Iceland** • 442 Holloway Rd

Map 62 · **Finsbury Park**

Finsbury Park used to be somewhere you passed through rather than lingered but with Stroud Green Road slowly being populated with numerous eating and drinking options and £5 million invested in tarting up the park, it really isn't that bad.

Coffee
- **Boulangerie Bon Matin** • 178 Tollington Park
- **The Deli at 80** • 80 Stroud Green Rd

O Landmarks
- **North London Central Mosque (Finsbury Park)** • 7 St Thomas's Rd

Libraries
- **N4 Library** • 26 Blackstock Rd

Nightlife
- **The Faltering Fullback** • 19 Perth Rd
- **WB Yeats** • 20 Fonthill Rd

Post Offices
- **Stroud Green Rd** • 97 Stroud Green Rd

Restaurants
- **Girasole** • 150 Seven Sisters Rd
- **Hana Sushi** • 150 Seven Sisters Rd
- **Le Rif** • 172 Seven Sisters Rd
- **Lulu's Caribbean Cuisine** • 84 Stroud Green Rd
- **Osteria Tufo** • 67 Fonthill Rd
- **Petek** • 96 Stroud Green Rd

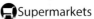
Shopping
- **The Deli at 80** • 80 Stroud Green Rd
- **The Happening Bagel Bakery** • 284 Seven Sisters Rd

Supermarkets
- **Tesco** • 105 Stroud Green Rd

Map 63 · **Manor House**

Manor House

Map 63

Don't hang out near the 'scummy round the edges' station as it can get pretty gruesome at night. You might chance upon a warehouse party round here, but walk south, dodge the rats around the reservoir, admire the faux turrets of **The Castle Climbing Centre**, and head to the **New River Café** for great fry-ups with views over the leafy oasis of Clissold Park.

Coffee

• **Boulangerie Bon Matin** • 178 Tollington Park
• **Fink's Salt & Sweet** • 70 Mountgrove Rd
• **Simply Organique** • 316 Green Lanes

O Landmarks

• **The Castle Climbing Centre** •
Green Lanes & Lordship Park

Libraries

• **Woodberry Down Library** • 440 7 Sisters Rd

Nightlife

• **The Brownswood Park Tavern** • 271 Green Lanes

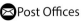

Post Offices

• **Woodberry Grove** • 107 Woodberry Grove

Restaurants

• **Fink's Salt & Sweet** • 70 Mountgrove Rd
• **New River Café** • 271 Stoke Newington Church St

Shopping

• **Bennet & Brown** • 142 Lea Bridge Rd
• **Sargent & Co.** • 74 Mountgrove Rd
• **Simply Organique** • 316 Green Lanes
• **Sylvanian Families** • 68 Mountgrove Rd

Map 64 · **Stoke Newington**

Stoke Newington

The richer cousin of Dalston and the poorer cousin of Islington, Stoke Newington has an inferiority complex-cum-swagger which explains why 90% of its inhabitants are creative types. The curvy Church Street is the port of call with its boutique shops (**Metal Crumble**) and aptly Nietzsche stacked bookshops. Great beer and atmosphere (**The Shakespeare**), curry (**Rasa N16**), Sunday roast (**Rose and Crown**), and check out the butterflies and bats at Park Cemetery.

O Landmarks

- **Newington Green Church** • 39 Newington Green

Libraries

- **Stoke Newington Library** • 184 Stoke Newington Church St

Nightlife

- **The Auld Shillelagh** • 105 Stoke Newington Church St
- **The Dalston Jazz Bar** • 4 Bradbury St
- **Londesborough** • 36 Barbauld Rd
- **Mascara Bar** • 72 Stamford Hill
- **Rose and Crown** • 199 Stoke Newington Church St
- **Ryan's Bar** • 181 Stoke Newington Church St
- **Ruby's** • 76 Stoke Newington Rd
- **The Shakespeare** • 57 Allen Rd
- **White Hart** • 69 Stoke Newington High St

Post Offices

- **Church Street** • 170 Stoke Newington Church St
- **Stoke Newington** • 150 Stoke Newington High St

Restaurants

- **Anglo Asian** • 60 Stoke Newington Church St
- **Blue Legume** • 101 Stoke Newington Church St
- **Rasa N16** • 55 Stoke Newington Church St
- **Sariyer Balik** • 56 Green Lanes
- **Yum Yum** • 187 Stoke Newington High St

Shopping

- **Ark** • 161 Stoke Newington Rd
- **The Beaucatcher Salon** • 44 Stoke Newington Church St
- **Belle Epoque Patisserie** • 37 Newington Green
- **Bridgewood & Neitzert** • 146 Stoke Newington Church St
- **Church Street Bookshop** • 142 Stoke Newington Church St
- **Metal Crumble** • 13 Stoke Newington Church St
- **Mind** • 11 Stoke Newington Church St
- **Of Cabbages & Kings** • 127 Stoke Newington High St
- **Ribbons and Taylor** • 157 Stoke Newington Church St
- **S'graffiti** • 172 Stoke Newington Church St
- **Sacred Art** • 148 Albion Rd
- **The Spence Bakery** • 161 Stoke Newington Church St
- **Stoke Newington Farmers Market** • Stoke Newington Church St & Stoke Newington High St

Supermarkets

- **Whole Foods Market** • 32 Stoke Newington Church St
- **Iceland** • 17 Green Lanes

139

Map 65 · **West Hampstead**

Hampstead's ugly sister, West Hampstead is a leafy suburb that has absorbed some of Kilburn's grittiness. Young urban nomads make up much of the population, as rent is moderate by London standards.

Coffee

- **Costa** • 203 W End Ln
- **Starbucks** • 201 W End Ln

Libraries

- **West Hampstead Library** • Dennington Park Rd

Nightlife

- **The Black Lion** • 274 Kilburn High Rd
- **The Czech and Slovak Bar** • 74 West End Ln

Restaurants

- **Kaipiras by Barraco** • 10 Kingsgate Pl
- **Small & Beautiful** • 351 Kilburn High Rd

Supermarkets

- **Sainsbury's** • 88 Kilburn High Rd
- **Sainsbury's** • 377 Kilburn High Rd

Map 66 · Finchley Road / Swiss Cottage

Mill Lane

West Cottages

West End Lane

Frognal

Frognal

Oak Hill Park Ms

Mount Vernon

Church Row

Holly Bush Hill Holly Wk Mt

Hampstead

Ellerdale Road

Oriel Court Perrins Wlk Perrins Ct Perrins La

Church Street

Cannon Hill

Lyncroft Gardens

Greencroft Gardens

Chesterford Gardens

Frognal Way

A41

Inglewood Road

Holmdale Road

Sumatra Road

Narcissus Road

Brook Rd

Dennington Park

Kingdon Road

B510

West End Lane

Fawley Road

Honeybourne Road

Frognal Lane

West End Lane

Langland Gardens

Frognal Close

Prince Arthur Road

Ellerdale

A

Dresden Rd Sndn Wd

Kingston Cl Mistletoe Cross

Lymington Road

Crediton Hill

Cumberland Lawn Tennis Club

Alvanley Gardens

Lindfield Gardens

Frognal

Fitzjohn's Avenue

B511

Hampstead Heath

West End Lane

B520

Blackburn Road

West Hampstead

Lymington Road

Hampstead Cricket Club

Crown Doul Ion Ms

Mint Ms Wlk Spode Wlk Wcr Ms

Bes Ms

Wcr Cl

Arkwright Road

WEST HAMPSTEAD

Netherhall Gardens

Lyndhurst Road

West Hmpstd Cl

◄ 65

Lithos Road

Rosemont Road

Frognal

Netherhall Way

Frognal Court

Netherhall Gardens

B511 Fitzjohn's Avenue

Wedderburn Rd

Lyndhurst

Broadhurst Gardens

Fairhazel Gardens

Broadhurst Close

Canfield Gardens

Frognal

Nutley Terrace

Gardens

Fitzjohn's Avenue

Belsize

Berlin Mews

Dobson Mews

Bel Pk Ms

Court

Prncess Ms

◄ 67 ►

Compayne Gardens

Canfield Gardens

Canfield Gardens

Finchley Road

Bump er Close

Netherhall Gardens

Maresfield Gardens

Dalham

Belsize Lane

Burdett Ms

Bel Court

Lyndhurst

Greencroft Gardens

SOUTH HAMPSTEAD

Greencroft Gardens

Finchley Road A41

Maresfield Gardens

College Crescent

Belsize Park

Belsize Park

Becos Square

Becos Square Bel

B

Aberdare Gardens

Goldhurst Terrace

Fairhazel Gardens

Marston Cl

Naseby

Belsize Lane

Belsize Park

Lancaster Grove

Lancaster Drive

Goldhurst Terrace

◄ 68

Coleridge Gardens

Fairfax Place

Fairfax Road

Priory Cl

Harben

Buckland Crescent

Adamson Road

Crossfield Road

Strathray Gdns

Belsize Road

B509

Belsize Rd Hilgrove Rd

Belsize Road

Dobson Close

Finchley Road

College Crescent

Eton Avenue

BELSIZE PARK

Wadham Gdns Kings College Rd

Marton Rd

Rowley Way

Alexandra Place

Alexandra Rd

Loudoun Rd

South Hampstead Rail Station

B509

Dorman Way

Eton Avenue

Swiss Cottage

Fellows Road

Eton Garages Eton Cl

Elsworthy Rd

Wnsworth Way

Boundary Rd

Rowley Way

Alexandra Rd

Ainsworth Way

A41

Adelaide Avenue Road

Winchester Road

Adelaide Road

Fellows Road

Hornby Court

King's College Rd

◄ 69 ►

Springfield Road

Clifton Hill

Ordnance Hill

Marlborough Hill

Elm Tree Rd

Wood Field

Hyde Wood Park

Adelaide Road

0.25 mile

0.25 km

Finchley Road/Swiss Cottage

With so much promise and surrounded by the likes of West Hampstead, Primrose Hill and Camden, the area is still inexplicably in need of resuscitation. A long list of shops not worth mentioning and a few restaurants whose existence defies dignity should not detract from the fact that **The Camden Arts Centre** is a jewel in this battered crown and well worth braving the surrounding boredom to visit.

 ## Cinemas
- **Odeon Swiss Cottage** • 96 Finchley Rd
- **Vue Finchley Road** • Finchley Rd & Blackburn Rd

 ## Coffee
- **Costa** • 98 Finchley Rd
- **Starbucks** • 255 Finchley Rd

 ## Libraries
- **Swiss Cottage Library** • 88 Avenue Rd

 ## Nightlife
- **Ye Olde Swiss Cottage** • 98 Finchley Rd

 ## Restaurants
- **Bradleys** • 25 Winchester Rd
- **Camden Arts Centre** • Arkwright Rd
- **Singapore Garden** • 83 Fairfax Rd

 ## Supermarkets
- **Sainsbury's** • 255 Finchley Rd
- **Waitrose** • 199 Finchley Rd

Map 67 • **Belsize Park**

Belsize Park

Map 67

There is a reason that Kate Moss, Jude Law, Chris Martin and Noel Gallagher (to name a few) all live here. It's less pretentious than neighbouring banker-filled Hampstead and far enough away from the Primrose set to be artistically elitist. Extraordinarily expensive shops and restaurants reign over the area but in at the celebrity-frequented **Washington** pub there's an excellent atmosphere and foodwise, Belsize Lane never disappoints.

Cinemas

• **Everyman Belsize Park** • 203 Haverstock Hill

Coffee

• **The Little One Coffee Shop** • 115 Regent's Park Rd
• **Starbucks** • 57 England's Ln
• **Starbucks** • 202 Haverstock Hill

O Landmarks

• **Freud Statue** •
  Fitzjohn's Ave, opposite Maresfield Gardens Junction
• **St Stephen's** • Rosslyn Hill

Libraries

• **Belsize Library** • Antrim Rd

Nightlife

• **The Washington** • 50 England's Ln

Restaurants

• **Retsina** • 48 Belsize Ln

Map 68 · **Kilburn High Road / Abbey Road**

Kilburn High Road/Abbey Road

FFS, "Let It Be!" Indeed, while the area's main attraction is a crosswalk and a dilapidated recording studio once home to the world's greatest band, the grime and urban decay that surround it hardly make it an "Octopus's Garden." But "Come Together" because "Here Comes the Sun."

 ## Coffee
- **Starbucks** • 1 Circus Rd

O Landmarks
- **Abbey Road Zebra Crossing** • 3 Abbey Rd

Libraries
- **Kilburn Library** • 12 Kilburn High Rd
- **St John's Wood Library** • 20 Circus Rd

 ## Nightlife
- **The Old Bell** • 38 High Road
- **Raw Brick** • 11 Kilburn High Rd

 ## Post Offices
- **Kilburn** • 79 Kilburn High Rd
- **St Johns Wood** • 41 Charlbert St

Supermarkets
- **Tesco** • 115 Maida Vale

Map 68

Map 69 · **St. John's Wood**

BELSIZE PARK

PRIMROSE HILL

1

2

66

67

68

70

76

Finchley Road A41

Adelaide Road A41

Adelaide Road B509

Avenue Road B525

Avenue Road B525

Avenue Road B525

Prince Albert Road A5205

Prince Albert Road A5205

Finchley Road

Finchley Road

A41

A41

A41

Kilburn High Road

Alexandra Place

Boundary Road

Loudoun Road

Dorman Way

Middle Field

Boundary Road

The Marlowes

The Marlowes

St. John's Wood Park

Queensmead

Queensmead

Queensmead

Queen's Grove

Queen's Grove

Wellpark Mews

Rossetti Mews

Norfolk Road

Norfolk Road

Wadesdon Road

Acacia Place

Ordnance Hill

Acacia Road

Henstridge Place

St. Ann's Terrace

Aquila Street

Cochrane Mews

Charles Lane

Allitsen Road

Allitsen Road

St. John's Wood Terrace

Radlett Place

Townshend Road

Barrow Hill Rd

Newcourt Street

Cochrane Street

Charlbert Street

Ordnance Hill

Mackennal Street

Salisbury St

Edmunds St

Titchfield Rd

Broxwood Way

St. Stephens Close

St. Stephen's Close

St. Edmunds Ter

St. Edmunds Terrace

St. James's Terrace Mews

Wells Rise

James's St

Ormonde Terrace

Elsworthy Terrace

Elsworthy Road

Elsworthy Road

Elsworthy Rd

Wadham Gardens

Harley Road

Hawtrey

King Henry's Road

Lower Merton Rise

Lower Merton Rise

King Henry's Road

Griffith Close

Eton Sq

Eton Avenue

Fellows Road

Fellows Road

Fellows Road

Hornby Close

Winchester Road

Merton Rise

Bruntisfield Close

Buckland Close

Chalcot Gardens

Primrose Hill Road

Primrose Hill

PAGE
348

Regent's Canal

Macclesfield Br.

Outer Circle

Outer Circle

Outer Circle

Regent's Park

PAGE
348

Winfield House Grounds

Swiss Cottage

Prince Albert Road

St. John's Wood High Street

Greenberry Street

Charlbert Street

Cavendish Ave

Kingsmill Terrace

Queen's Terrace

Stoughton Mews

Wilton Place

St. John's Wood Church Gardens

Regent's Park Road

London Zoo

0.25 mile

0.25 km

St. John's Wood

Map 69

Nouveau riche and bourgeois mix in this leafy salad of a suburb that, you guessed it, reeks of money. Pinned in between Primrose Hill and Regent's Park, there isn't much to do in this mainly residential area, unless you like to gawk at expensive houses.

Nightlife

• **The Duke of York** • 2 St Ann's Terrace

Restaurants

• **The Ivy** • 120 St John's Wood High St

Primrose Hill

Map 70

Primrose Hill is factory-packed with pretty young things and established actors mixing with models, designers and artistic types in an area that is London's low-key version of Beverly Hills. If you don't stumble across a celebrity or are disinclined to stalk one you can check out the trendy stores, grab a pint in the equally trendy **Lansdowne** or take in the views of London from the Hill itself.

Landmarks

• **3 Chalcot Square** • 3 Chalcot Sq

Libraries

• **Primrose Hill Community Library** • 14 Sharples Hall St

Nightlife

• **Cecil Sharp House** • 2 Regent's Park Rd
• **The Lansdowne** • 90 Gloucester Ave
• **Princess of Wales** • 22 Chalcot Rd

Post Offices

• **Regent's Park Road** • 91 Regent's Park Rd

Restaurants

• **Lemonia** • 89 Regent's Park Rd
• **Melrose and Morgan** • 42 Gloucester Ave
• **Odette's** • 130 Regent's Park Rd
• **Primrose Bakery** • 69 Gloucester Ave
• **Two Brothers** • 297 Regent's Park Rd

Shopping

• **Nicolas (off licence)** • 67 Regent's Park Rd
• **Press** • 160 Regents Park Rd
• **Primrose Hill Books** • 134 Regent's Park Rd
• **Primrose Newsagent** • 91 Regent's Park Rd
• **Richard Dare** • 93 Regent's Park Rd
• **Shepherd Foods** • 59 Regent's Park Rd
• **Shikasuki** • 67 Gloucester Ave
• **Sweet Pea** • 77 Gloucester Ave
• **Tann Rokka** • 123 Regent's Park Rd

Map 71 • Camden Town / Chalk Farm / Kentish Town (West)

Camden Town/Chalk Farm/Kentish Town (West)

Camden is still the musical heartbeat of London, and while the ratty-tatty venues of the '60s that solidified its reputation are long gone, or surgically modernized, the pavements still reverberate to a constant beat. The area is crowded during the week and jam-packed during the weekend but the cacophony of wacky stores, bric-a-brac stalls, and an eclectic selection of culinary treats mean London wouldn't be London without it.

Cinemas

- **Odeon Camden Town** • 14 Parkway

Coffee

- **Cafe La Cigale** • 41 Heath Road
- **Cafe Metro** • 178 Camden High St
- **Caffe Nero** • 7 Jamestown Rd
- **Camden Coffee House** •
  30 Camden Rd
- **The Coffee Jar** • 83 Parkway
- **Costa** • 181 Camden High St
- **Pret A Manger** •
  157 Camden High St
- **Pret A Manger** • 231 High St
- **Starbucks** • 4/6 Parkway

O Landmarks

- **Camden Market** • Camden Lock Pl
- **Grand Regents Canal** •
  Grand Regents Canal
- **The Roundhouse** •
  Chalk Farm Rd & Crogsland Rd

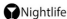 Libraries

- **Queen's Crescent Library** •
  165 Queen's Crescent

Nightlife

- **Barfly** • 49 Chalk Farm Rd
- **Dingwalls** • Middle Yard
- **The Dublin Castle** • 94 Parkway
- **Electric Ballroom** •
  184 Camden High St
- **The Enterprise** • 2 Haverstock Hill
- **Fiddlers Elbow** • 1 Malden Rd
- **Good Mixer** • 30 Inverness St
- **The Hawley Arms** •
  2 Castlehaven Rd
- **Jazz Cafe** • 5 Parkway
- **The Lock Tavern** •
  35 Chalk Farm Rd
- **Oxford Arms** • 265 Camden High St
- **Quinn's** • 65 Kentish Town Rd
- **The Underworld** •
  174 Camden High St

Post Offices

- **Camden High Street** •
  112 Camden High St
- **Queen's Crescent** •
  139 Queen's Crescent

Restaurants

- **Andy's Taverna** • 23 Pratt St
- **Anima e Cuore** •
  127 Kentish Town Rd
- **Bar Gansa** • 2 Inverness St
- **Cotton's** • 55 Chalk Farm Rd
- **Haché** • 24 Inverness St
- **Marathon Cafe** • 87 Chalk Farm Rd
- **Muang Thai** • 71 Chalk Farm Rd
- **My Village** • 37 Chalk Farm Rd
- **Woody Grill** • 1 Camden Rd

Shopping

- **Acumedic** • 103 Camden High St
- **All Ages Records** • 27 Pratt St
- **Cyberdog** •
  Stables Market, Chalk Farm Rd
- **General Eyewear** •
  Chalk Farm Rd & Castlehaven Rd
- **Graham and Green** •
  164 Regent's Park Rd
- **Melrose and Morganc** • 42
  Gloucester Ave
- **Oi Oi** • 454 Stables Market
- **Rokit** • 225 Camden High St
- **Traid** • 154 Camden High St
- **Whole Foods Market** • 49 Parkway

Supermarkets

- **Whole Foods Market** • 49 Parkway
- **Sainsbury's** • 77 Chalk Farm Rd
- **Sainsbury's** • 17 Camden Rd

Map 71

Map 72 · **Kentish Town**

Cars Road
Grafton Terrace
Dale Rd
Cress
Menu Close
Kingcroft
King's Place
Grafton Road

1

Carrol Close
Sanderson Close
Burghley Road
Oakford Road
Burghley Road

2

Junction Road
Tufnell Park

▲ **58**

Kentish Town City Farm

◀ **57**

Highgate Road
Evangelist Bungalow
Highley
Carker
Fortess Walk
Greenwood
Fortess
Balley Mews

Lady Somerset Road
Fortess Road A400
Raveley Road
Lupton Road
Osgrove
Countess
Ascham St
Dunollie Road
Dunollie Place
Lady
Montfemer Grove

Southcote Road
Falcon Road
Marquess

Brecknock Road

▲ **59**

A

Queen's Crescent
Woodyard
Gilles Street
Arctic St
Spring Place
Browns Lane
Warden Road
Athlone Street
Holmes Road
Wilkin Street
Alma Road
Willes Road
Perren Street
Inkerman Road
Raglan Street

Falkland Place
Leverton
Wilkes Row
Lady Margaret Road
Falkland
Falkland Road
Leverton Street
Wind Court

York Mews
Fortess Road A5200

Kentish Town ⇄

Frideswide Place
Islip Street
Wolsey Mews
Cavendish Street
Hammond Street
Angler's Lane

Leighton Road
Willey Farm
Leighton Grove
Long Meadow

Leighton Road A5200
Torriano Mews
Torriano Avenue
Grove
Torriano Cottages

B

Ospringe Road
Prince of Wales Road
Hadley Street
Grafton Crescent
Church Avenue
Kelly Street
Castle Road
Castle Place
Castle Street
Cedar Way
Lewis Street
Hartland Road
Clarence Way
Hawley Rd A502

Grafton Yard
Kentish Town Rd
Bartholo Rd
Bartholomew Villas
Lawford
Palsnut
Pitchill Road
Bartholomew Road
Rochester Road
Rochester Terrace
Rochester Square
Whitfield Place
Rochester Ms

Dartford Street
Islip
Pockhurst
Newport
Bartholomew Road
Caversham Road
Cardington
Osney
Oseney Crescent
Busby Place
Northport Square
Cantelowes Gardens
Camden Mews
Abbydom
Cantelowes Skatepark
Camden Road A503

KENTISH TOWN

▶ **73**

Torriano Avenue A5200
Brecon Mews
Hamp Mews
Brecknock Road

◀ **71**

Farrier Street
Jeffreys Street
Prowse Place
Jeffroyb
Ivor Place
St Pancras Way A5202

Wilmot Place
Rochester Ms
Rochester Place
Wilmot Place

Camden Mews
North Villas
Camden Square
Camden Villas
Camden Park Road A5200
Camden Mews
Cliff Road

Camden Ms
Camden Street
Rochester Square
Strafford Villas
Camden Square
Murray Mews
Camden Square
Cobham
St Augustines
Camden Terrace

Camden Crescent
Kentish Town Road A400
Hawley Rd A502
Camden Gardens
Bonny
Camden Road A5202
Randolph Street
Agar
Grove
Camden Road
College Street
Baynes Street

▼ **78**

Greenland Road
Camden Road

▼ **79**

St Paul's Crescent
St Augustines
St Paul's Crescent
Agar Grove
A5200

0.25 mile   0.25 km

Kentish Town

Kentish Town may be Camden's less-interesting and less-affected neighbour but this isn't necessarily a bad thing. The area is on the up and between the grubby, horrible collection of pound shops, charity shops, and industrial stores there are new venues springing forth that offer some of the most welcoming atmospheres in North London. **The Pineapple** is a great little pit-stop pub with an infectious atmosphere.

Libraries

• **Kentish Town Library** • 262 Kentish Town Rd

Nightlife

• **The Abbey Tavern** • 124 Kentish Town Rd
• **The Assembly House** • 292 Kentish Town Rd
• **The Bull & Gate** • 389 Kentish Town Rd
• **Ladies and Gentlemen** • 2 Highgate Rd
• **The Lion and Unicorn** • 42 Gaisford St
• **O2 Forum** • 9 Highgate Rd
• **The Oxford Tavern** • 256 Kentish Town Rd
• **The Pineapple** • 51 Leverton St
• **Rio's Health Spa** • 239 Kentish Town Rd

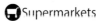

Restaurants

• **The Bengal Lancer**• 253 Kentish Town Rd
• **Cafe Renoir**• 244 Kentish Town Rd
• **Mario's Cafe** • 6 Kelly St
• **The Oxford** • 256 Kentish Town Rd
• **Phoenicia Mediterranean Food Hall** • 186 Kentish Town Rd

Shopping

• **Dots** • 132 St Pancras Way
• **Phoenicia** • 186 Kentish Town Rd

Supermarkets

• **Co-Op** • 250 Kentish Town Rd
• **EARTH natural foods** • 200 Kentish Town Rd
• **Iceland** • 301 Kentish Town Rd
• **Tesco/Esso** • 196 Camden Rd

Map 72

Holloway

Map 73

Holloway is best known for its women's prison and not much else. To the west of Holloway Road it feels a bit like a sprawling backyard to gentrified Camden, Islington, and King's Cross. Nevertheless, bars like **The Lord Stanley** have gone all gastro, so it doesn't quite have the gritty vibe that it once had.

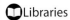 ## Libraries
• **Cat and Mouse Library** • 277 Camden Rd

 ## Nightlife
• **Aces and Eights Saloon Bar** • 156 Fortess Rd
• **The Big Red** • 385 Holloway Rd
• **The Lord Stanley** • 51 Camden Park Rd
• **The Depot** • 1 Carpenter's Mews

 ## Post Offices
• **Brecknock Rd** • 20 Brecknock Rd

 ## Shopping
• **Bumblebee Natural Foods** • 33 Brecknock Rd

 ## Supermarkets
• **Tesco/Esso** • 196 Camden Rd

Map 74 · **Holloway Road / Arsenal**

⊗N

1
2

Windsor Road · A103 · Thane Villas · Travers Road · Parkside · Quill St · Monsell Road · Pine Grove

Sutterton Road · A503 Seven Sisters Road · Mayton Street · Roden Street · Arthur · Annette · Kinloch Street · Thane Villas · Stacey Street · Steve Biko Rd · Steve Biko Rd · Citizen Road

62
61

Arsenal

Gillespie Park Local Nature Reserve

Gillespie Road

63

Elwood Road · Conewood

Tollington Road · A503 · Hertslet Road · Bavaria Road

A

Tollington Road · A503 · Hornsey Road A103 · Shelburne Road · Caedmon Road

Effort Road

Highbury Hill

Drayton Park

Aubert Park

Drakeley Court

Hamilton Park West

Elphinstone Street

Parmiter

Loraine Road · Lowman Road · Annette Road · Dunford Road · Jackson Road

Emirates Stadium – Arsenal F.C.
PAGE **376**

Stavordale Road

Hamilton Park

Highbury Hill

Leigh Road

Camden Road · A503 · A1 · Widdenham Road · Biddestone Road · Ringcroft St · Palm...

Holloway Road · A1 · Hornsey Rd

Queensland Road

Bryantwood Road

Martineau Road

Drayton Park Rail

Coach House Lane

Whistler

Highbury Hill

Framfield Road

Camden Road · A5203 · Freegrove Road · Stock Orchard Cres

Quemerford Road · Pollard Close · Hornsey Street · Sherwood Grove · Hertslet Road

Ⓔ **Holloway Road**

Rollit

Bavaria Road

Courtney Road

Drayton Park

Battledean Road

Arvon Road

Highbury Terrace Mews

Highbury

Caledonian Road · A5203 · Sturmer Way · Stock Orchard Street · Hedingham Close

Eden Grove · George's Road · Chillingworth Road · Eden Grove

LOWER HOLLOWAY

Ⓞ Gillespie Park

Witherington Road

Ronalds Road

Highbury Crescent

Battledean Road

Melgund Road

Ronalds Road

B

Ⓤ **Caledonian Road**

Cottage Rd · Piper Close · Watkinson Road · Roman Way

Adams Pl · Ⓔ · Mackenzie Road

Hartnoll St · Eastwood Cl · Palmer Place · Fieldway Cres

75

Highbury Fields

73

Paradise Park

Sheringham Road · Crossley Road

Morgan Road · Ringcroft Street · Madras Pl · Liverpool Road B515

✉

Liverpool Road Garden

Calabria Road

Market Road · Bemerton Estate · Belfont Road

Mackenzie Road · Jupiter Way · Vivian Way · Westbourne Rd · Atlas Mews · Bride Street

Lough Road · Loraine Rd · Furlong Road

Bride Street

Orleston Road · Orleston Ms

Highbury & Islington Ⓤ Ⓔ

Highbury St. Paul's Corner

Canonbury Road

79

Armour Cl · Cheney Rd · Vibart Wk · Rheidol · Freegrove Rd

Ellington Street

80

Ringcroft · Cort Gardens

Liverpool Road B515

Highbury Station Road

Comp... Compton Terrace

St James...

Kerwick Cl · Bradley Close

Wheelwright St · London Cl · Offord St · St Clements St

Arundel Square · Arundel Square Garden

Laycock Street

Laycock Street Park

Upper Street

Bradley Close

|—— 0.25 mile ——|

|—— 0.25 km ——|

Holloway Road / Arsenal

Much like the football team the area shares its name with, there is a lot of potential talent here that just needs some time to come to fruition. On match days the streets make a sardine tin look roomy. This area also includes the grotty stretch of Holloway Road. For something different try **Tbilisi** for cheap Eastern European eats.

Map 74

Coffee

- **Cafe Nero** • 384 Holloway Rd
- **Le Peche Mignon** • 6 Ronalds Rd
- **Vagabond N7** • 105 Holloway Rd

O Landmarks

- **Emirates Stadium**
- **Gillespie Park** • 191 Drayton Park

Libraries

- **Central Library** • 2 Fieldway Crescent

Nightlife

- **The Coronet** • 338 Holloway Rd
- **Hen and Chicken Theatre Bar** • 109 St Paul's Rd
- **The Horatia** • 98 Holloway Rd
- **The Relentless Garage** • 20 Highbury Corner

Post Offices

- **Highbury** • 12 Highbury Corner
- **Holloway Rd** • 118 Holloway Rd

Restaurants

- **El Rincon Quiteno** • 235 Holloway Rd
- **Kokeb** • 45 Roman Wy
- **Messi's Kitchen** • 128 Holloway Rd
- **Tbilisi** • 91 Holloway Rd
- **Wolkite Kifto** • 82 Hornsey Rd

Shopping

- **Vivien of Holloway** • 294 Holloway Rd

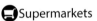Supermarkets

- **Waitrose** • 366 Holloway Rd

159

Map 75 · **Highbury**

HIGHBURY

CANONBURY

Canonbury
Rail

St. Paul's
Shrubbery

St. Paul's Road

Highbury &
Islington

Highbury Fields

0.25 mile

0.25 km

Map 75

A residential area close enough to Upper Street to keep you entertained and far enough away to keep you grounded, Highbury is blessed with the marvellous Highbury Fields, which during the summer is full of pretty things (in varying states of undress). Bordered by busy St Paul's Road and bustling Green Lanes, you'll never struggle for something to do here; try the **Snooty Fox** for a quiet drink.

O Landmarks

• **St Paul's Shrubbery** •
  St Paul's Rd & Northampton Park

Nightlife

• **Alwyne Castle** • 83 St Pauls Rd
• **The Hen and Chickens Theatre Bar** • 109 St Paul's Rd
• **The Snooty Fox** • 75 Grosvenor Avenue

Post Offices

• **Highbury Park** • 12 Highbury Park

Restaurants

• **Firezza** • 276 St Paul's Rd
• **Highbury Arts Club** • 73 Highbury Park
• **Prawn on the Lawn** • 292 St Paul's Rd
• **Primeur** • 116 Petherton Rd
• **Trullo** • 300-302 St Paul's Rd
• **Ustun** • 107 Green Lanes

Shopping

• **Cabbies Delight Auto Parts** • 9 Green Lanes
• **Highbury Vintners** • 71 Highbury Park
• **La Fromagerie** • 30 Highbury Park
• **Mother Earth** • 282 St Paul's Rd
• **Prawn on the Lawn** • 292 St Paul's Rd

Map 76 • Edgware Road / Marylebone (North)

Marylebone Road is noisy enough to have you running for the taps of the **Great Central Bar** straight away.

Coffee
• **Pret A Manger** • 120 Baker St

Emergency Rooms
• **Western Eye Hospital** • 173 Marylebone Rd

O Landmarks
• **Lord's Cricket Ground** • St John's Wood
• **Sherlock Holmes' House** • 221 Baker St

Libraries
• **Church Street Library** • 67 Church St
• **London Business School Library** • 117 Marylebone Rd
• **Marylebone Library** • 9 New Cavendish St

Nightlife
• **Great Central Bar** • 222 Marylebone Rd
• **The North London Tavern** • 374 Kilburn High Rd
• **Volunteer** • 245 Baker St

Post Offices
• **Edgware Rd** • 354 Edgware Rd

Restaurants
• **Sea Shell of Lisson Grove** • 49 Lisson Grove

Shopping
• **Alfie's Antiques Market** • 25 Church St
• **Archive Secondhand Books & Music** • 83 Bell St
• **Beatles London Store** • 231 Baker St
• **Lord's Cricket Shop** •
  Lord's Cricket Ground, Lisson Grove

Supermarkets
• **Tesco** • 94 Church St

Map 77 • Mornington Crescent / Regent's Park

London Zoo

70

71

Albert Road A5205

Outer Circle

Albert Lane

Park

Parkway A4201

Delancey

Street

A503

Camden High Street A400

Pratt Street

Pratt

St. Martin's Gardens

Greenland Road A503

Underhill Street

St. Martin's Close

King's

Miller Street

Plender Street

Plender

Bayham Place

Gloucester Gate

Gloucester Gate

Gloucester Gate

Albany Street A4201

Park Village East

A

Park West

St. Kath. pre

Camden Gate

Cumberland Terrace

Cumberland Terrace

Mornington Terrace

Mornington

Mornington Street

Arlington Road

Carlow Street

Carlow St. Ms

Bayham Place

Bayham Street

Beatty St

Albert Road

Hampstead Road A400

Mornington Crescent

Mornington Crescent

Crowndale Road

Regent's Park

PAGE 348

Outer Circle

Cumberland Terrace

Cumberland Terrace

Albany Street A4201

Park Village East

Mornington Pl

Mornington Crescent

Clarkson Row

Eversholt Street A400

Oakley Square

Oakley

REGENT'S PARK

Chester Pl

Cumb. Pl

Chester

Edward Ms

Little Edward Street

Redhill St

Redhill Street

Augustus Street

Granby Terrace

Greater London House

Lidington Place A400

78

Cranleigh

Bramley Street

Eversholt Street

Chester Road

Chester Road

Chester Terrace

Chester Close North

Chester CL N.

Ches. CL S.

Cumberland Market

Market

Cumb. MKT

Mack St

Stanhope Street

Harrington Street

Cumberland

Varndell Street

Hampstead Road A400

Hampstead Road

Cardington St

B

Outer Circle

Cambridge Gate

Cambridge Gate

Cambridge Terrace

Cambridge Ter. Ms

Chester Gate

Chester Terrace

Albany Street A4201

Little Albany Street

Robert Street

Clarence Gardens

Munster Square

Munster Square

Everton Bldgs

Netley Street

Robert Street

Colworth Grove

Cardington Street

St. James's Gardens

Euston Station

PAGE 410

Outer Circle

Park Square Gardens

Cambridge Gate Mews

Osnaburgh Terrace

Osnaburgh Ter

Longford Street

Laxton Place

Stanhope Street

Wybert Street

William Road

North Gower St

Drummond Street

Chalton St

Bidgs

Melton Street

Coburg Street

Doric Way

Drummond St

Regent's Park

Park Square East

Peto Place

Great Portland Street

Euston Tower

Euston Road A501

North Gower Street

Hampstead Road A10

Euston Square

Tolmer's Square

North Gower St

Euston Square

Regnart Bldgs

Stephenson Way

Euston Street

Euston Road A501

Euston Road A400

Euston Rd A400

Euston Road

Gower Place

Gower Court

3

4

Crescent Gardens

Marylebone Road A501

Park Cres

Park Square West

Park Crescent West

Outer Circle

Warren Street

Warren Street

Warren Street

Endsleigh Gardens

Gordon St

Mornington Crescent/Regent's Park

Map 77

Hemmed in by Regent's Park and Euston, this patch combines pretty streets with tower-block thoroughfares. Skip the din of Euston underpass for Drummond Street, Camden's 'little India'—hit up **Bhel Poori** for decent dosas and visit **Chutneys** for veggies. Wash it all down with mugs of Black Sheep Ale at **The Crown and Anchor** before mingling al fresco with **Edinboro Castle's** yuppier folk.

O Landmarks

- **Euston Tower** • 286 Euston Rd
- **Greater London House** • Hampstead Rd

Nightlife

- **The Crown & Anchor** • 137 Drummond St
- **Edinboro Castle** • 57 Mornington Terrace
- **Euston Tap** • 190 Euston Rd
- **Horse & Groom** • 128 Great Portland St

Restaurants

- **Chutneys** • 124 Drummond St
- **Diwana Bhel Poori** • 121 Drummond St
- **The Green Note** • 106 Parkway
- **Mestizo** • 103 Hampstead Rd

Shopping

- **Chess & Bridge** • 44 Baker St

Map 78 · Euston

Euston's first port of call for thousands of people each day, be it city workers from the Shires or pilgrims to the many erotic bookshops by the railway. Look beyond the station—an ugly grey cube that dominates the area—and you'll find a few gems. Students and bookish types head to the outstanding **library** (British that is) while beer aficionados head to **Euston Tap**.

Coffee

- **Origin Coffee** • 96 Euston Rd
- **Pret A Manger** • 296 Pentonville Rd
- **Pret A Manger** • 117 Euston Rd
- **Starbucks** • 296 Pentonville Rd

O Landmarks

- **The British Library** • 96 Euston Rd
- **Camden High Street** • Camden High St & Delancey St
- **Central Saint Martins** • 1 Granary Square
- **Cheney Road** • Cheney Rd & Weller's Ct
- **Euston Station** • Eversholt St & Doric Wy
- **Platform 9¾** • King's Cross Station
- **St Pancras** • Pancras Rd & Euston Rd
- **St Pancras Hospital** • 4 St Pancras Way

Libraries

- **The British Library** • 96 Euston Rd
- **Camden Town Library** • 218 Eversholt St
- **Wellcome Library** • 183 Euston Rd

Nightlife

- **The Camden Head** • 100 Camden High St
- **The Champagne Bar at St Pancras** • Pancras Rd
- **The Doric Arch** • 1 Eversholt St
- **The Euston Tap** • 190 Euston Rd
- **Lincoln Lounge** • 52 York Wy
- **The Royal George** • 1 Eversholt St
- **Scala** • 275 Pentonville Rd

Post Offices

- **Kings Cross** • 21 Euston St

Restaurants

- **Asakusa** • 265 Eversholt St
- **The Booking Office** •
  St Pancras Renaissance London Hotel, Euston Rd
- **Camino** • 3 Varnisher's Yard
- **Caravan** • 1 Granary Building
- **Dishoom** • 5 Stable St
- **Great Nepalese** • 48 Eversholt St
- **The Somerstown Coffee House** • 60 Chalton St

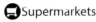## Shopping

- **All Ages Records** • 27 Pratt St
- **Housmans Bookshop** • 5 Caledonian Rd

Supermarkets

- **Sainsbury's** • 10 Camden High St

Map 79 · **King's Cross**

King's Cross

Map 79

No area in North London benefited more from the Olympic games than this crucial commuter hub. The once tawdry Kings Cross Station has a new face and a modern aura while **St Pancras** is as glorious a station as you'll find in Europe. Once London's seediest spot the KC is now full of rakish bars and clubs with excellent live music and some tasty eats up Caledonian Road.

Libraries

- **Lewis Carroll Children's Library** • 166 Copenhagen St
- **West Library** • Bridgeman Rd

Nightlife

- **The Big Chill House** • 257 Pentonville Rd
- **Central Station** • 37 Wharfdale Rd
- **Drake and Morgan** • 6 Pancras Sq
- **EGG** • 200 York Wy
- **Hemingford Arms** • 158 Hemingford Rd
- **The Lexington** • 96 Pentonville Rd
- **Lincoln Lounge** • 52 York Wy
- **The Parcel Yard** • Euston Road Kings Cross
- **Simmons** • 32 Caledonian Rd
- **Tarmon** • 270 Caledonian Rd

Post Offices

- **Caledonian Road** • 320 Caledonian Rd

Restaurants

- **Addis** • 42 Caledonian Rd
- **Euro Café** • 299 Caledonian Rd
- **Marathon** • 193A Caledonian Rd
- **The New Didar** • 347 Caledonian Rd

Supermarkets

- **Co-Op** • 303 Caledonian Rd
- **Iceland** • 259 Caledonian Rd

Map 80 · **Angel / Upper St**

N

74

75

Highbury &
Islington

Highbury
Corner

81

St. Paul's Road

Assata
Mews

John Spencer
Sq

Prior Bolton
Street
Hopping La

Canonbury
Sq

Canonbury Rd A1200

Compton Terrace

Canonbury Villas

Alwyne Lane

Highbury Station Road

Laycock
Street Park

Laycock Street

Compton Avenue

Canonbury Lane

Tyndale Ter

Tyndale
Lane

Braes Street

Canonbury Vs

Canonbury Road

A

BARNSBURY

Barnsbury Park

Islington Park Street

College Cross

Barnsbury Street

Richmond
Grove

Florence
St

Tress
Cl

Sebbon Street

Canon Vs

Essex Road

179

B515

Milner
Place

Waterloo Ter

Napier
Terrace

Battishill Street

Almeida Street

Hawes Street

Halton
Cros

Halton
Road

Richmond Avenue

Gibson Sq

Milner Street

Gibson Square

Moon Street

St. Mary's
Church
Gardens

Popham
Street

Britannia
Row

Essex Road A104

ISLINGTON

Cloudesley
Square

Theberton Street

Studd St

Gaskin St

Upper Street

Collins St

Duncan Terrace

Charlton Pl

Camden Passage

Colebrooke Row

B

Cloudesley Place

B515

Batchelor Street

Ritchie Street

Bromfield
Street

Bennett
Road

Upper Street

Islington A1173

Islington
Green

Camden Walk

Camden Passage

Gerrard Road

Noel Road

Noel Road

Grand Junction Wharf

The Bull

83

PENTONVILLE

Pentonville Road
A501

White Lion
Street

Chapel
Market

Angel

6

Angel

Angel
Station Roof

Upper Street

City Road A501

Goswell

Vincent Terrace

Colebrooke Row

City Road A501

Regent's Canal

0.25 mile

0.25 km

Angel / Upper St

A purpose-built playground for a twenty-somethings crowd that has to wake up for work in the morning. Whether it's the boutique shops, bars and restaurants that cater to any and all taste preoccupying Upper Street, the antique shops along **Camden Passage**, or an eclectic and vivid live music and theatre scene (Head to the **Kings Head Pub** for both), Angel has it all, and much more.

Map 80

Cinemas
• **Everyman Screen on the Green** • 83 Islington Green
• **Vue Islington** • 36 Parkfield St

Coffee
• **Estorick Gallery** • 39 Canonbury Sq
• **Euphorium Bakery** • 202 Upper St
• **Pret A Manger** • 27 Islington High St
• **Starbucks** • 7 Islington High St

Landmarks
• **Angel Station** •
• **The Bull** • 100 Upper St

Nightlife
• **69 Colebrooke Row** • 69 Colebrooke Row
• **The Angel** • 3 Islington High St
• **The Angelic** • 57 Liverpool Rd
• **Camden Head** • 2 Camden Walk
• **The Castle** • 54 Pentonville Rd
• **Compton Arms** • 4 Compton Ave
• **The Crown** • 116 Cloudesley Rd
• **The Drapers Arms** • 44 Barnsbury St
• **The Garage** • 20 Highbury Corner
• **Hope And Anchor** • 207 Upper St
• **Islington Academy** • 16 Parkfield St
• **The Islington Town House** • 13 Liverpool Rd
• **King's Head Theatre & Pub** • 115 Upper St
• **Little Bat** • 54 Islington Park St
• **Lucky Voice** • 173 Upper St
• **Old Red Lion** • 418 St John St
• **The Regent** • 201 Liverpool Rd
• **Union Chapel** • Compton Terrace

Restaurants
• **Afghan Kitchen** • 35 Islington Green
• **The Albion** • 10 Thornhill Rd
• **The Breakfast Club** • 31 Camden Passage
• **Candid Café** • 3 Torrens St
• **Casa Fabrizi** • 1 Chapel Market
• **Fig and Olive** • 151 Upper St
• **Fredericks** • 106 Camden Passage
• **Gem** • 265 Upper St
• **Indian Veg Bhelpoori House** • 93 Chapel Market
• **Le Mercury** • 140 Upper St
• **Mem & Laz** • 8 Theberton St
• **Ottolenghi** • 287 Upper St
• **Tortilla** • 13 Islington High St
• **Zaffrani** • 47 Cross St

Shopping
• **After Noah** • 121 Upper St
• **Camden Passage** • Camden Passage
• **Cass Art** • 66 Colebrooke Row
• **Gill Wing Kitchen Shop** • 190 Upper St
• **Monte's Deli** • 23 Canonbury Ln
• **Paul A Young Fine Chocolates** • 33 Camden Passage
• **Twentytwentyone** • 274 Upper St

Supermarkets
• **Iceland** • 62 Chapel Market

171

Map 81 · Canonbury

Canonbury

Map 81

The Canonbury area is a delicious cocktail of diversity with a heady mix of leafy spacious streets, multi-million-pound mansions, a dollop of tempered hipster abodes and some of London's poorest estates. Essex Road has a Banksy and quirky shops including the notable **Get Stuffed** for all your taxidermy needs. Foodies are well catered for with real butchers (**James Elliot**), bakers (**Raab's**), and great ethnic eateries.

O Landmarks
• **Gladiators Paving Slab** • 10 Canonbury St

Libraries
• **South Library** • 115 Essex Rd

Nightlife
• **The Canonbury Tavern** • 21 Canonbury Pl
• **Marquess Tavern** • 32 Canonbury St
• **Myddleton Arms** • 52 Canonbury Rd
• **The Lord Clyde** • 342 Essex Rd

Restaurants
• **Raab's Bakery** • 136 Essex Rd
• **Tierra Peru** • 164 Essex Rd

Shopping
• **Get Stuffed** • 105 Essex Rd
• **James Elliot Butchers** • 96 Essex Rd
• **Planet Organic** • 64 Essex Rd
• **Steve Hatt** • 88 Essex Rd

Map 82 · De Beauvoir Town / Kingsland

Ferntower Road

A105

Elton Place

Toman's Close

Stoke

Shackelwell

Pyrland Road

Beresford Road

A105

Newington Green Road

Aubert Grove

Woodfield Place

Mildmay Road

Arundel

Tavistock

Alvington

Sandringham

John campbell

64

Gillett Street

Beresford
Terrace

Grosvenor

Avenue

75

Heaven Tree
Close

Canonbury
Rail

A

St. Paul's Road A1199

CANONBURY

CANONBURY

Linden
Mews

Mildmay

Mildmay

North

Mildmay

Newington Green Rd

St. Paul's Place

Bingham Place

Mildmay St

Mildmay
Wk

Grove North

Grove South

King Henry's Wk Gdn

Oocwra's Bldgs

Bldgs

A104

Queen Margaret's Grove

St. Jude Street

Kingsbury Ter

Jewish
Burial
Ground

Hawthorne
Close

Kingsbury

Mildmay
Place

Bradbury
Street

Kings
Close

Burder
Close

Burder
Close

Burder
Rd

Kingsland High Street

Bole

Abbot Street

Colve

Dalston Lane

86

Balls Pond Road

Balls Pond Road A104

War Cl

Culford Mews

Toffenham

Eagle
Mews

Bent

Nim
Pas

KINGSLAND

Forest

A104

Essex Road

Douglas Rd

Culford Road

Wall
Street

Hertford Road

Baxter

Wakeham
Street

Mitchison Road

Buckingham
Road

Quainta
Mews

Richmond

Rich
Rd

Bee

Dove
Road

Hensall
Street

Southgate Road B102

81

Ockendon Road

Culford
Grove

Culford Road

Arthingham Road

Stamford Road

De Beauvoir Road

Kingsland Road A10

Freshfield

Englefield Road

Ufton Grove

Ufton Road

Englefield

Mortimer Road

Hertford Road

Rich

Oakley Road

Northchurch
Road

Elmore Street

Cleveland Road

Halford Road

Icon Ms

Dea

Southgate Gro

Orchard
Ms

W. Mill

Haines
Clo

Norm. Ter

De Beauvoir
Square

De
Beauvoir
Square

St. Peter's
Way

Enfield Rd

Middleton

B

Essex Road

Cassland
Court

Cleveland Road

Almorah Road

Avenue

Mortimer Road

Downham Road

Water
Cress
Place

Lan
caster
Close

Hertford

Arbutus
Street

Lee Street

Downham Road

Southgate Road B102

Park
Road

Benyon
Road

Rosa
St

DE BEAUVOIR TOWN

Baines Road

Kingsland Road A10

Frederick St

Dunston St

Dunston Rd

North Road

A1200

Shepperton Road

Rotherfield Street

Rosemary
Gardens

Dalliffes Road

De Beauvoir Crescent

Hertford

Baltic
Close

88

Wilton

Rydon St

83

Baring Street B102

New North Road

Canal Walk

Branch Place

Taplow St

84

Whitmore

Regent's Canal

Orsman Road

Suleymaniye
Mosque

Mill Row

Canal Path

Basire Street

Morton

Halcomb
St

Bridport St

Brighton

Penn Street

Hyde Rd

Phillipp St

Wiltshire Row

Hoxton

Kingsland Road A10

Win
Gdns

Whiston

Poole St

Gopsall St

Clinger
Street

Shoreditch

Grange Street

0.25 mile

0.25 km

De Beauvoir is the buffer zone where swanky Islington meets the self-regard of Dalston. As such it's an ideal place to get a reprieve from either side. To the west are quiet squares and gastropubs. Venture east and you'll be up-'til-dawn boozing, talking to individuals comic book writers couldn't dream up. When you're sick of both, sit in De Beauvoir Square (with its thousands of palm trees) and ponder life.

Coffee

• **2&4** • 4 Southgate Rd

O Landmarks

• **Suleymaniye Mosque** • 212 Kingsland Rd

Libraries

• **Mildmay Library** • 21 Mildmay Park

Nightlife

• **Dalston Boys Club** • 68 Boleyn Rd
• **Dalston Jazz Bar** • 4 Bradbury St
• **The Duke of Wellington** • 119 Balls Pond Rd
• **The Hunter S** • 194 Southgate Rd
• **Rosemary Branch Theatre** • 2 Shepperton Rd
• **The Vortex** • 11 Gillett Sq

Restaurants

• **Mother Earth** • 101 Newington Green Rd
• **Peppers and Spice** • 40 Balls Pond Rd
• **Stone Cave** • 111 Kingsland

Shopping

• **2&4** • 4 Southgate Rd
• **Mother Earth** • 101 Newington Green Rd
• **North One Garden Centre** • 25 Englefield Rd

Map 83 • **Angel (East) / City Rd (North)**

N

Rosemary
Gardens

Essex St
New North Road A1200
Shepperton Road

Greenman St
Tibberton Square
Rosemary St
Canal Walk

Hayes St
Shilling St
Hayman Road
Fowler Road
Hall's Cross Est
Maldon Cl
Popham Street
Ridge St
Wilton Sq
Wilton St
Baring St
Baring Street B102
Bridport Place

Mary's Church Terrace
Cross Street
Dibden Street
Pickering Pl
Elder Wlk
Halton Pl
Popham Street
Bishop Street
Basire St
Presland St
Coleman St
Rees St
Coleman Fields
Wiltshire Row
Buckland St
Shoreditch St
Nether Place

Britannia Row
Prebend Street
Struthland Cl
Canon St
Mary St
Elephant Lane
Arlington Ave
Coleman Avenue
New North Road A1200

HOXTON
Shoreditch
Park, (Sports
Grds.)

Mary's Church Path
Horse Yard
Wind sor Terrace
Packington Street
St Paul St
Union Square
Arlington St
Clock
Mews

Queen's Head St
Rheidol Ms
Chantry Street
St Peter's St
Dame Street
Gerald Street
Packington Square

Eagle Wharf Road B144
Sherborne St
Poole St
Baches St
Godwin St
Torsion St
Napier Grove
Purcell St
Cropley St
Fanshaw St
Wenlock St
Cavendish St

Essex Road A104
Colebrooke Row
Elliott's Pl
Charlton Pl
Camden Walk
Mews
St Peters Street
Devonia Road
Grantbridge Street
Danbury Street
Allingham St
Frome Street
St Peter's Street Mews
Rheidol Terrace
Close Court
Baldwin Terrace

Shepherdess Walk B144
Wharf Rd
Wenlock
Shaftesbury
Sturt Street
Micawber St
Windsor Terrace
Wimbourne Street
Underwood St

Wenlock Road
Eagle Wharf Road

80
82
84

Gerrard Road
Noel Road
Noel Road
Burgh Street

Vincent Terrace
Quick Street
Sudeley Street
Radcliffe St
City Rd
Graham Street
Grand Junction Wharf
Pickford's Wharf
Wharf Road

Colebrooke Row
Elia Street
Elia Mews
Nelson Place
Coombs St
Nagswick St
Garden Row
Micawber St
Windsor Terrace
Alford
Place
Murray Grove
Underwood Court
84

6
Duncan Terrace
Oakley Cres
Danbury St
Nile Street
Underwood Row
Wellesley
Terrace
Shepherdess Walk B144
Nile Street
Westland Place
Ebenezer St
Shepherd Place

City Road A501
Goswell Road A1
Sidney Grove
City Gdn Row
Wakley St
Hall Street
New Charles Street
Pickard St
Central St
City Road A501
Baltic Street
Bath Street B144

7
Moreland Street
Dingley Road
Hull Street
Lever Street B502
Galway Street

Goswell Road A1
Spencer Street
Northampton St
St John St
Friend St
Owen St
Chadwell St
Hermit St
Sebastian St
Goswell Road
Kings Square
Garden
King Square
Lever Street B502
Norman St

NSBURY

ST.
LUKE'S

0.25 mile   0.25 km

If you're bored of the bars on Upper Street or the ironic chic of Hoxton, the streets in between (along Essex Road or by the canal) are a better bet, with a more laidback atmosphere. The **Island Queen** (NFT London's official birthplace!) is a cosy local pub and well worth a visit. One day they'll just have to give us one of those blue plaques.

Nightlife

- **The Alpaca** • 84 Essex Rd
- **Barrio Angel** • 45 Essex Rd
- **The Bill Murray** • 39 Queen's Head St
- **The Duke of Cambridge** • 30 St Peter's St
- **Earl of Essex** • 25 Danbury St
- **The Narrow Boat** • 119 St Peters St
- **The Island Queen** • 87 Noel Rd
- **The Old Queens Head** • 44 Essex Rd
- **The Wenlock Arms** • 26 Wenlock Rd

Restaurants

- **Shepherdess Cafe** • 221 City Rd

Shopping

- **Flashback** • 50 Essex Rd
- **Past Caring** • 54 Essex Rd

Map 84 • Hoxton

Hoxton

The only constant in Hoxton is change: what passes as monthly rent now was a deposit on a pad a decade earlier. The vibe is special and the pulse of the area radiates out of Hoxton Square and its bedfellow Curtain Road. Shop at **Hoxton Monster Supplies**.

Emergency Rooms

• **Moorfields Eye Hospital** • 162 City Rd

O Landmarks

• **Hoxton Square** • Hoxton Sq
• **Village Underground** • 54 Holywell Ln

Libraries

• **Shoreditch Library** • 80 Hoxton St

Nightlife

• **Happiness Forgets** • 9 Hoxton Sq
• **Howl at the Moon** • 178 Hoxton St
• **Hoxton Square Bar and Kitchen** • 2 Hoxton Sq
• **The Macbeth** • 70 Hoxton St
• **The Old Blue Last** • 38 Great Eastern St
• **Red Lion** • 41 Hoxton St
• **The Stag's Head** • 55 Orsman Rd
• **Strongroom** • 120 Curtain Rd
• **Troy Bar** • 10 Hoxton St

Restaurants

• **The Barrel Boulangerie** • 110 Hoxton St
• **The Clove Club** • 380 Old St
• **Cocotte Shoreditch** • 8 Hoxton Sq
• **MEATliquor** • 15 Hoxton Market
• **RAPSA** • 100 Hoxton St
• **Blacklock Shoreditch** • 28 Rivington St

Shopping

• **Good Hood** • 151 Coronet St
• **Hoxton Street Monster Supplies** • 159 Hoxton St
• **SCP** • 135 Curtain Rd

Supermarkets

• **Co-Op** • 136 New North Rd

Map 84

179

ARCHWAY

BROWNSWOOD
PARK

FINSBURY
PARK

ST.
NEWI

Clissold
Park

Hampstead
Heath

ARSENAL

DARTMOUTH
PARK

Parliament
Hill

HOLLOWAY

HIGHBURY

HAMPSTEAD

LOWER
HOLLOWAY

KIN

KENTISH TOWN

BARNSBURY

CANONBURY

DE
BEAUV
TOW

CAMDEN
TOWN

ISLINGTON

PRIMROSE
HILL

London
Zoo

REGENT'S
PARK

PENTONVILLE

ANGEL

HO

The
Regent's
Park

FINSBURY

ST. JOHN'S
WOOD

EUSTON

ST. PANCRAS

CLERKENWELL

ST. LUKE'S

S

MARYLEBONE

FITZROVIA

FARRINGDON

BARBICAN

BRO

LISSON
GROVE

HOLBORN

SOHO

BLACKFRIARS

THE CI

TEMPLE

WEST END

MAYFAIR

THE
STRAND

Hyde
Park

SOUTH
BANK

BORO

SOUTHWARK

Buckingham
Palace
Gardens

KNIGHTSBRIDGE

WATERLOO

NEWINGTON

BELGRAVIA

WESTMINSTER

LAMBETH

ELEPHANT &
CASTLE

Map 85 · Stoke Newington (East)

N

1

2

Stamford Grove East

Stamford Grove West

Forburg Road

Common A107

Jess

Lynmouth Road

Reizel Close

Stamford Hill

Darenth Road

Kyverdale Road

Lynmouth Road

Filey Avenue

Gilda Crescent

Lampard Grove

Margaret Road

Alkham Road

Oldhill Street

Osbaldeston Road

Chardmore Road

Filey Avenue

Chardmore Road

Upper Clap

Margaret Bldgs

Kyverdale Road

Cazenove Road

Windus Road

Belfast Road

Station App

Stoke Newington Rail

Cazenove Road

Alkham Road

Kyverdale Road

Osbaldeston Road

Fountayne Road

Durlston Road

Hogan Way

Geldeston Road

Rossington

Cypress Cl

Chamb

A

164

Gibson Gdns

Briggeford Close

Abney Park Cemetery

Wilmer Place

Northwold Road A10

Northwold Road B111

Alconbury Rd

Geldeston Rd

Narford Road

Reighton Road

Garnham St

Garnham St

Sanford Ter

Stoke Newington Common

Benthal Road

Norcott Road

Maury Road

Evering Road

oke Newington hurch St B104

Lawrence Buildings

Cottage Walk

Smalley Close

Sanford Ter

Jenner Road

Brooke Road

87

B

Stoke Newington High Street A10

Manley Court

Dynevor Rd

Leswin Road

Brooke Road

Rectory Road A10

Oak Park Ms

Rectory Road Rail

Evering Road

Laurence Ln

Brooke Road

Walsingh

Dynevor Rd

Tyssen Road

Batley Place

Darville Road

Bayston Rd

Nile Close

Rendlesham Rd

Kenninghall Rd

Victorian Gro

Hollar Road

Batley Rd

Leswin Place

Rectory Road A10

Benthal Road

Monteagle Way

Muir Rd

Nolan Way

Victorian Rd

Glading Ter

Evering Road

Manse Road A10

Evering Road A10

Stellman Close

Stellman Close

Stellman Close

Rendlesham Rd

Monteagle Way

Muir Way

Coronation

Aysta

86

Victoria Sq

Stok

Sydney Road

Sydney Road

| 0.25 mile | | 0.25 km |

Stoke Newington (East)

Map 85

Stokey has turned into something of a Notting Hill of the east with all-terrain buggies taking up the pavement while the MILFs do their organic grocery shopping. It's resplendent in dining options but try **Testi** first. Various abolitionists and Salvation Army veterans are interred at the nineteenth-century **Abney Park Cemetery**, which doubles as an overgrown nature preserve and cruising spot.

O Landmarks

- **Abney Park Cemetery** •
  Stoke Newington High St & Rectory Rd
- **Kynaston Gardens** • 2 Kynaston Ave

Libraries

- **Clapton Library** • Northwold Rd

Nightlife

- **The Jolly Butchers** • 204 Stoke Newington High St
- **Royal Sovereign** • 64 Northwold Rd
- **White Hart** • 69 Stoke Newington High St

Post Offices

- **Stamford Hill** • 82 Stamford Hill

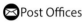Restaurants

- **19 Numara Bos Cirrik** • 34 Stoke Newington Rd
- **Bagel House** • 2 Stoke Newington High St
- **Café Z Bar** • 58 Stoke Newington High St
- **Testi** • 38 Stoke Newington High St
- **Thai Cafe** • 3 Northwold Rd
- **Three Crowns** • 175 Stoke Newington Church St

Shopping

- **Hamdys** • 167 Stoke Newington High St
- **Stoke Newington Bookshop** •
  159 Stoke Newington High St
- **Rouge** • 158 Stoke Newington High St

Map 86 · Dalston / Kingsland

85

64

Hackney
Downs

87

Centreprise

Dalston
Kingsland Rail

Hackney
Downs Rail

82

Balls Pond Road A104

Dalston Lane A104
Holy Trinity
The Clowns
Church
Dalston
Junction

89

88

0.25 mile

0.25 km

Bustling Ridley Road market is still the beating heart of Dalston, while Kingsland Road is like a Vice mag shoot with Nathan Barleys stalking up and down as though it were a catwalk. With hip bars like **Dalston Superstore** and **Ridley Road Bar**, it's no wonder, **Cafe Oto** is the experimental music cafe de jour.

Cinemas
• **Rio Cinema** • 107 Kingsland High St

Coffee
• **Dalston Eastern Curve Garden** • 13 Dalston Ln

O Landmarks
• **Holy Trinity, The Clowns Church** • Beechwood Rd & Kirkland Walk

Libraries
• **CLR James Library** • Dalston Sq

Nightlife
• **Café Oto** • 18 Ashwin St
• **Dalston Superstore** • 117 Kingsland High St
• **The Haggerston** • 438 Kingsland Rd
• **High Water London** • 23 Stoke Newington Rd
• **The Moustache Bar** • 58 Stoke Newington Rd
• **The Prince George** • 40 Parkholme Rd
• **Ridley Road Market Bar** • 49 Ridley Rd
• **The Shacklewell Arms** • 71 Shacklewell Ln
• **VFD** • 66 Stoke Newington Rd

Post Offices
• **Kingsland High Street** • 118 Kingsland High St

Restaurants
• **The Best Turkish Kebab** • 125 Stoke Newington Rd
• **Dalston Eastern Curve Garden** • 13 Dalston Ln
• **Evin Bar and Café** • 115 Kingsland High St
• **Mangal 1** • 10 Arcola St
• **Mangal 2** • 4 Stoke Newington Rd
• **Peppers and Spice** • 40 Balls Pond Rd
• **Somine** • 131 Kingsland High St
• **Stone Cave** • 111 Kingsland High St

Shopping
• **Dalston Mill Fabrics** • 69 Ridley Rd
• **Hackney Downs Studios** • 17 Amhurst Terrace
• **Healthy Stuff** • 168 Dalston Ln
• **LN-CC** • 18 Shacklewell Ln
• **Oxfam** • 514 Kingsland Rd
• **Party Party** • 9 Ridley Rd
• **Ridley Road Food Market** • Ridley Rd
• **St Vincent's** • 484 Kingsland Rd
• **Turkish Food Centre** • 89 Ridley Rd

Map 87 · **Hackney Downs / Lower Clapton**

85

Cypress Close
Mount Pleasant Lane
Brampton Close
Mt Pleasant
Southwold Road

Clapton Rail

Gunton Road
Cleveleys Road
Casimir Road

Lee Valley Park -
North Millfields
Recreation Ground

Narford Road
Rendlesham Road
Evering Road
Teighburgh Road
Brooke Road
Walsingham Road
Nightingale Road

Nicholson Street
Maury Road
Neville Road
Laura Grove

Upper Clapton A107

Proud Road

Lea Valley Park -
South Millfields
Recreation Ground

Bethnal Green
Evering Road
Clapton Way

A

Stellman Close
Montague Way
Muir Road

Kenninghall Road

Lea Bridge Road A104

Cotesbach Road
Thornby Road
Fletching Rd
Northiam St
Mildenhall

Rennscroft Way
Clapton Way
Midhurst Way
Worsley Grove

Muir Road
Della Path
Brackenfield
Napoleon Road
Nolan Way
Gliddon Drive
Mount Way
Tiger Way

Ferron Road
Charnock Road
Powell Road
Heyworth Road

Lower Clapton Road A102

Newick Road
Millfields Road
Rossae Street
Denne Place
Elderfield Road

Thistlewaite Road
Contemplation Ave

Wick Road
Downs Rd A104
Lower Clapton Rd

Casterton Street
Colenso Road

186

First Terrace
Downs Road

Hackney
Downs

Crickfield Road A104

Gaviller
Place

Apprentice
Way

Atherden Rd
Rushmore Road
Mayola Road
Landseer Rd

Downs Park Road
Queensdown Road

Rowhill Road

Laura Place

Century
Ms

Linscott Road

Blurton Road
Glenarm Road
Dunlace Road

B

Sandbrook Close
Bridge Close
Wren Terrace

Downs Park Road

Mothers
Sq

Tilia Road

Ruca
Ms

Andre Street
Amhurst Road

Pembury Road A104
Bodney Road

Goulton Road
Clarence Road

Anthony's
Close

Clarence Place

London
Orphan
Asylum

College Road
Median Road
Dulverton Walk
Allsibade
Close
Dean Clo

Langford Close
Wattisfield Road
Terrace Road

Sigdon Road
Wilton Way
Lushington Terrace
Pembury
Place

Shelness Rd
Hindrey Road
Tolsford Road
Orchard Place

Clarence Mews

Clarence Square
Clapton Passage

Lower Clapton Road A107

Rowe Lane
St John's
Church Road

Urswick Road

Median Road
Haldon Close
Waterloo
Close

Barton Close
Burrett Mews

90

Dalston Lane A107

Hackney
Downs Rail

Dalston Ln A104

Kreedman Walk
Wayland Avenue
Malvern Road

Amhurst Rd A107

Institute Pl
Marcon Place
Spurstowe Terrace

Bodney Road
Kenmure Road

Kenmure
Yard

Brett Road

Ashland
Mews

St John's
Church Road

The Strand
Building

Sutton Sq

Sutton Pl

Sutton House

Homerton
Barnabas Road
Furrow Lane

89

Cottrill Gdns
Navarino Grove
Fassett Square
Fassett Road

Poyston Road
Bohemia Place
Hackney
Cemetery
Path
Mehetabel Road

| 0.25 mile | | 0.25 km |

Hackney Downs/Lower Clapton

Hackney Downs/Lower Clapton

A few years ago you couldn't move for house gigs and secret raves around the Downs, but these days the area is devolving into the moody gangland it used to be whilst breeding the rioters of tomorrow. Lower Clapton, on the other hand, is ever on the up. Shop at **Umit's** for rare films and sweets. Food and coffee can be found at vegan punk paradise **Pacific Social Club**.

Coffee

- **Organic & Natural** • 191 Lower Clapton Rd
- **Pacific Social Club** • 8 Clarence Rd

Landmarks

- **London Orphan Asylum** • Lower Clapton Rd & Linscott Rd
- **The Strand Building** • 29 Urswick Rd
- **Sutton House** • 2 Homerton High St

Nightlife

- **Biddle Brothers** • 88 Lower Clapton Rd
- **The Crooked Billet** • 84 Upper Clapton Rd
- **The Pembury Tavern** • 90 Amhurst Rd
- **Star by Hackney Downs** • 35 Queenstown Rd

Post Offices

- **Dalston Lane** • 244 Dalston Ln
- **Hackney** • 400 Mare St

Restaurants

- **Mess Café** • 38 Amhurst Rd

Shopping

- **Kate Sheridan** • 02 Lower Clapton Rd
- **Oslo** • 1 Amhurst Rd
- **Palm 2** • 152 Lower Clapton Rd
- **The Pet Shop** • 40 Amhurst Rd
- **Salvation Army Clapton** • 122 Lower Clapton Rd
- **Umit & Son** • 35 Lower Clapton Rd

Map 87

Map 88 · **Haggerston / Queensbridge Rd** N

86

Mayfield Close

Grace Jones Close

St.

Englefield Road

Mortimer Road

Hertford Road

Kingsland Road St Market

Richmond Road

Richmond Road

Beehive Close

Buxted Road

Holly Street

Lomas Drive

Lenthall Road

Gayhurst Road

De Beauvoir Square

De Beauvoir Square

Glebe Road

Evergreen Square

Mapledene Road

Mapledene Road

St. Peter's Way

Freshfield Avenue

Mulberry Rd

Celandine Dr

Evergreen Square

Jacaranda Grove

Lavender Grove

82

Ernied Road

Oslo Road

Mayfield Close

Frederick Terrace

Albion Terrace

Albion Drive

Queensbridge Road B108

Ropewalk Ms

Middleton Rd

A

Lancaster Close

ess Place

Hertford Road

Kingsland Road A10

Arbutus St

Arbutus Street Park

Haggerston

Lee Street

Albion Square

Albion Drive

Livermere Road

Shrubland Road

89

Grand

Marlborough Avenue

Brougham Road

Acton Mews

Sean Street

Loanda Close

Clarissa Street

Scriven Street

Brownlow Road

Anna Close

Harriet Close

Byron Close

Johnson Close

Wilde Close

Dunston Street

Phoenix Close

Richardson Close

Garden Place

Samuel Close

Aitken Close

Letitia Close

Osborn Close

Magrian Close

Stephen Close

Baltic Place

Dunston Street

Seacole Close

Denne Terrace

Pownall Road

Regents Row

Canal Path

Mill Row

Pear Tree Close

Amber Wharf

Nursery

Laburnum Street

Regent's Canal

Gloucester Square

Whiston Road

Sister

Regents Row

Regent's Canal

Nichol Sportsman Street Mews

Sportsman Mews

Egan Street

Phillipp St

Wilmer Road

Nuttall Street

Dove Row

Hay St

Move

92

84

Kingsland Road A10

Tyler Close

Hows Street

Weymouth St

Kent St

Thirtle Road

Kent St

Haggerston Park

Boston St

Audrey St

Malard Sq

Goldsmith Row

B

Hare Walk

Ormsby St

Appleby Street

Weymouth Terrace

Teale Street

Sovereign Mews

Pearson Street

St Mary's Secret Garden

Weymouth St

Queensbridge Road B108

Boston St

Goldsmith's Row

Geffrye Museum Gardens

Hoxton

Crabtree Close

Dunloe Street

Dunloe St

Dawson St

Yorkton Street

Hackney City Farm

Geffrye Museum

Geffrye Street

Fellows Ct

Scawfell St

91

Hackney Road A1208

Shenfield St

Cremer Street

Stanway Place

Redvers Street

Stamp Place

Columbia Road

Ion Square Gardens

Warner Pl

Peter's Square

Shipton Street

With the opening of Haggerston Station and the Ginger Line, it seems Shoreditch is merging with Dalston to form one sprawling kingdom of hipdom. Stroll down to the gardens at the **Geffrye Museum** or Haggerston Park for some people-watching with a flat white from **Long White Cloud**.

Coffee
• **Long White Cloud** • 151 Hackney Rd

O Landmarks
• **Geffrye Museum** • 136 Kingsland Rd
• **St Mary's Secret Garden** • 30 Pearson St

🍸 Nightlife
• **Brilliant Corners** • 470 Kingsland Rd
• **The Jago** • 440 Kingsland Rd

✉ Post Offices
• **Kingsland Road** • 416 Kingsland Rd

Restaurants
• **Berber & Q** • Arch 338, Acton Mews
• **Chicks n Sours** • 390 Kingsland Rd
• **Fabrique Bakery** • 385 Geffrye St
• **Faulkner's** • 424 Kingsland Rd
• **Hackney City Farm** • 1 Goldsmiths Row
• **Uludag** • 398 Kingsland Rd
• **Song Que** • 134 Kingsland Rd
• **Viet Hoa Café** • 70 Kingsland Rd

🛍 Shopping
• **KTS The Corner** • 415 Kingsland Rd

London Fields/Hackney Central

Skip through London Fields, dip your toe in the **Lido**, and attempt to make your way through the throngs checking out their reflections in the shop windows on Broadway Market.

Coffee

- **Climpson & Sons** • 67 Broadway Market
- **Donlon Books** • 77 Broadway Market
- **Violet** • 47 Wilton Wy
- **Wilton's** • 63 Wilton Way

O Landmarks

- **London Fields Lido** • London Fields Westside

Libraries

- **Hackney Central Library** • 1 Reading Ln

Y Nightlife

- **Baxter's Court** • 282 Mare St
- **The Dove** • 24 Broadway Market
- **Draughts** • 41 Kingsland High St
- **The Old Ship** • 2 Sylvester Path
- **Pub on the Park** • 19 Martello St

Post Offices

- **London Fields** • 39 Broadway Market

Restaurants

- **Buen Ayre** • 50 Broadway Market
- **Cat and Mutton** • 76 Broadway Market
- **Hai Ha** • 206 Mare St
- **Okko** • 49 Broadway Market
- **Ombra** • 1 Vyner St
- **Pidgin** • 52 Wilton Wy
- **The Spurstowe Arms** • 68 Greenwood Rd

Shopping

- **Broadway Market** • Broadway Market
- **Burberry Factory Shop** • 29 Chatham Pl
- **Candle Factory** • 184 Mare St
- **E5 Bakehouses** • 395 Mentmore Terrace
- **L'eau a la Bouche** • 35 Broadway Market London
- **Viktor Wynd's Shop of Horrors** • 11 Mare St

Supermarkets

- **Iceland** • 150 Mare St
- **Tesco** • 55 Morning Ln

Map 90 • Homerton / Victoria Park North (N)

1

2

Redwald Road

Shalness Rd
Clarence Pl
Clarence Rd

Hindrey Road
Dunlace Rd
Colne

Tolsford Road
Clifden Road
Clifden Road

Orchard Place
Elderfield Road
Ashenden Road

Dalston Lane A107
Clifden Mews
Chelmer Road

Lower Clapton Road A107
Fisher Clo
Riding Road

Amhurst Road A107
Median Rd

Kenmure Rd
Rowe Ln
Dean Clo
Ambleside Clo
Symington Mews
Glyn Road

St. John's Church Road
Staveley Clo
Barton Clo
Cranby Place

Urswick Road
Waterloo Close
Hospital
Homerton Grove
Cranby Place

Sutton Sq
Burnett Clo
Homerton Row
Warlle Street
St. Barnabas Ter

Sutton Pl
87
Fenn Street
Ryder Ms
Homerton High Street A102
Marsh Hill B112

Graham Rd A1207
Mehetabel Road
Link Street
Sedgwick St
Mackintosh Ln
Crozier Terrace

Morning Ln B113
Chatsworth Road
Ram Place
Digby Road

Belsham St
Woodbine Ter
Stevens Avenue
Berger Road

Paragon Road
Retreat Place
Oriel Road
Homerton Rail

Darnley Road
Cresset Road
Daley St
Hassett Road

189
Collent Street
Anderson Rd
Ballance Road

Brenthouse Road
Milborne Street
Bentham Road
Wick Road B113

Loddiges Road
Valentine Rd
Kenton Road B113
Bramshaw Rd
Hartlake Road

Frampton Park Road
Poole Road
Queen Anne Rd
Bradstock Rd

Well Street
Cassland Road A106
Cassland Road
Meynell Rd

Meynell Gardens
Meynell Cres

Well Street A106
Church Crescent
Gerald Road
Meynell Rd

Balcorne Street
Groombridge Road
Well Street Common

Clarendon Close
Banbury Road
Victoria Park Road A106

Moulins Rd
Alpine Gro
Elderslie Road
Penshurst Road

Jackson Close
Lauriston Rd
Guinness Close

Southborough Rd
Victoria Park

Victoria Park Road A106
Lauriston Rd A1205
PAGE 356

St. Agnes Close
Connor St
Iveagh Close

Morpeth Grove
Hackney Cemetery (Jewish)
Wetherall Rd

Deer Park
Gore Road
Morpeth Rd

0.25 mile   0.25 km

Homerton/Victoria Park North

Aah, Hackney Village: leafy Lauriston Road and its surrounds would make a nice retreat from the madding crowd if everyone else didn't have the same idea. Nevermind, have a Sunday Roast at the **Royal Inn on The Park**. Whereas once one would only be seen in Homerton if one was going to the hospital (or going to the hospital because one was in Homerton), Chatsworth Road (just off map) is now the place du jour.

Emergency Rooms

- **Homerton University Hospital** • Homerton Row

Libraries

- **Homerton Library** • Homerton High St

Nightlife

- **Chats Palace Arts Centre** • 42 Brooksby's Walk
- **The Kenton** • 38 Kenton Rd
- **The Lauriston** • 162 Victoria Park Rd
- **Royal Inn on the Park** • 111 Lauriston Rd

Post Offices

- **High Street** • 226 Homerton High St
- **Victoria Park** • 112 Lauriston Rd
- **Well Street** • 188 Well St

Restaurants

- **Eat 17** • 64–66 Brooksby's Walk
- **The Empress of India** • 130 Lauriston Rd
- **The Fish House** • 126 Lauriston Rd
- **Well Street Kitchen** • 203 Well St

Shopping

- **The Ginger Pig** • 99 Lauriston Rd
- **House of Pets** • 135 Well St
- **Perlie Rides** • 137 Well St
- **Sublime** • 225 Victoria Park Rd
- **Work Shop** • 77 Lauriston Rd

Supermarkets

- **Tesco** • 180 Well St

Map 90

Map 91 • Shoreditch / Brick Lane / Spitalfields N

Throbbing with trend-lords on single-speed bikes, great curry houses, and alternative-lifestyle vomit, the trick is to sample Brick Lane and Shoreditch on market days for pure colour and bustle, but to avoid it on weekend eves. Shopping is abundant: **Beyond Retro**, and oodles of great little rag shacks. Head towards **Catch** for booze. For a dash of authenticity, leave your £1000 bike unlocked and watch what happens.

Cinemas

- **Ninety One Living Room** • 91 Brick Ln
- **Rich Mix Centre** • 35 Bethnal Green Rd

Coffee

- **Allpress** • 58 Redchurch St
- **Cafe 1001** • 91 Brick Ln
- **Leila's Shop** • 17 Calvert Ave
- **Nude Espresso** • 26 Hanbury St

Landmarks

- **Brick Lane Mosque** • 59 Brick Ln
- **Christ Church Spitalfields** • 2 Fournier St
- **Dennis Severs' House** • 18 Folgate St
- **Spitalfields Market** • 105 Commercial St
- **Sweet Toof Graffiti Alley** • Pedley St & Brick Ln
- **Ten Bells** • 84 Commercial St
- **Truman's Brewery** • 91 Brick Ln

Nightlife

- **93 Feet East** • 150 Brick Ln
- **Bar Kick** • 127 Shoreditch High St
- **The Birdcage** • 80 Columbia Rd
- **Browns** • 1 Hackney Rd
- **The Big Chill Bar** • Dray Walk off Brick Ln
- **Café 1001** • 91 Brick Ln
- **The Carpenters Arms** • 73 Cheshire St

- **Catch** • 22 Kingsland Rd
- **The Cocktail Trading Co.** • 68 Kingsland Rd
- **The Commercial Tavern** • 142 Commercial St
- **The Culpeper** • 40 Commercial St
- **The Golden Heart** • 110 Commercial St
- **Jaguar Shoes** • 32 Kingsland Rd
- **Uwl & Pussycat** • 34 Redchurch St
- **Pride of Spitalfields** • 3 Heneage St
- **The Redchurch** • 107 Redchurch St
- **The Royal Oak** • 73 Columbia Rd
- **Sager + Wilde** • 193 Hackney Rd
- **Shoreditch House** • Ebor St

Post Offices

- **Bethnal Green** • 223 Bethnal Green Rd
- **Hackney Road** • 178 Hackney Rd

Restaurants

- **Beigel Bakery** • 159 Brick Ln
- **Boundary** • 2 Boundary St
- **Brawn** • 49 Columbia Rd
- **Chez Elles** • 45 Brick Ln
- **The Culpeper** • 40 Commercial St
- **Dishoom** • 7 Boundary St
- **Ethiopiques** • Brick Ln
- **Frizzante** • 1 Goldsmith's Row
- **Hanoi Cafe** • 98 Kingsland Rd
- **Hawksmoor** • 157 Commercial St
- **Lyle's** • 56 Shoreditch High St

- **Marksman Public House** • 254 Hackney Rd
- **Mein Tay** • 106 Kingsland Rd
- **The Premises** • 209 Hackney Rd
- **Rosa's** • 12 Hanbury St
- **St John Bread and Wine** • 94 Commercial St
- **Tay Do Cafe** • 65 Kingsland Rd
- **Viet Grill** • 58 Kingsland Rd

Shopping

- **Beyond Retro** • 112 Cheshire St
- **Blackman's Shoes** • 46 Cheshire St
- **Brick Lane** • Brick Ln
- **Columbia Road Flower Market** • Columbia Rd
- **Columbia Road Market** • Columbia Rd
- **Dum Dum Donutterie** • 2–4 Bethnal Green Rd
- **The Grocery** • 54 Kingsland Rd
- **Labour & Wait** • 85 Redchurch St
- **Lily Vanillie** • 18 Ezra St
- **Luna and Curious** • 24 Calvert Ave
- **A Portuguese Love Affair** • 326 Hackney Rd
- **Rough Trade East** • 91 Brick Ln
- **Sunday (Up)Market** • Brick Ln
- **Taj Stores** • 112 Brick Ln
- **Taylor Taylor** • 137 Commercial St

Map 92 · **Bethnal Green**

Regents Row
Westgate Street
King Edwards Rd
B108
Thurne Way
Whiston Road
Duncan Street
Duncan Road
Dove Row
Warburton Street
Warburton Road
Whiston Road
Ada Place
Ada Road
Sheep Lane
Bush Road
Ash Grove
B108
Helena
Butler Road
Victoria Park Road A106
Northam Street
Christchurch
Square
Pennethorne
Close
Vicars Close
Vyner Street
Lyle St
Corridge Cres
Lark Row
Hare Row
Wadeson Street
Martha Court
Moulins Road
Bishops Way
93
B127

Haggerston
Park

Hackney
City Farm

Goldsmith's Sq
Teale Street
Marian
Sq
Marian
Pl
Emma Street

Hackney Road A1208

Ion Square
Gardens
St. Peter's Ave
St. Peter's Sq
St. Peter's Clo
Coate Street
Dfmont Street
Marian Street
Treadway
Cambridge
Centre
Street
Minerva St
Temple Street
Cambridge Heath Rail
Cambridge
Heath Road A107
West St Mill
Parmiter Street
Huddleston
Close
Robinson Road
Bonner Road
Edinburgh
Clo
Russia Lane
Approach Road

Warner Place
B108
Claredale Street
Sheldon St
Maple St
Winkley St
Crown Works
Tanners Yd
Clare Street

Wellington Row
Nelson Gdns

A
B118
Del Ta Way

91

Blythe St
Old Bethnal Green Road
St. Jude's Rd
Middleton Street
Clarkson Street
Pundersons Gdns

Cambridge Heath Road A107

Patriot Square
Peel Grove
Old Ford Road
B118
Cyprus St
Cyprus St
Museum
Gardens
Victoria Park Square

Old Ford Road
B118
Moravian St
Gawber
Street
Meynwyn St
Kirkwall
Place
Hartley
Street
Royston St

Bethnal Green Road B108
Squirries Street B108
Florida Street
Voss St
Voss St
Derbyshire Street
Ainsley Street

Mansford St
Pollard St
Wat P
Rushmead
Florida
Camlet Street

A1209
Viaduct
Place
Viaduct Street

Ravenscroft
Mape St
Fott St
Gales Gardens
Hollybush Gdns

Roman Road
London
Buddhist
Centre
Globe Road
B119
Digby Street

Ropley St
Bethnal
Green
Tube Station

Weavers
Fields
Kelsey St
Chester St
Vallance Road B108

Dunbridge Street
B135
Fakruddin Street

Bethnal Green
Rail
Three Colts Lane
B135

Corfield Street
Finnis Street
Vigor St
Suffolk St
Wilan Street
Herald St
Glass St
Cornwall Ave

Bethnal
Green
Gardens
Mantus Road
Wessex St
Hadleigh St
Portman Place
Globe Road B120

Tent Street
Scott St
Somerford Street
Cudworth Street
Barnsley St
Buckhurst Street

Brady
Street
Cemetery
(Jewish)

St. Bartholomew
Gardens
Mercerons Street

Malcolm Pl
Williams Bldgs.
Malcolm Road
Digby St
Colville
Coborn
Cephas St
Cephas Avenue
Cephas St

Cambridge Heath Road A107

Durward Street
Winthrop Street
96
Whit
Whitechapel Road A11
Mile End Road A11

0.25 mile

0.25 km

97

Vaudrey Close
Cleveland Gro
Mile End Rd
Stepney

Bethnal Green

Map 92

No longer the inner-city ghetto from days of yore, but you can still find some of the gor-blimey-lor-love-a-duck cockney cheekiness that one would expect in this hood. **E. Pellicci** is one of the oldest remaining greasy spoons in London, so head in for a Full Monty and a cuppa. If a lager and a burger down the **Sebright Arms** is not your thing, head down to the **Buddhist Centre** for a bit of instant karma.

Coffee

• **Hurwundeki Cafe** • 242 Cambridge Heath Rd

O Landmarks

• **Bethnal Green Tube Station** •
Bethnal Green Tube Station
• **London Buddhist Centre** • 51 Roman Rd

Libraries

• **Bethnal Green Library** • Cambridge Heath Rd
• **Idea Store Bow** • Roman Rd

Nightlife

• **Bethnal Green's Working Men's Club** • 44 Pollard Row
• **The Florist Arms** • 255 Globe Rd
• **Sebright Arms** • 31 Coate St
• **Satan's Whiskers** • 343 Cambridge Heath Rd
• **The Star Of Bethnal Green** • 359 Bethnal Green Rd
• **The Virgin Queen** • 94 Goldsmiths Row

Post Offices

• **Bethnal Green Road** • 365 Bethnal Green Rd
• **Cambridge Heath** • 481 Cambridge Heath Rd

Restaurants

• **Bistrotheque** • 23 Wadeson St
• **E Pellicci** • 332 Bethnal Green Rd
• **The Gallery Cafe** • 21 Old Ford Rd
• **Little Georgia** • 87 Goldsmiths Row
• **Mission** • 250 Paradise Row

Shopping

• **AP Fitzpatrick** • 142 Cambridge Heath Rd

Supermarkets

• **Tesco** • 361 Bethnal Green Rd

Map 93 · **Globe Town / Mile End (North)**

1

2

Pennathorne Close

Vicars Close

Rutland Road

Connor Street

Hackney Cemetery (Jewish)

Wetherall Road

Gore Road

Morpeth Gro

Morpeth Road

Waterloo Gdns

Sewardstone Road

Bishops Way B127

Bonner Road

Robinson Road

Approach Road

St James's Avenue

Sewardstone Road B127

Deer Park

Victoria Park

Victoria Park

PAGE 356

Lauriston Rd A1205

A

◀92

Elsden Mews

Old Ford Road B118

St James Avenue

Cyprus Street

Old Ford Road B118

Royal Victor Pl

Peachwalk Ms

Nightingale Mews

Chisenhale Road

Vivian Road

Zealand Road

Ellesmere Road

Driffield Road

Dalling Way

Cyprus Street

Miranda St

Gawber St

Wilmot St

Brierly

Royston St

Hartley St

Mace St

Cranbrook St

Twig Fnwy

Gathorne Street

Wennington Green

Kenilworth Road

Bunsen St

Roman Road B119

Lanfranc St

◀94

Globe St

Jersey

Peary Pl

Bonham St

Morpeth St

Knottisford

Usk St

Smart Street

Palmers Road

Roman Road B119

Vernon Road

Thoydon Road

Olga St

Olga St Ms

✉ **Roman Road**

Digby Street

Bullards Place

Wilton Rd

Grove Road A1205

Arbery Road

Strahan Road

Mile End Park

Meath Gardens

Morpeth St

Walter St

Meath Crescent

Haverfield Road

Antill Road

Cherrywood Drive

○ **Mile End Climbing Wall**

Lichfield Rd

Ashcroft Road

Alloway Rd

Rhondda Grove

Pembroke Rd

Bancroft Road

Portelet Road

Hartley Road

Bradwell Street

Leatherdale Street

Longnor Road

Grantley Street

B

Cephas Street

Massingham Street

Maple Street

Carlton Sq

Toilet St

Carlton St

Holton St

Globe Road

Boyton Rd

Sceptre Road

Portman Place

Alderney Road

Colman Close

CarWe Mews

Alderney Road Cemetery (Jewish)

Alderney Place

Frimley Way

Bancroft Road

Mile End Jewish Cemetery

Westfield Way

PAGE 346

Mile End Park

Clinton Road

Morgan St

Lawton Road

○ **Art Pavillion**

Aberavon Road

Mile End

A1205

Whitman Rd

Pembroke Mews

Wentworth Mews

Eric Street

◀99

Mile

Mile End Park

◀97

⊖ **Stepney Green**

B120

Louisa Street

Eastbury Terrace

Ernest Street

Cephas Ave

Evans Pl

Mile End Road A11

Sunda Walk

Toby Lane

Close

Canal

Union Drive

98

Mile End Road A1205

Burdett Road

Hamlets Way

Tomlins Terr

Cam...

Med...

0.25 mile

0.25 km

Globe Town / Mile End (North)

Map 93

Yeah Victoria Park is nice and all, but it's just a bunch of trees and grass innit? South of all that green sh** is an up-and-coming nabe with so many great little gems. So, **The Palm Tree** is the best pub in Britain. **The Victoria** is becoming a brilliant gig spot. We'd move here if we had the balls, in fact.

O Landmarks
- **Art Pavilion** • 221 Grove Rd
- **Mile End Climbing Wall** • Haverfield Rd & Grove Rd

Nightlife
- **The Approach** • 47 Approach Rd
- **The Lord Tredegar** • 50 Lichfield Rd
- **Morgan Arms** • 43 Morgan St
- **Palm Tree** • 127 Grove Rd
- **The Victoria** • 110 Grove Rd

Post Offices
- **Roman Road** • 138 Roman Rd

Restaurants
- **Greedy Cow Burgers & Steaks** • 2 Grove Rd
- **Morgan Arms** • 43 Morgan St

Map 94 • **Bow**

1 2

Victoria Park
PAGE 356

Jodrell Road

Ollerton Grn

River Lee or Lea

Waterside Close

Parnell Road

Candy Street

Barge Lane

Hornbeam Square

Cedar Clo

Ruston Street

Gunmakers Rd

Saw Yard

Bridsfield

Tree Cl Ln

Willow Mews

Hawthorn Ave

Alexandra Annexe

Old Ford Road

Old Ford Road B118

Empire Wharf B118

Chisenhale Rd

B118

Roach Street

Beale Road

Alice Lane

Pulteney Clo

Annie Besant Close

Lea Clo

Tamar Clo

Chariot Clo

Hadrian Clo

East Cross Route A12

A

Zealand Road

Ellesmere Road

Driffield Road

Daling Way

Ford Road

Ford Street

St Stephen's Road

Allen Road

Aberavon Road

McCullum Road

Libra Road

Armagh Road

Legion Terrace

Garrison Rd

Forum Clo

Tiber Clo

Vivian Road

Hewlett Road

Wrights Road

Beale Place

Roman Sq Market

Cladstone Place

Usher Road

Parnell Road B142

Hitchin Sq

Daling Way

Ford Clo

Roman Road

B119

St. Stephen's Road

Wyatt Place

Roman Road

Cardigan Road

Hewison Street

Ford Clo

93

Medway Buigs

Lyal Road

Norman Grove

Rose Bank Gdns

Bank Pl

Saxon Road

Anglo Road

Vernon Road

Tredegar Road

B112

Doune

Medway Road

Selwyn Road

Stafford Road

Shetland Road

Usher Road

Four Seasons Close

Stanfield Road

Athelstane Grove

Carlile Clo

Hereford Road

Ordell Road

Mostyn Grove

Matilda Gdns

Morville Street

Redwood Mews

Primrose Close

Arbery Road

Strahan Road

Antill Road

Cherrywood Close

Tredegar Road

Springwood Close

Lichfield Road

Malmesbury Road

B

Alloway Rd

Fern-brook Mews

Morgan Street

Tredegar Terrace

Tredegar Mews

Coborn Road

Benworth Street

Harley Grove

Alfred Street

Lawrence Close

Caxton Grove

Addington Road

Denmark Place

Hartford Terrace

Kitcat Terrace

Aberavon Road

A1205

Rhondda Grove

Tredegar Sq

Lyn Mews

Coborn Street

Regal Place

98

Mile End

99

Bow Road A11

Bow Road

Bow Church

0.25 mile 0.25 km

Map 94

What have the Romans ever done for us? Not much, you might think, walking down Roman Road. But look closer and you'll find not only one of the oldest, most authentically East End jellied eels and mash eateries of the city, but also a market so cheap it'll knock even the most die-hard bargain hunters right out of their Centurion sandals. Pint? The haughty-sounding combo of **The Young Prince** or **The Lord Morpeth**.

Nightlife

- **Coborn Arms** • 8 Coborn Rd
- **Lord Morpeth** • 402 Old Ford Rd
- **The Lord Tredegar** • 50 Lichfield Rd
- **Young Prince** • 448 Roman Rd

Post Offices

- **Roman Road (603)** • 603 Roman Rd

Restaurants

- **G. Kelly Noted Eel & Pie Shop** • 526 Roman Rd
- **Pavilion Victoria Park** • Old Ford Rd

Shopping

- **Roman Road Market** • Roman Rd

Head to **Wilton's Music Hall** for crumbling decadence and table tennis.

Coffee
- **Black Sheep Coffee** • 2 Leman St
- **Starbucks** • 45 Whitechapel Rd
- **White Mulberries** • 3 Ivory House

Nightlife
- **The Dickens Inn** • 1 St Katherine Docks
- **Simmons** • 61 Mint St
- **Wilton's Music Hall** • Graces Alley & Ensign St

Restaurants
- **Cafe Spice Namaste** • 1 Lower Dock Walk
- **The Empress** • 141 Leman St

Supermarkets
- **Waitrose** • Thomas More St & Nesham St

Map 96 • Whitechapel (East) / Shadwell (West) / Wapping

Ex-dockland Wapping now imports yuppies into its converted warehouses, less-gleaming Shadwell and Whitechapel keep more of the East End spirit alive. Wapping High Street is mainly residential, Whitechapel Road is more lively. **Tayyab's** is cracking—stick out the queues, or if curry's not your thing head to **Il Bordello**.

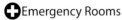Emergency Rooms

• **Royal London Hospital** • Whitechapel Rd & Vallance Rd

O Landmarks

• **Battle of Cable Street Mural, St George's Hall** • 236 Cable St
• **Blind Beggar Pub** • 337 Whitechapel Rd

Libraries

• **Idea Store Watney Market** • 260 Commercial Rd
• **Idea Store Whitechapel** • 321 Whitechapel Rd

Nightlife

• **Captain Kidd** • 108 Wapping High St
• **Town of Ramsgate** • 62 Wapping High St

Post Offices

• **Eastern** • 210 Whitechapel Rd
• **Philpot Street** • 12 Philpot St

Restaurants

• **Il Bordello** • 70 Wapping Wall
• **Lahore Kebab House** • 2–10 Umberston St
• **Needoo Grill** • 87 New Rd
• **Tayyabs** • 83 Fieldgate St

Supermarkets

• **Iceland** • 1/11 Watney St
• **Sainsbury's** • 1 Cambridge Heath Rd

Map 97 · **Stepney / Shadwell (East)**

Mercerone St

Beadman Street

Selby St

Nicholas Rd

Chicksand St

Old Montague St

Chilton St

Angel Alley

Vine Ct

Alderney Rd

Alderney Road Cemetery (Jewish)

1

2

93

Buckhurst St

Cleveland Way

Cambridge Heath Road

Durward Street

Winthrop Street

Mount Terrace

Vawdrey Close

Bellevue Place

Skinner's Rd

Globe Road B120

Trinity St

92

Stepney Green

Whitechapel

Whitechapel Road A11

Whitechapel Road A11

Mile End Road

A11

Alderney Rd

Ernest St

Raven Row

Adelina Grove

O'Leary Sq

Assembly Pass

Mile End High

Cressy Ct

Hayfield Yard

Louisa Street

Maria Ter

Eastbury Ter

Beaumont Sq

Shandy Street

A

Ashfield Street

Newark St

Sidney Street

Lindley Street

Wolsey St

Smithy Street

Beckman's Road

Cressy Rd

Imlay St

Bedford Sq

White Horse Lane

Trafalgar Gdns

Masters St

Varden Street

Nelson Street

Ford Square

Ashfield Ford

Aylward Ford

Clark Street

Clark Street

Stepney Way

Jamaica St

Wickham Clo

Ewhurst Close

Stepney Green Park

Redman's Road

Stepney Green B121

Garden Street

96

Musbury Street

Cornwood Drive

Aylward

Aylward Street

Seagrave Clo

Wellesley St

Rogers

Stepney Way

Stepping Stones Farm

98

Ben Jonson Road

Belgrave St B121

Salmon Lane

Matlock St

Timberland Road

Damien St

Anthony St

Burns St

Golding St

Watney Market

Mortor Close

Tarling Street

Ashfield St

Sidney St

Clearbrook Way

Arbour St

E Arbour St

Dunelm Street

Ashall Ter

Walter Terrace

Chudleigh Street

Bekesbourne St

Belgrave St

White Horse Road B121

Loddiges Row

Sutton St

Long Rydon

Oyster Row

Lucas Row

Emmott Close

Summercourt Way

Commercial Road A13

Marlow Mews

Head St

Ronald Street

Old Church Rd

Bromley Street

Lighterman Mews

Belgrave St

Southampton St

Cornwall St

Shadwell

Martineau Street

Johnson Street

Juniper Street

Devonport Street

Barnardo Street

Barnardo Gdns

Havering St

Aylward St

Adler St

Bower St

Ratcliffe Cross St

Butcher Row

Glasshouse St

Limehouse

Cable Street B126

Redcastle Close

Elf Row

Brodlove Lane

Glasshouse Fields

Schoolhouse La

Aldford Street

Bere St

Cranford Street

Branch Rd A101

Limehouse Cswy

B

The Highway A1203

Glamis Place

Glamis Road

The Highway A1203

Jardine Road

Horseferry Road

Narrow Street

West Gdns

Rum Close

Angel Mews

Chapman Street

Wapping Wall

Prospect Place

Milk Yard

Wapping Gdns

Newlands Quay

King Edward VII Memorial Park

Rotherhithe Tunnel

Limehouse Link

River Thames

0.25 mile

0.25 km

N

Cockney geezers run into hipsters and smart new developments sit next to rundown estates. No one quite knows where this area is going. We know where we're going, though—to **The George Tavern**, mainly, for impromptu theatre, blue-collar poetry and other arty madness, or **The Prospect of Whitby**, if we're feeling nostalgic.

Cinemas
• **Genesis Mile End** • 93 Mile End Rd

Nightlife
• **The Blind Beggar** • 337 Whitechapel Rd
• **Cable Street Studios** • 566 Cable St
• **The George Tavern** • 373 Commercial Rd
• **The Prospect of Whitby** • 57 Wapping Wall
• **Troxy** • 490 Commerical Rd

Post Offices
• **Globe Road** • 34 Globe Rd
• **Stepney** • 7 Westport St

Supermarkets
• **Co-Op** • 193 Mile End Rd

Map 98 · **Mile End (South) / Limehouse**

Mile End (South) / Limehouse

Scary desolate landscapes and urban decay? Cool! Authenticity and Edge go hand-in-hand 'round here until you get to the water, where it livens up and turns into a Foxtons wank fantasy. Still, **The Grapes**, **Kitchen on the River**, and **La Figa** are eats and drinks havens while the **Ragged School Museum** offers a glimpse of what it was like when it was really grim round 'ere.

O Landmarks

• **Ragged School Museum** • 46 Copperfield Rd

Nightlife

• **The Grapes** • 76 Narrow St

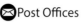Post Offices

• **Ben Jonson Road** • 52 Ben Jonson Rd
• **Mile End** • 13 Burdett Rd

Restaurants

• **Ariana** • 2 Midlothian Rd
• **Bread Street Kitchen on the River** • 44 Narrow St
• **La Figa** • 45 Narrow St
• **The Orange Room** • 63 Burdett Rd

Map 98

Map 99 · Bow Common

94

93

Bow Road

Bow Church

Mile End

98

Mile End Park

Mile End Stadium
Revolution Karting

A

B

100

101

Tredegar Sq

Morgan Street

Rhondda Grove

Aberavon Road

Lyn Ms

Coborn Road

Harley Grove

Tredegar Rd

Bromley High Street

Bow Road A11

Merchant St

Went Ms

Dublin Ms

Wentworth Mews

Eric Street

Southern Grove

Bromsley Street

Bristol Street

Fairfield Road

Bow Church

Campbell Road

Arnold Road

Tomlins Grove

Payne Road

Strudwick Walk

Arrow Road

Bruce Road

Reeves Road

Devons Road

Hamlets Way

English Street

Treby St

Ropery Street

Bow Common Lane

Archibald Street

Eleanor Street

Wellington Way

Coventry Street

Merchant St

Tower Hamlets
Cemetery Park

Fairfoot Road

Fillebrook Way

Tidworth Road

Swaton Road

Corby Way

Chiltern Street

Rounton Road

Devons Road

St. Andrews Way

Portia Way

Wager Street

Joseph Street

Maritime St

Cantrell Rd

Roberton Street

Ackroyd Dr

Bow Common Lane

Cantell Rd

Spanby Rd

Knapp Road

Fern Street

Whitehorn Street

Blackthorn St

Brock Place

Maddams Street

Watts Grove

Cranwell Close

Violet Road

Joseph Street

Weatherley Close

Bythorne Street

Holdith Street

Shakespeare Ct

Leopold St

Selsey Street

Bow Common Lane

Bellot Street

Yeley St

Devons Road

Cale Street

Furze Street

Copton Close

Yeo Street

Glaucus Street

Haven Mews

St. Paul's Way B140

Locksley Street

Turners Road

Rhodeswell

Booker Cl

Walwood Cl

Burgess Street

Celandine Cl

Killer

Bealmaland Ct

Cording Cl

Hawgood Street

Locksong Clo

Broomfield Street

Brabazon Street

Barchester Street

Morris Road

Chrisp Street

Rifle Str

Clifton Street

Langd

Clemence Street

Dora Street

Copenhagen Pl

Agnes Street

Burdett Road A1205

Thomas Road

Limehouse Cut

Coball Street

Upper North Street

Godalming Road

Cording

Norbiton Rd

Southwater Cl

Pixley Street

Stainsby Road

Bartlett Park

Arcadia Street

Northumbria St

Ellesmere Street

Grasshaven Way

Carron Close

Cardigan Road

Grafton Cl

Copenhagen Pl

Dod Street

St. Anne's Road

Tile Yard

Farrance Street

Old School St

Pigott Street

Lindfield Street

Hind Grove

Upper North Street

Flora Close

Augusta Street

Girauld St

Cavatina Cl

Cordelia Street

Southill

Canton Street

Ricardo Street

Grundy Street

Kerbey Street

Chrisp Street

Willis Street

100

West India Dock Road

East India Dock Road A13

Pekin Street

Nankin St

Saracen Street

Grenade Street

Three Colt Street

Gill Street

Oak Lane

Newell Street

Amoy Place

Annabel Close

Jeremiah Street

Duff Street

Plimsoll Close

East India Dock Road A13

101

All Saints

Morant Street

Poplar

0.25 mile

0.25 km

Bow Common

Map 99

Desolation Row pretty much. For hardy explorers kitted out with knives and/ or chastity belts, the wonderfully overgrown and sh**-your-pants scary **Tower Hamlets Cemetery Park** is great. In fact, keep the afore-mentioned kit on if you intend creeping through the boarded-up council estates and general doom.

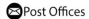 Post Offices
• **Poplar** • 22 Market Sq

Map 100 • **Poplar (West) / Canary Wharf (West)**

Poplar (West) / Canary Wharf (West)

Map 100

Now that we're officially out of the recession you can wander the wharf marveling at the 'scrapers without pesky ruined bankers landing on you. Ah yes, the smell of money has resurfaced around finance's engine room and the brilliantly futuristic landscape is once again replete with suits shopping at the bland mall under Cabot Square. They never left of course, they just got used to packed lunches like the rest of us.

Cinemas
• **Cineworld West India Quay** • 11 Hertsmere Rd

Coffee
• **Bagel Factory** • Jubilee Tube Station
• **Café Brera** • 45 Bank St
• **Café Brera** • Cabot Sq
• **Starbucks** • Unit 11, Jubilee Pl

O Landmarks
• **Canary Wharf Tower** • 1 Canada Sq
• **Canary Wharf Tube Station** • Canary Wharf

Nightlife
• **The Parlour** • 40 Canada Sq Pk

Post Offices
• **Canary Wharf** • 5 Chancellor Passage

Restaurants
• **Browns** • Hertsmere Rd
• **Plateau** • Canada Sq
• **Royal China** • 30 Westferry Circus

Supermarkets
• **Tesco** • 15 Cabot Sq
• **Waitrose** • N Colonnade & Canada Sq

Map 101 • Poplar (East) / Canary Wharf (East)

1

2

Grundy Street

Annabel Close

Jeremiah Street

Duff Street

Susannah Street

Follett Street

99

Sturry Street

East India Dock Road A13

East India Dock Rd

Black Wall Tunnel N App

Blackwall Tunnel N App A12

East India Dock Road A13

Numnery Cha

Poplar Bath St

Grove Villas

Ashton St

Bullivant St

Woodstock Terrace

Clove Crescent

Woolmore Street

Naval Ro

Poplar Recreation Ground

Wades Place

Hale Street

Cottage Street

Lawless St

All Saints

Newby Place

Bazely Street A1206

Cotton Street A1206

Robin Hood Lane

Robin Hood Gardens

Quixley Street

Hemp Street

St. Matthias Churchyard

Smythe St

Landon Walk

Montague Place

All Saint's Chyd

A

Sheppard Lane

Castor Lane

Simpsons Road

Poplar High Street

Harrow La

Ditchburn St

Blackwall

Poplar

Blackwall Tunnel

◄100

Aspen Way A1261

Aspen Way

Baffin Way

Blackwall Way

Preston's Rd

Yabsley Street

Fairmont Avenue

Boardwalk Place

Trafalgar Way

St. Lawrence St

Casilis Rd

Canada Square

Canada Square Park

Upper Bank Street

The North Colonnade

West India Docks

Landons Clo

Galleana Rd

Bridge House Quay

Blackwall Tunnel

Canary Wharf

Montgomery Street

Cold Harbour

Jubilee Park

Upper Bank Street

Clove Crescent Walk

Lightermans Walk

Nazario Place

Cold Harbour

Bank Street

Preston's Road

B

River Thames

South Quay

Lawn House Close

Glen Terrace

SW India Dock

Selsdon Way

Folly Wall

◄102

Marsh Wall

103

Millwall Dock

Chicka St

Harbour Exchange Sq

Manchester Rd A1206

0.25 mile

0.25 km

Poplar (East) / Canary Wharf (East)

Map 101

One day NFT lay down in the shadow of the Tower after a few in **The Greenwich Pensioner** and gazed up at the 'scraper, admiring its Philip K. Dickian splendour. A small plane buzzed by. Well-heeled bankers stuffed with pub grub from **The Gun** strode by us. Then we got pulled up by the dreadlocks by a rozzer and got hoofed out for not reading the *Financial Times*. Serves us right.

 Libraries

• **Idea Store Canary Wharf** • Churchill Pl
• **Idea Store Chrisp Street** •
  East India Dock Rd • 1 Vesey Path

Nightlife

• **Bar Salento** • 3 Clove Cres
• **The Greenwich Pensioner** • 28 Bazely Street

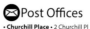 **Post Offices**

• **Churchill Place** • 2 Churchill Pl

Restaurants

• **The Gun** • 27 Coldharbour

Map 102 · **Millwall**

Ⓝ

King Street

Marsh Wall

Strafford Street

Harbour Exchange Square

Hutchings Street

The Quarterdeck

Havannah Street

Malabar Street

Mastmaker Row

Lightermans Road

Limeharbour

Alpha Grove

Cassilis Road

Indescon Court

Lanterns Court

Millharbour

Janet Street

Cheval Street

Mellish Street

Muirfield Cres
Pepper Street

Crossharbour & London Arena

Sir John McDougall Gardens

Westferry Road

Mellish Street

Tiller Road

Muirfield Cres

Turnberry Quay

Millwall Dock Road

Claire Place

Starboard Way

Greenwich View Place

East Ferry Road

Glengall Causeway

Seldon Way

Arnhem Place

Wateridge Close

The Docklands Sailing & Watersport Centre

Millwall Outer Dock

Millwall Inner Dock

Old Bellgate Place

Newton Pl

Charnwood Gdns

Severnake Close

Wheat Sheaf Close

Undine Road

Undine Rd

Mudchute

Crews Street

Claude Street

Barnsdale Avenue

Telegraph Place

Taeping Street

Taeping Street

Taeping Street

Undine Road

Mudchute

Cyclops Mews

Thames Cir

Epping Clo

Sherwood Gardens

Spindrift Avenue

Taeping Street

Homer Dr

River Thames

Masthouse Terrace

Ferguson Close

Ironmongers Pl

Barnfield Pl

Amb Sq

Cahir Street

Harbinger Road

Hesperus Cres

Hesperus Cres

Thermopylae Gt

103▶

Vulcan Square

Westferry Road A1206

Chapel House St

Gilliam Place

Lock Pl

Magellan Pl

Napier Ave

Cluny Ct

Tyndale Ct

Maritime Quay

Napier Ave

Wharf St

Wynan Road

Westferry Rd

Burrell St

Rainbow Ave

Pointer's Clo

Cel Place

St Davids Sq Ba

Blasker Walk

Lanterbourne

St Davids Sq

0.25 mile

0.25 km

Though Millwall has award-winning **Docklands Sailing Centre**, it doesn't really have much else. Bereft of tube, overground, or DLR, it doesn't even have Millwall FC anymore. Despite the potential of Canary Wharf on the doorstep and flush of luxury riverside apartments, it's still tainted with the whiff of BNP and football hooliganism. Buy now.

O Landmarks

• **The Docklands Sailing & Watersport Centre** •
235 Westferry Rd

Post Offices

• **Westferry Rd** • 367 Westferry Rd

Nightlife

• **Hubbub** • 269 Westferry Rd

Map 103 · **Cubitt Town / Mudchute**

N

Meridian Place

1

2

Marsh Wall

Lawn

Folly Wall

Harbour Exchange Sq

101

Chipka Street

East Ferry Road

Capstan Sq

River Barge Close

Rogerston Street

Limeharbour

High Roher Street

Over Close

Pierpa Street

Launch St

New Union Close

Manchester Street A1206

Millwall Inner Dock

Crossharbour & London Arena

Strathnodale St

Marshfield Street

Field Crescent

A

Pepper Street

Turnberry Quay

Glengall Grove

Amsterdam Road

Lenharn D

Rotterdam Drive

Rembrandt Close

Millennium Drive

102

Seldon Way

Friars Mead

Friars Mead

Millwall Inner Dock

East Ferry Road

Friars Mead Mews

Saltbord

Sam James Mews

Fair Circle

Olitfe Street

Chichester Way

Schooner Close

Mudchute Park

Blyth Close

Sextant Avenue

Undine Road

Mudchute Farm

Pier Street

Plymouth Wharf

Telegraph Place

Taeping Street

Taeping Street

Taeping Street

Undine Road

Undine Road

Undine St

Seyssel Street

Storers Quay

Mudchute

Kingfield Street

Caledonian Wharf

Spindrift Avenue

Billson Street

Saunders Ness Road

Empire Wharf

Seldonate Street

Sonage Street

Grosvenor Wharf

Thermopylae Gate

Macquarie Way

Millwall Park

Glengarry St

Glenaffric Ave

Cumberland Mills Sq

B

Chapel House Street

Tiller Road

Island Gardens

Cumberland

Harbinger Road

Undolo Court

Tobago Street

Tiller Court

Julian Place

Crockshall Place

Manchester Grove

Island Gardens

Livingstone

Westferry Road A1206

Manchester Road A1206

Wynan Road

Pointer Cl

Lang

East Ferry Road

Horseshoe Cl

Ferndale gdns

Livingstone Ferry Street

Saunders Ness Road

Midland

Bunker Walk

bourne Pl

St. Davids Square

PW

River Thames

| 0.25 mile |
| 0.25 km |

Cubitt Town / Mudchute

Map 103

Though shaded by the skyscrapers of Canary Wharf and a rash of luxury developments, this corner of the Island is blessed by the marvellous **Mudchute Farm and Park** (with the standout **Mudchute Kitchen** and equestrian centre), not one, not two, but three DLR stations, and a number of down-to-earth boozers like **Lord Nelson**. Who let the Isle of Dogs out?

O Landmarks
• **Mudchute Farm** • Pier St

Libraries
• **Cubitt Town Library** • Strattondale St

Nightlife
• **The Ferry House** • 26 Ferry St
• **The Lord Nelson** • 1 Manchester Rd

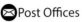Post Offices
• **Cubitt Town** • 15 Castalia Sq
• **Isle Of Dogs** • 159 Manchester Rd

Restaurants
• **Mudchute Kitchen** • Pier St

Supermarkets
• **ASDA** • 151 E Ferry Rd

Map 104 • **South Bank / Waterloo / Lambeth North**

1 **2**

Stony Place

Victoria
Embankment
Gardens

Waterloo Bridge A301

The pier
at OXO Tower

Oxo House by
the River

Upper Ground

Upper Ground

Rennie Street

Blackfriars Bridge

Blackfriars
Plaza

A3200

South

Low tide
at South Bank

South Bank
Book Market

The Television
Centre

Duchy Street

Broadwall

Stamford Street

A3200

Burrell St

River
Thames

Royal National
Theatre

Upper Ground

Colin Street

Stamford Street A3200

Aquinas St

Duchy Pl

Coin Street

Doon Street

Hatfields

Paris Garden

Colombo Street

105 ▶

Pitches

The Hayward Gallery

Meymott Street

Nicholas
St

Nicholson St

SOUTH BANK

Concert Hall Approach

Belvedere Road

**PAGE
352**

Waterloo Road

Stamford Street A3200

Theed Street

Secker St

Whittlesey St

Roupell Street

Joan Street

Brad Street

Windmill Walk

Isabella Street

Southwark

Blackfriars Road

A

Jubilee
Gardens

Tenison Way

Exton Street

Alaska Street

Wootton St

Sandell Street

Cornwall Road

Cons Street

The Cut B300

Webber Street

Mitre Road

Burrows Mews

Boundary Row

Chicheley Street

York Road A3200

Mepham St
Station Approach

Waterloo
Station

**PAGE
416**

Station Approach
Spur Road

Holmes
Terr Plaz Pl

Waterloo
Millennium
Green

Ufford Street

Chaplin Close

Valentine Place

The
London
Eye

Belvedere Road

Coral Street

Webber Street

Gray Street

Baylis Rd

Pontypool Pl

Webber Row

County
Hall

Graffiti Tunnel

Addington Street

Leake Street

Sturge St

Targett St

Sidoania

Frazier Street

Pearman Street

Cosser St

Gray St

Dodson Street

B

LAMBETH

A302 Westminster Bridge Road

◀ 131

Westminster Bridge Road A3200

Lower Marsh

Lambeth
North

Cooper's Cl

Cooper Cl

Westminster Bridge Road A23

St Georges Rd

A201

Upper Marsh

Carlisle Lane

Newnham
Terrace

Hercules Road

Murphy St

Greenham

Baylis Road B300

Burdett Street

Emery St

Gerridge Street

Frazier St

King Edward Walk

St Georges Circus

St Georges Road A302

Gladstone Street

Colnbrook St

Royal Street

Centaur Street

Virgil Street

Kennington Road A23

Lambeth
Palace
Gardens

Cosser Street

Sidford Place

McAuley St

Kennington Road A23

Geraldine Mary
Harmsworth Park

Geraldine Street

West Square

West
Temple
Mews

Lambeth Palace Road A3036

Norfolk Row

Pratt Walk

Sail Street

Lambeth Road A3203

Walnut Tree Walk

Kennington Road A3203

Ravey St

Brook Drive

Walcot Square

Harmsworth
Ms

Austral St

Cotton

112 ▼

A3203

0.25 mile   0.25 km

Hug the riverbank and you can culture 'til you puke. But you'll need stamina to survive; with such densely populated institutions your brain will give up long before your body.

Cinemas

- **BFI London IMAX** • 1 Charlie Chaplin Walk
- **BFI Southbank** • Belverdere Rd & Waterloo Rd

Coffee

- **Bagel Factory** • Waterloo Station
- **BFI Bar and Kitchen** • Belvedere Rd
- **ScooterCaffe** • 132 Lower Marsh
- **Starbucks** • 3 Belvedere Rd

O Landmarks

- **County Hall** • Westminster Bridge Rd & Belvedere Rd
- **The Hayward Gallery** • Southbank Centre
- **The London Eye** • Westminster Bridge Rd
- **Low Tide at South Bank** • Waterloo Rd & Upper Ground
- **National Theatre** • South Bank
- **The Pier at OXO Tower** •
  Barge House St & Upper Ground
- **South Bank Book Markct** • Under Waterloo Bridge
- **Waterloo Bridge** • Waterloo Bridge

Libraries

- **Imperial War Museum** • Lambeth Rd
- **Poetry Library** • Royal Festival Hall
- **Waterloo Library** • 1 Kennington Rd

Nightlife

- **The Anchor & Hope** • 36 The Cut
- **BFI Bar and Kitchen** • Belvedere Rd
- **Cubana** • 48 Lower Marsh
- **The Cut Bar** • 66 The Cut
- **Royal Festival Hall** • Belvedere Rd
- **Skylon** • Belvedere Rd

Restaurants

- **The Anchor & Hope** • 32 The Cut
- **The Cut Bar** • 66 The Cut
- **Giraffe** • Riverside Level 1
- **Marie's Cafe** • 90 Lower Marsh
- **Oxo Tower Wharf** • Barge House St
- **Skylon** • Belvedere Rd
- **Tas Cut** • 33 The Cut

Shopping

- **Calder Bookshop** • 51 The Cut
- **Calder Bookshop Theatre** • 51 The Cut
- **Greensmiths** • 27 Lower Marsh
- **Konditor & Cook** • 22 Cornwall Rd
- **ScooterCaffe** • 132 Lower Marsh
- **Southbank Book Market** • Under Waterloo Bridge

Supermarkets

- **Iceland** • 112 Lower Marsh
- **Marks & Spencer** • Waterloo Station
- **Sainsbury's** • 101 Waterloo Rd

Map 103 • **Southwark / Bankside (West)** N

Southwark / Bankside (West)

The **Tate Modern**, ladies and gents. It deserves all the praise it gets. And next door there's **Shakespeare's Globe**, the modern reconstruction of the Elizabethan playhouse where the Bard of Avon's works were contemporaneously produced. Both make this looked-after stretch of the Thames embankment a treasure for those hungry for culture.

Coffee

- **Pret A Manger** • 2 Canvey St
- **Starbucks** • Emerson St (Units 1–3 Benbow House)

O Landmarks

- **Buskers' Archway** • Southbank
- **Elephant & Castle** • Elephant & Castle
- **Michael Faraday Memorial** • Elephant & Castle
- **The Ring** • 72 Blackfriars Rd
- **Shakespeare's Globe** • 21 New Globe Walk
- **Tate Modern** • Bankside

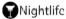 Nightlife

- **Albert Arms** • 1 Gladstone St
- **The Libertine** • 125 Great Suffolk St
- **The Lord Nelson** • 243 Union St
- **Ministry of Sound** • 103 Gaunt St
- **The Prince of Wales** • 51 St George's Rd
- **Union Theatre** • 229 Union St

Post Offices

- **Blackfriars Road** • 52 Blackfriars Rd

Restaurants

- **Mercato Metro** • 42 Newington Causeway
- **The Table** • 83 Southwark St
- **Tate Modern Restaurant** • Bankside
- **Terry's Cafe** • 158 Great Suffolk St

Map 106 • Bankside (East) / Borough / Newington

Thames

Bankside

New Globe Walk
Bear Gardens
Rose Alley

Sumner Street

Southwark Bridge Road

Park Street

Clink Street
Winchester
Palace

The Golden
Hinde

Montague
Close

Winchester
Square

Southwark
Cathedral

Duke Street Hill

London Bridge

The London
Tombs

A200

London
Bridge
Station

PAGE
412

The Shard

Porlock St
Gate
House
Sq

Perkins Sq

Maiden Lane

Zoar St

Thrale Street

Southwark Street A3200

Wardens Grove

America Street

Pepper St

Copperfield St

Union Street B300

O'Meara St

Ayres St

Union Street B300

Cross Bones
Graveyard

Little
Dorrit
Park

**THE
BOROUGH**

Marshalsea Road

Mint
Street
Park

Borough

St George
the Martyr

A200

St. Thomas Street

Old Operating
Theatre
Museum

Great Maze Pond Rd

Snowsfields

Hamilton
Square

Long Lane A2198

Bermondsey Market
Square

Leathermarket
Gardens

◄105

Borough Road A3202

Newington Causeway A3

Great Dover Street A2

Tabard
Gardens

107▶

Great Suffolk Street

Borough High Street

Trinity Street

Newington
Gardens

Dickens
Fields

Harper Road B240

Roman
Cemetery

Female
Gladiator

Great Dover Street A2

112▼

New Kent Road A201

County Street

County Street

113▼

New Kent Road A2

A Shoreditch for grown-ups, these parts have become a bit sudified lately—especially now that it's been reborn as 'London Bridge Quarter' under the Shard. Still, there's plenty of fun to be had. Gourmet-minded **Borough Market** draws the crowds on Saturdays, while the pubs and bars lining Borough High Street keep the party-minded happy throughout the week. Don't miss **The Rake** if you like (unusual) beer, **Brindisa** for Spanish tapas, and **Roast** if meat's your thing.

Coffee

- **Caffe Nero** • 3 Cathedral St
- **Costa** • 134 Borough High St
- **Pret A Manger** • 11 Borough High St
- **Pret A Manger** • 49 Tooley St

O Landmarks

- **Cross Bones Graveyard** • Red Cross Way & Union St
- **Female Gladiator** • 159 Great Dover St
- **The Golden Hinde** • Clink St & Stoney St
- **The London Tombs** • 2 Tooley St
- **Mint Street Park** •
  Southwark Bridge Rd & Marshalsea Rd
- **Old Operating Theatre Museum** • 9 St Thomas St
- **Roman Cemetery** • 165 Great Dover St
- **The Shard** • 32 London Bridge St
- **Southwark Cathedral** • Cathedral St & Montague Close
- **St George the Martyr** • Borough High St & Tabard St
- **Winchester Palace** • Clink St & Storey St

Libraries

- **John Harvard Library** • 211 Borough High St

Nightlife

- **The Anchor** • 34 Park St
- **Belushi's** • 161 Borough High St
- **Bunch of Grapes** • 2 St Thomas St
- **The George Inn** • 77 Borough High St
- **The Globe** • 8 Bedale St
- **Number 1 Bar** • 1 Duke St Hill
- **The Market Porter** • 9 Stoney St
- **The Rake** • 14 Winchester Walk
- **The Roebuck** • 50 Great Dover St
- **The Rose** • 123 Snowfields
- **The Royal Oak** • 44 Tabard St
- **Southwark Tavern** • 22 Southwark St

Post Offices

- **Great Dover Street** • 159 Great Dover St
- **London Bridge** • 19 Borough High St

Restaurants

- **Arabica Bar & Kitchen** • 3 Rochester Walk
- **Boot and Flogger** • 10 Redcross Wy
- **Champor-Champor** • 62 Weston St
- **Fish!** • Cathedral St
- **Nando's** • 225 Clink St
- **Roast** • The Floral Hall, Stoney St
- **Silka** • 6 Southwark St
- **Tapas Brindisa** • 18 Southwark St
- **Tas Borough High Street** • 72 Borough High St
- **Wright Bros Oyster Bar** • 11 Stoney St

Shopping

- **Borough Market** • 8 Southwark St
- **Brindisa Retail** • Borough Market

Supermarkets

- **Marks & Spencer** • London Bridge Station
- **Sainsbury's** • 116 Borough High St

Map 107 · **Shad Thames**

1

2

River Thames

HMS Belfast

City Hall

MORE LONDON

Potters Fields Park

Tower Bridge A100

Shad Thames

Design Museum

London Bridge Station

PAGE 412

Duke Street Hill A200

Meadow Row

Bailie Bridge Lane

Hay's Counter St

Abbots Ln

Vine Ln

Battle Bridge Lane

Weston Street

Bermondsey Street A2205

Morgan's Ln

Tooley Street A200

Magdalen St

Holyrood St

Shand Street

Barnham Street

Druid St A100

Potters Fields

Horselydown La

Shad Thames

Lafone St

Corlite St

Gainsford Street

Maguire Street

Queen Elizabeth St

St. Thomas Street A2205

Crucifix Lane

A2207

Snowsfields

Kirby Grove

Hardwidge St

Carmarthen Pl

Black Swan

White's Grounds

Brunswick Court

Druid Street

Roper Ln

Boss La

Gedling La

Fair Street

Colson Way

Bevington St

Millenium Sq

Shad Thames

Tooley Street A200

Tanner Street A200

Sweeney Cres

Mill Street

Jacob St

Dockhead

Floating Gardens

A

Mellior Street

Guy Street

Leathermarket Gardens

Ship and Mermaid Row

Tyers Gate

Fashion & Textile Museum

Morocco St

Tanner Street

Archie St

Druid Street A2207

Millstream Rd

Stanworth Street

Maltby Street

George Row

Bermondsey Wall

Enid Street

Porlock Street

Snowfields

Long Lane A2198

Leathermarket Street

Lamb Walk

Royal Oak Yard

Bluelion Pl

Weston Street

◀106

Market Yard Ms

Newhams Row

Tower Bridge Road A100

Pope St

Riley Road

Abbey Street B202

Bridewain St

108▶

Manciple Street

Tabard Gardens

Pardoner Street

Black Horse Ct Lane Street

Weston Street

Wild's Rents

Cluny Pl

Decima Street

Rothsay Street

Abbey Street A2198

Long Walk

Stevens St

Radcliffe Rd

Fendant St

Fendall St

Sqauero

Griggs Pl

Alwin Est

Grange Walk

The Grange

Grange Yard

Grange Road A2206

Spa Road

Bermondsey Spa

Great Dover Street A2

Potier Close

Hunter Cl

Alice St

Green Walk

Rephidim St

Raglingm St

Tower Bridge Road A100

Webb Street

Swan Mead

Leroy Street

Woods Pl

Crimscott Street

Bacon Grove

Curtis St

Curtis Way

Setchell Way

Willow Walk

Alscot Way

Alscot Road

Keyse Rd

Henley Close

Dunton Road B203

Fort Road

B

New Kent Road A2

Searles Road

Wooster Place

Manciple Street

Old Kent Road A2

Marlbut St

Leroy Street

Quarancie Close

Guinness Sqaure

Page's Walk

Stompie

Bartholomew Street

Bathurst

Mason St

Townsend Street

Preston Cl

Congreve Street

Chatham St

◀113

Mandela Way

114▼

Buttermere Close

Milton Close Dry

Shad Thames

The elitist's Bermondsey, Shad Thames is home to ultra-hip boutiques, glass balconies, and converted warehouses. No café dares exist without its own gallery. Bermondsey Street blossoms as an epicentre of creatives knocking out their latest bestseller over brunch, while the More London space by the Thames is an invigorating crowd-pleaser. Head to **The Scoop** for top free events.

Coffee

- **Caphe House** • 114 Bermondsey St
- **Fuckoffee** • 163 Bermondsey St

O Landmarks

- **City Hall** • Queen's Walk, More London Development
- **Fashion and Textile Museum** • 83 Bermondsey St
- **Floating Gardens** • 31 Mill St
- **HMS Belfast** • The Queens Walk
- **The Scoop** • The Queens Walk
- **Tower Bridge** • Tower Bridge Road

Nightlife

- **The Garrison** • 99 Bermondsey St
- **The Hide** • 39 Bermondsey St
- **Hilton London Tower Bridge** • 5 Tooley St
- **The Woolpack** • 98 Bermondsey St

Restaurants

- **Butlers Wharf Chop House** • 36 Shad Thames
- **Casse-Croute** • 109 Bermondsey St
- **José** • 104 Bermondsey St
- **Le Pont de la Tour** • 36 Shad Thames
- **M Manze Pie and Mash** • 87 Tower Bridge Rd

Shopping

- **Fine Foods** • 218 Long Ln
- **Fine Foods Locanda del Melo** • 218 Long Ln
- **Maltby Street Market** • Maltby St

Map 108 · **Bermondsey**

Bermondsey

Map 108

With its mixed bag of winding cobbled streets, council estates, and posh new builds, you can imagine the awkwardness when the new-to-the-neighbourhood clean shirt steps into the the adamantly local Bermondsey boozer. The old-timers are sticking to their guns, and there is a definite dirty side to this on-the-cusp part of town.

Libraries
• **Blue Anchor Library** • Market Pl

Post Offices
• **Jamaica Road** • 158 Jamaica Rd
• **Southwark Park Road** • 242 Southwark Park Rd

Restaurants
• **Brew by Numbers** • 79 Enid St

Shopping
• **The Kernel Brewery** • 11 Dockley Road Industrial Estate

Supermarkets
• **Co-Op** • 3 Mill St
• **Iceland** • 222 Southwark Park

Map 109 · **Southwark Park**

River
Thames

1 | **2**

Loftie Street
Bevington Street
Emba Street
Waterside Plaza
Janeway Place
Mangold Street
Wilson Grove
Cherry Garden Street
Pottery Street
Bermondsey Wall East
West Lane
Cathay Street
Paradise Street
Prospect St
Fulford Street

King Stairs Close
King's Stairs Gardens
Elephant Lane
St. Mary's Church
Mayflower Street
Cathay Street
Fulford Street
Rotherhithe Street
Railway Avenue
Western Street
Kenning Street
Rotherhithe

Major Rd
Bermondsey
John Roll Way
Keetons Road
Perryn Road
Brunel Road
Rotherhithe Tunnel
Albion Street
Elephant Lane
Neptune St
Renforth Street
Chack Court
Neptune St

Jamaica Road A200

A

Collett Road
Stalks Road
Webster Road
Tranton Road
Drummond Road
Southwark Park Road
Gataker Street
Slippers Place
Clements Road
Stalham St

◀108

Albin Memorial Garden
Lower Road A200
Culling Road
Ann Moss Way
Ann Moss Way
Gomm Road
Gomm Road
orange Place
Hotfield Place
Hithe Grove Gate

110▶

ROTHERHITHE
Canada Water
Surrey Quays Road
Deal Porters Way
Moodkee Street

Ca
Wa

Blue Anchor Lane
Bombay St
Banyard Rd
Layard Street
Layard Square
Frankland C
Southwark Park Road
Raymouth Road A2206
Almond Road
Aspinden Road
Neldale Road
Abbeyfield Road

Southwark Park

Canute Gdns
Hornet Cro
Hawkstone Road

111▶

Lower Ro
Rotherhithe Old Road

B

Tecla Rd
Anchor Street
Roseberry Street
Galleywall Road
Lynton Road
Hyson Rd
Russell Road
Sheppard Drive
Storks Drive
Concorde Way
Drive

Rotherhithe New Road A2208
Jarrow Road
Debnams Road
Corbetts Lane
Contents Passage
Silwood Street
Millender Walk
Wardour St
Rotherhithe New Road
Eugenia Road
Alpine St
St. Helena Road
Concorde Way
Island Road

116▼

0.25 mile | 0.25 km

Southwark Park

Map 109

Bordered by tower blocks and the unfortunate juxtaposition of a nursing home and undertaker's, you might toy with taking your picnic elsewhere. But step inside, because it's every bit the oasis that local hero Dr Salter hoped it would be. Well-spent investment has given it a boating lake, rose garden, wildlife area, and the inspired Café Gallery Projects. Nip to **The Angel** afterwards for cheap beers and river views.

Nightlife

- **Ancient Foresters** • 282 Southwark Park Rd
- **The Angel** • 101 Bermondsey Wall E

Map 110 · **Rotherhithe (West) / Canada Water**

Rotherhithe (West) / Canada Water

Map 110

If residential flats are your thing, you'll love Rotherhithe West. Not if bars are your thing though. Or shops. Or life. But among the warren of apartments is **The Mayflower**, one of the greatest historical pubs in London, with the grave of the Mayflower ship's captain in the churchyard opposite. Entertain your dad at the **Brunel Museum**, and jog or snog your way along this serene stretch of Thames path.

Coffee

• **Brunel Museum Café** • Railway Ave

O Landmarks

• **Brunel Museum** • Railway Ave & Rotherhithe St

Libraries

•**Canada Water Library** • 21 Surrey Quays Rd

Nightlife

• **The Mayflower** • 117 Rotherhithe St
• **Old Salt Quay** • 163 Rotherhithe St
• **The Ship** • 39 St Marychurch St

Post Offices

• **Lower Road Rotherhithe** • 142 Lower Rd

Restaurants

• **Mayflower** • 117 Rotherhithe St
• **The Rainbow** • 33 Brunel Rd
• **Simplicity** • 1 Tunnel Rd

Map 111 · **Rotherhithe (East) / Surrey Quays** N

River Thames **1** **2**

Sovereign Crescent

Rotherhithe Street

Road

Edward Square

St. Paul's Sports Ground

Lavender Road

Byron's Ave

St. Paul's Close

Braeside

Yalding

Lavender Pond Nature Park

Byways Place

Heron Place

Pilgrim Crescent

Rotherhithe Street

Foundry Close

Globe Pond Road

Staples Close

Bywater Place

Acorn Walk

Saltter Road B205

Fisher Athletic (London)

Stave Yard Road

Bucklers Rents

Farrins Rents

Brewhouse Walk

Silver Walk

Katherine Cl

Clarence Mews

Rotherhithe Street

Lagado Mews

Football Club Ground (Surrey Docks Stadium)

Fir Trees Cl

Russia Dock Road

Capstan Way

Byfield Close

Brunel Road

Timber Pond Road

Midship Close

Redwood Close

Silver Walk

Bryan Rd

Rotherhithe Street

Odessa Road

A

Surrey Water

Deal Porters Way

Sunfish

Gunwhale Cl

Marlow Way

Hull Close

Motlish Sports Ground

Task Close

Holyoake Court

Salter Road

Osiate Close

Dock Hill Ave

Fishermans Drive

Greenacre Square

Stave Hill Ecological Park

Downtown Road

Radley Ct

Baltic Ct

Stave Hill

Vaughan St

Surrey Docks Farm

Christopher Close

Poolmans Street

Carter Way

Archangel Street

Russia Dock Woodland

Somerton Way

Hamilton Close Way

Steers Way

Spence Close

Needleman Street

Albatross Way

Victory Way

Homers Way

Shipwright Road

Redriff Est

Elgar Street

Odessa Street

◄110

Canada Street

Roberts Close

Lovell Place

Oslo Square

Bergen Square

Gulliver Street

◄109

ROTHERHITHE

Quebec Way

Plough Way

Onega Gate

Norway Square

Finland Street

Canada Water

Teredo Street

Odessa Street

Surrey Docks Farm

A200

Redriff Road A2202

Brunswick Quay

Helsinki Square

South Sea Street

B

Surrey Quays Road

Surrey Quays

Lower Road A200

Worgan Street

Trundleys Road

Tawny Way

Greenland Dock

Sweden Gate

Rope Street

South Dock

▼118

◄116

Canada Gardens

Cope Street

Redriff...

Greenland Quay

Mayflower Street

Trident St

Plough Way B206

Odessa Street B206

▼117

Boat Lifter Way

Lighter Close

Dunnage Crescent

California Way

Hobner Gro

Grove

Plough Way

St. Georges Mews

St. George Square

0.25 mile	0.25 km

Rotherhithe (East) / Surrey Quays

Map 111

It still has some dodgy estates, but Rotherhithe East is blossoming in a clean-cut city-worker kind of way. The docks are delightful and have resisted the chain bars, instead allowing great little independents like **The Moby Dick** to flourish. Trying to be healthy? Enjoy lunch among the goats at wholesome **Surrey Docks Farm Café**, and visit **Decathlon** for sport equipment paradise.

 Cinemas

• **Odeon Surrey Quays** • Redriff Rd & Surrey Quays Rd

 Landmarks

• **Surrey Docks Farm** • Rotherhithe St

Nightlife

• **Blacksmith's Arms** • 257 Rotherhithe St
• **Moby Dick** • 6 Russell Place, off Greenland Dock
• **Ship & Whale** • 2 Gulliver St
• **Whelan's** • 11 Rotherhithe Old Rd

 Restaurants

• **Café East** • 100 Redriff Rw
• **Ma Po** • 176 Lower Rd

 Shopping

• **Decathlon** • Surrey Quays Rd

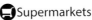 Supermarkets

• **Tesco** • Redriff Rd

Massive change is being promised in Elephant and Castle, although when and for whom is quite debatable. With masses of social housing lost with the closure of the Heygate Estate, the area could be set to become another drab luxury development a la Docklands.

O Landmarks

• **56A** • 56 Crampton St

Libraries

• **Brandon Library** • Cooks Rd
• **Durning Library** • 167 Kennington Ln

Nightlife

• **Brasserie Tolouse Lautrec** • 140 Newington Butts
• **Corsica Studios** • 5 Elephant Rd
• **Dog House** • 293 Kennington Rd
• **The Old Red Lion** • 42 Kennington Park Rd
• Prince of Wales • Cleaver Sq

Post Offices

• **Kennington Park** • 410 Kennington Park Rd

Restaurants

• **Brasserie Tolouse Lautrec** • 140 Newington Butts
• **Dragon Castle** • 100 Walworth Rd

Shopping

• **Recycling** • 110 Elephant Rd

Walworth

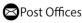 **Map 113**

Oh, Walworth. With all this about the Elephant and Castle redevelopment, why do we get the funny feeling you will never change? From the excessive amount of Gregg's bakeries along Walworth Road, to the 'who really buys these things?' tat at **East Street Market**, Walworth's lack of motivation is somehow endearing. **La Luna** for pizza is a find.

Coffee
• **Ranya Café** • 314 Walworth Rd

Landmarks
• **East Street Market** • Walworth Rd & East St
• **Heygate Estate** • Deacon Way & Heygate St

Libraries
• **Walworth Library** • 147 Walworth Rd

Nightlife
• **Red Lion** • 407 Walworth Rd

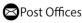Post Offices
• **Walworth Road** • 234 Walworth Rd

Restaurants
• **La Luna** • 380 Walworth Rd

Shopping
• **G Baldwin & Co** • 171 Walworth Rd

Supermarkets
• **Iceland** • 332 Walworth Rd

Map 114

Now that the 51-acre Burgess Park has been given an £8 million facelift (due to tireless community campaigning), locals have good reason to be smug as they enjoy the 30ft water fountains, 5k running track, or any of the other many new additions on their doorstep. For something different, stroll along the old canal and connect with ghosts of Peckham past.

O Landmarks

• **The Animatronic Fireman** • Old Kent Rd
• **Peckham Library** • 122 Peckham Hill St

Supermarkets

• **Tesco** • 107 Dunton Rd

Post Offices

• **Old Kent Road** • 240 Old Kent Rd

Map 115 · **Old Kent Road (East)**

Ⓝ

1
2

Weisford Street
Simms Rd
Simms Road
Beatrice
Camilla Road

Long way
Bushwood Drive
Long
Chaucer
Lynton Road
Cadet Drive
Ox
Monnow Road
Esmeralda Road
Kotree Way
Lynton Road

108

109

Chaucer Drive
Burn

Cadet Drive
Lynton Road
Peterson Park

Rolls Road
Oxley Close
Sheppard Dr
Rossetti Road

B204
Abercorn Way
Mason
Stevenson
Sheppard Dr

Borrowes Street
Avocet Close
Actris Close
Erasmus Drive
Stevenson Crescent
Crescent
Weald Close
Stubbs Drive

A
Brodie Street
Colgers Road
Fortune Pl
Palamond Ct
Rolls Road
Steven Cres
Steven Crescent
Steven Cres

116

Terrace
New Harmony Way
Mawbey Place
B204
Catlin Street B204
Masters Dr

Old Kent Road A2
Mawbey Place
Avondale
Sturge
St James's Road
Sherwood Gdns
Fern Wlk
Fellow Ct
Willow Wlk

Rotherhithe New Road
Masters Dr
Bike Rider Close
Birkdale Close
Ryder Drive

Terrace
Ainsdale Dr
Marlborough Grove
Argyle Way
Cul Close
Ryder Drive
Verney Road

Burgess Park
Waite Street
Ossory Road
Longrove Street
Verney Road

Waite Street
Old Kent Road A2

Glengall Terrace
Malt Street
Olmar Street
Canal Grove
Sandgate Street
Ruby Triangle
Ruby Street

114

Trafalgar Avenue B215
Surrey Linear Canal Park
Livesey Place
Hyndman Street
Murdock Street

Frensham Street
Old Kent Road A2

B
Pennack
Bianca Road
Leyton Square Park
Green Hundred Road
Edward Road
Pencraig Way

Davey Street
Latona Road
Alder Close
Bushell Close
Unwin Close
Glengall Road
Reddins Road
Malmore Street
Friary Road
Camelot Street

Willowbrook Road B215
Colegrove Road
Bird in Bush Road
Ledbury Road
Naylor Road
Commercial Way

Nutt Close
Peckham Park Road B216
Radnor Road
Bird in Bush Road
Broom Yd Ho
Cardine Mews

123

124

Rosemary Road
Rosemary
Peckham Hill Street
Lyndhurst Way
Corbett
Sylverdale Wlk
Lympstone Gdns
Lympstone Gdns
Commercial Way
Frary Road
Elcot Av
Nutcroft Road
Wates Wy

0.25 mile
0.25 km

Map 115

There must be something to this portion of Old Kent Road, as the Pearly Kings and Queens won't shut up about the whole thing. As far as we can tell, it's not that much more than a giant Asda. Walk along Bird In Bush Road to laugh at its name and over to Peckham Park Road for a damn good fry-up at **Roma Café**.

 Libraries

• **East Street Library** • 168 Old Kent Rd

 Supermarkets

• **ASDA** • Old Kent Rd & Ossory Rd

Restaurants

• **Roma Café** • 21 Peckham Park Rd

Map 116 · **South Bermondsey**

N

1 **2**

Banyard Rd

Southwark Park

Rotherhithe Old Rd A200

Surrey Quays

Lower Road

Rot. New Rd

A2206

Raymouth Road

A2206

Southwark Park Road

A2206

Hawkstone Road A2208

Canute Gdns

Rodnet Grove

Rotherhithe New Road A2208

A200

Abbeyfield Rd

Rot. N. Rd

A2208 Rotherhithe New Road A2208

A

Millender Walk

St. Helena Road

Concorde Way

Island Row

Corbetts Lane

Silwood Street

Eugenia Road

Goldsworthy Gdns

Alpine Road

Larnaburne Grove

Reculver Road

Sketchley Gdns

Jarrow Road

Corbetts Passage

◄ **108**

▲ **109**

South Bermondsey Rail

Silwood Street

Hyson Road

Sheppard Drive

Rosseth Road

Stubbs Drive

Stubbs Drive

Slippers Place

Weald Close

B204

Stubbs

Masters Dr

Howlett

Brian Gro

Del Rd

Delaford Road

Cranswick Road

Credon

Ryder

Drive

Birk Drive

Cal Dr

Dav

Ablett Street

Barkworth Road

Bolina Road

Ilderton Road

Millwall FC
(The Den)

117 ►

115 ◄

Verney

Road

Varcoe Road

Eagle Close

Varcoe Road

Gerards Ct

Zampa Road

Stockholm Road

Surrey Canal Rd

Bridge Meadows

B

Record Street

Hatcham Road

Rollins Street

Ormside Street

Ideas Road

Ilderton Road

Rollins Street

Lovelinch Close

Lovelinch Close

Sharratt Street

Sharratt Street

Lovelinch Close

Manor Grove

Devonshire Grove

Sylvan Grove

Hornshay Street

Bridge House Meadows

Old Kent Road A2

Wales Way

▼ **124**

Patterdale Road

John Williams

Hunsdon Road

Farrow Lane

0.25 mile 0.25 km

South Bermondsey

Map 116

There may be more to this area than we've listed, but the fact is we like you. We want to see you live to enjoy our favourite picks among these pages. If you make the wrong kind of eye contact as you tremble past the Millwall flags fluttering menacingly from the balconies, then we're worried we'll lose a much-loved reader. Swallow your valuables and back slowly away.

O Landmarks

• **Millwall FC Stadium** • Zampa Rd & Bolina Rd

Map 117 · Deptford (West)

Deptford (West)

Map 117

Apparently, developers have their eye on Deptford West. You've really got to hope so. The Blitz did its best, but the area came back with hastily built and charmless '60s tower blocks. Still, like the rest of Deptford it's going through a gradual regeneration as young buyers move in to make their money stretch.

Map 118 · Deptford (Central)

When Christopher Marlowe was murdered in a Deptford tavern, Deptford hit its nightlife peak. That was 1593. Today, while the rest of London turns everything into a pub, Deptford turns its pubs into churches. Without beer, you may want to drown your sorrows in the Thames, but even that is thwarted: here the Thames path breaks to take you through neglected residential areas instead. Escape!

 Post Offices

• **Evelyn Street** • 301 Evelyn St

Map 119 · Deptford (East)

River Thames

1

2

A

B

Glaisher Street

Glaisher Street

Twinkle Park

Borthwick Street

Trevithick Mews

Watergate Street

Caravel Mews

Benbow Street

Henrietta Close

St. Nicholas House

Hamilton Cresent

Basey Way

Basey Way

Glaisher Street

Greenwich Quay

Dacca Street

Prince Street

Prince Street

Frigate Mews

Deptford Green

Stowage

Creek Road A200

Norman Road

Thame

New King Street

Czar Street

Carrick Mews

Brig Mews

Copperas Street

Prince Street

Sanston Road

Evelyn Street A200

McMillan Street

Bruford Court

Berthon Street

Deptford Creek

Griming Place

Beech Cross

Larch Close

Lamerton Street

Albury Street

Deptford Church Street

Berthon Street

Bronze Street

Tarver

118

Walnut Close

Edward Street

Hyde Street

Mary Ann Gardens

St. Paul's Churchyard Gardens

Sue Godfrey Local Nature Reserve

120

Wotton Road

Edward Place

Payne Street

Hamilton Street

Hamilton Street

Crossfield Street

Ffinch Street

Resolution Way

A2209

Creekside

Deptford Rail

Adolphus Street

Adolphus Street

Octavius Street

Idonia Street

Rochdale Way

Giffin Square Market

Giffin Street

Frankham Street

Napia Close

Amersham Vale

Turnpike Close

Douglas Way

Stanley Road

Mornington Road

Margaret McMillan Park

Glenville Grove

Glenville Grove

Douglas Way

Street Market

Watson's Street

Vaughan Williams Close

Margaret McMillan Park

Deptford High Street

Deptford Street Market

Eg_lar Close

Baildon Street

Comet Street

Reginald Road

New Butt Lane

Reginald Square

Fletcher Path

Admiralty Close

Ravensbourne River

Mumford Mills

Greenwich High Road A206

Burgos Grove

Blackheath Road

126

New Cross

New Cross Road A2

Deptford Broadway

Deptford Bridge A2

Deptford Bridge

Broadway

0.25 mile

0.25 km

Deptford (East)

Map 119

If you're one for a bargain, then this is your place. Browse the charity shops for dresses rumored to be donated by local prostitutes, pick up all manner of junk from the market or visit one of the many fishmongers, who have been known to sell live eels and sharks. And if you want to fit in with the countless old punks drinking cider get yourself a face tattoo on Church Street.

Nightlife

- **The Bird's Nest** • 32 Deptford Church St
- **Bunker Club** • 46 Deptford Broadway
- **Dog & Bell** • 116 Prince St

Post Offices

- **New Cross** • 500 New Cross Rd

Restaurants

- **Chaconia Roti** • 26 Deptford High St
- **Manzes** • 204 Deptford High St
- **The Waiting Room** • 134 Deptford High St

Shopping

- **Deptford Market** • Deptford High St

Supermarkets

- **Iceland** • 112 Deptford High St

Map 120 · **Greenwich**

River
Thames

Cutty Sark
Gardens

Greenwich
Foot Tunnel

Naval
College
Gardens

Glaisher Street

Basevi Way

Greenwich Quay

Stowage

Bruford Court

Berthon Street

Bronze Street

Copperas Street

Deptford
Creek

Creekside

Thames Street

Norway Street

Woodwharf

Clavell Street

Welland
Street

Creek Road A200

Bardsley Lane

Norman Road B208

Thornham Street

Claremont Street

Roan Street

Terres Way

Straightsmouth

College
Approach

Durnford
Street

Thames Street

Greenwich Church Street

Cutty Sark

Roan Street

Randall Place

Churchfields

Nelson Road A206

King William Walk

Romney Road A206

Stockwell Street

National
Maritime
Museum Gardens

Greenwich
Park

PAGE
336

Greenwich

Greenwich High Road

Burney Street

Gloucester Circus

Peyton
Place

Circus Street

Prior Street

Crooms Hill

Crooms Hill
Grove

King George Street

Royal Hill B209

Greenwich High Road A206

◀119

Maitland Close

Welland Court

Kay Way

Egerton Drive

Ashburnham Place

Ashburnham Grove

Ashburnham
Retreat

St. Marks Close

Greenwich South Street A2211

Brand Street

Arlington
Place

Royal Hill

Royal
Place

Gerrard Place

Hawks Mews

Diamond Terrace

Cable Place

Hyde Vale
B209

Chesterfield Garden

Rangers Square

Clayton Mews

Burgos Grove

Mumford Mills

Catherine Grove

Devonshire Drive

Peabody
Close

Guildford Grove

Admirals Gate

Blissett Street

Winforton Street

Maidenstone Hill

Point Hill

Westgrove Lane

West Grove

Cade Road

Blackheath Road A2

Crossley Van

Franklin Place

John Penn Street

Franklin Close

Beck Close

Morden Street

Bennett Grove

Coldbath Street

Lewisham Road A21

Sparta Street

Robinscroft
Mews

Friendly
Place

Plumbridge Street

Lindsell Street

Trafalgar
Road

Dabin Crescent

Dutton Street

Hollymount Close

Blackheath Hill A2

Point Close

Dartmouth Hill

Dartmouth Row

Allison Close

Dartmouth Grove

Dartmouth Terrace

Shooters Hill Roa

Hare & Billet Road

West Tyler Road

Brookmill
Park

0.25 mile   0.25 km

With the **Cutty Sark** magnificently restored and Greenwich's status as an Olympic Borough, the area has been given a new, touristy lease of life recently. There's still plenty of quirky pubs and shops to let you escape the crowds though. And anyway, if you do want to do some proper sightseeing, what better place to do it?

Cinemas

• **Greenwich Picturehouse** • 180 Greenwich High Rd

Coffee

• **Paul Rhodes Coffee** • 37 King William Walk
• **Starbucks** • 54 Greenwich Church St

O Landmarks

• **Cutty Sark** • King William Walk & Romney Rd
• **Greenwich Foot Tunnel** •
  Greenwich Church St & Thames St

Libraries

• **West Greenwich Library** • 146 Greenwich High Rd

Nightlife

• **North Pole Bar and Piano** • 131 Greenwich High Rd
• **O2** • O2 Arena
• **Up The Creek** • 302 Creek Rd

Post Offices

• **Greenwich** • 261 Greenwich High Rd

Restaurants

• **Goddard's Pie Shop Booth** • 22 King William Walk
• **The Hill** • 89 Royal Hill
• **North Pole Bar and Grill** • 131 Greenwich High Rd

Shopping

• **Cheeseboard** • 26 Royal Hill
• **Mr Humburg** • Greenwich Market
• **Music & Video Exchange** • 23 Greenwich Church St

This slowly reviving segment of Camberwell brings together a minority of polite arty types in the crumbling-yet-quaint town houses of Camberwell New Road with take-no-prisoners urbanites as seen in the chaos of Denmark Hill and its pointless **Butterfly Walk** (why?). The neighbourhood good stuff includes killer Indian (**New Dewaniam**).

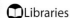

Libraries
- **Minet Library** • 52 Knatchbull Rd

Nightlife
- **The Joiners Arms** • 35 Denmark Hill
- **The Sun of Camberwell** • 61-63 Coldharbour Ln

Post Offices
- **Camberwell Green** • 25 Denmark Hill

Restaurants
- **New Dewaniam** • 225 Camberwell New Rd
- **Rock Steady Eddie's** • 2 Coldharbour Ln
- **Viet Cafe** • 75 Denmark Hill
- **Zeret Kitchen** • 216 Camberwell Rd

Shopping
- **Butterfly Walk Shopping Centre** • Denmark Hill

Supermarkets
- **Co-Op** • 177 Camberwell New Rd
- **Iceland** • 120 Camberwell Rd

Map 122 · **Camberwell (East)**

Camberwell (East)

Maybe it was Kevin Spacey moving to the Grove, maybe something else entirely, but this area of Camberwell, in particular Church Street, has become something of an eating and drinking mecca in recent years. Work through the mammoth selection of craft beers in **Stormbird** before soaking it up with excellent kebabs from **FM Mangal** or regional Chinese from **Silk Road**.

Coffee

• **Fowlds Cafe** • 3 Addington Square

Libraries

• **Camberwell Library** • 48 Camberwell Green

Nightlife

• **Grove House Tavern** • 26 Camberwell Grove
• **Hermit's Cave** • 28 Camberwell Church St
• **Stormbird** • 25 Camberwell Church St

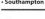## Post Offices

• **Southampton Way** • 156 Southampton Wy

Restaurants

• **Caravaggio** • 47 Camberwell Church St
• **Crooked Well** • 16 Grove Ln
• **Falafel** • 27 Camberwell Church St
• **FM Mangal** • 54 Camberwell Church St
• **Silk Road** • 49 Camberwell Church St
• **Theo's** • 2 Grove Ln
• **Wuli Wuli** • 15 Camberwell Church St

Shopping

• **Architectural Rescue** • 1-3 Southampton Way
• **Cowling and Wilcox** • 8-12 Orpheus St

Peckham

Map 123

As old pubs, pool halls, telephone boxes, and coal bunkers are converted into galleries faster than you can say 'fixed gear bicycle', it's safe to say Peckham is the epicenter of the new(ish) South London art scene. But don't be scared off—get the cheapest lunch for miles at **Manze's** or pay a visit to the art/music/religion/theatre behemoth that is **The Bussey Building**.

Coffee
• **Petitou** • 63 Choumert Rd

Libraries
• **Peckham Library** • 122 Peckham Hill St

Movie Theaters
• **Peckham Multiplex** • 95 Rye Ln

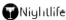
Nightlife
• **The Bussey Building** • 133 Rye Ln
• **The Four Quarters** • 187 Rye Ln
• **Frank's Cafe** • 95 Rye Ln
• **The Montpelier** • 43 Chomert Rd

Post Offices
• **Peckham** • 125 Peckham High St

Restaurants
• **Agrobeso African Cuisine** • 139 Peckham High St
• **Ganapati** • 38 Holly Grove
• **M. Manze Pie and Mash** • 105 Peckham High St
• **Miss Tapas** • 45 Choumert Road
• **Obalende Suya Express** • 43 Peckham High St

Shopping
• **Persepolis** • 20 Peckham High St
• **Primark** • 51 Rye Ln

Supermarkets
• **Iceland** • 74 Rye Ln

Map 124 • **Peckham East (Queen's Road)**

Although the local halfway house ensures the streets are filled with beggars, and the buses passing through en route to the continent make you wish you were somewhere else, this small pocket of Peckham isn't really so bad. Head for great African food at **805** or take a short walk to the incredible Victorian **Nunhead Cemetery**.

 Libraries

• **Nunhead Library** • Gordon Rd

 Restaurants

• **805** • 805 Old Kent Rd
• **Tops Caribbean Takeaway** • 173 Queens Rd

Map 125 • **New Cross Gate**

N

1   **2**

Rollins Street

Bridge Meadows

Myers Lane

Lovelinch Close

Bridge House Meadows

Mercury Way

Samuel Close

Juno Way

117

Rolt Street

Folkes Gard

Lovelinch Close

Sanford Walk

Knoyle Street

Chubworthy St

Whitcher

Cold Blow Lane

Sanford Street

Chifley St

Hornshay Street

John Williams Close

Coldblow Lane

Sterling Gardens

118

Cottesbrook Street

Nynehead

A   **116**

Hunsdon Road

Water Lane

Avonley Road

Edric Road

Monson Road

Joseph Hardcastle Close

Camplin Street

Baxtree

Farrow Lane

Pump Lane

Heathfield Ct

Wardalls Grove

Barlborough Street

Wrigglesworth Street

Leyland Road

Robert Lowe Close

Tarragon Close

Southern

Reaston Street

Ventnor Road

Auburn Close

Goodwood Road

Eckington Gardens

Casella Road

Egmont Street

Brockehurst Street

Hatfield Close

Billington Road

124

New Cross Road A2

Romney Close

Lubbock Street

Pankhurst Close

Hatcham Park Road

126

Nettleton Road

Harts Lane

Faulkner Street

Briant Street

Fishers Court

Kender Street A202

Kenwood Avenue

Besson Street A202

Hotcham Park Mews

New Cross Gate

Mylis Close

New Cross Road A2

Godley Close

Lanchester Way

Hatcham Gdns

Fullerby Street B2227

Pepys Road

Troutbeck Road

Jerningham Road

Queens Road A202

Waller Road

Erlanger Road

0.25 mile   0.25 km

Since the sad demise of the Montague Arms this strip has become even more of a no man's land—not quite New Cross but not quite Peckham. Apart from a semi-decent junk shop and a not-so-great retail park, there's not much to see. Do yourself a favor and stroll on into one of the aforementioned neighborhoods—or jump on the brilliant London Overground and be in Dalston in no time.

✉ Post Offices

• **New Cross Gate** • 165 New Cross Rd

🍴 Restaurants

• **Good Neighbor** • 58 Peckham Rye
• **La Boulangerie** • 258 New Cross Rd
• **Jin Jiang** • 36 Deptford Boardway
• **Ma Po** • 176 Lower Rd
• **The Rosemary** • 178 New Cross Rd

Map 126 · **New Cross**

N

Sanford Street

Nynehead Street

Bawtree Road

Ludwick Mews

Desmond Street

Bowerman Avenue

Milton Court Road

Achilles Street

1

Edward Street B207

Clifton Rise

Angus Street

Pagnell Street

Childeric Road

Fordham Park

Batavia Road

Clifton Rise

Achilles Street

Exeter Way

Amersham Gr

Edward Place

Payne Street

Napier Close

Royal Naval Place

Douglas Way

Amersham Vale

Turnpike Cl

Stanley Street

Mornington Rd

Comet St

2

Idonia Street

Adolphus Street

Hamilton Street

Octavius Street

Rochdale Way

Watson's Street

Douglas Way

Margaret McMillan Park

Elgar Close

Comet Street

Baildon Street

118

Glenville Grove

New Cross Rail

New Cross Road A2

Sanford Street

Tyrwhitt Way

Southerngate Way

Alexandra Street

Primrose Walk

Pearl Way

Auburn Close

Goodwood Road

South Gate

Way

A

New Cross Gate Rail

Batavia Mews

New Cross Road A2

Laurie Grove

St James's

Loring Road

Ben Pimlott Building

Dixon Road

Parkfield Rd

Lewisham Way A20

Mulberry Mews

Amersham Rd A20

119

Alpha Road

Florence Terrace

Florence Road B218

Heald Street

Omara Street

Heston Street

Wickham

Tanners Hill

Thornville Street

125

Goldsmiths College

St Donatts Road

Chestnut Close

Brindley St

St Donatts Road

Malpas Road

Cheshire Close

New Cross Gate Cutting Nature Reserve

B

Shardeloes Road

Barriedale

Sandbourne Road

Vesta Road

Malpas Road B218

Vesta Road

Vulcan Road

Luxmore Gardens

Luxmore Street

Rokeby Road

Upper Brockley Road

Wickham Road

Ley Road

Milncar

Alexandra Cottages

Tanners Mews

Friendly Gardens

Oscar Street

Ashby Road

0.25 mile   0.25 km

New Cross

Map 126

Once hailed as the new Shoreditch, this corner of Lewisham has managed to provide us with all the good stuff about hipsterville, while avoiding everything bad.

O Landmarks
• **Ben Pimlott Building** • University of London, New Cross

Libraries
• **Goldsmiths Library** • Lewisham Wy

Nightlife
• **Amersham Arms** • 388 New Cross Rd
• **Marquis of Granby** • 322 New Cross Rd
• **New Cross Inn** • 323 New Cross Rd

Post Offices
• **Lewisham Way** • 150 Lewisham Wy
• **New Cross Road** • 500 New Cross Rd

Supermarkets
• **Iceland** • 277 New Cross Rd
• **Sainsbury's** • 263 New Cross Rd

Map 127 • Coldharbour Lane / Herne Hill (West)

1 **2**

Serenaders Road

Peckford Place

Vila Road

Wiltshire Road

Lyndhurst Road

Max Roach Park

St. James's Crescent

Stanford Gardens

Millams Mews

Angell Road

Fenley Road

Styles Gardens

Major Close

121

Luxor Street

Loughborough Junction

Padfield Road

Bengeworth Road

Northway Road

Kemerton Road

Ridgeway Road

Hinton Road B222

Herne Hill Road

Milkwood Road

Wyck Gardens

Millbrook Road

Western Rd

Gresham Road

Blacktree Ms.

Barrington Road

Coldharbour Lane A2217

A

128

Pablo Neruda Close

Langston Hughes Close

Poplar Road

Deronda Road

Oakbank Grove

Frisby Road

Rus

Valentia Place

Brixton Station Road

Brixton

Atlantic Road B223

Electric Lane

Rushcroft Road

Saltoun Road

Jones Road

Sail Place

Wyck Rd

145

Clarewood Walk

Geneva Drive

Somerleyton Road

Corry Drive

Broughton Ct.

Calton Drive

Clifton Drive

Moorland Road

Loughborough Park

Codella Close

Shakespeare Road

Whitman Close

Dylan Rd

James Joyce Walk

Alice Walker Walk

Louise Bennett Close

Derek Walcott Close

Jessop Road

Fawnbrake Avenue

Brantwood Road

Danecroft Road

Ferndene Road

144

Marcus Garvey Way

Railton Road B223

Mervan Road

Effra Rd

Rattray Road

Bankton Road

Kellett Road

Probert Road

Jelf Road

Barnwell Road

Mayall Road

Robert Burns Mews

Gubyon Avenue

Regent Road

Milton Road

Mendora Close

Chaucer Road

Spenser Road

Milton Road

Herne Place

Railton Road

Herne Hill Rail

Coldharbour Ave

Kestrel Avenue

Oberne Road

150

Effra Road A204

Bailey Mews

Trelawn Road

Dalberg Road

Effra Parade

Rattray Road

Morval Road

Brixton Water Lane A2214

Mendora Road

Rushcroft Road

B

St Matthew's Gardens

Rus Gdns

St Matthew's Gardens

Dray Gardens

Crownstone Road

Tulse Hill A204

Brixton Water Lane

Josephine Avenue

Trinity Rise

Effra Rd

Regent Road

Milton Road

Dulwich Road A2214

Hurst St.

Runner St.

Half Mo

PAGE 328

Brockwell Park

0.25 mile   0.25 km

Coldharbour Lane / Herne Hill (West)

Map 127

There don't seem to be as many shootings on Coldharbour Lane as there used to be. Maybe the crack dealers are just quietly selling the stuff, as somebody on The Wire once sensibly advised. Or maybe they've all been converted by the pleasant conservatory at **The Florence**, invigorating swims at the **Brockwell Lido**, and handmade jams from the **Blackbird Bakery**. Yes, that's probably it.

Nightlife

- **The Commercial** • 210 Railton Rd
- **The Florence** • 133 Dulwich Rd
- **The Prince Regent** • 69 Dulwich Rd

Restaurants

- **Ichiban Sushi** • 58 Atlantic Rd
- **Naughty Piglets** • 28 Brixton Water Ln

Shopping

- **Blackbird Bakery** • 230 Railton Rd

Map 128 · Denmark Hill / Herne Hill (East) N

Denmark Hill / Herne Hill (East)

Map 128

There's something quaintly grounded about the leafy Victorian suburb of Herne Hill, where funky neo-hippies settle into dreadlocked nuclear families. Denmark Hill sits at its top, with its imposing Salvation Army training grounds, following on to Ruskin Park for ornamental ponds and Edwardian ruins. Half Moon Lane plays main drag—get lost in a book at **Tales on Moon Lane** and lost in a bowl of noodles at **Lombok**.

Emergency Rooms

• **King's College Hospital** •
Denmark Hill & Champion Park

Libraries

• **Carnegie Library** • 188 Herne Hill Rd

Post Offices

• **Crossthwaite Avenue** • 6 Crossthwaite Ave

Restaurants

• **Lombok** • 17 Half Moon Ln

Shopping

• **Tales on Moon Lane** • 25 Half Moon Ln

Supermarkets

• **Sainsbury's** • 132 Herne Hill

Map 129 · **East Dulwich**

N

1

2

▲ 122

▲ 123

▶ 130

Champion Park

A2214

Hill Rail

Champion Grove

Stories Mews

Stories Road

Camberwell Grove

Pelham Close

Nairne Road

Copleston Mews

Choumert Road

Danby Street

McDermott Road

Wingfield

Marbeth Road

Grove Hill Road

Mallott Rd

Avondale Rise

Bellenden Road

Ashby Road

Arnott

Denmark Hill

The Hamlet

Langford Grn

Champion Hill

Grove Lane A2216

Grove Hill Road

Albrighton Road

Bromar Road

Soames Street

Oglander Road

Marsden Road

Muschamp Road

Amott

Alderton Close

Champion Hill

Champion Hill

Albrighton Road

Pytchley Road

Oxenford Street

Everthorpe Road

Ondine Road

Falkirk Close

A

Arnould Avenue

Warley Road

Dog Kennel Hill

Quorn Road

Hayes Grn

Copleston Road

East Dulwich Road

Grove Vale

Goose Green

East D

Drivers

Kings College Sports Ground

A2216

St Francis Road

Besant Place

East Dulwich Rail

📚

Grove Vale

Wixham Road

Dulwich Hamlet Football Club Ground (Champion Hill Stadium)

Abbotswood Road

Burrow Road

Talbot Road

Dewell Grove

Elsa Road

Zenoria Street

Spurling Road

Greendale Playing Fields

Shaw Road

Jarvis Rd

Melbourne Grove

East Dulwich Grove A2214

Matham Grove

Frogley Road

Crawthew Grove

Nutfield Road

Archdale Road

Lacon Road

Naime Grove

Sunray Avenue

Gyncote Close

St. Olave's Recreation Ground

Trossachs Road

Tarbert Road

Glengarry Road

Tell Grove

Ashbourne Grove

Chesterfield Grove

North Cross Road

Sage Mews

Dudrich Mews

Bassano St

Shawbury Road

Hansler Road

Felbridge Road

Ulverscroft Road

B

◀ 128

Woodfarrs

Casino Avenue

Thorncombe Road

Hillsboro Road

Lytcott Grove

Lordship Lane

Bawdale Road

Great Dale Close

Green Dale

Playfield Crescent

Beckwith Road

Aysgard Road

Great Spilmans

Colwell Road

Whateley Road

Silvester Road

Pellatt Road

Woodside Mews

Landcroft Road

North Dulwich Rail

🚂

Village Way A2214

Gilkes Crescent

Calton Avenue

Townley Road

Rodwell Road

Heber Road

Jennings Road

Goodrich Road

Half Moon La

Pond Mead

Dovercourt Road

Beauval Road

Milo Road

Thompson Road

0.25 mile	0.25 km

East Dulwich is where your ex-flatmate finally settled down and now won't shut up about taramasalata, babies, and how he's only fifteen minutes from London Bridge by train over perfect cocktails. Dodge baguettes, pushchairs, and delis along Lordship Lane, just don't get sucked in.

Coffee
• **Caffe Nero** • 8 Lordship Ln

Libraries
• **Grove Vale library** • 18 Grove Vale

Nightlife
• **East Dulwich Tavern** • 1 Lordship Ln

Restaurants
• **The Palmerston** • 91 Lordship Ln

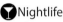
Supermarkets
• **Marks & Spencer** • 59 Lordship Ln
• **Sainsbury's** • 80 Dog Kennel Hill

Map 130 • **Peckham Rye**

N

1 **2**

123 124

Choumert Road
Costa Street
Sternhall Lane
A2215
Heaton Road
Ellerslie
Meridian Close
Consort Road

Danby Street
McDermon Road
Nigel Road
Wivenhoe Close
Wivenhoe Close
Monteagle Way

Wingfield Street
Bellenden Road
Amott Road
Bushey Hill Road
Philip Walk
Scylla Rd

Wingfield Mews
Howden Street
Bushpole Road
Huguenot Road
Vivian Sq
Scylla Road

Maxted Road
Niatbrook Street
Dewar Street
Krisdale Road
Nunhead Pass
Whorlton Road
Old James St
A2214

Amott Road
Consort Road
Nunhead Crescent
Nunhead Lane

Keston Road
Consort Road
Fenwick Grove
Peckham Rye A2215
Barforth Road
Garden Road
Linden Grove

A Ondine Road
Marsden Road
Hinckley Road
Fenwick Road
East Dulwich Road
A2214
Solomon's Passage
Waverley Ave

129
Goose
Green
East Dulwich Road A2214
Solway Road
Wellington Mews
Peckham Rye B219
Peckham
Rye Common
Peckham Rye

Zenoria St
Spurling Rd
Wingham Road
Crystal Palace Road
Haines Close
Kelmore Grove
The Gardens
The Gardens

Dulwich Grove A2214
Frogley Road
Crawthew Grove
Dahurst Grove
The Gardens
Straker's Road

Matham Grove
Ashbourne Grove
Nutfield Road
Almdale Road
Acre Drive
Ferris Road
Tyrrell Road
Barry Road

North Cross Road
Lacon Road
Upland Mews

Chesterfield Grove
Lordship Lane A2216
Shawbury Road
Ulverscroft Road

Sage Ms
Bassano Street
Hansler Road
Felbrigg Road
Crystal Palace Road
Darrell Road
Hindmans Road
Barry Road B219

Bawdale Road
Peckham
Rye Park

B Colwell Road
Whateley Road
Silvester Road
Landells Road
Friern Road
Hansiawe Road
Piermont Green
Piermont Road

Woodgale
Mews
Pellatt Road
Mulberry Close
Forest Hill Road B238

Rodwell Road
Heber Road
Upland Road
Marcus Garvey Mews
St Aidans Road
Dunstans Road

Jennings Road
Friern Road
St Aidans Road
Dovedale Road

|——— 0.25 mile ———| |——— 0.25 km ———|

Map 130

A noticeboard on Peckham Rye Common alleges that ancient British Queen Boudicca was finally defeated by the Romans here. Anyone suggesting that the very middle class streets around North Cross Road—with its market and lazy Sunday lunches at **The Angel Oak**—have anything to do with Peckham as we know it might get the same treatment.

Coffee

• **Old Spike Roastery** • 54 Peckham Rye

▼Nightlife

• **The Angle Oak** • 31 Peckham Rye
• **The Gowlett** • 62 Gowlett Rd

⚫Restaurants

• **The Angel Oak** • 31 Peckham Rye
• **Artusi** • 161 Bellenden Rd
• **Pedler** • 1 Canada Sq
• **Thai Corner Cafe** • 44 Northcross Rd

⚫Shopping

• **Flock and Herd** • 155 Bellenden Rd

Map 131 · **Vauxhall / Albert Embankment** Ⓝ

Westminster Bridge Road

1

Westminster Bridge Road A302

LAMBETH

104

Westminster Bridge

Upper Marsh

Lower Marsh

Grinnan Street

2

Bavil's Road

Frazier Street

Cottington

Cosser Street

Cornwall

Street

Murphy

Street

Greenham

Close

Emery

Street

Burdett

Street

Gerridge Street

Webber

Row

Cottesloe

Mews

Lambeth

North

St Georges Road

King's College

PAGE

366

Royal Street

Newham

Terrace

Centaur

Street

Carlisle Lane

Hercules Road

McAuley

Close

Maid Row

King Edward Street

Lambeth Road

Tenn

Cts

Cosser Street

Morton

Place

Geraldine Mary

Harmsworth Pk

Kennington Road A23

Victoria

Tower

Garden

River Thames

A3212

A

Lambeth Palace Gardens

Sports

Grd

Archbishop's

Park

Slaford

Place

Lambeth Road A3203

Brook Drive

Walcot Square

Walcot Square

Abingdon Street

Lambeth Palace Road A3036

Lambeth Palace

Norfolk

Row

Pratt Walk

Sail Street

Bishops

Terrace

Oakden

Street

St. Mary's

Gardens

St. Mary's

Gardens

Lambeth Bridge A3203

Thorney Street

A3212

Millbank

River Thames

Albert Embankment A3036

Lambeth High Street

Old Paradise

Street

Ingram

Close

Juxon Street

Bedlam

Mews

Hemball

Close

Walnut Tree Walk

Fitzalan Street

112

Wincott Street

Reedworth Street

Chester Way

Newport Street

Gibson Road

Lollard Street

Ustinger's

Street

Lambeth

Walk

Open Space

Lollard Street

Whitgift Street

Lambeth

Recreation

Ground

Lambeth Walk

Lambeth High Street

Salamanca

Place

Salamanca Street

Salamanca

Street

Lilac Place

Stroughton

Close

Distin Street

Kennington Road

Denny Street

White Hart

Cardigan Street

Randall

Row

Pedlars

Park

Randall

Place

Citadel

Place

Jonathan Street

Vauxhall Walk

Tyers Street

Beaufoy

Walk

Marylee

Way

Newburn Street

Black Prince Road

Hotspur Street

Kennington Road

A23

Cleaver Square

Cleaver Street

Bowden Street

Tinworth Street

Wickham Street

Vauxhall Street

Sancroft Street

Distin

Street

Stables

Way

Courtenay

Square

Bowden

Street

Nutmeg

Lane

Ravensdon Street

Glasshouse Walk

Worgan Street

Orsett Street

Dolland

Street

Wynyard

Terrace

Loughborough Street

Aveline

Street

Longville

Road

Courtenay Street

Wigton

Place

Mathiew

Place

Windmill

Row

B

Laud Street

St Oswald's Place

Tyers Terrace

Kennington Green

Chester

Way

Milverton Street

A202

New Spring

Gardens Walk

Spring

Gardens

Godling Street

Auckland

Street

Glyn Street

Vauxhall City Farm

Vauxhall

City

Farm

Durham Street

Vauxhall

Grove

Harleyford Road

Meadow

Road

Kennington Lane A3204

Kennington

Oval

Vauxhall Street

Montford Place

Claylands

Road

Stannary Street

Clayton Street

Secret Intelligence

Service HQ (MI6)

Bridgefoot A203

134

Vauxhall

Rail

⊖ Vauxhall

135

Feel like doin' the Lambeth Walk? You can. Right here. On Lambeth Walk, incidentally. Though nowadays 'doing the Lambeth Walk' is likely to have an entirely less innocent connotation if some of the area's kinkier gay clubs are anything to go by. This part of Vauxhall, under the watchful eye of MI6, is slightly less that way inclined, but maintains its share of hot spots. If you're after a sausage fest of another kind, get stuffed at **The Jolly Gardeners**.

Emergency Rooms

- **St Thomas' Hospital** •
  Westminster Bridge Rd & Lambeth Palace Rd

Landmarks

- **Lambeth Palace** • Lambeth Palace Rd & Lambeth Rd
- **Secret Intelligence Service HQ (MI6)** •
  85 Vauxhall Cross
- **Vauxhall City Farm** • 165 Tyers St

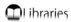

Libraries

- **Lambeth Palace Library** •15 Lambeth Palace Rd

Nightlife

- **Eagle London** • 349 Kennington Ln
- **The Jolly Gardeners** • 49–51 Black Prince Rd
- **The Royal Vauxhall Tavern** • 372 Kennington Ln

Post Offices

- **Westminster Bridge Road** • 125 Westminster Bridge Rd

Supermarkets

- **Tesco** • Kennington Ln

Battersea (West)

Map 132

With no tubes or trains to attract the hoi polloi, Battersea West sits smugly hugging the River Thames, happily cut off from the hustle and bustle of the rest of London. However, with the Imperial Wharf Overground not far away, the commute isn't as bad as it used to be and the masses flock—mostly for the spacious floor-to-ceiling glass apartments with killer river views. Take in a Sunday lunch at **The Prince Albert**.

Nightlife
• **Duke of Battersea** • 74 Battersea Bridge Road
• **The Prince Albert** • 85 Albert Bridge Rd
• **The Woodman** • 60 Battersea High St

Supermarkets
• **Sainsbury's** • 326 Battersea Park Rd

Post Offices
• **Battersea Bridge Road** • 72 Battersea Bridge Rd
• **York Road** • 583 Battersea Park Rd

Map 133 • **Battersea (East)**

Battersea (East)

Map 133

An odd slice of post-industrial London dominated by the derelict Battersea Power Station, there's naff-all here until someone decides what to do with the old hulk and its surrounding domain. In the meantime, try cycling around nearby Battersea Park. **The Mason's Arms** serves a decent beer.

O Landmarks

- **Battersea Dogs' Home** • 4 Battersea Park Rd
- **Battersea Park Gasometers** •
  Queenstown Rd & Prince of Wales Dr
- **Battersea Power Station** • 188 Kirtling St

Libraries

- **Battersea Park Library** • 309 Battersea Park Rd

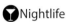 Nightlife

- **The Mason's Arms** • 169 Battersea Park Rd

Post Offices

- **Battersea Park Road** • 20 Battersea Park Rd

Shopping

- **London Recumbents** • Battersea Park

Map 134 · **South Lambeth**

South Lambeth

Map 134

With an overground, tube, and extensive bus station, Vauxhall's southern counterpart is remarkably well connected. But it offers a mixed bag. Gritty backwater estates intermix with middle class townhouses and no-nonsense gay clubs. For pastel de nata like nobody's business, hit up Little Portugal on South London Road. Bite into a fois gras toastie at the **Canton Arms** and wash it down with beer and amateur comedy at **The Cavendish Arms**.

 ## Coffee

• **Starbucks** • 2 S Lambeth Rd

 ## Libraries

• **South Lambeth Library** • 180 S Lambeth Rd

 ## Nightlife

• **Bar Estrela** • 113 S Lambeth Rd
• **The Battersea Barge** • Nine Elms Ln
• **The Cavendish Arms** • 128 Hartington Rd
• **Fire** • 38 Parry St
• **The Priory Arms** • 83 Lansdowne Way
• **The Vauxhall Griffin** • 8 Wyvil Rd

 ## Post Offices

• **South Lambeth** • 254 Wandsworth Rd

 ## Restaurants

• **A Toca** • 343 Wandsworth Rd
• **Bar Estrela** • 113 S Lambeth Rd
• **Brunswick House** • 30 Wandsworth Rd
• **Canton Arms** • 177 S Lambeth Rd
• **Tia Maria** • 126 S Lambeth Rd

Shopping

• **Fetish Freak** • 76 Bolton Crescent
• **LASSCO** • 30 Wandsworth Rd
• **New Covent Garden Market** • Nine Elms Ln
• **The Nine Elms Sunday Market** • New Covent Garden

 ## Supermarkets

• **Sainsbury's** • 62 Wandsworth Rd

Posh town houses rub shoulders somewhat uneasily with housing estates here, and there's no denying the walk from Oval Station can be dodgy, but if you're a fan of cricket, the presence of the Oval cricket ground more than makes up for it. When there's a match on, the area fills to the brim, but normally it's a modest and unimposing neighbourhood. Organic foodies delight in vegan ex-squat **The Bonnington Café**.

Map 135

O Landmarks
• **The Oval** • Kennington

Coffee
• **Bonnington Cafe** • 11 Vauxhall Grove

Nightlife
• **The Fentiman Arms** • 64 Fentiman Rd

Post Offices
• **Brixton Road** • 68 Brixton Rd

Restaurants
• **Adulis** • 44 Brixton Rd
• **Bonnington Café** • 11 Vauxhall Grove

Putney

Putney has a bit of a bipolar personality disorder. On the one side, it's suburban middle England with its rugby and rowing types, on the other, it's increasingly vibrant and hip. The High Street's a bit genteel by day and young-and-up-for-it at night.

Coffee

- **Artisan Coffee** • 203 Upper Richmond Rd
- **Caffe Nero** • 132 Putney High St
- **Grind Coffee Bar** • 79 Lower Richmond Rd
- **Pret A Manger** • 121 Putney High St

Libraries

- **Putney Library** • 5 Disraeli Rd

Movie Theaters

- **Odeon Putney** • 26 Putney High St

Nightlife

- **The Boathouse** • 32 Brewhouse Ln
- **Duke's Head** • 8 Lower Richmond Rd
- **The Jolly Gardeners** • 61 Lacy Rd

Post Offices

- **Putney** • 197 Upper Richmond Rd

Supermarkets

- **Sainsbury's** • 2 Werter Rd
- **Waitrose** • Putney High St & Lacy Rd

Map 137 • **Wandsworth (West)**

Dissected by the busy Upper and Lower Richmond Roads, this bit of Wandsworth is a bit lifeless though pleasant enough. The pretty, riverside Wandsworth Park is a huge plus and heaves with locals with the first sniff of sunshine.

 Restaurants

• **Miraj** • 123 Putney Bridge Rd

Map 138 · **Wandsworth (Central)**

River Thames

Carnwath Road

Wandsworth Bridge

Bridgend Road A217

Pier Terrace

Jew's Row

Marl Road

1

2

Bridgend Road A217

139

Swandon Way A217

Bridgend Road A217

River Wandle

A

Eastfields Avenue

Osiers Road

Enterprise Way

Osiers Road

North Passage

The Causeway

Smugglers Way

Swandon Way A217

Wandsworth Town Rail

Lovatt's Place

Ferrier Street

More Street

Edgel Street

Podmore Road

Ballantine Street

Dilhorne Street

Smardale Road

Coach House Yard

Elsley Street

Dighton Road

Coleford Road

Fullerton Road

Bloomsbur

East Hil

Northfields

Pulney Bridge Road

Point Pleasant

Pros. Cotts

Oakhill Place

Oakhill Road

Pennythorn Place

Adela Road

Sudlow Road

Fort Road

Dormay Street

Old York Road

Toksley Street

Tonsley Place

Tonsley Hill

Tonsley Road

Tonsley Street

Crockerton

Cricketers M

Fairfield Drive

Fairfield Street

137

Frogmore

Point Pleasant

Bridge Park

Armoury Way

Wandsworth Plain

Ram Street A217

Boardwatch Street

Shore

ham Close

Hendon Road

Knoll Road

Enfantine

146

Santos Road

Erickson Close

Chesterton Ro

Bush Cotts

Garters Yard

Alf Saints Pass

New Way

Wandsworth High Street

Oak Place

College Mews

Malva Close

Ribbmount Road

Astley Road

West Hill

05

Lebanon Gardens

Downs Ms.

Dutch

Tied Don Sq.

Hardwicke

Broomhill Road

New Yd.

Vintage Way

St.

B

Garrat Lane A217

Garratt Lane Grave Yard

Weirfield Close

Marius Terrace

Marius Road

Marcus Terrace

Dentoft Street

Borrodale Road

Iron Mill Road

Berisford Mews

Peatland Gardens

St. Ann's Hi

Gattid

Ringford Rd.

Southfields Road

Merton Road

Buckhold Road

Parkview Court

Neville Gill Close

Crescent Lane

Garrat Lane A217

Haldon Rd.

Jessatha Road

King George's Park

Wandsworth (Central)

Map 138

This is East Wandsworth's poorer, uglier cousin—and you've got to feel sorry for it. It's got a drab shopping centre and a four-lane traffic system brings noise and air pollution. On the plus side, plenty of chain stores (Gap, Uniqlo etc.) and a **Cineworld** make life a little easier. To get away from it all, hibernate in the Old York Road. For the best Nepalese food in London, hit **Kathmandu Valley**.

Cinemas

• **Cineworld Wandsworth** •
  Wandsworth High St & Ram St

Coffee

• **Caffe Nero** • Southside Shopping Centre

Nightlife

• **The Cat's Back** • 88 Point Pleasant
• **The Queen Adelaide** • 35 Putney Bridge Rd

Post Offices

• **Wandsworth** • 54 Wandsworth High St

Restaurants

• **Kathmandu Valley** • 5 West Hill

Supermarkets

• **Sainsbury's** • 45 Garratt Ln
• **Waitrose** • 66 Wandsworth High St

Map 139 · **Wandsworth (East)**

N

1 2

132

140▶

138◀

146

Clapham Junction

River Thames

York Gardens

Spencer Park

Wandsworth Common

Fairchild Close
Musjid Road
Afghan Road
Kambala Road
Heaver Road
McDermott Close
Hicks Close
Kerrison
Wye Street
Wolfencroft Close
Sullivan Close
Falcon
Mantua Street
Ingrave Street
Bridges Court
York Road
Lavender Road
Newcomen Rd
Meyrick Road
Bramand
Ganley Road
Livingstone Road
Winstanley Road
Winstanley Road
Cotton Row
Molasses Row
Cinnamon Row
Calico Row
Coral Row
Ivory Square
Gartons Way
York Place
York Pl
Gartons Way
Chatfield Road
Holgate Avenue
Wallis Close
Hope Street
Benham Close
Jensen Walk
Fowler Close
Camp
Close
John
Sq
Holli
Sq
Fenner
Sq
Thomas Baines Road
Weekley Square
Lother Rd
Grant Road
Mendip Road
Great Chart Street
Hibbert Street
Winter Street
Chillington Drive
Maysoule Road
Kernot
Cz
Beveley Close
Windmill Close
St. John's Hill
Jungert Drive
York Road A3205
Usk Road
Petergate
Effingham Street
Nantes Close
Harbut Road
Cologne Road
Plough Terrace
Oberstein Road
Brussels Road
Osborne Road
Strath Terrace
Strathblaine Road
Bridgend Road A217
Jew's Row
Bridgend Road
Trinity Rd
York Road A3205
Swandon Way
Swandon Way
Rochelle Close
Garrick Close
Tonsley Close
Bartholomew Close
Turenne Close
Garrick Close
Haydon Way
Marcilly Road
Harbut Close
St. John's Hill A3036
St. John's Hill Grove
Spencer Road
Sigmona Road
Yardley Close
Battersea Rise
A3
Bramford Road
Dalby Road
Balmoral Road
Dighton Road
Birchwild Road
Dempster Road
Anna Road
Fullerton Road
Elsynge Road
Spencer Park
Spencer Park B234
Polmore Road
Sendale Road
Coleford Road
Bloomsbury Place
East Hill A3
East Hill A3
Trinity Road A214
Woodwell
E Hill
Huguenot Place A3
Trinity Road A214
Wandsworth Common West Side
Menlo Road
Acris Street
Trefoil Road
Cicada Road
Jessica Road
Caroline Road
Ellandine Close
North Side Wandsworth Common A3
Sheanan Road
Whitehall Road
Arundel Close
Elmer Street
Tonsley Hill
Knoll Road
Rosehill Road
Eglantine Road
Ashley Road
Usury Rd
Wandsworth Road

Elba Place
Trinity Road A214
Trinity Road A214

Wandsworth (East)

Map 139

With London's new Overground network and Clapham Junction on its doorstep, this corner of Wandsworth, including what locals call 'the Toast Rack' on East Hill, is becoming more gentrified everyday. You'll hear your share of 'rah's at **St John's Tavern**, with its upscale gastro fare and nod to colonial Britain, while yummy mummies stuff their cake holes at **Cake Boy** and practice their French at **Gazette**. Stay true to the neighbourhood's roots with a less than picturesque view of the Thames at **The Waterfront**.

 ## Coffee

• **Birdhouse** • 123 St John's Hill
• **Caffe Nero** • Southside Shopping Centre
• **Story Coffee** • 115 St John's Hill

 ## Restaurants

• **Gazette** • 79 Chatfield Rd

 ## Libraries

• **York Gardens Library** • 34 Lavender Rd

 ## Shopping

• **Cake Boy** • 2 Kingfisher House, Battersea Reach

 ## Nightlife

• **St John's Tavern** • 147 St Johns Hill
• **The Waterfront** • Juniper Dr

Clapham Junction / Northcote Rd

Map 140

We have a newfound sense of respect for Clapham Junction after it rose like a determined phoenix from the ashes of the summer 2011 riots. Suffering extensive devastation from looters, the neighbourhood dusted itself off with help of volunteers from across the capital and was back in business almost instantly. Seeing the **Party Superstores** open again after nearly burning to the ground is a particular sight for sore eyes. All fancy dress party goers can breathe a sigh of relief.

Coffee

• **Caffe Nero** • 20 St John's Rd

O Landmarks

• **Northcote Road** • Northcote Rd

Libraries

• **Battersea Library** • 265 Lavender Hill
• **Northcote Library** • 155 Northcote Rd

Nightlife

• **B@1 Cocktail Bar** • 85 Battersea Rise
• **Blame Gloria** • 91 Battersea Rise
• **Humble Grape** • 2 Battersea Rise

Post Offices

• **Alfriston Road** • 99 Alfriston Rd
• **Battersea** • 202 Lavender Hill

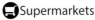 Restaurants

• **Gail's Bread** • 64 Northcote Rd
• **Jack's At The Junction** • 252 Lavender Hill
• **Mien Tay** • 180 Lavender Hill
• **Parisienne** • 225 Lavender Hill
• **Pizza Metro** • 64 Battersea Rise

Shopping

• **Huttons** • 29 Northcote Rd
• **Party Superstores** • 268 Lavender Hill
• **Space NK Apothecary** • 46 Northcote Rd
• **Sweaty Betty** • 66 Northcote Rd
• **TK Maxx** • 17 St John's Rd
• **TRAID** • 28 St John's Rd
• **Vintage Market Place** • Battersea Arts Centre
• **Whole Foods Market** • 305 Lavender Hill

Supermarkets

• **ASDA** • 204 Lavender Hill
• **Whole Foods Market** • 305 Lavender Hill
• **Sainsbury's** • Clapham Junction Shopping Centre

Battersea (South)

Map 141

Apart from the occasional house party, few have reason to go to Battersea South. You either live there, congratulating yourself on your nice Victorian conversion, or you pass through on the way to Clapham or one of the livelier bits of Battersea. The 'action' happens around Lavender Hill.

Coffee

• **Captain Corelli** • 132 Battersea Park Rd

Shopping

• **Battersea Car Boot Sale** • 401 Battersea Park Rd
• **Get A Grip Bicycle Workshop** • 19 Lavender Hill

Nightlife

• **Lost Society** • 339 Battersea Park Rd

Map 142 · **Clapham Old Town**

N

133

Qui

Broughton Street

Elms Road

leigh Road

Caroline Place

St. Philip Sq

Prairie Street

Bewick Street

Dickens Street

Coleridge Close

St. Rule Street

Morley Street

Heathbrook Park

Portslade Road

Erpingham St

Westbury Street

Pensbury Place

Pensbury Street

Bradmore Avenue

Braxbourne Avenue

Thackeray Road

Silverthorne Road

Frodie Street

Robertson Street

St. Rule Street

Wandsworth Road

St. Paul's Churchyard

Netherford Road

Braxbourne Avenue

Vespenalya

A

Stanley Grove

Ingelow Road

Queenstown Road

St. Philip Street

Tennyson Street

Montefiore Street

Gambetta Street

B224

Heath Road

Pearton Street

Turret Grove

Stone Close

141

Dunston Road

Wresham Way

Robertson Street

Heather Close

Heather Ct

Keith Connor Close

Heather Ct

Bell Court

M Close

Daley Thompson

Heath Road

Pearton Street

Rowby Street

North Street

B224

Iveley Road

Charles Barry Close

Jost Terrace

143

Audley Road

Beauley Road

Basnett Road

Millard Street

Redmore Mews

Mackay Road

Lambourn Road

Broadhinton Road

Bobbin Close

Stephen Place

Fitzwilliam Road

Otterden Road

By Crescent

Traven Mews

Crosland Place

Garfield Mews

Abbeney Mews

Garfield Mews

Turn chapel Mews

CLAPHAM

Victoria Rise

Hannington Road

Lillieshall Road

Charlotte Row

Flans Place

Rectory Grove

Liston Road

Freke Road

Cedars Road

A216

Macaulay Road

Orlando Road

Lydon Road

Sycamore Ms

Scout Lane

Kiln Ct

Slater Mews

Grafton Square

Grafton Square

Taybridge Road

Wickes Lane

Wilkinson Road

Wildet ness Mews

Macaulay Square

The Chase

The Polygon

Old Town

The

Downers Cottages

B

Freke Road

Lyncott Crescent

Willoughby Cedars Mews

Victoria Mews

Barker Mews

The Pavement B303

B224 The Pavement

Bromell's Road

Taybridge Road

Clapham Common North Side

B303

Clapham Common

PAGE 330

Cock Pond

Clapham Common

Clapham Common North Side   A3

Long Road   A3

Clapham Common South Side

B224

Map 142

The more genteel side of Clapham, Old Town hosts some fine restaurants (**Trinity**), good watering-holes (**The Prince of Wales**), and one of London's best butchers (**Moen's**), all bordered by the green of Clapham Common. If you need more, head to Queenstown Road for further classy dining establishments.

 Coffee

• **Starbucks** • 40 Old Town

 Libraries

• **Clapham Library** • 91 Clapham High St

 Nightlife

• **Prince of Wales** • 38 Clapham Old Town
• **The Sun** • 47 Old Town

Restaurants

• **Nardullis Ice Cream** • 29 The Pavement
• **The Sun** • 47 Old Town
• **Trinity** • 4 The Polygon

Shopping

• **Cult Furniture** • 811 Wandsworth Rd
• **M. Moen & Sons** • 24 The Pavement
• **Puppet Planet** • 787 Wandsworth Rd

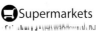 Supermarkets

• Sainsbury's • 199 Wandsworth Rd

Map 143 · Clapham High Street

N

1

2

Larkhall Park

134

Heathbrook Park

133

Wandsworth Road A3036

Wandsworth Road

A3036

St. Paul's Churchyard

A

Union Road

142

Clapham High Street Rail

144

Clapham North

Clapham High Street A3

✉

○ Clapham Common Air-Raid Shelter

Clapham Common

Clapham Common The Pavement

Clapham The Pavement

The Pavement B221

PAGE 330

B

Long Road A3

Clapham Common N Side

Clapham Common South Side A24

Clapham Park Road A2217

Clapham Park Road A2217

Bedford Road B221

Ferndale Road

Sandmere Road

Solon New Rd

Acre Lane A2217

150

King's Avenue

149

North Side

0.25 mile   0.25 km

Clapham High Street

Map 143

Clapham is a microcosm of Cath Kidston mummies and their token gay best friends—watch them jog and brunch around the common in all weather. Whatever you do, do not—we repeat, DO NOT—set foot in **Infernos**. We will find out and we will judge you.

Cinemas
• **Clapham Picturehouse** • 76 Venn St

Coffee
• **The Black Lab** • 18 Clapham Common South Side
• **Brickwood** • 16 Clapham Common South Side
• **Café Delight** • 19 Clapham High St
• **Caffe Nero** • 186 Clapham High St

O Landmarks
• **Clapham Common Air-Raid Shelter** • Clapham High St

Nightlife
• **The Alexandra** • 14 Clapham Common South Side
• **Bread & Roses** • 68 Clapham Manor St
• **The Clapham North** • 409 Clapham Rd
• **The Coach and Horses** • 173 Clapham Park Rd
• **The Falcon** • 33 Bedford Rd
• **Infernos** • 146 Clapham High St
• **The Railway** • 18 Clapham High St
• **Two Brewers** • 114 Clapham High St

Post Offices
• **Clapham Common** • 161 Clapham High St

Restaurants
• **Brickwood** • 16 Clapham Common South Side
• **The Pepper Tree** • 19 Clapham Common South Side
• **Tsunami** • 5 Voltaire Rd

Shopping
• **Apex Cycles** • 40 Clapham High St
• **M. Moen & Sons** • 24 The Pavement
• **Today's Living Health Store** • 91 Clapham High St

Supermarkets
• **Iceland** • 4 The Pavement
• **Sainsbury's** • 133 Clapham High St
• **Sainsbury's** • 33 Clapham High St

Map 144 · **Stockwell / Brixton (West)**

N

1
134
2

Larkhall Park

Lansdowne Way A3

Clapham Road

Pilory Grove

Priory Grove

Cranmer Road

Studley Road

Paradise Road

Landsdowne Way A3

South Lambeth Rd

Stockwell Terrace

Clapham Road

Durand Gardens

Liberty Street

Isabel Street

Sabel Street

Stockwell

Johnston Close

Hackford Road

Groveway

Wilkinson Street

Stockwell Park Rd

Clarence Walk

Lansdowne Way

Clapham High Street

Stockwell Road A203

Stockwell Gardens

Gordon Grove

Groveway

Lingham Street

Crossford Street

Burnley Road

St Michael's Road

St Martin's Rd

Stockwell Park Crescent

Lorn Road

Slade Gardens

McCall Close

Jeffreys Walk

Grantham Road

Ingram Road

145

Irving Grove

Stockwell Lane

Sidney Road

Robsart Street

Lidcote

A

Chatham Rd

Skoi Mews

143

Cambria Road

Rhodesall Road

Kaif Road

Landor Road

Broomgrove Road

Stockwell Green

Moat Place

Aytoun Road

Stockwell Park Road

Winians Walk

Wynne

Vil

Union Road

Kirkstall Road

Trigonment Road

Prideaux Road

Edithna Street

Kimberley Road

Meadow Road

Argyll Close

Combermere Road

Rumsey Road

Stockwell Park Walk A203

St John's Cr

Max R

Pa

Landor Road

Cottage Grove

Willington Road

Tasman Road

Ardales Road

Hubert Grove

Hargwyne Street

Morgan Street

Burgoyne Rd

Chantrey Road

Stansfield Road

Rothery Close

Gateley Road

Stockwell Road

Brixton Road

Western Road

Crescent

Bedford Road B221

Fenwick Place

Pulross Road

Bellefields Road

Beehive Place

Ferndale Road

Ferndale Road

Dolman Street

Belfont Street

Geneva Street

Ferndale Road

Dorrell Place

Brixton Station Road

B

Kepler Road

Solon Road

Sandmere Road

Solon New Rd

Solon New Road

Corrance R'ad

Ballater Road

Trent'ham Street

Duce Street

Melvin Street

Santley Street

Nursery Road

Tunstall Road

Barnwell Road

Saltoun Grove

Bernard's Street

Brixton

Atlantic Road

Effra Road

Coldharbour Lane

Brixton Vi
Mark

Hitherington Road

Ashmore Grove

Plato Road

Bellevue Road

Compton Str

Raeburn Street

Marlborough
Ms

Trinity Gardens

Brighton Terrace

Buckhall Close

Valentia

Electric
Ave

Brixton
Market

Vining Street

Acre Lane

150

Regis Place

Acre Lane A2217

Coldharbour Lane

A2217

Buckner Road

Brixton Hill A23

Rushcroft Road

Saltoun Road

Kellet Road

Barbes Road

0.25 mile

0.25 km

Stockwell / Brixton (West)

Map 144

Lift up the roof of **Brixton Market** on Thursday, Friday, and Saturday nights and underneath you will find rows of arcades teaming with all species of hipster. After years of almost being cool, this microcosmic neighbourhood beneath the train tracks has officially earned Brixton the title of hippest place in town.

Coffee

• **Federation Coffee** • 77–78 Brixton Village Market

O Landmarks

• **Brixton Market** • Electric Ave & Electric Ln
• **Brixton Village Market** • Coldharbour Ln
• **Electric Avenue** • Electric Ave

Nightlife

• **The Duke of Edinburgh** • 204 Ferndale Rd
• **Marquis of Lorne** • 49 Dalyell Rd
• **The Prince of Wales** • 469 Brixton Rd
• **The Queen's Head** • 144 Stockwell Rd
• **The Swan** • 215 Clapham Rd

Post Offices

• **Stockwell** • 1B Wynne Rd

Restaurants

• **Brixton Cornercopia** • 65 Coldharbour Ln
• **Falafel Van** • Station Rd
• **Honest Burgers** • 12 Brixton Village
• **Jeff the Chef** • 1 Brixton Station Rd
• **Mama Lan** • 18 Brixton Village Market

Shopping

• **Funchal Bakery** • 141–143 Stockwell Rd
• **The Old Post Office Bakery** • 76 Landor Rd

Supermarkets

• **Iceland** • 441 Brixton Rd
• **Iceland** • 314 Clapham Rd
• **Sainsbury's** • 425 Brixton Rd
• **Tesco** • 330 Brixton Rd

Map 145 · **Stockwell / Brixton (East)**

Things have changed a bit since The Clash sang 'The Guns of Brixton' in '79 and race riots were a regular occurrence. While the middle classes have infiltrated most parts of Brixton, this neighbourhood still retains a defiant edge. Community spirit and close-knit neighbourhoods take precedence over trendy bars and pricey restaurants. Live music rules here; the legendary **Brixton Academy** still draws the hordes, while **Jamm** offers an eclectic and worthy alternative.

O Landmarks

• **Stockwell Bowls** • Stockwell Rd & Stockwell Park Walk

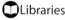Libraries

• **Anti-Slavery International Library** • Broomgrove Rd

Nightlife

• **Brixton Academy** • 211 Stockwell Rd
• **Jamm** • 261 Brixton Rd

Map 146 · Earlsfield

◀138
139
147▶

1
2

A

B

Spencer Park

Wandsworth Common

A214 A3

Trinity Road A214

Windmill Road

Spencer Park

Newtinson Close

John Archer Way

Short Close

Coates Avenue

Muir Drive

Fitzhugh Grove

Wandsworth Common

Wandsworth Common West Side

Cicada Road

Tretoli Road

Jessica Road

Melody Road

Quarry Road

Rosehill Road

Greenmee Road

Cicada Road

Dault Road

Wombe Road

Wcicada Road

Beresford Mews

Penford Gardens

Gordon Place

St Ann's Crescent

Killarney Road

Crieff Road

Kershaw Close

Heathfield Gardens

Marshall Close

Pentland Street

Allfarthing Lane

St Ann's Park Road

Barmouth Road

Cader Road

Ravensbury Road

Swanage Road

Westover Road

Daphne Street

Craickook Street

Assiart Street

Swaffield Road

Whitelead Chive Place

Cranbrook Road

St Ann's Hill B234

Bassingham Road

Brookelwalk Road

Bucharest Road

Wells Place

Waverton Road

Wilna Road

Dingwall Road

Chegwell Mews Road

Mexenhelen

Wilfrid Road

Inman Road

Heathfield Road

Heathfield Avenue

Alma Terrace

Doricote Road

Henderson Road

Baskerville Road

Nicosia Road

Carmichael Mews

Patten Road

Trinity Road A214

Heathfield Square

Heathfield Square

Wilde Place

Roath Road

Groom Crescent

Strickland Row

Magdalen Park Tennis Club

Lyford Road

Burcote Road

Milton Road

Wandsworth Cemetery

Magdalen Road

Ticehurst Road

Loxley Road

Elberton Road

Frewin Road

Wandsworth Common

Vanderbilt Road

Willow Tree Close

Caroll Road

Capron Road

Marville Road

Patten Road

Athelstane Road

Brightman Road

Titehurst Road

Godley Road

Fieldview

Herondale Avenue

Burntwood Grange Road

Collamore Avenue

Manor Gardens

Lingfield Gardens

Samlage Lane

Sir Walker John's Sports Ground

Ellet Lane

Heritage Place

Earlsfield Rail

Victoria Mews

Lickford Road

Headington Road

Openview

Bennett Rd

Burntwood Close

Guiners Road

Burntwood Lane B229

Faterbaum Road

Thornsett Road

Groton Street

Summerley Street

Smiths Yard

Skelbrook Street

St Andrew's Court

Tranmere Road

Sxeby Road

Townsend Road

Wayfield Street

Aldrich Terrace

Lidiard Road

Dawnay Road

Isis Street

Bodmin Street

Bramford Road

St Hilda's Close

St Andrews Close

St Peter's Close

St Edmunds Close

St Anthony Close

Central London Golf Centre

0.25 mile

0.25 km

Earlsfield

Map 146

Sleepy little Earlsfield tends to mind its own business. It's a pretty sedate kind of place, slightly cut off by the lack of a tube stop. The well-heeled locals seem happy enough and make the most of what's on offer. Try **Amaranth** for great noodles.

 Libraries

• **Earlsfield Library** • 276 Magdalen Rd

 Nightlife

• **Halfway House** • 521 Garratt Ln
• **Le Gothique** • Windmill Rd & John Archer Wy

 Restaurants

• **Cafe Amaranth** • 346 Garratt Ln

Map 147 • **Balham (West)**

N

1 2

The Avenue A3

Malmesbury Road
Bennerley Road
Salcott Road
Wakehurst Road

140

Northcote Road B229
Bellevue Road
Kelmscott Road
Bramfield Road
Ratham Close
Cobham Close
Darley Road
Honeywell Road

Chatham Road
Stormont Road
Wilna Road

Ashness Road
Burland Road
Dulka Road
Chatto Road

Winsham Grove

Broomwood Road
Kyrle Road

Broxash Road

Manchuria Road

Walsingham Place

Clapham Common
Clapham Common West Side
Sunburgh Road

Clapham Common
West Side A3

PAGE
330

Broomwood Road B229

Gorst Road
Denis Road

Chivalry Road
Wroughton Road

Hillier Road

Baskerville Road

Devereux Road

Roseneath Road

Nutwell Road

Holmside Road

Beddington Road

A

Blenkarne Road

Montrouge Road

Gayville Road

Thurleigh Road

Sudbrooke Road

Old Park Avenue

Fernemore Mews

Ramsden Road

Bramfield Road
Bracken Avenue

148

Wandsworth
Common

Bolingbroke Grove B229

Morella Road

Hendrick Avenue

Granard Road

Rusham Road

Nightingale Lane

Western Lane

Elsynge Road

Ainslie Road

Temperley

Linnet
Mews

Nightingale
Square

Oldridge Road

Balham Grove

Vicarage Road
Patten Road
Routh Road

Birchlands Avenue

Nightingale Road

Norgrove
Street

Old
Devonshire
Mews

B229

Wexford Road

Lyford Road

St James's Drive B237

Bellevue Road

Bradley Mews

Amers Road

Western Road

Nottingham Road

Ancroft Avenue

Mayford Road

Mayford Close

Nadarin Way

Airedale Road

Calbourne Road

Fernside Road

Gosberton Road

Ravensden Road

Mayford Road

Chestnut Grove

Churchcroft Close

Tantallon Road

Heathville Road

**Wandsworth
Common Rail**

Wandsworth
Common

B

Trinity Road A214

Balham Park Road

Chiseley Road

Sarsfeld Road

Boundaries Road

Hestor Road

Boundaries Road

Balham High Road A24

Sandford Lane
Burntwood Lane B229
Cathnor Avenue

146

**Sir Walker St.
John's Sports
Ground**

Timings Lane
Old Hos.
Cl.

Brodrick Road

Florence
Way

Sarsfeld Road

Sarsfeld Road

Hunter Close

Boreman Road

Franklin Road

151

Mavis Gardens

Watner Road

The Boulevard

Marius Passage

Marius Road

Balham High Road A24

0.25 mile 0.25 km

Balham (West)

Map 147

Ensconced between the livelier Clapham and Tooting, this is a gentle slice of residential Southwest London. Bellevue Road offers a number of places to eat and drink overlooking Wandsworth Common, climaxing with the stupendous **Chez Bruce**. Nightingale Lane is terribly twee and hosts a few opportunities to shop organically and **The Hope** serves up a healthy pint of Tribute.

 Coffee

• **Caffe Nero** • 137 Balham High Rd

 Restaurants

• **Chez Bruce** • 2 Bellevue Rd

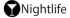 Nightlife

• **The Hope** • 1 Bellevue Rd
• **The Nightingale** • 97 Nightingale Ln

Balham (East)

Map 148

Balham is growing up to become the cooler, decidedly more understated little brother to nearby Clapham. Although it still oozes its own sense of character, evident in quirky mainstays like the **Balham Bowls Club**, the draw of its **Waitrose** risks losing its hip factor.

Coffee

- **Brickwood** • 11 Hildreth St
- **Camden Coffee House** • 208 Balham High Rd
- **M1LK** • 20 Bedford Hill

Libraries

- **Balham Library** • 16 Ramsden Rd

Nightlife

- **The Avalon** • 16 Balham Hill
- **Balham Bowls Club** • 7 Ramsden Rd
- **The Bedford** • 77 Bedford Hill
- **The Exhibit** • 12 Balham Station Rd
- **Hagen & Hyde** • 157 Balham High Rd

Post Offices

- **Balham Post Office** • 90 Balham High Rd
- **Cavendish Road** • 273 Cavendish Rd

Restaurants

- **Brickwood** • 11 Hildreth St
- **The Exhibit** • 12 Balham Station Rd
- **Hagen & Hyde** • 157 Balham High Rd

Shopping

- **Moxon's Fishmongers** • Nightingale Ln

Supermarkets

- **Sainsbury's** • 149 Balham High Rd
- **Sainsbury's** • 21 Balham Hill
- **Waitrose** • Balham High Rd & Ramsden Rd

Map 149 · **Clapham Park**

N

143

1 2

Clapham
Common
PAGE
330

Norwood Close
Tabbard Avenue
Almric Way
West Road
Kildoran Road
Kings
Mews
Margate
Maulen
Mand

Shakespeare
Mews
Longley Close
Waldo Close
Crescent Lane
Leppoc Road
Barnwood Road
Mayfield
Close
Park Hill
Allard
Gardens
Holm
Oak
Mews
Rye
Plaza

Windmill Drive
St Gerards
Close
Wakeford
Close
Calderdale Road
Franconia Road
Columb
Close

**CLAPHAM
PARK**

Clapham Common South Side A24
Cautley Avenue
Mandeley Road
Elms Road
Rodenhurst Road
Patio Close
Clarence
Maple Close
King's Avenue B221
Bynater
Close
Rosebery Road

A
Lessar Avenue
Lynette Avenue
King's Avenue
Rambell Road
Narbonne Avenue
Elms Crescent
Morten
Close
Clarence
Avenue
Thornbury
Road
Thorncliffe
Road

Cavendish Road
Shandon Road
Gowrie Road
Bonneville Gardens
Roseville Road
Trouville Road
Gassmore Drive
Headlam
Road
Heiby Road
Miller
Road
Bourke
Close

Englewood Road
Hazelbourne Road
Anchor
Mews
Hearnville
Road
Franmore
Road
Clarence
Avenue
Poynders Road A205
Thornecliffe
Road

148

Gaskarth Road
Cathles Road
Lynn Road
Belira Street
Grove
Place
Ruskin Road
Balham
Road
Honeybrook Road
Poynders Gardens
Honey brook Rd
Sudbrooke Road
Poynders
Road
Plummer
Road

Yukon Road
Dinsmore Road
Kenilford
Road

Atkins Road
Belthorn Crescent
Scrutton
Close
Atkins Road A205

Hanson
Close
Martindale
Road
Limerick
Close

Queensville Road
Parkholme
Road
Langholm
Close

Ravenswood Road
Balham New Road
Old Devonshire Road
Balham
Mews
Mrytle
Hoppers
Close
West Road
Foster
Road
Radbourne
Road
Rosethorn
Close
Thornton Road B221
Copthorne
Avenue
Barkwood
Close
Zennor
Road
Fury
Ct
Portingale
Gardens

B

**GRANGE
MILLS**

Ormeley Road
Redman
Street
Penning Road
Hydethorpe Road
Cambray Road
Midmoor Road
Laxton
Gardens
Thornton
Gardens
Kirkstall
Road

Laitwood Road
Sistova Road
Rossiter Road
Scholars Road
Bevericote
Road
Burnbury Road
Ravenhill
Road
Balham Hill
Road
Gilleston
Road
Ramsome
Road
Hyde
Farm
Mews
Selkirk
Road
Thornton Avenue B221
Kirkstall
Road
Telford Avenue

0.25 mile   0.25 km

This is where all the Claphamites settle down, have kids, move into their dream town house, and one-up their friends with dinner parties and barbecues every other weekend. All this domesticity has left the locals' only restaurant options north on Clapham High Street or south in Balham. Still, you need fodder for your friends, so gourmet food shopping is where it's at at **MacFarlane's**.

Restaurants

• **Bistro Union** • 40 Abbeville Rd

Shopping

• **MacFarlanes** • 48 Abbeville Rd

Map 150 · **Brixton**

N

STOCKWELL

BRIXTON

Brixton
Brixton

1 **2**

Atlantic Road
Coldharbour Lane A2217
B223
Electric Lane
Brixton Orchard
Rushcroft Road
Vining Street
Saltoun Road
Kellett Road

Ferndale Road
Sandmere Road
Rubens Place
Nursery Road
Stanton Road
Tunstall Road
Bernays Grove

144

143

Kenoa Road
Reet Road
Haslinge
Rope Place
Britannia Close
Northmoor Mews

Solon New Road
Keplet Road
Linom Road
Ashmere Grove
Holmewood
Plato Road
Solon Road

Corrance Road
Tintern Street
Duck Lane
Baldwin Street
Semley Street
Concanon Road

Brighton Terrace
Trinity Gardens
Buckland Gardens
Buckner Road
Poplar Road
Buckner Road

Delmare Road
Brixton Road B23

St. Matthew's
St. Matthew's Road

Mandeville Mews
Magnolia Place
West Road
Kings Mews

Clapham Park Road A2217

Acre Lane A2217
Baytree Road
Sudbourne Road

Mervan Road
Ranston Road

BRIXTON

Effra Road A204
Bailey Mews
Trelawn Road
Morval Road

A

Mayfield Close
Altard Gardens
Crescent Lane
Roden Road

Glenroy Road
Strathleven Road
Branksome Road
Horseshoe Mews
Kildoran Road
Margate Road
Mauleverer Road
Mandrell Road

Winslade Road
Winterwell Road
Haycroft Road
Prague Place

Bonham Road
Torrens Road
Horsford Road
Trent Road
Lambert Road

Hayter Road
Beverstone Road

Hickett Road
St Matthew's Rd
Hicken Rd

Rush Common
Dray Gardens

Brixton Water Lane A2214

Crownstone Road

127

Cossar Mews
Arlington Road

Holm Oak Mews
Lyham Road

Glanville Road
Halliwell Road
St. Saviour's Road

Blenheim Gardens

Josephine Avenue

Helix Gardens
Ardenne Road
Helix Road

149

Bedford Road B221

Ramilles Close
Windmill Gardens

Loats Road
Bowater Close
Rosebery Road
Thornbury Road

John Ashby Close
Rosebery Mews
Wigford Road

Windmill Park
Waterworks Road
Jebb Avenue

Raleigh Gardens
Fairmount Road

Calbre Close
Beachdale Road

Leander Road

Tulse Hill A204
Josie Walk
Bristol Close

Maple Close
Clarence Crescent
Helby Road

Bourke Close
Kingswood Road
Chale Road

Lyham Close
Dumbarton Road
Felsberg Road
Dovefield Road

Brixton Hill A23

Cherry Close
Greenleaf Close
Craignair Road

B

Headlam Road
Bowie Road

King's Avenue B221

Tilson Gardens
Frostal Road
Saxby Road
New Park Road

Rush Common
Upper Tulse Hill

Endymion Road
Elm Park
Medora Road

Dumbarton Road
Somers Road
Merredene Road
Aitchisons Road
Ostade Road
Calina Mews

Reading Wandart Road
Craster Road

Athlone Road
Claverdale Road
Maplestead Road

Harriet Leichenwald
Elstan Road

Atkins Road A205

Streatham

Morrish Road
Stilna Road
Holmleigh

Brixton Hill Place

Dalyngton Gardens
Palace Road
Delawnwood Gardens

Redlands Way
Holmewood Gardens
Brookmill Grove

Vibart Gardens

Saxonfield Close
Scobba Road

0.25 mile   0.25 km

Brixton is where it's at. Shoreditch: old news. Dalston: yawn. Any self-respecting hipster wouldn't be caught dead around these hot spots (too many hipsters) and so they've gravitated south of the river. For Brixton Village's other half, check out Market Row, with its killer katsu (**Kamome**).

Cinemas

• **Ritzy Picturehouse** • Coldharbour Ln & Brixton Oval

Libraries

• **Brixton Library** • Brixton Oval

Nightlife

• **The Dogstar** • 389 Coldharbour Ln
• **The Effra** • 38 Kellet Rd
• **Effra Social** • 89 Kellet Rd
• **Electric Brixton** • Town Hall Parade
• **Gremio de Brixton** • St Matthew's Rd
• **Hootananny** • 95 Effra Rd
• **Hope & Anchor** • 123 Acre Ln
• **Prince Albert** • 418 Coldharbour Ln
• **Satay** • 447 Coldharbour Ln
• **St Matthews Church** • Brixton Hill
• **Upstairs at the Ritzy** •
   Ritzy Picturehouse • Brixton Oval, Coldharbour Ln
• **The Windmill** • 22 Blenheim Gardens

Post Offices

• **Brixton Hill** • 104 Brixton Hill

Restaurants

• **Asmara** • 386 Coldharbour Ln
• **Boqueria** • 192 Acre Ln
• **Franco Manca** • 4 Market Row
• **Kamome** • 49 Brixton Station Rd
• **KaoSarn** • 96 Coldharbour Ln
• **Khan's of Brixton** • 24 Brixton Water Ln
• **Lounge** • 56 Atlantic Rd
• **Negril** • 132 Brixton Hill
• **Refill** • 500 Brixton Rd

Shopping

• **Bookmongers** • 439 Coldharbour Ln
• **Supertone Records** • 110 Acre Ln
• **Traid** • 2 Acre Ln

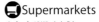
Supermarkets

• **Iceland** • 13 Winslade Rd

Tooting Bec

Map 151

Not quite the Bec of beyond, this Tooting is the home of Europe's largest lido and has a plethora of Asian grill bars for post-pub munchies. The best of the curry houses has to be **Al Mirage**, despite a popular following at **Mirch Masala**.

Coffee
• **Dee Light Bakery** • 14 Ritherdon Rd

Nightlife
• **The King's Head** • 84 Upper Tooting Rd

Post Offices
• **Upper Tooting** • 63 Trinity Rd

Restaurants
• **Al Mirage** • 215 Upper Tooting Rd
• **Meat and Shake** • 47 Upper Tooting Rd
• **Mirch Masala** • 213 Upper Tooting Rd
• **Royal Mahal** • 32 Upper Tooting Rd
• **Spice Village** • 121 Upper Tooting Rd

Shopping
• **Crazy Horse Bike Workshop** • 275 Balham High Rd
• **Russell's Trade & DIY** • 46 Upper Tooting Rd
• **Wandsworth Oasis HIV/AIDS Charity Shop** • 40 Trinity Rd

Map 152 · **Tooting Broadway**

Fishponds
Playing
Field

Fishponds Road
Fishponds Road

Rogers Road

Elmwood Road
Ashbrook Road

Rectory Lane

Broadwater Road

Gatton Road

Selkirk Road

Volna Road

Graveney Road

Greaves Place

Garratt Lane

Garbutt Road

Garratt Lane A217

Garratt Terrace

Gilbey Road

Coverton Road

Effort Street

Hoyle Road

Woodbury Street

Tooting Grove

Nutwell Street

Maybury Street

Aldis Street

Cardwell Street

Tooting High Street

A24

Mellow Mead
West Gardens

Waterfall Terrace

Carr Gardens

Devas Road

Blackshaw Road

Bertal Road

Clive Road

Warren Road

Marlborough Road

Rutland Close

Rutland Road

Wilton Road

Cavendish Road

Colliers Wood
Recreation Ground

Clarendon Road

Myrna Close

Taylor Road

Island Road

Fleming Mead

Hartswood Road

Coppetson Road

Fishponds Road

Hereward Road

Moffat Road

Letchworth Street

Kellino Street

St Cyprian's Street

Angel Court

Castle Mews

Garratt Lane

Longmead Road

Ashvale Road

Tooting
Broadway

Gala Bingo Hall

Ivy Road

Laurel Close

Bickley Street

Undine Street

Valnay Street

Franciscan Road

Dewey Street

Vant Road

Rookstone Road

Church Lane

Mellison Road

Himley Road

Chartnorth Road

Brightwell Crescent

Mitcham Road A217

Sellincourt Road

Trevelyan Road

Longley Road

Bickersteth Road

Loubet Street

Otterburn Street

Glasford Street

Renmuir Street

COLLIER'S
WOOD

Robinson Road

Lyveden Road

Grenfell Road

Warch Close

Harewood Road

Norman Road

Devonshire Road

Singlegate Close

Singleton Close

North Place

Flanders Crescent

Finborough Road

Shrewton Road

Arnold Road

Swains Road

Pitcairn Road

Crusoe Road

Kenmare Road

Priory Road

Figges
Marsh

Figges Road

St James Road

Dovedale Road

Ansell Road

Cowick Road

Blackshaw Road

Coteford Street

Chaseleigh Road

Cowick Road

Derinton Road

Lessingham Avenue

Lynden Road

Morva Road

Franchise Street

Gassiot Road

Erwin Road

Totterdown Street

Cheriton Court

Rams Court

St Bene dict's C

Chertsey Street

Alfriston Way

Hawthorn C

Carrington

St Anne's

Southview Close

St Nicholas Glebe

Byton Road

Stella Road

Naughton Mews

Ascot Road

Boscombe Road

Cromer Road

Deal Road

Eastbourne Road

Links Road

Seely Road

Southcroft Road

Croxborough

Inglecombe Close

Salterford Road

Freshwater Close

Ramsdale

Aldrich Gardens

Alderbury Road

Bruce Hall Mews

Groonfield Road

Lucien Road

151

Tooting

Station Grove

Stanley Gardens

Ashbourne Road

Harton Road

Thirsk Road

Stanley Road

Milton Road

St Barnabas Road

Gorringe Park Avenue

Ynysmaerdy Court

Finton Road

Bruce Road

Ajuga Court

Barrington Road

Woodmill Close

Inglemere Road

| 0.25 mile | | 0.25 km |

Decent rent, a Northern Line station and a grade one listed bingo hall: there's a lot here to like. Hit the High Street for curries and halal it all. Need anything else? Mitcham Road has the ticket.

Coffee

• **Caffee Manal** • 984 Garratt Ln

O Landmarks

• **Gala Bingo Hall** • 50 Mitcham Rd

Libraries

• **Tooting Library** • 75 Mitcham Rd

Nightlife

• **The Ramble Inn** • 113 Mitcham Rd
• **The Secret Bar** • 20 Totterdown St
• **Tooting Tram and Social** • 46 Mitcham Rd
• **Unwined** • 21 Tooting High St

✉ Post Offices

• **Amen Corner** • 1 Amen Cor
• **Tooting** • 2 Gatton Rd

Restaurants

• **Dosa n Chutny** • 68 Tooting High St
• **Jaffna House** • 90 Tooting High St
• **Radha Krishna Bhavan** • 86 Tooting High St
• **Rick's Restaurant** • 122 Mitcham Rd

Shopping

• **Tooting Market** • 21 Tooting High St

Supermarkets

• **Iceland** • 27 Tooting High St

General Information

Website: www.alexandrapalace.com
Phone: 020 8365 2121

Overview

If you fancy panoramic London views, exemplary Victorian architecture and an unrelenting stiff breeze to the face, the heights of Alexandra Park could be your cup of tea. With a fraction of the visitors of North London neighbours Hampstead Heath and Primrose Hill, Alexandra Park is nonetheless home to Ally Pally—Alexander Mackenzie's magnificent 1873 exhibition centre once renowned as the home of television after the BBC used it to broadcast the world's first high def transmissions in '36. It also boasts 196 acres of pristine, Green Flag-winning parkland, a two-hectare conservation area, and a fully functioning ice rink to boot.

Practicalities

Alexandra Park is well served by public transport: Alexandra Palace railway station is a short ride from King's Cross and Moorgate and sits directly next to the park's Wood Green entrance. You can also take the underground to Wood Green, catch the W3 direct to Ally Pally from just outside. You could also take advantage of the 2000 free parking spaces in the park itself if driving, though it's only a short walk from Muswell Hill town centre.

Nature

No doubt tempted by the reservoirs, 155 species of birds have been spotted in the park over the last 30 years. Nature fetishists should take in the two-hectare conservation area, which includes a wide array of animals including deer, donkeys, foxes and rabbits. In 1998, there was even a rare water vole sighting. There he was, large as life, like he owned the bloody place.

Architecture

For most Alexandra Park visitors it's all about the Palace, these days a thriving hub for exhibitions, concerts, farmer's markets and, uh, world darts tournaments. The Palace building itself was ravaged by fire in the 80s and has since been restored to its former glory, though nearby banqueting venue Blandford Hall succumbed to the same fate in 1971 and was completely destroyed. No matter: Ally Pally remains an impressive, domineering building well worth a nose-around. For the less active, admiring the view from sedentary perspective from the underrated Phoenix Bar (located in the south wing) is just as good.

Open Spaces

It's safe to say that Alexandra Park has more than enough grass to keep Cheech & Chong happy, being typified by the diverse range of landscaped grounds that can be found within. The Grove Garden actually pre-dates the park itself and there's also a good little café here if you fancy a quick bite. The Rose Garden is to the east side of the Palace and is even more aesthetically pleasing. Many newer small woodlands have been developing over the last few decades owing to the planting of large numbers of trees, producing an environment pleasing to both the rambler and runner.

Performance

The park often plays host to funfairs and circuses, but the Palace itself will usually be used at night for concerts. Its revival over recent years as a gig venue has led to the likes of the Arctic Monkeys and Paul Weller playing there, with its capacity being around 8,500, making it ideal for bands who've outgrown the Brixton Academy. Other parts of the Palace, such as the Great Hall, are used for classical music recitals.

More recently 'The Secret Cinema' took over the Palace for a screening of *Lawrence of Arabia*, attracting thousands of filmgoers clad in Bedouin attire. Some even brought a camel.

The Palace also houses a theatre, which was dormant for over sixty-five years until a performance took place in 2004. It is still being restored and should be reopened to the public for performances in the near future.

Check out Ally Pally's informative website (listed above) for a full calendar of upcoming events.

Sports

An indoor ice rink is housed within the Palace with a capacity of 1,250, with all manner of ice sports catered for (you can get further information by ringing 020 8365 4386). There is also a large boating lake with its own islands and fishing area (and even a smaller area for kids to boat on their own), with pedalos and rowing boats available for hire; being a seasonal facility, it's best to ring the operators Bluebird Boats Ltd. (020 7262 1330) beforehand. The boating pond is adjacent to a children's playground as well. For those who like golf with a view, the popular ten-hole pitch and putt course was recently revamped with an injection of Heritage Fund money: for prices and booking info see www.alexandrapalace.com/pitch-putt/book-now/ or call 020 8365 2121. Alexandra Palace Park is also popular with cyclists, with the Parkland Walk a particular favourite, being a disused railway line that links up with Finsbury Park. In summertime the park is also a great place to get embroiled in countless spontaneous games of football and Frisbee, or to gawp/hurl insults at joggers

(323)

General information

NFT Map: 7

Address: Barbican Centre, Silk St, London,
            EC2Y 8DS.

Phone: Box Office & Membership: 020 7638
            8891 (9 am-8 pm daily); Switchboard:
            020 7638 4141

Centre opening times:
            Mon-Sat: 9 am-11 pm; Sun & Public
            Holidays: 11 am-11 pm (although
            different parts of the centre may
            open at different times)

Website: www.barbican.org.uk

Overview

As terrifying as it is impressive, the Barbican
Centre is a one-stop shop for all things cultural.
At its best, the Barbican is utterly brilliant: a
rambling collection of cinemas, galleries, bars,
theatres, even a housing estate and a school. But
stay after dark, when the culture vultures have
left, and you can find yourself alone and lost in
this city-within-a-city.

That the centre is brutally ugly makes what's
inside even more splendid. The gallery space
hosts world-class exhibitions and the cinemas
show both mainstream and arthouse films.
There's a world, classical and jazz music
programme catering for everyone from scruffy
backpackers to bearded professors. Most are
sensible enough to leave before it gets too
spooky. But plan your exit route in advance just
in case.

Music

The heart of the Barbican monster is its music
hall. A mecca for lovers of cerebral music, the
centre's resident band is the London Symphony
Orchestra: classical heavyweights who play year-
round. The BBC Symphony Orchestra also has a
base here, and the stage attracts biggies from
around the world, including performances from
Yo-Yo Ma, the Vienna Philharmonic and Cesaria
Evora. But you don't need a high brow to find
something to like: a flick through their listings—
which last year included Sufjan Stevens, Sparks,

The Africa Express and Micachu—will soon have you clicking Book Now.

Festivals are another key draw: not the pot-and-portacabin type, but impassioned celebrations. The Mostly Mozart festival reaches sci-fi convention levels of fanaticism; the Great Performers Festival is an orgy of some of the world's most spectacular musicians; and the Jazz Festival will have you feeling über hip (then perhaps a bit perplexed. And then, if you're 100% honest, rather wishing it was over). African, Latin, Contemporary and Opera festivals also sell out the near-2000 capacity venue.

Film

The programme has an arty bias but is so diverse that you're bound to find something inviting on one of the three screens. Rule of thumb: silent films, in. J-Lo, out. Subtitles, in. Mighty Duck trilogy, out. But they do offer the screens for private hire, so if you really want you can stick it to 'em and have your own showing of Snakes on a Plane. The Barbican also hosts the annual Australian Film and London Children's Film Festivals, and runs constantly changing series. Recent favourites include the Bad Film Club for fans of the most reviled films, and Second Chance Sunday so you can see on the big screen films which you missed first time around.

Theatre and Dance

Don't be fooled by the Barbican's hulking exterior—the centre dabbles in the more delicate arts rather well. Its two theatres cater for both ends of the performance spectrum. The main room, a shared home for acting and dance, seats over 1,000 punters and attracts some of the biggest names in high culture. Deep in the Barbican's bowels the smaller Pit theatre is home to experimental and new acts. But be warned: with just 200 seats the Pit is small enough for anyone dozing off to be highly visible.

Art

Nowhere else at the Barbican is the idea of making culture accessible for all more apparent than their art spaces. The main gallery hosts temporary exhibitions, mixing all types of art into one cultural hot pot. In 2007, under the umbrella

of Art and Sex from Antiquity to Now, erotic Roman cutlery—that's right: erotic cutlery—shared a stage with impressionist paintings and an 11-minute film of someone's face as she was, ahem, attended to. Every first Thursday of the month the gallery opens for a nocturnal viewing, with talks, performances—burlesque dancers for the art and sex exhibition—and a themed bar. A second space, The Curve, winds its way round the ground floor where the exhibitions are generally free.

The Library

Libraries often get a bad press. They've got stuck with an image of frumpy, middle-aged women peering down their spectacles and telling youths to be quiet. But this couldn't be further removed from the reality of the Barbican Library. Alongside a decent array of books, there's a dazzling collection of live musical recordings. Some of these tracks are so rare that they can't be heard anywhere else in the world. Put some headphones on and rock out. Just don't get carried away and smash up the children's section.

How to Get There

By car: Parking is pricey with two hours costing £6.50 and each hour thereafter costing two or three quid more, though there's a flat weekend fee of £9 per day.

By bus: The 153 (which runs from Liverpool Street to Finsbury Park) stops directly outside the Barbican at Silk Street; the following buses run nearby: 8, 11, 23, 26, 35, 42, 43, 47, 48, 55, 56, 76, 78, 100, 133, 141, 149, 172, 214, 242, 243, 271, 344 (seven days a week); 4, (Mon-Sat); 21, 25, 521 (Mon-Fri). If none of these buses can take you home then consider yourself extremely unlucky. By tube: Barbican stations runs on the Circle, District and Hammersmith & City lines. Other stations nearby are Moorgate, St Paul's, Bank, Liverpool Street and Mansion House.

By train: The nearest overland stations are Liverpool Street, Farringdon and Blackfriars. City Thameslink services run through Barbican, Moorgate and Cannon Street.

Practical Information

NFT Map: 132, 133, & 141
Official opening time is 8 am, although the gates are usually unlocked a little earlier than this. The park closes at dusk.
Friends of Battersea Park:
www.batterseapark.org
Zoo: www.batterseaparkzoo.co.uk
Local council: www.wandsworth.gov.uk
(see also for information on the Pump House Gallery)
Cycle hire:
www.londonrecumbents.co.uk
BlueBird boat hire:
www.facebook.com/bluebirdboats1

Overview

Opened in 1858 with the aim of giving the Victorian working classes something to do other than drinking gin, Battersea Park has developed to become one of London's prettiest, most popular and most usable parks. Squeezing a range of gardens, cafes, animals, sports, cultural facilities and even a peace pagoda into its diminutive 200 acres, the park is popular with everyone from hordes of snotty little kids to wandering dog-walkers. It is also centrally located enough to be easy to get to but still far enough from Central London to retain a local feel.

The park is about two miles southwest from Westminster and occupies the spot on the south bank of the Thames between Albert and Chelsea bridges. Originally used for duelling, the Duke of Wellington famously discharged upon the Earl of Winchelsea on the site in 1829. Rather than the vast open and flat spaces that many London parks offer, Battersea is neatly divided into a number of features and sections, making it feel much larger than it is.

Sporting Activities

Battersea has an incredibly good array of sporting facilities. The 'Millennium Arena' is a 400m 8-lane running track situated in the northeast corner of the park; it hosts athletic meets and training sessions and it benefited from an expensive overhaul in, you guessed it, 1999. Next to the arena are ten tennis courts and an all-weather football pitch whilst there are further all-weather astro-turf pitches in the southeast corner of the park marked for both hockey and football. The park also boasts cricket pitches and practice nets, a bowling green, smooth wide paths for skating and enough open spaces to invite impromptu sessions of pretty much any other sport. If you consider attacking fish a sport, and have a permit and rod licence, the park's lake offers fishing for nine months of the year. Rowing boats and pedaloes can also be taken out on to the lake during July and August (adults £8/hour, children £4). Bicycles can be hired from the London Recumbents shop, which is next to the Millennium Arena on the park's East Carriage Drive—but be warned: bikes can only be used in the park itself, and as it takes just 15 minutes for a leisurely pedal around the parameter, an hour's hire can become a little Groundhog Day.

Art

Battersea has fostered a creative relationship with the arts and has a number of sculptures dotted about, its own public gallery and a biannual art fair. Taking pride of place next to the lake are two large Henry Moore and Barbara Hepworth sculptures, both of which are well worth rooting out. The Pumphouse Gallery is a grade II-listed building, originally used to power the park's water works, which has been restored and converted into a gallery and information centre with six exhibitions throughout the year. The Gallery, located northeast of the lake, is also available for private hire and even has a licence to hold civil weddings. The park has hosted the Affordable Art Fair since 1999, which has become a leading showcase for art priced under £3,000.

Performance

In summer music aficionados should head down to La Gondola al Parco, the café by the lake, for free live concerts every Tuesday and Friday from 7 pm. Entrance is free and there's also a BBQ and refreshments aplenty.

Nature and Children's Zoo

Battersea's varied landscapes ensure you stand a decent chance of seeing more than a rat or a pigeon while you saunter round. Squirrels, ducks and Canada geese are all too plentiful. More interesting potential sightings include woodpeckers, cormorants, Peregrine falcons, terrapins and, according to the RSPB, Pochards (whatever they are). If you don't come across any interesting wildlife, your only option is to cheat and visit the park's zoo. A five-minute stroll from the Chelsea Gate entrance, the zoo is aimed at children and has a cool collection of small mammals, including lemurs, as well as small farm animals and some excitingly named birds, such as some 'Peach-faced Love birds'. In case you do fall in love with any of the zoo's inhabitants, eight species are available for year-long adoption at £40. The zoo is open throughout the year and entry costs £10.95 for adults, £8.95 for children.

How to Get There

By tube: Sloane Square (on the Circle and District lines) is the nearest Underground station at just under a mile away. From the station walk down Lower Sloane Street, which becomes Chelsea Bridge Road and leads to the Thames. Walk over Chelsea Bridge and you will see the park on your right. Alternatively take bus no 319.

By bus: From central London, buses run to the park from Liverpool Street (number 344), Notting Hill (452), Oxford Circus (137), Sloane Square (319, 137), Victoria Station (44) and Vauxhall (344).

By train: Battersea Park station is within sight of the park, trains run to both Clapham Junction and Victoria at high frequency. Queenstown Road is around 300m from the park. Trains from this station run to Waterloo and Clapham Junction and depart less often than from Battersea Park.

General Information

NFT Map: 127
Brockwell Park: www.friendsofbrockwellpark.org/
Brockwell Park Lido: www.brockwelllido.com
020 7926 9000

Overview

Brockwell Park may not be a household name when it comes to London Parks but for many South Londoners—not least residents of neighbouring Herne Hill—it's the pick of the bunch, all the lovelier for its unconventionality, tattiness and relative anonymity. It's eclectic, it's quirky, and it's impossible not to fall in love with.

History

By the end of the 19th century the local population was large, growing and in need of a serious park. Brockwell was secured for use by the public after MP Thomas Bristowe got wind of a private country estate that seemed just the ticket. Still, he might have over-exerted himself in the process: having taken a Bill through Parliament to convert the land, led a committee to negotiate the price, and raised funds from across the community, Bristowe himself promptly collapsed and died on the steps of Brockwell Hall, moments after the opening ceremony in 1892.

Café

If that doesn't put you off your scones, nowadays, the ground floor of Brockwell Hall is a café where refreshments have been served ever since. Located at the top of the hill, it's a great place to stop for inexpensive cake, drinks etc. after some…

Activities!

There's heaps to do. A BMX track, tennis courts, bowling green, football and cricket pitches, basketball courts, outdoor theatre club, a children's play area and a paddling pool. Or you could chill by the ponds, in the walled garden, under the clock tower, at the picnic area, near the flower gardens, etc.

Brockwell Lido and Greenhouses

Built in 1937, Brockwell Lido is essentially an (unattractive) art deco building that replaced an old bathing pond. After experiencing financial difficulty it was restored and reopened in 2007. As well as a large outdoor pool, there is a gym and classes are held in yoga, pilates, tai-chi and meditation. For the under 5s, Whippersnappers have everything from acrobatics to puppets and African drumming. A Miniature Railway runs between Herne Hill Gate and the Lido. Run by a local enthusiast on a not-for-profit basis; it's only £1 for a round trip. May–Sept, Sat–Sun, 11am–5pm.

Brockwell also boasts a superb community greenhouse project open to volunteers. The greenhouses are open Sunday afternoons and give Londoners a rare chance to get green fingers and grow their own produce. Contact volunteer@brockwellgreenhouses.org.uk to get involved.

Annual Events

July: Lambeth Country Show is always good fun and involves medieval jousting, farm animals, live reggae/dub and rides, and there are homemade cake and jam contests, too. The Alternative Vegetable Animal Competition requires fruit and veg be crafted into a famous person or building with a very entertaining adult category.
September: The annual Urban Green Fair helps teach London to become more sustainable.
November: The big fireworks show on Guy Fawkes Night is worth braving the cold for.

How to Get There

By rail/tube/foot: The park is a short walk from the following overland and underground stations:

Herne Hill Rail Station—5 mins
Tulse Hill Rail Station—15 mins
Brixton Tube—20 mins
Clapham North Tube—30 mins

By bus: The following all stop at Brockwell Park—2, 3, 37, 68, 196, 322, 468, P15

Parks & Places · **Clapham Common**

Overview

Lively and happening; youngish, professional, and trendy (in a safe way). Clapham Common reflects the area well.

Popular all year round, the Common truly comes alive in summer. On a warm weekend you'll find the park overflowing with picknickers sipping champagne and just plain lookin' good. It's a lovely scene made better by the relaxed, friendly atmosphere. And, when the sun finally sets, you're left with a seriously impressive choice of bars close by.

As well as drawing the usual funky sophisticates, the park is also family-friendly with lots of little ones enjoying the space.

Plenty of organised (or not) sport, kite flying, model boating, Ultimate Frisbee, and even fishing happens here too, but while the common is safe as houses during the day, at night time it is best avoided.

History

Clapham began as a Saxon village. Back then it was called Clopp Ham, meaning the village (ham) by the short hill (clopp). The common was used by villagers to graze their livestock and as a source of firewood.

In the late 17th century the population began to grow as refugees arrived from the Great Plague of London (1665) and the fire of 1666. During this time, the rich gentry of London built a number of fine country houses around the common. When the railways were developed there was a sudden influx of commuters, driving the upper class away to somewhere less, um, common.

Today, the surrounding area is one of the more expensive in South London, partly because of its excellent transport links.

Clapham Sect

On the common is the Holy Trinity Church. This was a meeting place of the Clapham Sect, a group of 19th-century Evangelical Anglicans who fought for social reform. "Ugh" you say, but wait…

The Clapham Sect played a significant part in the abolition of slavery in England. They didn't stop there, going on to campaign for the eradication of slavery worldwide. They also fought for reform in the penal system, focusing on unjust sentencing and the dire prison conditions of the time.

Eateries

The Terrace (vegetarian-friendly)
10 Rookery Rd, SW49DD, 020 3468 0223

Three ponds

Mount Pond—is a fishing park pond about three acres in size. It contains carp, roach, gudgeon and eels. Suggested baits include pellet, maggot, meat, and boilies, it says here.

Eagle Pond—is a smaller pond with a little island. This one is also fishable. Stocks include carp, tench, bream, roach, rudd, perch, chub and gudgeon. Best baits are bread, pellet, maggot, hemp and castor, it goes without saying.

Long Pond—has a century-old tradition of use for model boating.

Activities

These days there are still some nice leafy pathways lined by mature trees left for the strollers to enjoy.

Sporty types can go for the football, rugby, cricket, softball, tennis, basketball, Aussie rules football, croquet (!) or bowling.

Events

Some of the annual highlights include:

Race For Life—Throughout the year: Race For Life—The girls take on the common in pink to raise awareness of cancer. One of the biggest Race For Life running events.

July: Ben 'n Jerry's Sundae On The Common—also goes down well. If it sounds horribly corporate, it's worth noting that a full restoration of the bandstand in '05/'06 was partly funded by proceeds from this festival. Or, just think of the free ice-cream…

August: The Clapham Common Metro Weekender—Two successful, quality festivals have joined forces. South West Four (progressive house, trance, and breaks) and Get Loaded In the Park (indie/dance) now happen side by side at the end of August.

November: The Bonfire Night Fireworks—it's as good as it gets here.

How to Get There

By train: Wandsworth Road Station (12 minutes), Clapham High Street Station (12 minutes)

By tube: Clapham Common (4 minutes), Clapham South (13 minutes)

By bus: 4, 35, 37, 88, 137, 155, 255, 345, 355, 417, G1

Overview

A lot is packed into this 54-acre park—mostly people. On a sunny day Clissold throngs with Stokenewingtonites; yummy mummies and three-wheeled buggies; gaggles of youths, with or without hoods; lads playing football; and assorted dog walkers. Visitors can see deer and goats in the animal enclosure, diamond doves and love birds in the aviary, and coots and moorhens in the nature ponds. Parents take little ones to the paddling pool (summer months only), toddlers group at the One O'clock Club or the well-equipped children's playground. The park hosts the usual hodgepodge of circuses and steam fairs as well as the famous arts festival, StokeFest, in the summer. On grey days, chilly days, or in the early hours, peace can be found—in the rose garden perhaps, or underneath one of the ancient trees.

Clissold House and Café

Phone:	0207 923 9797
Email:	www.venuehire@hackney.gov.uk
Website:	www.hackneyvenues.com/clissold-house
Hours:	Open daily.
Admission:	FREE

Clissold Mansion, the Grade II listed building just visible from Stoke Newington Church Street, is home to a large, child-friendly cafe. Herbal tea drinkers jostle with dripping ice-cream cone lickers on the sun trap front veranda and circular lawn. The large inside rooms are best avoided if you find children's chatter grating, but otherwise a lively spot to tuck into a plate of egg and chips. The building was constructed in the late 18th century on behalf of a Quaker family whose daughter was courted by a local reverend—Augustus Clissold. He wooed, then married her, and swiftly changed the name of the estate to Clissold Place. Where is Catherine Cookson when you need her?

A hundred years later when the land was up for redevelopment, two influential campaigners persuaded the Metropolitan Board of Works to create a public space, and Clissold Park was born on 24 July 1889. Now run by the London Borough of Hackney, Clissold is kept in check by the Clissold Park User Group, who recently secured a multi-million pound lottery bid to spruce the place up a bit and return it to its former 19th century splendour.

Sport in the Park

Year round you can hear the yells of football players churning up mud, the whine of iPods as joggers run in ever decreasing circles, the thwack of cricket ball against cricket bat, and the crunch of misthrown Frisbees hitting the litter bins. There is a basketball court and 10 tennis courts (two kiddies' sized) which are bookable by contacting the Park rangers (020 8800 0011) though they are impossible to get your hands on around Wimbledon—and they say TV doesn't affect our behaviour.

But one of the delights of this park is the more unusual sport that takes place. On misty mornings you can watch cotton-clad figures practice tai chi, and on warm weekends you can nearly always spot a group of hotties from the London School of Capoeira circling around each other. Then there is the occasional father/ daughter pair practising Taekwondo, or two dreadlocked crusties slinging up a line to get some tightrope practice in. Most recent addition to watchable sports in the park is run by 'Pushy Mothers'—groups of mums exercising with buggies. The buggy, with child on board, is pushed hither and thither by the panting parent. It's the ultimate in resistance training.

Nature and the Ponds

Hackney is one of the greenest inner-city boroughs and though relatively small, Clissold Park is still an important green, shady and watery spot for local wildlife, particularly waterfowl. The two nature ponds are named Beckmere and the Runtzmere in honour of the two principal

founders (Beck and Runtz, in case you were wondering). The third pond in front of the cafe is more of a 'canalette' and actually used to be part of the New River built in the early 1600s to supply drinking water to London.

The animal enclosure with its fuzzy-nosed deer, fluffy rabbits and bearded mini-goats are popular with visitors who stand stuffing chips and handfuls of poisonous leaves from nearby bushes through the fence directly under the signs saying: 'Please don't feed the animals—it will make them ill.'

Note: the paddling pool is not a nature pond and though you still can't let your dog in, hours spent gazing at its inhabitants are not looked on kindly.

How to Get There

By car: There isn't much in the way of parking. But if you really need to, from Newington Green head north along Green Lanes until you see a large green space with trees on your right. Or from the A10 turn left onto Stoke Newington Church St past all the cute shops and inviting pubs, until you get to the large church on your left. The park is on your right.

By tube: From Manor House, take exit 4 and walk south down Green Lanes for 10 minutes. The park is on your left.

By train: From Stoke Newington station, head south down the High St and turn right up Stoke Newington Church St, walk for 10 minutes until you see the park on your left just past Stoke Newington Town Hall.

By bus: The 341, 141, 73, 393, and 476 all stop at various entrances to the park

Additional Information

London Borough of Hackney
www.hackney.gov.uk/clissold-park.htm
Clissold Park User Group
www.clissoldpark.com

Lothair Rd. S
Camrose Rd
Alroy Rd
Endymion Rd
Hermitage Rd
Green Lanes
Earle Rd
Yale Rd
American Football Field

MAP 55

Dagmar Rd
Beatrice Rd
Cornwall Rd
Oakfield Rd

American Gardens Play & Picnic Area

New River

Rowley Grns

Finsbury Park

Woodberry Gro

Bowling Club

Track & Gym

Alpha Dog Club

Manor House

Upper Tollington Pk
Scarborough Rd
Carlisle Rd

Manor House Lodge & Garden

Green Lns

Basketball Courts

Boating Pond

Parkland Walk

Oxford Rd

Café

McKenzie Flower Gardens

Play & Picnic Area

Princes Ct
Portland Rise
Ursula M

Woodstock Rd

Tennis Courts

Skate Park

MAP 62

Seven Sisters Rd
Alexandra Gro
Adolphus Rd
Henry Rd

MAP 63

Gloucester Dr

Colthurst Cres

Morris Pl
Wells Ter
Stroud Green Rd

Wilberforce

Finsbury Park Rd

Queen's Dr

Mydleton Ave

Finsbury Park Railway Station

General Information

NFT Map: 55, 62, & 63
Website: www.haringey.gov.uk/libraries-
              sport-and-leisure/parks-and-
              open-spaces/z-parks-and-open-
              spaces/finsbury-park

Overview

Sculpted from what was once a large woodland area on the fringes of London, Finsbury Park was baptized officially in the mid 19th century as a green escape for increasingly urbanized North Londoners. Today's Finsbury Park has been revamped to the tune of £5 million in an attempt to shake off the cloak of urban grime which descended during the 1970s. Though it certainly has cleaned up its act, the park is still a barren tundra-esque plain compared to Hyde or Regent's Park. More of a green scab on the city landscape that surrounds it, the sparse shrubbery and token trees are more suitable for football or running away from Staffordshire Terriers. Delve a little deeper, however, and there are quaint eccentricities and little gems dotted around.

Practicalities

You can enter this veritable urban Oz at Endymion Road, Seven Sisters Road, Green Lanes and Stroud Green Road. Two tube stops serve Finsbury Park: Manor House and the eponymous Finsbury Park. There are also overland trains at Harringey Green Lanes (grab an opulent Turkish meal on the way) and at Finsbury Park Stroud Green Road. Buses 4, 19, N19, 29, N29, 106, N106, 253, N253, 254, N279, W3 and W7 all touch the park at some point. Bear in mind that if you wish to travel in the area during an Arsenal match day you'd better take a stun gun and a red scarf to navigate the crowds!

Attractions

Quaint Englishness and sweaty sporting pursuits abound within the perimeters of Finsbury Park. There are many activities you can partake in from tennis (seven courts are available on a turn up and play basis) to running in the London Heathside Athletics Club (020 8802 9139). There are even two American Football pitches. For a more twee time stroll up to the tiny boating pond and spend an hour in a beat-up boat circling the aviary island—home to exotic birds like ducks, some swans and, uh, ducks again. The kidz are catered for in the form of a skate park. Best of all is the amazing Parkland Walk, which snakes out from Finsbury Park to Alexandra Palace via Highgate.

Nature

The Arboretum and the Avenue of Mature Trees are the two main spots for tree watching. Granted, experienced botanists may find little to fire them up here, but on a mild Autumn day there are plenty of rich colours and textures that enrich any stroll through the park. There are no real 'wild' areas in the park, unlike Hampstead Heath, but there are some lovely quiet spots in the American Gardens which have been landscaped according to the original 19th century plans, with added kiddie play areas. There are some shrubs planted around the boating pond which Harringey Council calls the 'McKenzie Flower Garden' with capital letters which are barely merited.

Festivals

Recently the vast open spaces of the park have been used for music festivals and various other fairs. The Rise, Fleadh, and FinFest festivals are all fairly regular events. The park is also a popular venue for one off special music events—both the Sex Pistols and Morrissey have played controversial shows here. The steam and fun fairs are also worth going to for nostalgic or regressive fun.

Old Woolrich Rd

Romney Rd

Trafalgar Rd

Nelson Rd

Western Hemisphere

Eastern Hemisphere

Greenwich Park St

Maze Hill

Woodland Cres

National Maritime Museum

Burney St

Park Row

Park Vista

Boating Pond

Maze Hill Railway Station

Greenwich Meridian 0° Longitude

Westcombe Park Rd

Herb Garden

King George St

Croom's Hill

MAP
120

Conduit House

Flamsteed House

The Avenue

Old Royal Observatory

Queen Elizabeth's Oak

Roman Ruins

Maze Hill

Greenwich Park

Café

McCartney House

Great Cross Ave

Blackheath Ave

Vanbrugh Fields

Croom's Hill

Ranger's House

Ranger's Field

Bower Ave

Flower Garden

Lodge

The Wilderness (Deer Park)

Shooters Hill Rd

Goffer's Rd

Park Office

Charlton Wy

Prince Charles Rd

Maze Hill

Long Pond Rd

Shooters Hill Rd

Black Heath

Overview

Greenwich Park is the oldest enclosed Royal Park in Britain and has been an integral part of London life for centuries. Saxons built mounds here; Romans worshipped here; King Henry VIII and Anne Boleyn flirted here, and Charles II even built an observatory here. Then the modern day caught up and 2012 brought it to the world as an Olympic venue. It's now a playground for ageing eccentrics escaping London, yuppie families with new puppies, and heaps of tourists trekking up the staggeringly steep hill towards the iconic Royal Observatory.

And it's worth the trek. The sweeping views from the highest point are spectacular and beat the London Eye hands down. London is revealed in all its glory, from the jutting skyline of Canary Wharf, to the sinuous turns of the Thames and the seemed-like-a-good-idea-at-the-time Millennium Dome. All in stark contrast with the neoclassical architecture of the Old Royal Observatory, Royal Naval College, National Maritime Museum and the Queen's House in the immediate foreground.

A well sought-after spot throughout history, the park has belonged to the Royal Family since 1427, and in the early 1600s, under James I, the park was given a makeover in the French style, which gave it its well-groomed tree-lined pathways. He then had Inigo Jones build the missus the stately Queen's House.

The Royal Observatory and Flamsteed House

Address: Greenwich Royal Park, Greenwich, London SE10
Phone: 020 8312 6608
Website: www.rmg.co.uk/royal-observatory
Hours: 10 am-5 pm daily
Admission: Flamsteed House & Meridian Courtyard—£16 adults, £8 Children

Time begins, rather arbitrarily, here—on the Prime Meridian of the World, or Longitude 0°. Time all over the earth is based on a place's distance east or west from this imaginary line, outlined in metal so throngs of tourists can gawp at it. Thanks to Charles II's interest in science, Sir Christopher Wren was commissioned to build the Royal Observatory and Flamsteed House, the living quarters for the first Royal Astronomer. Time your visit to catch a workshop, talk, exhibition or planetarium show, which seek to give visitors a richer experience than simply straddling the Meridian with thumbs up.

Also notable is the Camera Obscura, which sits in a small building next to Flamsteed House. A predecessor to the modern camera, this small dark room displays a live image of the distant National Maritime Museum, projected using only a small hole in the roof.

National Maritime Museum

Address: Greenwich, London SE10 9NF
Phone: 020 8858 4422
Website: www.rmg.co.uk/national-maritime-museum
Hours: 10 am-5 pm daily
Admission: Free

Adjacent to the park's boundaries, this is a museum dedicated to all things nautical. It comprises the Royal Observatory as well as the Queen's House, but its main components are the Maritime Galleries. Highlights include a collection of ships' figureheads, navigational charts, maps, medals, flags and models. They also host relics from Sir John Franklin's ill-fated Northwest Passage expedition (1845-1848) including a pair of his very old-school sunglasses.

Nature

Amongst the well-mowed green are trees of infinite varieties. The scented herb garden is best enjoyed in the summer time. The fallen remains of the 900 year-old Queen Elizabeth Oak can still be viewed and lie as proof of Henry VIII's passion for these grounds, he was said to have danced around the younger tree with Anne Boleyn (before he had her executed, obviously).

How to Get There

The nearest DLR station is Cutty Sark. It's fun too: push the excitable children out the way so you can sit in the front and pretend to be the driver—always a winner with the ladies. By bus, the 53, 177, 180, 188, 199 and 286 will all get you to points of suitable proximity.

You can also take the Greenwich foot tunnel from the Isle of Dogs, which runs beneath the Thames and is open 24 hours a day. Ignore the ominous drips: it's been sturdy for over 110 years, and even if it does at last succumb to the pressure of 50 ft of river above it, then you'll not have time to worry about it. So relax and enjoy!

337

Overview

Hampstead Heath is 791 acres of rambling woods and idyllic meadows worthy of much frolicking. It's the fact that its wilderness seems so, well, wild that makes this London park deceptive. You can be merrily re-enacting the Brothers Grimm, only to be spat out rather rudely onto Parliament Hill and confronted with gob-smacking views of St Paul's and the Gherkin. The Heath is truly nothing short of heaven—until you stumble over George Michael up to no good in the bushes. You can swim naked in its ponds, stroll amongst its tall grasses without seeing another living soul for twenty minutes or more and engage in a little sex scandal amongst the greenery. The park's common theme is one of a hidden countryside retreat right in the middle of it all.

Most likely because it *is* countryside. It's just the rest of London that's gone all urban around it. Long-established hedgerows and ancient trees attest to its lengthy history. The range of wildlife on show is impressive—kingfishers, parakeets, 300 species of fungi and several types of bat, to name a few. All sorts of famous people have enjoyed its leafy company through the years. Boudicca's Mound near the men's bathing pond (hmm... sounds dirty), is said to mark the ancient queen's burial chamber. Karl Marx and his family had a picnic here every Sunday while he lived in London and writer Wilkie Collins used the park as a backdrop for The Woman in White. All in all, the Heath has been a much-loved place of social gathering and strolling for centuries, a place of peace and perspective amongst the greater hustle and bustle of the Big Smoke.

Ponds, Ponds and…Oh Yeah, More Ponds…

It might be argued that losing your Heath virginity consists of swimming in one of its famous outdoor bathing ponds. These are open throughout the year and attract throngs of dedicated swimming fans. On the eastern side—closer to Highgate—are a series of eight 17th and 18th century reservoirs dotted between Parliament Hill Fields and Kenwood House. Amongst these is one swimming pond for guys, another for gals, a toy boat pond, a wildlife reserve pond, and a lake for fishing. On the western side of the Heath are three more, including the 'mixed pond', where you can have some underwater flirtations, should you wish.

Kenwood House

Kenwood House is closed for refurbishment until Autumn 2013. However, the Brewhouse Café remains open and can be visited between 9am-5pm. Kenwood House, a 17th century manor in the middle of the park, adds nicely to the Heath's countryside effect. Its striking classically white walls and landscaped grounds play backdrop to summer jazz festivals as well as a few scenes in the movie Notting Hill. Purchased by brewing magnate Edward Cecil Guinness in 1925, Kenwood House is more than just a pretty façade. Thanks to Guinness's fortune and interest in art, the manor house is also a very noteworthy art gallery featuring works by the likes of Rembrandt, Turner and Gainsborough.

Golders Hill Park

Golders Hill Park is the younger brother to the bigger Hampstead Heath, adjoining it on the western side. Where the latter is an icon of epic proportions, the former is more of a good ol' neighbourhood park. Its large expanse of grass was created rather suddenly when a house that stood on the grounds was bombed during the Blitz. It has a lot to offer for its size though, with a formal flower garden, a deer park and a small zoo (with alpacas no less). If you're feeling sporty, there are tennis courts, putting greens and plenty of jogging paths.

How to Get There

The closest tube stations are Hampstead, Golder's Green and Archway on the Northern Line. Nearby overland stations include Hampstead Heath and Gospel Oak. Bus numbers running to the park are the 168, 268 and 210, which cuts through on Spaniard's Road (where you may want to stop for a pint at the historic Spaniard's Inn).

Additional Information

City of London
www.cityoflondon.gov.uk
Information and booking tickets for swimming:
020 7485 5757
Heath and Hampstead Society:
www.heathandhampsteadsociety.org.uk

Highgate Cemetery General Info

NFT Map: 51 & 59
Web: www.highgate-cemetery.org
Phone: 020 8340 1834

West Cemetery

The West Cemetery opened in 1839 and most of the original pathways and structures still exist. This part of the cemetery is a wild wonderland of creeping vines and eerie Victorian tombs. On weekdays, tours take place daily at 1:45 pm from March to November. There's a limit of 15 people so you'll need to book in advance on the number above. The weekends are a free-for-all with tours taking place hourly from 11 am until 4 pm April to November and until 3 pm December to March.

East Cemetery

The newer East Cemetery is located on the opposite side of the road to the West entrance. This side is open daily and for four pounds you get to roam unsupervised for as long as you please. It may not be as impressive as the West side, but it's still a place of breathtaking beauty. Although there are some well-trodden paths and proper walkways, large parts of the cemetery are almost completely overgrown, making it a wonderful place to go for a stroll.

Opening Hours
1st April to 31st October
Mon-Fri: 10 am-5 pm
Sat-Sun: 11 am-5 pm

1st November to 31st March
Mon-Fri: 10 am-4 pm
Sat-Sun: 11 am-4 pm

Famous Occupants

Quite a few notable people are buried here. The caretakers will be more than willing to inform you of the whereabouts of the following graves and plenty of others.

Douglas Adams, author. Most famous for the *Hitchhiker's Guide To The Galaxy* series of books.

George Eliot, English author and poet; also actually a woman.

Christina Rossetti, English poet.

Karl Marx. Philosopher; considered the father of communism.

Alexander Livinenko, Russian ex-spy, famously murdered by radiation poisoning in a Soho sushi restaurant in 2006.

A whole load of Charles Dickens' clan but not the man himself.

The Highgate Vampire

There have been numerous accounts of shapes, ghosts and supernatural figures seen on the cemetery grounds, and in the early 70s the media picked up on a theory involving a vampire and the legend of The Highgate Vampire was born. It caused quite a stir and soon mobs of 'vampire hunters' descended on the place (imagine something like the Thriller video, but with flares and tank tops). Finally, Sean Manchester, president

and founder of the Vampire Research Society, claimed to have killed the fiend in 1973, when he tracked it to a nearby house. Manchester was also, in his spare time, patron of the Yorkshire Robin Hood society, and remains, in this publication's estimation, the single most compelling reason not to wander around Highgate Cemetery after dark.

Waterlow Park Overview

Waterlow Park is a beautifully landscaped park located just next to the cemetery, making it a perfect spot for a pre- or post-gravespotting picnic. Often overlooked and overshadowed by nearby Hampstead Heath it is a charming and peaceful alternative. You can feed the ducks in one of the three ponds, hire tennis courts by the hour, admire the awesome view of London, wander in the rose garden, or just go and look at the cool hollow tree at the bottom of the park.

Lauderdale House

Address: Highgate Hill, Waterlow Park
London N6 5HG
Tel: 020 8348 8716
Web: www.lauderdalehouse.co.uk

Lauderdale House operates independently from the park, but is located on its grounds. The original house was built in 1582, but has gone through major alterations and restorations since then. In 1963 a major fire destroyed much of the old building and it was left untouched and unoccupied for 15 years. In 1978 it was finally repaired and reopened in its current incarnation. The house runs classes, concerts and exhibitions by local artists. There's also a small café. The House and the galleries are usually open all week 12 pm–4 pm, but you can always phone in advance to avoid disappointment.

How to Get There

Nearest tube station is Archway. Exit the station and turn left up Highgate Hill. Waterlow Park is about five minutes walk on your left hand side. To get to the cemetery, cross the park down to the Swain's Lane exit, which is adjacent to the East Cemetery gates.

General Information

Website: http://www.royalparks.org.uk/parks/
              hyde-park
Phone: 030 0061 2000

Overview

For over 370 years Hyde Park has been the 'Lungs of London'—the place to go for oxygen-starved Londoners to take a breath of fresh air. This park remains an essential part of the beating heart of London. As the city's grown, so has the desire to preserve this 350-acre mass of parkland and thankfully, Hyde Park has never been in better shape.

Eating

Perambulating through the park is bound to get that metabolism going, so stop off at one of the numerous food stalls to quench your thirst or down a plasticky hot-dog. Yum. For a more civilised affair check out one of the park's seated joints: the **Colicci Cafe** (which also has a paddling pool) or **The Serpentine Bar & Kitchen**.

Nature, Architecture & Sculpture

The Serpentine Lake attracts the usual assortment of ducks as well as some exotic additions, such as Egyptian Geese. **The Lookout Education Centre** holds informative talks about the park's wildlife. **The Grand Entrance** at Hyde Park Corner is an awe-inspiring arched construction of Greek influence, whilst the **Albert Memorial**, erected by Queen Victoria after her husband's death, is a true show of love. The **Diana, Princess of Wales Memorial Fountain**, remains one of the most visited areas in Hyde Park and is worth a look to satisfy curiosity, as is the **Peter Pan Memorial**. And pause to reflect at the heartbreaking 7 July Memorial, which pays tribute to each of the victims of the 2005 London Bombings.

Performance

The park attracts big musical events, and by big we mean Live 8 big. It's only the musical deities that get their own special Hyde Park treatment—Bruce Springsteen, Paul McCartney and Blur, but summer means festival time and the annual Wireless Festival and Hard Rock Calling. Brass band concerts are held throughout the summer at **The Bandstand**. **Speakers' Corner** is guaranteed to entertain. Since 1872 it's been the site of a verbal free-for-all stemming from the activities of the Reform League who marched for manhood suffrage in 1866. These days the topics aren't quite as revolutionary. Heather Mills sounded off here recently…ah, the injustice of having too much cash.

Sports

There are ample jogging paths, designated bike routes (see www.companioncycling.org.uk) and great naths for roller blading and walking. Even more fun is boating on **The Serpentine Lake** from March to

October. Informal games of rugby, football or cricket can be played on the **'Sports Field'** while **Hyde Park Tennis & Sports Centre** does exactly what it says on the tin. There's also a bowling green and horse riding at the **Manege**.

Kensington Gardens

The 111 hectares west of the Western Carriage Drive are known as Kensington Gardens. Annexed from the main park in 1689, the area retains a slightly more formal air, with regular tree-lined avenues to stroll down and less spaces for rambunctious sporting displays. This makes the Gardens an ideal spot for a picnic or a quiet ponder. Kensington Gardens also boasts the **Serpentine Gallery** (in between the Diana Fountain and the Albert Memorial), a toy-sized venue for renowned modern and contemporary art exhibitions, and the rather stunning **Kensington Palace**. Still a royal residence, the palace majestically confirms some of the most well ordered green spaces London has to offer.

Richmond Rd

Richmond Rd

Eleanor Rd

Ellingfort Rd

Gayhurst Rd

Tennis Courts

Lido

Playground

The Pub on the Park

London Ln

London Fields West Side

Sport Piches

Martello St

London Fields Railway Station

Wilman Gro

Gransden Ave

Martello Ter

MAP 89

Middleton Rd

London Fields

Lamb Ln

Mentmore Ter

Lamb Ln

Shrubland Rd

Sport Piches

Helmsley Pl

Bayford St

Sidworth St

London Fields East Side

Lansdowne Dr

Grand Union Cres

Exmouth Pl

Warburton Rd

Mare St

Dublin Ave

Playground

Warburton Rd

Triangle Rd

Trederwen Rd

Creston St

Dericote St

Westgate St

Westgate St

Broadway Mkt

Bocking St

Mare St

Overview

Best green space of the northeast? Victoria Park might still bag the accolade, but this relaxed, mid-sized park in the middle of Hackney is catching up. And quickly. It's lush and it's spacious and its latest addition, a smashing 50-metres Lido (see below), is hard to beat. Just off busy Mare Street and minutes from Regent's Canal, the park is easily reachable and easily manageable. There are two tennis courts, football, basketball and cricket pitches, and two well-equipped and well-maintained playgrounds, if you have kids in tow. London Fields does a nice job of attracting a pleasantly diverse mix of people, from Hoxton-refugee artists and rollie-smoking would-be philosophers, to pram-pushing mums and East End geezers with no teeth and big dogs. The architecture framing the tree-studded space is just as varied: bland high rises, pretty Victorians, depressing brick estates and fancy new developments, all modern Hackney is there.

The park's own drinking spot, imaginatively called Pub on the Park, is good for a relaxed outside pint, simple pub food or the footie. If you're after a slightly more refined meal, check the gastropub-ish Cat and Mutton at the park's bottom. This is also where Broadway Market begins, a traditional East End market street, now brimming with nice little shops, several pubs and original eateries. If the red wine you shared with your painter friends on their picnic blanket got you into serious party mood, head to the close-by (and late-night) Dolphin on Mare Street. Or just fall asleep in the shadows of those massive oak trees. Chances are, one of the dogs will lick you back to reality.

London Fields Lido

Address:	London Fields Westside, London E8 3EU
Phone:	020 7254 9038
Website:	www.hackney.gov.uk/london-fields
Hours:	6:30 am–9 pm every day
Admission:	£5.25 for adults, £3.05 for kids

You might say that in a city where, essentially, you have the choice between stomach-turningly grotty leisure centre pools and hopelessly overpriced member gym versions, any new public swimming basin would be a winner. Fair enough. But WHAT a winner. Having mouldered closed for almost two decades, a £2.5m effort has restored this art deco gem to its former glory. In fact, it's probably better than ever: the 50-metre basin is nicely heated all year round (25C when we last checked), the changing rooms are modern and clean, admission's okay. Come during the week for a few pre-work lanes, when steam mysteriously hangs over the water, or jump in on the weekend, followed by a Sunday roast in one of the pubs close-by or a picnic in the park. Sounds nice? We know.

Sports

There's no shortage of things to do. The park's two tennis courts can be booked for hourly slots (open 8.30 am–dusk; £6.00/h during peak times, £4.00/h off-peak; call 020 7254 4235 for more info). The Hackney Tennis Club (www.hackneycitytennisclubs.co.uk) also offers classes and joint sessions. The football pitch (run come and play) is located in the middle, the basketball space (ditto) towards the south. Follow the sound of children for the playgrounds, one in the north, one in the south. If cricket is your cup of tea, get in touch with the London Fields Cricket Club (londonfieldscc@gmail.com), who keep the park's long-standing tradition as a cricket pitch alive (which, incidentally, is said to go back to 1800).

How to Get There

By bus: Most buses stop on Mare Street (get off at the London Fields stop), a few minutes walk from the actual park. From Liverpool Street Station, take 48 and 55, from Mile End or Bethnal Green grab the D6. The 106 takes you here from Finsbury Park, the 277 from Highbury & Islington. Two buses stop directly at the bottom of the park: the 236 (connecting to Dalston, Newington Green, Finsbury Park) and the 394 (Hackney Central, Homerton Hospital, Hoxton, Angel).

By train: The train is a great option, since London Fields station is located right next to the park. Train operator National Express East Anglia (formerly known as One Railway) serves the central Liverpool Street Station (via Cambridge Heath and Bethnal Green) and connects the Victoria Line tube stations Seven Sisters and Tottenham Hale further north. You can travel using your Oyster Card, for timetables check www.greateranglia.co.uk.

Victoria
Park

Old Ford Rd

Hertford Union Canal

Grove Rd

Gunmakers Ln

Vivian Rd

Zealand Rd

Driffield Rd

Ellsmore Rd

Hewlett Rd

Roman Rd

St Stephen's Rd

Cardigan Rd

Vernon Rd

Mace St

Twig Folly Cl

Lanfranc Rd

Medway Rd

Lyal Rd

Norman Gro

Saxon Rd

Selwyn Rd

Athelstane Gro

Shetland Rd

Stafford Rd

Tredegar Rd

Roman Rd

Grove Rd

Arbery Rd

Strahan Rd

Antill Rd

Malmesbury Rd

Morpeth St

Meath
Gardens

Cherrywood Cl

Lichfield Rd

Merchant St

Harley Gro

Mile
End
Park

Ashcroft Rd

Clinton Rd

Morgan St

Rhondda Gro

Tredegar Sq

Coborn Rd

Meath Crescent

Bradwell St

Longnor Rd

Moody St

MAP
93

W Field Wy

Lawton Rd

Aberavon Rd

Mile End Rd

Tredegar Sq

Grantley St

Bancroft Rd

"The
Banana"

⊖ Mile End

Southern Grove

Brokesley St

British St

Alderney Rd

Mile End Rd

Grove Rd

Hamlets Wy

Eric St

Mossford St

English St

Treby St

Tower Hamlets
Cemetery

⊖
Stepney
Green

Solebay St

Mile
End
Park

Ropery St

Ropery St

Bow Common Ln

Ernest St

Commodore St

Canal Rd

White Horse Ln

Shandy St

Hartford St

Essian St

Ragged
School
Museum

Copperfield Rd

Wager St

Joseph St

Burdett Rd

Beaumont Sq

Duckett St

Bale Rd

Bohn Rd

MAP
98

Stadium

Aylward Dr

Ackroyd Dr

Burdett Rd

Stepney Green

Rectory Sq

Dongola Rd

Ben Jonson Rd

Rhodeswell Rd

Timothy Rd

Leopold St

Stepney
Green

Garden St

Hayley St

Alston Rd

Carr St

Rhodeswell Rd

St Paul's Wy

Whitethorne St

Salmon La

Hamlet's Wy

Lindfield St

Stepney Wy

Repton St

Overview

Bordered at the north by the chain-ridden fake-a-rama, Bow Wharf, to the east and south by rat runs, and to the west by the dank waters of the Regent's Canal, this strange elongated park doesn't appear to have a lot going for it. However, this 32-hectare wiggle of green is more a string of mini parks—divided up by roads and railway lines—and each segment has hidden treasures worth digging for. There is an adventure playground, an arts pavilion with weird orange-and-white sculptural seats by Leona Matuszczak, an ecology park with moths and all sorts, a terraced garden and a sheltered children's playground. Clever landscaping and inventive use of space creates pockets of peace, and when the sun comes out, sparkling on the canal, bouncing off the reflective jackets of the cyclists bombing past or laying its beams on niggling young couples, the park of many parts comes into its own.

It was created following the Second World War after the area was destroyed in the Blitz. The idea of Lord Abercombie, who envisioned a creepy-sounding 'finger of green' in amongst the rubble, Mile End really came into being in 1999 with Millennium Commission funding providing new areas, strange metal cross signage and an amazing green bridge—known by locals as the Banana. It actually has grass and shrubs taking walkers and cyclists over Mile End Road.

The remains of the Victorian terraces sit on the west side of the park, and one resilient pub, The Palm Tree, squats alone in the middle of a grey car park, a testament to the rows of two-up-two-downs which no longer flank the pub. This great local boozer is filled most nights with a mix of climbers and locals tucking into doorstep sandwiches and draft beer.

For those who want a bit more local history, The Ragged School Museum (www.raggedschoolmuseum.org.uk) on Copperfield St overlooks the southern tip of the park: a canal side slum that was transformed into a school for the local urchins by philanthropist Dr Barnado. It now has a mocked-up Victorian classroom and clunky little cafe. Only open Wednesday and Thursday and the occassional Sunday—check before you go.

Sports in the Park

The southern end of the park is a haven for sporty types with a refurbished stadium and ten all-weather pitches made from recycled car tyres, a go-kart track and the large Ikea-like Mile End Leisure Centre with all the usual sauna, gym, pool and verruca-infested changing rooms. Mile End Climbing Wall is housed in an old pipe engineering works in the middle of the park, and is one of London's 'big three' (The Castle and the Westway are the others). It was opened in the 80s and some of its users seem unaware of time's passage, judging by their fetching leggings.

How to Get There

By tube: Turn left out of Mile End station, cross Grove Rd and you'll find yourself at one of the entrances to the middle section of the park.

By car: The park can be easily accessed from Bow Road, Grove Rd, or Mile End Rd, though according to London Borough of Tower Hamlets, 'The local streets operate a resident's parking permit system and are regularly patrolled by traffic wardens. Limited parking is available at Bow Wharf.'

By bus: The, D6, D7, 25, 205, 277, 323, 339 and all take you to various entrances around the park.

Additional Information

London Borough of Tower Hamlets
www.towerhamlets.gov.uk/lgnl/leisure_and_culture/parks_and_open_spaces/mile_end_park/mile_end_park.aspx

Mile End Climbing Wall
www.mileendwall.org.uk

General Information

Website: www.royalparks.org.uk/parks/
the-regents-park
Park Tel: 030 0061 2300
London Zoo: www.zsl.org
Open Air Theatre: www.openairtheatre.com/

Overview

Whenever your quaint and backward country-dwelling friends are telling you the virtues of rural life, you can silence them with two words: Regent's Park. Let the yokels have their cleaner lungs, their maypoles and their children running barefoot and feral, because London may have its city drawbacks but it knows how to do a good park. When you stroll in Regent's Park, you're strolling on nothing less than Property of the Crown—you can see tigers and gorillas, play on the largest outdoor sports area in London, take in some Shakespeare, or, on a very good day, watch girls playing volleyball in bikinis. With 410 acres of parkland, you will always find a spot away from the (many thousands of) fellow visitors. It is the perfect space to take stock, step back and refresh, to sit in a deckchair with a good book, picnic with friends, breathe better air. Moreover, the same obnoxious people who wouldn't move down the tube to let you on or who pushed in the sandwich queue, are here relaxing with their families, lazing over a paper in a patch of sun, falling in love, throwing a Frisbee: it can be just what you need to re-bond with London when you're becoming jaded, and to get away from it all without leaving Zone One.

How to Get There

By tube:
Regent's Park—Bakerloo.
Great Portland St—Hammersmith & City, Circle, Metropolitan.
Baker St—Hammersmith & City, Jubilee, Metropolitan, Bakerloo.
St John's Wood—Jubilee.
Camden Town—Northern.

The Park is served by bus routes 2, 13, 18, 27, 30, 74, 82, 113, 139, 189, 274, 453 and C2.

Nature

The Park is a haven for the city's wildlife, thanks to a biodiversity which includes grassland, woodland, wetland, lakes and scrubs, as well as beautifully tended and fragrant gardens. Over 200 species of birds have been spotted in the Park, along with favourite garden mammals such as hedgehogs, squirrels and foxes. But if that's all just a bit too Beatrix Potter, you can get your fix of the more badass species at London Zoo in the Park's north-east end, where in addition to the normal enclosures, visitors can get closer to some of the animals with events like "Meet the Monkeys" or even help as a volunteer.

The Park's size and calm makes it a choice hangout for celebrities (not strictly nature, but dandelion schmandelion: spotting A-Listers doing tai chi in oversized sunglasses will impress more down the pub, and can there be a nobler calling?).

Performances and Events

The Park's permanent outdoor theatre is an absolute treat. The shows have a Shakespearian bias, but the venue also puts on non-bard performances, comedy nights and concerts. It is the experience more than the performance which will likely stay in your memory. Among the atmospheric trees of the park in the evening, with a bottle of wine and a blanket to snuggle up in (it is Britain after all—how many other theatres have an official "weather policy"?), it is a magical way to spend an evening. Outdoor does not mean free however: prices range from £10–£50 (Saturdays are the most expensive), and you pay theatre prices for food and drink. Cheaper to bring a picnic to enjoy in front of the theatre before the performance.

Regent's Park also hosts a number of big outdoor events. Notable regulars include Taste of London and the Frieze Art Fair London. Check the website for one-off listings.

Primrose Hill

To the north of Regent's Park sits Primrose Hill, which is a rather large hill, boasting corking views of much of Central and East London. It's also surrounded by some rather lovely eateries.

The former hunting ground for playboy king Henry VIII has a murky history, becoming the scene of a political feud in 1678, when magistrate Edmund Berry Godfrey was found dead there after being implicated in a plot to kill Charles II. In later generations Primrose Hill became the setting for duels: London lovers fought there over their ladies, while fops found it a good place to settle literary disagreements ("I say Dryden is naught but a one-trick satirist sir!" "Well then I say you are a cad and a scoundrel! Die you maggot!").

Celebrity voyeurs should keep 'em peeled for the likes of Kate Moss, old bumbles himself Mr Boris Johnson, and writer Alan Bennett, while Primrose Hill in winter is the ideal spot to check out panoramic views of fireworks across the city on Guy Fawkes Night (5 November).

Dawes Rd

High St

London Rd

Kew Palace

Café

Princess of Wales Conservatory

Kew Gardens

Palm House

Syon Park

Temperate House

Restaurant

Pagoda

Japanese Landscape

Queen Charlotte's Cottage

Royal Mid-Surrey Golf Course

Richmond Railway Station

Twickenham Rd

Sheen Rd

Kings Rd

Queen's Rd

Richmond Hill

Chiswick Railway Station

Kew Gardens

Kew Rd

Sandycombe Rd

Mortlake Rd

River Thames

Clifford Ave

Great Chertsey Rd

Lonsdale Rd

Barnes Bridge Railway Station

Mortlake High St

Barnes Railway Station

North Sheen Railway Station

Mortlake Railway Station

Upper Richmond Rd W

Roehampton Golf Course

Roehampton La

Park Office

Sawyer's Hill

Richmond Park

Roehampton Café

King Henry's Mound

Sidmouth Wood

Petersham Rd

Pembroke Lodge

Pen Ponds

White Lodge

Richmond Park Golf Course (Public)

Roehampton Vale

Ham Gate Ave

Richmond Rd

Queen's Rd

Isabella Plantation

Kingston Vale

Robin Hood Wy (Kingston Bypass)

Kingston Hill

Wimbledon Common

Overview

In 1625 Charles I brought his court to Richmond. He subsequently, with quite heroic selfishness, built a wall 'round a large expanse of open grassland, and created Richmond Park. These days the park is thankfully accessible to the public, opening at 7 am (or 7.30 in the winter) and closing at dusk every day. It's the biggest of the Royal Parks in London, and is an obvious choice for long horse rides, picnics, informal sports and other wholesome pursuits for your golden, happy days of youth. Oh, and there's deer.

Attractions

The park has a number of gardens and wooded areas, the most beautiful of which is probably the Isabella Plantation, an organic woodland garden that blooms with azaleas and rhododendrons. The Pen Ponds is another popular feature, as is Pembroke Lodge, the park's Georgian mansion, which can be rented out for weddings and conferences (www.pembroke-lodge.co.uk or call 020 8940 8207). The adjacent café also does a mean cream team.

Sports

There are three rugby pitches near the Roehampton Gate that are available for rental on weekdays during winter (contact the Rosslyn Park Rugby Club at 020 8948 3209), and two eighteen hole, pay and play golf courses (call 020 8876 1795 for info and booking). Between 16 June and 14 March you can purchase a fishing permit for the Pen Ponds (call 020 8948 3209 for information). Or for more extreme park-goers there is the option of Power Kiting, whatever the hell that is (www.kitevibe.com), and military-led Boot Camps to shape you up fast and mercilessly.

Kew

The Royal Botanic Gardens, Kew, begun in 1660, is not only easy on the eyes but is an important centre for horticultural research and a UNESCO World Heritage Site. Guaranteed to take place every year are the summer festival 'Kew the Music' (July) and ice-skating (Nov-Feb). Kew is a hugely popular day trip destination for schoolchildren and adults alike and contains such a surplus of sights and attractions that repeat visits are always surprising.

Attractions

Of course the main attractions here are the Gardens themselves. Between the formal gardens, smaller themed collections of plants and wildlife and conservation areas, there is enough walking and cooing to be done to justify any length of cake and sandwich sessions at one of the Gardens' eateries. There are also 39 Grade I and II listed buildings, all of which have some kind of historic significance. The 17th century Kew Palace (www.hrp.org.uk), is one of the most interesting of these, having previously been home to the notoriously 'mad' King George III. Other buildings in the gardens include the Chinese Pagoda of 1762, a traditional Japanese 'Minka' house and a number of museums. Decimus Burton's glasshouses (The Palm House and the Temperate) are iconic examples of this quintessentially Victorian architectural theme, and an essential part of any visit to Kew.

Events

Kew Gardens is run with great enthusiasm and has a packed programme of events throughout the year. These occur and change frequently so it's best to check the Kew website, which has comprehensive listings of everything that is going on in the Gardens, down to the blooming or blossoming of individual plant species: www.kew.org.

Several of the historic buildings, most spectacularly the Temperate Glasshouse, are available to rent for corporate and private parties.

How to Get There

Richmond station (overland trains, District Line) is a 20 minute walk from Richmond Park, or buses 371 and 65 both go from the station to the pedestrian gate at Petersham. Kew Gardens is (surprisingly) the closest station for Kew Gardens, London Overground trains stop here from across North and North West London. Trains from Waterloo stop at Kew Bridge station, a ten-minute walk from the gardens.

A large number of buses go from Hammersmith, Fulham, Clapham Junction, Wandsworth and Ealing to Richmond Park and to Kew Gardens.

351

River Thames

Blackfriars Bridge

Gabriel's Wharf

Oxo Tower Wharf

Upper Ground

Broadwall

Blackfriars Rd

Stamford St

Colombo St

Waterloo Bridge

National Theatre

The London Studios

Duchy St

Hatfields

Colombo Sports Centre

Victoria Embankment

Queen Elizabeth Hall Purcell Room

Coin St

Aquinas St

Meymott St

Hungerford Bridge

Hayward Gallery

Upper Ground

Doon St

Roupell St

Southwark

Royal Festival Hall

Stamford St

Exton St

Belvedere Rd

BFI IMAX

Waterloo East Railway Station

Union St

Jubilee Gardens

Mepham St

Cornwall Rd

The Young Vic

British Airways London Eye

York Rd

Waterloo Station

Waterloo Rd

The Cut

Ufford St

Pocock St

Chicheley St

The Old Vic

London Aquarium

Addington St

Station Approach Rd

Webber St

Blackfriars Rd

MAP 104

Westminster Bridge

Lower Marsh

Bayliss Rd

Pearman St

Morley St

Lancaster St

Westminster Bridge Rd

Waterloo Rd

Florence Nightingale Museum

Lambeth North

St George's Cir

Westminster Bridge Rd

Kennington Rd

Hercules Rd

London Rd

Lambeth Palace Rd

Lambeth Rd

Garden Row

St George's Rd

Archbishop's Park

Imperial War Museum

Lambeth Palace

Lambeth Rd

Lambeth Wk

Brook Dr

Haynes St

West Sq

Elliott's Row

Overview

A pedestrianised quarter formed of venues for theatre, music, cinema, art and various other artistically orientated entities, the South Bank is the realisation of a post-war dream of an arts-for-all hub in London. The area has its roots in 1951's Festival of Britain, a technicoloured marvel designed to showcase an optimistic future for Britons used to coal, Spitfires and fake mashed potato. The legacy of the Festival ensured that the surrounding area went on to grow into the playground that it has become today.

The South Bank Centre

The actual 'South Bank Centre' is officially formed of the Royal Festival Hall, the Queen Elizabeth Hall, the Purcell Room, the Hayward Gallery and the Saison Poetry Library, which are all concentrated in the centre of the South Bank. The Royal Festival Hall hosts a variety of musical and dance performances from its auditorium, whilst the Hall's foyer is an enormous and relaxed open-plan area with a bar, performance spaces and shop. The Queen Elizabeth Hall and Purcell Room offer further stages for musical recitals whilst the Saison Poetry Library houses a vast collection of poetry dating from 1912 onwards. The Hayward Gallery has an exterior of frightening ugliness, which shields a surprisingly spacious interior, devoted to exhibitions of the visual arts.

The National Theatre

The National Theatre is next-door to the South Bank Centre complex and is another gaping example of uncompromising architecture. Opened in 1963, it still looks slightly unhinged. The building consists of three theatres and puts on a range of productions from the established to the experimental. It also features an inviting foyer, and in the open spirit of the South Bank, offers back-stage tours, workshops, talks and costume and prop hire to Joe Schmo.

British Film Institute and IMAX

Nestling under Waterloo Bridge, the BFI promotes film and television through its archives, cinema screens, talks and festivals. It's a great alternative to the disgustingly over-priced and sticky-floored chain cinemas of central London and promotes an all-encompassing program from its three screens.

The Film Café and Benugo Bar & Kitchen do good pre- and post-flick munch. The BFI IMAX is the separate, rotund glass building situated around 200m south of the BFI. It shows films on Britain's biggest cinema screen accompanied by sound pumped from a gargantuan 11,600-watt sound system.

Everything Else

Beyond its theatres, music halls, galleries and cinemas, the South Bank has spawned a number of other attractions. The London Eye is an enormous Ferris wheel built in 2000 on the banks of the Thames adjacent to Westminster Bridge, it revolves at a leisurely 0.5 mph and offers brilliant views from its 135m-high seat. The London Aquarium is just opposite but with ticket prices roughly similar to the Eye, seeing big fish in small tanks starts to look a distinctly lame option. Less expensive attractions around South Bank include the open-air book market tucked under Waterloo Bridge and Gabriel's Wharf, a dinky enclave of small shops, bars and restaurants that offer succour to those cultured-out. Or you can ogle at the cool kids doing half pipes at the South Bank Skate Park..

Getting There

By tube: Nearest stations are Waterloo (Northern, Bakerloo, Jubilee and Waterloo & City lines) and Embankment (Circle, District, Northern & Bakerloo lines). From Waterloo, head 50m towards the river. Embankment station is at the northern foot of Hungerford footbridge.

By train: Nearest stations are Waterloo & Charing Cross. For directions from Waterloo, see 'By Tube'. From Charing Cross, walk 100m down Villiers Street towards the river and then walk across the Hungerford footbridge.

By bus: The South Bank is on numerous bus routes. Buses stop on nearby Waterloo Bridge, York Road, Belvedere Road, Stamford Street and Waterloo Station. Most coming from the North get to South Bank via Holborn, The Strand or Victoria. From the South they come via Elephant and Castle or Lambeth North.

By boat: Festival Pier is adjacent to the London Eye. Pleasure boats dock here on cruises, as do riverboat services which sail west as far as Tate Britain and east as far as Woolwich Arsenal.

General Information

NFT Map: 9 & 23
Website: www.royalparks.org.uk/parks/st-jamess-park
www.royalparks.org.uk/parks/green-park
Free guided walks: 020 7930 1793
Inn the Park Café and Restaurant
(St. James's Park): 020 7451 9999

Overview

With Trafalgar Square at one end and Buck Palace at the other, both St. James's and Green Park are slap-bang in the heart of picture-postcard London. When the belching fumes of the Hackney cab and hordes of Oxford Street shoppers threaten both health and sanity, there's only one place to go. Zip past the crowds and pigeons in Trafalgar Square and head under the grand curve of Admiralty Arch into the stately calm of St. James's Park. Stand yourself on the bridge that crosses the lake, take a deep breath and marvel at the history surrounding you in the city's oldest Royal Park, dating back to the days of Henry VIII.

The views: fairytale Buckingham Palace to the west, Downing Street, the seat of Parliament and Big Ben jutting out over Horse Guards' Parade to the east and the towers of Westminster Abbey to the south. There ain't nowhere else in London where you can view the icons of Church, State and Monarchy in one quick spin on your heels. Impressive. And when you're done marvelling, join the families, office workers, joggers and tourists in taking a stroll round the lake for pelican-spotting, duck-feeding, lunching and romancing.

A hop across the Mall and you'll find yourself in the rolling green of, yup, Green Park. Flowerbed free, this 53-acre patch of park with its aged plane trees is the more meditative of the two. A refuge from the noisy thoroughfare of Piccadilly and Hyde Park corner, its grounds soon fill with picnicking office-workers at the slightest suggestion of sun while the tree-lined Mall is the nearest you'll get to a Parisian boulevard.

Nature

The curving lake of St. James's park runs the length of the grounds and is perfect for indulging in some casual bird-spotting. Ever since the days of James I, the park has been home to an exotic menagerie, once including elephants, camels and even crocs.

While the crocs and ellies might be long gone, both Duck Island and the smaller West Island remain home to an impressive array of water birds. Beyond the humble duck and gulls, there are suitably stately black swans, rare golden eyes and the rather less-illustrious sounding shovelers, a close relative of the time-starved office-worker on lunch, we believe. But, with their gentlemanly swagger and mighty beaks, the five resident pelicans unquestionably steal the show. A gift from the Russian Ambassador in 1664, feeding time is worth a gander at 3pm daily in wait for their entertaining antics—like flying to Regent's Park Zoo on fish-stealing sprees—one caused a media storm when, clearly lusting after a menu change, it swallowed a live pigeon whole, flapping feathers 'n' all.

Take some old bread and the park's tame, tubby squirrels will feast from your hand. Hang around 'til dusk and the bats come out to play.

Architecture & Sculpture

As if housing ol' Queenie's Buckingham Palace wasn't enough, the parks are surrounded by two more palaces—Westminster, now the Houses of Parliament, and St. James's. From the Regency elegance of the Mall's Carlton House, home to the Institute of Contemporary Arts (ICA), to the impressive frontage of Horse Guard's Parade, the parks are hemmed in by grandeur.

Once a swampy wasteland for grazing pigs, it's a tale with humble beginnings for London's most royal park. While each passing King and Queen slowly improved St. James's Park, it was Charles II that really put the work in, getting trees planted, lawns laid and then opening it up for the first time to us commoners.

Sobering war memorials in St. James's Park abound, including world war icons Mountbatten and Kitchener in Horse Guards' Parade, and an overblown marble statue of Queen Victoria complete with glitter and gates. Oh, and that grand old Duke of York, best-known for marching his men up and down some hill? He's here too, in bronze atop a mighty pillar by the ICA.

The Parks in Season

St. James's in spring is carpeted with crocuses and daffodils. Come summer, they're quickly replaced with a carpet of sun-starved Tom, Dick and Sallys, laid bare as they dare to catch some rays. For an instant upgrade from the rabble, head to Green Park by the tube and hire a stripy deck-chair at £1.80 a pop from April to September.

Between May and August, add a dash of high-brow culture to your day with free concerts at the bandstand every lunchtime and early evening.

Autumn days might be chilly but clear skies make for impressive sunsets while wintry strolls are all the more head-clearing, especially after a night on the Soho tiles.

Sports

With cycling and ball-games banned—*entirely* inappropriate in such stately surrounds!—jogging, morning tai chi, leisurely strolls and pigeon chasing are as energetic as it gets. Sundays are best for strolling when Constitution Hill is closed to traffic.

The Mall and Constitution Hill are cycle-friendly and make a pleasant cut through the West End. Join the Serpentine running club for regular jaunts through St. James's. (www.serpentine.org.uk).

Enjoy the sedate pace with free lunch-time guided walks twice a month, discussing anything from horticulture to royalty (booking line: 020 7930 1793).

General info

NFT Map: 90, 93, & 94
Website: www.towerhamlets.gov.uk/lgnl/leisure_and_culture/parks_and_open_spaces/victoria_park/victoria_park.aspx
Information: 020 8985 5699

Overview

Look at all the joggers, skaters, cricketers and picnickers swarming in Victoria Park on any given weekend, and it seems hard to continue calling this 218-acres green space one of London's best-kept secrets. Yet, to many Londoners not living east, it still is. Lined by Regent's Canal in the south, London's third-largest cultivated green space is a nice blend of Regent's Park's beauty and the wilderness found in Hampstead Heath. It's also far enough off the Central London map to stay virtually tourist-free, while, at the same time, feeling reassuringly inner city urban, with the Gherkin and Canary Wharf's skyscrapers all in sight.

Divided into two handy bits by Grove Road, Victoria Park has much of what makes a park more than just grass and trees: excellent sporting facilities, ranging from athletics to rugby, several lakes, a deer enclosure, a secret garden—and plenty of decent drinking holes nearby. Designed in the 1840s to bring much needed greenery and breathing space to a soul-destroyingly grim East End, the "people's park" can also look back on an intriguing past of dissent, non-conformist rallying and all sorts of political mischief-making. And it's home to the oldest model boat racing club in the country. Come now, before the Olympics do. Once the squirrels start digging out amphetamines, the secret will be gone forever.

Nature

Ducks, swans, birds and god knows what else live around The Lake in the west, while deer and goats graze slightly further north. You're allowed to fish in the Old Lake, although we're not at all sure that there are really many fish in there. Pretty oak trees and hawthorns stud the whole place; colourful flowers and perfectly-groomed shrubs grow in the Old English Garden. It's a beautifully landscaped gem of a garden and one of this city's most peaceful spots—if you don't mind the odd greying philosopher, mumbling to himself.

Sports

Jogging and skating are popular and, thanks to wide pathways, possible throughout the park. There's a rugby pitch, a large dedicated football area, four tennis courts (call 020 7193 8933) and three all-weather cricket pitches, run by the esteemed Victoria Park Community Cricket League (www.vpccl.com/). The children's playgrounds are decent enough, and the athletic field is excellent. Get in touch with the park's own athletics association (www.vphthac.org.uk) for access to changing rooms, showers and its indoor training hall.

Architecture & sculpture

Rising in the middle of the park is a Grade-II listed drinking fountain erected by Baroness Angela Burdett-Coutts (England's wealthiest woman at some point, we're told), adorned by several half-naked marble boys, smiling cheekily. The Hackney Wick Great War Memorial, in the east part of the park is a reminder that this part of London was hit especially hard by the bombings of the Second World War. Close-by, you'll find two alcove-type fragments that survived the demolition of the old London Bridge Station. Fairly unremarkable, but good shelter when it's raining. Let's face it, no one comes here for architecture.

Festivals

The hazy days when The Clash whipped up a beer-can-throwing frenzy in the park—heralding a new era called punk along the way—might be over, but Victoria Park has kept its musical tradition alive. Slightly more tamed and organised, the festivals taking place these days range from the trendy, village-feel Field Day to the indie-and-electro-blending Lovebox Weekender, while big names (Radiohead for one) have also discovered a liking for the park's scenery and music-appreciating attitude.

Eat & Drink

The park's café, next to The Lake, is tiny, but the organic cakes are a tasty lot. That aside, you have to venture to the park's fringes for food and drink, but fear not: a tap is never far. Good Ales, a real fireplace, and up-marketish pub food make The Royal Inn on the Park, near the Royal Gates, the usually busy favourite.

General Information

Website: www.wpcc.org.uk

Overview

If London life starts to get you down, but trekking to the countryside is too much hassle, then Wimbledon Common provides the best of both worlds. Incorporating Putney Heath to the north, Wimbledon Common offers over 1000 acres of wild woodland, scrubland, heathland, ponds and well-tended, mown areas for sports and recreation. Bordered by the urban sprawls of Wimbledon, Putney and Richmond, the common has offered Londoners an escape from city life for centuries. Although thousands visit every weekend, the scale of the place is so vast that you can easily find a private haven for reading a book or a romantic picnic.

Unlike the micro-managed and perfectly structured central London parks, Wimbledon feels much more natural and random. Paths are unpaved and often little more than a muddy track leading off in unlikely directions. The untamed beauty of the common and the lack of traffic noise, or any noise for that matter, make it hard to believe you are still in London.

After a hard day of outdoor activity, or sunbathing, there are plenty of historic pubs to retire to in Wimbledon village. If you prefer your nature tamed or don't want to get your shoes dirty, head to the southeast corner of the common for Cannizaro House and gardens, a grand mansion converted into a boutique hotel and restaurant, with elegantly manicured gardens open to the public. In the summer, the friendly hotel bar opens onto a patio overlooking the grounds and makes a good spot for a sun-downer as you imagine being Lord or Lady of the Manor for the day.

Nature

The common is home to many animals including bats, badgers, and muntjac deer. It's also an important breeding ground for dragonflies and damselflies. For anyone wanting to find out more about the flora and fauna, the London Bat Group organises 'bat walks' while the London Wildlife Trust organises guided walks. You can also take a self-guided wander along The Windmill Nature Trail. 800 metres long, the trail has been created with accessibility in mind and begins right next to the Windmill car park. The visitors' centre behind the Windmill has wildlife exhibits and also tells the history of the common. It also sells maps and booklets giving the low down on the nature on offer.

Recreation

There is loads of space on the common for pick-up games of rugby, football, Frisbee and cricket. If you fancy a 'real game', you can hire tennis courts by the hour, cricket pitches by the day (from as little as £150) or enjoy a round of golf on the two available courses. The common is very popular with runners and steeplechase events have been held here since 1867. Various running clubs such as the South London Harriers and Hercules Wimbledon use the Common. If you've ever fancied trying horse riding, there are a number of stables that make use of the 16 miles of trails—or bring your own nag with you.

Golf
www.wcgc.co.uk
www.londonscottishgolfclub.co.uk

Horse Riding
Wimbledon Village Stables: 020 8946 8579

Rugby, Football and Cricket Pitch Hire
020 8788 7655

How to Get There

By public transport:
The Northern Line goes to South Wimbledon where you can take a bus to central Wimbledon then change or walk to the village and common. Wimbledon station is much closer. Take the District Line from central London or over ground trains from Waterloo or London Bridge. If you are feeling fit, a ten-minute walk up Wimbledon Hill takes you to Wimbledon village and beyond that, the edge of the common. Regular buses serve the village. Alternatively, you can access Putney Heath which joins up with Wimbledon Common. To do this, take the District Line to Putney Bridge or East Putney overground to Putney mainline station and take a bus up Putney Hill.

It's likely that at some point during your London residence, you've been seized with the romantic notion of floating your way round a London market—savouring the smells, laughing with a vendor, flirting your way to some freebies. If you have, then your attempts to live that dream almost certainly resulted in you silently fuming as you crawled among a crowd of thousands, trekking for a cashpoint because you forgot that stalls don't accept cards, and getting crapped on by a pigeon. Don't be put off!

At the markets you can buy some of the most unique, quirky, fresh, stylish, grungy, exquisite, unusual items in London. Sometimes you'll get brilliant bargains, sometimes you'll pay high for something you fall in love with. And sometimes, yes, you'll be driven near to homicidal rampage. But they're one of London's great strengths: use them while you can, because the developers have their evil, dollar-signed eyes on them.

For Groceries

The food in markets isn't necessarily locally grown, but you get a much more tempting choice than in most supermarkets. Expect fruit, veg, breads, cheeses, meats, spices and pastries, as well as stalls concocting irresistible snacks from around the world.

Borough (Map 106)

You don't come here for bargains: you come for ambiance, exquisite international foods, and to impress the person you woke up with. If you're rich and like the finer things in life, then head your weekly shop can consist of some of the freshest vegetables, plumpest fruit, sweetest patisseries and sockiest cheeses in London. If you're poor and just fancy a change from Saturday morning repeats of *Friends*, then head here for a hearty hog roast sandwich and to snaffle some free samples.

Broadway (Map 89)

As gorgeous as Borough, for a third of the price and a fifth of the crowds. It's a pain to get to, stuck in one of the city's remaining quaintly retro spots not closely served by the tube (London Fields), but you'll want to move here by the end of your visit.

Ridley Road (Map 86)

If the gourmet markets are too poncey for you, with their Bavarian organic rye bread and Malaysian honey from breast-fed bees, then get down the Ridley Road. Here, in a market which is bright, chaotic, grubby and bouncing to reggae, you can pick up an incredible array of Jamaican, Turkish, African, Indian and Chinese foodstuffs (and possibly e-coli).

For Market-Chic

You won't necessarily pay less than at the high street, but you will have a choice of original and irresistible items sold with passion and knowledge. Expect to leave these markets with a lighter pocket (though try to make sure it's not because of the pickpockets…).

Spitalfields (Map 91)

Mecca for anyone looking for ethnic-hip and well-priced clothes, bags and jewellery. Here you can often chat to the maker of the clothes you're eyeing up and learn the story behind their designs. Which is all very inspiring, until you try on their beloved creations, realise you're too fat for it, and reject it having slightly stretched it. Because then it's just awkward.

Greenwich (Map 120)

Craft-tastic: a great place to go for beautiful handmade gifts which people love to receive and then put in a cupboard for the rest of their useful life. Here you'll find a gorgeous range of items for home and lifestyle: pictures, antiques, candles, pottery, soft furnishings and clothes, as well as some great food stalls, and an above-average number of beautiful rich people than at most markets.

Portobello Road (Map 29)

Although famed for being the World's Largest Antiques Market, Portobello Road seems to sell *everything*. You'll need patience to work around its sprawling size and the crowds, but just about anything you're looking for is there somewhere or can be sourced by speaking to the right vendor. Stalls include clothes (from classy-vintage to student-cheap), jewellery, fabric, food, as well as 1500 antique stalls selling maps, medals, silverware, and things you never thought you needed (and which, after you've got them home, you realise you didn't).

Camden (Map 71)

Camden is actually home to six markets, though "chic" doesn't do any of them justice. Here you'll find a purse-emptying range of alternative fashions, vintage clothes, accessories, gifts, t-shirts, comedy hot water bottle covers, tie-dyed hippies, teeny-punks and chaps asking if you'd care for a nice bit of crack. Anything goes, and this open, free atmosphere makes it a major and exciting draw. Hit Camden Stables for brilliant international food stalls.

Fer Findin a Bit o' Laaandon Prop'a

If you're a Londoner who "just adores the city! But oh dear *no*, wouldn't *dream* of bringing kids up here" then chances are you don't mingle much with the Prop'a Laandoner. This hardy breed whose family history is a Dickensian yarn of blitzes, TB and chimney sweeps are the core of this city, and the gradual nudging out of their jellied eels and pub sing-songs is tantamount to ethnic cleansing. Find them at London's Propa Markets before they vanish.

Smithfield (Map 15)

Smithfield Market is in full swing at 4 am, which makes it the perfect place to stumble into on your way home from clubbing. Unless you're vegetarian, because while frying bacon may have you yearning for looser morals, the smell of this 800 year old meat market will have you retching over your recycled sandals. It's the best place in London to pick up any meat you could hope for, including, in the 1500s, a barbecued Protestant or a topside of William Wallace, this being the site of hundreds of executions in its time. Some of the local pubs hold special early licenses, so on your way to the office you can swing in for breakfast over a pint with some of the meat porters: they'd just *love* it if you did.

Columbia Road (Map 91)

There's something deeply touching about an exquisite flower market being manned by some of the burliest Cockneys you'll see outside a Guy Ritchie film. Get there first thing on Sundays for the best choice, or in a low-cut top for the best bargains. And if the crowds and cries of the "daffs, dahlin'?" become too much, just slip into the enchanting boutiques lining Columbia Road.

Billingsgate (Map 101)

For the largest selection of fish in London, outside the London Aquarium (where they frown on you if you try to fry the fish. Bloody bureaucracy.), head to Billingsgate. People were buying their fish here long before London went all yuppie, and much the same stock is available—winkles, cockles, potted shrimp and things which smell ungodly. Today you'll find alongside them almost any fish you could hope for (though don't ask for goldfish), as well as poultry, oils and snacks.

General Information

King's Cross Address: Granary Building,
1 Granary Square, London, N1C 4AA

Phone: 020 7514 7000

Website: www.arts.ac.uk/csm
or @CSM_news

Overview

Though hyped to infinity, and often lazily editorialised as the one vital source of all things up-and-coming in London, Central St Martins nevertheless has an undeniable history of producing graduates that tend to rocket to international fame upon leaving. The frequently cited list of alumni reads like a Who's Who of European art-and-design talent, and includes past superstars such as Alexander McQueen, Gilbert and George, and Anthony Gormley, as well as recent fashion darlings Christopher Kane, Gareth Pugh and Kim Jones, to name a few.

Central St Martins is part of the much larger University of the Arts London, made up of CSM, Chelsea College of Art, Camberwell College of Art, London College of Fashion, London College of Communication and Wimbledon College of Art. The school as it is today was formed in 1989 through the amalgamation of two prestigious 19th century institutions, the Central School of Arts and Crafts and St Martins School of Art. Since then it has annexed the Byam Shaw School of Art in Archway, and as a result offers a huge range of courses covering most areas of the visual and performing arts. St Martins has a particularly formidable reputation for fashion design—it is the only university to show student collections as part of London Fashion Week—but it is well respected in all departments for its hyper-progressive ethos (expect to hear words like 'challenging,' and 'risk-taking' liberally thrown around on open days). Whether you find the whole thing pretentious and overrated or are waiting in breathless anticipation for the next St Martins wunderkind, CSM is very difficult to ignore.

Campuses

The swish renovated warehouse building in Kings Cross, opened in 2011, centralises programs and student life in a way that was once difficult. The massive campus anchors the redevelopment of Kings Cross, formerly known for its transport links and general seediness. The facility allows students of art, fashion, design, and drama to be in one location, to interact cross-discipline, and form more of a united front rather than being scattered across the capital. Anyone who has walked the corridors of the old Charing Cross Road building will tell you that however charming the decaying archaic halls of academia may be, a brand spanking new building with technology to match is more than welcome. Occupying the Grade II listed Granary Building, architects Stanton Williams have integrated such wonders as an internal street, the Platform Theatre performance space, and an open-air terrace.

The Byam Shaw School of Art in Archway is a relatively recent addition (2003) to Central St Martins. Devoted solely to fine art, it runs a BA and a more skills-based 2 year FdA as well as a variety of short and post-graduate courses. CSM also has facilities in Richbell Place, Holborn.

College Culture

As is the case with most London institutions, the university community is massively subsumed by the bright lights of the city itself, but this is no bad thing. Though the college puts on frequent exhibitions, talks and events, there is no independent bar or central hub. The Student Union is not particular to Central St Martins but provides services for and represents all the art colleges in London (University of the Arts London) as a whole, and various services and societies (such as sports clubs) are run at this level. As far as the education part goes, it's not always easy being in the midst of the constant search for the next-big-thing, but at the same time the idiosyncratic slant of the teaching makes for a unique experience, and the generally high talent level of the students fosters a fantastic creative and social atmosphere.

Tuition

Fees are £9,000 a year for UK/EU applicants taking an undergraduate or Foundation level degree. Some courses require payment of an additional course fee for materials. International students can expect to pay approximately £16,000 depending upon the type of course taken.

Short Courses

Central St Martins also runs a large number of short courses for all aspirational (and rich) non-students wanting a piece of the action. Prices are high but the courses very popular, partly because of the college's reputation and partly because there are many interesting options to choose from. The courses run in evenings, weekends, or can be taken intensively as a Summer, Easter or Christmas school.

Phone Numbers:

Reception (Granary Building): 020 7514 7444

Drama Centre London: 020 7514 8760

Admissions—Degree Courses: 020 7514 7023

Admissions—Short Courses: 020 7514 7015

International Office: 020 7514 7027

Lethaby Gallery: 020 7514 9897

University of the Arts Students' Union: 020 7514 6270

Press Office: 020 7514 8098

General Info

Address: Northampton Square, London, EC1V 0HB
Phone: 020 7040 5060
Website: www.city.ac.uk or @CityUniLondon

Overview

In London, a place rich with academia, City University often gets overlooked. Unlike King's or LSE it has no grand halls, secret-handshakes or old-boys' networks. Its facilities are modest and its library short on fusty books. But it has carved out a reputation as a supplier of professionals, cementing its place in the top five for graduate employment.

Located on a pretty park on the edge of the City of London—the 'Square Mile' that itself has emerged at the centre of the global economy—the university is overwhelmingly diverse, with many coming from abroad to study at the Cass Business School. It's that section of the university that churns out workers for the finance industry—students who are so hell-bent on business success that they go to school in suits. The other five schools comprising City are the School of Arts & Social Sciences, School of Health Sciences, School of Mathematics, Computer Science & Engineering, School of Informatics, and The City Law School.

The university's first incarnation came in 1894 as an industrial college for the working classes. The on-site swimming pool was used when London hosted the 1908 Olympics, although it wasn't until 1966 that it gained full university status. It has maintained strong links with industry, with alumni including the founding father of budget Euro-travel, easyJet's Stelios (like Sting and Madonna he chooses to use only one name). Students at City may be lined up for good jobs when they graduate, but it comes at the cost of having to explain what their less well-known university is whenever they mention it.

Tuition

Annual undergraduate fees are £9,000. International undergraduate fees can be upward of £15,000.

Student Life

City offers on-campus housing, including a guarantee scheme for first-year undergraduates. The uni hosts some heavyweight lectures. The Students' Union offers limited clubs and societies with all the usual fare—tennis, chess, Christian Union. CitySport is City's state-of-the-art sports and fitness centre. 'Ten' (10 Northampton Square) is where the kids hang out, the social hub of City.

Departments

Cass Business School: 020 7040 8600
Admissions office (undergrad and postgrad): 020 7040 8716
Library: 020 7040 8191
CitySport: 020 7040 5656
Students' Union: 020 7040 5600

1 Gloucester Building
2 Innovation Centre
3 School of Social Sciences
4 College Building
5 Centenary Building
6 Drysdale Building
7 Refectory Building
8 University Building
9 Tait Building
10 Goswell Place
11 Myddelton Building
12 Parkes Building
13 Health Centre
14 Walmsley Building
15 Paramount House
16 Saddlers Sports Centre
17 Finsbury Residence Hall
18 Heyworth Residence Hall
19 Peartree Court Residence Hall

General Information

Address: Imperial College London,
South Kensington Campus, London SW7 2AZ
Phone: 020 7589 5111
Website: www.imperial.ac.uk or @imperialcollege

Overview

Imperial College really did have imperial beginnings with Prince Albert setting up the college as a research and learning centre of science, maths, medicine and engineering to enhance the image of the British Empire in 1887. In the Victorian age, and to this day, the college attracted the most enquiring of minds and was the central feature of what was once Prince Albert's successful push to create a centre of culture and learning, encompassing the nearby museums, Royal College of Music, Royal Geographical Society and the Royal Albert Hall. The university remains one of the best in the world, and as such remains one of the most selective institutions in the UK with the application to admissions ratio hovering around 7:1. Famous alumni include clever clogs Brian May (Queen), HG Wells and Alexander Fleming. In 2007 Imperial College became independent from the University of London and now awards its own degrees.

Departments

The pride and soul of the college are three faculties, each headed by a principal: engineering, medicine and natural sciences. Imperial also has a business school with Departments of Finance, Innovation & Entrepreneurship, and Management. The main purpose of the Humanities department is to provide elective subjects and language courses for the science students. For medical students Imperial is also associated with various London hospitals including St Mary's Hospital and Charing Cross Hospital.

Campus Culture

Imperial may have a 'heads down' atmosphere but there is still that unwritten rule that if you work hard you play hard. Imperial College Union (www.imperialcollegeunion.org) offers numerous clubs and societies from belly dancing to wakeboarding to backgammon. The Union Bar is also well used, and is particularly lively on an afternoon when a football or rugby match is screened. The free student paper, Felix (felixonline.co.uk), is a popular and useful resource for keeping up to date with campus life and aims to be independent from the College itself. Imperial also has its own student TV station, Stoic, and radio station ICRadio (www.icradio.com). There are also regular public lectures on a variety of subjects.

Facilities

Imperial's main campus in South Kensington is surrounded by many of London's best museums including the Natural History Museum, Science Museum and Victoria & Albert Museum. Being in the thick of it also means a close proximity to the shops and cafes of South Ken and High Street Kensington and being a stone's throw from Hyde Park.

The main campus boats some of the best facilities of the London universities. As well as the usual on-campus shops (including bookshop, cafes, travel agents and bank) there are some impressive sports facilities on offer. The Ethos sports centre contains not only a fully equipped gym but also an inside climbing wall, swimming pool, squash courts, sports hall and a treatment room offering massages and physiotherapy. On top of that there's a boathouse and a 60-acre athletic ground. Naturally, there's a well-stocked central library and various smaller departmental libraries.

Tuition

Home students' (UK/EU) annual fees are £9,000 for undergraduate programmes. International students pay upward of £25,000.

General Information

Address: King's College London, Strand,
London, WC2R 2LS
Phone: 020 7836 5454
Website: www.kcl.ac.uk or @KingsCollegeLon

Overview

Although it grants its own degrees, Kings College is one of the 18 colleges that make up the colossus that is the University of London. King's (or KCL, as otherwise known) has nearly 20,000 students and five campuses—the Strand, Guy's, Waterloo, St. Thomas' and Denmark Hill. In 2011 the school of law moved into the East Wing of the magnificent Somerset House. It has an excellent academic reputation and ranks among the top UK universities. Unlike some of the other University of London colleges, King's is equally well known for its arts and science courses.

Its religious affiliation is now less central, but back in 1829 King's was founded as a Church of England institution to counter University College London, or "the godless college in Gower Street."

The beautifully designed chapel at the Strand campus testifies to its pious beginnings, though few students would consider it a motivation for attending the college. The student body is diverse, as the societies list reflects—it includes a Catholic society, a Christian Union, a Krishna Consciousness group, and a Nomads society, among a myriad of others.

King's boasts a number of famous alumni. Keats studied apothecary there (he didn't like it much), and Florence Nightingale set up the world's first school of nursing at St. Thomas' Hospital, now the Florence Nightingale School of Nursing and Midwifery. In the 1960s, Archbishop Desmond Tutu spent time in its halls.

London prices may take their toll on the student purse, but King's students at least benefit from a prime location. As well as the nightclub, the college has two bars, one at Guy's Campus and one at the Strand. The Waterfront bar at the Strand looks directly onto the Thames, giving a view of everything from Westminster to the OXO Tower. It's also a great gig venue.

Sports

The college's sports facilities are impressive. It caters to almost anything—it has a swimming pool, gym, and even rifle range. Although King's cannot rival the Oxbridge rowing tradition, its sports do have a history—two of the men's rugby clubs, Guy's and St. Thomas', are the oldest in the world. To access the sports grounds students must leave Zone 1; the grounds are in Dulwich, Surrey, and South London.

Culture

Kings has numerous dramatic societies where amateur thespians can hone their skills. More unusually, its classics department stages a play in ancient Greek every year, and is the only classics department in the UK to do so. The college's religious origins are evident in its wonderful choral music. 25 choral scholars uphold this tradition.

Tuition

Annual undergraduate fees are £9,000. International undergraduate fees are upward of £18,000.

Contact Details

Admissions: 020 7848 7000
International Students: 020 7848 3388
Students' Union: 020 7848 1588

Colleges & Universities · LSE

General Information

Address: Houghton Street,
London WC2A 2AE
Phone: 020 7405 7686
Website: www.lse.ac.uk or @LSEnews

Overview

The London School of Economics and Political Science, or LSE as it is commonly known, is a single faculty college focused on the social sciences, world renowned for its highly prestigious programmes and distinguished alumni. Located amidst a hub of academic activity with UCL, King's College, SOAS and Birkbeck nearby, the college is affiliated with the University of London and stands apart due to its high proportion of postgraduate students.

LSE was founded in 1895 by the intellectual socialist movement the Fabian Society with the aim of bettering society through the education of Britain's business and political elite. Today it remains a strongly political institution, with considerable influence in government through both its research programmes and campaigns. Its alumni are also highly represented in business and law spheres. While best known for its economics and politics degrees, the broad range of social science programmes offered complements the international ethos of the school and it remains at the cutting edge in terms of research.

The college enrolls around 9,500 students from over 140 different countries; over half of these are postgraduates who rarely leave the library unless attending high-brow seminars on globalization and inequality. Its starry alumni includes Nobel laureates, international Heads of State, outstanding academics, and a notable proportion of British MP's. And of course Mick Jagger.

Campus Culture

Despite its reputation for academic excellence, LSE's social activities are mainly fuelled by a lively undergraduate population who also know how to enjoy themselves. With over 170 eclectic student societies ranging from Anime to Beekeeping to Catalan to Philosophy to Swing Dance, the broad international and diverse facets of the student population is encompassed. An atmosphere of work hard/play hard prevails and nightly events lure the undergraduates from the libraries and keep the campus buzzing. The large postgraduate population tends to shuffle by, however, holding on; the days of cheesy music, luminous drinks in shot glasses and ill-conceived experimental fashions behind them while they actually do some work. LSE also hosts numerous public lectures with acclaimed speakers at the forefront of the subject discussed. Past speakers have included Noam Chomsky, Kofi Annan, David Cameron and architect Richard Rogers.

Sports

Not to be let down by its central, and somewhat geographically limited campus, LSE manages to maintain a thriving sports culture through the Athletics Union. Football and rugby seem to top the bill, with provision for some of the less mainstream athletic pursuits such as capoeira and Ultimate Frisbee. The college makes use of its affiliation with the University of London Union, which broadens the scope for sports participation alongside students of other universities.

Tuition

2015/16 undergraduate fees are £9,000 and international undergraduate fees are upward of £18,400.

Contact

Undergraduate Admissions: 020 7955 7125
Graduate Admissions: 020 7955 7160
Library: 020 7955 7229
Students' Union: 020 7955 7158

General Information

Address: Gower Street, London WC1E 6BT
Phone: 020 7679 2000
Website: www.ucl.ac.uk or @uclnews

Overview

UCL, a constituent college of the University of London, has been a place of diversity from the word go—living very much up to its status as "London's Global University." University College London was founded in 1826 as a progressive alternative to Oxford and Cambridge's social exclusivity and religious restrictions. Thus, it was the first university in England to admit students of any race, class or religion and welcome women on equal standing with men. International students have been a part of the college's fabric since day one and it was the first English university to offer the systematic teaching of law, architecture and medicine. UCL is strongly associated with philosopher Jeremy Bentham, the university's so-called "spiritual father," perhaps in part because Bentham's clothed skeleton is on display in UCL's South Cloisters.

UCL consistently ranks among the top universities not only in the UK but also worldwide. The science, law and medical departments remain some of its strongest. 29 Nobel prizes have been awarded to UCL academics and students, a large portion of which in Physiology & Medicine. That said, UCL degrees in anthropology, history and the arts are also very highly regarded in their fields.

UCL's many networks of libraries are impressive and an easy place to get lost. The Main Library, designed by William Wilkins, who also designed the similar National Gallery building, focuses on arts and humanities, history, economics, public policy and law. The Special Collections include medieval manuscripts and first editions of works by George Orwell, James Joyce's *Ulysses*, Newton's *Principia* and Darwin's *Origin of the Species*.

There's no such thing as a typical UCL student, as it's such a diverse place. The only thing students have in common is their intelligence and London. Because it's a university with great academics right in the heart of Bloomsbury, it makes for some pretty interesting alums. Where else can you have such diverse graduates as Alexander Graham Bell, Mahatma Gandhi, Ricky Gervais, and all four members of Coldplay?

Tuition

Undergraduate home student (UK/EU) fees are £9,000 per year while International students should expect to pay upward of £17,000 (or upward of £20,000 for science-related programmes).

Sports

UCL's sports are as diverse as its students—everything from hockey, rowing and women's rugby to Kung Fu, skateboarding and water polo. The UCLU (University College London Union) is your one-stop shop for campus sports teams and clubs. If you're looking for football, The 90-acre UCL sports ground at Shenley, Hertfordshire, has very high quality pitches. Watford football club even train there. The Union gym (Bloomsbury Fitness) offers facilities for activities such as basketball and personal fitness programmes.

Culture

Being right in the centre of London means that you're never short of something cultural to do. However, UCL stands up quite well. It even has its own museum—the Petrie Museum of Egyptian Archaeology—accessible from the Science Library. Here you're even given your own torch to explore the collection of over 80,000 rare objects DIY (or Indiana Jones) style. UCL also has its own West End theatre, the Bloomsbury Theatre, wedged into the maze of main buildings. It's a must-stop for top comedian tours. Jimmy Carr and Ricky Gervais have been known to shoot their stand-up DVDs there. The UCL Union has access to the theatre for at least ten weeks a year, where it is dedicated to student drama and music society performances. Although neither drama, music nor dance are formally taught at UCL, this does not stop the Union's drama club from making it to the Edinburgh Fringe Festival. At UCL, despite the fact that students can really go out just about anywhere in London, many stay loyal to the bars within the Union, and it's usually a great place to meet before a bigger night out.

Contact

Admissions: 020 7679 7742
UCL Union: 020 7679 2500 or
www.studentsunionucl.org/
Bloomsbury Theatre: 020 3108 1000
Petrie Museum: 020 7679 2884

Colleges & Universities • SOAS

General Information

Address: Thornhaugh Street, Russell Square,
London WC1H 0 XG
Phone: 020 7637 2388
Website: www.soas.ac.uk or @SOAS

Overview

School of Oriental and African Studies is
a specialist college which focuses on the
languages, cultures, law and social studies of
Africa, Asia, and the Near and Middle East. SOAS,
as it is commonly known, is part of the University
of London and is the only institution of its kind
in the United Kingdom. It has an excellent
reputation as one of the leading authorities on
African and Asian studies in the world and ranks
highly in university charts on the strength of
its programmes. Originally founded in 1916 to
educate and inform British citizens bound for
overseas postings, the school began with an
Oriental studies focus and later incorporated
African studies. SOAS is nestled in the corner of
Russell Square, with another campus up close
to King's Cross; its diversity complements the
hotbed of academic activity that makes up this
part of London.

The college enrolls over 5,000 students, with
more than half coming from countries outside
of the UK. They are often seen sitting in Russell
Square eating their organic lunch, and chatting
(in Swahili) about their UNICEF internships.
SOAS's alumni include members of parliament
and royalty of a range of countries from Ghana
to Burma. The Crown Princess of Norway went
here. Well of course she did. The Norwegians are
so PC. Except for whale hunting.

Culture On Campus

One thing to be said about SOAS students is
they are serious. The Students' Union has a
reputation of leaning heavily to the left and
is very politically active. SOAS students have
been a notable presence at anti-war protests,
and they are also now rather concerned with
environmental causes—campaigning for the
reduction of carbon footprints, among other
issues. Societies at the college, unsurprisingly,
have a very international, 'right-on' flavour: the
Decolonising Our Minds Society, Student Action
for Global Internationalist Justice Society, Urdu
Conversation Society are just a few.

Tuition

Undergraduate home (UK/EU) fees are £9,000.
International undergraduate students can
expect to pay £16,090 per year.

Contacts

Undergraduate Admissions: 020 7898 4301
Masters Admissions: 020 7898 4361
Research Admissions: 020 7074 5117
Library: 020 7898 4163
Students' Union: 020 7898 4992
or soasunion.org

General Information

Address: Student Central,
Malet Street, WC1E 7HY
Phone: 020 7664 2000
Website: www.clubs-societies.london.ac.uk/
or @UoLondonSC

Overview

Students are the same the world over and in London they ain't no different. In amongst the banter over Bronte and misunderstandings about Marx stands beer, boogeying and burgers. Luckily, for over 120,000 of the University of London's students there's a central place to go to make your university years active and sociable—Student Central.

Formerly the student-run University of London Union, or ULU in 2014 the University of London took over the entity and renamed it Student Central. You will need to be a member of to get into some of the events, although grabbing a cheeky cheap sarnie in the café shouldn't pose too much of a problem for clued-up Londoners. There are 18 University of London colleges that are eligible for membership including Kings College and UCL, as well as ten other smaller institutions.

Practicalities

You cannot really get more central. There is a plethora of tube stations and lines within a five – to ten-minute walk, not to mention Oxford Street. The nearest tube, however, is Russell Square (Piccadilly Line) or Goodge Street (Northern Line).

Clubs & Societies (non-sport)

The range of clubs and societies on offer change more often than Europe's borders. Reason being the turnover of students and the lure from students' own colleges—all the more reason to get down there and sign up now! You've got the usual suspects such as Drama club but it would not be Londontown without a few obscure offerings—Revelation Rock Gospel Choir anyone? Hell, yeah.

Sports

Student Central has to cater to thousands of students, but also attract students away from sports clubs in their particular college. Sports, and the bar afterward, is the place to mix with students from the other colleges. Sportswise there's the usual fare—tennis, football, swimming and martial arts. There's also Energybase which contains a gym and pool. Amongst other things take your pick from salsa, breakdancing, fencing or rifle club. Now there's one for the CV…

Food & Bars

Lunch Box is Student Central's coffee shop, conveniently located on the ground floor for those who want to grab a quick (fair trade) coffee or a bargain meal deal. The Library is the main bar, with a lively atmosphere and live acts. The Gallery Bar is a low-key alternative to The Library, and also serves food. The Venue hosts a club night on Fridays, live music acts (up-and-coming unsigned bands as well as the odd better-known act) and cinema events during the week. For gigs enter Student Central on Byng Place.

Facilities

Copycats Print Centre will resolve all your reprographics and binding troubles. The Student Shop carries everything from lab coats to University of London-branded gear.

Learning in the capital has a long and venerable history. University College London (UCL) was the third university founded in England after Cambridge and Oxford and the first to admit students of any race or religion. Now there are hundreds of universities, colleges and adult education centres offering a mindboggling array of courses.

The first port of call for those with a lust for learning or even an empty Tuesday night to fill is Floodlight (www.findcourses.co.uk), which lists tens of thousands of courses. Fancy brushing up your motorbike maintenance skills at Hackney Community College, getting an NVQ in sugar modelling at the National Bakery School, learning how to create the ultimate kitchen garden at the English Gardening School or studying the nonsense verse of Lear and Carroll at City Lit? The sky is your oyster.

Continuing Education and Professional Development

University College London
Gower Street, WC1E 6BT
020 7679 2000
www.ucl.ac.uk or @uclnews

City University
Northampton Square, EC1V 0HB
020 7040 5060
www.city.ac.uk or @CityUniLondon

London South Bank University
103 Borough Road, SE1 0AA
020 7815 7815
www.lsbu.ac.uk or @LSBU

London Metropolitan University
166-220 Holloway Road, N7 8DB
020 7423 0000
www.londonmet.ac.uk or @LondonMetUni

University of East London
University Way, E16 2RD
020 8223 3000
www.uel.ac.uk or @UEL_News

University of Greenwich
Park Row, SE10 9LS
020 8331 8000
www.gre.ac.uk or @UniGreenwich

A Little Bit of Everything…

Birkbeck
Malet Street, WC1E 7HX
020 7631 6000
www.bbk.ac.uk or @BirkbeckNews

Open University
0300 303 5303
www.open.ac.uk

Bishopsgate Institute
230 Bishopsgate, EC2M 4QH
020 7392 9200
www.bishopsgate.org.uk or @BishopsgateInst

Arts and Lifestyle

University of the Arts London
272 High Holborn, WC1V 7EY
020 7514 6000
www.arts.ac.uk or @UniArtsLondon

Leiths School of Food and Wine
16-20 Wendell Road, W12 9RT
020 8749 6400
www.leiths.com or @Leithscooking

The London School of Journalism
126 Shirland Road, W9 2BT
020 7432 8140
www.lsj.org or @LSJournalism

English Gardening School
66 Royal Hospital Road, SW3 4HS
020 7352 4347
www.englishgardeningschool.co.uk

London School Of Beauty & Make-Up
18-19 Long Lane, London EC1A 9PL
020 7776 9767
www.beauty-school.co.uk or @londest

Institute Francais
17 Queensberry Place SW7 2DT
020 7871 3515
www.institut-francais.org.uk or @
ifru_london

London Buddhist Centre
51 Roman Road, E2 0HU
020 8981 1225
www.lbc.org.uk or @LDNBuddhist

The School of Life
70 Marchmont Street, WC1N 1AB
020 7833 1010
www.theschooloflife.com or @
TheSchoolOfLife

Athletics and Dance

National Centre for Circus Arts
Coronet Street, London, N1 6HD
020 7613 4141
www.nationalcircus.org.uk or @
NationalCircus

Tokei Martial Arts
28 Magdalen Street, SE1 2EN
020 7403 5979
www.tokeicentre.org

Regents Canoe Club
Regents Canal, 6-34 Graham Street, N1
8JX
www.regentscanoeclub.co.uk

Docklands Sailing & Watersport Centre
235a Westferry Road, E14 3QS
020 7537 2626
www.dswc.org or @dswcofficial

London School of Capoeira
1 & 2 Leeds Place, N4 3RF
020 7281 2020
www.londonschoolofcapoeira.com or @
londoncapoeira

General Information

NFT Map: 74
Website: www.arsenal.com or @Arsenal
Phone: 020 7619 5000
Box office: boxoffice@arsenal.co.uk
Location: Highbury House, 75 Drayton Park,
London N5 1BU

Overview

Arsenal is historically London's greatest club and holds numerous national records with a trophy room packed with more silver than any other, save Manchester United and Liverpool. T'was not always that course. From humble beginnings south of the river, Arsenal built themselves up from roots level, with glory years seeming to come in waves. The mid-80s saw the instatement of George Graham, a hugely popular former player, who begat a powerful, muscular side captained by local hero Tony Adams. Wenger brought a continental flavour to the team and an invigorating playing style—the once "boring, boring Arsenal" started playing "sexy football" which reached its zenith with the 2003–04 "Invincibles" who went the entire season without losing a game. Following Arsenal is not always an easy ride. It's surprising that so many people still flock to Emirates Stadium in Holloway given the stupendous ticket prices. If you're lucky enough to have the £1000s needed for a decent season ticket then you get to sit in a huge, soulless stadium named after an airline company to watch what are ostensibly a bunch of bloody foreigners. On the plus side, those bloody foreigners play some of the most dazzling football in Europe and you never know, this just could be the year Arsenal realizes its full potential (groan).

How to Get There

By Car: Unless you have a resident's permit to get around the Event Day Parking Scheme always in effect, it's impossible to park on-street. Which is to say, don't bother bringing a car.

By Public Transport: Arsenal (Piccadilly Line) is the nearest tube station, around three minutes walk from the ground. Finsbury Park (Victoria, Piccadilly Lines and Great Northern rail) and Highbury & Islington (Victoria Line, North London Line and Great Northern rail) stations are around a 10-minute walk—these should be slightly less crowded.

How to Get Tickets

Arsenal tickets are not easy to come by. However, in the new, swanky Emirates Stadium there is always going to be one or two no-shows or corporate tickets that have slipped into the wrong hands. Members have first dibs on tickets and snap them up but the less scrupulous ones sell them on to make a fast buck. Try Gumtree or matchday touts if you really must. To be honest, it's probably one of the rare instances where it really is worth the hassle.

General Information

Phone: 020 8333 4000
Website: www.cafc.co.uk or @CAFCofficial
Location: The Valley, Floyd Road,
Charlton, London SE7 8BL

Overview

Supporting Charlton is like being a drug addict without a healthy bank balance, the highs are amazing (when they come) but the lows are dark and lonely days. Back in 2007, The Addicks were mixing it with the big boys in the Premier League. But after several seasons in freefall, Charlton found themselves in football's third tier. During the dark days football's ugliest man, Iain Dowie took control and drunkenly drove the team off a bridge. He played a brand of football, which matched his grotesque looks, and got the boot (no, not to his face, that's just how he looks). Inexplicably, Les Reed got the job next—a man with no managerial experience. He lasted a month. That year they went down to the Championship. And guess what? They were relegated again, and finished 13th in League 1 (Third Division). In 2009 Phil Parkinson took over and things remained more or less the same. But during 2010 new ownership meant big changes, the effective but unremarkable Parkinson was given the boot in place of Charlton legend Chris Powell. After the 2010-11 season ended with mixed results the team had a spring clean, literally, Powell bought 19 new players and 2011-12 season ended with Charlton winning the Third Division and earning promotion to the Championship. Subsequent seasons saw the club underperform and Powell was sacked. Perhaps coming years under new owner Thomas Sandgaard should see the darkness lifted from the club and the ground reflect Charlton's reputation as a family club, rather than a stadium full of recovering addicts.

How to Get There

By Car: You can leave the M25 at Junction 2 in order to access the A2, heading towards London. When the A2 becomes the A102 (M), take the right hand exit at the roundabout into the A206 Woolwich Road. After passing the major set of traffic lights at the junction of Anchor and Hope Lane and Charlton Church Lane, turn right at the second roundabout into Charlton Lane. Go over the railway crossing then take the first right into Harvey Gardens, with the road leading to the ground. From central London, travel along the A13 until it becomes the East India Dock Road, then take the A102 through the Blackwall Tunnel. Come off at the second junction and take the first exit at the roundabout, then go along the A206 Woolwich Road into Charlton Lane as detailed above. Thanks to the local residents' parking scheme, you'll be hard pushed to find a parking space; try Westmoor Street, Eastmoor Street, Warspite Road and Ruston Road.

By Public Transport: The ground is within walking distance of Charlton railway station, with the Southeastern line running services from mainline stations Charing Cross and London Bridge and services from Cannon Street on Saturdays. You can also take the Jubilee Line to North Greenwich, and then take a short ride on buses 161, 472 or 486 to get to the Valley. Moderate masochists can walk from the tube station.

How to Get Tickets

For years Charlton couldn't give their tickets away. Now, interest ebbs and flows depending on how close the club is to being relegated, but seeing a match is by no means impossible. Tickets can be ordered by phone from the Box Office, via the internet at the club's website or in person at The Valley.

General Information

NFT Map: 43
Phone: 020 7958 2190
Website: www.chelseafc.com
or @ChelseaFC
Location: Stamford Bridge,
Fulham Road, London, SW6 1HS

Overview

Stamford Bridge, home to one of the Premiership's 'big four' clubs, is now one of Europe's most glamorous stadiums. However, 'The Bridge' was once an unappealing and daunting shit-hole more used to hosting pitch invasions and fighting hooligans than the well-heeled city types and Russian oligarchs of today. In the '70s and '80s, it was the violent 'headhunters' that made the club unpopular, but as 'The Blues' never won anything, no one took much notice. In recent years, Chelsea have succeeded in wrestling the mantle of most-hated team in England away from Manchester United, largely due to winning things with the never-ending supply of money from Roman Abramovich. The hooligans have all but gone, either priced out or grown up, but the antics of Prima Donna players and their sitcom private lives have been placing cement shoes on the club's image of late. While Chelsea's coffers have meant they've been able to import expensive foreign players, leading to back-to-back title wins in 2004–2006, their homegrown players have spent more time on tabloid front covers than on football pitches. John Terry and Ashley Cole's bed-hopping adventures will make a great airport novel one day but they've left a lot of fans disappointed in the meantime. These are troubling times indeed for the Blues; after the departure of celebrated manager Mourinho (his first stint with the club) the top position saw its own share of turbulence. With superstar coach Scolari sacked and the silverware drying up it seems money can't buy you everything. However, after two seasons of relative anonymity and a parade of failed managers, unlikely hero Roberto Di Matteo took over the reins of the club during 2012, managed to win both the FA Cup and the Champions League final (and then was sacked as well). Mourinho returned in 2013 and led them to the Premiership title in 2014–15 and they added another under Antonio Conte two years later.

How to Get There

By Car: It is possible to drive to Stamford Bridge on match days but it's pretty pointless to do so. Traffic snarls up badly and the effects are felt throughout Southwest London. If you do brave the traffic, remember that Fulham Road is closed off on match days. Parking is a nightmare with most zones given over to residents. Gangs of eager traffic wardens are on hand to make your Saturday afternoon miserable.

By Public Transport: Stamford Bridge is a two-minute stroll from Fulham Broadway tube station. Regular district line underground trains deliver the hordes from central London in a matter of minutes. If the idea of a packed train full of sweaty football fans isn't your idea of heaven, many fans descend at Ealing Broadway and take the ten-minute walk to the stadium instead.

How to Get Tickets

With so many competitions and cups, getting tickets is easier than you might think. The 'big' fixtures—London derby's, Man U, Liverpool and the later cup stages are either impossible to get or crazily priced, but tickets for the less glamorous ties can be picked up from the Chelsea website or box office. Otherwise, cheeky geezers will be on hand to fleece you on match day. You will probably end up in the West Stand alongside Japanese and American tourists, but that might be preferable to a fat skinhead in the 'Shed.

General Information

NFT Map: 47
Tickets: 0843 208 1222
Website: www.fulhamfc.com or @FulhamFC
Location: Craven Cottage, Stevenage Road,
London SW6 6HH

Overview

Fulham like to think of themselves as a family club. They have a quaint little stadium by the Thames and they play in Fulham for God's sake. (Now about that "Cottagers" nickname…easily the most off-color in all of football.) When Roy Hodgson took the reins in 2008 they were doomed. But he rescued The Cottagers from relegation and in 2009 guided them into Europe, before taking over football's worst job (England manager) in 2012. Mark Hughes took over the team and inexplicably quit before the season finished which, tossed Fulham into turmoil, until the steady hand of Martin Jol took control and ensured business as usual. The club is owned by Shahid Khan, the Pakistani-born embodiment of the American Dream who also owns the NFL Jacksonville Jaguars franchise. (Mohamed Al-Fayed, the club's previous owner, once owned Harrods; he's the father of Dodi Fayed, who died in Princess Diana in Paris in 1997.) The club has been in flux in recent years, and was relegated to the Championship in 2014. They have been up and down between the Championship and Premiership several times since. All that aside, Craven Cottage is still one of the nicest grounds in London and tickets are relatively easy to come by. Just be wary of that hole in the gents.

How to Get There

By Car: Craven Cottage sits in a leafy, riverside suburb of Fulham. Parking is relatively easy around the ground with plenty of parking meters, although reaching the ground could be difficult as weekend traffic in London is never fun to negotiate.

By Public Transport: Putney Bridge on the District Line is your best bet. Putney also has a mainline station with connections from Clapham Junction and direct trains from Waterloo. Cross the road opposite Putney station and hop on any passing bus. Alternatively, a ten-minute walk down the high street and over the river will get you to the ground.

How to Get Tickets

One of the 'joys' of watching Fulham is that tickets are easy to get your hands on. Many games are available on general sale through the club website. For the biggest matches, priority is given to members but persevere and you should be rewarded. If you can't get a ticket legitimately, you can always take your chance with a tout on match day. Try haggling; due to Fulham's fortunes, you could get lucky.

General Information

NFT Map: 76
Main switchboard: 020 7616 8500
Ticket Office: 020 7432 1000
Lord's website: www.lords.org
or @HomeOfCricket
England Cricket Board:
www.ecb.co.uk or @ECB_cricket
Middlesex County Cricket Club:
www.middlesexccc.com
or @Middlesex_CCC
Location: St John's Wood,
London NW8 8QN.

Overview

Even if you know nothing about cricket, don't be put off coming to Lord's. Yes, some games last for five days, and yes, it can still be a draw at the end of it. But as much as anything else Lord's is a fabulous place to come and have a drink. On a hot day the ground is paradise. The sunburnt crowd get slowly boozed up and by the time the players break for tea—yes, tea—few people are concerned at what's going on in the middle. With the polite hum of chatter building up to full-blown drunken singing, it's worth going to Lord's for the atmosphere alone. But when the rabble have calmed down, Lord's is a very genteel place. It's widely seen as the Home of Cricket, and used to house the international governing body. It hosts a heap of England games every year and it's the home ground of county side Middlesex. There's also a year-round gym—you don't even have to be posh to use it—and an indoor training centre. There's even a museum to amuse you when rain stops play. And, rest assured, at some point rain WILL stop play. At the moment, Lord's holds two Test matches (the marathon international five-dayers) and occasional England one-day games. These are the ground's showpiece events, where the crowd are at their most boisterous. Middlesex games rarely attract many spectators, and unless you're an old man or a dog you may be in a minority.

How to Get There

By Car: There's little parking around Lord's so, as you'll be parked up all day, public transport will always be cheaper. If you must drive, the ground is off the A4, which turns into the M4.

By Public Transport: The nearest station is St John's Wood (Jubilee Line). Marylebone (Bakerloo) and Baker Street (Bakerloo, Jubilee, Hammersmith and City, Metropolitan and Circle) are both nearby. Marylebone mainline station serves the north and west of the country. London Paddington is a short bus ride away. Dozens of buses run to Baker Street, and many of which stop right outside the ground.

How to Get Tickets

Getting your hands on England tickets can be tricky. The first few days of a Test match tend to sell out months in advance, though tickets for the last day never go on pre-sale (as the game could be over by then). Similarly, One Day Internationals are normally sell-outs, so it does take a little planning to get in. Check the website over the preceding winter and you might get lucky. If there are less than ten overs in a day due to rain, or if the game's already over, you can claim the full ticket price back. If the weather limits play to between 10.1–24.5 overs (in English, that's up to 149 balls played) you get a 50 per cent refund. Any more than that and you're deemed to have got your money's worth. Middlesex games rarely sell out, however, so you can just rock up on the day, beers in hand, and enjoy the Lord's village.

General Information

NFT Map: 135
Telephone: 0844 375 1845
Website: www.kiaoval.com or @surreycricket
Location: The Kia Oval,
Kennington, London, SE11 5SS

Overview

What better way to while away a sunny summer's day than at The Oval cricket ground, typically alongside hundreds of other shirkers who also called in sick? The Oval is one of London's twin icons of the game, alongside Lord's in North London, and boasts a rich history stretching all the way back to 1846, when it was converted from cabbage patch to cricket pitch. It now plays host to Surrey County and international test matches, including the biennial England-Australia slugfest "The Ashes." Live international cricket remains a boozy, good natured affair with English fanbase 'The Barmy Army' typically belting out salty chants and cheering occasional streakers. County cricket is a mellower, no less enjoyable event, with readily available tickets and a good portion of the crowd more interested in today's paper than the action in front of them. Taxing it ain't.

How to Get There

By Car: Driving to the Oval is not ideal, because parking is near impossible. Should you be willing to risk it, it's situated on the A202, near the junction with the A3 and A24, south of Vauxhall Bridge. As ever with London driving, you'll need your A to Z and nerves of steel.

By Public Transport: The Oval boasts its own, eponymous tube stop on the Northern Line, from which the stadium is a few hundred yards walk. Determinedly overground travellers should alight at Vauxhall, from which Oval is a ten-minute jaunt, tops. Buses 36, 185 and 436 stop right outside the ground, too.

How to Get Tickets

Tickets for Surrey county matches are relatively easy to get hold of, though seats for some fixtures can only be bought on site on the day of the match. International matches tend to sell out very quickly indeed—touts or online sales sites like eBay and Gumtree are usually the best option, at a price.

General Information

NFT Map: 32
Telephone: 020 8743 0262
Tickets: 0844 477 7007
Website: www.qpr.co.uk
or @QPRFC
Location: Loftus Road Stadium, South
Africa Road,
Shepherd's Bush, W12 7PJ

Overview

Once-itinerant football club Queens Park Rangers have called Loftus Road (now known as Kiyan Prince Foundation Stadium)—based, confusingly, in Shepherd's Bush—home since 1917, give or take a few seasons. Their footballing fortunes have yo-yoed through the decades: once a whisker away from winning Division One in the years before it became the Premiership; they finished the 2011-12 season just above the relegation zone, but gave us what undoubtedly was the game of the season after losing a 2–0 lead in stoppage time to gift moneybags Man City the Premier League title. New ownership, including pint-sized F1 oligarch Bernie Ecclestone, injected some much needed glamour into the club (prior to the takeover, Pete Doherty was the Hoops' most famous fan). But, amid wacky boasts of Euro domination, Bernie was cut down to size; Ecclestone has since sold his stake in the team, and at a healthy profit. The years following the sacking of their Italian boss De Canio has seen the Hoops' top spot resemble a revolving door in a busy brothel. Though different managers and caretakers have come and gone, resulting in turmoil on and off the pitch, the erratic QPR are definitely and defiantly worth watching live.

How to Get There

By Car: Whether you're approaching Loftus Road from the North (from the M1 through the A406 and A40), East (via the A40(M)), South (from the A3 and A219) or West (up the M4 via the A315 and A402 on a wing and a prayer), all routes lead through White City. Once there, turn right off Wood Lane into South Africa Road. Don't even set off without proper navigation tools, or emergency rations.

By Public Transport: The majority of QPR fans are local and rely either on nearby tube stops (White City on the Central Line, Shepherd's Bush on the the Hammersmith and City Line), any of buses 72, 95, or 220 to White City Station, or overground train to Acton Central, followed by a quick bus ride.

How to Get Tickets

Getting tickets for a QPR game is harder than you might expect. The team has a loyal fan base and is quickly becoming a guilty pleasure (due mainly to moments of madness) for casual spectators. However, getting tickets for a run-of-the-mill mid-season game should be a cinch, either via the Rangers' ticket website or by phone. You can also visit the Loftus Road box office on match days.

White City

South Africa Rd

South Africa Road Stand

Y1

A B C D E F G

HU

AL BL CL EL FL GL

HL JU

West Paddock East Paddock

Z1

Y2 Z2

JL KU

School End Stand (Visitors Only)

Y3 Z3

KL LU

Y4 Z4

LL MU

Y5 Z5

ML NU

Loftus Road End Stand

Y6 Z6

NL PU

PL PU

Loftus R

Y7

X W V T S R

QU

Ellerslie Road Stand

Ellerslie Rd

Shepherd's Bush

General Information

Website: www.englandrugby.com/twickenham
Phone: 020 8892 8877
Location: Twickenham Stadium, Whitton Road, Twickenham, TW2 7BA

Overview

The home of English rugby, Twickenham is a behemoth of a stadium. An ugly chunk of concrete seemingly dumped from a great height onto a quiet London suburb, Twickenham lacks the charm and character of Ireland's Landsdowne Road and Scotland's Murrayfield, and has been all but pushed to the sidelines by the magnificent Millennium Stadium in Wales. However, the stadium has largely remained a fortress when it comes to England Internationals. Cheered on by 82,000 well-spoken, white-shirted fans booming out 'Swing Low Sweet Chariot' probably helps. Maybe the England players absorb the unfussy and uncompromising nature of their surroundings into their psyche on match days. Critics would argue that their style of rugby is as ugly and bland as the stadium they play in. This would be harsh if England hadn't consistently underperformed after carrying off the Rugby World Cup in 2003. Twickenham also hosts a series of Rugby tournaments and exhibition matches, including the famous 'Sevens', in addition to the occasional Premiership fixture. Outside the Rugby season, the stadium is given over to rock concerts for international bands like U2, Bon Jovi and Lady Gaga. The World Rugby Museum, located in the East Stand at the stadium, is a collection of over 25,000 items related to the history of the sport. Tours of Twickenham are also available.

How to Get There

By Car: Twickenham is very accessible by road—if you live in the South. The M3 motorway turns into the A316 that passes the stadium, carrying on into central London. Certain roads get closed down on match days so drivers should allow plenty of time. Parking at the stadium is extremely limited and should be booked in advance. Resident permits are helpfully required for all roads bordering the stadium so the best thing to do is park in the general vicinity and walk the rest of the way.

By Public Transport: Mainline trains run to Twickenham station from Waterloo and Reading. London Underground runs to Richmond on the District Line where shuttle buses will take fans to the stadium (50p outbound, free return) Hounslow is an alternative Underground station but shuttle buses only run from Twickenham to Hounslow station so you will have to make it to the stadium under your own steam. Bus numbers 281, 267, 481, 681 and H20 all have regular services passing close to the stadium.

How to Get Tickets

England rugby tickets are hot property, commanding higher prices than top football games. As competition games are relatively infrequent, tickets sell out well in advance so keep checking the website for updates on ticket releases. Premiership tickets and friendly matches are easier to come by but will generally sell out. If you don't get lucky in advance, rugby touts (slightly less aggressive than their football cousins) will happily make your wallet lighter for you. Ticketmaster is the best option for concerts or Gumtree and Craigslist for re-sales and swaps.

General Information

Phone: 0800 169 2007
Website: www.wembleystadium.com
or @wembleystadium
Location: Wembley Stadium,
Wembley HA9 0WS

Overview

Wembley Stadium enjoys a strange position in the British psyche. For football fans it's most significant as the scene of England's only World Cup win back in 1966, as well as numerous pitch invasions by angry/jubilant Scottish fans whenever their national team came down to play. Plus, a generation of British bands have grown up dreaming of the day they'd bellow: "hello Wem-ber-ley, are you ready to rock?!!" to tens of thousands of people who've just paid a fiver for a chewy patty of minced spleen 'n' testicles in a dry bun. For these sentimental reasons, then, very few people complained that the National Stadium was a bit of a crap-hole stuck in an inaccessible suburb of West London. By the late '90s the place was looking a bit battered, so they knocked it down and then very, very slowly, and at tremendous, tabloid-scandalising expense, built a replacement on the same site. The result is, just about, worth it. There are none of the blind spots for spectators that the old stadium used to have, plus it has far greater leg-room for 90-thousand-plus people and much more comfortable seating. It also looks fantastically imposing as you walk out of Wembley Park tube with its massive arch curving into the sky. A trip here might not make your knees go "all trembly" as fans used to sing but for football lovers it's one of the world's great venues. They also have a special removable running track for athletics and, to the disgust of "soccer" purists, they've even let American "football" teams play here, too.

How to Get There

By Car: Short of hiring snipers to pick drivers off as they approach the mighty arch, the Stadium could hardly do more to discourage visitors from driving. "Wembley Stadium is a public transport destination. Please leave your car behind," the website primly advises. However, if you are some kind of die-hard, planet-raping petrol-head you'll see signs pointing to the stadium from Great Central Way onwards. There are very few parking spaces at the Stadium itself and these need to be booked in advance. On match days, or when there's anything else happening, the local area becomes residents' parking only, too. Yes, they really don't want you to bring your car.

By Public Transport: The nearest Tube is Wembley Park on the Metropolitan and Jubilee line. Wembley Central (on the Bakerloo line) is about 10–15 minutes walk and there's also Wembley Stadium mainline train station with links all over the country. If you're travelling from outside London there are National Express coaches from 43 different towns and cities.

How to Get Tickets

Easier said than done. 'Club Wembley' have kindly created a 'ten year seat licence'—no doubt to re-coup the massive overspend that accompanied completion of the stadium. These licences give owners access to all major events hosted at Wembley and its worth going on the website to laugh at the ridiculous prices. A 'one-off licence fee' starts at £172 per person per event. Annual season tickets are on top of that. Cloud Cuckoo Land. 'Normal' people can buy tickets to England games through the FA (you need to be a member), for football and rugby cup games through the respective clubs and tickets for one off events and shows through Ticketmaster. It's always worth checking Gumtree.com as you never know who might be flogging off a golden ticket to the highest bidder.

Practice Courts

Aorangi Pavilion

Buses

Aorangi Terrace ("Henman Hill")

No. 1 Court (see right)

Court 18

Court 19

Court 14

Court 15

Court 16

Court 17

Museum

Church Rd

Wimbledon Park

The Wimbledon Shop

Newstead Wy

Millennium Building

Centre Court (see right)

Long & Lawn Buffet

Car Park 3

Somerset Rd

Covered Courts/ Car Park 2

Court 3

Court 4

Court 5

Court 6

Café Pergola

Car Park 5

Car Park 1

Court 7

Court 8

Court 9

Court 10

Court 11

Wimbledon Park

Court 12

No. 2 Court

Maryat Rd

Buses

No. 1 Court

43 1
39 41 36 2
37 34 3
32 4
35 30 8
33 28 26 9
31 24 10 11
29 A 12
27 25 22 20 18 13
23 21 16 14
17 15
19

Centre Court

509 510 511
508 308 309 310 512
507 307 205 206 207 311 513 514
506 306 204 105 107 108 109 208 312 515
505 305 203 104 106 110 209 314 516
504 304 103 111 210 315 517
503 303 202 101 112 518
502 201 113 519
501 Royal Box 212 114 520
302 211 115 521
301 318 316 522
317 523

General Information

Telephone: 020 8971 2473
Website: www.wimbledon.com
or @Wimbledon
Location: The All England Lawn Tennis
and Croquet Club, Church Road,
Wimbledon, SW19 5AE

Overview

New balls please! If it's not pissing it down—which is a big if—Wimbledon's All England Tennis and Croquet Club is the place to witness the world's finest tennis players do battle on rye grass courts, home as it is to the oldest major Championship in the game each June/July. But this is also a place to be seen and to be merry—sure, it's about the tennis, but it's also about strawberries and cream (of which 62,000 pounds and 1,540 gallons worth are sold each year respectively), the free-flowing champagne, the celebrity crowd, and the Ralph Lauren-designed ballboy and ballgirl outfits. If you can't actually get a ticket for the tournament—the All England Club makes approximately 1,500 of them available each day, and more importantly, if you're not prepared to camp out overnight in the queue—you can always sit yourself on Murray Mound (formerly Henman Hill) at the northern end of the complex, where a vast television screen allows you to watch British players systematically eliminated in typically heartbreaking fashion. Really, we should stick to darts.

How to Get There

By Car: During the tournament, traffic and parking are nightmarish propositions, and you're better off using public transport. Nonetheless, the determined will need to take the A219 from the A3, and turn off left onto Church Road once in Wimbledon itself.

By Public Transport: Wimbledon railway station is a short journey from both Waterloo and Clapham Junction, and is otherwise serviced (Vicar!) by trains from towns right across the South of England. From here, board the London General shuttle bus straight to the grounds; they depart every five minutes or so during the tournament. Tube users should head for Southfields on the District line, from where a London General shuttle also operates. Those who prefer to saunter can mosey on down Wimbledon Park Road heading south for ten minutes or so, and you can also walk it from Wimbledon Park tube station, heading north-west.

How to Get Tickets

You can (legally) come by tickets to Wimbledon in two ways—one, apply in advance to the public 'ballot', via the website, in the hope you are selected at random to purchase tickets (closing date end of December). Two, join the serpentine, overnight queues for on-the-day tickets, of which five hundred are usually made available for each of Centre, Number One and Number Two Courts. Then, of course, there are all the other methods of which you're already no doubt aware.

Any bowling buff will tell you that there are two types of bowling in this country. Ten-pin bowling, the ghastly Americanized import, is by far the most popular among Londoners and the generally disrespectful Youth Of Today. Crown Green Bowling is a far more serene, (elderly) gentlemanly pursuit complete with its own rules and rituals.

London's ten pin bowlers are spoiled rotten. As it's now a trendy pastime shot through with irony, there are plenty of old, large basements converted into pristine bowling alleys designed to look retro. There's no chavs in tracksuits on speed around here: the **All Star Lanes** franchises **(Map 4, 91)** are heaving with immaculately dressed trendos and hen/stag nights drunkenly bowling and singing in the karaoke booths. However, at a peak rate of £10.95 per person per game (your average game is a mere 10 minutes) and an off-peak rate of a laughably similar £8.50 per game, you'll have to access whether it's worth blowing the rent money on one night of fun. **Bloomsbury Bowling Lanes (Map 4)** does the American chic thing a bit better and its lanes are £45 an hour, which works out cheaper in a group. They also host cool gigs and DJs occasionally.

For families and the penniless, London has plenty of more 'traditional' British bowling lanes. By this, of course, we mean cavernous warehouses with pumping chart music, scary underage drinkers and sticky air hockey tables. Try the classic **Rowans (Map 62)** which at its priciest is a mere £5.20 per person per game or **Queens Ice & Bowl (Map 30)** which has also has an ice rink to cool off those skittle blues.

And what of Green Bowling? Well, being an outdoor pursuit in Britain, it's safe to say it is primarily a summer affair. When the sun is out you'll find bowling greens in all the major parks; Hyde Park offers lanes for £18–22 per 2 people an hour.

After suffering at the hands of boho and cheapo ten-pin bowling facilities you may find that there can be no better way to waste an afternoon than to sit around a bowling green in Finsbury Park with a beer in hand, laughing at your idiot friends' attempts to hit the 'jack.' Maybe those elderly gentlemen are on to something…

Bowling	Address	Phone	Map
All Star Lanes	95 Brick Ln	020 7426 9200	91
All Star Lanes	Victoria House, Bloomsbury Pl	020 7025 2676	4
Bloomsbury Bowling Lanes	Bedford Way	020 /183 19/9	4
Hyde Park	Hyde Park	020 7262 3474	n/a
Queens	17 Queensway	020 7229 0172	30
Rowans	10 Stroud Green Rd	020 8800 1950	62

Nothing combines relaxation and hypertension quite like golf, nor indeed knee-length socks, spats and flat caps. For golfing Londoners, opportunities to play must be sought towards the outskirts of the capital, where the city shore is lapped once more by greenery and open space. You can, of course, take your one wood out onto London's pavements and practise your fade drive there, but you're odds on to be arrested if you do.

You'll be better received moving clockwise around London from the north, at establishments such as the **Highgate Golf Club** and **Muswell Hill Golf Club**. Both are highbrow member institutions with epic fairways, open nonetheless to the public, as long as that public is wearing a decent shirt. Eighteen holes at each are in the £30-45 range, which is also the case at the **Hampstead Golf Club**, home of one of England's toughest front nines. Nearby **Finchley Golf Club** is similarly priced for visitors but also offers some neat specials such as winter green fees under £30 and knockdown prices for twelve holes of 'twilight golf'. A little farther north, **Mill Hill Golf Club** is a shade cheaper though no less satisfying.

In the south-east, the **Royal Blackheath Golf Club** positions itself as the oldest in the world, which might be why playing eighteen holes as a visitor requires a small trust fund, at £60 during summer. **Royal Wimbledon Golf Club** terms itself a 'very private' club—visitors are welcome but will be required to apply in writing, prove handicap and, in all likelihood, undergo some kind of permanently scarring initiation ritual. Access to each of these Wimbledon clubs kicks off at a chokingly high £70 for eighteen holes. You could buy a second-hand Playstation for that. The **London Scottish Golf Club** on Wimbledon Common is much more like it, in the range of £20-30 a round, though a pillar-box red top is compulsory for all. Out west, **Dukes Meadows Golf Club** in Chiswick offers nine three-par holes, a driving range and function rooms, all at a reasonable price.

For golfers who really are determined not to leave Zone One, there is one option after all. **Urban Golf (Map 15)** Smithfield location is the last word in golf simulation, with the chance to play, virtual-style, some of the world's top courses. It also boasts well-stocked bars and chic lounge areas. You just know the purists will loathe it.

Golf Clubs	Address	Phone	Map
Dukes Meadows Golf Club	Dukes Meadow	020 8994 3314	n/a
Finchley	Frith Ln	020 8346 2436	n/a
Hampstead Golf Club	82 Winnington Rd	020 8455 0203	n/a
Highgate Golf Club	Denewood Rd	020 8340 1906	n/a
Holland Park	Ilchester Pl	077 6610 5594	34
London Scottish Golf Club	Windmill Rd	020 8789 1207	n/a
Mill Hill Golf Club	100 Barnet Way	020 8959 2339	n/a
Muswell Hill Golf Club	Rhodes Ave	020 8888 1764	n/a
Royal Blackheath Golf Club	Court Rd	020 8550 1795	n/a
Urban Golf	12 Smithfield St	020 7248 8600	15

Remember the Levi's ad in the pool hall? The one which had The Clash's "Should I Stay Or Should I Go?" as the soundtrack? Yeah, that one. It conjured up a pretty cool image, right? Unfortunately London's pool halls have not had the retro revamp (is that an oxymoron?) that bowling is currently enjoying (**All Star Lanes**, **Bloomsbury Bowling**) so it's rare to actually find a place where you can stand around looking like James Dean, kissing your teeth, chewing on a tooth pick, and generally inviting any hustler to take you on without like, really being taken on by someone from the Russian/Turkish mafia. We also inextricably link shooting some pool with having a drink or two, but it is often the lesser red and yellow-balled "pub" pool table (funnily enough) rather than the greater spotted (and striped) genuine American pool table which is found within the confines of the few remaining non-chain traditional pubs in London. **19:20 (Map 6)** in Clerkenwell has more of a pool hall feel with media types taking their game a little more seriously at the end of the working day. If you do fancy something a little more louche, there are many a pool and snooker hall to be found on the edges of central London which can offer a grittier atmosphere.

Pool & Snooker	Address	Phone	Map
19:20	20 Great Sutton St	020 7253 1920	6
Number 1 Bar	1 Duke Street Hill	020 3291 3251	106
Riley's	16 Semley Pl	020 7824 8261	19
Rowans	10 Stroud Green Rd	020 8800 1950	62

Tennis

Ah…the other beautiful game, beloved of park fence jumpers and upper class grunters alike. Like many popular sports, tennis may have originated in Britain, but we're pretty consistent in our ineptitude at it. This is not for the lack of trying: the country's capital is packed full of tennis clubs, outdoor park courts and large sports complexes.

Tennis is certainly not as exclusive as it once was, with an hour's playing a lot cheaper than ten-pin bowling, for example. You can mince about amidst leafy surroundings in Hyde Park (Hyde Park Tennis and Sports Centre, 020 7262 3474), flail in the dark depths of Finsbury Park on a turn-up-and-play basis, or in the luxury of the historic Queens Club (www.queensclub.co.uk, 020 7386 3429 for membership Information). Also commendable are the Paddington Sports Club (psclondon.com or 020 7286 8448) in Maida Vale and the courts in Regent's Park: go to www.urbanpadeltennis.com/ for information on, uh, playing tennis in parks. Indicative of the new equalitarian nature of the game are Tennis London International (www.facebook.com/groups/1129021643865931/) who take pride in being 'the largest gay and lesbian tennis group in the UK.' But it's not all democratic: there's always Wimbledon (www.wimbledon.org, which due to the jaw-dropping ticket prices, still is as exclusive as it's always been. If you still want to get caught up in the annual tennis frenzy, head to Henman Hill, or Murray Mound, or whatever it's called these days. Outside Centre Court, here you can sit on the grass and watch the action on video screens with all the other poor proles who don't have any kidneys left to trade for a ticket.

Squash

Like some weird secret society, squash players spend their time locked indoors, organised into little private clubs and engaged in an activity which will eventually mess them up. Squash is hard—just ask your poor knees. The squash court is a high-octane containment tank swimming in adrenalin, which explains why Londoners have taken to it with such gusto. A court at Sobell Leisure Center (020 7609 2166) in Finsbury Park for example, is near impossible to book at peak times. Be warned—a lot of sports centres don't have squash facilities, but somewhere like the Oasis Sports Centre (020 7831 1804) in Tottenham Court Road is a church to all things sweaty and squashy…and you can go for an outdoor swim afterwards, too. For a quirkier option try Maiden Lane Youth Club (020 7267 9586)—a community centre in a housing estate, which has one beat-up court for an hourly fee. If there isn't a yoga class in progress, that is.

Badminton/Table Tennis

They may be worlds apart in many ways, but badminton and table tennis are usually offered in the same place, and both are 'genteel' sports in which it is almost acceptable to be beaten by the opposite sex (whichever sex you are). Badminton is especially popular across the board, with almost all sizeable sports centres offering courts and equipment. However, if you've any experience in attempting to book a court at most public sports complexes you'll know of the often depressing amount of phone wrangling and frustration that arises from these exchanges. Chief perpetrator is Kings Hall Leisure Centre (020 8985 2158) in Lower Clapton, who will test your patience to inhumane limits. The Brixton Recreation Centre (020 7095 5100) caters to badminton and squash players but always sound like they can't wait to get you off the phone; their rates are £11.65 for badminton, which is pretty competitive. The Sobell Centre, as mentioned above, also caters for table tennis (doesn't "ping pong" sound nicer?) and badminton. The best strategy is to phone your local centre to ascertain which racquet sports they cater for and then prepare yourself to be either double-booked, misinformed or given a free session depending on the ability of the desk assistant!

Overview

As the nascent city of 'Londinium' was being named by the Romans in AD 43, in Asia the practice of yoga was entering its third or fourth millennium. Nineteen hundred years on, at last it found its way out west, and London's yoga establishments have flourished ever since. Essentially, the capital's schools can be divided into those concerned primarily with physical fitness—often the larger institutions offering a range of styles—and those with a more spiritual bent. Of the latter, popular Triyoga centres in Primrose Hill and Covent Garden are one-stop holistic shops for the upwardly mobile set. More specialised centres include Fierce Grace Hot Yoga - North in Kentish Town, and its partner Fierce Grace Hot Yoga - City—bring water and a towel for hard wearing, specially heated sessions—and the Iyengar Yoga Institute in Maida Vale, which offers a free introductory class. Special mention also goes to The Power Yoga Company, a newish venture offering all sorts including, unnervingly, 'power yoga'. Still, entering the peaceful surroundings of Power Yoga is, according to one client, like getting a hug. Those more spiritual schools include the wonderful Sivanada Yoga Centre, an oasis of serenity in the midst of Putney boasting resident yogi teachers, and the Satyananda Yoga Centre in Clapham with its deep focus on yoga-meditation techniques. Shanti Sadam, out west, is also more concerned with inner stillness than downward dogs. And hidden away in Archway, the Kriya Centre runs a series of kundalini yoga classes in humble but hospitable surroundings—Ohm tastic!

There's nothing quite like an obesity epidemic to make a city sporty. We're constantly being told that we're swelling to huge new levels. The message is worrying: buck up fatties, or you won't even fit into your own coffin. Unlike the majority of celebrations that take place in the capital, the 2012 Olympic Games didn't leave us dry mouthed and heaving on the floor with a national hangover. Instead the summer games littered our fair city with a legacy of leading sports venues, and lower-level sport has benefited the most with increased involvement citywide. London's sizeable ethnic communities have also brought weird and wonderful games with them (American Football? In London? They keep threatening…). Dozens of leagues, in dozens of sports, gather every evening to try and beat the bulge.

General Tips

A good starting point is the Gumtree website (www.gumtree.co.uk). Their sports and community section is full of ads trying to fills gaps in sports teams. And as it was started by born-to-sweat Aussies, it never lets up in sheer quantity of athletic opportunities. The local press is also a decent bet. All London boroughs have their own newspapers, who cover amateur sports with as much enthusiasm as the professionals. You may never make it in the big leagues, but at least you can be a hero in Camden. But one area where London struggles is with the concept of pick-up games. Perhaps it's part of our reserved nature, but it's unusual to just rock up at a park and challenge whoever's there. By all means try, but you may get rebuked by a stiff upper lip.

Football

Sunday league football in London used to have a reputation of being rough. For many years it was the preserve of hungover builders, who wanted ninety minutes letting off steam by kicking people around. But it's moved on slightly from those days, with a more general acceptance of skill and less emphasis placed on pain. The spiritual home of recreational football is Hackney Marshes. The East London site has a whopping 80-plus pitches—so many leagues and teams play there that it's worth just turning up and asking around. If you draw a blank there, then the FA website (www.thefa.com) has a club locator search. Regardless of where you live, you'll get a mammoth list of clubs. The hardest part of finding a team in London is narrowing down who it is you want to play for. Five-a-side football is also booming in London. In the city centre, where space is at a premium, it's often the only way of getting in a game. Powerleague (www.powerleague.co.uk) organise leagues around the capital, though these can be pricey. A cheaper option is to head to a leisure centre with a five-a-side pitch. They often run leagues and are less profit-driven than the private companies. Lists of leisure centres can be found on specific borough's website (such as Islington's www.islington.gov.uk).

Rugby

Don't mind drinking pints of your team-mates' urine? Enjoy a good eye-gouging? Then you must be a rugby fan! The Rugby in London website (www.visitlondon.com/things-to-do/whats-on/sport/rugby) is a Bible for lovers of casual violence, as it lists hundreds of clubs, contact details and even training venues and times. Female fans of egg chasing are also well represented. Most teams play any other Southwest London, though there's a few more dotted around the city. A full list is on the RFU Women's website (www.englandrugby.com/england/senior-women#index). If you don't fancy the full-on ear-biting code of the sport there's a flourishing touch rugby scene in London. In this form of the game tackling is represented by tagging your opponent. It's an altogether less bloody type of rugby, although you're still allowed to indulge in the booze-fuelled rituals that the contact players enjoy. In2Touch (www.in2touch.com) lists a few of these leagues.

Cricket

As a sport that takes up plenty of space, you have to head to the leafier parts of London such as Hampstead, Putney, and Dulwich to find cricket clubs at play. But with more green space than any other London borough, Hackney has embraced the gentleman's game, and the thwack of leather on willow can oft be heard on London Fields during the summer months where the North East London Cricket League (nelcl.leaguerepublic.com) has established itself. Victoria Park also has a Community Cricket League (www.vpccl.co.uk). The Play-Cricket website (www.play-cricket.com) has a full rundown on London clubs

Athletics and the London Marathon

Every spring, London's runners dust down their gorilla costumes and tackle the London Marathon. If you feel up to it then you have to plan ahead; places are limited and dished out via a ballot. If you need a helping hand in the run up to the race, consider a jogging and/or roadrunning club associated with British Athletics (www.britishathletics.org.uk): as well as getting you in shape, so you don't die after 20 miles, they can help you get a spot in the starting line-up. And if you catch the bug of competitive athletics, there are six clubs who compete in the London Inter Club Challenge (see London Athletcis at www.londonathletics.org).

Miscellaneous

For fans of all things Irish, there's the London Gaelic Sports Association (www.londongaa.org); American footballers can get their fix with the British American Football League (www.britishamericanfootball.org); and if tight shorts and sleeveless shirts are your thing there's the British Aussie Rules Association (www.aflengland.org; or you could just join the navy).

General Information

Address: Gatwick Airport,
West Sussex, RH6 0NP

Airport Code: LGW

General Information: 0844 892 0322

Lost Property: 01293 503162
or gatwick.lostproperty@excess-baggage.com

Website: www.gatwickairport.com
or @Gatwick_Airport

Overview

The UK's second-largest airport (behind Heathrow) and "the most efficient single-runway airport in the world" (seems to repeat the negative, that), Gatwick is not terribly flashy, but not so bad to deal with, and getting better and better. Located 28 miles south of London, Gatwick is not linked by the Tube, but the airport is served by a mostly painless 30-minute train ride from Victoria Station. Gatwick is a much nicer place than it once was ("high-summer sweat-filled free-for-all check-in zones for budget flights to Spain" sounds about right) but after BAA sold the airport to Global Infrastructure Partners (of London City Airport fame), GIP undertook an initial £1.2 billion overhaul of the airport and its services to better position itself as a go-to European hub. And there is even talk of a second runway—good news for Gatwick and especially whichever single-runway airport is the second-most efficient in the world.

Gatwick has two terminals: the South Terminal and the North Terminal. Trains arrive at the South Terminal, and there are more shops there, but if your flight is out of the North Terminal, a free automated train will take you on the five-minute transfer.

As far as amenities go, the usual suspects are all present, with convivial times available at Britain's premier diluting station, J.D. Wetherspoons, and the glamour of Knightsbridge miraculously squeezed into one of those little airport branches of Harrods—just in case you feel the need to inflict one of their god-awful teddy bears on another country. As far as eating's concerned, there are several Jamie Oliver outlets, a Comptoir Libanais and other spots catering to varied tastes and dietary restrictions, including vegetarian and gluten-free options. For shopping there are the usual wide range of shops befitting an airport as destination: Boots but also outlets like Zara, Ray-Ban, and BOSS.

Getting There

The Gatwick Express (www.gatwickexpress.com) runs from Victoria Station in London to the South Terminal at Gatwick in 30 minutes. First trains run at 3:30, 4:30 and then every fifteen minutes thereafter with the last trains at 00:01 and 00:32. If you're near the rail hubs it is by far the most pleasant way to get there—though a single journey is going to set you back around £20. Thameslink (www.thameslinkrailway.com) run trains to Gatwick from Blackfriars, City Thameslink, Farringdon and St Pancras International stations for £19. Easybus (www.easybus.com/en) coaches offer service to London with prices starting from £2 each way; travel takes about an hour.

To drive to Gatwick from the M25 you need to leave at Junction 7 and carry on southwards along the M23, following the signs. Leave the M23 at Junction 9 and again, follow those handy signs to get to the appropriate terminal.

Parking

Short stay car park rates start at £5 for the first half hour, £8 up to one hour, £13 up to two hours, £15 up to three hours, and climb steadily toward £45 for a 24 hour period. For long stays there are several parks located 5-15 minutes away (via bus transfers) from the airport. These are best booked in advance. For the official Gatwick car park, charges are £25 for the first day and £20 per day thereafter, and may be booked in advance online at www.parking.gatwickairport.com/.

Car Hire

The Gatwick on-airport car rental partners are Hertz, Avis, Europcar, Sixt, National, Alamo, Enterprise and Budget. The Gatwick Airport website also offers its own online car rental feature, with special rates.

Hotels

Gatwick has several hotels on site with varying levels of service. Keep in mind that the North and South Terminals are connected via a free five-minute transfer. In the South Terminal there is the 245-room BLOC hotel, the Hilton London Gatwick, and the economical YOTEL, which offers 46 cabins (available for four hour blocks or overnight) in a choice of premium (full-size double bed) or standard (large single). In the North Terminal, there is a Hampton by Hilton close to the airport check-in desks, the Premier Inn directly opposite the main entrance, and a four-star Sofitel. The full-service hotels feature amenities such as salons, restaurants, business facilities, and 24-hour gyms.

Airline/Terminal

Aegean Airlines: South
Aer Lingus: South
Afriqiyah Airways: South
Air Astana Wamiti: South
Air Baltic: South
Air Dolomiti: South
Air Europa: South
Air Malta: South
Air Transat: South
Aurigny: South
Belavia Belarusian: South
British Airways: North
Caribbean Airlines: North
easyJet: North/South
Emirates: North
Flybe: South
Freebird: South
Gambia Bird: South
Garuda Indonesia: North
Germania: South
Icelandair: North
Iraqi Airways: South
Meridiana Airlines: North
Monarch: South
Norwegian: South
Royal Air Maroc: North
Ryanair: South
Swiss International Air Lines: South
TAP Air Portugal: South
Thomas Cook: South
Thomson Airways: North
Titan Airways: South
Tunis Air: South
Turkish Airlines: North
Ukraine International Airlines: South
Vietnam Airlines: North
Virgin Atlantic: South
Vueling: North
WOW Air: South

General Information

Address: Hounslow, Middlesex, TW6
Airport Code: LHR
General Information: 0844 335 1801
Lost Property: 0844 824 3115 or missingx.com
Website: www.heathrowairport.com or @HeathrowAirport

Overview

Ah, Heathrow—London's main link to the outside world, resplendent in all the main airport offenders: infinite queues, bad food, draconian security and the acrid scent of 'the British on holiday.' Or as PM Hugh Grant once noticed, "Whenever I get gloomy with the state of the world, I think about the arrivals gate at Heathrow Airport." Or something like that.

Indeed, ex-London mayor Ken Livingstone once accused Heathrow of keeping people "prisoner" in its "ghastly shopping mall" but there does seem to be slow, gradual improvement. Heathrow has undergone years of seeming perpetual change, resulting in vastly improved transport services and upgraded motorway access. Terminal 1 is a thing of the past and the new Terminal 2 has eclipsed the old Terminal 2 in people's memory. Terminal 5 picked up the baton following a chaotic opening in 2008, taking the annual passenger count to upward of 70 million, and placing the airport in contention for busiest in the world. For years Heathrow has been stretched beyond its capacity, which has resulted in a campaign for a controversial third runway. The local residents might not like it but at least they don't have to suffer an hour on the tube to catch a flight.

Terminals

The terminals are organised around airline networks: Star Alliance, Oneworld, SkyTeam, with the non-aligned airlines wedged in where possible. Terminal 5 is the domain of British Airways.

Departures

Busy and security conscious, Heathrow demands travelers get there early—they suggest three hours before departure for long-haul and El Al flights, two hours for European flights, and a full 90 minutes for flights to the UK and Ireland. Makes you appreciate coach travel. Check-in is on the first floor of Terminal 4, the ground floor in Terminal 3, and the top floor of Terminals 2 and 5. When you arrive look for your check-in zone on the information screens near the entrance; check-in zones are marked by illuminated yellow cubes. If you are travelling through Heathrow, transfers are available between Heathrow Airport's four terminals. Terminals 2 and 3 are a short walk from each other (10–20 minutes) while Terminals 4 and 5 are served by free trains and buses.

Arrivals

As for the romance of the arrivals gate at Heathrow, arrivals areas are located on Level 1 at Terminal 2, the ground level of the Arrivals building at Terminal 3, and the ground levels of both Terminals 4 and 5. Official airport meeting points are marked. There are information screens in the arrivals area with flight status information and status codes: 'Expected' means the flight hasn't landed yet and Heathrow Airport Holdings Limited encourages you to indulge in a spot of shopping, 'Landed' means that you should expect 30–40 minutes for passengers to clear passport control, baggage reclaim and customs (longer at busy periods), and 'Baggage in hall' means that passengers should be in the arrivals area shortly. The Heathrow website also has live flight status information.

Hotels

In addition to the handful of area hotels that cater to Heathrow travellers, there are several hotels at the terminal, accessible by foot. The 605-room luxury Sofitel London Heathrow is located at Terminal 5 and the four-star Hilton London Heathrow Airport is located at Terminal

4. Both hotels offer requisite hotel amenities such as restaurants and business and fitness centres. The No.1 Traveller Lounge after the security lines in Terminal 3 offers day rooms, both twin bunks and singles.

Getting There

The cheapest option is London Underground's Piccadilly Line, which gets you to central London in less than an hour for £6. The wait time for a train is generally no more than 10 minutes. Heathrow has three underground stations; one serving both Terminals 2 and 3, and one each for Terminals 4 and 5.

The fastest option is Heathrow Express (www. heathrowexpress.com), a non-stop train between the airport and Paddington station—"in 15 minutes, every 15 minutes." It stops at Heathrow Central near Terminals 2 and 3, and also at Terminal 5. On-board fares are £25 one way and £47 for a return (£5 less if bought online, from ticket offices or ticket machines). TFL Rail follows the same route into west London, but serves intermediate stations making its journey time 25 minutes. At half the price of the Express though, it's probably worth the added minutes. TFL Rail trains depart Paddington every 30 minutes and reach Terminals 2 and 3 (travellers from Terminal 4 and 5 should use the free transfer). Fare is £10.10 one way to Paddington Station, less to intermediate stations. Both these trains run between approx 5 am–12 am.

National Express (www.nationalexpress.com) offers coach service from points around London to Heathrow. Tickets start at £10.

Driving from Central London takes about 45-60 minutes depending on traffic. To Terminals 2 and 3, exit the M4 (Junction 4) or M25 (Junction 15) and follow signs. When leaving Terminals 2 and 3, follow exit signs to the access/exit tunnel. Then follow signs to the M4 motorway, which will eventually bring you into London. Terminals 4 and 5 have separate entrances. If driving, exit M25 at Junction 14 and follow signs (if coming from the M4, leave at Junction 4B and follow the M25 south to Junction 14). A taxi to central London takes 45-60 minutes and costs £35-plus; note that there is no set fare from the airport.

Car Parking

There are short-term and long-term car parks, and both are expensive. Up to 30 minutes at the short stay is £3.80 (£4 for Terminal 4). An hour at the short stay is £7 (£7 at Terminal 4), two hours is £11.30 (£11 at Terminal 4), then rising steadily to £59.50 for 24 hours. The long stay car park is about 10 minutes away by courtesy bus and the standard drive-up price is £34.70 for the first day, then £27.90 each day thereafter. A peak surcharge is in effect for Easter, Christmas and some summer weeks.

Airline/Terminal

Aegean Airlines: 2
Aer Lingus: 2
Aeroflot: 4
Aeromexico: 4
Air Algerie: 4
Air Astana: 4
Air Canada: 2
Air China: 2
Air France: 4

Air India: 4

Air Malta: 4
Air Mauritius: 4
Air New Zealand: 2
Air Serbia: 4
Alitalia: 4
American Airlines: 3
ANA: 2
Arik Air: 4
Asiana Airlines: 2
Austrian: 2
Avianca: 2
Azerbaijan Airlines: 4
Biman Bangladesh Airlines: 4
British Airways: 5 (some 3)
Brussels Airlines: 2
Bulgaria Air: 4
Cathay Pacific Airways: 3
China Eastern: 4
China Southern: 4
Croatia Airlines: 2
Delta Air Lines: 3 & 4
Egypt Air: 2
El Al: 4
Emirates: 3
Ethiopian Airlines: 2
Etihad Airways: 4
EVA Air: 3
Finnair: 3
Germanwings: 2
Gulf Air: 4
Iberia: 5
Icelandair: 2
Iran Air: 3
Japan Airlines: 3
Jet Airways (India): 4
Kenya Airways: 4
KLM-Royal Dutch Airlines: 4
Korean Air: 4
Kuwait Airways: 4
Libyan Airlines: 4
LOT Polish Airlines: 2
Lufthansa: 2
Malaysia Airlines: 4
MEA: 3
Oman Air: 3
Pakistan International Airlines: 3
Philippine Airlines: 4
Qantas: 3
Qatar Airways: 4
Royal Air Maroc: 4
Royal Brunei Airlines: 4
Royal Jordanian: 3
SAS-Scandinavian Airlines: 2
Saudia: 4
Singapore Airlines: 2
South African Airways: 4
Sri Lankan Airlines: 3
Swiss International Airlines: 2
TAM: 4
TAP Portugal: 2
Tarom: 4
Thai Airways: 2
Transaero: 4
Tunisair: 4
Turkish Airlines: 2
Turkmenistan Airlines: 3
United Airlines: 3
US Airways: 3
Uzbekistan Airlines: 4
Vietnam Airlines: 4
Virgin Atlantic: 3
Virgin Atlantic Little Red: 2
Vueling: 3

General Information

Address: Hartmann Road,
London, E16 2PX

Airport Code: LCY

General Enquiries: 020 7646 0088/0000

Website: www.londoncityairport.com
or @LondonCityAir

Overview

With its one wee runway squeezed over the water between the old George V and Royal Albert Docks, City is London's smallest and most central airport (six miles from the City of London, 22 minutes from Bank station). Where once stevedores ate pie and mash, stockbrokers are now whisked off to lunchtime meetings on dinky short takeoff jets. Primarily used by business types, its small size and short runway means city serves mainly European destinations, with BA's New York service (including a stop off) being the one exception. Still, this means much faster check-in times and fewer delays than at the comparative behemoths of Heathrow and Gatwick.

Amenities at London City Airport include some above-average food options and complimentary WiFi. LCY also has a "silent airport policy," meaning no announcements are made, which also means you definitely shouldn't zone out too far away from your gate (you've been warned).

Getting There

In 2005 someone, somewhere, saw the light and extended the DLR (Docklands Light Railway) to City. The airport now couldn't be simpler to get to by public transport: get on the DLR at Bank; make sure you take a train destined for the King George V branch (these are marked "via City Airport"); and you'll arrive at the airport's station in under 25 minutes. A slightly quicker route is to take the Jubilee Underground line to Canning Town and take the DLR a mere three stops westbound from there. There is a taxi rank directly outside the terminal exit, expect to pay at least £40 for a black cab to go to or from the West End. Don't expect the journey to be much faster than on the DLR/Underground. Pre-booked cabs should be a little cheaper; bookings are available via www.minicabit.com.

If you're driving, given its central location there's no obvious route to City. A useful general rule is to point your wheels at the eastern end of Central London and then keep going that way from Tower Hill on the A1203 (East Smithfield/The Highway). The airport is signposted from this road. If you're getting there from the South East, head through the Blackwall tunnel and follow signs once you emerge into the daylight. If you're near the M25 and like traffic jams, crawl your way to junction 30 and take the Thames Gateway to the airport from there.

Parking

Short stay is directly next to the terminal and rates start at £13 for the first 30 minutes, £16 for one hour, £21 for two hours, and steadily increasing up to £60 for 24 hours. The long stay carpark is a short walk from the terminal and costs £45 per day. Pre-booking long stay parking results in drastically reduced rates; check online for more. All of which is to say, parking is expensive. If you still feel the need to park and can book in advance, get in touch with BCP airport parking for a (slightly) cheaper option at www.parkbcp.co.uk.

Car Hire

On-site car hire desks for Avis, Europcar and Hertz are located next to the terminal. Travellers can book cars through the London City Airport website.

Airlines

Air France
Alitalia
British Airways
Blue Islands
CityJet
Flybe
KLM Royal Dutch Airlines
Lufthansa
Luxair
Sky Work
Sun-Air
Swiss International Airlines (SWISS)

General Information

Address: Navigation House, Airport Way, Luton, Bedfordshire LU2 9LY

Airport Code: LTN

General Enquiries: 01582 405100

Lost Property: 01582 395219 or lostproperty@ltn.aero

Website: www.london-luton.co.uk or @LDNLutonAirport

Overview

You have to admire branding at work: appending "London" to "London Luton Airport" is perhaps slightly wishful thinking, seeing as the facility is located 35 miles north of Central London. That said, it's not impossible to get to the airport and parking is reasonable, but everyone knows why they're flying out of Luton: those ridiculously cheap budget tickets to the Spanish coast.

Luton debuted in 1938, was put to good use during WWII and quickly became a top airport for package holiday travel. Charter trips comprised the majority of flights in and out of Luton until the 1980s, when Ryanair began using Luton for short-haul flights. In the 1990s Luton was reborn as the go-to for no-frills budget air carriers flying in and out of the London area. Thus, the £2.99 flight to the Canary Islands with every other stag or hen party travelling that weekend.

Luton features the requisite airport amenities: Boots, Dixons, et al. plus light meals. For assistance in leaving the airport to wherever it is you're headed, the Onward Travel Centre is located on the main concourse in the terminal building and is open 24 hours a day, seven days a week.

Getting There

Unless you live in North London, getting to and from Luton by public transport isn't quite seamless. It consists of taking a half-hour train service from St Pancras or London Bridge to Luton Parkway. After your train journey you'll be met at Luton Parkway by a shuttle bus. Be sure to purchase your rail tickets with London Luton Airport as your final destination.

Luton is served by rail via the Luton Airport Parkway Station. From there a ten-minute shuttle bus takes you to the terminal. Keep in mind that while rail service from Luton Airport Parkway Station to central London is frequent (and through the night via Thameslink service), the shuttle only operates between 5 a.m. and midnight. Which is to say, if your plane is delayed past midnight—not out of the question with budget carriers—consider coach alternatives.

Coach services, such as the 757 Greenline, easyBus and National Express are good alternatives that will at least get you home if your flight comes in late. Greenline (www.greenline.co.uk/757 or 0844 801 7261) is probably your best bet, and it offers pick-up and drop-off points on Buckingham Palace Road, Marble Arch and Baker Street, as well as free WiFi. Fares to London Victoria are £10 and it takes about an hour, but it runs pretty regularly through the night. The National Express service A1 operates 60 departures a day between Luton and London Victoria, with free WiFi as well.

London Luton Airport is somewhat accessible from both the M1 and M25. If you have a choice, go for the M1, as the airport is only about five minutes from Junction 10. Without traffic, it can take about 45 minutes from central London. This can sometimes be longer when there are extensive road works, which tends to be always. When using Sat Nav systems, use the postcode LU2 9QT.

How to Get There—Really

Seriously. You've paid next to nothing for your airfare, splash out on a private cab. If you book a licensed mini-cab ahead of time, the service is often cheaper than the equivalent black cab fare and definitely easier, as they'll meet you at the arrivals hall. If you leave it to the last minute, and must take a black cab, get ready to shell out at least £85 (with their meters, this can increase with traffic) plus a meeting fee if you want them to wait for you. Cab rides from central London usually take about an hour.

Parking

Short Term Parking is pricier but situated closest to the terminal, with prices ranging from £9.50 for 30 minutes or £67.50 per day drive-up. Mid-term parking is ideal for stays of around five days and is about a five-minute transfer by bus. Mid term is £35 per day drive-up with significant savings if booked well in advance. Long-term parking is about 10 minutes from the terminal by bus, and costs £30 per day, with hefty discounts for booking in advance.

Rental Cars

Car hire desks are located at the Onward Travel Centre on the main concourse in the terminal building. Lots are connected to the airport via free shuttle service. On site companies are Avis, Europcar/National/Alamo, Hertz and Enterprise.

Hotels

There is no hotel at Luton but there are four hotels near the airport: Ibis Hotel (01582 424488), Holiday Inn Express (01582 589100), and Hampton by Hilton (01582 798477).

Airlines

Air Nostrum
AtlasGlobal
Blue Air
easyJet
El Al
La Compagnie
Monarch
Ryanair
SunExpress
TAROM
Thomson
Wizz Air

General Information

Address: Stansted Airport, Essex CM24 1QW

Airport Code: STN

General Enquiries: 0844 335 1803

Lost Property: 0844 824 3109
or stn.lostproperty@bagport.co.uk

Website: www.stanstedairport.com
or @STN_Airport

Overview

It might be tucked away on a former Roman burial site in the middle of the dull Essex countryside, but Stansted Airport has one thing going for it—it's amazingly simple. One terminal (and quite a nice one too, Norman Foster saluted), one check-in area, one security gate. Take that, Heathrow. Nearly 20 airlines, most of them budget, fly nearly 18 million passengers per year from here to a growing list of mainly domestic and short-haul destinations.

Stansted dates to WWII, and was a base for the RAF and the US Air Force during the war. Post-war Stansted was used for charter flights, then eventually scheduled flights. The Norman Foster-designed main terminal opened in 1991, considered one of the most modern airports at the time. During the 2000s annual passenger traffic doubled from about 12 million to nearly 24 million by 2007 before leveling off to about 17-18 million per year.

A word about amenities. As far as shopping is concerned, Stansted offers Boots and Dixon outlets plus the usual selection of 'small airport shops' more aimed at passing the time than serious purchases. Stansted, like the other area airports, has made efforts to provide nicer dining options (then there's the Burger King); feel free to settle in for a few pints and then grab a sandwich on the run once you hear your name being called for the third time; gingerly avoid screaming children and/or singing hen-night crowds on the way. You could also try the Escape Lounge where, for about the price of an easyJet fare, one can enjoy an open bar, complimentary dishes and free WiFi. Speaking of WiFi, travellers get 60 free minutes per device throughout the airport.

Getting There

Stansted might seem a long way from London, but getting there by public transport is surprisingly easy. All you have to do is choose between the train (fast) and the bus (cheap). Several train operators serve the airport from Liverpool Street Station. But before you start struggling with too many timetables for trains that stop at too many stops, opt for the dedicated Stansted Express (www.stanstedexpress.com). The service runs every 15 minutes and takes you to the airport in just over 45 minutes. Tickets start at £19 for a standard single ride between Stansted and London Liverpool Street. Buses will take an hour to take you to the airport, and longer if there's a lot of traffic, but single tickets go for between £8 and £10.50 (potentially even less for easyBus). A number of operators fight for your custom, the main ones are: Terravision (www.terravision.eu), which leaves from Liverpool Street Station and Victoria Station; the slightly more expensive National Express (www.nationalexpress.com) connects to the same stations but some buses also stop in Stratford and Golders Green; and easyBus (www.easybus.com/en) gives you the intimacy of a small mini-van, stopping in Baker Street and Old Street in the City. If you're traveling during the rush hour, take a book. Whitechapel Road is one of London's most bustling streets, but it will get boring at some point.

Driving

If you're fortunate enough to have a car, or managed to convince your dad-in-law to lend you his, find your way out of the city via Stratford and hit the M11. It's a straight drive from here and amid Essex' greenery, the airport is hard to miss. Cab drivers will know how to get you to the airport, but will probably charge you a small fortune for it.

Parking

Short-term parking rates start at £10 for the first 30 minutes and rise in steps to £62 for 24 hours. Long-stay will cost you £21.50 a day. If you're in for a weekend trip, opt for the mid-stay car park, which is closer to the terminal than the long-stay option and charges £30/day drive-up. Valet parking is available and can be pre-booked. Once there, drop your car at the end of Set Down Lane; the pickup point is next to the Fast Track car park. Book online before you head off for discounts on all Stansted parking options.

Car Rental

Hertz, Avis, Europcar, Budget, National, Alamo, Enterprise and Sixt all have desks at Stansted.

Hotels

There are three hotels either next to or within the perimeter of the airport. The four-star Radisson Blu (01279 661 012) is connected to the airport via a covered walkway. The Premier Inn (0871 527 9352) and Hilton London Stansted Airport (01279 680 800) are both located within the perimeter of the airport and connected by a short shuttle bus ride.

Airlines

Aegean Airlines	FlyBe
Air Berlin	Freebird Airlines
Air Moldova	Germanwings
Atlantic Airways	Pegasus Airlines
Atlasjet	Ryanair
Aurigny	Tangney-Tours
Belle Air	Thomas Cook
Cyprus Airways	Thomson Airways
easyJet	

General Information

TfL Customer Services: 4th Floor,
14 Pier Walk, London SE10 0ES

Phone: 0343 222 1234

Website: www.tfl.gov.uk/modes/tube
or @TflTravelAlerts

Overview

If the Underground had a motto it wouldn't be "Mind the gap" but "Sorry for any inconvenience caused." But as we grumble and ponder if anyone is ever actually sorry for squeezing you 30m below the surface, in a sweat-box held together by dust, rust and expensive fares, the magnificence of the 'Tube' network should really be appreciated. Across its 250-odd miles of track the Underground will take you to 270 stations spread the length and breadth of London (although with disproportionately few lines reaching into south London). The system is well integrated with the bus and overground train networks which share a common ticketing system with the Oyster card.

When fully functioning, the Underground will get you across town quicker than the bus and without the complicated timetables and schedules of overground trains. When it is struck by signal failures and breakdowns, which is very often, it can be excruciatingly slow and get very overcrowded, very quickly. In conclusion: the Underground won't necessarily get you anywhere on time, in style or in comfort, but it will (eventually) get you pretty much anywhere.

Fares

The vast majority of the network is divided into concentric fare rings or zones (1-6). Zone 1 covers central London, zone 6 covers the outskirts of London. Fares are dependent on how many zones your journey includes and there's a premium for travelling in zone 1. Peak fares (Monday to Friday from 6.30-9.30 am and 4-7 pm) are from 50p to a few pounds more than off-peak, although journeys limited to zone 1 do not benefit from the off-peak discount. Your best bet is to get an Oyster Card—lowest zone 1 single fare is £2.50 instead of £6.30 if you pay by cash. Oyster cards are available for just £5 from vending machines. It's a total no-brainer: the total amount that can be deducted from your Oyster card is also capped over a 24-hour period to match the equivalent cost of a one day travel card. So the fare system is complicated, but if you take £2.50 (which will get you a single journey within zone 1 with an Oyster card) as a base rate, and add to this the further out of zone 1 you travel, things become clearer. If you feel the need to marvel at the full intricacy of the fares and ticketing system, give yourself eye-strain at Transport for London's website.

Frequency and Quality of Service

The vast majority of centrally located stations will have a train at least every three minutes most of the day. At the very beginning and end of the day service frequency tails-off and can get as low as eight minutes between trains. Trains are also much less frequent at the farther reaches of some lines—the Metropolitan line has trains only every 20 minutes from its most north-western stations, even during peak times. Almost all lines have a reduced frequency on Sundays. First trains are 05:00-05:30, last trains are between midnight and 12.30. Last trains are generally safe; expect a slightly raucous mix of pickled after-workers and overly obsequious rough-sleepers rather than any real troublemakers, especially after booze was banned in 2008. The whole network had £5bn thrown at it for the 2012 Olympics, but the only noticeable improvement was increased cleanliness in many of the stations.

Lines

Bakerloo: (Brown coloured on maps) Runs from Harrow & Wealdstone in the north west to Elephant & Castle in the south east.

Central: (Red) Runs from West Ruislip in the west to Epping in the far north east. The central section is buried under Oxford Street and has four stops on the street, the quietest usually being Bond Street.

Transport · Underground

Circle: (Yellow) Notoriously slow, unreliable, and not strictly a circle—even more so now that a tail reaches down to Hammersmith. For this reason Edgware Road is now the end of the line. Shares almost all of its track and stations with other lines so don't necessarily bother waiting specifically for a dedicated Circle Line train. Look out for the 'Platform for Art' as you pass Gloucester Road station.

District: (Green) One of the few lines to serve deepest south London, branches run into Richmond and Wimbledon in the southwest and also to Ealing. The line continues up to Upminster in the northeast. Almost all of the branches of this fragmented line come together at Earls Court from where they run in one continuous mess, so plan ahead if changing there.

Hammersmith & City: (Pink) Starts at Hammersmith in the west of the city before heading north to Paddington and continuing east to Barking. Take it to Ladbroke Grove if heading to the Portobello market.

Jubilee: (Silver) Silver coloured as it opened in the year of the Queen's Silver Jubilee in 1977, the line serves northwest, central and east London, including the Canary Wharf business district. The section east of Green Park is the most recent addition to the network (it opened in 1999) and has a number of architecturally exemplary stations.

Metropolitan: (Dark Purple) The oldest of all the lines, this granddaddy of metropolitan underground railways strikes far out in the suburbs and countryside northwest of the city from its central root at Aldgate.

Northern: (Black) Presumably given black as its colour to reflect the dark mood of anyone unlucky enough to have to commute on it, the Northern line is the overcrowded spine of London, covering vast swathes of the city centre, the north and the south.

Piccadilly: (Dark Blue) From Cockfosters in the far northeast this line trundles all the way to Heathrow airport, with some of the most popular tourist spots in between. It's a very cheap way to the airport but is also the slowest. Southgate and Arnos Grove stations are both 1930s modernist brilliance.

Victoria: (Light Blue) Runs from Walthamstow in the north to Brixton in the south. This musty line is currently undergoing refurbishment and will feature new trains and track by 2011. In the meantime, check for early closing and shutdowns, particularly during weekends.

Waterloo & City: (Turquoise) No-one has ever met anyone who has been on this line. Fun, it has two stations, Waterloo and Bank, and is designed for suited and booted commuters coming in by train from Waterloo. No trains on Sundays.

London Overground: (Orange) TfL took over part of the overground rail network, notably the somewhat shabby and North London Line which now runs from Richmond to Stratford This has now been merged with what was the East London Line, which connects East, Southeast and Northeast London. Just think of it as an extension to the tube network.

Bicycles

Bicycles are generally only allowed on the tube outside peak hours and only from stations outside central London. They are not permitted on the Victoria or Waterloo and City lines at all. Folding bicycles can be taken on all sections of the Tube free of charge.

Transport • **The DLR**

General Info

TfL Customer Services: 4th Floor,
14 Pier Walk, London SE10 0ES

Phone: 0343 222 1234

Website: www.tfl.gov.uk/modes/dlr/
or @LondonDLR

Overview

Not quite a tram, tube or train, it's simply the Docklands Light Railway, a nifty little thing that makes getting to places like Greenwich Village and City Airport easy and cheap. Launched in 1987 with a modest 11 trains and only 15 stations, the regeneration of the Docklands area has seen it grow to seven lines covering 45 stations and counting, serving over 100 million passengers a year. Serving the east and Southeast of the city, it is pretty much as pleasant as London public transport gets. It's reliable, less noisy than the tube, generally less crowded and it's pretty well air-conditioned. The DLR is also fully automated and most of the time there is no driver, meaning that you can take the front seat and pretend that you're actually driving the thing.

The DLR provides a key service for London's suits, with the Bank to Canary Wharf journey taking just over ten minutes. For normal people, Canary Wharf also makes an interesting/unusual weekend destination. Almost completely deserted, a stroll amongst the abandoned skyscrapers is a strangely satisfying way to spend a Sunday afternoon.

Fares

As on the rest of London's public transport you're best off with an Oyster card. One thing to remember is that there are no barriers at DLR stations and instead Oyster readers are located at station exits and entrances. To avoid getting slapped with a fine and to ensure you're charged the right amount, remember to touch in and out correctly. The prices are similar to the tube, so cash works out more expensive (though not as expensive as the tube's cash single).

Hours

The DLR runs 5.30 am–12.30 am (Sundays 7.00 am–11.30 pm), with train frequencies depending on the time of day. On weekdays, trains run as often as every three-and-a-half minutes during peak times, and every five to ten minutes during off-peak times and weekends. The DLR is closed Christmas.

Transport • **Overground Trains**

General Information

National Rail: www.nationalrail.co.uk
or @nationalrailenq
Eurostar: www.eurostar.com or @Eurostar
TfL London Overground:
www.tfl.gov.uk/modes/london-overground/

Overview

The railways are one of the great British inventions but, unfortunately, the Victorians who built the network in this country did slightly too good a job. Every generation since has taken one look at the massively expensive task of modernising them and scuttled back into their Ford Fiestas. So, while France, Germany and Japan got on with building super-speed bullet trains Britain was stuck with an uneasy compromise between the technologies of 1950 and 1969. This doesn't mean that you shouldn't use trains. It just means that it's probably best to avoid them at peak times. That's when London plays a cruel trick on people who choose to live in places with names like 'Gravesend' and 'Slough' by making them lurch slowly with less personal space than the legal minimum

for cattle. During off-peak times train travel can, in contrast, be positively pleasant. It's a great way to see the countryside, every city and major town in the country is connected, and, if you book far enough in advance and shop around on sites like www.megatrain.com or www.thetrainline.com it can be less expensive than you'd think. In London itself, Transport for London manages four suburban rail routes that use the pay as you go Oyster system.

Stations

Broadly speaking, Euston and King's Cross stations serve the north of the country, Liverpool Street the east, Victoria the south, Paddington and Marylebone the west.

Eurostar

The King's Cross area is also home to the splendid St Pancras—the terminal for the Eurostar train service which connects Britain with the rest of Europe. Since November 2007 it's been possible to get from here to Paris or Brussels in around two hours—with connecting trains to Siberia and beyond.

Charing Cross Station

NFT Map: 24

Address: The Strand, London, WC2N 5HF

Station Code: CHX

General Station Enquiries: 03457 11 41 41

Lost Property: 020 7930 5444

Southeastern: www.southeasternrailway.co.uk
or @Se_Railway

Overview

Perched at the top of the Strand amidst popular tourist attractions such as Trafalgar Square and with the majestic 1865 Charing Cross Hotel being part of the station, you may presume that a cornucopia of ornate delights lies within. Well, it's a dump; the chances of Brief Encounter being remade here are pretty slim. But your chances of being barged by a curmudgeonly office worker are very good, what with it being one of the busiest rail terminals in London. Still, can you blame them for wanting to get out of the place so quickly?

Tickets

There is a small ticket office open some 20 hours per day, and three banks of ticket machines on or around the concourse.

Services

If you're in need of a quick bite, there's a decent variety of food outlets to cater for all tastes, from Burger King to a M &S Simply Food outlet. Indulge your Schadenfreude by watching the beleaguered information guy having to dispense a plethora of poor excuses as to why the 17.34 to Margate was cancelled. There is both a Boots and a WHSmith and cash machines can be found on the concourse and in the front entrance.

Public Transport

The station is easily accessible by Charing Cross station (Northern & Bakerloo lines) and also the adjoining Embankment station (Circle & District lines). The nearby Trafalgar Square is a major hub for buses—especially night buses for post-West End madness—which inch their way out to places as far apart as Harrow and Crystal Palace.

Euston Station

NFT Map: 78

Address: Euston Road, London, NW1 2RT

Station Code: EUS

General Station Enquiries: 03457 11 41 41

Lost property: 0207 387 8699

Website: www.networkrail.co.uk/communities/
passengers/our-stations/london-euston/
or @NetworkRailEUS

Overview

Easily the ugliest station in London, Euston creeps up as you nervously edge along Euston Road. The first inter-city terminal built in London, it was originally constructed in 1837, and the lovely original was demolished to make way for the monstrous concrete-and-glass coffin which now squats next to the mail depot. Since privatisation the interior has become an identi-kit British rail station with more chain businesses per head than is morally decent.

It's not all doom and gloom, however. Within this architectural eyesore you'll find a scarily concise summation of human nature. Like most busy stations, there's plenty of eccentricity and electricity here: abandoned Tube tunnels; stressed-out coffee-guzzling power-commuters; fresh-faced backpackers sprawled out on the floor; and the infamous beggar who—to the delight of football lovers everywhere except in Manchester—was arrested for punching Manchester Utd manager Sir Alex Ferguson.

The station is London's gateway to the north west of England and Scotland, and also North Wales. As such it is the point of entry for Scousers, Mancunians, Glaswegians and more. Avanti trains (www.avantiwestcoast.co.uk) to Glasgow can take as little as 4 hrs 30 mins.

Tickets

The ticket cashiers may have the glazed look of Kafka-esque zombies but the cleaning staff are often more helpful. Just use the Fasttrack machines!

There's plenty of eating and drinking options, all of the 'chain' variety. If you're an aficionado and determined to hang around, check out the Doric Arch (1 Eversholt St; 020 7383 3359), a little boozer with train memorabilia lining the walls. The left luggage office is at the top of the ramp to platforms 16–18 and is open between 7 am–11 pm.

Public Transport

As an actual railway station it is adequate. Served by two Tube lines and nine bus routes, it's nothing if not convenient.

King's Cross Station

NFT Map: 78

Address: Euston Rd & Pancras Rd, London, N1 9AL

Station Code: KGX

General Station Enquiries: 03457 11 41 41

Lost property: 020 7278 3310

Website: www.networkrail.co.uk/communities/passengers/our-stations/london-kings-cross/

Overview

Previously a dingy playground for prostitutes, drug dealers, and all sorts of similarly bad kids, King's Cross Station scrubbed up a bit, thanks to lots of chin scratching and typically panicked spending on the government's part. Built in 1852 on the site of a former smallpox hospital, it is one of the busiest and most well-connected stations in the country: running trains to Edinburgh; Newcastle; the East coast; as well as six Tube lines. Zany trivia about the station includes the fact that it is supposedly built on top of legendary Fembot-Queen Boudicea's grave (most probably a total lie) and that it has a tacky little shrine to Harry Potter at what has been designated 'Platform 9 3/4' (oh God).

Nearly all long distance train services leave from the overground platforms under the arches straight ahead of you as you enter from Euston Road. The Tube is also accessible from steps at this entrance and at what used to be the Thameslink station next to the Scala on Pentonville Road. From the main Tube entrance there is a pedestrian subway that comes up on the other side of Euston Road just outside Macdonald's. This is handy for crossing the road at busy times, and of course for getting chips.

Tickets

Tube tickets, including Oyster top ups and season tickets, can be purchased from the machines in front of the Tube entry gates, located just at the bottom of both sets of stairs at the station. For railcard discounts and more specific enquiries you'll have to queue at the manned ticket desks next to the machines. For all other tickets go to the upstairs ticket hall which is to the left of the main Euston Road entrance.

Services

With the renovations, the quality of services has significantly improved. But with the excellent Eat St literally round the corner, ditch the station completely and sample the wares of London's best street food traders. And for the basics, the trusty newspaper kiosk underneath the awning is still going strong.

Public Transport

King's Cross crosses more Tube lines (six) than any other station, and is serviced by at least twice as many buses, many of which run all night.

Liverpool Street Station

NFT Map: 8

Address: Liverpool St, London, EC2M 7PY

Station Code: LST

General Station Enquiries: 03457 11 41 41

Lost property: 020 7247 4297

Website: www.networkrail.co.uk/communities/passengers/our-stations/london-liverpool-street/

Overview

It's not that Liverpool Street is particularly ugly, but if it's architectural beauty you're after, you're much better off heading to Paddington or the new, improved St. Pancras International. In comparison to these two icons of British station design, Liverpool Street is extremely modest, boring even. Clean, modern and easy to navigate around, it is simply a good train station. With the markets, bars and restaurants of Spitalfields and Brick Lane just around the corner, the station is the perfect starting point to explore east London. First opened to the public in 1874, it is one of the busiest stations in London. With 18 platforms, the station mainly serves destinations in the east of England, including daytrip favourites such as Cambridge and Southend on Sea.

It is also the home of the Stansted Express, providing easy airport access with departures every 15 minutes. If you're travelling with a group of people a taxi might work out slightly cheaper, but the train is much quicker and more reliable. The Tube station, with its main entrance centrally located on the main concourse, makes all of London easily accessible with the Central, Hammersmith & City, Circle and Metropolitan lines all passing through. Being one of the busiest stations on the underground network, rush hour can get nasty and is best avoided.

Tickets

The ticket office is located on the main concourse, on your left hand side if entering from Bishopsgate. Ticket windows are open during station opening hours. There are also several express ticket machines scattered throughout the station. Tickets for the Stansted Express can be purchased from designated ticket machines opposite platforms 5-6. A cluster of cash machines can be found by the stairs leading up to the Old Broad Street exit. There are payphones on both levels and most are located on the Bishopsgate side of the station.

Services

With Brick Lane just around the corner, eating, drinking and shopping here should really be a last resort. The regular big-chain fast food joints are scattered throughout the station (some of them repeatedly) with the usual selection of coffee, burgers, sandwiches and sweets. The main shopping area is on the lower level around the Broadgate and Exchange Square exits, offering everything from toiletries and birthday cards to Italian silk ties and double-glazed windows.

Passengers are invited to wait for their trains in the so-called "food court," which really isn't much more than a few cramped tables near the Burger King. There's a small but nicer waiting lounge located adjacent to platform 10. Here you also find the left luggage, a bureau de change, a less busy cash machine and access to the main taxi rank. Smoking is prohibited at all times throughout the station.

Public Transport

The main bus station is located on the upper level of the station (Broadgate end), and provides a large number of services to destinations throughout London. Plenty of buses also stop on the street just outside the Bishopsgate exit.

London Bridge Station

NFT Map: 106

Address: Station Approach Road, London, SE1 9SP

Station Code: LBG

General Station Enquiries: 03457 11 41 41

Lost property: 03451 27 29 20 (Southern Railway)

Website: www.networkrail.co.uk/communities/passengers/our-stations/london-bridge/

Overview

Around in one form or other since 1836, when steam trains filled the air with smoke, London Bridge is the city's oldest station. It's a good starting point for weekend trips to Kent's countryside or days on Brighton's beach. Operators Southeastern and Southern cover the south east, while Thameslink operates (little-known) connections to the airports Gatwick and Luton. The station couldn't be better connected to public transport, with two Tube lines and a plethora of buses at the doorstep. The catacombs underneath the station—said to be haunted—have been turned into the museum-cum-gore-fest London Bridge Experience, adding to the spooky entertainment already provided by the London Dungeon next door—just in case a cancelled or delayed train leaves you with too much time on your hands. Does happen, we're told.

Tickets

The main office is located next to the main entrance (London Bridge Street) or there are machines situated throughout the station.

Services

The main concourse is lined with eating and shopping options. Grab Cornish pasties, sandwiches, donuts; and the usual burgers from the usual chains, with Borough Market just over the road though, you'd be mad to waste your money on these. M &S and WH Smith lead the list of practical, but terribly unexciting shop names. The caverns connecting the Underground station with the national trains is teeming with better food options however—some even non-chain.

Public Transport

Connections are excellent. London Bridge Station is served by the Jubilee Line and the Bank branch of the Northern Line. Escalators take you down from the main concourse. Step outside the main entrance for the massive bus station, where buses leave in all directions of the city, except its far western reaches.

Marylebone Train Station

NFT Map: 76

Address: Great Central House,
Melcombe Place, London, NW1 6JJ

Station Code: MYB

Lost Property: 08456 005 165

Overview

Despite Monopoly-board notoriety, Marylebone railway station fell into neglect in the mid – to late-twentieth century, spurned as a rundown piggy-in-the-middle wedged haplessly between neighbours Paddington and Euston. But it's an aimless drifter no more. A refurb' in the 90s and again in 2006 saw Marylebone reinvigorated, with a thorough sprucing up and two new platforms. Servicing the Midlands, it now threads as far as Birmingham, Shakespeare's Stratford-Upon-Avon, Leamington Spa, Aylesbury, and High Wycombe, amongst others. It remains the runt of the London train station litter, but is a popular location for television filming (Doctor Who; Magnum PI; Green Wing; Peep Show) at a fraction of the price of King's Cross. In its bowels, Bakerloo Line trains rumble through an underground station of the same name.

Tickets

Rail ticket windows are to the north of Marylebone's relatively petite concourse and open Monday-Saturday 06.30–22:10 or Sunday 07.30–21.40. As with all mainline train stations, self-service ticket machines are in abundance should ticket offices be closed or queues too long. Sturdy padded-barriers ensure buying tickets on board the train, or getting away without them, is not an option. Underground tickets can be purchased from windows or machines alike within the Tube station itself.

Services

The usual plethora of railway station chains are on hand: newsagent WH Smith, baguette bakers Upper Crust, supermarket Marks & Spencer, and pasty purveyors the West Cornwall Company among them. More individually, Marylebone also hosts AMT Coffee, a cafe with a seating area at the centre of the concourse, the nifty flower stand on the south wall, and The V &A free house in the west passageway—an old man's boozer in the classic, wood panelled style. Cash points and payphones are in this same walkway, and toilets are situated on the south wall.

Public Transport

Marylebone underground station lies directly beneath Marylebone overground, and is serviced (Matron!) by the Bakerloo Line, while buses 2 and 205 stop directly outside the main entrance. A taxi stand is also situated out front. Baker Street and Edgware tube stations are a short walk away.

Paddington Station

NFT Map: 31

Address: Praed Street, London, W2 1HQ

Station Code: PAD

General Station Enquiries: 03457 11 41 41

Lost property: 020 7262 0344

Website: www.networkrail.co.uk/paddington
or @NetworkRailPAD

Overview

If you're in that small minority of people who love stations, then Paddington's paradise. Designed by engineering legend Isambard Kingdom Brunel—his middle name is Kingdom for God's sake, of course his work's going to be magnificent—this barn-like structure harks back to an era when train travel retained a little glamour. If it wasn't for the on-site Burger King you could easily imagine tearful ladies waving silk handkerchiefs at dapper gents.

The station also occupies a unique place in literary heritage. Every British child in the last half-century knows the tales of Paddington Bear. From "deepest darkest Peru", he was left unattended at the station; but a kind family picked him up, took him in, and named him after it. No other station name can inspire such genuine warmth. It certainly wouldn't have worked if he'd been found at Clapham Junction.

Heathrow Express

The super-fast link to Heathrow from Paddington takes just 15 minutes to Terminals 1, 2 and 3. Be warned, though; it's far from cheap (www.heathrowexpress.com).

Tickets

A ticket office and machines are located near platforms 9-10, and there are other machines and an information point near the Eastbourne Terrace entrance and also underneath the mezzanine.

Services

If you have any money left from your ticket—unlikely at today's prices—there are plenty of sharks who can take it off you. Burger King and Upper Crust will overcharge you for burgers or baguettes and there's an 'offie' (off-license) for expensive booze. There are also other ways of staying amused; as it's the main portal for commuters entering London from the west and

Wales) there's WiFi, a supermarket, a bookshop and curiously, a lingerie shop. Just what sort of a job do you have if you get to the station and realise: "Bollocks! No suspenders!"? Certainly not one compatible with Paddington's place in children's lit, that's for sure.

Public Transport

The Bakerloo, Circle, District, and Hammersmith & City Tube lines all stop at Paddington. Buses serve west and north west London.

St Pancras International

NFT Map: 78

Address: Euston Road, London, N1C 4QP

Station Reception: 020 7843 7688

Lost Property: 020 7837 4334

Website: stpancras.com or @StPancrasInt

Overview

St Pancras station has been generating waves of breathless excitement ever since its opening ceremony in 2007, which was by all accounts a pretty histrionic affair. This "Cathedral of Transport" situated next door to King's Cross station is now home to the Eurostar international train service and has domestic connections (via Thameslink trains) to Luton Airport, Bedford and Brighton; as well as Midland Mainline connections to places like Leicester and Sheffield. As the first major project of a huge scheme to redevelop the area, St Pancras has been marketed as so-much-more-than-a-station. Alongside its rail platforms it features Europe's longest Champagne bar, a farmers market, and an arcade of pointedly classy shops. All this is housed within beautiful listed buildings dating from 1868, with an extension for the long Eurostar trains designed by British starchitect Norman Foster.

Tickets

The Eurostar ticket office and travel centre is located at the Euston Road end of the long arcade, while self-service machines (for collecting pre-booked tickets) can be found outside the Eurostar departure lounge further along the arcade and to the right. For National Rail services, you will need to buy tickets from machines, or a manned ticket desk at the designated area at the far end of the Arcade, next to that horrific kissing statue.

Services

At St Pancras International there are dozens of places to eat, drink and shop, with a fair number of chain stores as well as some exclusives. Best of all is the Booking Office bar, which serves some of the best cocktails in the city. The station has its own dedicated shopping arcade with branches of classic London stores like Hamleys, as well as a market area and another brace of shops at the north end of the station ('The Circle'). Everything is shiny, new and upmarket, so expect your money to vanish pretty damn quickly. The Betjeman Arms pub—named after the famous poet whose petition saved the listed buildings from the same fate as Euston's arch—hosts beer festivals and music/literature events.

Public Transport

St Pancras can be reached by Tube (via adjacent King's Cross station) on the Victoria, Hammersmith & City, Circle, Piccadilly, Northern and Metropolitan Lines. A large number of buses also stop along Euston Road day and night.

Victoria Station

NFT Map: 20

Address: Buckingham Palace Road, London, SW1E 5ND

Station Code: VIC

General Station Enquiries: 03457 11 41 41

Lost property: 020 7963 0957

Website: www.networkrail.co.uk/communities/passengers/our-stations/london-victoria/ or @NetworkRailVIC

Overview

80 million people use London Victoria per year, making it one of the UK's busiest stations. Hit it at rush hour and it will feel like those 80 million are all there with you. Built a century ago for a less populous, less rushed and less demanding city, it struggles with crowds of commuters who jostle for platform space. Now it enforces crowd-control measures at peak times: prepare to be patient. Nevertheless, it is well laid-out with services clearly sign-posted, and a major upgrade is planned to improve its capacity.

Victoria's main train operators are Southeastern, Southern and Gatwick Express, who between them will whisk you to Brighton, Portsmouth, Hastings and Gatwick, among other Southeastern towns. Or if you're looking for a romantic break and the Victoria route to Bognor Regis is just a little too obvious for you, you can earn yourself brownie points and a hefty overdraft by taking the Orient Express from this station.

The building itself is impressive: look above the modern shop fascias to enjoy century-old architecture. But if that is all a little too high-brow, look up anyway, as the entrance to the South East building sports four caryatids: columns shaped like women, whose tunics saucily hang open so a gratuitous nipple can pop out to cheer the commuters. Rule Britannia!

Tickets

If you haven't booked in advance (why? Why?!), then head for the 24 hour ticket office in the central concourse, where you will queue for anything up to a year to buy your journey for much more money than you'd have paid online a week earlier. If you don't require assistance from a ticket officer, use the automated machines dotted round the concourse: their queues always move faster (unless the person in front of you is a newbie who can't figure out the buttons, which is guaranteed if you have less than five minutes to catch your train). Keep your ticket handy as all platforms are guarded by ticket barriers, and add a few extra minutes to reach platforms 15–19.

Services

All the predictable station fare is available in the main concourse for your journey's usual sandwich, loofah and tie needs. Food options have mercifully diversified so in addition to the obligatory artery-cloggers you can now grab sushi from the Wasabi stand or maintain your body's temple-status at the Camden Food Co. If it's a meal you're after and you must remain at the station, head up to the food court via Victoria Place for a choice of what could charitably be described as restaurants. Victoria Place itself boasts the ubiquitous high street shops to help you kill time or for any last minute gifts (as long as you don't really like the person you're buying for). Station loos are 30p—even up in the food court you can't pee for free—and showers are available if you're getting a bit ripe. Victoria also has a left luggage service, WiFi (charged) and photo booths.

Public Transport

Victoria is on the Victoria, Circle and District lines: entrance to the underground is opposite platform 7. The bus terminus is just outside the main entrance. It is also next door to London's national bus depot for cheapo travel to/from other parts of the UK. The main taxi rank is outside the main entrance, but if it has a heart-sinking queue then head up to the Plaza exit for an alternative rank.

Waterloo Station

NFT Map: 104

Address: Station Approach Road,
London, SE1 8SW

Station Code: WAT

General Station Enquiries: 03457 11 41 41

Lost property: 020 7401 7861

Website: www.networkrail.co.uk/communities/
passengers/our-stations/london-waterloo/

Overview

Until 2007, Waterloo was the first port of call for 'Europeans' arriving by train. Thousands of chic foreigners, clutching manbags and sporting huge sunglasses, would arrive at the station every week. But not any more. Nearly 200 years after the British triumphed in the first battle of Waterloo—a town in Belgium—the French got their revenge. Last November Eurostar gave the two fingers to the British Waterloo and promiscuously buggered off to St Pancras. Rumour has it that ex-PM Margaret Thatcher had specifically ordered that Eurostar terminate at a station named after a famous French defeat; but things have moved on a little since the "Iron Lady" left office. We're all Europeans now…

In truth, perhaps it's not that bad a thing. Even though no other British station covers as much space, Waterloo feels like it's at its bursting point. Even without the Eurostar it has a whopping 19 platforms—in almost constant use—and four Tube lines; it's the busiest station in Britain. It's calmed down slightly since the international terminal was put out to stud, but it's still pretty manic.

The station services London's south western suburbs (as can be seen by the swathes of well-dressed commuters) and, farther afield, the towns south west of the capital.

Waterloo East

NFT Map: 104

Address: Sandell St, SE8 8H

General Station Enquiries: 0800 783 4524

Overview

If the south west isn't your bag, you can disappear to England's south east—Kent, Sussex and SE London—from Waterloo East (station code: WAE). There's an escalator next to Burger King, opposite platform 12, that makes a trip to the south east look far more alluring than it really is; an elevated walkway over Waterloo Road connects Waterloo East with its larger cousin. The facility, considered its own terminal, is operated by Southeastern. The main entrance is on Sandell St.

Tickets

The main office is opposite platforms 16–17. And it's open 24 hours—so why not charm them into giving you a free ticket after a few drinks? They can't have heard it before, right?

Services

A delay is just unplanned "me time", so make the most of it by buying a newspaper, eating your own weight in overpriced pasties and cookies; then wash it down with a few pints of generic football-sponsorlager in the pub before buying your loved-one a novelty tie/'cute' socks to make up for being late. And drunk. And flatulent. And tasteless. There's a left luggage office between platforms 11-12.

Public Transport

Waterloo is served by four underground lines: Bakerloo, Jubilee, Northern, Waterloo & City; and numerous bus routes.

Overview

If there's one thing that screams London, it's big red buses—loads of 'em—preferably passing beneath Big Ben for maximum iconic impact. There was an almighty roar from Londoners when the Routemaster was scrapped: panoramas viewed from the Oxo tower were dotted with fists clutching rolled-up Time Outs shaking at the mayoral offices. The accordion buses which replaced them were met with similar anger but they've now been phased out: one can only guess at the amount of revenue lost by fare dodgers.

Whatever you think of the death of the bendy bus and Boris' reinvention of the Routemaster (also known as the "New Routemaster") one thing is certain: you're going to spend a lot of time on buses, around them, dodging them or moaning about them. Let's have a quick rundown of things to drop in a London bus convo: 'Drivers take pleasure in driving off just as you get to the stop,' 'Why do they always drive so fast/slow?' They're earning up to £500 a week? Why are they so grumpy all the time?' ad infinitum. As a Londoner, your list of hobbies and interests now includes transport: deal with it.

There are a variety of different operating companies, but to us they're all the same, all the way out to the frontiers of Zone 6. Get on at the front, get off at the middle. After the old double-decker buses were retired in 2005, Thomas Heatherwick's all-new Routemaster launched in Spring 2012. Just like the classic version there is an open rear platform for hopping on and hopping off. If you do want to live out your 1940s film fantasies, you can still catch the quaint old Routemasters doddering along the Heritage Route 15 during the day, a shorter version of the full route.

Fares

In a further move towards the cashless society, cash is not accepted on buses. A single fare costs £1.65 with an Oyster card, contactless card or one-day paper Travelcard. A bus and tram pass costs £21 per week. The Oyster ("The world's your…"—geddit?) is an electronic swipe card that can be bought at all Tube stations and thousands of other outlets such as newsagents and corner shops. The card can carry a mixture of travel passes (travelcards) and pay-as-you-go value. Note that if you choose pay-as-you-go, and you end up making more journeys than you anticipated; once it reaches the equivalent cost of a one-day travelcard, it will cap itself so you don't spend more. When you get on, don't forget to push your card against the scanner by the drivers' window. Sure, you're on camera 300 times per day, and every journey you make is recorded. But if you're paranoid, try another city, because they are watching you here.

24-Hour Services

You'll not hear London referred to as "the other city which never sleeps". Partly because it's unwieldy, but mostly because it's not true. After a hard night's binge-drinking and fighting in taxi ranks, we like our kip. But for those of you that are hardcore no-sleep-till-Brockley types, there is a network of 24-hour services. There are also a large number of night buses. They're just like day buses, except the route number is prefixed by a large 'N' and the view is less interesting.

Information

TfL's website (tfl.gov.uk) is an essential reference. Fare information and travel updates are available, plus PDFs of routes and timetables. As you get closer to central London, many routes operate on a frequency-basis rather than at fixed times. The main reason to visit TfL's site is the useful Journey Planner: enter your start and end points and it will (usually) calculate the best options. A word of warning though, computers are fallible and some route maps are schematics—so do check your own map and use common sense. Like those idiots that follow their GPS even when it tells them to drive into a river, it's frustrating to take three buses in a big circuit then realise you could have walked it in five minutes…

Safety

Like all big cities, London has its fair share of oddballs and criminals. And then a few institution-loads more in case things ever get boring. But CCTV in every bus and the creation of Safer Transport teams is having an effect—and not just on the share price of video camera manufacturers. Also, bus crime is concentrated in particular areas on particular routes. And you'll soon get to know the 'usual suspects' so don't worry. Night buses can get a bit lairy, so follow a few tips to make sure the only stress you suffer is traffic-related. Gangsters may wish to laugh at the following; Mother Theresas may wish to tattoo it on the inside of their eyelids: Avoid top decks where necessary. Sit on the left so the driver can see you (he has a radio link to base). Don't fall asleep. Use the same stop at night and know your surroundings so you can be confident. Keep your belongings close to you and be switched on. Get to know the 'hot spots' so you can be aware.

Overview

Although convenient and cost effective, coaches are traditionally associated with the grimier side of travel. But when it comes to budget travel, grime is in the eye of the beholder. So if your impression of coaches includes cold turkey junkies showering sick on unsuspecting passengers or if you maintain a general aversion to getting within three coach lengths of the portal of hell that is the coach toilet, then perhaps this mode of travel is not for you. That said, coach travel enjoys a long tradition across the UK, and it's much, much better here than many other places.

For years, National Express (www. nationalexpress.com), the UK's biggest coach company, has been trying to shake its image as a purveyor of seedy transport. Having rebranded itself as quick, comfortable and green, their fleet of coaches are shiny and the drivers slightly less grumpy than they used to be. National Express' nemesis is Megabus (www.megabus.co.uk), the £1 people (of course they release only a handful of these tickets for each journey and then the fare rises the closer you get to your preferred date). It hasn't always been this way, but Megabus coaches are now pretty much as good as National Express. Megabus Plus (www.megabusplus.com) combines bus and rail travel for selected destinations. At the same time, National Express started its own super cheap ticket campaign.

Victoria Coach Station (Buckingham Palace Road, London, SW1W 9TP) is the main coach hub is near Victoria train station. You can buy tickets for both Megabus and National Express—the two main operators who run from Victoria Coach Station—from the same booths just inside the station. But, like plane tickets, (only without that last shred of glamour that air travel still has) if you buy in advance, you can get some super-cheap prices. National Express has an office on the road between the train and bus stations. Victoria Coach Station is also a hub for other bus companies serving the continent, some of which can be very cheap.

London's other main hub is Golder's Green. This is the last stop for services heading north (or the first stop for buses coming down into London). If you live in north London, it's worth jumping off here, as it's on the Northern Line and can shave an hour off the trip.

There's also a healthy trade in coaches to Oxford. The Oxford Tube (www. oxfordtube.com) competes with National Express on the route from Victoria; travelling via Marble Arch, Notting Hill and Shepherd's Bush. Tickets normally cost about £15 and you can buy on board. They also run through the night—so if you get drunk and have the urge to go on an impromptu holiday—well, Oxford it is.

Beyond Tooting, Croydon's trams will take you from places like Wimbledon to shop—lemming-like with the locals—at the Ampere Way IKEA. The trams accept Oyster and use a similar charging scale to buses. Once you get back on the map, your flatpacked sideboard will win admiring glances but few friends as you trail home on busy tubes.

General Information

Transport for London: www.tfl.gov.uk

London Cycling Campaign: lcc.org.uk
or @london_cycling

Overview

There's a war going on out there, one with real casualties and collateral damage. When David Cameron was spotted going through a red light on his bicycle, it threw into sharp relief a low-level conflict which has been going on for decades. Bikes v. Cars: with hapless pedestrians caught in the middle.

Cycling around London is not for the faint-hearted, but municipal improvements (especially during Boris Johnson's tenure) and the hard work of the London Cycling Campaign, are encouraging people to drop their Oyster cards and jump on their bikes. London continues to implement its system of Cycle Superhighways providing safer routes (and some dedicated lanes) into Central London and across the city. The city's cyclehire program, Santander Cycles (formerly sponsored by Barclays and also known as 'Boris Bikes'), is a brilliant system based on European models in which users pick up a bike and then drop it off when finished at a suitable point in the city. If you want to explore London this way, note that Transport for London has some fun leisure routes detailed on its website. Transport for London offers great free cycling maps (order via the TfL website); some of the 14 routes have become so popular, cycling along them is like taking part in the Tour de France (albeit slower and with slightly fewer drugs). The maps give colour-coded help; look for the brown routes (separate from the traffic) or even better the green routes (separate from the traffic and passing through parks, beside canals or rivers.)

But cycling does hold some risks. As well as the nightmare of walking around all day with 'helmet hair' you've got accidents and theft. LCC's website has details of road-confidence training and lists local cycling groups who run social events and cycle maintenance classes. They will sometimes cycle your new route to work with you to help you negotiate the difficult bits. Aren't they nice?

For those new to cycling on London's roads, basic rules include: stay a door length (or stride) away from the pavement or parked cars; watch out for distracted office drones leaping into the road and into black cabs; don't undertake bendy-buses or HGVs; don't use your phone while moving; and if in doubt on a tricky junction, transform yourself into a pedestrian—get off and push your bike wherever you need to go.

Bolt-cutting 'tea-leaves' steal thousands of bikes every year. You have three options to reduce this particular risk. One, buy a rubbish bike that no-one would want to steal and lock it with one lock. Two, get a decent bike, carry around a D-lock and two other locks and spend 20 mins each time you stop. Three, get a shit-hot bike and never take it out.

Where to Ride Bikes

There are plenty of great rides around town and a happy cyclist is one who has been able to incorporate one into their commute. Good options are the short but scenic Parkland Walk Nature Reserve, which links Finsbury Park to Highgate via an abandoned railway line; a Saturday morning cycle takes you to one of Highgate's wonderful pubs for lunch and a lazy pint. The City, normally snarled with cabs, buses and kamikaze pedestrians, is a dream on a Sunday morning.

Though not continuous, the path along the Regent's Canal linking Paddington with Canary Wharf takes cyclists away from traffic and along some surprisingly gorgeous stretches of canal (which also sport some top-notch graffiti)—as well as some godawful, festering dumps. A useful section of the canal links the west side of Regent's Park with Paddington via Lisson Grove and Warwick Avenue. Watch out for super-fast cyclists determined to slice a second off their PB, especially where the path narrows under bridges or around ramps.

A jaunt through any of the capital's great parks seems an obvious choice, but beware, some parks (notably Hampstead Heath) ban bikes on almost all paths, thanks to selfish cyclists of the past who went too fast and frightened the jumpy pedestrians.

RideLondon (www.ridelondon.co.uk/) is a fun two-day riding festival built on the success of the earlier FreeWheel event include a family ride along closed central London roads, a 100-mile ride, and a Grand Prix for pros.

Bike Shops	Address	Phone
Apex Cycles	40-42 Clapham High St, SW4 7UR	020 7622 1334
Bikefix	44 Emerald St	020 7405 1218
Brick Lane Bikes	118 Bethnal Green Rd, E2 6DG	020 3022 3002
Brixton Cycles	296 Brixton Rd	020 7733 6055
Condor Cycles	51 Gray's Inn Rd, WC1X 8PP	020 7269 6820
Cycle Docs	70 Holloway Rd	077 2974 1137
Decathlon	9 Maritime St	020 7394 2000
K's Bicycle Workshop	248 Archway Rd	078 8325 2225
London Recumbents	Battersea Park	020 7228 6843
ReCycling	110 Elephant Rd, SE17 1LB	020 7703 7001
Velorution - Islington	123 Essex Rd, N1 2SN	020 7148 5573

To consider taking a taxi in London you either need (a) a trust fund, or (b) to be drunk. If you are both, congratulations: prepare to be taken for a ride in more ways than one.

Dating back to the mid-17th Century (kind of), London's 'black cabs', or 'Hackneys', are the world's oldest taxi service and are as representative of London as Routemasters, Big Ben and robbery. They are the most visible, the most iconic and probably the most expensive taxi service in London. While this flag-down option is great (they are the only company licensed to pick up on the street) budgeting for a black cab is tricky. Their prices are designed to confuse passengers into parting with huge wads for what often feels like a round-the-block trip. A whole range of metaphysical problems contribute to that huge sum waiting to be paid at journey's end; all fares start at £2.40 and are based on three types of tariffs— higher tariffs apply on evenings, weekends and late nights. Fares are also affected by traffic. In general, as a very broad guideline, expect to pay around £9 for up to one mile, £14 for up to two miles, and £22 for up to four miles. Fares between Heathrow and Central London are anywhere between £45–£85. A £4 surcharge applies during the days around Christmas and New Year. There's also a 'puke charge' of £40 if you soil the cab and the driver has to take it out of service to clean it; keep it in!

Black cabs are operated by many different companies who are all regulated and licensed by the Public Carriage Office (PCO). Generally speaking, the service you receive doesn't vary much from company to company, though some boast little add-ons to capture your fare. Big, well organized companies like Dial-A-Cab (020 7253 5000) and Radio Taxis (020 7272 0272) offer carbon neutral trips and friendly service. All black cab drivers must pass 'The Knowledge' test to get their license, so every driver will have a labyrinthine understanding of London and most will not be shy in sharing this with you.

Though a cheaper option, going private can be a minefield. Since 2001 all taxi services in London are required by law to be licensed by the PCO: this includes the city's thousands of private-hire minicabs. Private hire companies are everywhere you look and often take the form of nicotine-stained, shoddily built little offices with lots of bored men milling about. Every neighbourhood has plenty of local services and it's really trial and error to find one that doesn't rip you off or drive barely roadworthy chariots of rust. The drivers of these little companies can be pretty eccentric—you can be regaled by tales of times past, given essential life advice or simply receive the disdainful silent treatment. The 'private taxi sector' does go upmarket, however. By far the most efficient and elegant service is that offered by Addison Lee, (www.addisonlee.com; 020 7407 9000) who text you twice, have huge gleaming six-seaters, and perfectly-manicured drivers. Fares are pretty cheap over longer distances but the minimum is around £10. Transport for London (tfl.gov.uk) has a useful online tool for locating licensed black cabs and minicabs, as well as an app (Cabwise). Another option is Uber (www.uber.com/cities/london), with its handy app and account-based system.

A word of warning: London is awash with rogue taxi-drivers who are not licensed and who will attempt to pick you up from outside a club or theatre. These guys will either charge you more than you agreed upon, not know where they are going, or they will be driving beat-up death-traps. If a ride hasn't been booked with a licensed minicab company, then there is no record of your journey, meaning also that if there is a problem, your driver cannot be traced. There are also many stories of attacks on women, so if in doubt, don't get in!

London Heliport

020 7228 0181

www.londonheliport.co.uk or @LondonHeliport

SW11's very own heliport! Includes aerial tours of London and airport transfers (Heathrow in ten minutes). The nearest tube is Clapham Junction.

EBG Helicopters

01737 823 282

www.ebghelicopters.co.uk or @ebgheli

Running helicopter tours of London and charter flights from Redhill Airport in Surrey, 10 minutes by car from Gatwick Airport. £140 will get you 35 minutes over London, the only downside is getting to Surrey. Also offers charters for weddings and corporate events and air taxi service starting from £650 for up to three passengers.

Elstree Aerodrome

www.londonelstree.com/

A variety of charters operate out of Elstree offering sky tours, as well as flight academies for those who want to take the wheel. On site is a restaurant, plus it's close to the M1.

Ferries/Boat Tours, Rentals & Charters

London River Services (LRS)
020 7941 2400
www.tfl.gov.uk/modes/river/

Provides commuter river transportation on the Thames. This runs in the East from Masthouse Terrace Pier to Savoy Pier at Embankment. In peak hours services run to Woolwich Arsenal with a further service from Blackfriars Millenium Pier in the City to Putney Pier in the west costing £21.30 return. WiFi is available on boats serving Woolwich. Services run every 20 minutes. All are wheelchair friendly.

Thames Clippers
0870 7815049
www.thamesclippers.com

London's answer to the NYC water taxis, primarily serving the O2 stadium from Waterloo, Embankment and Tower Bridge. Conveniently runs later than the Tube meaning you can actually stay right to the end of a show without the worry of being stranded on the south side of the river. Single tickets cost between £7-13 with Oyster Card holders getting 1/3 off. Boats leave every 15 minutes.

Bateux London
020 7695 1800
www.bateauxlondon.com/

Dinner, lunch and charter cruises from Embankment Pier. Yes, there's even a jazz cruise.

Westminster Passenger Services Association
020 7930 2062
www.wpsa.co.uk

One of the only popular charters to offer services upriver to Kew, Richmond and Hampton Court.

City Cruises
020 7488 0344
www.citycruises.com.

Hop on hop off services primarily aimed at tourists and with tourist prices. Tickets start from £11.75

return for adults from Greenwich to Westminster/Waterloo Pier.

Heritage Boat Charters
01932 224 800
www.heritageboatcharters.com

For something different, try messing about on the river in one of these historic wooden numbers. On offer are skippered cruises down the Thames starting at £825. Formal dinner on board is available.

Silver Fleet Woods River Cruises
020 7759 1900
www.silverfleet.co.uk

Luxury chartered boats. Particularly good at putting on top-notch corporate events.

Thames Cruises
020 7928 9009
www.thamescruises.com

Two words—disco cruise. Hot pants are not required for dinner cruises.

Marinas/Passenger Ship Terminal

Chelsea Marina
07770 542 783
www.harbourguides.com/
harbours/chelsea_harbour

Despite being in upmarket Chelsea, the prices for mooring your boat here are incredibly generous—£2 per metre a night or £300 a year with space for 60 boats. Secure subterranean parking also available.

Chiswick Quay Marina
020 8994 8743
www.chiswickquay.com/marina

Great, secluded spot for West Londoners near Chiswick Bridge. A little far from a tube station, yet Chiswick overland station is within walking distance with services to Waterloo. Prices are on an annual basis at £162 per metre including a resident harbourmaster, shower block, mains water and electricity.

Gallions Point Marina
020 7476 7054
www.gallionspointmarina.co.uk

In London's Docklands and therefore perfect for those working in the city.

St Katharine Haven
020 7264 5312
skdocks.co.uk

One of London's best marinas. Great location by Tower Bridge, close to the quayside bars and restaurants and reasonable prices at £2.60 per metre, per day.

Welcome Floating Terminal in Greenwich
01474 562 200
www.pla.co.uk/

Built in 2004 and believed to be the world's first floating terminal. Welcome has on-site immigration and custom services for cruise ship passengers entering or leaving London.

London Cruise Terminal at Tilbury
01375 852 360
www.capitalcruising.co.uk/

The most popular regional departure point for passenger liners is 25 miles from Central London in Essex. Its close proximity to the M25 makes it easy for Londoners to get to. Current destinations from here include Scandinavia and continental Europe.

General Information

TfL Traffic News: tfl.gov.uk/trafficnews
or @TfLTrafficNews

Parking Information for Cars: www.londoncouncils
.gov.uk/services/parking-services

Parking Information for Motorbikes and
Scooters: www.cityoflondon.gov.uk/services/
parking/motorcycles-and-bicycles

AA Route Planner:
www.theaa.com/route-planner

Overview

With London's Congestion Charge, Low Emission
Zone, pricey parking, kamikaze bus drivers,
dreaded speed bumps, 20 mph limits, speed
cameras and a road layout that would give Spock
the night terrors—"it's so illogical Captain"—
driving around town is something to be avoided.
Combine this with over 7.5 million people who
just want to get from A to B without anyone
getting in their frickin' way, and you can see
where problems arise.

That said, there are times when a four-wheeler
is the only option, in which case the more you
know… To start, pedestrians can become an
infuriating lot, at least those who love striding
purposefully into the road with nary a thought
for their safety; keep a weather eye out, one
foot over the brake and one hand over the horn.
Then there are the cyclists, an ever-increasing
number—give them plenty of space and
remember for the one speedhound jumping
the lights there are hundreds of law abiders that
you just don't notice; for your own sanity, try to
focus on them. As for the mechanized obstacles,
remember that motorbikes and scooters are not
all ridden by leather-clad Hells Angels or Jamie
Oliver clones—most just want to get about and
avoid the Congestion Charge; as with cyclists,
give plenty of space and check your blind spots.
A special danger are the black cabs, those roving
London landmarks that have been known, on
occasion, to pull up to the curb, do a 'U-ie' and
even advertise the FT without sufficient warning.
And finally, a word about traffic wardens, which
are also known as 'council revenue generating
units': make sure you avoid illegal parking—
unless you are an ambassador. Fines are not
cheap.

Indeed, most of the stress caused by driving in
London, apart from the sheer volume of traffic,
is caused by lack of consideration for others—
usually as drivers are running late. So make sure
you leave PLENTY of time for your journey, try not
to block junctions, and let people out if you have
a chance. And try to avoid rush hour: remember
that morning rush lasts from 7 am to 10.30 am,
lunch rush from 11 am to 2.30 pm, school run
rush from 2.45 pm to 4.15 pm and afternoon rush
from 4.30 pm to 8.45 pm. Bonne chance…

Driving in the Congestion Charge Zone and the Low Emission Zone

The Congestion Charge Zone, introduced in 2003, is a surcharge for driving in Central London between 7 am and 6 pm Monday through Friday (except Bank Holidays). Huge red Cs in circles alert drivers to the start of the zone, if you miss them you should consider a swift visit to your optician. There is ongoing debate over the actual impact of the charge, although it has raised money for public transport.

The charge is £15 and there is no extra charge for driving in and out of the zone. Drivers who use the Congestion Charge Auto Pay (CCAP) system receive a £1 discount; Auto Pay keeps a tally of how many days a car was driven and charges your card at the end of the month. Drivers can pay in advance or by midnight on the day of travel. For £14 you have until midnight the following day to pay the charge. Payments are accepted by phone, online, by regular mail, and by text. Exemptions and discounts exist for motorbikes and residents living in or near the charge zone. Penalty charges are steep: £160 penalty charge (reduced to £80 if paid within 14 days).

The Low Emission Zone (LEZ) was introduced in February 2008 to deter everything from pickup trucks and van to buses, coaches and large lorries from dragging their belching exhausts through town. It covers a much larger area than the Congestion Charge: almost all of London within the M25 and applies 24/7. The charge varies between £100 and £200 a day. Best leave your concrete mixer at home.

Red Routes

The red double lines along a roadway indicate a "red route," part of the Transport for London Road Network (TLRN), and amounting to a special enforcement zone patrolled by Transport for London agents. No stopping rules are strictly enforced, as are yellow box junction infractions, banned turns, and unauthorized use of bus lanes. Although only five percent of London's roadways, the TLRN carries 30 percent of the city's traffic. As such the point of the oversight is to keep traffic moving. The rest of the roads are managed by local councils.

Key Roads

A1

Running straight north from St Paul's Cathedral in the City through Islington, Archway, Highgate and beyond, this old Roman Road has some freer stretches allowing the frustrated drive to accelerate to 43 mph for 3 seconds, get a speeding ticket and then slam on the brakes. Ends (eventually) in Princes Street, Edinburgh, Scotland.

North Circular/South Circular (A406)

This is the M25's angrier and twisted little brother. Circling Outer London it has some of the busiest stretches of road in London and even includes a ferry across the river at Woolwich. The way dwindles to one exhausted lane in certain sections, causing great clots of traffic every day in rush hour. See left for rush hour times.

Euston Rd/Marylebone Road (A501)

Running east-west past King's Cross and Euston, this wide road skirts the northern edge of the congestion zone. It gets very crowded, because it's a feeder road to the relatively breezy start of the A40 heading out of London.

Embankment

The view as you drive along the Embankment along the north bank of the Thames is breathtaking. It needs to be to keep you occupied as you inch forward for hours. Runs from Chelsea (A4) to Tower Bridge.

Vauxhall Bridge Rd/Grosvenor Place/Park Lane/Edgware Rd (A5)

Running roughly north-west from Vauxhall Bridge Rd, around Victoria, past Hyde Park Corner and Marble Arch and out to join the A40, this route is a free corridor through the Congestion zone—free from charge rather than free from traffic. Be prepared—it's rammed.

Old Kent Rd/New Cross Rd/Lewisham Way/etc. (A2/A20)

Running south-west from The Bricklayers Arms roundabout and eventually down to Dover, where you catch the ferry to France; the Old Kent Rd, despite being the cheapest Monopoly property, is totally free from traffic at all times. No wait—that can't be right.

A3

Starting at London Bridge, this road eventually ends up in Portsmouth, but you have to struggle past Elephant and Castle, Clapham Common and Wimbledon Common along with everyone else trying to get to Guildford.

Traffic Hot Spots

Angel, Elephant and Castle, Hanger Lane Gyratory, Vauxhall Gyratory, Trafalgar Square, Parliament Square, Hammersmith Gyratory, everywhere else.

Car Share

The great thing about being a Londoner is there's really no need to have a car. Except on those few occasions where you're cursing yourself for hauling a flat-packed Ikea coffee table on the shitty Croydon tram service. This is where joining a membership-based carsharing company, such as such as Zipcar (www.zipcar.com/en-gb or @ZipcarUK), Enterprise CarShare (www.enterprisecarshare.com or @carshare) or Hertz 24/7 (www.hertz247.com or @Hertz247). When you need to move the band, there's also Zipvan (www.zipvan.com).

The membership services are convenient and easy: self-service cars and vans billable by the hour, day, week or month. The vehicles are parked in town, which means you don't have to hike to a car rental centre, stand in a queue or deal with annoying upselling at a counter. Plus, if you get thrown out of your girlfriend's flat at 2 am and need a ride, you're in luck. After signing up for a modest membership fee (less than £100 a year), all you have to do is unlock the car with an entry card or fob, grab the keys from the glovebox and away you go. Cars have hourly rates (in general between £5–10 depending on the plan and type of vehicle) on top of the membership fee. Fuel and insurance are included.

General Information • **Calendar of Events**

January

- **New Year's Day Parade** • Big Ben to Piccadilly Circus • Marching bands and thousands of kids. How better to cure a hangover?
- **London Boat Show** • ExCel Exhibition Centre • Like we always say: you can never have too many yachts.
- **Russian Winter Festival** • Trafalgar Square • Magical Russian Winterland replaces the normal Pigeon-Crap Land.
- **London Art Fair** • Over 100 galleries and thousands of artists under one roof.
- **The London Bike Show** • ExCel Exhibition Centre • The best of the best of modern cycling equipment pandering to over-indulged cyclists.
- **London International Mime Festival** • Southbank Centre • Even weirder when you see it for real.
- **The London Outdoors Show** • ExCel Exhibition Centre • The country's biggest collection of outdoor goods—ironically hosted indoors.
- **Charles I Commemoration Ceremony** • Trafalgar Sq • St James' Palace • Thousands of uniformed Cavaliers confuse the tourists.
- **TNA Wrestling** • Wembley Arena • Strange men in spandex faux-fighting in front of drunken man-children.
- **Walking with Dinosaurs** • The O2 • Get your prehistoric freak on with twenty life-size dinosaurs (not literally) freaks!

February

- **British Academy Film Awards (BAFTA)** • Royal Opera House • Britain's finest film and television talent take a bow.
- **Chinese New Year** • West End • Party like it's 4707.
- **Destinations: Holiday and Travel Show** • Earls Court Exhibition Centre • Chase away the Winter Blues.
- **Live Tudor Cookery** • Hampton Court Palace • Glutinous Tudor food prepared in classic Tudor fashion. It's OK the New Year's

resolutions will be long dead by now.
- **London Fashion Week** • Somerset House • Far Too Thin.
- **National Wedding Show** • Olympia • Perfect day out for a first date.
- **Professional Beauty** • ExCel Exhibition Centre • Pay to get pretty with the latest developments in modern cosmetics.
- **Lifted** • Harrods • A bizarre annual exhibition inside Harrod's lifts.
- **The Great Spitalfields Pancake Race** • Old Truman Brewery • Pancake race in wacky clothes. No, London. Just, no.
- **Blessing the Throats** • St Ethelreda's Church, Ely Place • Lemsip not working? Sore throats cured by holy candle.
- **Clowns' Service** • Holy Trinity, Dalston • Because God likes clowns too.
- **Kinetica Art Fair** • P3• Carnivorous lampshades and pole-dancing robots? We're there.
- **BAFTAs** • London Palladium • Ten points per autograph.

March

- **Affordable Art Fair** • The Marquee, Battersea Park • Now even The Great Unwashed can buy art!
- **Affordable Art Fair** • The Marquee, Battersea Park • Now even The Great Unwashed can buy art!
- **Easter Egg Hunt** • Kew Garden's • Delightful Easter affair, perfect for the kids, don't forget to check out the animal farm.
- **Ideal Home Show** • Earls Court Exhibition Centre • Make your home ideal (or a bit less grotty).
- **St Patrick's Day Parade** • Park Lane • Shamrocks, river-dancing, big fluffy Guinness hats: true Irish tradition.
- **London Drinker Beer & Cider Festival** • The Camden Centre • Get rat-arsed on Pressed Rat & Warthog.
- **La Dolce Vita** • Business Design Centre • Get your sampling face on

- **Men's Afternoon Tea** • Mandeville Hotel • Because nothing is manlier than an exclusive tea, champagne and cake afternoon.
- **Move It** • Olympia • Put on your dancing shoes.
- **The International Food & Drink Event** • Olympia • This gorge-fest happens biannually, so start starving yourself now.
- **The Country Living Spring Fair** • Business Design Centre • For those with time for wooden chicken eggs
- **JobServe Live!** • Olympia • Career ideas and thousands of vacancies.

April

- **Cake International** • ExCel Exhibition Centre • Decorate and glutinously devour delicious cakes.
- **Oxford & Cambridge Boat Race** • River Thames • Hole up in a pub by the river and cheer over a beer.
- **Virgin London Marathon** • Greenwich – The Mall • 35,000 pairs of bleeding nipples.
- **London Book Fair** • Earl's Court • The publishing industry's main event. Occasionally stuff for free.
- **Alternative Fashion Week** • Old Spitalfields Market • Huge range of cutting edge fashion. And fetishwear.
- **Queen's Birthday Gun Salute** • Hyde Park • Who said the monarchy is archaic?
- **St George's Day** • Covent Garden / Cenotaph / Shakespeare's Globe • Brush up your Morris dancing skills.
- **The Real Food Festival** • Earl's Court Exhibition Centre • Real Food: much nicer than fake food
- **Hot Cross Bun Service** • St Bartholomew-the-Great, Smithfield • Widows get a free hot cross bun. Worth losing the husband.
- **London Independent Film Festival** • Various West and Central Cinemas • Cool celebration of cinematographic indieness without The Man. Or something.

May

- **Freedom of the City** • Central London • Frequently awesome improv and experimental festival attracting top names.
- **Baishakhi Mela** • Brick Lane • Celebrate the Bengali New Year in the British tradition: vindaloo.
- **Bathing the Buddha** • Leicester Square • Buddha gets a birthday bath.
- **Mind, Body, Spirit Festival** • Royal Horticultural Halls • Make up for all the time in the pub.
- **Camden Crawl** • Throughout Camden • If you're not crawling by the end, you haven't done it right.
- **Chelsea Flower Show** • Royal Hospital Chelsea • You'll go for the flowers. You'll stay for the Pimms.
- **Chelsea Flower Show** • Royal Hospital Chelsea • You'll go for the flowers. You'll stay for the Pimms.
- **Greenwich Beer & Jazz Festival** • Old Royal Naval College • An odd paring that somehow works.
- **London Pet Show** • Earls Court Two – The cute, odd, scary and weird bring their pets and show them off.
- **Sci-Fi Festival** • London Apollo • The UK's only Sci-Fi Festival. Thank god.
- **Interiors London** • ExCeL Centre • For those rich enough to treat their homes like art.
- **The Drag Olympics** • The Way Out Club • Drag Queens are put through their pedicured, high-heeled paces.

June

- **City of London Festival** • The City • Bringing High Culture to a bunch of bankers.
- **Field Day** • Victoria Park • A pseudo hippy music festival with a lighthearted vibe.
- **Start of Open Air Theatre season** • Regent's Park • Ignore the climate and take in an outdoor play.
- **Taste of London** • Regent's Park • The best picnic in the world.

- **Wimbledon** • All England Lawn Tennis and Croquet Club • Short skirts and grunting. Marvellous.
- **Trooping the Colour** • Horse Guard's Parade • Hundreds of chaps in uniforms. Ohhhhh yes.
- **Meltdown Festival** • Southbank Centre • Eclectic music festival curated by major musicians.
- **Royal Academy Summer Exhibition** • Royal Academy • Lots and lots and LOTS of art.
- **Arts Festival Chelsea** • Chelsea • The artists formerly known as 'The Chelsea Festival'.
- **Naked Bike Ride** • Hyde Park • Don't think about the bums on seats.
- **Polo in the Park** • Hurlingham Park • Its turbo-nah dahhling, pass the Pimms.
- **Shakespeare Globe Season** • • To be or not to on that is the question.

July

- **Dogget's Coat & Badge Race** • Thames; London Bridge to Chelsea • Intense boat race to win a badge. Hardly seems worth it.
- **Pimms Urban Regatta** • Finsbury Square • People full of Pimms race on land in bottomless boats. Bloody Ozzies.
- **Pride London** • Trafalgar Square • One of Britain's biggest, funnest street parties.
- **The British 10k London Run** • Hyde Park · Whitehall • Work off the pies.
- **Hampton Court Palace Show** • Hampton Court • Stock up your garden / flowerpot / imagination.
- **The Chap Olympiad** • Bedford Square Gardens • Olympics for gentleman—no sportswear please.
- **Uprise Festival** • Islington • Celebrating the best of multicultural London, for free.
- **Swan Upping** • River Thames • Census of swans. For goodness sake.
- **Opening of Buckingham Palace** • Buckingham Palace • The Plebeians allowed in to see how their taxes (and steep entrance fees) are spent.

- **Wireless Festival** • Hyde Park • Big names vibrate the Serpentine.
- **Shoreditch Festival** • Shoreditch. • Because you can never have too many local festivals. Apparently.

August

- **Innocent Smoothies Festival** • Regent's Park • You wouldn't think fun could be this wholesome.
- **Great British Beer Festival** • Earls Court Exhibition Centre • A festival that puts the Great in Britain.
- **Trafalgar Square Festival** • Trafalgar Square • 3 weeks of music, theatre, dance and art.
- **Carnaval del Pueblo** • Royal Victoria Docks • Thousands of Latino lovelies. That's all you need to know, right?
- **Camden Fringe** • Camden People's Theatre • Wonderfully weird, hilariously funny and light on the wallet.
- **London Triathlon** • Docklands • Marathons are for pussies.
- **London Mela** • Gunnersbury Park • Partaaaay, Asia-style.
- **Metro Weekender** • Clapham Common • Dance music Saturday, bands on Sunday, chilled all weekend.
- **Notting Hill Carnival** • Ladbroke Grove • Party till your wallet gets nicked.
- **Parliament Tour Season** • Westminster • Go see first hand where it all goes so wrong.
- **Kids Week** • West End • West End shows free for kids. Soooo unfaaaaiiiir.
- **Tiger Beer Singapore Chilli Crab Festival** • Truman Brewery • Cold beer, hot food and cool sounds.

September

- **The Great British Duck Race** • The Thames • Like the Oxbridge boat race. But with 165,000 rubber ducks.
- **Horseman's Sunday** • Hyde Park Crescent • London's horses say their Hail Maries. Yes, really.

General Information · **Calendar of Events**

- **Oyster & Seafood Fair** • Hays Galleria • The romance of oysters with the unholy stink of kippers.
- **Thames Festival** • Tower Bridge • Westminster • Fireworks, costumes, river races, carnivals. Kids like it.
- **Last Night of the Proms** • Royal Albert Hall • Camp overnight if you want tickets.
- **London Duathlon** • Richmond Park • It's like a triathlon… for people who can't swim.
- **London Tattoo Convention** • Old Truman Brewery • Who cares if it looks crap when you're 80?
- **Spitalfields Show & Green Fair** • Buxton Street • Who has the biggest marrow?
- **Open House Weekend** • Various around London • Over 600 architectural landmarks open for a nosey.
- **Fashion Week** • Summerset House • The September instalment of the famous frockfest.
- **Great Gorilla Run** • Start at London Underwriting Centre • Raise £400 for the Gorilla Organisation and the costume's yours.
- **Vintage Fashion Fair** • Primrose Hill • For those with a passion for vintage fashion.

October

- **The Big Draw** • Museum of Childhood • Pencils, not guns. Unfortunately.
- **Down Under Live** • Olympia • For those contemplating emigrating to warmer climes.
- **'Original Pearly Kings & Queens Association Harvest Festival** • Church of St Martin-in-the-Fields Affordable Art Fair.
- **International Halloween Festival** • Queen Mary College • Witches, druids and shamans unite for Europe's biggest Pagan festival.
- **Halloween** • London Dungeon • Trick Or Treating is for pussies.
- **Frieze Art Fair** • Regent's Park • Air kisses all round.

- **London Film Festival** • BFI Southbank • Two weeks of the best new films and lectures from A-Listers.
- **Metro Ski & Snowboard Show** • Olympia • London hosts the world's biggest winter sport show. Naturally.
- **Veolia Entertainment Wildlife Photographer of the Year (exhibition opens, for 6mths)** • Natural History Museum Puts your arty market photos to shame.
- **The Yoga Show** • Olympia • Bendy people upon bendy people. Literally.
- **Turner Prize Exhibition** • Tate Britain • Get to know the next Hirst or Emin.

November

- **London's Christmas Ice Rinks** • Venues across London • Much more romantic in your head than in reality.
- **Brighton Veteran Car Run** • Starts Hyde Park • Century-old bangers potter their way to Brighton.
- **Erotica Show** • Olympia • 31,000 horny adults pretend they're just browsing.
- **Barclays ATP World Tour Finals** • O2 Arena • Very rich tennis players make more money at this entertaining but unimportant tournament.
- **Bonfire Night** • Venues across London • Hundreds of thousands of pounds go pop.
- **Country Living Christmas Fair** • Business Design Centre • For those dreaming of a posh Christmas.
- **Royal British Legion Festival of Remembrance** • Royal Albert Hall • Take tissues.
- **Lord Mayor's Show** • Central London • Running for over 800 years and yet still a bit crap.
- **London Jazz Festival** • South Bank Centre • Start practising your jazz hands.
- **Winter Wonderland** • Hyde Park Grottos and Glühweins galore.

December

- **Satan's Grotto** • London Dungeon • Tortured elves and spit-roasting robins.
- **Trafalgar Square Christmas Tree** • Trafalgar Square • The only thing everyone knows about Oslo.
- **Aegon Masters Tennis** • Royal Albert Hall • Former World No.1s wheeze their way through a tournament.
- **Peter Pan Cup** • Serpentine Lido, Hyde Park • Freeze your nipples off on Christmas morning.
- **Great Christmas Pudding Race** • Covent Garden • We're mad, us! What are we like? Crazy!
- **Christmas Carol Sing-along** • Royal Albert Hall • Belt out your favourites and get in the mood.
- **Christmas Carol Sing-along** • Royal Albert Hall • Belt out your favourites and get in the mood.
- **Taste of Christmas** • ExCel Exhibition Centre • Tasty tips for making Christmas that little merrier.
- **Midnight Mass at St Paul's** • St Paul's • Eats the other Midnight Masses for breakfast.
- **New Year's Eve Fireworks** • Jubilee Gardens • Ooooooh. And, of course, aaaaaaah.

Tactics

Finding somewhere to live in London is a ruthless and cutthroat business. Make sure you have plenty of red bull, cigarettes and patience. However, places go in the blink of an eye so it's important to move quick. Take a week off and hire a driver, if you can.

Ok, so these precautions aren't completely necessary, but you will have to work in mysterious and multifarious ways if you don't want to spend the next six months paying through your gullible nose for mice and verrucas. A good place to start by harassing your friends, your friends' friends, and your friends' friends' friends. Send out a group email and hope it gets passed around and make sure you Tweet like mad about it. Twitter is a great place to get your request passed around. Who knows? Stephen Fry might have a room to let. Estate agents (see below for a list) will invariably try and rip you off but, then again, so will everyone else, so it's worth registering with all the big ones, as well as any where office you see in the street, or you spot in newspapers, on TV or the internet. After uncovering a fair few completely brazen lies in the property listings on www.gumtree.com you will find that many of the smaller businesses place adverts for (sometimes fake) properties here. Don't be put off by the lies though, because this can be a good way of finding an agent (or getting in direct contact with a landlord) who is keen to make a deal with you, or who will try and match the prices advertised, even if they have nothing that fits the bill at the exact moment of lying. Of course, some of these listings are also genuine, and a good way to find rooms/apartments at lower than usual rates. Just bare in mind that a LOT of people use this site.

General sites

www.gumtree.com
www.craigslist.org
www.rightmove.co.uk
www.spareroom.co.uk
www.zoopla.co.uk

Estate Agents

There are hundreds of Estate Agents and Letting Agents across the city, some of the larger players (good and bad) include:

www.keatons.com - Offices all over London.
www.blackkatz.com - Lettings only agency, numerous offices.
www.fjlord.co.uk - Numerous offices, specialise in uncooperative staff.
www.nelsonsales.com - South and central London.
www.atkinsonmcleod.com - City and Docklands.

If you do end up using an agent, they will of course want to charge you an additional fee beyond any deposits or advance rent required by the landlord. But, as many of the agents in central London are close together, it's possible that they may be competing with each other to sell/rent the same properties. This will enable you to get a better deal. So shop around, be devious, and backstab as much as possible.

Council Tax

Council Tax is an annoying hidden cost that always comes as a bit of a surprise. It is worked out by your local council and is based on the value of your house/flat, which the council will already have placed in to one of 8 tax bands (bands are A–G, G covering the most valuable properties).There are several ways to determine the value of a property, but the easiest is probably to go to the website of the valuation office at www. voa.gov.uk. Having done that, it's possible to weigh up the benefits of different areas by comparing the council tax in equivalent bands charged by different local councils. It's fairly laborious, but worth it in the long run, if you can be bothered.

Because council tax is based on the property, not the people inside it, the rate is constant no matter how many people live in the house. This means that it's much cheaper to live in a big house with lots of people to split the tax with, than on your own, when you are liable for the full amount. Students do not have to pay council tax at all, but if they are sharing with one or more non-students then there will still be council tax to pay. A single non-student in a house full of students receives a 25% discount on his/her council tax bill, but if there is more than one non-student then all non-students are liable to pay full whack.

Deposit Information

The deposit is the necessary bank drain of every new tendency agreement. Typically deposits range from one – three months rent in advance, but if you pay over a two-month deposit you are entitled to special privileges including the right to sublet your space. If you can't afford the financial outlay there are other options available to you; it is possible to get involved with the Deposit Guarantee Scheme (you will need to contact your local council for more information), or independent agencies offer a similar service for a 10% - 20% fee. While not all landlords in London are Ebenezer Scrooge pre hallucination-esque you'll still hear your fair share of horror stories. Make sure you use the Deposit Protection Scheme (DPS) www.depositprotection.com to protect your cash. For a comprehensive overview on deposit information and your rights visit the Direct Gov website at www.gov.uk.

Alternative Options

In a city where house prices have been soaring through it's roof for some time now (although it's calmed down somewhat recently), of course people do things like squat, have dreadlocks and go vegan. If you're not willing to go the whole way but fancy an adventure, or simply don't have much money, then it might be worth taking a look at being a guardian for Camelot. This company aims to fill vacant properties with responsible people who will prevent them from being abused. You must have good references, a job, and be over eighteen, as well as be ok with sharing with an indeterminate number of strangers, but the benefits are the unusual properties (e.g. schools, disused churches), the often large spaces and the ridiculously cheap rent (£25–60 pw inclusive of all bills). Of course loads of people want to do this and properties in London are not always available, but it's nevertheless a good idea to keep an eye on their site if the idea excites you: website: www.cameloteurope.com.

WAREHOUSES

As with Starbucks and obesity, us Brits have finally caught on to the American craze for warehouse 'live/work' spaces. Okay we may have had the likes of Tracey Emin and other artists living in old carpet factories since the YBA days, but recently a whole crop of established estate agents have been refurbishing lofts and factories for letting at a premium. Any established warehouser will tell you the way to go is independent, through enthusiastic urban explorers who renovate and convert these old buildings for love and enjoyment. Often the only way into this secret brotherhood of the leaky roof is by simply ending up at a huge party at 4am in one of these spaces and asking the residents politely. The freedom of living in these places can be exhilirating if you've spent years toeing the line with grumpy neighbours and grumpier landlords.

CANAL-BOATS

If all this land lubbing is bringing you down, there's always the option of dropping anchor at Little Venice or the Lea Valley Harbour and sampling London's canal networks. More and more skint artsy fartsy folk are squeezing their possessions into canal boats and living a romantic life on the water. A casual stroll down Regent's Canal may convince you this is the way to live, but bare in mind the hidden cons of London nautical life: mooring fees, fuel, unlit walks down leafy paths frequented by degenerates…Don't say we didn't warn you!

The Best of the Best

London is full of interactive children's pursuits, and nothing beats discovering all the joys that the city has to offer to the little ones, so we thought we'd give you some inside tips on what there is!

- **Best Rainy Day Activity:** The Science Museum (Exhibition Road, SW7 2DD, 0870 870 4868) is great fun and one of London's most interactive museums. Don't miss the Launchpad gallery, which is full of hands-on exhibits to tinker with, simulators and a face morphing machine. The museum's occasional Science Nights are activity filled, with overnight camping in the building included. Entry is free. Open 7 days a week from 10am to 6pm.

- **Coolest Cinema:** The BFI London IMAX Cinema (1 Charlie Chaplin Walk, SE1 8XR, 020 7902 1234) has the largest screen (20 metres) in the country, as well as an 11,600-watt digital surround sound system with which to deafen your children. With most of the cinema's 3D programming dedicated to children's films, they'll be spoilt rotten by the whole experience; even the entrance to the place is cool, with futuristic blue lighting paving your way through the tunnels.

- **Goriest Tourist Haunt:** The London Dungeon (The Queen's Walk, SE1 7PB, 033 3321 2001) specialises in the darker side of English history and has a preponderance of gruesome waxworks, theme rides and costumed staff to scare the bejesus out of your children, which they'll love (unless you've brought them up to be soft). Open all week from 11am to 5pm.

- **Best Tour For Budding Media Moguls:** The BBC Television Centre Tour (Wood Lane, W12 7RJ, 0870 603 0304) provides a chance for children 9 and over to take a behind the scenes look at the world of TV, as well as a chance to play in an interactive studio. A separate tour (ages 7 and over) entitled "The CBBC Experience" is based on the BBC's kids' channel and offers visitors the chance to roam around the Blue Peter garden, amongst other things. Regular tours are conducted every day except Sunday.

- **Best Ice Cream:** It's no secret that kids love ice cream, but the plethora of dodgy "Mr Whippy" vans selling their frozen wares in London can be improved upon. For outstanding homemade gourmet sorbets and exotic ice cream cones, there is no better place than the kiosk to the side of Golders Hill Park Refreshment House (North End Road, NW3 7HD, 020 8455 8010); prices are very reasonable and the park is a gorgeous setting within which to consume such tasty delights.

- **Best Inner City Farm:** Hackney City Farm (1a Goldsmiths Row, E2 8QA, 020 7729 6381). You don't want your child to be the one hiding on the bus on their first fieldtrip because they've never seen a cow. Hackney City Farm gives children and adults alike the chance to experience farming first-hand, interact with the animals and understand sustainable living, all of this in the heart of Hackney.

- **Best Eatery For Families:** Maxwell's (34 King St, WC2E 8JG) lies deep in the heart of Covent Garden and specialises in burgers (does any child not like burgers?) which won't break parents' banks. A kids' menu is provided, as well as activities and games.

Rainy Day Activities

Especially for when the infamous London weather puts a dampener on outdoor activities…

- **Cartoon Museum** (63 Wells St, W1A 3AE, 020 7580 8155) This fascinating place archives the development of cartoon art in Britain, from the 18th century through to the present day; best of all, the Young Artists' Gallery lets children try their hands at animation and claymation.

- **London Aquarium** (County Hall, Westminster Bridge Road, SE1 7PB, 020 7967 8000) One of the largest aquariums in the world, over 400 species of aquatic life (including the only zebra sharks in the U.K.) can be found within this building. With three floors, piranhas, and pools where you can prod things, there's more than enough to keep even the most jaded parent happy.

- **London Eye** (Jubilee Gardens, South Bank, SE1 7PB, 020 7967 8021) This 135-metre high riverside Ferris wheel offers breathtaking views of London in up to 25 miles in each direction, all from the vantage point of an air-conditioned glass pod. Book online to beat the queues.

- **Natural History Museum** (Cromwell Road, SW7 5BD, 020 7942 5000) Ever wanted to see a replica skeleton of a 26-metre long Diplodocus dinosaur? It's one of the 70 million items housed within this excellent museum, which also includes the Darwin Centre, a must for any budding paleontologists; non-nerds should love it too.

- **Madame Tussaud's** (Marylebone Road, NW1 5LR, 087 1894 3000) Infamous exhibition of waxworks, with recently introduced interactive exhibits giving you the chance to score a goal for England or sing with Britney Spears (she'll be the one lip-syncing). Worth booking online to avoid the often long queues.

- **Museum Of London** Currently closed but set to reopen in 2026 at Smithfield Market as the London Museum.

- **Peter Harrison Planetarium** (Royal Observatory Greenwich, Greenwich Park, SE10 9NF, 020 8312 6608) Open since 2007 and the only planetarium in London seats 120 and uses the latest technology to take you on an armchair tour of the universe. Children aged 4 and under will not be admitted.

- **Queens Ice And Bowl** (17 Queensway, W2 4QP, 020 7229 0172) An ice rink, ten pin bowling alleys and a pizza restaurant, it's the perfect opportunity for kids to stuff their faces whilst watching their Dad break a bone on the rink. Children's skating classes available.

- **Topsy Turvy World** (Brent Cross Shopping Centre, Prince Charles Drive, NW4 3FP, 020 8359 9920) A huge indoor playground in the middle of one of London's busiest shopping centres. There's more to this place than just bouncy things and over-excitement, it also offers baking activities (might as well get your children cooking for you early) and various classes.

- **Tower Of London** (Tower Hill, EC3N 4AB, 020 3166 6000) A cornucopia of royal history and English culture lies within the Tower's ancient walls, with royal jewels aplenty. Good for the whole family, and under 5s get in free. Avoid the queues by booking ahead.

- **Young V&A** (Cambridge Heath Road, E2 9PA, 020 8983 5200) This lesser known gem of the Victoria & Albert Museum houses the national childhood collection, which basically means it's full of toys, games, dolls, dollhouses, nursery antiques and children's costumes. There's no shortage of activities and events going on here to keep your kids occupied, and it's free.

Classes

A recent resurgence in the amount of out of school programmes being implemented in the capital means that there's more for your kids to do than ever before.

- **Art Club** (Orleans House Gallery, Riverside, TW1 3DJ, 020 8831 6000) A rare opportunity for 5-10 year olds to work with practicing artists and explore new techniques and materials. Every Wednesday and Thursday from 3.45-5pm.

- **Brixton Recreation Centre** (27 Brixton Station Road, SW9 8QQ, 020 7095 5100) Recently refurbished, this centre includes The Energy Zone (ages 5-15) for ball games and The Fitness Zone (ages 8-15) with SHOKK fitness equipment specifically designed for the younger body builder/steroid abuser.

- **Camden Square Play Centre** (Camden Square, NW1 9RE, 020 7485 6827) After school (and school holiday) centre with fun activities for children aged 4-12.

- **Camden Swiss Cottage Swimming Club** (Swiss Cottage Leisure Centre, Winchester Road, NW3 3NR, 020 7974 5440) Swimming lessons for children aged 4 and upward.

- **Chang's Hapkido Academy** (27 Blackfriars Rd, SE1 8NY, 07951 535876) Martial arts school with classes for ages 12 and upward.

- **The Circus Space** (Coronet Street, N1 6HD, 020 7613 4141) Prepare your children for a life in the circus with The Circus Space's variety of classes and workshops for all ages.

- **Crazee Kids** (Jackson Lane Community Centre, Archway Road, N6 5AA, Tuesdays), (Union Church & Community Centre, Weston Park, N8 9TA, Saturdays) 020 8444 5333, Weekly term-time dance, drama and music classes. Summer workshops.

- **Harringay Club** (Hornsey YMCA, 50 Tottenham Lane, N8 7EE, 020 8348 2124) A range of things to do for those aged up to 15, including a pre-school programme, gymnastics, ballet, street dance and kickboxing.

- **Kite Art Studios** (Priory Mews, 2B Bassein Park Road, W12 9RY, 020 8576 6278) Courses and workshops on painting, pottery and jewellery making amongst other fun activities for kids of all ages. Mother and toddler sessions too.

- **London Irish Centre** (50-52 Camden Square, NW1 9XB, 020 7916 7222) Irish dancing classes for beginners upwards, every Monday at 6pm, courtesy of the Barrett Semple-Morris School.

- **The Little Angel Theatre** (14 Dagmar Passage, Cross Street, N1 2DN, 020 7226 1787) Children's theatre offering after-school courses in puppet making, the art of puppetry performance and a Saturday Puppet Club.

- **The Little Gym** (Compass House, Riverside West, Smugglers Way, SW18 1DB, 020 8874 6567) Gymnastics and skills development within a relaxed environment for children aged up to 12.

- **Music House For Children** (Bush Hall, 310 Uxbridge Road, W12 7LJ, 020 8932 2652) Whether it's instrumental or singing lessons, this wonderful place can provide individual and group tuition and even caters for 1 year olds!

- **Painted Earth** (Arch 65, The Catacombs, Stables Market, NW1 8AH, 020 7424 8983) Ceramic arts classes supervised by staff. Children can make their own mugs and plates.

- **Pirate Castle** (Oval Road, NW1 7EA, 020 7267 6605) Kids can canoe or Kayak around Camden's only castle at this outdoor adventure club, which moonlights as a school and youth services centre.

- **Richmond Junior Chess Club** (ETNA Community Centre, 13 Rosslyn Road, TW1 2AR, 07720 716336) Chess classes with a mixture of instruction and play for those up to the age of 18.

- **Sobell Leisure Centre** (Hornsey Road, N7 7NY, 020 7609 2166) No need to book, just turn up for coached sessions in basketball, badminton, football and ice hockey amongst other sports. Children aged 7 and under must be accompanied by an adult.

- **Tricycle Theatre** (269 Kilburn High Road, NW6 7JR, 020 7328 1000) Not just a theatre/cinema/gallery, the Tricycle also runs term-time workshops in drama, storytelling and music.

- **Triyoga** (57A Jamestown Road, NW1 7DB, 020 7483 3344) Let the kids get their Zen on at after school yoga classes for ages 5 and over.

Babysitting/Nanny Services

- **Nannies Unlimited** 11 Chelveton Road, SW15 1RN, 020 8788 9640

- **Nanny Search** 1st Floor, 1 Shepherds Hill, N6 5QJ, 020 8348 4111

- **Sleeptight Nannies** 20 Nursery Road, N14 5QB, 020 8292 2618

- **Top Notch Nannies** 1st Floor, 85 Great Portland St, W1W 7LT, 020 7101 4232

Where to Go for More Info

www.dayoutwiththekids.co.uk

Shopping Essentials

- **Balloonland** 12 Hale Lane, NW7 3NX, 020 8906 3302 – Balloons and party supplies.

- **Benjamin Pollock's Toyshop** 44 The Piazza, Covent Garden WC2E 8RF, 020 7379 7866 – Toys.

- **Bonpoint** Chic clothes.
  197 Westbourne Grove, W11 2SE – 020 7792 2515
  256 Brompton Road, SW3 2AS – 020 3263 5057
  400 Oxford St, W1A 1AB – 020 7499 6952
  52 Marylebone High St, W1U 5HR – 020 7487 2512
- **Burberry** 21-23 New Bond Street, W1S 2RE, 020 7980 8425 – Clothes.
- **Caramel** 291 Brompton Road, SW3 2DY, 020 7589 7001 – Cool clothes.
- **Children's Book Centre** 237 Kensington High Street, W8 6SA, 020 7937 7497 – Books.
- **Disney Store** – Disney merchandise.
  350-352 Oxford St, W1C 1JH – 020 7491 9136
- **The Farmyard** 63 Barnes High Street, SW13 9LF, 020 8878 7338 – Toys for younger children and babies.

- **Hamley's** 188-196 Regent Street, W1B 5BT, 020 7153 9000 – Toys galore, tourists galore.
- **Happy Returns** 36 Rosslyn Hill, NW3 1NH, 020 7435 2431 – Toys again!
- **International Magic** 89 Clerkenwell Road, EC1R 5BX, 020 7405 7324 – Magic shop.
- **Little Stinkies** 15 Victoria Grove, W8 5RW, 020 7052 0077 – Dolls' houses, toys and puppet theatres.

- **Patrick's Toys & Models** 107 Lillie Road, SW6 7SX, 020 7385 9864 – Outdoor games and equipment.

- **Patrizia Wigan** 91 Brick Lane, E1 6QL, 020 3051 7933 – Clothing boutique.

- **QT Toys** 90 Northcote Road, SW11 6QN, 020 7223 8637 – Toys, games and gifts.

- **The Shoe Station** 12 Station Parade, TW9 3PZ, 020 8940 9905 – Shoes and footwear.

- **So Tiny London** 64 Titchfield Street, W1W 7QH, 020 7636 2501 – Funky children's clothes.

- **Soup Dragon** 27 Topsfield Parade, Tottenham Lane, N8 8PT, 020 8348 0224 – Toys and clothes.

- **Trotters Childrenswear** 84 Turnham Green Terrace, W4 1QN, 020 8742 1195 – Clothes boutique.

- **Tulip & Nettle** 53 Godfrey St, SW3 3SX, 020 7349 8829 – Children's clothes.

For many, the Internet is *the* key to the city. Before the dawning of the Internet, we Dickensian scamps had to scurry around in the filth foraging for information in 'books' and by talking to actual 'people'. Now that the future is here, Londoners can navigate their city's streets, explore its dark history, organise a debauched weekend in Chiswick or, as is more likely, peer over the shoulder of men in raincoats in Internet Cafes.

Internet Cafes are everywhere. In fact you probably live in one. They can range from the dimly lit 'Money Transfer' shacks that have an air of illegality, to chains that dominated the market before home internet use skyrocketed in the late 90s. To be fair, internet use in these places is usually criminally cheap: as low as 50p per hour in the non-tourist areas. For a large list of London internet cafes check out: www.allinlondon.co.uk/directory/1166.php.

London was one crowned WiFi capital of the world, owing to its astronomical rate of increase in WiFi networks in 2007. Today, it is difficult to move in your local cafe without catching the edge of a laptop. An alternative to those of you who have joined the growing legion of smartphone users and don't want the commitment of a long-term contract try **Gifgaff** (www.giffgaff.com). For £10 you can get 250 minutes, unlimited texts and unlimited data for a month with no additional cost incurred. They offer a best in business rate for the Internet addicts among you.

Useful and/or Fun London Links

www.royalparks.org.uk
www.tfl.gov.uk
www.londonist.com
www.onlondon.co.uk/author/onlondon
www.shadyoldlady.com
www.derelictlondon.com
www.hidden-london.com/
www.london-underground.blogspot.com
www.twitter.com/ifancyapint
www.gumtree.com
www.timeout.com
www. wildinlondon.blogspot.com
www. westlondonblogger.blogspot.com
www. dalstonoxfamshop.blogspot.com
www.londonreviewofbreakfasts.blogspot.com
www.beerintheevening.com
www.london-se1.co.uk
londoncabby.blogspot.com

The doom-sayers have less cause to complain about the decline of Gayhood in London recently, what with **Heaven** (London's self-proclaimed most famous gay club) hanging on and new nights popping up everywhere. Yes, popular indie disco **Rebel Rebel** has relocated but we are so in love with 'polysexual' club **Dalston Superstore** at the moment. Of course every time one door (read: gay club) closes another one opens, and let's face it, the latter will probably open later and sell you even cheaper Red Bull and vodka.

One of the most exciting developments in the past few years has been the advent of what has been dubbed London's new 'Gay Village'—the cluster of clubs, saunas and after-hours hangover incubators that have sprung up in Vauxhall. Now it's possible, though still just as inadvisable, to party from Thursday through to Monday without stopping to reapply deodorant, or think about the consequences of what you're doing—hooray. The small outcrop of gay and 'polysexual' nights in the East End, is still thriving, and offers another refreshing alternative to Soho for those in search of an aggressive fashion consciousness and a less cruisy atmosphere. This said, if you can handle bright lights, pop music, tight t-shirts and a lot of hair gel, you'll still have massive amounts of fun around Soho and Old Compton Street, the traditional central London gay epicentre. This area is always buzzing, day and night, and is a great place to sit back and do some people watching as well as to go out and, y'know, go crazy.

For girls there is still room for improvement, with options fewer and less centralised, but **The Minories'** new Girls' night is a blast and the continuing women-only nights at **Village** is cause for celebration. Many mixed and polysexual nights also draw large female crowds, and though dedicated lesbian bars and clubs are few and far between, there is enough going on in the city to make any day of the week a possible night out.

Websites

http://scene-out.com - Comprehensive mainstream scene guide.
www.gingerbeer.co.uk - Lesbian guide to London.

www.gmfa.org.uk - Gay men's health charity.
www.patroc.com/london/clubs.html-Great source for upcoming gay events.

Publications

The following are all free listings/scene magazines that can be found in most gay shops and venues (anywhere on Old Compton Street should have some copies lying around!)

Boyz Magazine - Weekly scene news and listings, out Thursdays. www.boyz.co.uk

Qx Magazine - Gay men's mag. www.qxmagazine.com

Shops

Gay's the Word, 66 Marchmont Street, WC1N 1AB, 020 7278 7654, www.gaystheword.co.uk/, The only dedicated Gay and Lesbian Bookshop in London, recently threatened by rising rent. Visit whilst it's still there!

Prowler, 5–7 Brewer Street, W1F 0RF, 020 7734 4031, The ultimate gay men's shop, stocking everything from (skimpy) clothes to sex toys plus mountains of lube, pornography, and the other usual suspects.

Sh! Women's Erotic Emporium, 35 Pitfield St, N1 6HB, 033 3444 4005, http://www.sh-womenstore.com/, London's only female-orientated sex shop, run by women, for women.

Sexual Health

A comprehensive list of London clinics that offer same day HIV testing and PEP treatments for gay/bisexual men is available at www.lgbthero.org.uk/pages/category/gmfa. CLASH, on the next page, is particularly recommended.

CLASH (Central London Action on Street Health), 11 Warwick Street, W1B 5NA, 020 7734 1794, Friday night clinic for gay men, with incredibly friendly staff who will offer comfort and advice. Same day (often instant) HIV testing, PEP treatment. Fridays, 5 - 8.30pm, call for an appointment.

Support Organizations

Again, a more comprehensive list can be found at the GMFA website: www.gmfa.org.uk/londonservices/support-groups/index

Stonewall, 192 St John St, EC1V 4JY, 020 7593 1850, www.stonewall.org.uk, Gay rights charity and lobbying group.

PACE Youthwork Service, Camden Square Play Centre, Murray St, NW1 9RE, www.paceforall.com/, Support organization for gay and lesbian youths under 25. Organizes regular social events and offers one to one consultations with advisors: phone or visit the website to get involved.

London Friend, 86 Caledonian Road, N1 9DN, 020 7833 1674, www.londonfriend.org.uk, Voluntary organization which runs several helplines, group workshops and social events, as well as offering advice on reporting hate crime.

London Lesbian and Gay Switchboard, 0300 330 0630, www.switchboard.lgbt/about-us/, Counselling and information service.

Naz Project London, 30 Black's Rd, W6 9DT, 020 8741 1879 www.naz.org.uk, Charity that organizes support and sexual health services for black and ethnic minority communities in London. Various services, including free one-on-one counselling and support groups are available, phone or check website for details.

GALOP, 356 Holloway Rd, N7 6PA, 020 7697 4081, www.galop.org.uk, Charity specialising in advice about reporting hate crime.

Annual Events

Pride London, www.prideinlondon.org/, Large pride festival, takes place every July.

GFEST – www.gaywisefestival.org.uk, London's premier cross-arts festival, GFEST features a variety of established and new LBG&T artists. The festival promotes the queer arts scene while keeping LBGT human rights the underlying focus of proceedings.

London Lesbian and Gay Film Festival, www.bfi.org.uk/llgff, Film festival at the BFI on South Bank, March–April.

London LGBT History Month, www.lgbtplushistorymonth.co.uk/, Nationwide awareness month, with various talks and events staged in London, every February.

Gay/Mixed Venues

Soho:

The Admiral Duncan, 54 Old Compton Street, W1D 4UB, 020 7437 5300

Comptons, 53–57 Old Compton Street, W1D 6HN, 020 7096 5470, Crammed gay pub.

Duke of Wellington, 77 Wardour Street, W1D 6QA

G-A-Y Bar, 30 Old Compton Street, W1D 5JX, 020 7494 2756, Poptastic bunker. Video walls and cheap drinks.

G-A-Y Late, 5 Goslett Yard, WC2H 0ER, 020 7437 0479, Cheap drinks and pop videos wipe out brain functions 'til 3am.

Halfway to Heaven, 7 Duncannon Street, WC2N 4JF, 020 7484 0736.

Heaven, Under the Arches, Villiers Street, WC2N 6NG, 020 7930 2020, Legendary gay club. An institution.

Ku Bar, 30 Lisle Street, WC2H 7BA, 020 7437 4303, Newly relocated bar for the young and clueless.

The Village, 81 Wardour Street, W1D 6QD, 020 7478 0530, Tacky, flirtatious bar spread across two floors.

North:
Central Station, 37 Wharfdale Road, N1 9SD, 020 7278 3294. Pub/club with ominously blacked out windows.

East:
Bistrotheque, 23–27 Wadeson Street, E2 9DR, Jonny Woo's restaurant, great food and drag acts.
The Black Horse, 40 Leman St, E1 8EU, 020 7488 1406

South:
Eagle London, 349 Kennington Lane, SE11 5QY, 020 7793 0903
Fire, South Lambeth Road, SW8 1RT, 020 3242 0040, The quintessential Vauxhall club. Open pretty much forever, bulging muscles everywhere.
Royal Vauxhall Tavern, 372 Kennington Lane, SE11 5HU, 020 7820 1222
The Two Brewers, 114 Clapham High Street, SW4 020 7819 9539
Union Nightclub, 66 Albert Embankment, SE11 7TP, Sister club of Area, with a more cruisy vibe.

Recommended Nights

DTPM, www.ra.co/promoters/63941, Legendary event, no longer with a fixed location. See site for details of upcoming parties.
Horsemeat Disco, Sundays @ Eagle London, Italo and 70s Disco bring all sorts to this fantastic night, originally a bear love club.
Matinee, monthly (check site) @ Fabric, 77a Charterhouse Street, EC1M 3HN, 020 7335 8898, www.fabriclondon.com, Irregular gay night at this enormous club in Farringdon.
Trailer Trash, Fridays @ Basing House, 25 Kingsland Road, E2 8AA, 020 7688 0339, The dirtiest electro and the drunkest you've ever been. Crammed with sweating fashionistas.

Lesbian Venues

The Star At Night, 22 Great Chapel Street, Soho, W1 8FR, 020 7494 2488, Mixed cocktail bar with a predominantly female crowd.

Recommended Nights

100% Babe, Bank Holiday Sundays @ The Roxy, 3 Rathbone Place, W1P 1DA, 020 7255 1098, Irregular party for fans of funky house, R&B, old skool and electropop.

Girls on Girls, Wednesdays @ Village, 81 Wardour Street, W1D 6QD, 020 7478 0530

Play, irregular night @ Bar Rumba, 35 Shaftesbury Ave, W1D 7EP, 020 7287 6933, www.barrumbalondon.com/

Rumours, last Saturday of the month @ The Minories, 64 Minories, EC3N 1JL, 020 7703 1658

Stickier Options

Club Fukk, second Fridays @ Central Station, 37 Wharfdale Road, N1 9SD, 020 7278 3294, www.centralstation.co.uk or www.woteverworld.com/id12.html, Predominantly Lesbian fetish/play club. One of many sex/cruising nights at the venue – check site for details.

Hard On, monthly @ Union Nightclub, 66 Albert Embankment, SE1 7TW, www.hardonclub.co.uk, Rubber and fetish sex club for gay and bisexual men and women.

Nudity, first Fridays @ Hidden, Union Nightclub, 66 Albert Embankment, SE1 7TW, Nude men's dance/play club.

Sailors, 574 Commercial Rd, E14 7JD, 020 7791 2808, Gay sauna.

London Timeline

A timeline of significant events in London's history.

50: The Romans found Londinium, building the first London Bridge.

61: Queen Boudicca burns Londinium down.

100: Londinium becomes the capital of Roman Britain.

200: The Romans build the London Wall.

410: Roman occupation ends and Londinium is largely abandoned for many years.

604: King Aethelbert of Kent completes the first St Paul's Cathedral.

700: The Saxons build Lundenwic a mile to the west of old Londinium.

851: The Vikings burn Lundenwic down (starting to see a pattern, here?)

878: Alfred The Great defeats the Vikings and establishes a new settlement within the Roman Walls.

1013: The Viking King Canute besieges London.

1066: William The Conqueror becomes the first king to be crowned at Westminster Abbey.

1088: William The Conqueror builds the Tower Of London.

1097: William Rufus builds Westminster Hall—later part of the Houses Of Parliament.

1176: The wooden London Bridge is replaced by a stone structure.

1343: 'The Canterbury Tales' author Geoffrey Chaucer is born in London.

1348: The Black Death wipes out between a third and half of London's population in 18 months.

1381: Peasants revolt, storming the Tower Of London.

1599: William Shakespeare's theatre company The Chamberlain's Men build the Globe Theatre.

1605: Guy Fawkes' Gunpowder Plot fails to blow up the Palace Of Westminster.

1635: Hyde Park opens to the public.

1649: King Charles I is beheaded at Whitehall.

1665: The Great Plague kills a fifth of London's population (starting to see another pattern, here?)

1666: The Fire of London destroys 60% of the city, including St Paul's Cathedral, but wipes out the plague. This really must have been a great year.

1708: The new St Paul's Cathedral is completed by Sir Christopher Wren.

1732: Downing Street becomes the home of the Prime Minister.

1750: Westminster Bridge is built.

1814: Lord's Cricket Ground is opened.

1829: Robert Peel establishes the Metropolitan Police force, policemen known as 'Bobbies' or 'Peelers'.

1831: London becomes the world's biggest city.

1834: The Houses Of Parliament are built.

1843: Nelson's Column is completed in Trafalgar Square.

1851: Six million people gawp at newfangled technology and design at The Great Exhibition.

1858: The Great Stink inspires the 19th century's biggest civil engineering project—London's sewerage system.

London Timeline

1863: The first London Underground line is built.

1876: The Albert Memorial to Queen Victoria's husband Prince Albert is completed.

1877: The first Wimbledon Championship takes place. A Brit wins, but only Brit's are playing.

1884: An imaginary line through Greenwich Royal Observatory is internationally accepted as the Prime Meridian. Except by the French.

1887: Arthur Conan Doyle publishes the first Sherlock Holmes story 'A Study In Scarlet.'

1888: Jack The Ripper's first victim, Mary Ann Nichols, is murdered.

1908: London hosts the Olympics for the first time.

1915: German Zeppelin airships launch first air raids on London, ultimately killing over 700 people.

1923: Wembley Stadium is built in 300 days, costing £750,000.

1940: The Blitz begins—German bombs kill over 30,000 Londoners by the end of WW2 and destroy large areas of the city.

1946: Heathrow Airport opens for commercial flights.

1948: The second London Olympics is held.

1951: The Royal Festival Hall is built as part of the Festival Of Britain.

1952: The Great Smog, caused by a combination of fog and coal smoke, kills 4000 people in five days.

1956: The Clean Air Act puts an end to London's smog problems.

1965: The Notting Hill Carnival is established by West London's Caribbean community

1966: England win the FIFA World Cup at Wembley stadium, better still, against Germany.

1969: The Beatles play their last ever gig on the roof of the Apple building.

1976: The Sex Pistols play at the first 'International Punk Festival' at the 100 Club on Oxford Street.

1981: The first London Marathon.

1983: Six people are killed when the IRA bombs Harrods.

1991: London's tallest building, One Canada Square (better known as Canary Wharf), is completed.

2000: Ken Livingstone becomes London's first directly-elected Mayor.

2005: 52 people are killed by four suicide bombers on Underground trains and a bus.

2007: The rebuilt Wembley Stadium is completed after four years, costing £778 million.

2008: Boris Johnson defeats Red Ken in the London Mayoral Election with a promise to re-instate the Routemaster.

2011: Royal Wedding mania.

2012: London's third Olympics held; Danny Boyle adapts NHS as West End spectacular.

2012: Queen Elizabeth II celebrates her Diamond Jubilee with a rainy-day boat show.

2013: Prince George of Cambridge born.

London is an egotist—it just *loves* to talk about itself. As you might expect, there's a vast array of print and online publications, not to mention radio stations, designed to let the city do exactly that. Single-handedly forcing the environmental movement back twenty years are freebie dailies **The Metro** and the more fiscally orientated **City A.M.** Free weeklies to look out for include **Stylist** on Wednesday's for girls and **ShortList** on Thursday's for boys. The Aussies are pushing **TNT** at tube stations on Monday, but it lacks the wider appeal. A newer addition to the freesheet line-up is the substantial **Evening Standard**, which went free in January 2009, and is the preferred news-roundup du jour of suburbanites and city types alike, if only for the sudoku and quick crossword puzzles. Online, **www.thisislocallondon.co.uk** condenses forty local newspapers into 'one online voice. On the wireless, **Capital** croon nonstop an irksome parade of popular hits and frenetic DJs, whilst **Heart** and **Magic** corner the market on lip-trembling power ballads, mid-paced chart rock and wacky quizzes. All of the British Broadcasting Corporation's national radio stations—including the snazzy, young(ish) **Radio 1** and ovaltine-drinkers' choice **Radio 2**—are based in London, as is (surprisingly) **BBC London**, a decent option for weekend sports coverage. Cooler, urban types are more likely to be tuning into **Kiss FM** (dance, hip hop), **Smooth FM** (jazz, soul) or **Choice** (dancehall, roots), while alternative rockers tune their dials anguishedly to **XFM**, and the talkative indulge in unreserved subjectivity over at **LBC**. Of course, the undisputed king of alternative London broadcasting is Resonance FM, a 'community run' station. Expect everything from 'Calling All Pensioners' to live psycho-geographic wanders around city's warped dark streets. Un-licensed and illegal pirate radio stations offer a slightly un-hinged ear into the fringes of London's musical society. Twiddle your dials around the extreme ends of the FM spectrum for pirate stalwarts **Rude FM** and **Kool FM**. On the telly-box, the latest news is spoon-fed to you on ITV's **London Tonight** show and delivered in short slots at the end of the BBC and ITV national news programs. For those actually risking going outside, **Time Out** remains the socialite's sacred text.

Print

The Evening Standard Northcliffe House, 2 Derry Street, W8 5TT, 020 7938 6000, Newly reinstated as a freesheet, it continues to be London's favourite journey home read.

Metro Northcliffe House, 2 Derry Street, W8 5TT, 020 7651 5200, Free underground daily from same stable.

City AM 130 Fenchurch St, EC3M 5DJ, 020 3201 8900, Free morning business bulletin for city-goers.

TimeOut London 172 Drury Ln, WC2B 5QR, 0207 813 3000, Listings & reviews across the city. Pretty damned comprehensive.

London Gazette PO Box 3584, NR7 7WD, 033 3200 2434, Capital's oldest paper—official journals record of the government.

The London Magazine 11 Queen's Gate, SW7 5EL, 020 7584 5977, Bi-monthly Arts reviews.

TNT London 14a St, RL EC1V 2NY, 020 8050 4546, Info and opinion for the antipodean set.

Loot 114 Strand, WC2R 0AG, 020 8900 4331, Classifieds: flats, bought/sold and lonely hearts.

The Voice GV Media Group Ltd, Northern & Shell Tower, 6th Floor, 4 Selsdon Way, E14 9GL, 020 7510 0340, African-British national.

Polish Express 40 Bloomsbury Way, WC1A 2SE, 020 8190 0441, News and info for the Polish community.

Live Listings Magazine Keith Villa (House), 102 Mallinson Rd, SW11 1BN, 020 7207 2734, Guide to what's on in multicultural London.

ShortList 4 Prince Albert Rd, NW1 7SN, 020 7242 5873, A Thursday freebie for metrosexuals.

Stylist 185 Fleet St, EC4A 2HS, 020 7400 1036, London's first free women's glossy. Handed out on Wednesdays.

Public Radio

FM

89.1 BBC Radio Two: Middle-aged music and chat.
91.3 BBC Radio Three: Classical.
93.5 BBC Radio Four: Current affairs, comfort listening.
94.9 BBC London: Chat, sport.
95.8 Capital FM: Chart, capers.
96.9 Choice FM: Hip Hop, R&B.
97.3 LBC: Phone in, chat.
98.8 BBC Radio 1: Pop, rock, more pop.
100.0 Kiss FM: Dance, urban.
100.9 Classic FM: Classical.
102.2 Smooth FM: Jazz, soul.
102.6 Essex FM: Audible in East London.
103.3 London Greek Radio: Um, Greek.
103.5 BBC Essex: Audible out East.
104.4 Resonance FM: Always bizzare,
always brilliant.
104.9 Xfm: Alternative, rock.
105.4 Magic: Pop, slush.
105.8 Virgin Radio: Pop, rock.
106.2 Heart: Chart, pop.
106.6 Time: West London only.
107.3 Time: South East London only.

AM

252 Atlantic: Rock.
558 Spectrum International: Multi-ethnic.
648 BBC World Service: Global.
720 BBC Radio Four: Spoken word.
909 BBC Radio Five Live: Sport, phone in.
963 Liberty Radio: 70s, 80s pop.
1035 Ritz: Country.
1089 talkSPORT: Sports phone in.
1152 LBC News: News, weather.
1215 Virgin Radio: Pop, rock.
1305 Premier Radio: Christian.
1458 Sunrise: Asian.
1548 Capital Gold: Rock 'gold', sport.
1584 London Turkish Radio: Turkish community.

Essential London Books

The Diary of Samuel Pepys (1825): Samuel Pepys: eyewitness accounts of the Restoration, Great Plague and Fire of London from noted sixteenth century scribbler.

Oliver Twist; Hard Times; Great Expectations (1837, 1854, 1860): Charles Dickens: any Dickens novel paints Victorian London at its most exacting.

The Strange Case of Dr. Jekyll and Mr. Hyde (1886): Robert Louis Stevenson: the book that enthralled a city unnerved by Jack the Ripper.

The Adventures of Sherlock Holmes; The Hound of the Baskervilles (1892): Arthur Conan Doyle: classic whodunits featuring Holmes and Watson.

The Inimitable Jeeves (1923): P.G. Wodehouse: prewar upper-class tomfoolery in London Town.

Mrs Dalloway (1925): Virginia Woolf If you know London, you can follow Clarissa Dalloway every step of the way – in real time.

Londinium: London in the Roman Empire, John Morris (1982): London's rise from a Roman outpost into a debauched medieval mecca.

V For Vendetta (1982-1989): Alan Moore, The world's greatest comic writer blows up London in a fit of Anarchist fantasies.

London Fields (1989): Martin Amis: post-modern jaunt through London at the end of the millennium.

London – The Biography, and **Illustrated London** (2000): Peter Ackroyd: definitive, eight hundred page mother lode of remarkable city history, and lavish pictorial version.

London's Disused Underground Stations (2001): JE Connor: documenting forgotten, ghostly tube stations beneath the pavements.

London Orbital and Hackney That Rose Red Empire (2002): Iain Sinclair: London's premier scribe continues to fill our brains with joy despite being ripped off by devotee Peter Ackroyd.

The Clerkenwell Tales (2003): Peter Ackroyd: corking murder mystery set in the time of Chaucer.

Brick Lane (2003): Monica Ali: award winning coming-of-age tale centred on Brick Lane's Muslim community.

Art Deco London (2003): Colin Michael Hines: Wistful but enjoyable stroll around London's Art Deco heritage.

Intimate Adventures of a London Call Girl (2005): Belle de Jour: steamy, real-life shenanigans ahoy.

From Here to Here (2005): Simmons, Taylor, Lynham, Rich: 31 top notch short stories about Circle Line destinations, includes Simon Armitage.

Secret London: Exploring the Hidden City, with Original Walks and Unusual Places to Visit (2006): Andrew Duncan: an explorer's dream.

The London Bombings: An Independent Inquiry (2006): Nafeez Mosaddeq Ahmed: balanced, subtle overview of 2005 Underground bombings.

Around London with Kids   60 Great Things to See and Do (3rd edition; 2006): Eugene Fodor: should keep the little rascals from breaking into cars.

I Never Knew That About London (2007): Christopher Winn: Well, did you?

The London Encyclopaedia (2008): Ben Weinreb and Christopher Hibbert: London's history and culture documented in minutest detail

Derelict London (2008): Paul Talling: The urban explorers' bible!

Essential London Songs

Lambeth Walk, Noel Gay/Douglas Furber (1937): All together! *Doing the Lambeth Walk!* Oi!

A Nightingale Sang in Berkeley Square, Judy Campbell (1940): Wartime cheer made famous by Vera Lynn.

London Pride, Sir Noel Coward (1941): Written during the Blitz, this sensational ballad gave comfort to Londoners being bombed nightly.

Maybe It's Because I'm a Londoner, Hubert Gregg (1944): Pearly Queen favourite crammed with WWII spirit.

A Foggy Day (In London Town), Ella Fitzgerald (1956): Definitive recording of Gershwin classic.

Waterloo Sunset, The Kinks (1967): Timeless paean to the nation's capital.

Consider Yourself, Lionel Bart (1968): Oliver Twist hoodwinked into a life of crime by the Artful Dodger, the rascal.

Primrose Hill, John and Beverly Martyn (1970). Folk rock's ▓▓▓▓▓▓ ▓▓▓▓▓▓ ▓▓▓▓ ▓▓▓ ▓▓ ▓▓ ▓▓▓ Nick Drake and Kate Moss they were watching the sun set, did they?

Streets Of London, Ralph McTell (1974). Cool folk dude destroys credibility forever with international monster hit.

Baker Street, Gerry Rafferty (1978): Feel that sax line, air that guitar.

London Calling, The Clash (1979): Joe Strummer paints an apocalyptic vision of a city in post-punk London.

Electric Avenue, Eddy Grant (1983): Roots-rock champion name checks 80s Brixton scene.

London, The Smiths (1983): Morrissey lugubriously debates a trip south. Miserable shite.

West End Girls, Pet Shop Boys (1986): East London working class meets West London affluence in electro-pop classic.

Pump Up London, Mr. Lee (1988). Squelchy Chicago House dude makes London sound amazing whilst name checking every British town he can think of: Leeds! Manchester! Scatland!

Parklife, Blur (1994): Home counties-boys get cockney makeover while eyeing London's jogging scene.

Sunny Goodge Street, Donovan (2002). Folk crooner sings of a hippy London goneby.

The London Underground Song, Amateur Transplants (2005): Sweary, infectiously catchy and a comical ballad to the tube, rings painfully true.

Sheila, Jamie T (2006): Mr. T delivers an excellent poetic diatribe on what being young and hopeless in London is like.

Hometown Glory, Adele (2007): This song will make you fall in love with the city all over again.

Essential London Films

The 39 Steps (1935): Hitchcock adaptation of John Buchan novel.

Pygmalion (1938): Leslie Howard as Henry Higgins and Wendy Hiller as Eliza Doolittle prove Shaw's classic comedy does very well without music.

Great Expectations (1946): Rare Richard Attenborough acting outing in classic Dickens comedy.

The Ladykillers (1955): Superb black comedy from the Ealing canon, with pre-Obi Wan Alec Guinness.

One Hundred and One Dalmations (1961): Innocent pelt-seeker tortured by 101 belligerent pups. For shame.

Mary Poppins (1964): Notable for Dick Van Dyke's confounding, lanky turn as cockney chimney sweep.

A Hard Day's Night (1964): Classic, swinging 60s' comedy from the Fab Four.

Alfie (1966): Caine in much-lauded role as audience-addressing lothario.

Carry On Doctor (1967): Critically-panned, guilty-pleasure raunchfest from Pinewood Studios.

The London Nobody Knows (1967): The greatest film about London ever. Period.

▓▓▓▓ ▓▓▓ ▓ ▓▓▓▓ ▓▓▓▓▓ ▓▓ ▓▓ ▓▓▓ classic.

A Clockwork Orange (1971) Kubrick's dystopian masterpiece was set in Thamesmead, which is still, "Feeling a bit shagged and fagged and fashed."

The Elephant Man (1980): John Merrick 'accepted' by London's polite Victorian-era society in David Lynch masterpiece.

An American Werewolf in London (1981): US student attacked on moors; gets haunted; romps with Jenny Agutter; becomes werewolf; slaughters innocents; is shot in alley; credits roll.

My Beautiful Launderette (1985): Hanif Kureishi's controversial depiction of cross-culture, same-gender love in the Thatcher-era.

Muppet Christmas Carol (1992): That Michael Caine, he sure can act. But he sure can't sing.

London (1994): Patrick Kellier's abstract ramble through 'the most unsociable and reactionary of cities.'

Lock, Stock and Two Smoking Barrels (1998): East End crime capers from Madonna's (not from the East End) husband.

Notting Hill (1999): Hugh Grant as mumbling, bumbling, lovesick fop.

Bridget Jones's Diary (2001): Rene Zellweger goes Sloane in adaptation of Helen Fielding novel.

28 Days Later (2002): Us Londoners finally erupt in pandemic rage at how slow tourists are on the tube.

Love Actually (2003): Expansive Richard Curtis romcom with Grant in slightly-less mumbly, slightly-more bumble form.

Shaun of the Dead (2003): Fighting off zombies at the local pub. Hilarious.

The Kings Speech (2010): A stuttering King finds his voice and wins a few Academy Awards for his efforts.

There can't be anything worse than the inconvenience of trying to find a convenience when nature takes an unexpected hold of your nether regions; you may choose to follow the lead of many a Saturday evening reveller and use a public doorway, but is it really worth the £80 fine that will be levied if caught in the act (and let's face it, it's hard to conceal the evidence)?

Unfortunately, London has seen a recent decline in the provision of public toilet facilities, as local councils seem to have decided that they are under no obligation to provide such a service; you'll also be hard pushed to find a toilet attendant manning a lavatory these days, and the dubious goings-on in some loos may not be quite what you had in mind, unless your name has a "Michael" in it. Most surviving public toilets seem also to emit their own particular aroma of…well, you don't really have to use your imagination. But don't get down in the dumps!

The most obvious place to go to when in need is McDonald's. Despite what some may say about their food, their outlets are the place to go when caught short and not wishing to pay to pee. Usually maintained and cleaned throughout opening hours, they can also be used inconspicuously and without purchasing anything; and let's face it, you can't move without the glow of those golden arches following you across London. It's also a safe bet to use Starbucks, Caffe Nero and Costa Coffee bars, although they often have a policy of access to toilets by key only, which can be a bit of a bummer (groan).

It may seem like a good idea to visit pubs or bars solely for their toilets, but you might find yourself being hauled out by an irked landlord mid-act. Furthermore, don't expect luxury; pub toilets are usually fairly scummy and often not furnished with toilet paper. It's also unlikely to find a men's cubicle that will have a working lock in it; do you really wish to have an unwanted visitor whilst on the throne? Exceptions are the Wetherspoon's chain, which prides itself on having toilets cleaned on the hour, and the nicest of gastro pubs, which can offer commodious and clean facilities (at least during the day). Otherwise, if desperate, at least go for a pub or bar that's busy.

Also bear in mind that if you find yourself in need in the City of Westminster, you can use a toilet text service from your mobile phone! Known as SatLav, texting the word 'Toilet' to 80097 will result in a message being sent to your phone informing you of the nearest public convenience. It may prove to be the most relieving 25p you'll ever spend in London…

A good and extensive list of London public toilets can be found at www.cityoflondon.gov.uk/services/streets/clean-streets/community-toilet-scheme-cts.

If none of the afore-mentioned places are available, there are other options:

Other street public toilets—yes, those bizarre futuristic looking structures on some of London's central streets are toilets. Known as sanisettes or "superloos", there is a charge to use them and once in, you've got 15 minutes before the door automatically opens (don't get extended stage-fright). They're self-cleaning, which usually means that they're in a right state, and are also quite popular with junkies and prostitutes, so best saved for when extremely desperate.

There are also a few pop up toilettes which, although intended for the right use, unfortunately stink like hell and fortunately return back there during the day. These are only suitable for (drunk) men and rise to the challenge of channelling away an evening's excesses from 7pm to 6am. Located at notorious 'wet spots' in the West End, they are linked to the main sewerage system; taking the piss, indeed…

Stations—including almost all large railway stations and a few central London tube stations. There will usually be a cost for these facilities though (around 30p).

Department Stores—All the large ones, including John Lewis, Selfridges, Debenhams and Harrods. Smaller shops rarely have toilets for public use.

Supermarkets—many larger branches of Sainsbury's and Marks & Spencer.

Museums—the majority of London's large museums and galleries are free to enter (erm, and have toilets).

Libraries—most libraries will have an area of salvation for the needy.

Universities and Colleges—and you get to pass yourself off as a student or lecturer (in need of the loo).

Hospitals—you can also drop in on that relative that you always meant to visit, or maybe leave a stool sample; just try not to leave with a superbug.

Parks—not on the grass, please.

Hotels—larger hotels shouldn't pose a problem.

London has some of the finest hospitals in the world, attracting top-notch specialists who carry-out state-of-the-art procedures—the trick is, getting in to see one of them. An appointment at a specific hospital, or with a specialist, requires a referral from your GP and plenty of patience. In an emergency go to your nearest A&E—bring a book and some earplugs. On the weekends after eleven, waiting times for non-urgent problems can be measured in aeons, but rest assured, if something is seriously wrong you'll be seen very quickly—lucky ol' you. For non serious injuries or illnesses, find your nearest Minor Injuries Unit or Walk-in Centre on www.nhs.uk. You'll spend less time hanging around and free up A&E for critical cases and over-cidered teens needing stomach pumps. The ever-friendly 24 hr NHS Direct 0845 4647 is also always available for advice.

If you have the money, numerous private sector hospitals and clinics are available to cure what ails you, or to pander to your hypochondriacal needs. You won't necessarily get better treatment, but there'll be less waiting, more pampering and more grapes by your bedside. For information, start at www.privatehealth.co.uk.

A & E	Address	Phone	Map
Charing Cross Hospital	Fulham Palace Rd & St Dunstan's Rd	020 3311 1234	41
Chelsea and Westminster Hospital	369 Fulham Rd	020 8746 8000	43
Homerton University Hospital	Homerton Row	020 8510 5555	90
King's College Hospital	Denmark Hill & Champion Park	020 3299 9000	128
Moorfields Eye Hospital	162 City Rd	020 7253 3411	84
Royal Free Hospital	Pond St & Fleet Rd	020 7794 0500	57
Royal London Hospital	Whitechapel Rd & Vallance Rd	020 7377 7000	96
St Mary's Hospital	Praed St & Winsland St	020 3312 6666	31
St Thomas' Hospital	Westminster Bridge Rd & Lambeth Palace Rd	020 7188 7188	131
University College Hospital	235 Euston Rd	020 3456 7890	4
Western Eye Hospital	173 Marylebone Rd	020 7886 6666	2
Whittington Hospital	Magdala Ave	020 7272 3070	59

Other Hospitals	Address	Phone	Map
Bupa Cromwell Hospital	162 Cromwell Rd	020 7460 5700	35
Capio Nightingale Hospital	11 Lisson Grove	020 7535 7700	76
Charing Cross Hospital	Fulham Palace Rd & St Dunstan's Rd	020 3311 1234	41
Chelsea and Westminster Hospital	369 Fulham Rd	020 3315 8000	43
City Medical	17 St Helen's Pl	0845 123 5380	17
Eastman Dental Hospital	47 Huntley St	020 3456 2300	5
Elizabeth Garrett Anderson Hospital	25 Grafton Way	020 3456 7890	4
Fitzroy Square Hospital	1 Fitzroy Sq	020 7725 0880	3
Gordon Hospital	Bloomburg St & Vauxhall Bridge Rd	020 8746 8733	21
Great Ormond St Children's Hospital	34 Great Ormond St	020 7405 9200	5
Guy's Hospital	Great Maze Pond & St Thomas St	020 7188 7188	106
Heart Hospital	16 Westmoreland St	020 3456 7890	2
Highgate Private Hospital	17 View Rd	020 8341 4182	51
Homerton University Hospital	Homerton Row	020 8510 5555	90

Other Hospitals	Address	Phone	Map
Hospital For Tropical Diseases	Martimer Market & Capper St	020 3447 5959	4
Hospital of St John and St Elizabeth	60 Grove End Rd	020 7806 4000	68
King Edward VII Hospital For Officers	5 Beaumont St	020 7467 4344	2
King's College Hospital	Denmark Hill & Champion Park	020 3299 9000	128
Lambeth Hospital	108 Landor Rd	020 3228 6000	144
Lister Hospital	Chelsea Bridge Rd	020 3993 7566	20
London Bridge Hospital	27 Tooley St	020 3553 9022	106
London Independent Hospital	1 Beaumont Sq	020 7780 2400	97
London Welbeck Hospital	25 Welbeck St	020 7224 2242	2
Marylebone Consulting Rooms	10 Bulstrode Pl	020 8872 3838	2
Maudsley Hospital	Denmark Hill & Champion Park	020 3228 6000	104
Mile End Hospital	Bancroft Rd & Alderney Rd	020 7377 7000	93
Moorfields Eye Hospital	162 City Rd	020 7253 3411	84
National Hospital for Neorology and Neurosciences	Queen Sq & Great Ormond St	020 3456 7890	5
Portland Hospital For women and Children	209 Great Portland St	020 3993 3972	3
Princess Grace Hospital	42 Nottingham Pl	020 3131 2549	2
The Rosenheim Building	25 Grafton Way	020 3456 7890	4
Royal Brompton Hospital	Sydney St & Cale St	020 7352 8121	45
Royal Free Hospital	Pond St & Fleet Rd	020 7794 0500	57
Royal London Homeopathic Hospital	60 Great Ormond St	020 3456 7890	5
Royal London Hospital	Whitechapel Rd & Vallance Rd	020 7377 7000	96
Royal Marsden Hospital	Fulham Rd & Sydney Close	020 7352 8171	45
Royal National Orthopaedic Hospital	51 Bolsover St	020 8954 2300	3
Royal National Throat, Nose and Ear Hospital	47 Huntley St	020 3456 2300	5
St Bartholomew's	West Smithfield & Hosier Ln	020 7377 7000	15
St George's at St John's Therapy Center	162 St John's Hill	020 8812 4000	139
St Mary's Hospital	Praed St & Winsland St	020 3312 6666	31
St Pancras Hospital	4 St Pancras Way	020 7530 3500	78
St Thomas' Hospital	Westminster Bridge Rd & Lambeth Palace Rd	020 7188 7188	131
University College Hospital	235 Euston Rd	020 3456 7890	4
Wellington Hospital	8 Wellington Pl	020 3733 5344	76
Western Eye Hospital	173 Marylebone Rd	020 3312 6666	2
Whittington Hospital	Magdala Ave & Dartmouth Park Hill	020 7272 3070	59

Overview

Librarians love nothing more than a warm cardigan and a complex cataloguing system, nevertheless, they've done themselves proud with London's libraries. London boasts an enormous, if somewhat eccentric and confusing, network of over 360 libraries. In 2009 the Chief Librarians initiative passed and 4,000 libraries in England, Wales and Northern Ireland can now be easily accessed and used for all library services including checking out books, as long as you have an existing library card and proof of address. This excludes the elite British institutions (see below) and all books must be returned to a library in the same area.

London's libraries vary enormously in subject, range and facilities, with some accessible for free, some for a fee, some with an appointment and some only if you are very very nice and give the curator a chocolate digestive. But the treat of such a large network, apart from the world-class breadth, depth and quality of collections, is that many of the libraries have a unique personality to make them a treasured part of London. For example, £10 will get you a day's membership to the **London Library (Map 23)**, an atmospheric labyrinth where you can browse alongside ghosts of past members including Dickens, Tennyson and Darwin, and feel several IQ points higher than before you went in. In Tower Hamlets, libraries are now "Ideas Stores" **(Map 92, 101, 96)**, because Tower Hamlets is, like, cool. In addition to the books, magazines, music and internet facilities which are available at most public libraries, these superb spaces also offer activities such as free PopLaw legal advice clinics, homework clubs and jazz classes. The borough has built four of these wonders; find them in Bow, Whitechapel, Canary Wharf and

on East India Dock Road. London linguists are spoiled with the excellent **French Institute (Map 36)**, **Instituto Cervantes (Map 19)** and the **Goethe Institut (Map 37)**, while more cunning linguists may prefer the eye-opening gynaecological collection among the 2.5 million medical-related works in the **Wellcome Library (Map 4)**. Poets should meander their way to the **Saison Poetry Library (Map 104)**, ensconced within the South Bank Centre, for a little inspiration. Artists will enjoy the **National Art Library (Map 36)**, which nestles within the V&A Museum. You can use many of London's academic and specialist libraries through the Inspire London scheme, which grants one-day reference access to collections throughout London; ask your local library to refer you.

However, the Daddy of them all is the **British Library (Map 78)**. This behemoth receives a copy of every publication printed in the UK and Ireland, and requires 625km of shelving space to accommodate its 150million items. But it's just such a tease. You cannot borrow books, and to even access the collections you need to obtain a Reader Pass, via an introductory discussion to establish why you need it and whether you're likely to doodle on the books. This requires two forms of ID, no compromise: refer to www.bl.uk for the latest guidelines. Once you have your pass you can access the Reading Rooms, albeit with your personal belongings in a clear plastic bag (or stored in a locker). But if you just fancy seeing the Magna Carta, Shakespeare in Quarto or some Beatles manuscripts, you can access the book-free visitor areas without appointment and still gain an impressive look at one of the world's greatest information resources.

General Information

Important phone numbers:
All emergencies: 999
Non-emergencies: 101
Anti-terrorism hotline: 0800 789 321
Crime Stoppers: 0800 555 111
Neighbourhood Watch: 020 79934709
Missing Persons: 0500 700 700
Complaints: 08453 002 002
Websites:
www.met.police.uk
www.cityoflondon.police.uk (Separate police force specifically covering the Square Mile).
www.btp.police.uk (Separate police force specifically covering public transport).

Statistics* (Greater London)

	2008/09	2009/10	2010/2011
Murder	146	113	124
Rapes	2,177	2,839	3279
GBH	11,212	10,525	8374
Burglary (res)	59,176	60,909	60803

* all sourced from the MPS Crime Website http://content.met.police.uk

Police Stations

	Address	Phone	Map
Albany Street Police Station	60 Albany St	030 0123 1212	77
Battersea Police Station	176 Lavendar Hill	030 0123 1212	132
Bethnal Green Police Station	12 Victoria Park Sq	030 0123 1212	92
Charing Cross Police Station	Agar St & Strand	030 0123 1212	24
Chiswick Police Station	209 Chiswick High Rd	030 0123 1212	38
Fulham Police Station	Fulham Rd & Heckfield Pl	030 0123 1212	42
Hammersmith Police Station	226 Shepards Bush Rd	030 0123 1212	33
Hampstead Police Station	21 Fortune Green Rd	030 0123 1212	56
Holborn Police Station	10 Lamb's Conduit St	030 0123 1212	5
Holloway Police Station	284 Hornsey Rd	030 0123 1212	61
Islington Police Station	2 Tolpuddle St	030 0123 1212	80
Kennington Police Station	49 Kennington Rd	030 0123 1212	104
Kensington Police Station	72 Earl's Court Rd	030 0123 1212	35
Kentish Town Police	12 Holmes Rd	030 0123 1212	72
Lavender Hill Police Station	176 Lavender Hill	030 0123 1212	140
Peckham Police Station	177 Peckham High St	030 0123 1212	123
Stoke Newington Police Station	33 Stoke Newington High St	030 0123 1212	64
Tooting Police Station	251 Mitcham Rd	030 0123 1212	152
Walworth Police Station	12 Manor Pl	030 0123 1212	113
Wandsworth Police Station	146 Wandsworth High St	030 0123 1212	138

Overview

London hotels can be sources of hopelessly romantic creativity. In 1899 Claude Monet painted the Houses of Parliament from his balcony at the Savoy hotel. About 100 years later, Fay Weldon moved in with her typewriter as writer in residence. If you've got visitors in town, fancy giving Claude a run for his money, or just can't face going back to your dump of a flat, you'll need the services of a hotel. When choosing your hotel, think carefully about what kind of London you're looking to experience and whom the room is for. We've identified a few of the usual suspects for whom you may find yourself booking a hotel room, and heartily offer you our best suggestions for each. Just don't expect to emerge from any of them clutching a masterpiece penned overnight.

Only the Best, Daah-ling

So you need to find a hotel for a VIP client who will accept nothing but the best. Where to start? Since you don't have to cover the bill yourself, here is where you can really dig into London hospitality at its most deluxe. Start by trying to book **The Ritz (Map 9)**, with its amazing views of Green Park, Rococo detailing and killer high tea. **Brown's (Map 9)** is a stunning five-star and was the first hotel in London to have a lift. There is also the **Dorchester (Map 9)**, and its neighbour the **Hilton Park Lane (Map 9)**, where you may see a celebrity stumbling back to their quarters at four in the morning, if you're very, very lucky. **The Landmark (Map 76)** is a wonderfully Victorian retreat in the centre of ritzy Marylebone and has a rather fine atrium. But the granddaddy of luxury London must be the **Savoy (Map 24)**. This elegant old-timer stunk of old money until its temporary closure in 2007 for a £100 million spruce-up. It was built on the location of the Savoy Palace, which burned down during the Peasants' Revolt in 1381. We say let them eat cake (and tea).

A Dirty Weekend

This can be any weekend where a Londoner decides booze-goggled sex and/or quick-to-bed access after a night of clubbing is worthy of dishing out the dosh on an über-chic central hotel. It's one (giant) step up from splurging on a taxi and is the realm of the London boutique hotel where location is everything. **Hazlitt's (Map 12)** is right in the middle of Soho yet still wonderfully intimate. **Andaz Hotel (Map 8) (formerly Great Eastern Hotel)** is in the heart of the City, with funky Shoreditch on its doorstep, whilst the 'modern English' style of the **Charlotte Street Hotel (Map 3)** is painfully hip and sophisticated.

The Tea-and-Crumpet Tourist

Then there's the hotel for your sweetly naïve cousin that sees London through rose-tinted Ray Bans: full of scones, Mary Poppins and the chimes of Big Ben. You wouldn't want to burst her cute little bubble, would you? Not to worry, there are plenty of hotels to satisfy the Harrods tourist. **San Domenico House London (Map 46)** is a Chelsea boutique hotel that is about as warm and cuddly as a cup of sugary tea. **The Rookery (Map 15)**, built amongst a row of once derelict Georgian townhouses in Clerkenwell, is cluttered with museum-worthy furniture, open fires and ye oldey worldey frippery. Or, if she can't bear to be too far away from Buckingham Palace, there's the nearby **Windermere (Map 20)**.

General Information · **Hotels**

Parents in Town?

If your parents have spent their nest egg on bailing you out of your London-induced debt, they will probably want to get the most out of London for the least money possible. But if the hotel you pick for their stay is anything short of perfect, you'll never hear the end of it. If they have loyalty cards with any of the bigger hotel chains, now is a good time to use them. **The London Bridge Hotel (Map 22)** is an independent four-star that usually has good deals and is conveniently close to Borough Market and London Bridge station. Gower Street has a wealth of small family-run hotels at reasonable prices, including the **Cavendish (Map 23)**, within stumbling distance of the British Museum, as is the nearby **Crescent Hotel (Map 4)**, next to Russell Square. If you miss home cooking, get your 'rents a serviced apartment with a kitchenette. Marlin Apartments and Think London have a few different properties, often ripe for the celeb sighting as pop stars are known to hitch up their wagons during drawn-out tours.

In Lieu of a Couch to Crash On

Then you get your university friend still in strong denial of the real world, who refuses to get a real job. The amount of times this sponger has crashed on your sofa has been enough to send your might-be-the-one girl/boyfriend packing. Instead of blaming him/her for your future life of loneliness, banish them from the flat and call in the services of one of London's cheapies. They do exist, you just have to look hard. The **Hoxton Hotel (Map 84)**, an urban cheap boutique founded by the owner of Pret a Manger, is famous for its £1 hotel room sales. Cheap but cheerful chain Premier Inn (multiple locations) boasts rooms from £29 a night. Sometimes short-term rental companies, like **Airbnb** (www.airbnb.com), offer shared facility flats at very cheap prices. This is perfect if a guest is wishing to stay for a week or more. Airbnb has over 9,000 listings in London, which start as low as £10 a night. This can be a necessary and friendly alternative to endless weeks of friends imposing on your hospitality.

Where to Stick Your Best Friend From School
(And Her Husband, Two Perfect Kids and a Dog)

Unfortunately, for some people visiting London, a dodgy guesthouse isn't going to cut it. You want to show them how your city can be just as perfect as their countryside home and how not jealous you are of them! Of course, they don't see the point in paying tons either. This is where the few and far between bed and breakfasts come out of the woodwork. Most of these are small, so book in advance. London's best is the warm and welcoming **Bay Tree House and Annex B&B (Out of coverage)**. Great for families or singletons alike, it's in New Southgate (about 25 minutes by tube from central London) but can be a relaxing retreat. **Barclay House (Map 43)** is a hidden gem in Fulham Broadway (make sure you write down the address as it's not signposted and can blend in). **Aster House (Map 45)** is a bit pricier but close enough to posh High Street Kensington to give a glimpse of how the other half live.

With all these hotels, compare prices online, ask for their best rate and/or call for last minute deals, you may be surprised at the reductions available. Good offers mean you can pay less than you'd think for the best, and London does really have the best.

457

As you might expect from a site constantly inhabited since the Roman invasion of Britain, and probably before, London has managed to assemble a vast array of good, bad and ugly landmarks. The city is, in fact, stuffed with them, and the following is a slightly subjective rumination on a small proportion of some of the most noteworthy.

Historical

London gracefully bears a massive weight of history, and many of its landmarks reflect this. One of the oldest is the remains of the **Temple of Mithras (Map 16)** on Walbrook, built by the Romans when London was Londinium. Parts of the **London Wall (Map 18)**, also originally built by the Romans, still exist, the best fragments are around Tower Hill station. In Medieval times London became a bustling place; celebrate one of its most beautiful churches by visiting the oddly named **St Giles' Cripplegate (Map 7)**, which is ensconced within the brutal **Barbican Centre (Map 7)**, a landmark itself. By the 1600s, London was bustling so hard it got the plague and then some idiot burnt the entire city down in 1666. Celebrate three days of the Great Fire by climbing to the top of the 202 feet high **Monument (Map 18)**, before visiting post-fire architect Christopher Wren's masterpiece, **St Paul's Cathedral (Map 16)**. Into the 18th century, things became a little more sophisticated and some of London's prettiest domestic architecture bloomed. Stroll down Bloomsbury's **Doughty Street (Map 5)**, stopping at Charles Dickens' House, for perfectly proportioned Georgian elegance. The Victorians had a huge impact on London, with whole tracts of the city bearing the stamp of the starched times of chimney sweeps and empire bashing. For the lighter side of Victorian London, poke about the museums quarter from the **Victoria & Albert Museum (Map 37)** up to the **Albert Memorial (Map 36)**. For the darker, dodge the elderly at the **St Pancras Hospital (Map 78)**, an ex-workhouse.

Tourist Bait

London has a host of over-exposed landmarks that are honey to the swarms of tourist worker-bees but over-rated in the eyes of many Londoners. We don't necessarily share this view, but if you want to venture beyond the crowds at **Big Ben (Map 22)**, try some of the following. The aforementioned **St Paul's Cathedral (Map 16)** is an absolute wonder, although try the smaller **Southwark Cathedral (Map 106)** for a more intimate option. **The British Museum (Map 4)** is a beauty made fairer by its recent courtyard renovation; peruse the library to see where Marx pondered upon 'Das Kapital'. **The Burlington Arcade (Map 10)** is how shopping should be. The crypt under **St Mary-le-Bow Church (Map 16)** is 11th century weirdness complete with its own vegetarian restaurant. The Thames is long enough to provide you with your own spot of riverside tranquillity. If you're scared of bridges, burrow under the river at the **Greenwich Foot Tunnel (Map 120)**, or chug across it on the free Woolwich Ferry. For a weekend mooch, try the **Grand Regent's Canal (Map 71)**.

Modern Landmarks

The 20th century blessed the city with some opinion splitting contributions. **The Hayward Gallery (Map 104)** and **National Theatre (Map 104)** are both concrete frighteners which we are learning to love. Despite originally housing a power station, **Tate Modern (Map 105)** has been more graciously received. Meanwhile, further down the river, long abandoned **Battersea Power Station (Map 133)** will be undergoing major developments in 2013 and will be replaced by some form of flashy money-without-substance monstrosity. The **BT Tower (Map 3)** is like a 1960s lighthouse for central London drunks. **The Lloyds Building (Map 18)** and **Tower 42 (Map 18)** are both absorbing odes to the banker and glare menacingly at new rival **One Canada Square (or Canary Wharf Tower) (Map 100)**. A more recent contribution to the city is the **Canary Wharf Underground Station (Map 100)**. Until at least 2014 the 150-year squabble over what to put in **Trafalgar Square's (Map 24)** fourth and only empty plinth rages on. Expect modern, classic and performance art in this space for the time being, at least, until they add a statue of Britain's future supreme commander Rupert Murdoch strangling Lady Justice in 2014.

Lowbrow

In these clean times of starchitects, steel and glass, a few minutes spent gawping at **Elephant and Castle (Map 105)** shopping centre is enough to remind anyone how awry a landmark can go. Even a quick squizz at the nearby **Faraday Memorial (Map 105)** may not lift your gloom, largely as it now forms the body of a clogged roundabout. However, London can do lowbrow with the best of them, starting with the **Westway Flyover (Map 31)**: a noisy, dusty shard of concrete to remind you that the car is still king. The disused **Kingsway Tram Tunnel (Map 4)** is a forgotten piece of prime underground real estate and **Centre Point (Map 4)** and **Millbank Tower (Map 21)** are good examples of dodgy skyscrapers that no-one needed. **Battersea Park Gasometers (Map 133)** are imposing monsters, whereas **Lots Road Power Station (Map 50)** is fast becoming London's trendiest disused power station. If you must jump upon band wagons, keep your eyes peeled around east London for art left on walls by Banksy. Mobile lowbrow starts with a trip on a Routemaster, despite the buses being withdrawn in 2005, two heritage routes are still running. Lowbrow (along with logic, aesthetic quality and planning) finishes with **Euston Station (Map 78)**, which is, simply, disgusting.

Map 1 · Marylebone (West)

Marble Arch	Oxford St & Park Ln	Randomly plonked gateway to nowhere.
Speakers' Corner	Cumberland Gate & Park Ln	It's easy—stand on the corner and listen to the 'speeches.'

Map 2 · Marylebone (East)

Hertford House	Manchester Sq & Hinde St	Terribly twee home of the Wallace Collection.
Jimi Hendrix Memorial Blue Plaque	23 Brook St	Jimi lived here. Some bloke called Handel lived next door.

Map 3 · Fitzrovia

BT Tower	60 Cleveland St	A 574 foot tall official government secret until 1993.
Charlotte Street	Charlotte St	Restaurant strip for the advertising in-crowd.
Middlesex Hospital	Mortimer St & Cleveland St	Closed-down and spooky-looking.
Pollock's Toy Museum	1 Scala St	Brimming with delightful, traditional toys and Dickensian atmosphere.
Sinner Winner Man	216 Oxford St	Are you a sinner? Or a winner? London's top preacher's patch.
Tottenham Court Road	Tottenham Ct Rd	Buy your electronics 'ere, innit?

Map 4 · Bloomsbury (West)

The British Museum	Great Russell St & Museum St	Newly-covered Great Court is architectural manna.
Centre Point	101 New Oxford St	Ugly skyscraper looking kinda out of place.
Kingsway Tram Tunnel	Theobalds Rd & Southampton Row	Spooky remnant of London's defunct Tram network.
SOAS	Thornhaugh St	University focused on Africa, Asia and the Middle East.
Senate House	Malet St & Torrington Sq	Ominous art deco building; Orwell's Ministry of Truth.
Tavistock Square	Tavistock Sq	Has a statue of Gandhi looking as cool as ever.
University College London	Gower St	London's "Global University," upholding progressive ideals since 1826.

Map 5 · Bloomsbury (East)

The Dickens House Museum	48 Doughty St	Unassuming from the outside, mecca for Dickens' fans on the inside.
Doughty Street	Doughty St & Guilford St	Exquisite Georgian street in heart of literary land.
Gray's Inn Field	Theobald's Rd	Holborn Hideaway.

Map 7 · Barbican / City Road (South)

Barbican Centre	Silk St & Whitecross St	An architectural eyesore. Bloody good events though.
Bunhill Fields	38 City Rd	120 thousand dead people, including William Blake. All buried, luckily.
Church of Saint Bartholomew the Great	6 Kinghorn St	Stroll in for your daily dose of frankincense and choir song.
LSO St Luke's	161 Old St	Home to the London Symphony Orchestra. Peaceful gardens for relaxation.
St. Giles-without-Cripplegate	Fore St & Wood St	Medieval church which defied the Blitz. Catch an organ recital.

Map 8 · Liverpool Street / Broadgate

Fulcrum at Broadgate	Broadgate	Richard Serra's overwhelming steel megalith.

Map 9 · Mayfair / Green Park

50 Berkeley Square	50 Berkeley Sq	The most haunted house in all of London town!
Apsley House	149 Piccadilly	"Number One, London,"—former hip address of Duke of Wellington.
Buckingham Palace	The Mall	Unofficial HQ for Fathers For Justice.
Down Street Station	Down St & Piccadilly	Bricked-up Underground station. The Turtles didn't live here.
Hard Rock Cafe	150 Old Park Ln	Original location; check out free Vault memorabilia collection downstairs.

Map 10 · Piccadilly / Soho (West)

Burlington Arcade	Burlington Arcade & Piccadilly	Welcoming shoppers since 1819.
Carnaby Street	Carnaby St	Will anything innovative ever come from here again?
Kingly Court	Kingly St & Foubert's Pl	Flash the cash to cut a dash.
Statue of Eros	Piccadilly Circus	God of Love, smothered in pigeon crap: a cautionary tale.

General Information · **Landmarks**

Map 11 · Soho (Central)

Huge Tree In Pub (Waxy O'Connor's)	14 Rupert St	No, you're not drunk, it really is a tree.
John Snow Water Pump	Broadwick St	Source of 1854 Cholera outbreak identified by Snow.
Berwick Street Market	Berwick St & Rupert St	Arrive early for traditional Cockney trader songs / off-duty hookers.

Map 12 · Soho (East)

Denmark Street	Denmark St & Charing Cross Rd	Guitar land. 'Enter Sandman' forbidden in most stores.
FA Headquarters	25 Soho Sq	Home of English football's top brass.
Old Compton Street	Old Compton St	Dubious gay hub.
The Phoenix Garden	21 Stacey St	A beautiful green mini-oasis in the middle of the city.
Soho Square	Soho Sq	Great atmosphere on hot summer days.

Map 13 · Covent Garden

Oasis Lido	32 Endell St	A lido in central London! In a 50s housing estate!
Seven Dials	Upper St Martin's Ln & Earlham St	Slum area in the past. Now great for shopping!

Map 14 · Holborn / Temple

Aldwych tube station	Strand & Surrey St	Creepy abandoned tube station. With a photo booth... of doom?
BBC Bush House	Aldwych & Kingsway	London calling the world, since 1940.
Hatton Garden	Hatton Garden	Historic jewelry and diamond district
Inner Temple Garden	Inner Temple	A peaceful oasis where the lawyers look relaxed.
Lincoln's Inn Fields	High Holborn & Chancery Ln	Largest public square in London.
The Old Curiosity Shop	13 Portsmouth St	The oldest shop in London is truly Dickensesque.
Royal Courts of Justice	Strand & Bell Yard	Witness justice meted out to all, even the McCartneys.
Sir John Soane's Museum	13 Lincoln's Inn Fields	Spooky museum dedicated to the great 18th century architect.
Site of Sweeny Todd's Barber Shop	186 Fleet St	Swing by for a demon haircut and lovely pie.
Somerset House	Strand	18th century palace, beautiful fountains; has various modern functions.

Map 15 · Blackfriars / Farringdon

Daily Express Building	121 Fleet St	Art Deco sleeper.
Millennium Bridge	Millennium Bridge	Footbridge famous for wobbling alarmingly when it was opened.
Postman's Park	King Edward St & Little Britain	Tile memorial for 'average' people who did really cool things.

Map 16 · Square Mile (West)

The Guildhall	Gresham St & Basinghall St	Big, posh, old... Like Prince Phillip but less entertaining.
St Mary le Bow Church	Cheapside & Bow Ln	A historic place for City tycoons to save their souls.
St. Paul's Cathedral	St. Paul's Church Yard & Cannon St	Magnificence since 604AD.
Temple of Mithras	Queen Victoria St & Queen St	3rd century Roman temple foundations. Discovered 1954 and moved here.

Map 17 · Square Mile (East)

Bank of England	Threadneedle St	The 'Old Lady' still churns out the pounds.
London Stone	111 Cannon St	Possibly used by Romans to measure all distances in Britannia.
Threadneedle Street	Threadneedle St & Prince's St	London's original Grope Cunt Lane. Seriously, it's a true story.

Map 18 · Tower Hill / Aldgate

The Gherkin	30 St Mary Axe	Phwoar.
Leadenhall Market	Leadenhall Market	Designed by Horace Jones (Billingsgate and Smithfield Markets)
The Lloyds Building	1 Lime St	Dystopia's nicer side.
London Wall	Cooper's Row & Trinity Sq	Ruins, should be re-built to keep Northerners out.
The Monument	Monument St & Fish St Hill	Climb 311 coronary-inducing steps for unique, unsung London views.
Pudding Lane	Pudding Ln	Starting point for Great Fire of 1666. No smoking.
Royal Raven Lodgings	Wakefield Tower	Want to upgrade your pokey flat? Become a raven.

(461)

General Information · Landmarks

Soup Kitchen for the Jewish Poor	Brune St & Tenter Ground	The kitchen's gone; the stunning ornate façade is still there.
Thames Clipper	Tower Pier	
Tower 42 (Natwest Tower)	25 Old Broad St	One of London's skyscrapers. Great view (and restaurant) at top.
Tower of London	The Tower of London	Kings and Queens. Surprisingly insightful, annoyingly expensive.

Map 20 · Victoria / Pimlico (West)

| Little Ben | Victoria St & Vauxhall Bridge Rd | Big Ben's runty kid brother. |
| Westminster Cathedral | 42 Francis St | Yep, impressive. |

Map 21 · Pimlico (East)

| Millbank Tower | 21 Millbank | Ugly sore thumb. And Labour Party HQ! |

Map 22 · Westminster

Big Ben	House of Commons	The world's most famous clock and pretty damn cool.
Bolan Rock Shrine	Queen's Ride, Putney	Memorial shrine where 70s rock star Marc Bolan died.
Field of Remembrance	Victoria St & Dean's Yard	Sea of crosses and poppies to honour veterans.
New Scotland Yard Sign	8 Broadway	It spins!! Just like on the telly!!
Smith Square	Smith Sq	Square with great concert venue--watch out for MPs.
UK Parliament	Victoria St & Abingdon St	Parliament buildings where you can watch government debates.
Westminster Tube Station	Bridge St & Victoria Embankment	A daunting, soulless, engineering playground. Good and bad both extinct here...

Map 23 · St. James's

Economist Plaza	25 St James's St	Rotating sculpture installations from bratty young artists.
Giro the Nazi Dog	9 Carlton House Terrace	London's sole Nazi memorial. You'd think there'd be more…
Leicester Square	Leicester Sq	Tragic, tacky, always inexplicably heaving. Avoid.
TKTS	Leicester Square & St Martin's St	Cheapo tickets to sometimes worth-seeing shows.

Map 24 · Trafalgar Square / The Strand

10 Downing Street	10 Downing St	The Prime Minister's house.
The Actors' Church	29 Bedford St	Somewhat hidden and unique church long-associated with thesps.
The Banqueting House	Whitehall & Horse Guards Ave	Unsullied Renaissance cum-shot. Still does private parties.
Cleopatra's Needle	Embankment	Ancient-Egyptian Empire esoterica, with additional Luftwaffe-era 'distressed' styling.
Eleanor Cross	Charing Cross Station, The Strand	A mourning King's tribute to his expired Queen.
Jane Austen Residence	10 Henrietta St	The first Bridget Jones' bachelorette crashed here for a time.
Right-hand Drive Street	Savoy Ct	Britain's only right-hand-drive street. Like being on holiday! (Ish)
Sewer Lamp	Carting Lane & Strand	Lit by the power of your bowels.
St Martin-in-the-Fields	St Martin's Pl & Duncannon St	Was indeed surrounded by fields once. Just TRY to imagine!
Top Secret Tunnels	6 Craig's Ct	Government's WWII tunnels, 100ft below London. But shhh: top secret.
Trafalgar Square	Trafalgar Sq	Hardly an oasis but space to sit, look and think.

Map 25 · Kensal Town

| Trellick Tower | 5 Golborne Rd | Grade II listed 1960s council estate inspiring love/hate reactions. |

Map 29 · Notting Hill Gate

| Portobello Road Market | 223 Portobello Rd | Antiques, clothes, food and more. A London institution. |

Map 31 · Paddington

Paddington Bear Statue	Paddington Station	The statue's pleasant. But they're milking it with the crap shop.
Tony Blair's house	Connaught Square & Seymour St	Promise not to do anything naughty now.
Westway Flyover		Coolest car route into London

General Information · **Landmarks**

Map 33 · Shepherd's Bush

BBC Television Centre	Wood Ln & Ring Rd	Treasure it before the BBC moves out in 2013.

Map 34 · West Kensington / Olympia

Kyoto Garden (Holland Park)	100 Holland Park Ave	Traditional Japanese Garden in Holland Park offering peace and tranquility.

Map 35 · Kensington

Kensington Palace Gardens	Kensington Palace Gardens	Billionaire's Row. Stunning street to amble down and gawp at the mansions.

Map 36 · South Kensington / Gloucester Rd

Albert Memorial	Kensington Gardens	The shiniest balding head in town.
Royal Albert Hall	Kensington Gore	One stunner of a music hall, inside and out.

Map 37 · Knightsbridge

Holy Trinity Brompton	Brompton Rd & Knightsbridge	Historic HTB is home to the Alpha course. Even Guy Ritchie's been!
Victoria & Albert Museum	Cromwell Rd & Thurloe Pl	Victorian treasure trove, building a beauty itself.

Map 42 · Baron's Court

Empress State Building	Lillie Rd & North End Rd	Awesome Art Deco building now a scary cult center.

Map 43 · West Brompton / Fulham Broadway / Earl's Court

Stamford Bridge	Fulham Road & Moore Park Rd	That's not sweat you smell but money at Chelsea FC's HQ.

Map 46 · Sloane Square

Saatchi Gallery	Duke of York HQ, King's Rd	See rich dude's great art collection, for free.

Map 48 · Fulham

Putney Bridge Tube Pill Box	Putney Bridge Station	"We will fight them on the platforms!"

Map 50 · Sand's End

Lots Road Power Station	27 Lots Rd	Pint-sized power station, now disused.

Map 51 · Highgate

Highgate Cemetery	1 Swain's Ln	Eerily gothic home to Karl Marx and The Highgate Vampire.
Karl Marx's grave	Highgate Cemetry	Exactly what it says on the tin.

Map 52 · Archway (North)

Parkland Walk Nature Reserve	Parkland Walk	Hedgehogs and graffiti to be spotted along this abandoned railway.
Suicide Bridge	Hornsey Ln & Archway Rd	Former London entry point, now very much an exit point.

Map 53 · Crouch End

Abandoned Warehouse	Parkland Walk & Crouch End Hill	Dereliction galore along one of the best walks in London.

Map 55 · Harringay

Railway Fields Nature Reserve	381 Green Lanes	Calm oasis at former railway depot near Green Lanes station.

Map 56 · Hampstead Village

Hampstead Observatory	Lower Terrace & Hampstead Grove	The highest point in London, and open to the public!

Map 57 · Hampstead Heath

John Keats House	38 Heath Hurst Rd	Here lived a writer whose name was writ with water.
Lawn Road Flats	Lawn Rd & Garnett Rd	c.1934 modern living. Learn to love concrete.

General Information · **Landmarks**

Map 60 · Archway

Banksy's Hitchhiking Charles Manson	Tally Ho Corner (off Highgate Hill)	Early stencil by internationally renowned graff artist.
Dick Whittington's Cat	89 Highgate Hill	Small stone statue of obscure Mayor's cat.

Map 62 · Finsbury Park

North London Central Mosque (Finsbury Park)	7 St Thomas's Rd	New name, ethos for once controversial, now myth-dispelling, mosque.

Map 63 · Manor House

The Castle Climbing Centre	Green Lanes & Lordship Park	Fake castle, real climbers.

Map 64 · Stoke Newington

Newington Green Church	39 Newington Green	'ERECTED 1708, ENLARGED 1860'...well, it made us laugh.

Map 67 · Belsize Park

Freud Statue	Fitzjohn's Ave, opposite Maresfield Gardens Junction	Statue by Oscar Nemon near the psychoanalyst's Hampstead home.
St Stephen's	Rosslyn Hill	Gothic awesomeness. Currently being restored to its former glory.

Map 68 · Kilburn High Road / Abbey Road

Abbey Road Zebra Crossing	3 Abbey Rd	Go on. Take THAT photo. You know you want to.

Map 70 · Primrose Hill

3 Chalcot Square	3 Chalcot Sq	Home of poet Sylvia Plath, 1960-61.

Map 71 · Camden Town / Chalk Farm / Kentish Town (West)

Camden Market	Camden Lock Pl	Shop, hang, drink, listen, pose, watch, chill, rock, laugh.
Grand Regents Canal	Grand Regents Canal	London's best bike lane. Or canoe to Birmingham.
The Roundhouse	Chalk Farm Rd & Crogsland Rd	Prominent round building and historic performance venue.

Map 74 · Holloway Road / Arsenal

Gillespie Park	191 Drayton Park	Weird and wonderful nature park along the train tracks.

Map 75 · Highbury

St Paul's Shrubbery	St Paul's Rd & Northampton Park	All Monty Python jokes welcome, in fact, positively encouraged.

Map 76 · Edgeware Road / Marylebone (North)

Sherlock Holmes' House	221 Baker St	It's elementary my dear Watson!

Map 77 · Mornington Crescent / Regent's Park

Euston Tower	286 Euston Rd	Quite an impressive erection.
Greater London House	180 Hampstead Rd	Crazy Art Deco building.

Map 78 · Euston

The British Library	96 Euston Rd	Prestigious research library with unmatched collection.
Camden High Street	Camden High St & Delancey St	'Alternative' tourist mecca.
Cheney Road	Cheney Rd & Weller's Ct	"Chaplin, 'Alfie' and many more were filmed on these cobbles.
Euston Station	Eversholt St & Doric Way	So ugly it's oogly.
Platform 9¾	King's Cross Station	This Harry Potter thing has gone way too f'ing far.
St Pancras Station	St Pancras Way	Listed Gothic frontage, massive modern Eurostar hangar behind.
St Pancras	Pancras Rd & Euston Rd	Ex-Victorian workhouse turned superbug den.

Map 80 · Angel / Upper St

Angel Station Roof	Angel	You can get on the roof here, you epic teens.
The Bull	100 Upper St	Hands up: who loves beer?

Map 81 · Canonbury

Gladiators Paving Slab	10 Canonbury St	Logo of fighty telly show built into pavement. Me neither.

General Information · Landmarks

Map 82 · De Beauvoir Town / Kingsland

Suleymaniye Mosque	212 Kingsland Rd	Striking minaret silhouetted against Shoreditch Church spire and Broadgate Tower.

Map 84 · Hoxton

Hoxton Square	Hoxton Sq	Great in summer. Buy some cans and join the hipsters.
Village Underground	54 Holywell Ln	How did they get the trains up there?
White Cube	48 Hoxton Sq	Jay Jopling's homage to modern art

Map 85 · Stoke Newington (East)

Abney Park Cemetery	Stoke Newington High St & Rectory Rd	Egyptian revival-style, spooky nature reserve.

Map 86 · Dalston / Kingsland

Centreprise	136 Kingsland High St	Multi-cultural art centre, cafe, bookshop and venue.
Holy Trinity, The Clowns Church	Beechwood Rd & Kirkland Walk	Every Feb, clowns mourn Grimaldi. In full costume.

Map 87 · Hackney Downs / Lower Clapton

London Orphan Asylum	Lower Clapton Rd & Linscott Rd	Grandiose remains of historic site now beloved of environmental artists.
The Strand Building	29 Urswick Rd	Beautiful Art Deco building, NOT the subject of Roxy Music song.
Sutton House	2 Homerton High St	Music and arts in the oldest house in East London.

Map 88 · Haggerston / Queensbridge Rd

Geffrye Museum	136 Kingsland Rd	English interior design from 1600 to today.
St Mary's Secret Garden	50 Pearson St	A bit calm amongst the bees and the butterflies.

Map 89 · London Fields / Hackney Central

London Fields Lido	London Fields Westside	Open-air swimming for hardy Hackney folk.

Map 91 · Shoreditch / Brick Lane / Spitalfields

Brick Lane Mosque	59 Brick Ln	The area's changes reflect on the building – once a synagogue, now a mosque.
Christ Church Spitalfields	2 Fournier St	Star architect Nicholas Hawksmoor's pretty masterpiece.
Dennis Severs' House	18 Folgate St	Candle-lit cellar, parlour, smoking room - step 300 years back in time.
Spitalfields Market	105 Commercial St	No bargains but certainly one-of-a-kind fashions.
Sweet Toof Graffiti Alley	Pedley St & Brick Ln	Signature sweeties and skulls – just off Brick Lane.
Ten Bells	84 Commercial St	Where Jack the Ripper got his victims.
Truman's Brewery	91 Brick Lane	Beautiful old building now a hip weekend market. That's progress...

Map 92 · Bethnal Green

Bethnal Green Tube Station	Bethnal Green Tube Station	Scene of the worst civilian loss of the Second World War.
London Buddhist Centre	51 Roman Rd	Get your freak om.

Map 93 · Globe Town / Mile End (North)

Art Pavillion	221 Grove Rd	Arts center seemingly designed by the Teletubbies.
Mile End Climbing Wall	Haverfield Rd & Grove Rd	Classic climbing centre - one of London's big three.

Map 95 · De Beauvoir Town / Kingsland

The Sun HQ	1 London Bridge St	It's probably not legal to stake out Page 3 girls.

Map 96 · Whitechapel (East) / Shadwell (West) / Wapping

Battle of Cable Street Mural, St George's Hall	236 Cable St	Celebrating an almighty multi-faith bashing of a 1930s fascist march.
Blind Beggar Pub	337 Whitechapel Rd	A killing here finally led to Ronnie Kray doing porridge.

Map 98 · Mile End (South) / Limehouse

Ragged School Museum	46 Copperfield Rd	Barnado's school 'for the deserving poor' turned East End museum.

465

General Information • **Landmarks**

Map 100 • Poplar (West) / Canary Wharf (West)

Canary Wharf Tower	1 Canada Sq	You can smell the money yards away. Look, don't touch.
Canary Wharf Tube Station	Canary Wharf	Norman Foster's Jewel in the Jubilee Line Extension.

Map 102 • Millwall

The Docklands Sailing & Watersport Centre	235 Westferry Rd	Award-winning sailing centre.

Map 104 • South Bank / Waterloo / Lambeth North

County Hall	Westminster Bridge Rd & Belvedere Rd	One of London's most historical and vast buildings.
The Hayward Gallery	Southbank Centre	Revered and reviled bruiser.
The London Eye	Westminster Bridge Rd	Two words: Tourist. Trap. Nice view though.
Low Tide at South Bank	South Bank	Go for a walk on the exposed riverbed.
National Theatre	Waterloo Rd & Upper Ground	South Bank centre-piece, looked like it was from 2050 in 1960.
The Pier at OXO Tower	Barge House St & Upper Ground	Screw OXO! Have a picnic on the pier instead.
South Bank Book Market	Under Waterloo Bridge	Little-known outdoor market; heaps of vintage and second-hand reads.
Waterloo Bridge	Waterloo Bridge	When tired with London, come here and watch the sunset.

Map 105 • Southwark / Bankside (West)

Buskers' Archway	Southbank	Excellent acoustics make the decorated tunnel a coveted buskers' spot.
Elephant & Castle	Elephant & Castle	Everything that was wrong with 60s town planning. Concrete hell.
Michael Faraday Memorial	Elephant & Castle	He gave us electromagnetism, we gave him a roundabout.
The Ring	72 Blackfriars Rd	London's first boxing ring was here; now a characterful pub.
Shakespeare's Globe	21 New Globe Walk	The Bard's famous playhouse reconstructed.
Tate Modern	Bankside	Herzog and de Meuron dazzler.

Map 106 • Bankside (East) / Borough / Newington

Borough Market	8 Southwark St	London's best food market. Enjoy the free samples.
Cross Bones Graveyard	Redcross Way & Union St	Medieval resting place for London's ladies of the night.
Female Gladiator	159 Great Dover St	1st cenruy AD grave of London's very own Xena.
The Golden Hinde	Clink St & Stoney St	Amazing replica of Francis Drake's Tudor war ship.
The London Tombs	2 Tooley St	Lesser known Tower experience—beware the plague pits.
Mint Street Park	Southwark Bridge Rd & Marshalsea Rd	Open space on the site of the old Evelina Children's Hospital.
Old Operating Theatre Museum	9 St Thomas St	Macabre ancient operating theatre, with gallery for eager spectators.
The Shard	32 London Bridge St	72-storey Renzo Piano glass pyramid along the river.
Southwark Cathedral	Cathedral St & Montague Close	Worth the diversion to see Chaucer and Shakespeare's stomping grounds.
St George the Martyr	Borough High St & Tabard St	Look for the homage to Dickens.
Winchester Palace	Clink St & Storey St	Random 13th century ruins with remarkable rose window.

Map 107 • Shad Thames

City Hall	Queen's Walk, More London	Dubbed 'The Testicle' by Mayor Ken Livingston. Nice.
Design Museum	224 Kengsington High St	Fairly unsatisfying shows - drool-worthy bookshop.
Fashion and Textile Museum	83 Bermondsey St	DAH-ling, it's just fabulous!
Floating Gardens	31 Mill St	Gardens. Mad tramps. On Boats. What else do you want?
HMS Belfast	Morgan's Lane & Tooley St	Floating WW2 killing machine, much beloved of children.
Stompie	Mandela Way & Page's Walk	Sounds like a baby elephant. But it's a Soviet tank.
Tower Bridge	Tower Bridge Road	Messing about on the water.

Map 110 • Rotherhithe (West) / Canada Water

Brunel Museum	Railway Ave & Rotherhithe St	Where engineering geeks can seek refuge from being picked on.

Map 111 · Rotherhithe (East) Surrey Quays

Surrey Docks Farm	Rotherhithe St & Salter Rd	Show the kids what their bacon used to look like.

Map 113 · Walworth

East Street Market	Walworth Rd & East St	Gloriously useless stuff.
Heygate Estate	Deacon Way & Heygate St	A testament to urban planning gone horribly wrong.

Map 114 · Old Kent Road (West) / Burgess Park

The Animatronic Fireman	Old Kent Rd	Be afraid. Be very afraid.
Peckham Library	122 Peckham Hill St	Groundbreaking modern architecture or huge, carelessly dropped Tetris block?

Map 116 · South Bermondsey

Millwall FC Stadium	Zampa Road & Bolina Rd	A football mecca for somebody?

Map 120 · Greenwich

Cutty Sark Gardens	King William Walk & Romney Rd	Where the Archbishop of Canterbury was murdered in 1012.
Greenwich Foot Tunnel	Greenwich Church St & Thames St	Walk/crawl/skip/limp under the Thames.

Map 126 · New Cross

Ben Pimlott Building	University of London, New Cross	A building of cheerful, decay-warped, modern fascist fun

Map 131 · Vauxhall / Albert Embankment

Lambeth Palace	Lambeth Palace Rd & Lambeth Rd	Where the Archbishop of Canterbury lives; no, not in Canterbury, stupid.
Secret Intelligence Service HQ (MI6)	85 Vauxhall Cross	Real life James Bonds in a not-so-secret location.
Vauxhall City Farm	165 Tyers St	So that's where an egg comes from.

Map 133 · Battersea (East)

Battersea Dogs' Home	4 Battersea Park Rd	Re-house a pooch. Now does cats too.
Battersea Park Gasometers	Queenstown Rd & Prince of Wales Dr	Rusting monsters.
Battersea Power Station	188 Kirtling St	The world's most beautiful power station, surely.

Map 140 · Clapham Junction / Northcote Rd

Northcote Road	Northcote Rd	Middle-class marketing-types mecca.

Map 143 · Clapham High Street

Clapham Common Air-Raid Shelter	Clapham High St	The depths of government paranoia.

Map 144 · Stockwell / Brixton (West)

Brixton Market	Electric Ave & Electric Ln	Caribbean flavours, smells and sounds.
Electric Avenue	Electric Ave & Brixton Rd	First shopping area in Britain lit by electricity, in 1880.

Map 145 · Stockwell / Brixton (East)

Stockwell Bowls	Stockwell Rd & Stockwell Park Walk	70's concrete skatepark, take quads and get beaten-up.

Map 152 · Tooting Broadway

Gala Bingo Hall	50 Mitcham Rd	Bingo hall with Grade One listed interior.

MAP 37

Level 6

137 138 139 140 141 142 143 144 145

118 118a
119
120
220 221 220 225 225
121 122 123 125

level 4

128a
127 128 129 131

Europe
Asia
Modern
Materials & Techniques
Special Exhibitions

81 87 94 95
82 88 96
70a 65 66 67 68 69 89 88a 97
70 90 98
71 90a 102 99
72 84 101 100
73 85 109 107 108
74 National Art Library

level 3

111

40a

113 114a 114b 114c 114d 114e
116 117 112

52 52b
52
53 53b
54
54a 56a 58b
55 56 57 58

level 2

156
151

Level 1

11 16a
17 27
18 Shop
19 26 38a
20
51 21 21a 22 23 24 25 32 33

Special Exhibitions

40 41 42 44 45 46a 46 46b
47a 47b 47c 47d 47e 47f 47g
48a 49 50a 50b

1
2
3
4 5 6 7 8 9

Level 0

General Information

NFT Map: 37
Address: Cromwell Road
              London SW7 2RL
Phone: 020 7942 2000
Website: www.vam.ac.uk
Hours: 10am – 5.45pm daily. Select areas
              open until 10pm every Friday.
              National Art Library open 10am –
              5.30pm Tuesday through Saturday
              and 6.30 on Fridays. Check website
              for areas/ activities that require
              booking. Closed 24th, 25th and
              26th of December.

Admission: Free to the permanent collection.
There is a charge for temporary exhibitions.
Tickets have an allotted time slot and
although they can be purchased on the day,
it is recommended you book ahead of time
by phone or online, especially with the more
popular exhibitions.

Overview

The Victoria and Albert Museum, or the V&A,
calls itself the world's greatest museum of art
and design and nowhere has there ever been
such an eclectic collection of objects inducing
so many 'ooooohs', 'aaaaahs' and 'holy shits!'.
With a permanent collection of over 4.5 million
objects, pretty much all on display in the 145
galleries, you can go everyday for a lifetime and
be blown over by something you hadn't noticed
before. For the tourist and non-tourist alike, the
V&A is a wonderful maze of cultural ramblings.
You'll get lost, overwhelmed and flustered, but
we promise you won't get bored.

The V&A is a cabinet of curiosities of gargantuan
proportions, boasting 5000 years of art and
design, in every medium imaginable (from wax
dioramas to a little black dress made of bras),
spread over seven levels and organised by five
themes—Asia, Europe, Materials & Techniques,
Modern and Exhibitions. The trouble is where to
start. You'll no doubt spend the first 10 minutes
mesmerised by the glass Chihuly chandelier
over the information booth, but what you do
afterwards depends on how much time you
have. Got hours? Avoid structure and just
wander. Got an hour? Take a look at the map,
see what strikes your fancy and head straight
there. Just don't forget to hit up the gift shop
afterwards—it's killer.

The Greatest Hits

There's no real method to the V&A's madness.
Despite their best efforts to categorise
everything, Vivienne Westwood gowns are just a
stumble away from 1000 year-old Buddhas. But
this is a great thing. The best advice is really to
ditch the guidebook and go with your instincts.
To make sure you take in the best stuff, start in the
basement (having arrived through the Tunnel
Entrance from the tube station), where you'll
find the 17th century **Cabinet of Curiosities**—
predecessors to the modern museum—which
will get you in the right mind set. Weaving past
bits and pieces of **Versailles**, you emerge onto
the ground floor (Level 1) which covers fashion,
Asia and both Medieval and Renaissance
Europe. Highlights of which include the **cast
courts**, which boast a life-size replica of **Trajan's
Column** in plaster, then onto ancient **samurai
swords** and spectacular **kimonos** in Asia, the
Ardabil Carpet—the largest and most amazing
Islamic carpets in existence dating from 1539
(lit up on the hour and half-hour), an extensive
costume room covering everything from **18th
century crinolines** to **Juicy Couture** worthy of
Paris Hilton, and lastly, **Raphael's cartoons**—
massive sketches for a 1515 commission of
tapestries that now hang in the Vatican. Before
heading on, stop for a tea in the **Morris, Gamble
& Poynter Rooms** café for teacakes in 1860s
arts and crafts surroundings. Level 2 consists
of the tucked away **British Galleries**, including
the **Great Bed of Ware** as well as the endearing
Lord and Lady Clapham dolls bedecked in
miniature turn-of-the-18th century outfits. Up
again on Level 3, you'll find the Materials &
Techniques rooms, with its vast collections of
silver, ironwork and musical instruments, as
well as some dynamite paintings. Don't miss
Rossetti's The Daydream and then **Ron Arad's
Chair** in the modern rooms. This floor also
houses the **National Art Library**—an art history
student's research dream (you have to get a
reading pass to study here though). Level 4 has
a wonderfully tactile display of **glasswork**, as
well as architecture and more **British galleries
from 1760-1900**. If you've made it this far, you
deserve a knighthood.

MAP 4

Upper Floors

94 93 92
91 90
66
61 62 63 64 65
59 58 57 56 55 54 53
73 52
72 Restaurant 51
71 50
70 49
69a 69 36 40 41
68 37 38 39
47 46 45
48

Ancient Greece & Rome
Middle East
Asia
Egypt
Enlightenment
North & Central America
Africa
Exhibitions and changing displays
Europe
⊠ Lift
||| Stairs

Main Floor

67
Montague Place Entrance
34
33a 33
33b
24
26 27
20 21
18 19 9
22
17 23 8 4
16
15 10 1
14
13
12 11 6
5 3
Restaurant
Main Entrance Great Russell Street
Paul Hamlyn Library
35
Reading Room
Great Court

Lower Floor

78 77
25 25 25
25
Clore Education Centre
Ford Centre for Young Visitors

General Information

NFT Map: 4

Address: Great Russell Street, WC1B 3DG

Phone: 020 7323 8299 (information) or
        020 7323 8181 (exhibition tickets)

Website: www.britishmuseum.org

Hours: The galleries and the Great Court
        are open daily 10 am–5 pm and
        until 8.30 pm on Fridays. Check
        website for planned maintenance
        causing gallery closures. Closed 1st
        of January and 24th, 25th and 26th
        of December.

Admission: Free, with a charge for some
            special exhibitions.

Overview

Unless you're Indiana Jones, combining archaeological expertise with the swashbuckling energy to defeat obnoxious school groups, then do not attempt to cover the British Museum in a day. With 13 million items covering two million years of human history in almost 100 permanent and temporary galleries, you are better off treating yourself to different sections when the mood takes you—a perk of having one of the world's largest museums on your doorstep and open for free.

At 250 years, it is also the oldest museum in the world, but forget preconceptions of dusty urns and endless Roman coins—they're there if that's your bag, but this is a very modern organisation. The permanent displays include some of the world's most fascinating treasures, while the temporary exhibitions bring London a chance to break and lose artefacts which have seen some of the greatest moments of history, such as the recent display of drawings by Michelangelo, Raphael, Leonardo, and some other Renaissance scribblers who didn't make Ninja Turtle status.

However, while preserving artefacts to inspire its visitors, the Museum can also be seen as a testament to the great British pastime of looting. Some of the shining lights of its collection were acquired under the shadiest of circumstances, and the countries which were plundered so that snotty kids could chortle at the genitalia of their sculptures are increasingly vocal about getting the items back. For example the Elgin Marbles, rechristened with their pleasantly playful English name after the earl who helped himself to them, are huge slabs hacked from the 2500 year old Athenian Parthenon (albeit Elgin's entire nose later rotted off due to syphilis: a gratifying example of one-upmanship by nature). The legality of this move is hotly debated, but apart from the damage to the Parthenon, the Marbles undeniably suffered when they were cut into smaller pieces for transport to Britain, and when rowdy schoolboys bopped the leg off a centaur in 1961. The Museum holds firm that returning debated items would empty the museums of the world, but it has extended the occasional olive branch to ease the controversy; compensation was paid for the display of drawings stolen by Nazis, and they returned the Tasmanian Ashes (aboriginal human remains) to Australia after a 20-year battle.

The Greatest Hits

The **Great Court** is not just a Greatest Hit of the Museum, but of London as a whole. Being "the world's largest covered public square" may sound too niche an accolade to be impressive, but it really is stunning. The 150 year old **Reading Room** at its centre is a delight, both for the excellent library and for the wall-mounted list of major historical figures who have sought inspiration within its round walls. Whatever your ethics on plunder, some of the most morally-dubious exhibits are among the absolute must-sees: the **Elgin Marbles** in Room 18 are remarkable, while the **Rosetta Stone** in Room 4 gives you the irresistible buzz of seeing something so legendary up close, or as close at the backpacked hordes will allow, in your own town. A whole **Moai Statue** from Easter Island is in Room 24, the **Lewis Chessmen** set is in Room 42, and the **Mausoleum of Halikarnassos** exhibition displays some of the last remaining fragments of one of the Seven Wonders of the World. However, it is the stories of heartache, adventure, mystery and passion behind the items which bring them to life. Asking the steward of Rooms 62-3 how the **mummies** came to be in the museum, or seeing the pages from **The Book of the Dead** which recorded lives of the deceased, is a fascinating way to gain insight into people around the world and throughout time. And if that's a bit too deep, just head to one of the four **shops** for a mummy-shaped pencil case or replica Rosetta Stone.

General Information

NFT Map: 36
Address: Cromwell Road, SW7 5BD
Phone: 020 7942 5000
Website: www.nhm.ac.uk
Hours: Daily 10 am–5.50 pm
               (Last admission 5 pm)
               "After Hours" events run on the
               last Friday of each month
               during Nov–Apr.
               24–26 Dec: closed.
Admission: Free access to most of the
               Museum. Fee charged for
               some special exhibitions
               (free to Members).

Overview

Visiting the Natural History Museum is like reading National Geographic, if it was edited by JK Rowling. As imagination-tingling to adults as it is to kids, you can mull over serious questions about genetic modification and the environmental cost of modern life, while walking inside a termite mound or knocking on a petrified tree.

With more than 70 million specimens in their collection, you simply won't see it all at once, or for most of us—ever. But with free entry, regularly refreshed exhibits and unforgettable special exhibitions, it's worth dropping in when you have the opportunity. Grab a free map at the entrance to work out your route, which is colour-coded for a (slightly) easier life: Red Zone for the planet and forces of nature; Green for ecology and the environment; Blue for dinosaurs, mammals and biology; and Orange for the Wildlife Garden and behind-the-scenes peeks.

Weekends are inevitably heaving with hyperactive button-pressing families, spellbound tourists and Londoners trying to rebuild the brain cells they killed off with the night before's drinking; weekdays are amok with school groups. But don't let this put you off. If there's a queue outside the main entrance on Cromwell Road, and you don't fancy killing time by spotting all the different creatures carved around the entrance arch, pop 'round the side to Exhibition Road entrance and you'll fast-track yourself in. You can go early or late for fewer crowds, or stick with the permanent exhibitions, which are superb but not as sexy as the world-class special exhibitions which draw in the masses. Or, if all else fails, just shove the kids out the way: they're smaller than you and the buttons are *so much fun* to press.

The Greatest Hits

Anyone who didn't see the **Dinosaur Exhibition** as a child really missed out: run here and rectify the situation immediately if you haven't been, or revisit and enjoy the modernised exhibits if you have. The **Mammals Exhibition** will get you wondering exactly *how* someone stuffs a giraffe, and gives you a chance to get close to the gaping jaws of a hippo. For a different perspective on this room, go up to the balcony around it: watching people stare agog at the brilliantly-displayed **blue whale** is as entertaining as the exhibits themselves. For proof that even history geeks can make the earth move for you, visit the **Power Within** exhibition which recreates an earthquake (though don't expect a Universal Studios experience. The will is there, bless, but the budget just isn't…). Watch blushing parents introduce their kids to the birds and the bees in the **Human Biology** section, where an 8-times-life sized model of a **foetus** will put you off pregnancy forever. The **Wildlife Garden** is an oasis of serenity open from April–October, or you can impress a date (or not, depending on your coordination) by **ice-skating** next to the stunning Victorian building from November–January.

The Museum's Special Exhibitions are superb—check the website for current information. The annual **Veolia Wildlife Photographer of the Year**, October–April, is utterly inspirational, while a varying daily programme of events includes **lectures, behind the scenes tours** of the botany department, and **fossil workshops** for kids. Due to the success of the children's version, the museum is now running Dino Snores sleepovers for adults, which includes a three course meal, life drawing classes and an all night monster movie marathon. So if you fancy yourself as Ben Stiller in Night at The Museum start saving, as the stay will cost you a whopping £175.

Like the creatures it displays (except for the Dodo—you'll find one in the Green Zone), the museum keeps evolving. Aptly, the latest major development is the Darwin Centre, where you can stoke your nightmares by checking out the giant tarantulas, experience life in a cocoon (like life in a London flat, but more spacious), and watch scientists at work. You might not think that watching scientists analysing and cataloguing bits of plant would be much of a spectator sport, but an hour in the centre will whiz by and leave you bursting with new knowledge to irritate your mates with.

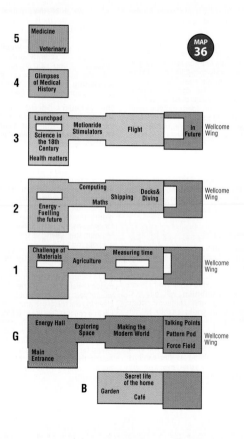

5 Medicine · Veterinary

MAP **36**

4 Glimpses of Medical History

3 Launchpad · Science in the 18th Century · Health matters · Motionride Stimulators · Flight · In Future · Wellcome Wing

2 Computing · Energy – Fuelling the future · Maths · Shipping · Docks & Diving · Wellcome Wing

1 Challenge of Materials · Agriculture · Measuring time · Wellcome Wing

G Energy Hall · Exploring Space · Making the Modern World · Talking Points · Pattern Pod · Force Field · Main Entrance · Wellcome Wing

B Garden · Secret life of the home · Café

General Information

NFT Map:	36
Address:	Exhibition Road, South Kensington, London SW7 2DD.
Phone:	033 0058 0058
Website:	www.sciencemuseum.org.uk
Hours:	Open 10 am–6 pm every day except 24 to 26 December. check website for special school holiday and summer opening hours.
Admission:	Free, but charges apply to IMAX 3D Cinema, simulators & a few special exhibitions.

Overview

Museum and Science. Two words known to strike fear into the heart of many a child. And many a grown-up, come to that. But the Science Museum is one of the most visited museums in London. How so? Perhaps it's the heady mix of mildly erotic pistons and shafts; 60s room-sized computers and Bakelite ashtrays; special effects simulators and the mighty IMAX theatre? Or maybe it is the multitude of buttons; red and blue and green actual buttons, as well as Minority Report-style touch screens? We know they're aimed at kids, but we like. Oh and levers, did we mention levers?

The museum has its origins in the popular Great Exhibition of 1851. Prince Albert (no laughing in the back please) suggested the extra cash made by the Exhibition be used to found a number of educational establishments. Following a number of building moves and expansions the Science Museum as we know and love it opened in 1885.

The Greatest Hits

The museum's 300,000 gidgets, gadgets and gizmos attract 2.5 million visitors a minute or something, but venture above the third floor, to the **medical floors**, and you will have the place almost to yourself. The most popular area is the main drag along the ground floor which includes **Exploring Space** hung with real life space probes and other relics that look like they've come from the Doctor Who costume and props department, and **Making of the Modern World** featuring **Stephenson's Rocket**, to titillate your dormant trainspotter.

The third floor's **Launchpad** area has as many interactive displays as an 8-year-old could ever want. Parents hope their little darlings are actually learning something as they race from exhibit to exhibit whirling wheels, spinning liquids in plastic tubes and grimacing through head-sized lenses till tiredness or RSI sets in. For younger kids the tactile **Pattern Pod** on the ground floor makes up for its lack of buttons by its immensely pleasing shape.

The museum has its own Imax to impress the grown-ups and to make whimpering children cower as 3D Rexes loom into their faces. Don't even think about going in with a hangover. A huge silver hoop joins the **Energy exhibition** on the second to the ground floor. Answer a question on a nearby monitor, (don't worry they are easy) and watch your initials and age whiz around the inside of the ring. But what's that BUZZ? Like a huge electric fly killer? It's the inspired **'don't touch' display**—irresistible for the naughtiest in the class, one small electric shock later, the rest of the lemmings race over for a turn. Hilarious.

Tate Modern

7
Bar
East Room

6
Members Room

5
8 9 10 11 12 | 11 10 9 8
7 2 | 3 7
6 5 4 3 1 | 1 2 4 5 6

4
Espresso Bar

3
6 7 2 9 10 | Scale | 9 8
8 | 7 6
5 4 3 2 1 | 2 3 1 | 4 5

River Entrance

2
Café | Seminar Room | Starr Auditorium | Gallery

1
Shop
Gallery
Main Entrance

MAP 105

Level 5
States of Flux
Energy and Process
Conceptual Models

Level 4
Exhibitions

Level 3
Poetry and Dream
Material Gestures

|||| Stairs
Escalators

Tate Britain

5 4
6 3
2
Duveen Galleries
1
8
28 27
9 Octagon | Art Now | 26
10 11 24 25
12 23
14 22 21 | T4 T5 | T8
18 | T1 T3 | T7
15 19 20 | T2 T6 | T9
16 17
T10

Millbank Entrance

MAP 21

Manton Entrance (Atterbury St)

Restaurant | Cafe

Auditorium
Sculpture Court
Clore Entrance

Level 3
Level 2
Level 1

Arts & Entertainment · **The Tates**

General Information

Tate Britain:
NFT Map: 21
Address: London SW1P 4RG
Phone: 020 7887 8888
Website: www.tate.org.uk/visit/tate-britain
Hours: Open 10am – 6pm every day. Last
              admission to special exhibitions is
              30 minutes before closing time.

Tate Modern:
NFT Map: 105
Address: London SE1 9TG
Phone: 020 7887 8888
Website: www.tate.org.uk/visit/tate-modern
Hours: Open 10am–6pm daily. Last
              admission to special exhibitions is
              30 minutes before closing time.

Overview

In a city renowned for its galleries and museums, London's Tate galleries shine from the banks of the Thames. The first Tate was founded in 1897 as the National Gallery of British Art, but was renamed soon afterwards after its main patron Henry Tate—he of Tate and Lyle and the sugar cube. Originally on the site of the former Millbank Prison (where Tate Britain remains), the gallery gradually expanded and divided its collection over the four sites, two in London, one in Liverpool and the last in St Ives. In London, Tate Britain houses British art dating from 1500 to the present day, while Tate Modern was created to house—yes you've guessed it—more modern work from 1900 to the present day, and is reportedly the most visited modern art gallery in the world.

The two Tates carry the same trendy Tate logo and the shops contain much of the same avant-garde merchandise with a great range of children's stuff available in both. But while the more traditional Tate Britain more closely resembles the National Gallery in architectural and artistic flavour, Tate Modern has a very hip feel and draws a slightly broader audience, in part due to its location on the increasingly buzzy South Bank.

Both museums have popular restaurants and cafes, but to encourage those without a membership to sign up, each offers an exclusive members' room. These provide the best views, nicest toilets, and quieter and ever so slightly self-important customers, and are always a safe bet to impress a date.

Tate Modern

Based in the former Bankside Power Station, Tate Modern has proved to be an extremely popular attraction for tourists and Londoners alike since its opening in 2000. It houses the national collection of modern art, so expect plenty of inspirational and challenging works alongside exhibits that look like your cat sicked them up. The temporary art installations of the five-storey tall Turbine Hall provide much of the draw to the gallery. This huge space displays specially commissioned works from October to April of each year—a programme which was intended to run for only five years, but was extended due to its popularity. Quirky exhibitions fill the vast Turbine Hall, like Olafur Eliasson's 'Weather Project' which encouraged visitors to lie back on the floor in their thousands, gazing at the shadows cast by the synthetic sun. Ai Wei Wei's Sunflower Seeds, in 2010/11, was probably his most ambitious and attention-grabbing work before going MIA—ironically and probably due to the unwanted exposure it brought to the Chinese government. That and the fact punters had to be forbidden from walking on the seeds due to the fine dust the porcelain they were made from produced which could have been inhaled and damage the lungs. Again, ironically. As always, we await with baited breath who will fill the Turbine Hall and with what. If it all seems like you could have created better art yourself, then try one of the gallery's excellent workshops or courses and give it a go.

Tate Britain

The Tate Britain boasts the most comprehensive collection of British art in the world, and is home to the annual and unmissable Turner Prize show. Stone steps lead up to the portico and once inside, the Duveen Galleries' ethereal sculptures lie straight ahead, giving the first taste of a breathtaking collection of artwork. Tate Britain's collection is divided chronologically and dedicates space exclusively to notable artists, such as Turner, Blake and Constable. The gallery also includes significant works by William Hogarth, Stanley Spencer and Francis Bacon. Look out for the themed guides to suit your mood, such as "The I've Just Split Up", "The I'm In A Hurry" and "The I Haven't Been Here For Ages" collections: a highly endearing way ease you through the 500 years of exhibits.

General Information

NFT Map: 24
Address: Trafalgar Square
London WC2N 5DN
Phone: 020 7747 2885
Website: www.nationalgallery.org.uk
Hours: 10 am–6 pm daily,
Fridays until 9 pm.

Admission: Free to the permanent collection and temporary exhibitions in the Sunley Room, Room 1 and The Space on Level 2. There is a charge for temporary exhibitions held on Level 2 in the Sainsbury Wing. Tickets have an allotted time slot and although they can be purchased on the day, it is recommended you book them ahead of time online, especially with the more popular exhibitions.

Overview

The National Gallery is home to one of the best and largest collections of Western European painting in the world, coming in at around 2100 paintings on display at any one time. An emphasis on *Western* and *painting* is needed. If you're looking for Roman antiquities or Persian miniatures, head for the British Museum or the V&A—this is not where you're going to get it. Furthermore, if you're into anything post-Impressionist, make an about face for the Tate Britain. This is a celebration of the arts of Europe in all their old-school occidental glory. Taking the surprisingly manageable tour around the galleries (most of which are on one floor) will leave you wowed by how many works of art you will recognise. This is a collection that has been branded deep into your subconscious—with its oh-yeah-that-one Turners, Hogarths, Rembrandts and Leonardos. Bring a date and even the most culturally challenged will be able to impress.

The collection came into being in 1824 when the House of Commons paid £57,000 for 38 paintings belonging to a banker, using his Pall Mall home as the exhibition space. Compared to the Louvre, calling a few paintings in some guy's house the National Gallery was a little too embarrassing for the British public. So the great and the good demanded the Government pull their finger out and get to work on a purpose-built gallery worthy of a national art collection. In 1832, architect William Wilkins was given the job, constructing the recognisable porticoed façade in an up-and-coming area known as Trafalgar Square, called by one trustee 'the very gangway of London'. The most recent addition to the gallery is the Sainsbury Wing, designed in 1991 by leading contemporary architects Robert Venturi and Scott Brown after much controversy. Prince Charles, notoriously fussy when it comes to architecture, dismissed one suggested design as "a monstrous carbuncle on the face of a much-loved and elegant friend".

The National Gallery can be tackled in one exhausting afternoon, if you put your mind to it. Take advantage of the fancy benches, as many of the more epic paintings are best viewed from a distance. Be sure to get lost in the many smaller galleries, which house some dynamite, lesser-known, works. If you're feeling hungry, the National Dining Rooms is a critically acclaimed (read: expensive) restaurant, serving up the best in British fare. If you're feeling like a little culinary nationalism, the more casual National Café serves a very good cream tea.

The Greatest Hits

Starting with the Sainsbury Wing, the collection snakes around, covering European painting in chronological order from 1250 to 1900. There are a lot of paintings and it can get slightly overwhelming, so if you're pressed for time and want to make sure you've 'done' the National Gallery, try one of their 60 minute taster tours or pick up their guide to the 30 must-see paintings. Don't miss the **Arnolfini Portrait** (signed with 'Van Eyck was here' above the mirror hilarious), **Botticelli's Venus and Mars**, **The Wilton Diptych**, and Uccello's **The Battle of San Romano**. Moving onto the 1500-1600 range, you'll recognise **Leonardo's cartoon of The Virgin and Child with St Anne and St John the Baptist**, 'The Ambassadors' by Hans Holbein the younger (the one where you have to crouch to see the skull), the still-hilarious portrait of **A Grotesque Old Woman** by Quinten Massys (a 1664 example of the classic conundrum—a 64 year-old trying desperately to look 16) and **Titian's Bacchus and Ariadne**. Moving on, the collection houses a rather large collection of Dutch masters, including **Rembrandt, Rubens and van Dyck**. If you're sick of 2-D, a rather cool contraption is **Samuel von Hoogstraten's peepshow**. Peer through the peep hole in this painted box for an eye-popping view of the interior of a Dutch house. Very cool. A trip to the museum is never complete without viewing a **Gainsborough, Turner and Hogarth**, all of which are housed in the 1700-1900 galleries. Do not miss Hogarth's **Marriage a la Mode** a comical rendition of an 18th century arranged marriage—in a series of six paintings. Last but not least, onto the juxtaposition of three epic 19th century history paintings depicting corporal punishment with chilling realism—**Manet's Execution of Maximillian**, Delaroche's **Lady Jane Gray** and Puvis de Chavanne's **Beheading of St John the Baptist.** What a way to end it all, quite literally.

General Information

Address: Peninsula Square,
             London, SE10 0DX
Website: www.theO2.co.uk
General Information: 020 8463 2000
Tickets: 0871 984 0002

Overview

Exactly how the Millennium Dome transformed itself from national embarrassment and vortex for millions of taxpayers' money to the slick new home of groovy events is a bit of a mystery. Or maybe it's blindingly obvious—suits are better than politicians at this kind of thing. Anyway, on the outside it looks the same— the oversized lovechild of a jellyfish and hedgehog. Inside, gone are the attractions and concepts of 1999, aimed at celebrating all things British, so visionary that visitors stayed away in droves. Instead, the contents of an above-average high street have been stuffed inside—generic bistro food and wine bars, a multi-screen cinema. Whoope-doo you might think. But hold on—people come for the music. No really, they do.

Enter the O2 Arena or its little sis, the IndigO2 (see what they did there?) and be very impressed. The Arena has been engineered to provide sight lines that older venues can only dream of. The air conditioning—usually a rarity at London gigs, actually works. The acoustics have to be heard to be believed. It might not be a destination venue for mosh-loving purists and those who like the sweat and beer to fly, but if you like your music with a bit of comfort and luxury, you know, like toilets that work and don't stink of piss (548 of them!) then the 02 is well worth a look. Wheelchair users are catered for with fully accessible facilities. London seems to have its first venue that feels like some real thought has gone into its creation. If the organisers get their act together and diversify the bands appearing, including more that veer away from mainstream bands then it could become unstoppable.

How to Get There—Driving

Driving to the O2 isn't as daft as it might sound considering its location—previously un-chartered industrial wastelands of south east London. 2,000 parking spaces can be reserved in advance. With decent road links, traveling after rush hour should be bearable. The A102 linking north and south London runs through the Blackwall Tunnel, right next to the venue.

How to Get There—Mass Transit

In theory, the O2 has excellent transport links no matter how you travel. In practice, there's a good chance that your gig coincides with engineers digging up the precise bit of track you need to travel on. Check www.tfl.gov.uk before you travel. But when everything is working, then the Jubilee line at nearby North Greenwich connects directly with Waterloo and London Bridge. The Docklands Light Railway is one stop away and several bus routes drop off right outside. But the best way to arrive has to be by boat— the high speed Thames Clipper runs every 20-30 minutes. from several piers including Greenwich, Embankment and Waterloo. It's not only relaxing, but you get to see London at its best on the trip.

How to Get Tickets

Ticketmaster. Naturally. Try Gumtree and Craigslist for swaps, unwanted tickets and scum-of-the-earth touts.

Life in London can sometimes seem like one continuous, eventful film, but if you like your plots to take place on screen then the city has a lot to offer. Going to catch a flick in London can often unravel like some kind of Indiana Jones-esque adventure—the Holy Grail being a reasonably-priced ticket in a clean, comfortable theatre, that can only be sought after battling hundreds of tourists and fellow Londoners all with the same thought. Every year 164 million people visit London's cinemas; now that's a fair few ticket stubs.Thankfully, by leaving The Twilight Zone (a.k.a. the tourist trap of the West End) there are plenty of cinematic treasures to be plundered. Whatever genre of film takes your fancy, whatever time of night and whether you want a velour seat and popcorn or a leather chair and glass of champagne, you are sure to find it in the nation's capital.

For those who are desperate to catch Spielberg's latest offering, and are crazy enough to stick it out in the West End, chain cinemas abound. You'll find **Odeon** (Maps 1, 4, 23, 30, 35, 61, 66, 71, 111 & 136), **Vue** (Maps 12, 33, 43, 66 & 80) and Cineworld (Maps 100 & 138) theatres all over London. If you're brave, or just fancy seeing a star or two at one of the regular premiers, **Odeon Leicester Square** (Map 23) (made up of two separate theatres) could be for you. Another monster on the square is the historic **Empire** (Map 11), seating an impressive 1,300 patrons is a landmark in itself, although she is a slightly faded leading lady these days. Beware though. While the price of a cinema ticket in the big smoke is normally enough to make you choke on your Butterkist, wandering into any of the theatres in Leicester Square may force you to re-mortgage with prices as high as £22.50 a ticket at peak times. **Vue Piccadilly Circus** (Map 23) on Lower Regent Street was formerly the home of Paramount Pictures in the UK but now houses five small, luxurious theatres showing the latest flicks on general release.

It's not hard to find cinemas offering art house and independent films in London. Finding a good one, however, can be more of a challenge. **The Barbican** (Map 7) is always a good bet, and you can take in an exhibition before your film to really beef up your grey matter. We highly recommend the **Curzon Soho** (Map 11) offering not only a wide range of cinematic gems but

also a plush bar to loosen you up for that three hour Kurasawa number. Remember if the queue is snaking along the pavement, tickets can be bought at the bar downstairs too. Check out the cinema's cousin in **Mayfair** (Map 9) as well as the slightly shabby **Curzon Bloomsbury** (Map 5) in Brunswick Square. **Everyman Chelsea** (Map 45) on the lustrous King's Road is one of London's premier art houses with two-seaters available for the perfect smooching experience. **The Gate** (Map 29) in Notting Hill was created from a restaurant in 1911 and now offers independent releases in a luxurious setting. **BFI Southbank** (Map 104) specializes in film through the ages as well as hosting frequent events. Who would have thought old Charlie would help us save our pennies? **The Prince Charles Cinema** (Map 11) off Leicester Square sits in a perfect location and offers revivals, cult and foreign language films for as low as £1.50. Now that's a bloody bargain. For those with a penchant for 'le cine' courtesy of our French neighbours visit **Cine Lumiere** (Map 36) in South Kensington. Uber-cool Clapham has an equally trendy art house cinema, the **Clapham Picturehouse** (Map 143), Dalston's Art Deco gem the **Rio Cinema** (Map 86) is worth a look, while Bloomsbury offers up **The Horse Hospital** (Map 4)—the name's almost as avant-garde as the films they show. Just leave Dobbin behind.

There are some wonderful cinematic experiences to be had too. **BFI IMAX** (Map 104) is housed in a curious circular building, south of Waterloo Bridge, with the biggest screen in the UK—the size of five double-decker buses. Then there are those three magic words—**The Electric Cinema** (Map 29) on Portobello Road. Grab a Pinot Grigio, rest your derriere on a soft leather seat and munch away at home-made ice cream all the way from sunny Hampshire while catching the latest Polish release. And treat your mates to another round and a packet of crisps, because there are increasing numbers of mini-cinemas in pubs and bars such as **The Garrison** (Map 107) and **The Roxy** (Map 106).

Cinemas	Address	Phone	Map
Aldwych Film	1 Aldwych	020 7300 0400	14
Barbican Centre Cinema	Silk St & Whitecross St	020 7638 4141	7
BFI London IMAX	1 Charlie Chaplin Walk	033 0333 7878	104
BFI Southbank	Belverdere Rd & Waterloo Rd	020 7928 3232	104
Cine Lumiere	17 Queensberry Pl	020 7871 3515	36
Cineworld Leicester Sq	5 Leicester Sq	033 0333 4444	11
Cineworld Wandsworth	Wandsworth High St	0871 220 8000	138
Cineworld West India Quay	11 Hertsmere Rd	033 0333 4444	100
Clapham Picturehouse	76 Venn St	087 1902 5747	143
Curzon Bloomsbury	1 Brunswick Sq	033 3321 0104	5
Curzon Mayfair	38 Curzon St	020 7495 0501	9
Curzon Soho	99 Shaftesbury Ave	020 7292 1686	11
The Electric Cinema	191 Portobello Rd	020 7908 9696	29
Empire Cinemas Haymarket	63 Haymarket	087 1471 4714	23
Everyman Baker Street	96 Baker St	012 3355 5642	1
Everyman Belsize Park	203 Haverstock Hill	012 3355 5642	67
Everyman Chelsea	279 King's Rd	012 3355 5642	45
Everyman Hampstead	5 Hollybush Vale	012 3355 5642	56
Everyman Screen on the Green	83 Islington Green	012 3355 5642	80
The Exhibit	12 Balham Station Rd	020 8772 6556	148
Frontline Club	13 Norfolk Pl	020 7479 8950	31
Fulham Road Picturehouse	142 Fulham Rd	020 7326 2649	43
Gate Picturehouse	87 Notting Hill Gate	020 7018 3629	29
Genesis Mile End	93 Mile End Rd	020 7780 2000	97
Greenwich Picturehouse	180 Greenwich High Rd	087 1902 5747	120
Hackney Picturehouse	270 Mare St	0871 90 25 734	89
ICA Cinema	The Mall & Horse Guards Rd	020 7930 3647	23
Notting Hill Coronet	103 Notting Hill Gate	020 3642 6606	29
Odeon Camden Town	14 Parkway	033 3014 4501	71
Odeon Holloway	419 Holloway Rd	033 3014 4501	61
Odeon Leicester Square	24 Leicester Sq	033 3014 4501	23
Odeon Panton Street	11 Panton St	033 3014 4501	23
Odeon Putney	26 Putney High St	033 3014 4501	136
Odeon Surrey Quays	Redriff Rd & Surrey Quays Rd	033 3014 4501	111
Odeon Swiss Cottage	96 Finchley Rd	033 3014 4501	66
Odeon Tottenham Court	30 Tottenham Ct Rd	033 3014 4501	4
Peckham Multiplex	95 Rye Ln	084 4567 2742	123
Phoenix Cinema	52 High Rd	020 8444 6789	na
Prince Charles Cinema	7 Leicester Pl	020 7494 3654	11
Rich Mix Centre	34 Bethnal Green Rd	020 7613 7490	91
Rio Cinema	107 Kingsland High St	020 7241 9410	82
Ritzy Picturehouse	Coldharbour Ln & Brixton Oval	020 7326 2649	150
Riverside Studios	Crisp Rd & Queen Caroline St	020 8237 1111	41
Vue Finchley Road	Finchley Rd & Blackburn Rd	034 5308 4620	66
Vue Fulham	Fulham Rd & Cedarne Rd	034 5308 4620	43
Vue Islington	36 Parkfield St	034 5308 4620	80
Vue Piccadilly Circus	19 Regent St	034 5308 4620	23
Vue Shepherds Bush	Shepherds Bush Green & Rockley Rd	034 5308 4620	33
Vue West End Cinema	3 Cranbourn St	034 5308 4620	12

It seems that every pub, bench and bridge in London has a tale to tell of past literary greats mulling over their troubles, weeping over lovers lost or launching themselves into the Thames. Ours is a city saturated in literary history and literature-lovers, with an abundance of bookshops and diversity of readers. While so many other retailers are homogenising, our independent bookshops—with their knowledgeable staffs and their often narrow focus—remain as eclectic and enthusiastic as ever. As well as a great selection of specialist independent stores, London is also home to dozens of second-hand bookshops, book markets, a literature festival, a major international book trade fair, and Europe's largest bookshop.

General

The **Foyles** flagship store on Charing Cross Road (Map 12) is a London institution, with a history as eccentric as its stock. Along with mainstream books and best-sellers, it offers a good range of second hand and out-of-print books, as well as a specialist Antiquarian department and a chilled jazz café. Venerable **Hatchard's (Map 10)** has been hawking books for over 200 years, making it London's oldest bookstore. The **London Review Bookshop (Map 4)** offers a huge range of constantly updated books with an intellectual bent and intellectual staff. Kids can find a bookshop wonderland in **Tales on Moon Lane (Map 128)**. The excellence of the independent stores has meant the chains have had to up their game—and loath though we are to say it, some, such as academic specialists **Blackwells (Map 12)** has gotten it very right indeed. In particular, **Waterstone's** in Piccadilly (Map 23) attracts all sorts of excitable superlatives, being the largest bookshop in Europe, running a range of literary activities to complement their stock, and even hosting a bar with some of the finest views of London.

Second Hand

Sadly, the world-renowned status Charing Cross Road used to command as the Mecca of second-hand bookstores is fading, and those who go looking for the genteel expertise immortalised in Helene Hanff's bestseller *84 Charing Cross Road* will find a "Med Kitchen" (shudder) at number 84. Many shops still cling to their ideals however, such as **Any Amount of Books (Map 12)** selling titles from as little as £1 and offering a leather-binding service so your books can furnish your room as well as your mind. Good places to start if you are scouting for quality second-hand bookshops are: the tardis-like **Village Bookshop (Map 129)** staffed by bookworms who have read *everything* (or so it seems) and can always help you find a gem; **John Sandoe (Map 46)** for true bookshop charm (rickety staircases, passionate staff, enchanting atmosphere); and the **Trinity Hospice (Map 136)** and **Oxfam Bookshops (Maps 58, 51, 88)**—not only an astonishingly cheap and broad collection of works, but all for charidee.

Specialist

Finding a bookshop devoted to your passion is like finding a club of old friends, and London caters for all tastes. Bored of cheese toasties? **Books for Cooks (Map 29)** smells as good as the recipes look, as they're tested in their kitchen first, while in-store cooking workshops teach new skills to avid customers. Sci-Fi nerds will be in their element at **Forbidden Planet (Map 179)**. **Gekoski (Map 4)** stocks a good range of modern first editions, or for older and rarer first editions try **Henry Sotheran (Map 10)**: a unique, but pricey, treat for any enthusiast. Head to **Atlantis (Map 4)** for all your occult needs (though no doubt the Spirits had already tipped you off on that one). Arty types are extensively catered for: **The Photographers' Gallery (Map 3)**, a treat in itself, has a substantial shop stocking photography titles, artists' monographs and unusual cameras; the **ICA Bookshop (Map 23)** is a great destination for art and film fans, and you can take in an exhibition while you're there; **Travis & Emery (Map 24)** stocks a vast range of music books and scores; comic geeks can get their fix at **Gosh! (Map 11)**. And for those with a passion for passion, pop along to the book section of **Coco de Mer (Map 13)**. Head to **Artwords (Map 84)** for books on—nope, I'll see if you can guess. **Motor Books (Map 24)**, surprisingly London's only shop dedicated to motoring, rail, aviation and military books, is the ideal repository for your menfolk when you need some peace.

Travel

Feeling lethargic? Head to one of the city's superb travel bookshops to have your energy restored. **Stanford's (Map 13)** has been inspiring London for 150 years, with its enormous collection of travel books and maps. A bookshop for travellers who like to read, **Daunt Books (Maps 2, 28, 57 & 67)** arranges all its books by geographical location, so even its fiction, cookbooks and history are shelved by country. Or to learn any of over 150 languages, head to **Grant & Cutler (Map 10)**, the UK's largest foreign-language specialist.

Politics

Bookmarks (Map 4) stocks left-leaning works on a huge range of issues and takes a lively role in political activism, giving it a real and infectious sense of purpose. Also hugely right-on, both representing and driving several lefty social movements, is **Housmans (Map 78)**.

Talks and Events

Publishing is a cut-throat business, and many writers have to sell their soul to get noticed. For them, it means an endless round of book signings and talks; for us, it means a fabulous chance to hobnob with our favourite authors. Most bookshops host occasional signings, but for regular events from the most celebrated authors, the big boys predictably have all the clout. **Foyles (Maps 12 & 104)** and **Waterstone's (see p.489)** attract huge names: recent guests have included JK Rowling, Louis de Bernières, Salman Rushdie and AS Byatt. **Stanford's (Map 13)** offers opportunities to hear well-known travel editors, writers and photographers for an inspirational and sometimes career-changing evening. For intellectually stimulating debates and literary discussions, check out the **London Review Bookshop (Map 4)** and **Bookmarks (Map 4)**. Some events are free, some as much as a theatre ticket, but all should be booked in advance to ensure a place.

Bookshops	Address	Phone	Map
Any Amount of Books	56 Charing Cross Rd	020 7836 3697	12
Artwords	20 Broadway Market	020 7923 7507	89
Atlantis	49 Museum St	020 7405 2120	4
Blackwells	50 High Holborn	020 7292 5100	12
Bookmarks	1 Bloomsbury St	020 7637 1848	4
Books for Cooks	4 Blenheim Crescent	020 7221 1992	29
Coco de Mer	23 Monmouth St	020 7836 8882	13
Daunt Books	83 Marylebone High St	020 7224 2295	2
Daunt Books	193 Haverstock Hill	020 7794 4006	67
Daunt Books	51 S End Rd	020 7794 8206	57
Daunt Books	112 Holland Park Ave	020 7727 7022	28
Donlon Books	77 Broadway Market	020 7684 5698	89

Bookshops	Address	Phone	Map
Forbidden Planet	179 Shaftesbury Ave	020 7420 3666	12
Foyles	107 Charing Cross Rd	020 7437 5660	12
Foyles	Southbank Centre	020 7440 3212	104
Foyles	22 Waterloo St	020 3859 9254	104
Gay's the Word	66 Marchmont St	020 7278 7654	5
Gosh! Comics	1 Berwick St	020 7437 0187	11
Hatchard's	187 Piccadilly	020 7439 9921	10
Henry Sotheran	2 Sackville St	020 7439 6151	10
Housmans Bookshop	5 Caledonian Rd	020 7837 4473	78
ICA Bookshop	The Mall	020 7930 3647	23
John Sandoe	10 Blacklands Terrace	020 7589 9473	46
Librairie La Page	7 Harrington Rd	020 7589 5991	7
London Review Bookshop	14 Bury Pl	020 7269 9030	4
Magma	29 Short's Gardens	020 7240 7970	12
Oxfam	80 Highgate High St	020 8340 3888	51
Owl Books	209 Kentish Town Rd	020 7485 7793	72
Pages of Hackney	70 Lower Clapton Rd	020 8525 1452	87
The Photographers' Gallery	16 Ramillies St	020 7087 9300	10
Southbank Book Market	Under Waterloo Bridge	020 3879 9555	104
Stanford's	7 Mercer Walk	020 7836 1321	13
Stoke Newington Bookshop	159 Stoke Newington High Street	020 7249 2808	85
Tales on Moon Lane	25 Half Moon Ln	020 7274 5759	128
Travis & Emery	17 Cecil Ct	020 7240 2129	24
Trinity Hospice Bookshop	147 Putney High St	020 8780 0737	136
Village Books	1 Calton Ave	020 8693 2808	129
Waterstone's	82 Gower St	020 7636 1577	4
Waterstone's	9 Garrick St	020 7836 6757	13
Waterstone's	1 Whittington Ave	020 7220 7882	18
Waterstone's	206 Piccadilly	020 7851 2400	23
Waterstone's	Trafalgar Square	020 7839 4411	24
Waterstone's	158 King's Rd	020 7351 2023	45
Waterstone's	255 Finchley Road	020 7433 3299	66
WHSmith	Fenchurch Street Station	020 7480 7295	18

Yep you've heard the news. Theatre in the capital is all commercial. Predictable. Repetitive. Uncontroversial. If you believe the whingers, it's all boring stuff. Don't, because it's not. Yes, the West End, that heartland of commercial theatre around Shaftesbury Avenue, is filled with tourist-grabbing, crowd-pleasing musicals. Yes, there are more star-dominated, tried-and-tested plays than ever. Yes, the Mousetrap is still taking up the space at St Martin's after 58 years of we-bloody-well-know-whodunit.

But all that's only half the story. To find the other half, look beyond the glittering billboard signs to find the daring, small West End theatres, such as the **Donmar Warehouse (Map 13)**, bringing the innovative and unusual to Theatreland. There are the Off-West End theatres that proudly fly the flag for new writers, unafraid of being political, controversial and in-yer-face: **The Royal Court (Map 19)**, **The Soho (Map 11)**, **The Bush (Map 33)**. There are the unconventional, anarchic ensemble companies, such as PunchDrunk, shaking up things all the way from these fringe to the West End, while innovative short-play evenings are popping up at pubs across the city (see below).

But let's not forget the cracking double-whammy of the **National Theatre (Map 104)** and **The Old Vic (Map 104)**, two artistic powerhouses currently going from strength to strength. At the National, the unstoppable Nicholas Hytner brings original works to this Southbank concrete colossus (coupled with a £10-tickets offer) while down the road, Hollywood-star-turned-theatre-connoisseur Kevin Spacey is returning the Old Vic into its former glory. The refurbished **Young Vic (Map 104)**, meanwhile, is one of the best places to see fresh, new theatre (and get drunk afterwards). And, whatever you do, you're never far from a good Shakespeare production.

Keeping It Real in the West End

The **Donmar Warehouse (Map 13)**, the West End's smallest theatre, has gained a reputation for being one of Theatreland's most innovative, yet still crowd-pleasing houses. It's quite common for good new plays that have successfully kicked off at a fringe or Off-West End venue to transfer to the West End, such as Tom Stoppard's guitars-meet-politics cracker Rock'n'Roll. **Dean Street's Soho**

Theatre (Map 11) hunts out some of the most original, fearless or hilarious theatre around, while the **Harold Pinter Theatre (Map 23)** may play it a little more safe but packs its shows with jaw-dropping casts. The West End is also a great place to catch up on those classics you always wanted to see but never got round to: from Beckett to Shakespeare.

Off-West End & The Fringe—The Best

The underground-led, breakneck guerrilla heyday must be over, but theatre outside the West End is in rude health. Head to rough-around-the-edges Dalston, where the **Arcola Theatre (Map 86)** continues to thrive in its scruffy ex-factory home, thanks to eclectic programming, an early-fringe-days feel and heaps of creative energy. The tiny **Bush Theatre (Map 33)** has long been a fierce champion of new work, and after being rescued by a star-studded tantrum in the face of funding cuts in 2008 it will doubtless continue to discover exciting new talent. So will **The Royal Court (Map 19)** on Sloane Square, which is one of London's finest. For new, innovative work, also keep your eyes on the **Battersea Arts Centre (Map 140)**, to watch what others will pay £50 to see next year (such as its premiere of Jerry Springer The Opera while other theatres nervously wrung their hands.)

Theatre can't change society? Try telling that to the conviction-led crew of Kilburn's **The Tricycle (Map 65)**—easily London's most radical and most dedicated, political theatre. Islington's **Almeida (Map 80)** is far more conventional, but pretty—and that's got to count for something. If you're up for a laugh, check **The Hackney Empire (Map 87)**, a turn-of-the-century music hall, hosting some of London's best variety shows. **The Old Red Lion (Map 80)**, home inside an Islington pub, stubbornly clings to its unconventional, ale-fuelled fringe attitude, while **Battersea's Theatre 503 (Map 132)** is as provocative as ever. Be surprised.

If the thought of being in a theatre at all is too bourgeois for you, then you're still well catered for. London thesps it up wherever it can so you're never too far from a performance and its sometimes unwitting audience. Recent outings have included an opera about domesticity and flatpack furniture in the Wembley Ikea, and a thriller performed in an office while the audience watch with binoculars and audiophones from the terrace opposite.

Tickets

If you know what you're after, check the theatre's website—they will either have their own system, a link to a ticket selling site, or provide a phone number. If not, check www.officiallondontheatre.co.uk, which lists shows by name, theatre and genre. The site also displays shows that are just opening, or just closing, and links straight to the appropriate ticketing website, once you have made your mind up. There's a handy map of all West End venues, too.

Fancy a bargain? The iconic TKTS ticket booth on Leicester Square, sells, on the day, tickets for most big shows, half-price. The queue can be mind-boggling, so go early. There's a £2.50 booking fee, but it's included in the price shown. Many theatres also have their own discount schemes. If you don't mind standing, you can get Royal Court tickets for as little as 50p. Yes, that's 50p. Just show up between 6 pm and 6.30 pm on the day of the performance. The National has £5 standing tickets for all shows, but the view ain't always great.

Exciting & New

Enter the ensemble. They are multi-skilled, imaginative and are shaking the cosy, venue-obsessed Theatreland with a vengeance. Ensemble companies like PunchDrunk and Kneehigh are touring their way through London's venues in vigorously anarchic fashion. The result is increasingly physical, increasingly unconventional—and increasingly exciting theatre, which you'd be mad to miss.

PunchDrunk (punchdrunk.com) have gained a reputation for site-specific productions, inviting the audience to walk around and follow actors and themes as they please. Their 2006 treatment of Goethe's Faust at the National Theatre was widely hailed as one of the best things to have happened to British theatre in years. The award-winning Cheek by Jowl (www.cheekbyjowl .com), which have been producing Shakespeare

and European classics since 1982, keep discovering hot names—and ways to innovate.

If that's not grassroots enough, visit one of the themed short-play evenings that are popping up across town. Bringing together writers, actors and directors for twenty-minutes-or-so mini-shows, they have become a popular theatre alternative. Take your pick: Established organisers Nabokov have found a West End home at the **Trafalgar Studios (Map 24)** and relative newcomers DryWrite have made Whitechapel's **The George Tavern (Map 97)** their own. The message is spreading. What you thought was a boozer, really is a stage. The possibilities are endless.

Contemporary Dance

From small company shows to big stage spectacles, contemporary dance is having one hell of a ride. **Sadler's Wells (Map 6)** (www. sadlerswells.com), the grand old lady of dance venues, is still doing a fine job bringing some of the world's best dance to London. Check their Sadler's Wells Sampled programme, showcasing dazzling future talent for as little as £10. **The Barbican (Map 7)** (www.barbican.org.uk) has established itself as a reliable source of powerful dance performances, while the **Royal Festival Hall (Map 104)** attracts increasingly bold and interesting works to its refurbished riverside location. For London's most innovative dance performances, check **The Place (Map 4)**, a stylish venue that combines performance, training and dance education (www.theplace.org.uk).

Theatres	Address	Phone	Type	Map
Adelphi Theatre	The Strand	020 3725 7060	West End	24
The Albany	Douglas Way	020 8692 4446	Performing Arts	119
Aldwych Theatre	49 Aldwych	034 5200 7981	West End	14
Almeida Theatre	Almeida St	020 7359 4404	Fringe	80
Ambassadors Theatre	West St	033 3009 6690	West End	12
Apollo Theatre	Shaftesbury Ave	033 0333 4809	West End	11
Apollo Victoria Theatre	17 Wilton Rd	033 3009 6690	West End	20
Arcola Theatre	24 Ashwin St	020 7503 1646	Fringe	86
ArtHouse	159 Tottenham Ln	020 8245 3099	Performing Arts	54
Arts Theatre	6 Great Newport St	020 7836 8463	West End	12
Barbican Centre	Silk St & Whitecross St	020 7638 4141	Performing Arts	7
Barons Court Theatre	28 Comeragh Rd	020 8932 4747	Fringe	42
Battersea Arts Centre	Lavender Hill & Theatre St	020 7223 2223	Fringe	140
Bloomsbury Theatre	15 Gordon St	020 3108 1000	Fringe	4
Brixton Academy	211 Stockwell Rd	020 7771 3000	Performing Arts	145
Bush Theatre	7 Uxbridge Rd	020 8743 5050	Fringe	33
Cadogan Hall	5 Sloane Terrace	020 7730 4500	Performing Arts	19
Cambridge Theatre	Earlham St	020 7087 7745	West End	13
Chats Palace Arts Centre	42 Brooksby's Walk	020 8533 0227	Performing Arts	90
Criterion Theatre	218 Piccadilly	020 7839 8811	West End	10
The Dogstar	389 Coldharbour Ln	020 7733 7515	Fringe	150
Dominion Theatre	268 Tottenham Court Rd	020 7927 0900	West End	4
Donmar Warehouse Theatre	41 Earlham St	020 3282 3808	West End	13
Duchess Theatre	Catherine St	033 0333 4810	West End	14
Duke of York's Theatre	St Martin's Ln	033 3009 6690	West End	24
Etcetera	265 Camden High St	020 7482 4857	Fringe	71
Eventim Apollo Theatre	Queen Caroline St	020 8563 3800	West End	41
Fortune Theatre	Russell St	033 3009 6690	West End	13
Garrick Theatre	Charing Cross Rd	033 0333 4811	West End	24
Gate Theatre	26 Crowndale Rd	020 7229 0706	Fringe	29
The George Tavern	373 Commercial Rd	020 7790 7335	Fringe	97
Gielgud Theatre	Shaftesbury Ave	034 4482 5151	West End	11
Greenwich Theatre	Crooms Hill & Nevada St	020 8858 7755	Fringe	120
Hackney Empire	291 Mare St	020 8985 2424	Fringe	89
Hampstead Theatre	Eton Ave	020 7722 9301	Fringe	66
The Harold Pinter Theatre	Panton St	033 3009 6690	West End	23
The Hen & Chickens Theatre Bar	109 St Paul's Rd	020 7354 8246		109
Her Majesty's Theatre	Haymarket	020 7087 7762	West End	23
Indigo at the O2	205 Peninsula Sq	020 8463 2000	Performing Arts	na
Jermyn Street Theatre	16 Jermyn St	020 7287 2875	Fringe	23
Kiln Theatre	269 Kilburn High Rd	020 7328 1000	Fringe	65
King's Head Theatre & Pub	115 Upper St	020 7226 4443	Fringe	80
Koko	1 Camden High St	020 7388 3222	Performing Arts	71
Leicester Square Theatre	5 Leicester Pl	020 7734 2222	West End	11
Little Angel Theatre	14 Dagmar Passage	020 7226 1787	Performing Arts	80
London Palladium	Argyll St	020 7494 5020	West End	10
Lyceum Theatre	21 Wellington St	033 3009 6690	West End	14
Lyric Theatre	29 Shaftesbury Ave	033 0333 4812	West End	11
National Theatre	South Bank	020 3989 5455	West End	104

Theatres	Address	Phone	Type	Map
New London Theatre	Drury Ln	020 7557 7300	West End	13
Noël Coward Theatre	St Martin's Ln	034 4482 5151	West End	24
Novello Theatre	Aldwych	034 4482 5138	West End	14
Old Red Lion	418 St John St	020 7837 7816	Fringe	6
The Old Vic Theatre	103 The Cut	084 4871 7628	West End	104
Palace Theatre	Shaftesbury Ave	033 0333 4813	West End	12
Park Theatre	Clifton Terrace	020 7870 6876	Fringe	62
Phoenix Theatre	Charing Cross Rd	033 3009 6690	West End	12
Piccadilly Theatre	16 Denman St	033 3009 6690	West End	10
The Place	17 Duke's Rd	020 7121 1000	Performing Arts	4
Playhouse Theatre	Northumberland Ave	033 3009 6690	West End	24
Prince Edward Theatre	28 Old Compton St	084 4482 5151	West End	12
Prince of Wales Theatre	Coventry St	084 4482 5115	West End	11
Queen Elizabeth Hall	South Bank Centre	020 7960 4200	Performing Arts	104
Sondheim Theatre	51 Shaftesbury Ave	034 4482 5151	West End	11
RADA Studios	16 Chenies St	020 7307 5060	Fringe	4
Riverside Studios	Crisp Rd & Queen Caroline St	020 8237 1111	Fringe	41
Ronnie Scott's	47 Frith St	020 7439 0747	Performing Arts	12
The Roundhouse	Chalk Farm Rd & Crogsland Rd	030 0678 9222	Performing Arts	71
Royal Albert Hall	Kensington Gore	020 7589 8212	Performing Arts	36
Royal Court Theatre	Sloane Sq	020 7565 5000	West End	19
Royal Festival Hall	Belvedere Rd	020 3879 9555	Performing Arts	104
Royal Opera House	Bow St	020 7240 1200	Performing Arts	13
Sadler's Wells	Rosebery Ave	020 7863 8000	Performing Arts	6
Savoy Theatre	The Strand	033 3009 6690	West End	24
Scala	275 Pentonville Rd	020 7833 2022	Performing Arts	78
Shaftesbury Theatre	210 Shaftesbury Ave	020 7379 5399	West End	13
Shakespeare's Globe	21 New Globe Walk	020 7902 1400	West End	105
Shepherd's Bush Empire	211 Shepherd's Bush Green	020 8354 3300	Performing Arts	33
Soho Theatre	21 Dean St	020 7478 0100	Fringe	11
Southwark Playhouse	77 Newington Causeway	020 7407 0234	Fringe	106
The Space	269 Westferry Rd	020 7515 7799	Fringe, Performing Arts	na
St John's	Smith Square	020 7222 1061	Performing Arts	22
St Martin's Theatre	West St	020 7836 1443	West End	12
Sutton House	2 Homerton High St	020 8986 2264	Performing Arts	87
Theatre 503	503 Battersea Park Rd	020 7978 7040	Fringe	132
Theatre Royal Drury Lane	Catherine St	020 7557 7300	West End	13
Theatre Royal Haymarket	18 Suffolk St	020 7930 8890	West End	23
Toynbee Studios	28 Commercial St	020 7247 5102	Fringe	91
Trafalgar Studios	14 Whitehall	020 7321 5400	West End	24
Vaudeville Theatre	404 Strand	033 0333 4814	West End	24
Victoria Palace Theatre	79 Victoria St	034 4482 5151	West End	20
Wembley Stadium	Wembley Hill Rd	080 0169 9933	Performing Arts	na
Wigmore Hall	36 Wigmore St	020 7935 2141	Performing Arts	2
Wilton's Music Hall	Graces Alley & Ensign St	020 7702 2789	Fringe	95
Wyndham's Theatre	32 Charing Cross Rd	034 4482 5151	West End	12
The Young Vic Theatre	66 The Cut	020 7922 2922	West End	104

There are many great things about London's vibrant art world. The best? It's free. Granted, if you want to see some of the big show-stopping exhibitions that pass through the **Tates (Maps 21 & 105)**, **British Museum (Map 4)**, **National Gallery (Map 23)** and **Royal Academy (Map 2)** you'll have to pay quite a hefty sum, but overall, you can experience visual arts throughout the capital without coughing up much dough. This might be a contributing factor to London's sprawling art scene, as it is so easy to duck in and out of the capital's 300+ museums and galleries on a lunch break.

Of course, there are concentrations of art in locations around Piccadilly and Bond Street (check out Cork Street for its galleries, such as **Messum (Map 10)** and the **Adam Gallery (Map 10)**, running parallel with Savile Row), the East End (funkier affair and an artistic hipster breeding ground—check out Vyner Street in Bethnal Green), South Kensington/Chelsea (a major culture scene as a result of the Great Exhibition of 1851) and various institutions dotted along the Thames (as seen from the Tate to Tate boat service). If your feeling really adventurous/ bored pretend you're really in the know and head to the New Cross, Peckham and Camberwell areas of South London where artists and galleries are pushing new boundaries in creativity/ pretentiousness. Great art is all over this city, so get out your Oyster Card, and get ready to cover a lot of ground.

Starting with London's modern art, the **Tate Modern (Map 105)**, with its massive smoke stack, has become a major London landmark. This is despite it only existing as a separate entity from the **Tate Britain (Map 21)** since 2000. Check out its spacious Turbine Hall, with often spectacular installations.

It's not surprising that the Tate Modern is often the London tourist's first stop these days, as the city has become well-known for contemporary art. Due in part to the too-cool-for-school London art scene of the 1990s, which saw the establishment of Turner Prizers Tracy Emin, Rachel Whiteread and Damien Hirst, and made a major mark under Saatchi's guiding light. This light has faded somewhat, as the movement's personalities have slowly sold out a little (Emin designing for Longchamp is a case in point). But certain London galleries remain as monuments to this explosion of counter-culture, and, in addition to the **Saatchi Gallery (Map 46)**, these include the **Serpentine Gallery (Map 30)** and **Victoria Miro (Map 31)**. Other inspiring alternatives include the **Riflemaker (Map 10)**, **South London Gallery (Map 122)**, **Camden Arts Centre (Map 66)**, the **White Cube** at Mason's Yard **(Map 23)**, Hoxton Square **(Map 84)**, and Bermondsey **(Map 107)**.

London is a city with a lot on offer, and if you're looking for something a bit more traditional, start with the **National Gallery (Map 24)** in Trafalgar Square, moving onto the National Portrait Gallery **(Map 24)** next door, which presents you with a who's who of British culture past and present. Stroll up Charing Cross Road to the awesome **British Museum (Map 4)** with its jaw-dropping two acre roof over the Great Court (yet another example of Norman Foster's obsession with glass and geometry). Be sure to take in the Parthenon Marbles, aka Elgin Marbles, before the Greek government makes any attempt to get them back. Then over to the not-nearly-praised-enough **Wallace Collection (Map 2)** behind Selfridge's for some tea and Watteau action. A traditional art-lover's tour of London is not over without a trip to the **Royal Academy (Map 2)** with its epic exhibitions and finally to the **Tate Britain (Map 21)**, where the Pre-Raphaelites reign supreme.

Feeling a little non-conformist? London has a brilliant array of cultural institutions that offer more than just marble and canvas. From ceramics to dolls houses, kimonos to plaster casts of just about every great sculpture in the world—the V&A has it all (not to mention an awesome gift shop). Other alternatives to the mainstream include **The Photographers' Gallery (Map 13)** by Leicester Square, which not only squeezes in the best photographic exhibitions in town, but also boasts the best bookshop on the subject. Odd in its own way is the **London Museum (Map 7)**, which walks you through the history of the city from prehistoric times to the present day. Recent London museum gems also include the newly renovated **London Transport Museum (Map 24)**, **Fashion and Textile Museum (Map 107)**, **Museum of Brands, Packaging and Advertising (Map 29)** and the **Design Museum (Map 34)**, with cars and video games in case you're stuck entertaining your nephew. Or check out one of London's hidden glories, from the The Vault at The Hard Rock Café (Map 9) by Hyde Park, or the mind blowing **Hunterian Museum (Map 14)** for fans of fetuses in jars and other macabre wonders (although be warned, do not go suffering from a weak stomach). The Horniman (*snigger*) Museum is a legacy of Victorian curiosity, starring an overstuffed walrus whose taxidermist didn't realise that walruses are supposed to have wrinkles.

The Museum of the Home (Map 88) is a good one to check out when you're in Shoreditch and tired of being hip. Just up Kingsland Road from **Flowers (Map 91)** (a good British contemporary art gallery), this museum of domestic interiors runs through the history of Britain one living room at a time. Somewhat forgotten are the weird and wonderful **Sir John Soane's Museum (Map 14)**, **Leighton House (Map 35)** and **Dennis Severs' House (Map 91)**—but we'll let you discover these gems for yourself.

So forget Pret a Manger—feed your soul in one of London's many museums and galleries. They certainly have more to offer than one of those crappy no bread sandwiches, anyway.

Museums & Galleries	Address	Phone	Map
Apsley House	149 Piccadilly	020 7499 5676	9
Arsenal Museum and Stadium Tour	Drayton Park	020 7704 4504	74
Bank of England Museum	Threadneedle Street	020 7601 5545	17
The Banqueting House	Whitehall & Horse Guards Ave	020 3166 6000	24
Benjamin Franklin House	36 Craven St	020 7925 1405	24
The British Library	96 Euston Rd	084 3208 1144	78
The British Museum	Great Russell St & Museum St	020 7323 8299	4
Brunel Museum	Railway Ave & Rotherhithe St	020 7231 3840	110
Brunswick House	30 Wandsworth Rd	020 7720 2926	134
Burgh House	New End Square	020 7431 0144	56
Camden Arts Centre	Arkwright Rd	020 7472 5500	66
Cartoon Museum	35 Little Russell St	020 7580 8155	4
Chelsea FC Museum and Stadium Tour	Stamford Bridge	087 1984 1955	43
Chelsea Physic Garden	66 Royal Hospital Rd	020 7352 5646	45
Churchill Museum and Cabinet War Rooms	King Charles Street	020 7416 5000	24
Clink Prison Museum	1 Clink St	020 7403 0900	106
Clockmakers' Museum	Aldermanbury	020 7998 8120	16
Dennis Severs' House	18 Folgate St	020 7247 4013	91
Design Museum	224 Kensington High St	020 7967 5001	44
The Dickens House Museum	48 Doughty St	020 7405 2127	5
Dr Johnson's House	17 Gough Square	020 7353 3745	15
Emery Walker Trust	7 Hammersmith Terrace	0208 741 4104	39
Fan Museum	12 Croom's Hill	020 8305 1441	120
Fashion and Textile Museum	83 Bermondsey St	020 7407 8664	107
Florence Nightingale Museum	2 Lambeth Palace Rd	020 7188 4400	131
Flowers Gallery	82 Kingsland Rd	020 7920 7777	91
Foundling Museum	40 Brunswick Square	020 7841 3600	5
Grant Museum of Zoology	21 University St	020 3108 9000	4
Guards Museum	Birdcage Walk	020 7414 3428	22
Handel House Museum	25 Brook St	020 7495 1685	2
Hayward Gallery	Belvedere Rd	020 3879 9555	104
Horniman Museum & Gardens	100 London Rd	020 8699 1872	n/a
Imperial War Museum	Lambeth Road	020 7416 5000	104
Institute of International Visual Arts	16 John Islip St	020 7630 1278	21
Jewish Museum	129 Albert St	020 7284 7384	71
Kirkaldy Testing Museum	99 Southwark St	013 2233 2195	105
The Library and Museum of Freemasonry	60 Great Queen St	020 7395 9251	13
Linley Sambourne House	18 Stafford Terrace	020 7471 9158	35
London Canal Museum	12 New Wharf Rd	020 7713 0836	79
The London Dungeon	The Queen's Walk & Chicheley St	033 3321 2001	104
London Museum	Smithfield Market	020 7001 9844	7

(continued)

Museums & Galleries	Address	Phone	Map
London Sewing Machine Museum	293 Balham High Rd	020 8767 4724	151
London Transport Museum	Covent Garden Piazza	034 3222 5000	24
Marylebone Cricket Club Museum	St John's Wood Rd	020 7616 8656	76
Messum	28 Cork St	020 7437 5545	10
Museum in Docklands	Hertsmere Road	020 7001 9844	100
Museum of Brands, Packaging and Advertising	111 Lancaster Rd	020 7243 9611	29
Museum of Fulham Palace	Bishops Avenue	020 7736 3233	48
Museum of Garden History	Lambeth Palace Road	020 7401 8865	131
Museum of the Home	136 Kingsland Rd	020 7739 9893	88
Museum of Immigration and Diversity	19 Princelet St	020 7247 5352	91
Museum of Methodism & Wesley's Chapel	49 City Rd	020 7253 2262	7
Museum of the Order of St John	26 St John's Ln	020 7324 4005	15
Museum of the Royal Pharmaceutical Society	1 Lambeth High St	020 7572 2210	131
National Army Museum	Royal Hospital Road	020 7730 0717	46
National Gallery	Trafalgar Square	020 7747 2885	24
National Maritime Museum	Park Row	020 8858 4422	n/a
National Portrait Gallery	St Martin's Place	020 7306 0055	24
National Trust	2 Willow Road	020 7435 6166	56
Natural History Museum	Cromwell Rd	020 7942 5000	36
The Old Operating Theatre, Museum & Herb Garret Venue	9 St Thomas St	020 7188 2679	106
Petrie Museum of Egyptian Archaeology	Gower St	020 7679 2884	4
Pollock's Toy Museum	1 Scala St	020 7636 3452	3
Ragged School Museum	46 Copperfield Rd	020 8980 6405	98
Riflemaker Gallery	74 Beak St	077 9462 9188	10
Rotherhithe Picture Research Library	82 Marychurch St	020 7231 2209	109
Royal Academy of Music Museum	Marylebone Rd	020 7873 7443	2
The Royal College of Surgeons of England	35 Lincoln's Inn Fields	020 7405 3474	14
Saatchi Gallery	King's Road	020 7811 3070	46
Science Museum	Exhibition Rd	033 0058 0058	36
Serpentine Gallery	Kensington Gardens	020 7402 6075	30
Sherlock Holmes Museum	221 Baker St	020 7224 3688	76
Sikorski Museum	20 Princes Gate	020 7589 9249	37
Sir John Soane's Museum	13 Lincoln's Inn Fields	020 7405 2107	14
South London Gallery	65 Peckham Rd	020 7703 6120	122
Spencer House	27 St James's Pl	020 7514 1958	23
St Bartholomew's Hospital Museum	West Smithfield	020 3465 5798	15
Tate Britain	Millbank	020 7887 8888	21
Tate Modern	Bankside	020 7887 8888	105
Tower Bridge Exhibition	Tower Bridge	020 7403 3761	107
Victoria & Albert Museum	Cromwell Rd & Thurloe Pl	020 7942 2000	37
Victoria Miro Gallery	16 S Wharf Rd	020 7336 8109	31
Wallace Collection	Manchester Square	020 7563 9500	2
Wellcome Collection	183 Euston Rd	020 7611 2222	4
Westminster Abbey	Parliament Square	020 7222 5152	22
White Cube	26 Mason's Yard	020 7930 5373	23
White Cube	144 Bermondsey St	020 7930 5373	107

Overview

Stumbling out teary-eyed into the light, pallid skin wrecked by long hours in darkness and surrounded by strangers, it's hard to believe that this time last year we were counting out our coppers and begging our friends to buy us another drink. Okay, so we're not completely in the red and London's cash registers may not be overflowing with moolah as they once were but we've managed to open new bars, forget about old ones, sing ourselves raw in amateur karaoke sessions, break a few bones dancing in scary clubs we shouldn't be in—you know, the usual. What is scary though is how fast the night-time landscape is changing around us. These days walking around Soho is like picking your way through a war zone; with The Astoria and its surrounding area now bulldozed, it sometimes feels the heart of London's soul has been ripped out by greedy developers. Maybe it has, but we're not dwelling on all those bad vibes: we're too busy digging amateur folk in Stokey, or quaffing luxurious cocktails in the depths of Old Street, or down the front at some dingy gig hellhole in the depths of Brixton having the time of our sorry little lives. As you may have gathered by now, London's options are as endlessly varied as her tastes. And being children of the post-modern age (or is that post-post-modern age?) we've given up caring about tribalism and consistency and have dived head-first into everything at once. Economy, what economy?

Local Pubs for Local People

North to South, East to West, whether in Zone 1 or Zone 6 the London 'local' encapsulates the city itself. That calm beating heart of the old geezer talking of times gone by in Limehouse or the adrenaline-fuelled racing heart of the City's next 'big thing' in Farringdon—all around a city that tells its stories, shares its woes and gets itself together over a pint of 'Pride' in the local boozer. The cavernous bowels of Dickens' favourite local **Ye Olde Cheshire Cheese (Map 15)** now provide tourist-free shelter for City folk. Borough's **George Inn (Map 106)**, with a dazzling selection of ales, is as ancient as they get. **The Lamb (Map 14)** is where to go after your office job if you want to pretend you're a writer, while the Grade-II-listed **Princess Louise (Map 4)** is sparkling with old man-ness but in

the heart of London. In Hampstead, it's got to be the pretty, and pretty hidden, **Holly Bush (Map 56)**. And while it's been gentrified since it was run by the Kray's mum, **The Carpenter's Arms (Map 91)**, is still a great, tiny little foreign beer-heaven. You can eyeball woodworm in the brilliant **The Compton Arms (Map 80)**. The old-timers in Rotherhithe's dream-of-your-dad **The Mayflower (Map 109)**, and Brixton's **The Effra (Map 150)** will have never heard of the 'Inter-web', never mind Facebook. Way out west, **The Dove (Map 40)** draws the local collective with its cosy fire, relaxed chatter and river spectacular.

Keep-It-Real Ale

The Carling brigade can take a hike, this town takes Price (sic) in its real brews. The **Wenlock Arms (Map 83)** proves we can do down-to-earth ale-enthusiast and **The Jerusalem Tavern (Map 3)** shows we can do fake ye olde times with amazing beer selection as well as any Lancashire local. Borough's **Market Porter (Map 106)** has a great selection, and is full of market traders counting their cash. Lovers of the Belgian stuff (and trendy Hackney-ites) will feel at home in **The Dove (Map 89)** and those after an even greater selection of European ales without the pretentiousness should head to **Quinns (Map 71)** in Camden. Too fancy? For great ale selections, there's **The Royal Oak (Map 106)** also in Borough, where the taps come courtesy of the Harveys brewery. Pitfield, Freedom and St Peter's, meanwhile, supply Islington's **Duke of Cambridge (Map 83)** with organic ale, if you like that kind of stuff. In Parson's Green **The White Horse (Map 49)** is a Victorian gem and the **Roebuck (Map 38)** provides Chiswick with an ever changing selection of local and national brews.

Good Mixers

While our ale keeps us down to earth, it's the lure of the cocktail that causes us to show off. Shaken or stirred, it doesn't matter. It's all about looking good with a long glass of the colourful sugary stuff dressed to the nines, glace cherry 'n all. For aesthetic hedonism we love **Lounge Bohemia (Map 8)**. Martinis? You'll find us at the **Charlotte Street Hotel (Map 3)**. At **5th View (Map 9)** there's vistas of Big Ben with your Kir Royal.

See also the plush Art Deco heaven that is **Claridge's Bar (Map 2)**. If you find yourself on Clapham High Street then you could do a lot worse than heading to **The Loft (Map 143)**—a modern, lush escape. One can feel studious while nursing a punch bowl at **The Cinnamon Club (Map 22)**, nestled perfectly inside the old serenity of the Old Westminster Library.

Weirdos

Let's face it, sometimes the booze just isn't enough to keep you entertained. Destroying your internal organs with the stuff is just sometimes a little boring, right? **The Windmill (Map 150)** of Brixton is a handmade weirdo magnet and **The Battersea Barge (Map 134)** is a friendly old pub—on a very thin barge. **The Coronet (Map 74)** in Holloway has a desolate, nostalgic charm as does perhaps the weirdest pub of them all, the **Palm Tree (Map 93)**, a celebration of British antiquity with crooners of a certain age most nights.

Smoker-Friendly

If the merciless prohibition regime of 2007 hasn't resulted in reluctant surrender, don't despair: from provisionally erected patios to all-year beer gardens to secret backdoors, London's ban-bashing creativity knows no boundaries. Great fag spots include the barbeque-and-beer-can courtyard of **93 Feet East (Map 91)** and the tree-shaded garden of the **Edinboro Castle (Map 77)**. Hang out in front of Highgate favourite **The Flask (Map 51)**. For clubbing, consider **Egg (Map 79)**, where you're allowed to smoke in the massive garden. **The Owl & Pussycat (Map 91)** is not just a surprisingly pleasant pub in Shoreditch, it's also got a surprisingly nice garden, where smoking is not just allowed, dear friends, but encouraged.

We're Raving, We're Raving

Over at superclub **Fabric (Map 15)** the cool kids of the capital are bringing down the house with ... er, a bit of House music. The ever-so-eclectic **Notting Hill Arts Club (Map 29)** continues to come up with exhilarating and inventive nights,

as does Brick Lane's 93 **Feet East (Map 91)**. **Cargo (Map 84)** is for those who like a deep seated couch with their DJ while **Madame Jojo's (Map 11)**. As long as lip fuzz is still trendy there's always the **Moustache Bar (Map 86)** in Dalston, natch. For serious rockabilly, find **Ye Olde Axe (Map 91)** gentlemen's club on Hackney Road, where the rock 'n' roll starts as soon as the last naked girl has disappeared behind the big-mirrored wall.

Great Bars

George Orwell's ideal pub was all about "draught stout, open fires, cheap meals, motherly barmaids and no radio." These days we'd maybe add music straight from a blog, handmade decor and a dangerous vibe. For some if not all of these try up-beat **Jaguar Shoes (Map 91)**, **Freud (Map 13)** or the **French House (Map 11)** in the West End are also solid contenders for boho schlock. But there's so much more: crawl from **Barrio North's (Map 80)** caravan to the country-house of **Lost Society (Map 142)**. We like standing next to (would-be) artists at the **ICA Bar (Map 23)** and actor types on the terrace of **The Cut Bar (Map 104)**. Later on, you'll find us nibbling cheese in Dalston's **Jazz Bar (Map 82)**.

Best of the Rest

Want to feel exclusive? Members-only clubs are not only becoming ever more popular, but also ever more accessible. So there. Escape Shoreditch's terrifying hordes to the rooftop swimming pool of **Shoreditch House (Map 91)** or the boredom of Shepherd's Bush to the underground ex-toilets that have become **Ginglik (Map 33)**. Of course, most of those in the know will drag you to the various warehouse raves that fire up every weekend. People like **Real Gold** (http://wearerealgold.com) are a good place to start if you fancy some of this awfulness. Remember it's not who you know but, oh wait, it is who you know.

To create your own entertainment and/or embarrass yourself, **Lucky Voice (Maps 10, 80)** is one of many joints offering private karaoke booths and you and some people who will most probably cease to be your friends after they hear you massacre 'Time After Time.' Shoreditch's exposed brick joint **The Book Club (Map 8)** has a bit of 'Social Athletics' on the bill—ping pong, old chap? If relying on that notoriously joke-cracking ex-friend of a friend for your evening's amusement sounds a bit risky, consider these alternatives: The standard-setting **Comedy Store (Map 11)** (book in advance) and **Covent Garden Comedy Club (Map 24)**, or, at the pub end of things, **The Bedford (Map 148)** and the **Camden Head (Map 78)**. If you think that YOU should in fact provide the evening's amusement, well, the **Poetry Café (Map 13)** gives you the stage. Or stay at home and talk to yourself; it's cheaper.

Music, Sweet Music

London's veins are pumped by its mellifluous melodies, the driving sound of grime, the sneers of angry young men and the coos of folkie maidens. Whether you're dub-stepping in the dark or jamming along at folk night there'll be something to hear at any given time of the week.

Strummin' Mental

This city's music scene is in a constant state of flux with bands, venues and styles falling in and out of cool lists quicker than a Ramones song. What never changes though is that there always is a scene and with that scene comes the venue. The good news is that there are so many great places to do this in. Yes we've got our share of corporate megaliths (that means you **O2**) but for every church of Carling there are two or three brilliant dives like the punky **Grosvenor (Map 145)** or the ever-mobbed **Stag's Head (Map 84)**.

For the sweatily inclined there are infinite choices. Bethnal Green's **Star of Bethnal Green (Map 92)** (formerly the Pleasure Unit), Highgate's **Buffalo Bar (Map 80)** and Angel's **Lexington (Map 79)** are as pant-wettingly indie as they come but if you like harder or weirder stuff the **Camden Underworld (Map 71)** does all the metals while **Cafe Oto (Map 86)** handles experimental and improv. **The MacBeth (Map 84)** is very popular yet somehow suffers from a fun bypass but **Monto Water Rats (Map 5)** is an

unshakeable legend. The refurbished **Old Blue Last (Map 84)** or Vice Magazine party HQ has surfed to the crest of the trend wave fueled by young kids attempting to be sexually harassed by older men like in their favourite adverts for American Apparel. Mid-sized venues for mid-fame bands? The **Scala (Map 78)** is a brilliant converted cinema. The **ICA (Map 23)** is the 'art-space' par excellence for all artistes who insist on that 'e' at the end of 'artist.' The **Amersham Arms (Map 126)** is a good place to watch some twonks you've been told to like by Dazed. The city's electronic music scene generally piggy-backs the guitars, but check out **Lightbox (Map 134)**.

As for the classics, the **Shepherd's Bush Empire (Map 33)** and the breathtakingly beautiful **Bush Hall (Map 32)** remain west London's finest, while Camden stalwart **Koko (Map 71)** keeps rocking in the free world. The north London show is being stolen by Roundhouse (Map 71), though boasting a healthy "I am Legend"-attitude and some bloody horrible Anthony Gormley statues waiting to jump from the top. **Brixton Academy (Map 145)** might be slightly overrated, but its sky-like ceiling remains awesome. If you have to do stadium-size, do stadium-size in style and get your seat in the **Royal Albert Hall (Map 36)**, which is increasingly luring good non-classical acts. The refurbishment of the **Royal Festival Hall (Map 104)**, meanwhile, has kick-started more pop-oriented programming on the South Bank.

Arts & Entertainment • **Nightlife**

A World of Jazz and Blues

Camden's intimate **Jazz Café (Map 71)** seems to have no intention of stopping its relentless stream of first-rate jazz performances, getting in more soul, funk and pop at the same time, while **Ronnie Scott's Jazz Club (Map 12)**, London's undisputed grandaddy of jazz original continues to offer up an eclectic programme of past and present. For some of the freshest jazz, alongside great contemporary folk and world music, head to Dalston, where the plush **Vortex (Map 82)** is a-buzz with free-spirited legends. On the other side of town, Fulham's small but perfectly formed **606 Club (Map 50)** sets the tone with crammed, small tables within slobbering distance from the saxes. For world music, the **Barbican Centre (Map 7)** leads the pack, but is easily beaten in atmosphere stakes by the **Union Chapel (Map 80)**, an Islington church doubling as one of London's most beautiful venues and in scummy stakes by **Dingwalls (Map 71)** who continue to expand their programming. The home of folk is the brilliant **Cecil Sharp House (Map 70)**. If classical music floats your boat, look beyond the obvious venues and settle amid the great acoustics of Chelsea's **Cadogan Hall (Map 19)**, the historical brilliance of Hackney's **Sutton House (Map 87)** or the magnificent **Wigmore Hall (Map 2)**, in Mayfair.

Map 1 · Marylebone (West)

Duke of York	45 Harrowby St	020 7723 1966	The ideal local.

Map 2 · Marylebone (East)

Claridge's Bar	55 Brook St	020 7629 8860	Posh and plush and Art Deco. More champagne!
Gunmakers	33 Aybrook St	020 7935 5291	Nice boozer on quiet street.
Inn 1888	21 Devonshire St	020 7486 7420	Quiet pint perfection.
The Phoenix	37 Cavendish Sq	020 7493 8003	A quirky gem amidst an ocean of crappy chain bars.
Purl	50-54 Blandford St	020 7935 0835	Victorian themed experimental cocktail bar.

Map 3 · Fitzrovia

100 Club	100 Oxford St	020 7636 0933	Ancient club that's seen off Nazi bombs and Sex Pistols.
The Albany	240 Great Portland St	020 7387 0221	Swanky, but nice. And the music's good.
Bourne & Hollingsworth	28 Rathbone Pl	020 7636 8228	Fine Fitzrovian basement boutique.
Bradley's Spanish Bar	42 Hanway St	020 7636 0359	60's rock joint with awesome jukebox and disgusting toilets.
Bricklayers Arms	31 Gresse St	020 7636 5593	Advertising types take no-nonsense boozing.
Charlotte Street Hotel	15 Charlotte St	020 7806 2000	Dirty gossip over dirty martinis.
The Cock	27 Great Portland St	020 7631 5002	Cheap, cheerful and central.
The Fitzroy Tavern	16 Charlotte St	020 7580 3714	Sam Smith's, anyone?
Hakkasan	8 Hanway Pl	020 7927 7000	Sleek, blue-lit boudoir. For saketinis and rose petal martinis.
The Holy Tavern	55 Britton St	020 7490 4281	A tiny old wooden gem of a pub. And organic ale.
Market Place	11 Market Pl	020 7079 2020	Warm buzz. Hot crowd. Cool prices.
The Northumberland Arms	119 Tottenham Court Rd	020 4524 9875	Cosy, old-style bar with a local feel.
The Remedy	124 Cleveland St	020 3489 3800	Deep dive into wine, with food pairings, too.
Rising Sun	46 Tottenham Ct Rd	020 7636 6530	Bordering studentland and Fitzrovia; pretty name, less pretty pub.
The Roxy	3 Rathbone Pl	020 7255 1098	Hip subterranean hangout. More chicks than dicks.
Shochu Lounge	37 Charlotte St	020 7580 6464	Japanese-styled cocktails underneath Roka restaurant.
The Social	5 Little Portland St	020 7636 4992	Fab music, nonchalant surroundings and plenty of trendsters.
Yorkshire Grey	46 Langham St	020 7636 4788	Upstairs is perfect when Oxford Street's pissing you off.

Map 4 · Bloomsbury (West)

All Star Lanes	Bloomsbury Pl	020 7025 2676	You'll be bowled over. Oh yes you will.
Bloomsbury Bowling Lanes	Bedford Way	020 7183 1979	As cool as bowling gets.
Marquis Cornwallis	31 Marchmont St	020 7278 8355	Chilled couches.
The Old Crown Public House	33 New Oxford St	020 3904 2744	After-work bar that takes itself very seriously.
The Plough	27 Museum St	020 7636 7964	Fancy a bite? London Vampyre Society meetings held here monthly.
The Princess Louise	208 High Holborn	020 7405 8816	Victorian gin palace now serving cheap but good lager.

Map 5 • Bloomsbury (East)

The Blue Lion	133 Grays Inn Rd	020 7405 4422	Pool table!
Calthorpe Arms	252 Gray's Inn Rd	020 7278 4732	Impressive old man pub.
The Clerk & Well	156 Clerkenwell Rd	020 7837 8548	You and a hundred cycle couriers.
The Perseverance	63 Lamb's Conduit St	020 7405 8278	Bustling, young and semi-trendy.
Pimp Shuei	59 Mount Pleasant		Kung fu-themed bar.
The Water Rats	328 Grays Inn Rd	020 7833 3312	No rats here, only the best up-and-coming bands.

Map 6 • Clerkenwell

1920	19 Great Sutton St	020 7253 1920	Classic American pool hall with occasional DJ events.
Bandstand Busking	Northampton Square		Free acoustic gigs in summer. Dreamy.
The Betsey Trotwood	56 Farringdon Rd	020 7253 4285	Thoroughly likable Shepherd Neame pub renowned for live music.
Café Kick	43 Exmouth Market	020 7837 8077	Creaky, Latin American table football cafe.
The Dovetail	9 Jerusalem Passage	020 7490 7321	Small, but perfectly formed Clerkenwell sister to Broadway Market's The Dove.
The Harlequin	27 Arlington Way	020 7833 1129	Livingroom boozer.
Old Red Lion	418 St. John St	020 7837 7816	Theatre pub legend.
The Slaughtered Lamb	34 Great Sutton St	020 7253 1516	Dimly-lit pub that's still packing in the Clerkenwell crowd.
The Three Kings	7 Clerkenwell Close	020 7336 7234	Quirky pub that dies on weekends.
The Wilmington Arms	69 Rosebery Ave	020 7837 1384	Staff have 'arsehole' tattooed on their foreheads.

Map 7 • Barbican / City Road (South)

Nightjar	129 City Rd	020 7253 4101	Like Fat Sam's Grand Slam.
The Two Brewers	171 Whitecross St	020 7502 7591	Traditional English pub with a young hip crowd.

Map 8 • Liverpool Street / Broadgate

The Book Club	100 Leonard St	020 7684 8618	All day food and drink venue with outdoor space and basement club.
Callooh Callay	65 Rivington St	020 7739 4781	Not-so-secret cocktail bar in The City; enter through a wardrobe.
Lounge Bohemia	1 Great Eastern St	077 2070 7000	Vintage martinis make up for neo-avant-garde pretenses.
Red Lion	1 Eldon St	020 7247 5381	Drinkers near Moorgate can't be choosers. So there.
Worship Street Whistling Shop	63 Worship St	020 7580 1960	Wet your whistle.
XOYO	32 Cowper St	020 7608 2878	Concrete music bunker with quality acts and a buzzing vibe.

Map 9 • Mayfair / Green Park

Chesterfield Arms	50 Hertford St	020 7499 3017	For drinking within Shepherd's Market.
Mahiki	1 Dover St	020 7493 9529	Crushingly tropical cocktail bar. Pineapples a-go-go.
The Wine Bar at Fortnum & Mason	181 Piccadilly	020 7734 8040	Empty Fortnum & Mason's wine cellar.

Map 10 • Piccadilly / Soho (West)

5th View	203 Piccadilly	020 7851 2433	Spill Bloody Marys over books in full view of Big Ben.
Ain't Nothing But...	20 Kingly St	020 7287 0514	Bracingly raw music in a tiny frontroom.
The Blind Pig	58 Poland St	020 7993 3251	Challenging cocktails above Social Eating House.
Courthouse Bar	19 Great Marlborough St	020 7297 5555	Drink where Oscar Wilde was in the clink.
The John Snow	39 Broadwick St	020 7437 1344	Yet another cheap, old school boozer from Samuel Smith Brewery.
Lucky Voice	52 Poland St	020 7439 3660	Why is this London's best karaoke bar? The dress up box.
The Red Lion	14 Kingly St	020 7734 4985	Amazingly cheap for such a central spot.
The Windmill	6 Mill St	020 7491 8050	Fab beers on tap but you come here for the pies.

Map 11 • Soho (Central)

Blue Posts	22 Berwick St	020 7437 5008	Unreformed, scuzzy boozer.
The Blue Posts	28 Rupert St	079 2133 6010	Hey, a decent pub in Soho.
The Comedy Store	1 Oxendon St	020 7024 2060	It ain't world famous for no reason, chuckles.

De Hems	11 Macclesfield St	020 7437 2494	Dutch bar with brain-cell-annihilatingly strong beer. Hic!
Experimental Cocktail Club	13 Gerrard St	020 7434 3559	The modern-day speakeasy: reservation by email only.
Freedom	66 Wardour St	020 7734 0071	Neon green cocktail kitsch.
The French House	49 Dean St	020 7437 2477	Boho Soho hang-out for eccentrics.
The Lyric	37 Great Windmill St	020 7434 0604	Charming Victorian pub with many draughts.
Village	81 Wardour St	020 7478 0530	Tacky, flirtatious Soho gay bar.

Map 12 · Soho (East)

Bar Termini	7 Old Compton St	07860 945018	Italian coffee and cocktails; efficiently scheduled.
Cafe Boheme	13 Old Compton St	020 7734 0623	Beautiful bar to prop up and people watch.
Comptons	53 Old Compton St	020 7096 5400	Crammed gay pub.
G-A-Y Bar	30 Old Compton St	020 7494 2756	Poptastic gay bunker.
G-A-Y Late	5 Goslett Yard	020 7437 0479	Cheap drinks and pop videos wipe out brain functions 'til 3am.
Garlic & Shots	14 Frith St	020 7734 9505	Drunken vampires beware.
Jazz After Dark	9 Greek St	020 7734 0545	Tunes and cheap drinks, until LATE.
Karaoke Box	18 Frith St	020 7494 3878	A bit gritty but one of London's cheaper karaoke bars.
Ku	30 Lisle St	020 7437 4303	Newly relocated gay bar for the young and clueless.
The Montagu Pyke	105 Charing Cross Rd	020 7287 6039	Cheap beer—in the West End.
Orange Yard Soho	Orange Yard	020 7734 5547	Cool basement club, bizarrely got up in Tex-Mex decor.
Ronnie Scott's		020 7439 0747	Original, and still the best.
The Royal George	133 Charing Cross Rd	020 7734 8837	Busy, but the crowd's nice. Board games and food.
The Three Greyhounds	25 Greek St	020 7494 0953	Recall glory days of Soho hunting grounds with real ale.
The Toucan	19 Carlisle St	020 7437 4123	Small and snug central bolthole for Guinness.

Map 13 · Covent Garden

Compagnie Des Vins Surnaturels	8-10 Neal's Yard	020 7734 7737	Encyclopedic wine bar with French-Italian focus.
The Cross Keys	31 Endell St	020 7836 5185	Tiny old-school boozer.
Freud	198 Shaftesbury Ave	020 7240 9933	Intimate basement bar that used to be Alex of Blur's living room. Literally.
Lamb and Flag	33 Rose St	020 7497 9504	Cobbled lane leads to a crowded but gloriously timeless inn.
Poetry Cafe	22 Betterton St	020 7420 9888	Eat, drink, write, listen or, yes, PERFORM!

Map 14 · Holborn / Temple

Bar Polski	6 Little Turnstile	020 7831 9679	With 50 types of vodka, even beetroot soup tastes good.
Bounce	121 Holborn	020 3657 6525	Anyone for (table) tennis?
Cittie of Yorke	22 High Holborn	020 7242 7670	Soe olde it's name has a real e's. A marvellouse pube.
The Craft Beer Co.	82 Leather Ln	020 7404 7049	Beer drinkers heaven, albeit with a scramble to get served.
The Enterprise	38 Red Lion St	020 7404 8461	More Captain Cook than Captain Kirk.
The Lamb	94 Lamb's Conduit St	020 7405 0713	Legendary little place with Victorian touches.
The Seven Stars	53 Carey St	020 7242 8521	Tiny, slightly dusty bar frequented by barristers.

Map 15 · Blackfriars / Farringdon

Fabric	77 Charterhouse St	020 7336 8898	Debauched club mecca for gurners of all persuasions.
Fox and Anchor	115 Charterhouse St	020 7250 1300	Amazing interior and the tankards make up for the wankers.
The Hat and Tun	3 Hatton Wall	020 7242 4747	Home of the original politically incorrect 100 shooter list.
Ye Olde Cheshire Cheese	145 Fleet St	020 7353 6170	Get tanked up where Dickens used to. Historic.
Ye Olde Mitre	1 Ely Pl	020 7405 4751	Elizabeth I used to dance here, don't you know?!

Map 16 · Square Mile (West)

Planet of the Grapes	9 Bull's Head Passage	020 7929 7224	The clue is in the name.
The Samuel Pepys	Stew Ln	020 7489 1871	Find it and be rewarded with Thames views.
Ye Olde Watling	29 Watling St	020 7248 8935	Squeeze in.

Map 17 · Square Mile (East)

The Counting House	50 Cornhill	020 7283 7123	A truly magnificent (former) bank. That sells beer now.

Map 18 · Tower Hill / Aldgate

Dion	65 St. Paul's Churchyard	020 7248 8880	Veuve Clicquot La Grande Dame Rose, anyone?
Kenza	10 Devonshire Sq	020 7929 5533	Belly-dancers, cocktails & couscous.
The Minories	64 Minories	020 7702 1658	Cavernous boozer by day, thumping disco by night.
Revolution	140 Leadenhall St	020 7621 9955	Vodka-drenched, vault-like DJ bar that couldn't care less about the revolution.

Map 19 · Belgravia

The Blue Bar	Wilton Pl	020 7235 6000	It's blue. Mindbogglingly so.
The Nag's Head	53 Kinnerton St	020 7235 1135	No mobiles allowed. Says it all.
The Plumber's Arms	14 Lower Belgrave St	020 7730 4067	Tradesman's pub from days of yore. Ask about Lord Lucan.
The Wilton Arms	71 Kinnerton St	020 3903 6222	A Shepherd Neame pub? In Belgravia?

Map 20 · Victoria / Pimlico (West)

The Cask & Glass	39 Palace St	020 7834 7630	Teeny tiny, English country garden-esque drinking hole. Flower-festoned frontage, real ale.
The Warwick	25 Warwick Way	020 7834 4987	Gastropub with fine selection of booze.
Windsor Castle	23 Francis St	020 7834 7260	Easier to like than to find.

Map 21 · Pimlico (East)

Morpeth Arms	58 Millbank	020 7834 6442	Where Millbank prisoners used to escape to.

Map 22 · Westminster

The Albert	52 Victoria St	020 7222 5577	Distinguished, well-preserved period pub. Tourist haunt but rightly so.
The Cinnamon Club	30 Great Smith St	020 7222 2555	Cocktail classiness inside the Old Westminster Library. Try finding it.
The Speaker	46 Great Peter St	020 7222 4589	Good after-worker with guest ales.
St. Stephen's Tavern	10 Bridge St	020 7925 2286	Tiny pub with character, despite being on tourist trail.
Two Chairmen	39 Dartmouth St	020 7222 8694	Public servants galore! Decent pub for this area though.

Map 23 · St. James's

Dukes Hotel	35 St James's St	020 7491 4840	Channel 007 and have a martini at Ian Fleming's haunt.
Institute of Contemporary Arts	The Mall	020 7930 3647	Cutting edge arts complex/bar, weirdly stuck on the upper-crust Mall.

Map 24 · Trafalgar Square / The Strand

The Chandos	29 St Martin's Ln	020 7836 1401	All Trafalgar Square pubs tourist traps? Think again.
The Coal Hole	91 Strand	020 7379 9883	Genuine old style.
Covent Garden Comedy Club	The Arches	079 6007 1340	Good acts play to a friendly crowd drinking awful beer.
Gordon's Wine Bar	47 Villiers St	020 7930 1408	Candle-lit vaults. Romantic perfection.
The Harp	47 Chandos Pl	020 7836 0291	Covent Garden's secret spot for sausage and a good brew.
Heaven	The Arches	020 7930 2020	Epicentre of London's late night gay scene.
Maple Leaf	41 Maiden Ln	020 7240 2843	Just don't ask which State they're from.
Punch & Judy	The Covent Garden Piazza	020 7379 0923	Naff, naff, naff. 'Nuff said?
Retro Bar	2 George Ct	020 7839 8760	Chilled gay bar, hiding from Charing Cross in a small alley.
The Sherlock Holmes	10 Northumberland St	020 7930 2644	Unintentionally sinister, must-see Holmes waxwork upstairs. Expect bad dreams.
The Ship and Shovell	1 Craven Passage	020 7839 1311	A pub made of two pubs, both obsessed with Sherlock Holmes.
Zoo Bar & Club	13 Bear St	020 3325 9739	Wake up with someone new.

Map 26 · Maida Hill

The Union Tavern	45 Woodfield Rd	020 7286 1886	A pub that bakes its own bread! Oh, and it's canal side...

Map 27 · Maida Vale

The Bridge House	13 Westbourne Terrace Rd	020 7266 4326	Canal views and comedy. Lovely.
The Warwick Castle	6 Warwick Pl	020 7266 0921	Down-to-earth drinking in Maida Vale. Indeed.
The Waterway	54 Formosa St	020 7266 3557	Try not to fall into the canal.

Map 28 · Ladbroke Grove / Notting Hill (West)

Julie's Restaurant & Champagne Bar	135 Portland Rd	020 7229 8331	Pleasantly posh wine bar full of pleasantly posh ladies.

Map 29 · Notting Hill Gate

Notting Hill Arts Club	21 Notting Hill Gate	020 7460 4459	Indie cave with bands, lurid projections and teenagers.
Sun in Splendour	7 Portobello Rd	020 7792 0914	Notting Hill denizens' choice.
Trailer Happiness	177 Portobello Rd	020 7041 9833	Step back in time.
Uxbridge Arms	13 Uxbridge St	020 7792 1362	Warm little place full of eccentric old toffs.
Windsor Castle	114 Campden Hill Rd	020 7243 8797	A wood-panelled piece of pub history.

Map 30 · Bayswater

All Star Lanes	Ariel Way	020 3167 2401	Glitzy bowling madness.
The Cow	89 Westbourne Park Rd	020 7221 0021	Lovely pub. Let down by braying trustafarians.

Map 31 · Paddington

The Victoria	10 Strathearn Pl	020 7724 1191	British pub straight from a Richard Curtis film. Simply perfect.

Map 32 · Shepherd's Bush (West)

Bush Hall	310 Uxbridge Rd	020 8222 6955	The red carpet, the ornate walls...the sheer beauty!
White Horse	31 Uxbridge Rd	020 8723 4531	Did you call my pint a slag? Outside, now!

Map 33 · Shepherd's Bush

The Defector's Weld	170 Uxbridge Rd	020 8749 0008	Tarted up boozer.
O2 Shepherd's Bush Empire	Shepherd's Bush Green	020 8354 3300	Still among London venueland's finest.

Map 34 · West Kensington / Olympia

The Cumberland Arms	29 North End Rd	020 7371 6806	Where long hard days become good again.
Famous 3 Kings (F3K) Bar	171 North End Rd	020 7603 6071	Brilliant atmosphere for big matches especially rugby. Pool tables too.
Society Bar	380 Kensington High St	020 7856 1980	Dying for a drink in Kensington? Well there.

Map 35 · Kensington

The Builders Arms	1 Kensington Ct Pl	020 7937 6213	Boozy haven from High Street Kensington's shopping madness.
The Devonshire Arms	37 Marloes Rd	020 7937 0710	Warm and cosy for a roast on a rainy Sunday.

Map 36 · South Kensington / Gloucester Rd

The Queen's Arms	30 Queen's Gate Mews	020 7823 9293	South Ken's secret drinking spot. Close to the Royal Albert Hall.

Map 38 · Chiswick

George IV	185 Chiswick High Rd	020 8994 4624	Fullers pies, real ale and a comedy club on the High Road? Sweet.
Packhorse & Talbot	145 Chiswick High Rd	020 8994 0360	A Chiswick institution. Proper British pub...with live jazz?! Truly.
The Roebuck	122 Chiswick High Rd	020 3978 2162	Best pub in West London. Unpretentious charm, killer Sunday roast.

Map 39 · Stamford Brook

The Raven	375 Goldhawk Rd	020 8748 6977	A bit grubby on the outside but £4 handmade pies are part of the appeal.

Arts & Entertainment · **Nightlife**

Map 40 · Goldhawk Rd / Ravenscourt Park

The Dove	19 Upper Mall	020 8748 9474	So perfect for dates that Charles II brought Nell Gwynne here.

Map 41 · Hammersmith

Brook Green	170 Shepherd's Bush Rd	020 7603 2516	Lost between Hammersmith and Shepherd's Bush? Fear not.
The Distillers	64 Fulham Palace Rd	020 8747 6167	Chandelier clad pub-bar with ace live music and comedy in The Regal Room.
Eventim Apollo	45 Queen Caroline St	020 8563 3800	Still West London's best music venue.
The Hampshire	227 King St	020 8748 3391	Relaxing spot for a Pinot Noir after a hard day.
Lyric Hammersmith	King St	020 8741 6850	Hammersmith's hottest home of hentertainment.

Map 42 · Baron's Court

Colton Arms	187 Greyhound Rd	020 3500 7921	If you're not already a regular, you'll wish you were.
The Curtains Up	28 Comeragh Rd	020 7386 7543	Pub which keeps actors in the basement.
The Fulham Mitre	81 Dawes Rd	020 7386 8877	Young, trendy Fulhamites like it. We don't.

Map 43 · West Brompton / Fulham Broadway / Earls Court

The Blackbird	209 Earl's Court Rd	020 7835 1855	Proper London local amidst the chaos of Earl's Court Road.
Chairs & Coffee	512 Fulham Rd	075 4553 3239	Friday is aperitivo night.
The King's Head	17 Hogarth Rd	020 7373 5239	Tucked away with British style tapas. Who knew!
Prince Of Teck	161 Earl's Court Rd	020 7870 2276	Locals and tourists receive a friendly welcome in this pub.

Map 44 · Chelsea

Brinkley's	47 Hollywood Rd	020 7351 1683	Enter the cougar's lair.
The Drayton Arms	153 Old Brompton Rd	020 7835 2301	Low-lit Victorian pub with mismatched chairs and a great beer selection.
The Duke of Clarence	148 Old Brompton Rd	020 7373 1285	All leather seats and wooden floors. Cool spot for a drink after work.

Map 45 · Chelsea (East)

The Anglesea Arms	15 Selwood Terrace	020 7373 7960	4th Best Pub in the UK, says The Morning Advertiser Industry.
Chelsea Potter	119 Kings Rd	020 7352 9479	Chelsea old school.

Map 47 · Fulham (West)

The Crabtree	Rainville Rd	020 7385 3929	The Thames view from the garden is reason alone to visit.

Map 49 · Parson's Green

Amuse Bouche	51 Parsons Green Ln	020 7371 8517	Fizzy fun.
Duke on the Green	235 New King's Rd	020 7736 2777	If only all pub food was this good (but half the price).
The White Horse	1 Parsons Green	020 7736 2115	Victorian pub and a beer drinker's heaven. Book a table.

Map 50 · Sand's End

606 Club	90 Lots Rd	020 7352 5953	Great jazz venue. If you like ten minute sax solos.

Map 51 · Highgate

The Angel Inn	37 Highgate High St	020 8341 5913	Lively local with board games and unusual beers.
The Boogaloo	312 Archway Rd	020 8340 2928	Not as cool as it thinks it is.
The Flask	77 Highgate West Hill	020 8348 7346	Great beers, great food, great place. Really, it is.
Prince of Wales	53 Highgate High St	020 8340 0445	Friendly local for posh Highgaters and their even posher dogs.
The Woodman	414 Archway Rd	020 8340 3016	Reformed fight club with gastropub intentions.
The Wrestlers	98 N Rd	020 8340 4297	Branded "best pub in Highgate" by residents.

Map 53 · Crouch End

King's Head	2 Crouch End Hill	020 8340 1028	Plenty of funny business.
The Queens	26 Broadway Parade	020 3978 2154	God save the Queens.
The Shaftesbury	534 Hornsey Rd	020 7272 7950	Family-friendly local with hearty food menu.
Stapleton Tavern	2 Crouch Hill	020 7272 5395	Super laid-back local.

Map 54 · Hornsey

McCafferty's Crouch End	128 Tottenham Ln	020 8341 3182	Proper local.

Map 55 · Harringay

The Beaconsfield	359 Green Lanes	020 8826 5200	Friendly local. The footy's always on!
Brouhaha	501 Green Lanes	020 8348 8563	Friendly, laid back atmosphere and varied clientele.
Jam In A Jar	599 Green Lanes	020 8347 0655	Reliably good local watering hole.
The Salisbury	1 Green Lanes	020 8800 9617	A local's secret...no longer! Exceptional.

Map 56 · Hampstead Village

Duke of Hamilton	23 New End	020 7916 0595	Lovely local, nicely tucked away.
The Flask	14 Flask Walk	020 7435 4580	Hampstead alleyway classic that's been refitted. But nicely so.
The Freemasons Arms	32 Downshire Hill	020 7433 6811	Lovely beer garden.
The Holly Bush	22 Holly Mount	020 7435 2892	It's hidden. It's a gem. Really.
The Horseshoe	28 Heath St	020 7431 7206	Birthplace of Camden Town Brewery.

Map 57 · Hampstead Heath

The Garden Gate	14 S End Rd	020 7435 4938	Nice pub with garden for those sunny days. (yeah right)
Roebuck	15 Pond St	020 7435 7354	Somewhere between cosy pub and stylish bar. And good at it.

Map 58 · Parliament Hill / Dartmouth Park

The Bull and Last	168 Highgate Rd	020 7267 8955	Good place for a post-Heath pint.
The Southampton Arms	139 Highgate Rd	073 7575 5539	Best pub in the area. A real ale lover's dream.

Map 59 · Tufnell Park

Aces And Eights Saloon Bar	156 Fortress Rd	020 7485 4033	Rock n roll n pizza.
Boston Arms	178 Junction Rd	020 7272 8153	Ferociously scruffy but friendly Irish pub, with rock pit attached.
The Lord Palmerston	33 Dartmouth Park Hill	020 7485 1578	Gone a bit plastic, but still worth it.
Siorai Bar	114 Junction Rd	020 7561 0779	LGBT friendly karaoke, drag shows, and guest DJ nights.

Map 60 · Archway

Mother Red Cap	665 Holloway Rd	020 7263 7082	Begorra! Bejesus! Be better off going to another boozer!

Map 61 · Holloway (North)

The Owl & Hitchhiker	471 Holloway Rd	020 8161 0150	Into bad U2 cover bands? Then you'll love it here.
The Swimmer	13 Eburne Rd	020 7281 4632	No running, diving in the shallow end, or heavy petting.

Map 62 · Finsbury Park

Faltering Fullback	19 Perth Rd	020 7272 5834	Tardis-like local. Avoid match nights unless you're a Gooner.
The Night Owl	5 Station Pl	020 3722 1060	Mix-and-match music, edgy vibe, and very cheap drinks.
WB Yeats	20 Fonthill Rd	020 8617 3400	Good selection of craft beers.
The World's End	21 Stroud Green Rd	020 7281 8679	Football and live music, sometimes at the same time.

Map 63 · Manor House

The Brownswood	271 Green Lanes	020 8802 0494	Enter, before Manor House drives you mad.

Map 64 · Stoke Newington

Auld Shillelagh	105 Stoke Newington Church St	020 3556 0688	The best Guinness in London; you won't leave standing up.
The Londesborough	36 Barbauld Rd	020 7254 5865	Stokey trendies on leather sofas.
The Rose and Crown	199 Stoke Newington Church St	020 7254 7497	Sunday roasts to die for and step-back-in-time décor.

Ruby's	76 Stoke Newington Rd		Underneath the cinema sign.
Ryan's Bar	181 Stoke Newington Church St	020 7275 7807	Boho cafe and venue with a noise limiter! Pussies.
The Shakespeare	57 Allen Rd	020 7254 4190	The Bard would be proud.
White Hart	69 Stoke Newington High St	020 7254 6626	Huge pub, huge beer garden—really it's huge.

Map 65 • West Hampstead

The Black Lion	274 Kilburn High Rd	020 7624 1424	Popular local since the 6th century.
Czech and Slovak Bar	74 West End Ln	020 7372 1193	Go Czech.

Map 66 • Finchley Road / Swiss Cottage

Ye Olde Swiss Cottage	98 Finchley Rd	020 7722 3487	What can we say.

Map 67 • Belsize Park

The Washington	50 England's Ln	020 7722 8842	Monday night is pub quiz night.

Map 70 • Primrose Hill

The Albert	11 Princess Rd	020 3301 5867	A local. Cosy and relaxed.
Cecil Sharp House	2 Regent's Park Rd	020 7485 2206	Sword dancing and Olde Stuffe.
The Lansdowne	90 Gloucester Ave	020 7483 0409	Home of the beautiful people.
The Princess of Wales	22 Chalcot Rd	020 7722 0354	Traditional pub with occasional jazz performances.
Sir Richard Steele	97 Haverstock Hill	020 7483 1261	Friendly local with quirky decor.

Map 71 • Camden Town / Chalk Farm / Kentish Town (West)

Brewdog	113 Bayham St	020 7284 4626	Original London branch of the Fraserburgh craft beer renegades.
Camden Town Brewery Bar	55 Wilkin Street Mews	020 7485 1671	Where better for a pint of Camden Ink.
Dingwalls	Middle Yard	020 7428 5929	Camden Lock's guitar-smashing heartland.
The Dublin Castle	94 Parkway	079 4957 5149	Famous, small, LOUD.
Electric Ballroom	184 Camden High St	020 7485 9006	Scruffy but essential rock haunt, perennially threatened by developers.
The Enterprise	2 Haverstock Hill	020 7485 2659	Literary Irish pub with tiny indie venue upstairs.
Fiddler's Elbow	1 Malden Rd	020 7485 3269	Live music venue pub sans pretention.
The Good Mixer	30 Inverness St	020 3076 0002	Ah, remember those halcyon days of Britpop?
The Grafton	20 Prince of Wales Rd	020 7482 4466	Hosts regular DJs from renowned Dirty Water Club.
The Hawley Arms	2 Castlehaven Rd	020 7428 5979	The Hawley will rise from the ashes. Camden needs it.
The Jazz Cafe	5 Parkway	020 7485 6834	A relentless stream of excellent gigs.
KOKO	1 Camden High St	020 7388 3222	From Charlie Chaplin to Lenny Kravitz, playing Koko still kicks ass.
The Lock Tavern	35 Chalk Farm Rd	020 7482 7163	Great gigs, Sunday roasts and (unpainfully) hip clientele.
Oxford Arms	265 Camden High St	020 7267 4945	Theatre pub where you may stumble upon Amy Winehouse, stumbling.
Quinn's	65 Kentish Town Rd	020 7267 8240	More German beer than you can pronounce.
The Underworld	174 Camden High St	020 7267 3939	Throbbing pit of angry rock and even angrier metal.

Map 72 • Kentish Town

The Abbey Tavern	124 Kentish Town Rd	020 7267 9449	Fairy-lit, casual beer garden with talented DJs on Saturdays.
The Assembly House	292 Kentish Town Rd	020 7485 2031	Massive pub with friendly atmosphere.
Club Fandango @ The Bull & Gate	389 Kentish Town Rd	020 7704 0187	A gigging institution.
The Forum	9 Highgate Rd	020 3362 4110	Good venue for medium-sized bands.
Ladies and Gentlemen	2 Highgate Rd	079 5674 9793	Once a disused Victorian lav, now a gin palace.
The Lion and Unicorn	42 Gaisford St	020 7267 2304	Old school pub, with upstairs theatre space.
The Pineapple	51 Leverton St	020 7284 4631	Backstreet Victorian with good beers and Thai grub.
Rio's	239 Kentish Town Rd	020 7485 0607	Bored of your wife? Swap her here.

Arts & Entertainment · **Nightlife**

Map 73 · Holloway

The Depot	1 Carpenter's Mews	020 3218 0083	Warehouse-style venue good for large groups.
The George Shillibeer	Carpenter's Mews	020 3218 0083	For relaxed drinking on comfy couches.
The Lord Stanley	51 Camden Park Rd	020 7284 3266	Dark wood, Edwardian interior, fireplace and secret walled garden.
The Unicorn	227 Camden Rd	020 7485 3073	Venue for the brilliant club Garageland.

Map 74 · Holloway Road / Arsenal

The Coronet	338 Holloway Rd	020 7609 5014	The smell of old men's piss is abound, but it's cheap!
The Garage	20 Highbury Corner	020 7619 6720	Bad sound and a guaranteed black hole in your evening.
Hen and Chickens	109 St. Paul's Rd	020 7354 8246	All the best pubs have theatres. Fact.
The Horatia	98 Holloway Rd	020 7682 4857	Forward thinking live music gem, packs a sexy crowd.

Map 75 · Highbury

The Alwyne Castle	83 St. Pauls Rd	020 7359 7351	Alright for a pint
Snooty Fox	75 Grosvenor Ave	020 7354 9532	Strangely empty—shame for such a great pub.

Map 76 · Edgware Road / Marylebone (North)

Great Central Bar	222 Marylebone Rd	020 7631 8000	Grand is the word.
The Volunteer	245 Baker St	020 7486 4091	Grand old Victorian taphouse great for a lively post-work pint.

Map 77 · Mornington Crescent / Regent's Park

The Crown & Anchor	137 Drummond St	020 7383 2681	A pub makeover masterpiece.
The Edinboro Castle	57 Mornington Terrace	020 7255 9651	Huge outdoors bit, great BBQ on summer weekends.
Euston Tap	190 Euston Rd	020 3137 8837	Post journey boozer with an award winning variety of beer.
Queen's Head & Artichoke	30 Albany St	020 7916 6206	The pinchos are addictive. We have warned, friends.

Map 78 · Euston

The Camden Head	100 Camden High St	020 7485 4019	Pre-gig/post gig boozer.
The Doric Arch	1 Eversholt St	020 7383 3359	Impressive range of all things ale
Lincoln Lounge	52 York Way	020 7837 9339	Arty, quirky and cool. Does King's Cross proud.
Scala	275 Pentonville Rd	020 7833 2022	Historic venue with plush edges. If these walls could talk...
Searcys St Pancras Grand Brasserie	Pancras Rd	020 7870 9900	Miss your train!

Map 79 · King's Cross

The Big Chill House	257 Pentonville Rd	020 7427 2540	Allow staff 28 working days to process your drinks order.
Central Station	37 Wharfdale Rd		Ominous looking cabaret bar-cum-cruise emporium. Check site first.
EGG	200 York Way	020 7871 7111	Big club, big garden, big night out.
The Hemingford Arms	158 Hemingford Rd	020 7607 3303	Full of local aleheads.
The Lexington	96 Pentonville Rd	020 7837 5371	Come and support your boyfriend's shit band.
Simmons	32 Caledonian Rd	020 3879 9243	The bar Alice goes when Wonderland's closed.
Tarmon	270 Caledonian Rd	020 7833 2630	Character. Lots of character.

Map 80 · Angel / Upper St

The Angel	3 Islington High St	020 7837 2218	Students. The elderly. The unemployed.
The Angelic	57 Liverpool Rd	020 7278 8433	A sophisticated local.
Camden Head	2 Camden Walk	020 7359 0851	Comedians debut new gags upstairs. Cheap—and mostly cheerful.
The Castle	54 Pentonville Rd	020 7713 1858	Needs breaking in.
The Compton Arms	4 Compton Ave	020 7354 8473	Islington's only real pub—or so they say.
The Crown	116 Cloudesley Rd	020 7837 7107	Jovial spot for a quiet pint and Sunday roasts.
The Drapers Arms	44 Barnsbury St	020 7619 0340	Celeb backlash against new CCTV. Big Brother really is watching.
Hope And Anchor	207 Upper St	020 7354 1312	Scuzzy pub with even scuzzier bands in the basement.
King's Head Theatre Pub	115 Upper St	020 7226 4443	Proper, good-time boozer.
Little Bat	54 Islington Park St	020 7359 6070	This boutique pub offers an escape from hedonistic Upper Street.
Lucky Voice	173 Upper St	020 7354 6280	Singing in private? Like a bathroom with beer.
O2 Academy	16 Parkfield St	020 7288 4400	Grubby live music. Slap on some skinny jeans first.
The Regent Pub	201 Liverpool Rd	020 7700 2725	Good news: it's finally starting to fray.
Union Chapel	Compton Terrace	020 7226 1686	God's favourite music venue. Hell, everyone's.

Map 81 · Canonbury

The Lord Clyde	342 Essex Rd	020 7288 9850	Like boozing in Land of Leather.
Marquess Tavern	32 Canonbury St	020 3441 5688	Scruffy locals live on, despite gastro revolution.
Myddleton Arms	52 Canonbury Rd	020 7226 4595	Don't those people have, y'know, jobs?

Map 82 · De Beauvoir Town / Kingsland

Dalston Jazz Bar	4 Bradbury St	075 3942 4208	Kitschy cool and not suffocatingly trendy, but no jazz, figure?
The Duke of Wellington	119 Ball's Pond Rd	020 7275 7640	Nice little boozer, as they say.
The Hunter S	194 Southgate Rd	020 7249 7191	As Hunter says, "Buy the ticket, take the ride."
The Northgate	113 Southgate Rd	020 7359 7392	Reliable local despite being—gasp!—a gastro.
Old Cholmeley Boys Club	68 Boleyn Rd		Keep your eyes peeled for gigs at this place.
Rosemary Branch Theatre	2 Shepperton Rd	020 7704 2730	Theatre pub with great selection of ales and hearty fare.
The Vortex	11 Gillett Sq	020 7254 4097	Dalston's only real jazz bar.

Map 83 · Angel (East) / City Rd (North)

Barrio North	45 Essex Rd	020 7749 3940	Groovy little bar with friendly international vibe. And a caravan!
The Duke of Cambridge	30 St. Peter's St	020 7359 3066	Feel self-righteous in the world's first organic pub.
The Earl of Essex	25 Danbury St	020 7424 5828	For drinking in the day. In the dark.
Island Queen	87 Noel Rd	020 7354 8741	Where NFT planned the London guide. Sweet.
The Narrow Boat	119 St Peters St	020 7400 6003	Cheerful canal-side pub for lazy pints and people watching.
The Old Queen's Head	44 Essex Rd	020 7354 9993	Trendier than the name suggests.
The Wenlock Arms	26 Wenlock Rd	020 7608 3406	Threadbare, battered old boozer with a magnificent range of real ales.

Map 84 · Hoxton

Colours	2 Hoxton Sq	020 7613 0709	Snotty bands and doormen. Wear something uber.
Happiness Forgets	9 Hoxton Sq	020 7613 0325	No door policy just no wallies.
Howl at the Moon	178 Hoxton St	020 7688 1970	Chuffing good little pub serving burgers.
The Macbeth	70 Hoxton St	020 7749 0600	Hot new bands love it. And so do we.
The Old Blue Last	38 Great Eastern St	020 7739 2892	Until the bass drum WILL bring down that pub ceiling.
Red Lion	41 Hoxton St	020 7729 7920	Stay forever if you bag the chaise lounge...
The Stag's Head	55 Orsman Rd	020 7739 5186	Run down boozer currently being used for hip gigs.
Strongroom	120 Curtain Rd	020 7426 5103	Shoreditch's last stronghold of unpretentiousness?
Troy Bar	10 Hoxton St	079 5829 8607	A semi-hidden gem with soul and funk music most nights.

Map 85 · Stoke Newington (East)

The Jolly Butchers	204 Stoke Newington High St	020 7249 9471	Revamped but unpretentious pub with great beer selection.
Royal Sovereign	64 Northwold Rd	020 8806 2449	Drink with the locals.

Map 86 · Dalston / Kingsland

Cafe Oto	18 Ashwin St	020 7923 1231	Mysterious new venue importing music from the hinterlands of psychedelia.
Dalston Superstore	117 Kingsland High St	020 7254 2273	Uber hip polysexual squelch-a-thon.
The Haggerston	438 Kingsland Rd	020 7249 7625	Artist-run flea pit. Chaotic crowd surfing most nights.
High Water London	23 Stoke Newington Rd	078 0923 5359	A slice of weirdness with wacked out DJing and drinking.
Moustache Bar	58 Stoke Newington Rd	020 8013 1893	Follow the moustache (sticker) trail to this trendy/grimy subterranean bar.
The Prince George	40 Parkholme Rd	087 1934 1384	Buzzing local favourite. Renowned Monday quiz night, great jukebox.
Ridley Road Market Bar	49 Ridley Rd		A contender for best little bar in Dalston.
The Shacklewell Arms	71 Shacklewell Ln	020 7249 0810	Relive your punk youth.
VFD	66 Stoke Newington Rd	020 7126 8462	The latest place to Vogue.

Map 87 • Hackney Downs / Lower Clapton

Biddle Brothers	88 Lower Clapton Rd	020 8985 7052	Almost trendy oasis for the trendy in an eccentric neighbourhood.
The Crooked Billet	84 Upper Clapton Rd	020 3058 1166	Proof that Clapton can still be f***ing terrifying.
The Pembury Tavern	90 Amhurst Rd	020 8986 8597	Large selection of microbrews.
Star by Hackney Downs	35 Queenstown Rd	020 7458 4481	Fun, circus themed pub.

Map 89 • London Fields / Hackney Central

Baxter's Court	282 Mare St	020 8525 9010	A chain pub, okay, okay. But check the ladies' toilets!
The Dove	24 Broadway Market	020 7275 7617	Belgian beer paradise.
Draughts	41 Kingsland High St	079 3093 6237	A library of 500 board games to choose from.
The Old Ship	2 Sylvester Path	020 8986 2732	Nicely refurbed ex-dive.
Pub on the Park	19 Martello St	020 7923 3398	Tap for London Fields.

Map 90 • Homerton / Victoria Park North

Chats Palace	42 Brooksby's Walk	020 8533 0227	Fantastic community arts venue—Hackney classic.
The Kenton	38 Kenton Rd	020 8533 9492	Local favourite.
The Lauriston	162 Victoria Park Rd	020 8985 5404	As vamped up as its would-be-village surroundings.
Royal Inn on the Park	111 Lauriston Rd	020 8985 3321	Victoria Park's prime boozer.

Map 91 • Shoreditch / Brick Lane / Spitalfields

93 Feet East	150 Brick Ln	020 7770 6243	Enthusiastic, trendy club (to impress out-of-towners).
Bar Kick	127 Shoreditch High St	020 7739 8700	Lemon-yellow table football gaff.
The Big Chill Bar	Dray Walk	020 7392 9180	Still among Brick Lane's better drinking spots.
The Birdcage	80 Columbia Rd	020 7739 5509	Karaoke! Til 3am!
The Blues Kitchen	134-136 Curtain Rd	020 7490 4789	Nice wallpaper, free music. Who's complaining?
Browns	1 Hackney Rd	020 7739 3970	Now really. What would your mother say?
Café 1001	91 Brick Ln	020 7247 6166	Like a house party. But one where cans cost £3.
The Carpenters Arms	73 Cheshire St	020 7739 6342	No longer run by the Kray twins' mother, still felonious fun.
Catch	22 Kingsland Rd	020 3325 9745	Reliable active dancefloor, reliable silly hats, reliable good fun.
The Cocktail Trading Co.	68 Bethnal Green Rd	020 7427 6097	Mixologically compelling drinks; fun attitude.
The Commercial Tavern	142 Commercial St	020 3137 9563	Quirky Shoreditch traditional.
The Culpeper	40 Commercial St	020 7247 5371	Used to be The Princess Alice. Beautiful interior.
Golden Heart	110 Commercial St	020 7247 2158	Has it all: fires, pints and a lazy resident dog.
Jaguar Shoes	32 Kingsland Rd	020 7683 0012	Happy hipsters behind wide windows.
The Owl & Pussycat	34 Redchurch St	020 3487 0088	Crooked little place, tucked in the folds of Shoreditch's blubber.
The Pride of Spitalfields	3 Heneage St	020 7247 8933	The only East End boozer left on Brick Lane.
The Redchurch	107 Redchurch St	020 3325 9743	Late, loud DJ box.
The Royal Oak	73 Columbia Rd	020 3437 0131	Gentrifying, gentrifying...gentrified.
Sager + Wilde	193 Hackney Rd	020 8127 7330	Get yer wine on.
Shoreditch House	Ebor St	020 7739 5040	Last one in the rooftop pool buys the drinks!
The Ten Bells	84 Commercial St	020 7247 7532	Jack The Ripper's local. An oddly nice place for an evening drink.
Ye Olde Axe	69 Hackney Rd	020 7729 5137	Rockabilly-only weekends. That's right: rockabilly-only. Occasional gentleman's club.

Map 92 • Bethnal Green

Bethnal Green Working Men's Club	44 Pollard Row	020 7739 7170	Saucy amateur burlesque that still confuses the resident Working Men's.
The Florist Arms	255 Globe Rd	020 8981 1100	The Camel's naughty little sister.
Satan's Whiskers	343 Cambridge Heath Rd	020 7739 8362	Devilishly good cocktails.
Sebright Arms	31 Coate St	020 7729 0937	Meantime lager and Lucky Chip burgers.
The Star Of Bethnal Green	359 Bethnal Green Rd	020 7458 4480	Formerly the Pleasure Unit. Still Bethnal Green's live music best.

Map 93 • Globe Town / Mile End (North)

The Approach	47 Approach Rd	020 8980 2321	Great if you can tolerate the ironic haircuts crew.
Morgan Arms	43 Morgan St	020 8980 6389	Grab a pint with some gourmet food.
Palm Tree	Haverfield Rd	020 8980 2918	Brass walls and retired crooners! Amazingly old-fashioned boozer.
The Victoria	110 Grove Rd	020 8712 5125	Coolified old man's boozer turned hipster joint.

Map 94 • Bow

Coborn Arms	8 Coborn Rd	020 8980 3793	Nice ales, nice beer garden.
Lord Morpeth	402 Old Ford Rd	020 8980 3012	Bow boozing's best.
The Lord Tredegar	50 Lichfield Rd	020 8983 0130	Trusty local boozer.
Young Prince	448 Roman Rd	020 8980 1292	If on Roman Road...

Map 95 • Whitechapel (West) / St Katharine's Dock

The Dickens Inn	St Katharine's Way	020 7488 2208	Proof that an awesome location can conquer all.
Simmons	61 Mint St	020 3879 9249	Reliable good time place.

Map 96 • Whitechapel (East) / Shadwell (West) / Wapping

Captain Kidd	108 Wapping High St	020 7480 5759	Pub with nice Thames-side beer garden.
Town of Ramsgate	62 Wapping High St	020 7481 8000	Get nautical.

Map 97 • Stepney / Shadwell (East)

The Grange Tavern	373 Commercial Rd	020 7790 7335	Old men, hipsters and blue-collar poets in imperfect harmony.
The Prospect of Whitby	57 Wapping Wall	020 7481 1095	Ye olde pub(e) on ye Thame s(e).
Troxy	490 Commercial Rd	020 7790 9000	Glorious art deco palace.

Map 98 • Mile End (South) / Limehouse

The Grapes	76 Narrow St	020 7987 4396	True to its roots East End boozer—natural survivor.

Map 101 • Poplar (East) / Canary Wharf (East)

The Greenwich Pensioner	28 Bazely St	020 7987 4696	No pensioners and not in Greenwich.

Map 102 • Millwall

The SpaceBar	269 Westferry Rd	020 7515 7799	Oasis in Docklands desert.

Map 103 • Cubitt Town / Mudchute

The Ferry House	26 Ferry St	020 7537 7813	Beer-drenched docks time capsule.
The Lord Nelson	1 Manchester Rd	075 3791 5737	Can I have a half, Nelson?

Map 104 • South Bank / Waterloo / Lambeth North

The Anchor & Hope	36 The Cut	020 7928 9898	For that intellectual pre-theatre/dinner chat.
Benugo Bar & Kitchen	Belvedere Rd	020 7401 9000	Long tables, sofas, soft lighting. Sup cocktails, feel cultured.
Cubana	48 Lower Marsh	074 7496 8275	Still riding the mojito trend. But good at them.
The Cut Bar	66 The Cut	020 7928 4400	Enjoy the outdoor terrace with trendy media types and thesps.
Royal Festival Hall	Belvedere Rd	020 3879 9555	Increasingly exciting programming amid nicely refurbished surroundings.
Skylon	Belvedere Rd	020 7654 7800	Impress someone with the view, then split the bill.

Map 105 • Southwark / Bankside (West)

Albert Arms	1 Gladstone St	020 7928 8224	Where yuppies meet students meet blow-ins meet locals.
The Libertine	125 Great Suffolk St	020 7378 7877	Pizza and beer, what more do you want?
Lord Nelson	243 Union St	020 7207 2701	Like a student union.
Ministry of Sound	103 Gaunt St	020 7740 8600	The sound really IS amazing.
The Prince of Wales	51 St George's Rd	020 7582 9696	Cheap local with downright scary karaoke.

Map 106 • Bankside (East) / Borough / Newington

The Anchor	34 Park St	020 7407 1577	Did Samuel Johnson have to battle this many tourists?
Belushi's	161 Borough High St	020 7939 9710	Drunk Antipodeans. Karaoke. General carnage.
The George Inn	77 Borough High St	020 7407 2056	Grab a home brew in the dazzlingly ancient George Inn.
The Globe	8 Bedale St	020 7407 0043	Bridget Jones' home? Do we care?
The Market Porter	9 Stoney St	020 7407 2495	Market traders and suits neck real ale. Smell the testosterone.
The Rake	14 Winchester Walk	020 7407 0557	Tiny place with a hundred different beers. Honestly, a hundred.
The Roebuck	50 Great Dover St	020 7357 7324	Cool but calm drinkerie for a pre-night-out drink.
The Rose	123 Snowfields	020 7403 0168	Backstreet boozer full of human oddities.
The Royal Oak	44 Tabard St	020 7357 7173	Possibly the friendliest landlords in London.
Southwark Tavern	22 Southwark St	020 7403 0257	Traditional ambience and ordinary fare in ye olde Southwark Tavern.

Map 107 • Shad Thames

The Hide	39 Bermondsey St	020 7403 6655	Slightly odd vibe, but cracking drinks.
Hilton London Tower Bridge	5 More London Pl	020 3002 4300	Super-chilled, low lit relaxation zone for the wealthy.
The Last Talisman	171 Bermondsey St	020 8189 9546	Wine buffs and cocktail lovers will lap it up.
The Woolpack	98 Bermondsey St	020 3437 0139	Filling lunches, comfy sofas, great garden. Job done.

Map 109 • Southwark Park

The Ancient Foresters	282 Southwark Park Rd	020 7394 1633	Surprise charmer in an otherwise grimy area.
The Angel	101 Bermondsey Wall E	020 7394 3214	Sam Smith pub with great views across the river
The Mayflower	117 Rotherhithe St	020 7237 4088	Used to be The Shippe from whenst the Mayflower departed

Map 110 • Rotherhithe (West) / Canada Water

Old Salt Quay	163 Rotherhithe St	020 7394 7108	Pub-by-numbers, but the riverside patio of dreams.
The Ship	39 St Marychurch St	020 7237 4103	Sunny day? Settle in with a beer and a sarnie.

Map 111 • Rotherhithe (East) Surrey Quays

The Blacksmith's Arms	257 Rotherhithe St	020 7231 8838	Good enough for the Queen Mum: good enough for us.
The Moby Dick	6 Russell Pl	020 7231 6719	Once here, it's hard to leave. Because it's really far from the tube.
The Ship & Whale	2 Gulliver St	075 9465 5816	So good we even come for breakfast.
Whelan's	11 Rotherhithe Old Rd	077 1385 3650	Looks rough around the edges, but you could do worse.

Map 112 • Kennington / Elephant and Castle

Brasserie Toulouse Lautrec	140 Newington Butts	020 7582 6800	Eclectic music venue in the Belle Epoque tradition.
Corsica Studios	5 Elephant Rd	020 7703 4760	Sweaty music venue with 'home-made' vibe.
The Dog House	293 Kennington Rd	020 3643 8982	Like your scruffy, unpretentious younger brother. Made for chill-axing.
The Old Red Lion	42 Kennington Park Rd	020 7735 4312	Best pub in the area.
Prince of Wales	Cleaver Sq	020 7735 9916	Stuart's favourite pub in Kennington.

Map 113 • Walworth

Red Lion	407 Walworth Rd	020 7703 7075	They'll look at you funny, but you'll be welcome enough.

Arts & Entertainment · **Nightlife**

Map 119 · Deptford (East)

The Bird's Nest	32 Deptford Church St	020 8692 1928	Hilarious 'locals vs. trendies' vibe. Go for monthly Flesh Dunce!
The Bunker Club	46 Deptford Broadway	020 8691 0000	The name tells all.
The Dog & Bell	116 Prince St	020 8692 5664	Now why can't ALL pubs in Deptford be like this?

Map 120 · Greenwich

The O2	O2 Arena	020 8463 3359	The grandaddy of mainstream live music.
The Old Brewery	Pepys Building	020 3437 2222	Get the excellent range of Meantime beers direct from the source.
Up The Creek	302 Creek Rd	020 8858 4581	Comedy club (plus comedy dancing at the disco)

Map 121 · Camberwell (West)

The Joiners Arms	35 Denmark Hill	020 7703 1654	Friendly local with occasional Irish dancing.
The Sun of Camberwell	61-63 Coldharbour Ln	020 7737 5861	Same owners and decor as nearby Tiger. Great beer garden.

Map 122 · Camberwell (East)

Grove House Tavern	26 Camberwell Grove	020 7703 8910	By far the best of the Grand Union chain.
Hermit's Cave	28 Camberwell Church St	020 7703 3188	Log fire and Deuchars on the pump.
Stormbird	25 Camberwell Church St	020 7708 4460	Insane selection of beers makes the bland décor bearable.

Map 123 · Peckham

The CLF Art Cafe	133 Rye Ln	020 7732 5275	Ex-cricket bat factory hosting galleries, studios and exciting new stuff.
The Four Quarters	187 Rye Lane	079 4336 6002	Arcade games bar: Hadouken!
Frank's Cafe	95 Rye Ln	075 2860 0924	Cheap Campari cocktails in a multi-story car park. Pure class.
The Montpelier	43 Chomert Rd	020 7635 9483	Cosy pub with free regular and eclectic film nights.

Map 126 · New Cross

Amersham Arms	388 New Cross Rd	020 8691 9506	Art school hipdom in grimy New Cross's coolest venue.
Marquis of Granby	322 New Cross Rd	020 8692 3140	Lovely old corner pub with mix of students and oldtimers.
New Cross Inn	323 New Cross Rd	020 8469 4382	Someone's gotta keep "the scene" going.

Map 127 · Coldharbour Lane / Herne Hill (West)

The Commercial	212 Railton Rd	020 7733 8783	Roaring fire and mulled wine in winter. Fits like a glove.
The Florence	133 Dulwich Rd	020 7326 4987	Microbrewery on premises.
The Prince Regent	69 Dulwich Rd	020 7274 1567	Life drawing on Wednesdays to titillate posh diners.

129 · East Dulwich

East Dulwich Tavern	1 Lordship Ln	020 8693 1316	Jeremy Clarkson was once thrown out for nefarious activities.

Map 130 · Peckham Rye

The Gowlett	62 Gowlett Rd	020 7635 7048	Shabby local serving pizzas famous across the area.
The Rye	31 Peckham Rye	020 7639 5397	For lazy lunches on summer Sundays.

Map 131 · Vauxhall / Albert Embankment

Eagle London	349 Kennington Ln	020 7793 0903	Fur on tap throughout the week. Sundays recommended.
The Royal Vauxhall Tavern	372 Kennington Ln	020 7820 1222	Fun gay pub with trashy cabaret.
The Jolly Gardeners	49 Black Prince Rd	020 7967 7327	German gastropub with uber-extensive collection of beer and sausages.

Map 132 · Battersea (West)

Duke of Battersea	74 Battersea Bridge Rd	020 7228 6482	A great pub well worth the trek.
The Prince Albert	85 Albert Bridge Rd	020 7228 0923	Enjoy a regal roast with a view of the park.
The Woodman	60 Battersea High St	020 7228 2968	A nice Fire. Pint of Badger. Luverleee.

509

Map 133 • Battersea (East)

The Mason's Arms	169 Battersea Park Rd	020 7622 2007	Perfect local boozer with quality Sunday roasts.

Map 134 • South Lambeth

Bar Estrela	113 S Lambeth Rd	020 7793 1051	Portugal transplanted to South London. Beer, tapas and football.
The Battersea Barge	Nine Elms Ln	020 7582 1066	Bouncy, buoyant, thrilled to see you—the Labrador puppy of venues.
The Cavendish Arms	128 Hartington Rd	020 7498 7464	Shabby, unpretentious pub with comedy nights and a cool streak.
Fire	38 Parry St	020 3242 0040	Legendary gay terrordrome with LED ceiling.
Lightbox	6 S Lambeth Pl	020 3242 0040	15,000 LED lights. Enough to give us all seizures.
The Priory Arms	83 Lansdowne Way	020 7622 1884	Renowned for their excellent selection of proper, geeky real ales.
The Vauxhall Griffin	8 Wyvil Rd	020 7498 5598	Theme nights to knock your socks off

Map 135 • Oval

The Fentiman Arms	64 Fentiman Rd	020 7793 9796	The staff believe that smiles kill kittens.

Map 136 • Putney

The Boathouse	32 Brewhouse Ln	020 8789 0476	Riverside pub with loadsa outdoor space.
Duke's Head	8 Lower Richmond Rd	020 8788 2552	Typical gastro pub upstairs. Dark DJ bar downstairs.
The Jolly Gardeners	61 Lacy Rd	020 8789 2539	Like all good pubs. And sock monkey classes on Wednesdays.

Map 138 • Wandsworth (Central)

The Cat's Back	88 Point Pleasant	020 3441 2232	Atmospheric and busy with loadsa obscure decoration.

Map 139 • Wandsworth (East)

St John's Tavern	147 St Johns Hill	020 7450 6457	Like stepping into a colonial Victorian plantation.
The Waterfront	Juniper Dr	020 7228 4297	No Marlon Brandos here. Not much of a view either.

Map 140 • Clapham Junction / Northcote Rd

B@1 Cocktail Bar	85 Battersea Rise	020 7978 6595	Be at one with a cocktail menu the size of a book.
Humble Grape	2 Battersea Rise	020 3620 2202	Unpretentious wine bar—hurray!

Map 141 • Battersea (South)

The Lost Angel	339 Battersea Park Rd	020 7622 2112	Put this in your pipe and smoke it, Shoreditch.

Map 142 • Clapham Old Town

Prince of Wales	38 Old Town	020 7622 4964	Eccentric, friendly. Run by a magpie.
Rose & Crown	2 The Polygon	020 7978 2417	For the CAMRA purists.
The Sun	47 Old Town	020 7622 4980	Nice pub. Ruined by surfeit of twats.

Map 143 • Clapham High Street

The Alexandra	14 Clapham Common South Side	020 7627 5102	Join an up-for-it crowd as multinational as the sport here.
Bread and Roses	68 Clapham Manor St	020 7498 1779	Surprisingly pleasant socialist boozer. Without Clapham tossers.
The Clapham North	409 Clapham Rd	020 7274 2472	A bit 'Clapham', but pretty likable really.
The Coach and Horses	173 Clapham Park Road	020 7498 6308	Honest little boozer.
The Falcon	33 Bedford Rd	020 7274 2428	"I told Daddy. I've nowhere to even PARK a CT!!"
Infernos	146 Clapham High St	020 7720 7633	Oh God no.
The Railway Tavern	18 Clapham High St	020 7622 4077	Half-trendy, half-local, three-quarters cool.
Two Brewers	114 Clapham High St	020 7819 9539	Club nights, gay cabaret, lots of fu-un!

Map 144 · Stockwell / Brixton (West)

The Duke of Edinburgh	204 Ferndale Rd	020 7326 0301	Warm, traditional pub with massive beer garden.
Marquis of Lorne	49 Dalyell Rd	020 7771 9408	A dying breed.
Plan B	418 Brixton Rd	020 7733 0926	Has made a name for itself, but pretty lame really.
The Prince of Wales	469 Brixton Rd	020 7095 1978	Behind dealers chanting skunk lies a nothin' special pub.
The Queen's Head	144 Stockwell Rd	020 7737 3519	Bastion of true Brixton.
The Swan	2 Stockwell Rd	020 7978 9778	Don't worry about spitting on the floor.

Map 145 · Stockwell / Brixton (East)

Brixton Academy	211 Stockwell Rd	020 7771 3000	Overrated, but still a tad awesome.
Jamm	261 Brixton Rd	020 7274 5537	The real deal a little way out.

Map 146 · Earlsfield

Halfway House	521 Garratt Ln	020 8946 2788	Slinky, chardonnay-swilling pub with terrific terrace.
Le Gothique	Windmill Rd & John Archer Wy	020 8870 6567	The answer to: "Open a bar! What could go wrong?"

Map 147 · Balham (West)

The Hope	1 Bellevue Rd	020 8672 8717	Consider nearby Wandsworth Common an extension of the beer garden.
The Nightingale	97 Nightingale Ln	020 8673 1637	Untrendified local. Long may it stay so.

Map 148 · Balham (East)

The Avalon	16 Balham Hill	020 8675 8613	Beer garden for lazy Sunday lunches and, er, Japanese whisky.
Balham Bowls Club	7 Ramsden Rd	020 8673 4700	A pub. In a bowling club circa 1950. Genius.
The Bedford	77 Bedford Hill	020 3976 8007	Music and comedy pub with great bands but crappy beer.
The Exhibit	12 Balham Station Rd	020 8772 6556	Bar with indie cinema attached
Hagen & Hyde	157 Balham High Rd	020 8772 0016	Popular boozer.

Map 150 · Brixton

The Dogstar	389 Coldharbour Ln	020 7733 7515	The burritos are great, but leave before the tunes get cheesy.
The Effra	38 Kellett Rd	020 7274 4180	A slice of the real Brixton.
Effra Social	89 Effra Rd	020 7737 6800	Retro pub in former Brixton Conservative Club.
Electric Brixton	Town Hall Parade	020 7274 2290	DJs and live music venue in former Fridge space.
Gremio de Brixton	St. Matthew's Rd	020 7924 0660	Spanish tapas bar in church crypt.
Hootananny	95 Effra Rd	020 7737 7273	Great gigs—many for free
Hope & Anchor	123 Acre Ln	020 7274 8794	Come for the tiki shacks and burgers.
Prince Albert	418 Coldharbour Ln	020 7274 3771	It's charming, trust us. In a not too obvious kindaway.
Satay	447 Coldharbour Ln	020 7684 5566	Cocktails to suit the snobbiest of drinks connoisseurs
Upstairs at the Ritzy	Brixton Oval	020 7733 2229	Where Brixton sparkles. Cinema, bar, café and free live music.
The Windmill	22 Blenheim Gardens	020 8671 0700	Rough-edged weirdo magnet. Unique and brilliant.

Map 151 · Tooting Bec

The King's Head	84 Upper Tooting Rd	020 8767 6708	Former gin palace brings yesteryear flair to the wasteland.

Map 152 · Tooting Broadway

The Little Bar	145 Mitcham Rd	020 8672 7317	It's a bar and it's little
The Ramble Inn	223 Mitcham Rd	020 8767 4040	Irish/locals bullcrap-free boozer.
The Secret Bar	20 Totterdown St	078 5758 0731	Convivial Portuguese bar.
Tooting Tram and Social	46 Mitcham Rd	020 8767 0278	Cavernous, funky and cool without trying.
Unwined	21 Tooting High St	020 3583 9136	Pop up turned permanent providing excellent wines.

British food and British chefs had a pretty bad reputation until fairly recently; greasy piles of stodge topped off with gravy was the general consensus for what to expect in a London restaurant. A couple of years back France's premier chef Alain Ducasse upped the ante for the London dining scene by declaring it the 'restaurant capital of the world.' While there are still numerous naff cafes around they're far outnumbered by brilliant bistros, bountiful brunch places, bodacious BBQs and boatloads of other badass eateries.

As one of the most multicultural cities in the world, London is packed with cuisine from around the world, with some areas dedicated to a signature cuisine. We've got Jewish, Indian, Peruvian, Mexican, Vietnamese, Moroccan, hell even Mongolian. Visitors don't even have to look at a Yorkshire pudding, roast beef, a full English, or fish & chips if there're not so inclined but anyone would be a fool to miss out on some of the better English places.

Foodie trends come and go in this dusty old town so if you really want be down with the urban gourmands you'll need to know what's hot right now. It would be terribly embarrassing to be caught nibbling on sushi when munching on king ribs is the in thing. Then there's the staple and stable cool places that manage to keep the hungry masses happy no matter what's cool.

What you spend on food is as flexible as British weather too; street food provides some of London's most famed snacks and old English favourites like **The Ritz** stick to the traditional-type menu its customers expect. For everyone else in between there's everything else in between. London even does Vegetarian, apparently.

Eating for Britain

In a country whose national dish is reportedly a Chicken Tikka Masala, pin-pointing what British cuisine actually is doesn't come easy. Taking a traditional approach we've got those archetypal dishes like the Sunday Roast, Full English, Fish & Chips, and Jellied Eels; if visitors believed every stereotypical image of the British it would stand to reason that these dishes make up our standard diet, along with bucket loads of builder's tea, of course.

Delve a little deeper though and you'll find a revolutionised British menu brought about by the demand of a newly sophisticated palate. We still do the soggy seaside favourite but you're just as likely to find grilled mackerel with potato salad on a chip-shop menu as you are a battered saveloy which is what you'll see at **Poppie's** in Spitalfields (Map 91). We still do Sunday lunch but you're more likely to be served the rarest of beef, a whole Poisson, or tenderloin pork than a leathery piece of gravied meat. Breakfast is a class of its own and though we're still to see a food revolution hit the East End pie shops, some things are best left as they are like the centuries-old **F.Cooke** (Map 89) on Broadway Market.

We're partial to a fusion, too; it's not unusual to see British tapas on a pub menu – expect things like mini toad-in-the-hole, bite sized beef wellington, and pork belly squares served with apple sauce. We're seeing things like whole Indian menus that are made entirely of British ingredients to keep the eco-warriors happy, and we're munching on American-style pulled pork that is smoked over English craft ales.

Our adopted second cuisine award goes to the Indian sub-continent whose spicy dishes us Brits consider to be synonymous with a night out on the tiles or a night in front of the telly. Samosas as a snack, bhajis on the way home from work, and a five course special of a Sunday eve; it's all good.

Hold the Pesticides

You'd think that with all the smog the city creates, and the pollution that's pumped around this place that Londoners would have come to accept the pesticides and chemicals often found in food; you would, of course, be wrong. London loves a good farmer's market and all organic café, and a good serving of local produce and meat. Weekly farmer's markets like those in Islington (**Map 00**), London Fields and Borough (**Map 106**) are credited with starting the trend for street food in London, a few years back. The vendors would cook each other's produce to sell to hungry shoppers which in turn created a demand for top end, tasty, chemical-free food.

Any café worth its salt uses free-range eggs, bacon from British pigs, lamb (from Wales not New Zealand), apples from Somerset orchards and oysters from Whitstable. There's certainly no crime in sticking to produce form British soils, serving misshapen tomatoes, and purple carrots, just be aware that more than a handful of 'organic' places like to charge over the odds for the pleasure of non-tainted meals.

Breakfast & Lunch—Brunch

Any good Londoner values their weekend days off like a dog loves his bone. The working week leaves time for no more than coffee and a croissant at breakfast time which is why we revel so much in a weekend brunch time. Be it with a lover, a group of rowdy friends, or visiting family members, we've developed the act of brunching into an art form in its own right.

You'll still see the off greasy spoon around, serving lukewarm baked beans, fatty bacon, and pebbly scrambled eggs but chances are that the dove grey (or Victorian green) painted shop two doors down will be packed to the proverbial rafters with a convivial young crowd of foodies and hipsters. There's a lot to be said for the Full English; it's a world-famous classic, and done well, it's the breakfast of kings. We've even branched out into providing grease-free breakfasts for the more delicate morning palate.

Pavilion Café (Map 93) in Victoria Park is a close contender for feeding the east's foodies – kippers with potato cakes and poached eggs is a fantastic Irish classic. **Caravan (Map 6)** has enjoyed its time at the top for a City brunch and it looks set to stay in the number one spot for some time; the chefs here are renowned for mixing up exotic flavour and creating elixical hangover cures. For American treats **The Breakfast Club (Map 80)** is a firm favourite and with three locations there's a seat for everyone.

Street Is Sweet

Eating on the street might mean using a plastic fork and sitting on a kerb but it certainly doesn't mean dissecting your way through a soggy sarnie or pulling half-eaten burgers out of the bin. It does mean queuing for a while to eat at the best places, trying to decide which of the tempting street stalls to eat from, and possibly dripping mustard down your best top.

You can literally find everything on the streets of London; from cockroaches to sleeping people, dog shit and hypodermics. Quite delightfully you can also find the much more attractive options of food from all over the world – we've got Peruvian, Polish, Vietnamese, Mexican, French, and pretty much everything else you can think of.

The humble burger has enjoyed huge acclaim over the past year with stalls like **Lucky Chip** reinventing the British BBQ classic to resemble something much more palatable. **Bahn Mi** is a travelling Vietnamese baguette specialist that keeps chiming in reward for serving the best pork rolls in town, and the East.St collective have a permanent spot at Kings Cross where they present the baying public with **Engine** and its haute-gourmet Hot Dogs. Even city centre workers have taken the bait for their bait though there is a heavy lean towards superfood salads and sushi in the city, the current bento leader is also perfectly positioned for visitors; right outside of Liverpool Street Station, **Wasabi** has a stall where you can pick up a salad, a couple of bits of sushi, and a delicious miso soup for less than a fiver.

Camden Market food used to be famous for all the wrong reasons; overcooked noodles, oily fried chicken, watery curry and cardboard pizzas, there's still plenty of that around but a newer set of stalls also caters to more refined tastes. What's on offer can be interchangeable but there are a few stalwarts that are worth a go. There's a French stall that does mushrooms and sauté potatoes in a Roquefort sauce and there's no exceptions made just because the chefs are serving from a stall instead of inside a restaurant; these things are literally sit-down-white-table-cloth standard.

The absolute upside to street food stalls, which we've cleverly held back 'til last, is the ability to enjoy top-notch, amazing food for a fraction of the price that a restaurant would charge for the same dish. We're talking £5-6 for a main meal that might be paella, Moroccan tagine, Goan curry, or an Argentinian steak. A little cake for afters should knock you back a couple of quid and will round off your stand-up meal quite nicely —**Violet's (Map 89)** lemon drizzle cake makes the proverbial icing on your day.

Doffing Hats to a Trend

The London food scene can be a fickle thing. One day it's Gin and Venison that's the reigning king of the food world and the next it's knocked off its perch by a BBQ rib and a craft beer. See, once the masses have caught onto a top secret food trend, the gourmands move on to new pastures where The Guardian is yet to report, and a license is yet to be passed.

We've lately seen some foodie revolutions, the death of others, and the birthing of a few. While the burger has surely enjoyed its time, one of the new kids on the block, Peruvian, is sticking around for a while, and crawling across the city like a drunk crab – the **Last Days of Pisco** pops up in venues across the city which can be a bit pesky if you turn up the day after it has moved on but their ceviche is possibly one of London's best new additions. Out in the West, the aptly named **Ceviche (Map 12)** does more of the fish-cooked-with-citrus thing and complements each dish with lashing of Peruvian firewater, Pisco which comes on its own, in dessert, and as a range of cocktails.

Onto another trend which is set to stay; the French have hors d'oeuvres the Spanish have tapas, the Swedish have smorgasbord and now the British have small plates, and we love them. Russell Norman's **Polpo (Map 10)** restaurants will remain as popular as ever to serve up shareable small plates in a New York diner-style setting. Expect to see things like Anchovy & Chickpea Crostini, Spicy Pork & Fennel Meatballs, and Rabbit & Chicory Salad, all made in perfect proportions whether you're planning to take a couple for yourself or share a load with friends.

Yauatcha (Map 10) is Soho's answer to the small plate influx where head chef Tong Chee Whee is renowned for combining complicated flavours and adding delicate notes to create things like Venison Puffs. **Brawn (Map 91)** on Columbia Road is in a class of its own when it comes to creating meaty feasts; the restaurant shamelessly rejoices in all things pig and waives any requests for a veggie option. The menu is dependent on season and on what the chefs feel like cooking; you might find salted ox tongue, pork scratching, or pickled wild boar here and it will all be delicious and meaty.

Pop-Up, Pop-Down

Providing a location for these pop up restaurants and supper clubs can be a challenge, mainly because the very nature of them means that most don't stay in the same place for too long, instead choosing to change venues every 3-6 months, allowing each little part of insular London to enjoy the experience.

Some of the more business-inclined places choose to pop in the same place, say, once a month, which makes it easier to pinpoint them but harder to actually get a table. Other that started as a travelling-circus version of a restaurant have settled into grown-up, permanent accommodation, or at least rented a kitchen to become semi-perm tenants.

Pay for What You Eat

It seems only sensible and fair that you should only pay for what you eat, right? Think about how much of your evening dining bill is often down to the sheer amount of booze you've put away though. Now imagine that you don't have to pay for that portion of the bill.

London has its fair share of bring your own bottle restaurants and the best part is that they're not all of one vein i.e Oriental, dingy, or in one place; even high-end Mayfair has BYOB bottle restaurants. There does seem to be a higher than normal number of BYOB eateries in the east but that's just because hipsters are skint, preferring to spend their cash on purple leggings and (il) legal highs.

By day **Hurwendeki (Map 92)** is a standard little coffee shop, tucked in a railway arch with a unique terrace, by night it is a Korean restaurant with perfect ambiance a brilliant, affordable menu and a BYOB policy. **Little Georgia (Map 92)** is a darling of a place; pretty pale green with a warm, inviting basement, and hearty portions of Georgian food is what to expect here. Kingsland Road is scattered with Vietnamese places where u can BYOB and while they're all fairly good **Mien Tay (Map 91)** is always packed out.

Key: £ : Under £10 / ££ : £10–£20 / £££ : £20–£30 / ££££ : £30–£40 / £££££: £40+
* : Does not accept credit cards./ † : Accepts only American Express / ††: Accepts only Visa and Mastercard
Time listed refers to kitchen closing time on weekend nights

Map 1 • Marylebone (West)

Daisy Green	20 Seymour Street	020 3887 9488	££	Aussie style easy eating.
Locanda Locatelli	8 Seymour St	020 7935 9088	££££ 11.30 pm	Outstanding Italian food.
Maroush Express	56 Edgware Rd	020 7724 8197	££ 12 am	Wax philosophical while smoking a hookah out front.
Twist	42 Crawford St	020 7723 3377	£££	Italian-focused small plates.

Map 2 • Marylebone (East)

Chiltern Firehouse	1 Chiltern St	020 7073 7676	£££ 12 am	Delicious food and celeb-spotting.
Comptoir Libanais	65 Wigmore St	020 7935 1110	£ 8 pm	Uncompromisingly cheap and cheerful mezes.
Dinwan	31 Thayer St	020 7935 2445	££	Lebanese gorge spot.
Fischer's	50 Marylebone High St	020 7466 5501	£££ 11 pm	Pitch-perfect Viennese cafe.
Galvin Bistrot de Luxe	66 Baker St	020 7935 4007	£££ 11 pm	Veloutés, ballotines, tartares and escargots. Delicieux? Mais oui.
The Golden Hind	73 Marylebone Ln	020 7486 3644	££ 10 pm	Fish and chips from the top-drawer. Can do BYOB
Goodman Mayfair	24-26 Maddox St	020 7499 3776	£££££	London steak institution.
Hush Brasserie	8 Lancashire Ct	020 7659 1500	£££ 11 pm	European food al fresco. Go on a lunch hour holiday.
Meat Liquor	37 Margaret St	020 7224 4239	£ 12 am	Best burgers and chilli cheese fries in town.
Patty & Bun	54 James St	020 7487 3188	£	Exactly what a burger should be. Be prepared to wait.
Pollen Street Social	8 Pollen St	020 7290 7600	£££££	The mighty Jason Atherton's flagship restaurant.
Royal China	24-26 Baker St	020 7487 4688	£££	Cantonese culinary powerhouse flagship; dim sum mandatory.
Royal China Club	40-42 Baker St	020 7486 3898	££££	More upscale iteration of Cantonese culinary powerhouse; dim sum mandatory.
Trishna	15 Blandford St	020 7935 5624	££££	Starred Indian cuisine highlighting the subcontinent's coastal regions.
Zoilo	9 Duke St	020 7486 9699	££££	Haute Argentine transcending beef-industrial complex.

Map 3 • Fitzrovia

Archipelago	53 Cleveland St	020 7637 9611	£££££ 10.30 pm	London's best, alright only, chocolate-covered scorpions and crocodile steaks.

Key: £ : Under £10 / ££ : £10–£20 / £££ : £20–£30 / ££££ : £30–£40 / £££££: £40+
* : Does not accept credit cards./ † : Accepts only American Express / †† : Accepts only Visa and Mastercard
Time listed refers to kitchen closing time on weekend nights

Barrica	62 Goodge St	020 7436 9448	£££		Tapas and sherry-forward bar.
Berners Tavern	10 Berners St	020 7908 7979	£££	10:30 pm	One for special occasions.
Brazilian Gourmet	70 Cleveland St	020 7018 0879	£	6 pm	Authentic and friendly.
Govinda's	10 Soho St	020 3687 0617	£*	8 pm	Cheap Krishna food. You know the deal.
Hakkasan	8 Hanway Pl	020 7927 7000	£££££	12 am	Soho's sexiest subterranean Chinese. China-chic dining for the beautiful people.
Iberica	195 Great Portland St	020 3026 5118	££	4 pm	Jamon Jamon
Italiano Coffee Co.	46 Goodge St	020 7580 9688	£	11 pm	Zen it is not—but who cares at £3.50 a pizza?
Kin Cafe	22 Foley St	020 3589 5185	£	5:30 pm	Father and son team cooking fresh and healthy.
Koba	11 Rathbone St	020 7580 8825	£		A Korean delight! Set lunch is a bargain.
Naroon	60 Great Titchfield St	020 7436 0934	£	6 pm	Parisian meets Persian
Portland	113 Great Portland St	020 7436 3261	££	11 pm	For when you want to impress the parents.
Ragam	57 Cleveland St	020 7636 9098	££	10.45 pm	Can't dis these dosas (potato crepes) at very decent prices.
The Riding House Cafe	43 Great Titchfield St	020 7927 0840	££		Ignore the stuffed squirrels and focus on the buttermilk pancakes.
Roka	37 Charlotte St	020 7580 6464	£££	11 pm	Dazzling Izakaya concept Japanese.
Salt Yard	54 Goodge St	020 7637 0657	£££	11 pm	Intimate and sexy. Take a date. Get laid. Possibly.
Sardo	45 Grafton Way	020 7388 4874	££	10 pm	Hit after hit. Try the crab pasta.
Thai Metro	38 Charlotte St	020 7436 4201	££	11 pm	Thai food, cooked well, served well, job done.
Yalla Yalla	12 Winsley St	020 7637 4748	£	11:30 pm	Shawarma-rama.

Map 4 · Bloomsbury (West)

Alara	58 Marchmont St	020 7837 1172	£££	7 pm	Hardcore veggie/vegan mecca, surprisingly good.
Bi Won	24 Coptic St	020 7580 2660	£	10 pm	Manhandling staff but great food.
Savoir Faire	42 New Oxford St	020 7436 0707	££	10.30 pm	Sweet little rustic restaurant, a stroll from Soho.

Map 5 · Bloomsbury (East)

Banh Mi Bay	4-6 Theobalds Rd	020 7831 4079	£		One of the originator's of London's bahn mi craze.
Ciao Bella	86 Lamb's Conduit St	020 7242 4119	££	11 pm	Authentic, rustic feel Italian complete with piano.
Fryer's Delight	19 Theobald's Rd	020 7405 4114	£*	10 pm	No frills chippie; big portions of chunky, salty, greasy tastiness.
Honey & Co	54 Lamb's Conduit St	020 7388 6175	£	10:30 pm	Husband and wife run.

Itadaki Zen	139 King's Cross Rd	020 7278 3573	£	10 pm	Get your zen on.
The Lady Ottoline	11 Northington St	020 7831 0008	£££		Great gastropub from owner's of Shoreditch's Princess.
Mary Ward Centre	42 Queen Sq	020 7269 6000	£*	5 pm	Hippy educational centre with a great organic cafe.
Paolina Snack Bar	181 King's Cross Rd	020 7278 8176	£*	10 pm	Grotty exterior disguises this diamond of cheerful authentic Thai.
The Perseverance	63 Lamb's Conduit St	020 7405 8278	££	10.30 pm	Good quality gastropub food.
You Me Sushi	180 Gray's Inn Rd	020 7278 8699	£££		Burgeoning sushi empire; good for takeout.

Map 6 • Clerkenwell

Caravan	11 Exmouth Market	020 7833 8115	£		Exceptional coffee and food.
Dans Le Noir	69 St John St	020 7253 1100	££££	9 pm	Blind waiters serve in pitch darkness: don't wear white.
The Eagle	159 Farringdon Rd	020 7837 1353	££	10.30 pm	London's first gastro pub—just look what they started.
Morito	32 Exmouth Market	020 7278 7007	£££		Moro's tapas-mezze sister restaurant.
Moro	34 Exmouth Market	020 7833 8336	££££	11 pm	DO believe the hype.
Pham Sushi	159 Whitecross St	020 7251 6336	£££		Central independent sushi for great healthy lunch.
The Sandwich Man	23 Easton St	020 7833 9001	£*	2.30 pm	Office delivery returns. Gourmet—and just 65p. Best lunch in London.
Sushi Tetsu	12 Jerusalem Passage	020 3217 0090	££££		Tiny, unpretentious, and world class.

Map 7 • Barbican / City Road (South)

| Carnevale | 135 Whitecross St | 020 7250 3452 | ££ | 11 pm | veggie on the cheap. |
| Nusa Kitchen | 9 Old St | 020 7253 1084 | £* | 5 pm | People queuing? For ages? For soup? Now I've seen everything. |

Map 8 • Liverpool Street / Broadgate

Duck & Waffle	110 Bishopgate	020 3640 7310	£££		Remarkably good value for such an 'elevated' dining experience.
Gaucho Broadgate	5 Finsbury Ave	020 7256 6877	££££	11 pm	Divine, ohmigod, melt-in-your-mouth steak. Oops, drooling!
Hoxton Grill	81 Great Eastern St	020 7739 9111	£££		Very sexy. Very nice. Very expensive.
The Princess of Shoreditch	76 Paul St	020 7729 9270	££		Gastropub and drinking hole for city workers and slackers.

Map 9 • Mayfair / Green Park

Alain Ducasse at The Dorchester	53 Park Ln	020 7629 8866	££££	10 pm	Better known for its extortionate prices than michelin-starred food
Burger & Lobster	29 Clarges St	020 3205 8960	££		Burger or lobster or both? Greedy!
Corrigan's	28 Upper Grosvenor St	020 7499 9943	£££££		When in Rome/ Mayfair...
The Drawing Room at Brown's	33 Albemarle St	020 7493 6020	££££	11 pm	Ah, so that's what a £48 cup of tea tastes like.
El Pirata of Mayfair	5 Down St	020 7491 3810	££	11.30 pm	Don't be put off by stuffy location—this is f'ing good tapas.
Galvin at Windows	22 Park Ln	020 7208 4021	£££££	11 pm	Art Deco French overlooking Buckingham Palace. We're not worthy!
Gymkhana	42 Albemarle St	020 3011 5900	£££		Posh four-star Indian with slightly disarming colonial flourishes.

Arts & Entertainment • **Restaurants**

Key: £ : Under £10 / ££ : £10–£20 / £££ : £20–£30 / ££££ : £30–£40 / £££££: £40+
* : Does not accept credit cards./ † : Accepts only American Express / †† : Accepts only Visa and Mastercard
Time listed refers to kitchen closing time on weekend nights

Kitty Fisher's	10 Shepherd Market	020 3302 1661	£££		Mediterranean-British in cozy digs.
L'Autre	5 Shepherd St	020 7499 4680	££££	11 pm	Polish meets Mexican. Surprisingly well.
Nobu	19 Old Park Ln	020 7447 4747	£££££	12 am	Rob a bank on the way as it's bloody expensive!
The Ritz	150 Piccadilly	020 7493 8181	£££££	10 pm	High tea amidst ornaments and swank—resist temptation to swipe towels.
Theo Randall	1 Hamilton Pl	020 7318 8747	£££££	11 pm	Sincere and stylish cuisine unfortunately hidden behind a hotel façade.

Map 10 • Piccadilly / Soho (West)

Bao	53 Lexington St		££		Scrumptious meat-filled buns.
Bob Bob Ricard	1 Upper James St	020 3145 1000	£££	11.30 pm	Proper posh British diner serving Cornish crab cake and...Ribena.
Bodean's BBQ	10 Poland St	020 7287 7575			Resistance is futile. Soho Special—great way to end a night.
Brasserie Zedel	20 Sherwood St	020 7734 4888	£		Service so-so, atmosphere tres Parisian. Great value.
Cecconi's	5 Burlington Gardens	020 7434 1500	££££	11.15 pm	All day menu for the spoilt. Delicious breakfasts.
Dehesa	25 Ganton St	020 7494 4170	£££	11 pm	Faux-rustic protein-rich tapas, sweetie.
Dishoom	22 Kingly St	020 7420 9322	££		All-day Parsi cafe straight outta Bombay.
Kulu Kulu	76 Brewer St	020 7734 7316	£	10 pm	Great, fresh, fast sushi for people on the go. Sit down in 45 minutes only.
Mildred's	45 Lexington St	020 7494 1634	££	11pm	Even non-vegetarians are fans.
The Photographers' Gallery	16 Ramillies St	020 7087 9300	£*	5.30 pm	Artsy coffee spot with photos on view.
Ping Pong	45 Great Marlborough St	020 7851 6969	££	11 pm	Don't leave without trying a char sui bun!
Polpo	41 Beak St	020 4537 4341	£		Venetian-style bacaro.
San Carlo Cicchetti	215 Picadilly	020 7494 9435	£££		Seasonal Italian; fresh ingredients; all-day menu.
Sartoria	20 Saville Row	020 7534 7000	£££££	11 pm	The pick of the Conran restaurants.
Sketch	9 Conduit St	020 7659 4500	££	1 am	Colossally trendy kitsch palace.
Social Eating House	58 Poland St	020 7993 3251	££££		Fun, creative cuisine with studiously low-key vibe.
Taro	61 Brewer St	020 7734 5826	££	10.30 pm	Where London's Japanese locals eat sushi.
Yauatcha	15 Broadwick St	020 7494 8888	£££££	11.45 pm	Traditional Chinese tea-house meets star-spangled media haunt.
Yoshino	3 Piccadilly Pl	020 7287 6622	££	10 pm	Back alley bentos so good you'll pretend they were your discovery.

Map 11 • Soho (Central)

Ba Shan	24 Romilly St	020 7287 3266	££		User-friendly Szechuan from Barshu folks.
Balans	60 Old Compton St	020 7439 2183	££	3 am	Share a 4am breakfast with the likes of Amy Winehouse.
Bar Bruno	101 Wardour St	020 7734 3750	£*	10 pm	Hidden Italian cafe gem. Authentically loud and friendly.
Blanchette	9 D'Arblay Street	020 7439 8100	££		Three French brothers bring modern bistro to Soho.
Bocca di Lupo	12 Archer St	020 7734 2223	£££	12 am	Italian for 'break a leg'; authentic fare gets your bocca watering.

Bone Daddies	31 Peter Street	020 7287 8581	£	11:30pm	Tonkotsu ramen, slurp.
Busaba Eathai	110 Wardour St	020 7255 8686	£££		Never mind the shared benches, the food's too yummy.
Copita	27 D'Arblay St	020 7287 7797	£££		Continually changing tapas menu and full bar.
Ember Yard	60 Berwick St	020 7439 8057	£££		Tapas-y charcoal-grilled meats and charcuterie via Spain & Italy.
Gelupo	7 Archer St	020 7287 5555	£		Grab a granita, close your eyes and you're in Sicily.
Jazz Club	10 Dean St	020 7437 9595	£	11 pm	Surprisingly, jazz takes the mediocre chain up a notch.
Jerk City	189 Wardour St	020 7287 2878	£	10 pm	Jamaican fast food. In doubt? Go for ackee and saltfish.
Leong's Legends	4 Macclesfield St	020 7287 0288	££	11 pm	A Chinatown legend.
Maoz	43 Old Compton St	020 7851 1586	£*	1 am	Falafeltastic!
The Palomar	34 Rupert St	020 7439 8777	££££		Open-kitchen gastroexperimentation.
Pizzeria Malletti	174 Clerkenwell Rd	020 7713 8665	£*	3 pm	Amazing! Use your mobile and you won't get served.
Randall & Aubin	16 Brewer St	020 7287 4447	£££	11 pm	Over-indulgently carnal seafood delights which only call for champagne.
Soho Joe	34 D'Arblay St	020 7287 1777			Darn good pizza with the locals that won't break the bank.
St Moritz	161 Wardour St	020 7734 3324	££££	11.30 pm	Swiss cheese heaven.
Tamarind Kitchen	167 Wardour St	020 7287 4243	£	11 pm	Tapas + curry. Fusion gone insane but somehow works.
Thai Sqmp	16 St. Annes Ct	020 7287 2000	££	11 pm	Thai with a good range. In set meals—go for star in HOT dinner!
Tokyo Diner	2 Leicester St	020 7287 8777	£		One of London's best for katsu curry. No tipping!
Wong Kei	41 Wardour St	020 7437 8408	££	10 pm	AKA Wonky's: institutionally rude service, cheap fast Chinese.

Map 12 • Soho (East)

10 Greek Street	10 Greek St	020 7734 4677	£££		Farm—and sea-to-table; courier font and slate.
Baozi Inn	24 Romilly St	020 7287 6877	£		No frills, quality Szechuan.
Bar Italia	22 Frith St	020 7437 4520	££	4.30 am	Soho institution; perfect for people watching at any hour.
Barrafina	26 Dean St	020 7813 8016	££	11 pm	Seriously, the best (and hippest) place for tapas.
Barshu	28 Frith St	020 7287 8822	£££		Hot 'n' heavy Szechuan in well-appointed digs.
Bi Bim Bap	11 Greek St	020 7287 3434			Cheap and healthy Korean rice bowls.

Arts & Entertainment · **Restaurants**

Key: £ : Under £10 / ££ : £10–£20 / £££ : £20–£30 / ££££ : £30–£40 / £££££ : £40+
* : Does not accept credit cards./ † : Accepts only American Express / †† : Accepts only Visa and Mastercard
Time listed refers to kitchen closing time on weekend nights

Cafe Boheme	13 Old Compton St	020 7734 0623	£££	11.45 pm	You want frites with that? Deliciously snobby comfort food.
Ceviche	17 Frith St	020 7550 9364			Brining Peruvian to the perverted.
Garlic & Shots	14 Frith St	020 7734 9505	££££	1 am	Garlic, garlic and more garlic. No-go zone for vampires.
Haozhan	8 Gerrard St	020 7434 3838	£££	11 pm	Can't pick? This is the one.
Imperial China	25 Lisle St	020 7734 3388	££		Solid dim sum option.
The Ivy	1 West St	020 7836 4751	£££		Dining experience that will prove memorable.
Koya	49 Frith St	020 7434 4463	£		Blink and you'd miss London's worst-kept udon secret.
La Bodega Negra	16 Moor St	020 4580 1186	££		Shh, it's a secret! Mexican food underneath a Soho sex shop.
La Porchetta Pollo Bar	20 Old Compton St	020 7494 9368	£££	12 am	Cheap and cheerful Italian. In the West End? Well, exactly.
Le Beaujolais	25 Litchfield St	020 7836 2955	££	10 pm	Get insulted by a Frenchman here in London—Mai oui!
Sartori	15 Great Newport St	020 7836 6308	££		Hit and miss service but all is forgiven with metre long pizzas.
Taro	61 Brewer St	020 7734 5826	££	10.30 pm	Like Taro Brewer Street. But gayer, obviously.

Map 13 · Covent Garden

Battersea Pie	28 The Market	020 7240 9566	£	6 pm	Who ate all the pies?
Café Mode	57 Endell St	077 5437 3597	££	11.30 pm	Pizza, pasta, salad. No fuss.
Flesh & Buns	41 Earlham St	020 3019 3492	£££		Fun izakaya and bun spot from folks behind Bone Daddies.
Kulu Kulu Sushi	76 Brewer St	020 7734 7316	££	10 pm	Tiny conveyor belt sushi joint. Bang on the money.
Lima Floral	14 Garrick St	020 7240 5778	££££		Elegant Peruvian, the way it's meant to be.
Mon Plaisir	21 Monmouth St	020 7836 7243	£££	11.15 pm	Not up to typical Paris standards, but still tres bon!
Punjab	80 Neal St	020 7836 9787	£££	11:30 pm	Relive the days of the Raj in this old-school curry house.
Rock & Sole Plaice	47 Endell St	020 7836 3785	£££	11 pm	London's oldest chippie. Est. 1871. On-street, fairy-lit picnic benches. Huge portions.
Rossopomodoro	50 Monmouth St	020 7240 9095	£	12 am	Chain Italian with very tasty pies. Cutlery prohibited!
Sarastro	126 Drury Ln	020 7836 0101	££	11.30 pm	Hilarious over-the-top decor; includes fornicating cherubs.
Souk Medina	27 Litchfield St	020 7240 1796	££	11 pm	Atmospheric Morrocan joint. Free refills on mouthwatering £20 set menu.

Map 14 • Holborn / Temple

Asadal	227 High Holborn	020 7430 9006	£££	10.30 pm	Go on—venture down those stairs—it's worth it.
Indigo	1 Aldwych	020 7300 0400	£££	11 pm	Sunday brunch and a movie—all in the same place!

Map 15 • Blackfriars / Farringdon

Beppe's Sandwich Bar	23 W Smithfield	020 7236 7822	££	3 pm	As classically Italian as oversized sunglasses. Only much, much better.
Bleeding Heart	Bleeding Heart Yard	020 7242 8238	£££	10.30 pm	Historic, hard to find, eccentric beauty.
Le Cafe du Marche	22 Charterhouse Sq	020 7608 1609	£££	11 pm	Wonderful French cuisine in delightful venue. Tucked away in Charterhouse Square.
Poncho 8	11 Queens Head Passage	020 7248 6744	£		St. Paul's branch of the Mexican restaurant.
Smiths of Smithfield	67 Charterhouse St	020 7251 7950	£££	10.45 pm	Overflowing with yuppies and trendy types; pricey but tasty.
St John	26 St John St	020 7251 0848	£££	11 pm	This place is ALL about the offal.
Tinseltown	44 St. John St	020 7689 2424	£	24 hrs	Funky diner serving great late-night milkshakes.
Vivat Bacchus	47 Farringdon St	020 7353 2648	£££	9.30 pm	Three wine cellars and a cheeseroom. A ROOM of cheese.

Map 16 • Square Mile (West)

Plaat of the Grapes	9 Bull's Head Passage	020 7929 7224	££	12 am	Finally, a reason to go to the Square Mile.
Sweetings	39 Queen Victoria St	020 7248 3062	£££	4 pm	Old fashioned institution for nostalgia trips. Lunch only

Map 17 • Square Mile (East)

Gaucho City	1 Bell Inn Yard	020 7626 5180	££££	11 pm	The best steakhouse in the city. Located in former gold vaults.
The Mercer	34 Threadneedle St	020 7628 0001	££	9.30 pm	Proper British grub in a light contemporary atmosphere.
Nusa Kitchen	2 Adams Ct	020 7628 1149	£	4 pm	Fresh soup made daily.
Simpson's Tavern	38 Ball Court Alley	020 7626 9985	££		Perfectly cooked classics in a pub full of history.

Arts & Entertainment · **Restaurants**

Key: £ : Under £10 / ££ : £10–£20 / £££ : £20–£30 / ££££ : £30–£40 / £££££: £40+
* : Does not accept credit cards./ † : Accepts only American Express / †† : Accepts only Visa and Mastercard
Time listed refers to kitchen closing time on weekend nights

Map 19 · Belgravia

Amaya	Motcomb St	020 7823 1166	££££	11.30 pm	Where the trendies go for their curry fix.
Boisdale	15 Eccleston St	020 7730 6922	£££££	11 pm	Posh Scottish nosh. No deep-fried Mars Bars, sadly.
Noura	12 William St	020 7235 5900	££	11 pm	Frequently orgiastic Lebanese pig-outs, habibi.
The Pantechnicon	19 Motcomb St	020 7034 5425	£££££		One to impress the parents.

Map 20 · Victoria / Pimlico (West)

Grumbles	35 Churton St	020 7834 0149	££	11 pm	Unfashionably unfussy Brit/French home-cooking. Gorgeous pies, no grumbles.
Pimlico Fresh	86 Wilton Rd	020 7932 0030	££		Best bet for a quality bite before your show.

Map 21 · Pimlico (East)

Regency Cafe	17 Regency St	020 7821 6596	£*	7 pm	Proper British fry-ups and atmosphere in this 1940's cafe.
The Vincent Rooms	76 Vincent Sq	020 7802 8391	£££	7 pm	Brilliant food served by awkward catering students.

Map 23 · St. James's

Laduree	71 Burlington Arcade	020 7491 9155	£££	10 pm	Grande Dame of Parisian tearooms and purveyor of cult macaroons.
The Wolseley	160 Piccadilly	020 7499 6996	££	12 am	Step back in time for an elegant afternoon tea.

Map 24 · Trafalgar Square / The Strand

Cafe in the Crypt	Trafalgar Sq	020 7766 1158	££	10 pm	Spooky sandwiches and fruit crumble.
India Club	143 The Strand	020 7836 4880	£	11 pm	Quirky run-down BYOB eaterie; more character than Brick Lane equivalents.
J Sheekey	28 St. Martin's Ct	020 7240 2565	££££	11 pm	Old-fashioned seafood haven that the celebs still love.
Portrait Restaurant	St Martin's Pl	020 7312 2490	£££	10.30 pm	Exceptional view over London; dinner Thursday and Friday only.
Rules	35 Maiden Ln	020 7836 5314	£££££	10.30 pm	London's oldest restaurant with old-fashioned comfort food to match.
Thai Pot	1 Bedfordbury	020 7379 4580	££	11 pm	Busy but fast with fresh and generous helpings. Delicious Massaman curry.
Wahaca	66 Chandos Pl	020 7240 1883	£££	11 pm	Tasty Mexican market food/tapas. Always busy.

Map 25 · Kensal Town

Boom Burger	272 Portobello Rd	020 8960 3533	££	11 pm	Jamaican burgers, jerk chicken and red snapper. Irie.
Lowry and Baker	339 Portobello Rd	020 8960 8534	££		Top notch eggs benedict.
Thai Rice	303 Portobello Rd	020 8968 2001	££	10.30 pm	Jaw-dropping food in sterile, bland enviornment.

Map 26 · Maida Hill

Mosob	339 Harrow Rd	020 7266 2012	£	11:30pm	Fresh, spicy home-cooked food.

Map 29 · Notting Hill Gate

Beach Blanket Babylon	45 Ledbury Rd	020 7229 2907	££££	12 am	Maze of baroque nooks and crannies where celebs nibble discreetly.
Cafe Diana	5 Wellington Terrace	020 7792 9606	£	10.30 pm	Creepy, kitsch shrine to Princess Diana with so-so food.
The Elgin	96 Ladbroke Grove	020 7229 5663	££		Gussied up pub classics.
Osteria Basilico	29 Kensington Park Rd	020 7727 9957	£££	11.30 pm	Quaint, buzzing and full of Italian rustic charm. A local hot spot.
The Shed	122 Palace Gardens Terr	020 7229 4024	£££		Best of British seasonal.
Taqueria	141 Westbourne Grove	020 7229 4734	££	11 pm	Wash down these fresh mini-tacos with a good tequila.

Map 30 · Bayswater

Al Waha	75 Westbourne Grove	020 7229 0806	££		Highly regarded Lebanese.
The Cow	89 Westbourne Park Rd	020 7221 0021	£££	9.45 pm	Top end bar food. Smart restaurant upstairs.
Tiroler Hut	27 Westbourne Grove	020 7727 3981	££££	1 am	Dementedly kitsch Austrian madhouse with lederhosen-clad waiters.

Map 31 · Paddington

Bonne Bouche	129 Praed St	020 7724 5784	£	4.30 pm	Deli counter is popular with local workers for sandwiches.
Casa Malevo	23 Connaught St	020 7402 1988	££££		Warm, welcoming Argentine steakhouse.
Ranoush Juice Bar	43 Edgware Rd	020 7723 5929	£		Stalwart late night Lebanese cafe.

Map 32 · Shepherd's Bush (West)

Abu Zaad	29 Uxbridge Rd	020 8749 5107	£	11 pm	A colourful Syrian welcome. Posh Kebabs.
Esarn Kheaw	314 Uxbridge Road	020 8743 8930	£	11.30 pm	Outstanding Thai. Transport your taste buds to Bangkok.
Vine Leaves Taverna	71 Uxbridge Rd	020 8749 0325	£	1 am	Friendly staff, traditional grub, huge portions.

Map 33 · Shepherd's Bush

Busaba Eathai	Westfield Shopping Centre	020 3249 1919	££		Westies can now chow down on great Mussaman closer to home.
Jasmine	16 Goldhawk Rd	020 8743 7920	££	11 pm	Awesome Thai.
Mr Falafel	15 Uxbridge Rd	073 0763 5548	£		Contender for best falafel in the city.
Popeseye	108 Blythe Rd	020 7610 4578	££££	10.30 pm	London's ONLY member of the Aberdeen Angus Society.
Tian Fu	39 Bulwer St	020 8740 4546	£		Steam rising, Nihao at the door. China right here in SheBu.

Arts & Entertainment • **Restaurants**

Map 35 • Kensington

Byron	93 Old Brompton Rd	020 7581 6460	££	10 pm	London's best burger? Locals in the know say so.
Cable Bar and Cafe	8 Brixton Rd	020 8617 9629	£		Charming 50s style hangout. Cocktails at night.
Clarke's	124 Kensington Church St	020 7221 9225	££	10 pm	Elegant, English fine dining. Perfect brunch spot if feeling refined.
Maggie Jones's	6 Old Court Pl	020 7937 6462	£££	10.30 pm	A British culinary time warp, but we like it anyway.
Yashin	1 Argyll Rd	020 7938 1536	£££		Sushi that's Japanese fresh, venue that's London cool.

Map 36 • South Kensington / Gloucester Rd

Da Mario	15 Gloucester Rd	020 7584 9078	£££	11.30 pm	Apparently Princess Di's local Italian Pizzeria. Affordable and A+ pizza.
Jakobs	20 Gloucester Rd	020 7581 9292	££	10 pm	Brave the slow service for delicious veggie dishes and fresh juices.
Kensington Creperie	2 Exhibition Rd	020 7589 8947	£*	11 pm	The best sweet and savoury crepes in London.
Oddono's	14 Bute St	033 3800 0480	£	11 pm	Gelato fix for homesick Italians and ice-cream freaks alike.
Zack's Deli	115 Gloucester Rd	020 7373 2221	£		More cafe than deli but has tasty home-cooked food.

Map 37 • Knightsbridge

Daquise	20 Thurloe Square	020 7589 6117	£££		Haute Polish cuisine.
Ognisko	55 Prince's Gate	020 7589 0101	£££		Schmancy Polish.
Zuma	5 Raphael St	020 7584 1010	£££	12 am	If your gal likes sushi, ideal for a romantic night out.

Map 38 • Chiswick

Chris' Fish Bar	19 Turnham Green Ter	020 8995 6743	£*	12 am	It's all British-ness wrapped in warm, greasy paper.
Foubert's	2 Turnham Green Ter	020 8994 5202	£	11 pm	Little Italian owned cafe. Excellent ice cream and gelato.
Franco Manca	144 Chiswick High Rd	020 8747 4822	££	10 pm	London's best pizza with longer opening hours.
High Road Brasserie	162 Chiswick High Rd	020 8742 7474	££	11 pm	As good as it looks. The continent comes to the High Road.
Kalamari	4 Chiswick High Rd	020 8994 4727	££	12 am	For those with a feta fetish.
La Trompette	5 Devonshire Rd	020 8747 1836	£££	10.30 pm	Unpretentious French restaurant with excellent service and set menus.
Zizzi	235 Chiswick High Rd	020 3302 2126	££	11.30 pm	Skip the mains—cut straight to the heavenly Apple Crumble.

Map 39 · Stamford Brook

Azou	375 King St	020 8563 7266	££	11 pm	Chilled, candle lit place in amongst a heap of other places. Great tagines.
The Carpenter's Arms	89 Black Lion Ln	020 8741 8386	£££	11 pm	As gastropub as it gets.
Lola & Simon	278 King St	020 8563 0300	££		Cosy and welcoming Kiwi-Argentine eatery serving a great brunch.
Saigon Saigon	313 King St	020 8748 6887	££		Inside and outside are charming, the pho and welcome authentic.
Tosa	332 King St	020 8748 0002	£	10 pm	Low-key authentic yakitori (fried skewered meat) joint. Easy on the wallet.

Map 40 · Goldhawk Rd / Ravenscourt Park

Mahdi	215 King St	020 8563 7007	££	12 am	Truly authentic, unpretentious Iranian place—menu in Arabic 'n all. Tasty!
Sagar	157 King St	020 8741 8563	££	11 pm	Yummy South Indian veggie food at a great price.

Map 41 · Hammersmith

The Gate	51 Queen Caroline St	020 7833 0401	££££	10 pm	Light and airy by day, cosy at night. Lovely food.

Map 43 · West Brompton / Fulham Broadway / Earls Court

Bodean's BBQ	4 Broadway Chambers	020 7610 0455	£££	11 pm	Stuff yourself on BBQ pulled-pork sandwiches. Yee haw!
Chutney Mary	73 St James St	020 7629 6688	££££	11.30 pm	Get cuddled over a curry (at a price), Michelin-starred
The Harwood Arms	Walham Grove	020 7386 1847	£££		cheese and Guinness on toast and a pint!
Megan's Deli & Restaurant	571 King's Rd	020 3468 0220	£		Boiled eggs in the calm and beautiful courtyard. Ah, bliss...
Pizza@Home	86 Lillie Rd	020 7244 8080	£*	10 pm	Maybe London's most authentic Italian pizza. Fast and cheap as chips!!
Vingt-Quatre	325 Fulham Rd	020 7376 7224	£	24 hrs	24 hour booze! Incidentally, the food is very good.

Map 44 · Chelsea

Bluebird Chelsea	350 King's Rd	020 7559 1000	£££	10.30 pm	So it seems you can get a bacon butty and look cool on the Kings Road.
Haché	329 Fulham Rd	020 7823 3515	£		Top notch gourmet burgers—check out the £1 lunch voucher!

Map 45 · Chelsea (East)

Big Easy	332-334 King's Rd	020 4580 1171	££		Tuesdays are all you can eat shrimp, Louisiana style.
Made In Italy	249 King's Rd	020 7352 1880	££	11 pm	"Food Mama used to Make." Unless you're not Italian, obviously.
My Old Dutch Pancake House	221 King's Rd	020 7376 5650	£	11.30 pm	Sweet or savory pancakey goodness in the heart of Chelsea.

Key: £ : Under £10 / ££: £10–£20 / £££ : £20–£30 / ££££ : £30–£40 / £££££: £40+
*: Does not accept credit cards./ †: Accepts only American Express / ††: Accepts only Visa and Mastercard
Time listed refers to kitchen closing time on weekend nights

Map 46 · Sloane Square

The Admiral Codrington	17 Mossop St	020 7581 0005	£££	10.30 pm	Go for simplicity here. Even the chips they get exactly right.
Bibendum Restaurant & Oyster Bar	81 Fulham Rd	020 7581 5817	£££££	11 pm	French institution with a cool (literally) oyster bar.
Restaurant Gordon Ramsay	68 Royal Hospital Rd	020 7352 4441	£££££	11 pm	Mmmmmm...debt...

Map 47 · Fulham (West)

The River Café	Rainville Rd	020 7386 4200	£££	11 pm	Fine dining by the Thames for champagne socialists.

Map 48 · Fulham

Fisher's Fish & Chips	19 Fulham High St	020 7371 5555	£	10 pm	Quality chips AND quality punning. It's why Britain's Great.
Fulham Palace Cafe	Bishop's Ave	020 7736 3233	£	5 pm	A historical and elegant spot for a cup of Earl Grey and a scone.
Royal China	805 Fulham Rd	020 7731 0081	£££		Cantonese culinary powerhouse; dim sum mandatory.

Map 50 · Sand's End

The Sands End	135 Stephendale Rd	020 7731 7823	£££	10 pm	Hearty, rustic Irish fare. Nowt much else around but makes the grade.

Map 51 · Highgate

The Bull	13 N Hill Ave	020 8341 0510	£££	12 am	Chic eatery with perfectly positioned front terrace.
The Red Lion & Sun	25 North Rd	020 8340 1780	££££	10 pm	Excellent Sunday roasts.

Map 53 · Crouch End

Jai Krishna	161 Stroud Green Rd	020 7272 1680	£	11pm	Super delicious vegetarian Indian food.
Wow Simply Japanese	18 Crouch End Hill	020 8340 4539			Naff name, good food.

Map 54 · Hornsey

Ridge Cafe	97 Tottenham Ln	077 3305 0375	£		Good place for quick lunch or just a caffeine boast.

Map 55 • Harringay

Antepliler	46 Grand Parade, Green Lanes	020 8802 5588	££		Turkish pide pizzas and grilled meat. Lots of it.
Bun & Bar	553 Green Lanes	020 8348 5111	££		Burgers & live music.
Devran	485 Green Lanes	020 8340 2288	£	2 am	Complementary baklava (if you have any room left!)
Gokyuzu	26-27 Grand Parade, Green Lanes	020 8211 8406	££		Wear stretchy trousers.
Hala	29 Grand Parade	020 8802 4883	£	2am	Delicious Turkish breakfast.

Map 56 • Hampstead Village

Jin Kichi	73 Heath St	020 7794 6158			Great range of reasonably priced Japanese favourites.
La Creperie De Hampstead	77 Hampstead High St	020 7445 6767	£*	11 pm	No crap crepes at this sublime French street stall.
Louis Patisserie	32 Heath St	020 7435 9908	£	6 pm	Tea and gorgeous cakes beloved of elderly Eastern European gentlemen.

Map 57 • Hampstead Heath

Mimo La Buffala	45 South End Rd	020 7435 7814	£££		Charming neighborhood Italian.
Paradise	49 S End Rd	020 7794 6314	£££		Excellent Indian with a modern twist.
Polly's	55 S End Rd	020 7431 7947	£	5 pm	Sometimes you just fancy a sarnie and a cuppa.

Map 58 • Parliament Hill / Dartmouth Park

Bistro Laz	1 Highgate West Hill	020 8342 8355		11 pm	Lovely meze. Or order in pizza if next door's full.
Lalibela	137 Fortress Rd	020 7284 0600	££		Steaming pots of Ethiopian stew mopped up with injera.

Map 59 • Tufnell Park

Rustique Cafe	142 Fortress Rd	020 7692 5590	££	8 pm	Damn those tasty tasty cookies for being so small.
The Spice	161 Fortress Rd	020 7267 7430	££	11.30 pm	Top-notch curries

Map 60 • Archway

500 Restaurant	782 Holloway Rd	020 7272 3406	££		Excellent homemade gnocchi.
Il Mio Mosaic	24 Junction Rd	020 7272 3509	££	10.30 pm	Head for the back garden sun-trap in Summer.
Nid Ting	533 Holloway Rd	020 7263 0506	£££	11.15 pm	Bigger, meatier portions than most Thai restaurants.
St John's Tavern	91 Junction Rd	020 7272 1587	££££	11 pm	Gastro pub oasis stranded among the pound-shops of Archway.

Map 61 • Holloway (North)

El Molino	379 Holloway Rd	020 7700 4312	£	11 pm	One of those, and those, and that..oh and that!
The Landseer	37 Landseer Rd	020 7281 2569	££	9.30 pm	Gastropub extraordinaire.
North Nineteen	194 Sussex Way	020 7281 2786	££		A bright spark in an area of surrounding darkness.

Key : £ : Under £10 / ££ : £10–£20 / £££ : £20–£30 / ££££ : £30–£40 / £££££ : £40+
* : Does not accept credit cards / † : Accepts only American Express / †† : Accepts only Visa and Mastercard
Time listed refers to kitchen closing time on weekend nights

Map 62 • Finsbury Park

Girasole	150 Seven Sisters Rd	020 3802 5462	£		Parmigiana like mama used to make.
Hana Sushi	150 Seven Sisters Rd	020 7281 2226	££	11pm	Authentic sushi.
Le Rif	172 Seven Sisters Rd	020 7263 1891	£*	10 pm	Essential for all your banter and microwaved Tagine needs.
Lulu's Caribbean Cuisine	84 Stroud Green Rd	020 7263 9690	£	11 pm	Caribbean food done just right. Irie.
Osteria Tufo	67 Fonthill Rd	020 7272 2911	££	11 pm	Delicious authentic Italian.
Petek	96 Stroud Green Rd	020 7619 3933	££	10.45 pm	Classy but cheap Turkish.
Pizzeria Pappagone	131 Stroud Green Rd	020 7263 2114	££		Has NFT's very own Italian seal of approval.

Map 63 • Manor House

Fink's Salt & Sweet	70 Mountgrove Rd	020 7684 7189	££	11pm	Restaurant/deli/wine/coffee/everything you could want.
New River Cafe	271 Stoke Newington Church St	020 7923 9842	£	11 pm	Steamy windows and top hangover cure fry-ups.

Map 64 • Stoke Newington

Anglo-Asian Tandoori	60 Stoke Newington Church St	020 7254 9298	££	11.30 pm	Classic curry house right down to the free sherry.
The Blue Legume	101 Stoke Newington Church St	020 7923 1303	£	11 pm	Dreamy eggs benedict, served under a giant aubergine.
Rasa N16	55 Stoke Newington Church St	020 7249 0344	££	11.30 pm	Vegetarian-style Indian cooking at its mouth-watering best.
Yum Yum	187 Stoke Newington High St Mussaman.	020 7254 6751	£££	11 pm	Tasty tasty, Thai Thai. Go for the Kang

Map 65 • West Hampstead

Barraco Cafe	10 Kingsgate Place	020 7604 4664	£	11 pm	Boteca bar frequented by Brazilians.
Small & Beautiful	351 Kilburn High Rd	020 7328 2637	£		Small and beautiful indeed, as is the bill.

Map 66 • Finchley Road / Swiss Cottage

Bradleys	25 Winchester Rd	020 7722 3457	£££	11 pm	Your friendly face in the neighbourhood that loves wine.
Camden Arts Centre	Arkwright Rd	020 7472 5500	£	6 pm	Excellent food in buzzing artistic setting.
Loft Coffee Company	4 Canfield Gardens	020 7372 2008			Simple, tiny cafe, with brilliant coffee.
Singapore Garden	83 Fairfax Rd	020 7624 8233	££	11 pm	Surprising flavours make a welcome alternative on a night out.

Map 67 • Belsize Park

Retsina	48 Belsize Ln	020 7431 5855	£££	11 pm	Lively Greek—grilled meat galore!

Map 68 • Kilburn High Road / Abbey Road

Geamos	122 Boundary Rd	075 4047 7982	£££		Proper Georgian winter food.

Map 70 · Primrose Hill

J Restaurant	148 Regent's Park Rd	020 7722 4924	££	11 pm	Excellent food, especially brunch. Tempestuous service.
Lemonia	89 Regent's Park Rd	020 7586 7454	£££	11.30 pm	Fancy a real Greek meal?
Manna	4 Erskine Rd	077 8883 5892	££	11.30 pm	Aesthetically gorgeous veggie restaurant, serving scrumptious food.
Melrose and Morgan	42 Gloucester Ave	020 7722 0011	£	8 pm	Scrumptious food and coffee. Good for solo snacks.
Odette's	130 Regent's Park Rd	020 7586 8569	£££	1 am	Delectably dainty restaurant, high-class service.
Primrose Bakery	69 Gloucester Ave	020 7483 4222	£	6 pm	A delectably dinky bakery. These cakes can't be missed.
Tandis	73 Haverstock Hill	020 7586 8079	££		Iranian food with a touch of elegance.

Map 71 · Camden Town / Chalk Farm / Kentish Town (West)

Andy's Taverna	23 Pratt St	020 7485 9718	££	11 pm	Big Greek restaurant with a garden.
Anima e Cuore	129 Kentish Town Rd	075 9042 7171	££		BYOB affordable fan-favorite Italian.
Bar Gansa	2 Inverness St	020 7267 8909	££	12 am	More buzzing and pleasurable than a Rampant Rabbit.
Bento Ramen	29 Parkway	020 7485 9933	££	11 pm	Exquisite Japanese food at very reasonable prices.
Cafe Chula	89 Camden Lock Pl	020 7284 1890	££		Mexican, for brunch?! Si, si si! A+ Huevos Rancheros.
Cottons	55 Chalk Farm Rd	020 8037 9555	££	10 pm	No hustle and bustle, just chill Jamaican style.
Haché	24 Inverness St	020 7485 9100	££	10.30 pm	Burger heaven for both vegetarians and carnivores.
Marathon Kebab House	87 Chalk Farm Rd	020 7485 3814	£*	4 am	Legendary late-night venue serving kebabs, chips and beer.
Muang Thai	71 Chalk Farm Rd	020 7916 0653	£	11 pm	Quiet vibe, tinkly music, reliably decent food.
My Village	37 Chalk Farm Rd	077 3789 2812	£	9 pm	Cute ethnic organic shop serving food, tea and coffee.
Thanh Binh	Stables Market	020 7267 9820	£*	11 pm	Once you pass the Spanish Inqusition, some excellent slop.
Woody Grill	1 Camden Rd	020 8616 9587	£*	12 am	Late night post-alcohol food without salmonella poisoning.

Map 72 · Kentish Town

Bengal Lancer	253 Kentish Town Rd	020 7485 6688	£££		The best (and priciest) Indian in the area.
Cafe Renoir	244 Kentish Town Rd	020 7485 7186	£		Nice and bright with simple food and decent coffee.
Mario's Cafe	6 Kelly St	020 7284 2066	£*	10 pm	Saint Etienne's local greasy spoon.
The Oxford	256 Kentish Town Rd	020 7485 3521	££	9.45 pm	Smug comfort eating.
Phoenicia	186 Kentish Town Rd	020 7267 1267	£	10 pm	Coffee 'n baclava, falafel, meze. All a steal.

Arts & Entertainment · **Restaurants**

Key: £ : Under £10 / ££ : £10–£20 / £££ : £20–£30 / ££££ : £30–£40 / £££££: £40+
*: Does not accept credit cards./ † : Accepts only American Express / †† : Accepts only Visa and Mastercard
Time listed refers to kitchen closing time on weekend nights

Map 74 • Holloway Road / Arsenal

El Rincon Quiteno	235 Holloway Rd	020 7700 3670	££		A ray of South American sunshine on bleak Holloway Road.
Kokeb	45 Roman Way	020 7609 9832	£	10 pm	Getenesh will look after you.
Wolkite Kifto	82 Hornsey Road	020 7700 3055	£	11 pm	Good veggie options as well as kitfo.

Map 75 • Highbury

Firezza	276 St. Paul's Rd	020 7359 7400	£		Up market-esque stone baked pizza joint.
Highbury Arts Club	73 Highbury Park	07826 899499	££	11 pm	Cosy space with live events.
Prawn on the Lawn	292 Saint Paul's Rd	020 3302 8668	£££	12 am	As fresh as it gets.
Primeur	116 Petherton Rd	020 7226 5271	£££		Fun, fresh European menu with French focus.
Trullo	300-302 St Paul's Rd	020 7226 2733	£££		Well-done rustic seasonal Italian.
Ustun Lahmacun	107 Green Lanes	020 7704 0360	£*	10 pm	Very nice lamachun.

Map 76 • Edgware Road / Marylebone (North)

The Sea Shell Lisson Grove	49 Lisson Grove	020 7224 9000	££	10.30 pm	Pescatarians will love this place—sorry, carnivores!

Map 77 • Mornington Crescent / Regent's Park

Chutneys	124 Drummond St	020 7388 0604	££	11.30 pm	Flavoursome, no-frills, fill-yer-boots affair. Bargainous buffet colossal.
Diwana Bhel Poori House	121 Drummond St	020 7387 5556	££	11 pm	South-Indian veggie with tasty dosai and puris.
Mestizo	103 Hampstead Rd	020 7387 4064	£££	11 pm	Great. The margarita is made by the devil himself.
York & Albany	127 Parkway	020 7592 1227	£££	11 pm	Gordo on a budget.

Map 78 • Euston

Asakusa	265 Eversholt St	020 7388 8533	£££	11.30 pm	Authentic Japanese.
The Booking Office	St Pancras Renaissance London Hotel, Euston Rd	020 7841 3566	££		Where the lucky few have pre Eurostar cocktails and snacks.
Camino Cruz del Rey	3 Varnisher's Yard	020 7841 7330	££	12 am	Sophisticated Spanish restaurant in Kings Cross. Seems wrong, somehow.
Caravan	1 Granary Building	020 7101 7661	££	11:30 pm	Industrial space serving food and awesome coffee.
Great Nepalese	48 Eversholt St	020 7388 6737	££	11 pm	Really the only option in the area.
Kerb	Lewis Cubitt Sq		£		Ever changing market showcasing best in London street food.
The Somers Town Coffee House	60 Chalton St	020 7387 7377	££	10 pm	Bistro food in grade II listed pub. Excellent set menu.

Map 79 · King's Cross

Addis	42 Caledonian Rd	020 7278 0679	££	11 pm	Lovely food with convivial sloth-like service.
Euro Café	299 Caledonian Rd	020 7700 6644	£	10 pm	Loveable caff with some unusual specials.
Marathon	196 Caledonian Rd	020 7837 4499	££	12 am	Raw meat, ritualistic coffee and crazed dancing.
New Didar	347 Caledonian Rd	020 7700 3496	£	12 am	Friendly staff willing to strike deals. Haggling gets you everywhere.

Map 80 · Angel / Upper St

Afghan Kitchen	35 Islington Green	020 7359 8019	£££*	10.45 pm	Only a few tables; Islington's smallest—and biggest—Afghan place.
The Breakfast Club	31 Camden Passage	020 7226 5454	££	9.30 pm	Not just breakfast, not a club. But just so gooood.
Candid Café & Courtyard	3 Torrens St	020 7837 4237	£	10 pm	Laid-back, arty cafe for dreamy types. Candle-lit. Perfect for lingering.
Casa Fabrizi	97 Chapel Market	020 7837 8330	£	4 pm	This, guv'nor, is a proper tea'n'two slices caff. Alright?
Desperados	67 Upper St	020 7226 5055	££	11.30 pm	Garish. More like the Mexico of MTV than the real world.
Fig and Olive	151 Upper St	020 7354 2605	££	11 pm	Incredibly busy at weekends which can affect service and quality.
Fredericks	Camden Passage	020 7359 2888	££	11 pm	Swanky Euro-flash bistro.
Gem	265 Upper St	020 7359 0405	£££	4 am	A good vibe is precious.
Indian Veg Bhelpoori	93 Chapel Market	020 7837 4607	£	10 pm	Honest all-you-can-eat Indian. Veggie propaganda on walls.
Le Mercury	140 Upper St	020 7354 4088	££	1 am	This place will seduce you AND your mother.
Mem & Laz	8 Theberton St	020 7704 9089	££	11 pm	Mediterranean chaos by candlelight.
Ottolenghi	287 Upper St	020 7288 1454	££	10 pm	Staff you'll want to take home to meet your mum.
Pera	170 Upper St	020 7704 6888	££		It's all about the Turkish brunch in this friendly joint!
Tortilla	13 Islington High St	020 7833 3103	££	10 pm	Damn good burritos!
Zaffrani	47 Cross St	020 7226 5522	££	11 pm	Thinking man's curry.

Map 81 · Canonbury

Raab's Bakery	136 Essex Rd	020 7226 2830	£	6 pm	Use your loaf sunshine.

Map 82 · De Beauvoir Town / Kingsland

Mother Earth	101 Newington Green Rd	020 7359 7353	£	8 pm	Wholesome cafe food.
Peppers and Spice	40 Balls Pond Rd	020 7275 9818	£*	10.30 pm	The real deal: jerk, oxtail, festival, plantain, ackee. Everytin irie.

Key: £ : Under £10 / ££ : £10–£20 / £££ : £20–£30 / ££££ : £30–£40 / £££££: £40+
* : Does not accept credit cards./ † : Accepts only American Express / †† : Accepts only Visa and Mastercard
Time listed refers to kitchen closing time on weekend nights

Map 83 · Angel (East) / City Rd (North)

The Shepherdess	221 City Rd	020 7336 6655	£	5 pm	Cafe offering no-frills traditional English fare.

Map 84 · Hoxton

The Clove Club	380 Old St	020 7729 6496	££££		Nu British tasting menus in grand setting.
Hoxton Barrel Pizza	110 Hoxton St	020 7683 0353	£	10 pm	Local favourite spot for pizza.
MEATliquor	15 Hoxton Market	020 7739 8212	£	12 am	Sister restaurant to Meat Liquor.
Rivington Grill	28 Rivington St	020 7729 7053	££	11 pm	Emin on the walls, meat in the buns.

Map 85 · Stoke Newington (East)

19 Numara Bos Cirrik	34 Stoke Newington Rd	020 7249 0400	££	10 pm	Meat, meat, meat—oh and onion, pomegranate and turnip salad.
Addie's Thai Cafe	3 Northwold Rd	020 7249 2618	££		Deceptively pokey, unimaginatively named, yet brilliant.
The Bagel House	2 Stoke Newington High St	020 7249 3908	£*	10 pm	Bagels to rival Brick Lane and without the queues.
Cafe Z Bar	58 Stoke Newington High St	020 7275 7523	£*	11 pm	Popular grease-shop/hangover center for Stokey Lefties.
Testi	38 Stoke Newington High St	020 7249 7151	£££	12 am	It's the dog's bollocks.
The Three Crowns	175 Stoke Newington High St	020 7241 5511	££		Impressive Victorian pub that's undergone gastropubification.

Map 86 · Dalston / Kingsland

The Best Turkish Kebab	125 Stoke Newington Rd	020 7254 7642	£*	12 am	Feed your soul. Always buzzing.
Dalston Eastern Curve Garden	13 Dalston Lane		£	11pm	Check website for days when food is served. this one.
Evin	115 Kingsland High St	020 7254 5634	££	11 pm	Fantastic Turkish place without the grease factor. Speciality is gozleme.
Mangal 1	10 Arcola St	020 7275 8981	£*	12 am	May the grill's smoke guide you, meat-loving friends.
Mangal 2	4 Stoke Newington Rd	020 7254 7888	££	12 am	Gilbert & George aren't the only ones loving this one.
Shanghai	41 Kingsland High St	020 7254 2878	££	10.30 pm	Tasty, good-value Chinese hiding behind the facade of a dingy old Kaff.
Somine	131 Kingsland High St	020 7254 7384	£*	24-hrs	Reanimating red lentil soup, Turkish style. Around the clock.
Stone Cave	111 Kingsland High St	020 7241 4911	££	12 am	Cave look and cave feel. Up-scale(ish) Turkish. And great.
Voodoo Ray's	95 Kingsland High St	020 7249 7865	£		All American late night pizza from folk behind Dalston Superstore.

Map 87 • Hackney Downs / Lower Clapton

Mess Café	38 Amhurst Rd	020 8985 3194	£*	5 pm	All manner of breakfast all the time.

Map 88 • Haggerston / Queensbridge Rd

Berber & Q	338 Acton Mews	020 7923 0829	£££		BBQ meets mezze under railroad arches.
Chicks n Sours	390 Kingsland Rd	020 3620 8728	££	10:30pm	Fried chicken and cocktails. Of course.
Fabrique Bakery	385 Geffrye St	020 7033 0268	£		Great Nordic bakery and cafe.
Faulkners	424 Kingsland Rd	079 7636 4076	£	10 pm	Legendary and traditional with traditional opening times.
Hackney City Farm	1 Goldsmith's Row	020 7729 6381	££	4.30 pm	Animals! In Hackney! And some overpriced fry-up.
Song Que	134 Kingsland Rd	020 7613 3222	££	11 pm	Still Little Vietnam's queen. An authentic, no-nonsense affair.
Uludag	398 Kingsland Rd	020 7241 1923	£		Great falafels and a bit of a nutter hub to boot.
Viet Hoa Cafe	70 Kingsland Rd	020 7729 8293	£	11.30 pm	Bland looking cafe hides gorgeous delicacies.

Map 89 • London Fields / Hackney Central

Buen Ayre	50 Broadway Market	020 7275 9900	££££	10.30 pm	Vegetarians take note—run for the hills.
The Cat and Mutton	76 Broadway Market	020 7249 6555	££	10 pm	Gastropub without the gastropub nastiness.
Hai Ha	206 Mare St	020 8985 5388	££*	11 pm	Brilliant BYO Vietnamese cafe.
Ombra	1 Vyner St	020 8981 5150	£		Neighbourhood Italian, good honest food.
Pidgin	52 Wilton Wy	020 7254 8311	£££		Ever-changing seasonal set menus, charming digs.
The Spurstowe Arms	68 Greenwood Rd	020 7249 2500	££	11 pm	Suntrap beer garden, good wine selection and gamey menu. Marvellous.

Map 90 • Homerton / Victoria Park North

Eat 17	64-66 Brooksby's Walk	020 8986 6242	££		Convenience store, burger bar, restaurant, florist, bakery, off licence, etc.
The Empress	130 Lauriston Rd	020 8533 5123	££	10 pm	Spiffy menu from brekkie through to dinner in Hackney Village.
Fish House	126 Lauriston Rd	020 8533 3327	££	9.45 pm	Not as cheap as chips but still very good.
Well Street Kitchen	203 Well St	020 8533 6275	£	5 pm	Good honest caff food.

Map 91 • Shoreditch / Brick Lane / Spitalfields

Beigel Shop	155 Brick Ln	020 7729 0616	£*	24 hrs	For 3am cravings; salted beef bagel from the Beigel Shop.
Boundary	2 Boundary St	020 7729 1051	£££	10.30 pm	Warehouse conversion, great view, some major boxes being ticked here.
Brawn	49 Columbia Rd	020 7729 5692			No pig left unturned.
Chez Elles	45 Brick Ln	020 7247 9699	£££		Out-Frenches most actual French bistros, and does it deliciously.
The Culpeper	40 Commercial St	020 7247 5371	££	2 am	Seasonal and local food.
Dishoom	7 Boundary St	020 7420 9324	££		All-day Parsi cafe straight outta Bombay.
Ethiopian Food Stall	Brick Ln		£*		One of many great food stalls, get Brazilian desert after!
Frizzante	1 Goldsmith's Row	020 7739 2266	££		All the Italians go to Agriturismo night (Thurs) just sayin'.

Arts & Entertainment · **Restaurants**

Key: £ : Under £10 / ££ : £10–£20 / £££ : £20–£30 / ££££ : £30–£40 / £££££ : £40+
* : Does not accept credit cards./ † : Accepts only American Express / ††: Accepts only Visa and Mastercard
Time listed refers to kitchen closing time on weekend nights

Hanoi Cafe	98 Kingsland Rd	020 7729 5610	££	11 pm	Cosy Viet joint, where the whole family's around.
Hawksmoor	157 Commercial St	020 7426 4850	£££	10.30 pm	France and America forget their differences for some serious steakage.
Issho-Ni	185 Bethnal Green Rd	020 7366 0314	£*	11.30 pm	Half the normal price; double the normal portions. Come hungry.
Lyle's	56 Shoreditch High St	020 3011 5911	££££		Modern British.
Marksman Public House	254 Hackney Rd	020 7739 7393	£££		Cut-above pub grub.
Mien Tay	106 Kingsland Rd	020 7739 3841			Kingsland's supreme Vietnamese.
Poppies	6 Hanbury St	020 7247 0892	£		The Great British dish served '50's style.
The Premises	209 Hackney Rd	020 7684 2230	££	11 pm	Bistro swarming with musicians thanks to next door's recording studio.
Rosa's	12 Hanbury St	020 7247 1093	££	11 pm	Quirky, warm little Thai place.
St. John Bread and Wine	94 Commercial St	020 7251 0848	£££	11 pm	Minimalist and meaty. Anyone for deep-fried pig's head?
Tay Do	65 Kingsland Rd	020 7729 7223	£	11 pm	Squish 'em in, feed 'em quick variety of cheap & filling Vietnamese cuisine.

Map 92 · Bethnal Green

Bistrotheque	23 Wadeson St	020 8983 7900	££	11 pm	Brunch, burlesque and pianist playing Smells Like Teen Spirit. Fabulous.
E. Pellicci	332 Bethnal Green Rd	020 7739 4873	£	4.30 pm	Challenge your hangover to survive their fry-ups.
The Gallery Cafe	21 Old Ford Rd	020 8980 2092	£	9 pm	Veggie/vegan haven.
Little Georgia	87 Goldsmiths Row	020 7739 8154	££	10 pm	Hearty fayre from the former Soviet State. No drinks licence.

Map 93 · Globe Town / Mile End (North)

| Greedy Cow Burgers & Steaks | 2 Grove Rd | 020 8983 3304 | $$ | | Burger and exotic meat taste explosion. |
| Morgan Arms | 43 Morgan St | 020 8980 6389 | £££ | 12 am | Which joker invented the term "gastropub"? This is one of them. |

Map 94 · Bow

| G. Kelly Noted Eel & Pie Shop | 526 Roman Rd | 020 8980 3165 | £ | 7 pm | Servin' 'ot 'ome-made pies, jellied eels 'n mash since 1937. |
| Pavilion Victoria Park | Old Ford Rd | 020 8980 0030 | | | Kippery breakfast with a view |

Map 95 · Whitechapel (West) / St Katharine's Dock

| The Empress | 141 Leman St | 020 7265 0745 | £ | 11.45 pm | Forget Brick Lane. This is where it's at. |

Map 96 · Whitechapel (East) / Shadwell (West) / Wapping

Lahore Kebab House	2-10 Umberston St	020 7481 9737	$		Pakistani grub gives new insight to 'eyes bigger than stomach'.
Needoo Grill	87 New Rd	020 7247 0648	££		For when Tayyabs queue is just too long.
Tayyabs	83 Fieldgate St	020 7247 9543	£	12 am	Lipsmacking seekh kebabs alone are worth the queues.

Map 98 · Mile End (South) / Limehouse

Bread Street Kitchen on the River	44 Narrow St	020 7592 7950	£££	11 pm	Gordon Ramsay's nod to gastropubs—cracking views.
The Orange Room	63 Burdett Rd	020 8980 7336	£££	11.30 pm	Tasty, fresh Lebanese food in a wasteland of stodgy takeaways.

Map 100 · Poplar (West) / Canary Wharf (West)

Browns	Hertsmere Rd	020 7987 9777	£££	11 pm	Always reliable.
Nicolas	1 Canada Sq	020 7512 9092	££	10.30 pm	Micro French restaurant and vintners in one.
Plateau	Canada Pl	020 7715 7100	££££	10.30 pm	Striking views and truffle gnocchi.
Royal China	30 Westferry Circus	020 7719 0888	£££		Cantonese culinary powerhouse; dim sum mandatory.

Map 101 · Poplar (East) / Canary Wharf (East)

The Gun	27 Coldharbour	020 7519 0075	£££	11 pm	Enjoyed by 18th century dockers and city workers alike.

Map 103 · Cubitt Town / Mudchute

Mudchute Kitchen	Pier St	074 4776 2691	££	5 pm	Food companion to the farm bit. Chi chi children.

Map 104 · South Bank / Waterloo / Lambeth North

The Anchor & Hope	36 The Cut	020 7928 9898	£££	10.30 pm	Fresh, seasonal, hearty. Long wait though.
The Cut Bar	66 The Cut	020 7928 4400	£££	11 pm	Brilliant chips. A cut above the rest.
Giraffe	Riverside	020 7042 6900	££	10.45 pm	Good crowd pleaser. Though too much world music and balloons.
Marie's Cafe	90 Lower Marsh	020 7928 1050	£	10.30 pm	Greasy spoon by day, a no-frills, super-yum BYO thai by night.
OXO Tower Wharf	Barge House St	020 7803 3888	££££	11 pm	You may have to rob a bank, but the view's amazing.
Skylon	Belvedere Rd	020 7654 7800	££££	10.45 pm	Expensive but staffs' uniforms and view make up for it.
Tas	33 The Cut	020 7928 2111	££	11.30 pm	Blink and you'll miss it. Buzzing Turkish cafe—best hummous in London.

Map 105 · Southwark / Bankside (West)

Restaurant at Tate Modern	Bankside	020 7887 8888	££	6 pm	Stunning views, crap food, clueless staff.
The Table	83 Southwark St	020 7401 2760	£*	10.30 pm	Go and find out why we're all obsessed.
Terry's Cafe	158 Great Suffolk St	020 7407 9358	£	2 pm	Mom & Pop British fare including mushy peas.

Arts & Entertainment · **Restaurants**

Map 106 · Bankside (East) / Borough / Newington

Arabica Bar & Kitchen	3 Rochester Walk	020 3011 5151	££		Fresh, fun, game-upping Middle Eastern cuisine.
The Boot and Flogger	10 Redcross Way	020 7407 1184	££	8 pm	Splendidly gentleman's club-esque—all savile row suits and chesterfield sofas.
Champor-Champor	62 Weston St	020 7403 4600	£££	10.15pm	Jaw-droppingly inspired high-end Malaysian cuisine. Totally impressive.
Elliot's Cafe	12 Stoney St	020 7403 7436	£££		Rumoured by some to serve London's best burgers.
Fish!	Cathedral St	020 7407 3803	££	10.30 pm	Great fish. Simple. Let it have its exclamation mark.
Nando's	225 Clink St	020 7357 8662	££	11 pm	Peri-peri madness underneath the arches.
Roast	Stoney St	020 3371 3120	££	9.30 pm	Meat, glorious meat. High-end food. Fab location.
Silka	6 Southwark St	020 7378 6161	£££	11.30 pm	Curry house that won't damage your arse in the morning.
Tapas Brindisa	18 Southwark St	020 7357 8880	££	11 pm	If you can bear the crowds; lovely market-bordering eatery.
Tas	72 Borough High St	020 7403 7200	££	11 pm	Reduce your carbon footprint: come here and feel 1000 miles away.
Wright Bros Oyster & Porter House	11 Stoney St	020 7403 9554	£££	10.30 pm	Tastebuds say no, but libido says YES.

Map 107 · Shad Thames

Butlers Wharf Chop House	36 Shad Thames	020 7403 3403	£££	11 pm	What better place for British best than under Tower Bridge?
Casse-Croute	109 Bermondsey St	020 7407 2140	£££		Fun French bistro with chalkboard menu.
Jose	104 Bermondsey St	020 7403 4902	££	10:15 pm	The real deal for tapas.
Le Pont de la Tour	36 Shad Thames	020 7403 8403	£££££	11 pm	Blair & Clinton's rendezvous. Posh but gosh!
M. Manze Pie and Mash	87 Tower Bridge Rd	020 7407 2985	£	2.30 pm	As English as it gets. Try it once.
Pizarro	194 Bermondsey St	020 7378 9455	£££		A slice of Spain south of the river, top Menu del Dia.

Map 109 · Southwark Park

The Mayflower	117 Rotherhithe St	020 7237 4088	£££		The pub Sunday Lunch was invented for.

Map 110 · Rotherhithe (West) / Canada Water

Simplicity	1 Tunnel Rd	020 7232 5174	££	10:30 pm	Boldly goes where no restaurant has gone before: Rotherhithe.

Map 111 · Rotherhithe (East) Surrey Quays

Cafe East	100 Redriff Rd	020 7252 1212	££	Best Vietnamese pho this side of the Kingsland Road.

Map 112 · Kennington / Elephant and Castle

Brasserie Tolouse Lautrec	140 Newington Bts	020 7582 6800	££££	French cuisine as excellent as the owners are eccentric.
Chatkhara	84 Walworth Rd	020 7701 8899	£	Possibly the best value lunch deal in the city.
Dragon Castle	100 Walworth Rd	020 7277 3388	££	11 pm	Odd locale for such a curious pocket of culinary authenticity.
Mamuska	9 Addington St	020 3602 1898	£		Hearty polish grub to stave off winter blues.

Map 113 · Walworth

Aobaba and Longdan Express	128-132 Walworth Rd	020 7701 2566		Canteen serving proper bahn mi, with adjoining oriental supermarket.
Bagel King	280 Walworth Rd	020 7277 4060	£	Refuge in the night.
La Luna	380 Walworth Rd	020 7277 1991	££	11 pm	Ignore exterior. It's the garlic bread inside that counts.

Map 115 · Old Kent Road (East)

Roma Café	21 Peckham Park Rd	020 7639 7730	£	10 pm	Escape Peckham and enjoy a good fry-up here.

Map 119 · Deptford (East)

Chaconia	26 Deptford High St	020 8692 8815	£		Lip-tingling rotis made by the Trinidadian version of your Granny.
The Waiting Room	134 Deptford High St	020 3601 0100	£	7 pm	Veggie and vegan heaven

Map 120 · Greenwich

Goddards at Greenwich	22 King William Walk	020 8305 9612	£	6 pm	Pie n' mash n' eels. Only at the weekend.
Greenwich Tavern	1 King William Walk	020 8858 8791	£££	10 pm	Kobe steak burgers. Nuff said.
The Hill	89 Royal Hill	020 8691 3626	£££	10 pm	Bistro food. Local favourite.
The Langos Company	5 Greenwich Market	020 8269 5096	£		Deep fried flatbread like no other.
North Pole Bar and Grill	131 Greenwich High Rd	020 8853 3020	£££££	2 am	Fish swim in the chandeliers. Get the idea?

Map 121 · Camberwell (West)

New Dewaniam	225 Camberwell New Rd	020 7703 9318	£	12 am	Mouth-watering Indian takeaway for a tenner.
Rock Steady Eddie's	2 Coldharbour Ln	020 7326 0621	£		Where Elvis would eat if he was born in King's College.
Zeret Kitchen	216 Camberwell Rd	020 7701 8587	£	11 pm	Order the special to try a bit of everything.

Map 122 · Camberwell (East)

Caravaggio	47 Camberwell Church St	020 7207 1612	£	11 pm	Cheap Italian with impressive fare. Stands out from the rest.
Crooked Well	16 Grove Ln	020 7252 7798	££££		A damn fine taste of the genteel side of Camberwell.
Falafel	27 Camberwell Church St	079 1000 0108	£		Better bet for an evening snack than stale friend chicken.
FM Mangal	54 Camberwell Church St	020 7701 6677	££		Book a taxi because the monstrous portions seriously hinder mobility.
Silk Road	49 Camberwell Church St	020 7703 4832	££		As far away from chicken chow mein as Chinese gets.
Wuli Wuli	15 Camberwell Church St	020 7708 5024	££		Go for the regional Sichuan dishes.

Map 123 · Peckham

Agrobeso African Cuisine	139 Peckham High St	020 7732 3721	£		For anyone mad enough to try honeycomb tripe.
The Begging Bowl	168 Bellenden Rd	020 7635 2627	£££		Great food, outstanding cocktails.
Ganapati	38 Holly Grove	020 7277 2928	£	10:30 pm	Influenced by street food of South India.
M. Manze Pie and Mash	105 Peckham High St	020 7277 6181	£		One of the only remaining original pie and mash shops.
Miss Tapas	45 Choumert Rd	020 3689 5050	£		Andalucian fare.

Map 124 · Peckham East (Queen's Road)

805	805 Old Kent Rd	020 7639 0808	£££	12 am	West African oasis. In Peckham.
Pedler	169 Queen's Rd	020 3030 5015	£	11pm	Vibrant neighbourhood eatery.
Tops Carribean Takeaway	173 Queens Rd	020 7635 4442	£		Eat incredible fried dumplings under a massive Obama mural.

Map 125 · New Cross Gate

Smokey Jerky	158 New Cross Rd	079 4623 3176	£		Some of the best, messiest jerk in South London.

Map 127 · Coldharbour Lane / Herne Hill (West)

Ichiban Sushi	58 Atlantic Rd	020 7738 7006	£	11 pm	The bee's knees.
Naughty Piglets	28 Brixton Water Ln	020 7274 7796	££		Nouveau bohemian French cafe-inflected menu.
New Fujiyama	5 Vining St	020 7737 6583	£	10.30 pm	This place blows Wagamama's out of the water.

Map 128 · Denmark Hill / Herne Hill (East)

Lombok	17 Half Moon Ln	020 7733 7131	£££	10.30 pm	From Stir-fries to curries, a no-fuss pan-Asian standby.

Map 129 · East Dulwich

The Palmerston	91 Lordship Ln	020 8693 1629	££££	10 pm	Gastropub that's a lot more gastro than pub.

Map 130 · Peckham Rye

Artusi	161 Bellenden Rd	020 3302 8200	££	10 pm	Italian-inspired seasonal menu.
Thai Corner Cafe	44 North Cross Rd	020 8299 4041	££*	11 pm	Tiny, laidback neighbourhood cafe.

Map 134 · South Lambeth

A Toca	343 Wandsworth Rd	020 7627 2919	£££		Football on numerous screens, as if you were in Lisbon!
Bar Estrela	113 S Lambeth Rd	020 7793 1051	£	11 pm	Like mama used to make. Probably.
Brunswick House	30 Wandsworth Rd	020 7720 2926	££	12 am	Opulent setting.
Canton Arms	177 S Lambeth Rd	020 7582 8710	£££	10 pm	Recently acquired by Anchor & Hope folks. Bring on the yuppies.
Tia Maria	126 South Lambeth Rd	020 3642 5337	£	1 am	Known for its tapioca wraps.

Map 135 · Oval

Adulis	44 Brixton Rd	020 7587 0055	£	11 pm	C'mon, it's yummmy and cheap. And we can't cook Eritrean.
Bonnington Café	11 Vauxhall Grove	075 5247 5535	£*	10.30 pm	Wonderful vegetarian meals in a communified (ex-squat) environment.
Grill 32	32 Clapham Rd	020 7735 1898	£*	10 pm	Fancy a doner kebab? Go nowhere else.

Map 136 · Putney

Enoteca Turi	87 Pimlico Rd	020 7730 3663	£££		Aperol Spritz followed by some homemade ravioli.
Pinto Thai Putney	320 Upper Richmond Rd	020 8780 5103	££	10.30 pm	Thai-ny, family-run restaurant with Thai supermarket, cooking classes and Thai regulars.

Map 137 · Wandsworth (West)

Miraj	123 Putney Bridge Rd	020 8875 0799	£	10 pm	Curry in a hurry? Cheap, tasty take away joint.

Map 138 · Wandsworth (Central)

Kathmandu Valley	5 West Hill	020 8871 0240	££	11.45 pm	Nepalese is the new black (read: curry).

Map 139 · Wandsworth (East)

Gazette	79 Chatfield Rd	020 7223 0999	££		Unpretentious French brasserie fare that is tres sophistique.

Map 140 · Clapham Junction / Northcote Rd

Gail's Bread	64 Northcote Rd	020 7738 2915			Clapham branch of North London artisanal chain.
Jack's At The Junction	252 Lavender Hill	020 7228 9111	£		There's only one rule here—be a very hungry Jack.
Mien Tay	180 Lavender Hill	020 7350 0721			Kingsland Road stalwart brough to Lavender Hill.
Parisienne	225 Lavender Hill	020 7924 5523	£	5 pm	Massive sarnies and baked potatoes.
Pizza Metro	64 Battersea Rise	020 7228 3812	£££		Pizza by the metre!

Map 142 · Clapham Old Town

Nardullis Ice Cream	29 The Pavement	020 7720 5331	£		Real Italian gelato to smear over your chops.
Trinity	4 The Polygon	020 7622 1199	£££	10.30 pm	How to do local dining really quite fantastically well.

Map 143 · Clapham High Street

Brickwood	16 Clapham Common South Side	020 7819 9614	£	6.30 pm	Top brunch.
The Pepper Tree	19 Clapham Common South Side	020 7622 1758	£*	11 pm	Speedy Thai with soul.
Tsunami	5 Voltaire Rd	020 7978 1610	££££	10.30 pm	The new Nobu. Unbelievable. Unfortunate name.

Map 144 · Stockwell / Brixton (West)

Bellantoni's	81 Granville Arcade	078 7294 5675	££		Artisan homemade pasta for date night at Brixton Village.
Falafel Van	Station Rd		£		Tasty falafel from a man with a nice Muhammad Ali portrait.
Honest Burgers	12 Brixton Village	020 3148 2970	££		Best British burgers in Brixton. Not gonna lie.
Jeff the Chef	Station Rd				Proper oil drunk jerk and fresh coconuts.
Mama Lan	18 Brixton Village Market	020 7733 7279	£		Slap-up corner joint selling nom noodle soups and dumplings.

Map 146 · Earlsfield

Amaranth	346 Garratt Ln	020 8874 9036	££*	10 pm	Rarefied, bustling restaurant with tacked-on takeout element.

Map 147 · Balham (West)

Chez Bruce	2 Bellevue Rd	020 8672 0114	££££	10.30 pm	Worth its fancy-pants (read Michelin) star.

Map 148 · Balham (East)

Brickwood	11 Hildreth Street	020 8772 6818	£	6 pm	Top brunch.
The Exhibit	12 Balham Station Rd	020 8772 6556	£££	2 am	Cool event space; friendly, laid back vibe.
Hagen & Hyde	157 Balham High Rd	020 8772 0016	££	2 am	Modern British pub food.

Map 149 · Clapham Park

Bistro Union	40 Abbeville Rd	020 7042 6400	£££		All-day bistro featuring well-crafted modern fare.

Map 150 · Brixton

Asmara	386 Coldharbour Ln	020 7737 4144	££	11.15 pm	Disconcerting but delicious curry with pancakes to mop it up.
Boqueria	192 Acre Ln	020 7733 4408	£££		Insanely good croquetas de jamon. Excellent value too.
Duck Egg Cafe	424 Coldharbour Ln	020 7274 8972	££		Unassuming brunch. Go duck eggs, ginger beer and hash browns.
Franco Manca	4 Market Row	020 7738 3021	££	10 pm	London's best pizza? Eclectic concoctions of sour dough goodness comes west.
Kamome	49 Brixton Station Rd	020 7326 1399	£££		Katsu curry that makes Wagamama's taste like a crying shame.
KaoSarn	Coldharbour Ln	020 7095 8922	££		The beating heart of Brixton Village. Half-chicken or bust.
Khan's of Brixton	24 Brixton Water Ln	020 7326 4460	££	11 pm	Great curry, and BYO to boot. Have it!
Lounge	56 Atlantic Rd	020 7733 5229	£	10 pm	A local favourite for breakfast, recovery and hanging on weekends.
Negril	132 Brixton Hill	020 8674 8798	£	10 pm	Tasty Carribean with veg options (which are joy).
The Phoenix	441 Coldharbour Ln	020 7733 4430			Old school institution. Good bubble and squeak.
Refill	500 Brixton Rd	020 7274 5559	£		24 hour with suprisingly good patties and jerk sandwiches.

Map 151 · Tooting Bec

Al Mirage	215 Upper Tooting Rd	020 8772 4422	£	10.30 pm	Better than Mirch Masala? We think so.
Mirch Masala	213 Upper Tooting Rd	020 8672 7500	£	12 am	Cheap, no frills, award-winning curries. Sublime.
Spice Village	121 Upper Tooting Rd	020 8672 0710	£	11 pm	Go for grilled.

Map 152 · Tooting Broadway

Dosa n Chutny	68 Tooting High St	020 8767 9200	£		Breakfast, South Indian style. Amazing.
Jaffna House	90 Tooting High St	020 8672 7786	££	12 am	Mediocre curry fare beneath flourescent bulbs.
Radha Krishna Bhavan	86 Tooting High St	020 8682 0969	££	11.30 pm	Busy, buzzing, bhavan of South Indian curry.
Rick's Restaurant	122 Mitcham Rd	020 8767 5219	£££	11 pm	Tooting's best kept culinary secret.

So are we still in the Recession? Who knows? Who cares? We're getting used to this boom and bust cycle but we've cut up all our credit cards. When it comes to retail, people will always spend whether money or no (that's how we got in this fine mess remember Stanley?), it's just that with little of the stuff about, people are more discerning about what they spend their hard earned cash/State Benefits on. And of course if we didn't spend we would never collectively crawl out of this endless dirge of gloom. As the well-observed slogan on the reusable eco-shopping bag from Modern Toss (available at **Magma, Maps 5, 12**) says, "Buy More Shit Or We're All Fucked". Indeed. But if the economic crisis is teaching us anything it's to be more picky about what we purchase and for retailers not just to deliver the goods but also all the extras that we, as polite English people, so foolishly see as just "extras". Primarily what we mean is, that intangible thing that contributes to a satisfying shopping experience and brings a customer back to the same store again and again: excellent service—helpfulness, genuine smiles and interest in the product and the customer. Beautiful packaging, loyalty cards, discounts, samples, invites to in-store events all help, too. In an adverse way, consumers have never had more power than now to demand what they want—as important—don't want. So just make sure you buy more cool shit as opposed to any old shit.

The British High Street is certainly changing and support for independent shops is growing. A leaning towards handmade items and crafts which support local designers and artisans—Columbia Road and Cheshire Street are hotspots for this kind of thing. Yes there are a lot of these shops cropping up that purely sell "beautiful things" like **Of Cabbages And Kings (Map 64)** and (if it's a beauty of a decaying kind you're looking for) **Viktor Wynd's Shop of Horrors (Map 87)** name just a couple (and we like them). But when it comes to fashion we also like to know that a little bit of love has been sprinkled into the making of an item. Special mention here must go to **Vivien of Holloway (Map 74)** who has built a real niche following but whose fabulous 1950s tailoring would make any gal feel like a doll. Both have gorgeous, well-fitted, unique shop spaces, too. For blokes, **Folk (Map 5)** are renowned for their limited

collections, particularly shoes which are hand-stitched (hence the price tag).

Part of this trend is Pop-Up Shops which are installed for a few months at a time sometimes displaying the work of a single designer/company or else a co-operative of independent designers. Not only is this a thrifty way of setting up shop in these uncertain times, it also provides a showcase for new young things so always worth a look. These tend to appear around Carnaby Street and Spitalfields, especially in the summer.

The Big Boys

When it comes to department stores, **Selfridges (Map 2)** is without a doubt the daddy of them all—arguably, (and the emphasis is on that word depending on your budget) you can just get everything you need from here but if you're strapped, at least go and marvel at the window displays. **Harvey Nics (Map 37)** and **Harrods (Map 37)** are very much for ladies who lunch, and the Knightsbridge set use them like corner shops—that's not to say they don't have their uses. For a more personal touch, **Fenwick (Map 2)** and **Liberty (Map 10)** are wonderful British institutions which take you far from the madding crowd. If all these close-quarters encounters get up your nose head to **Whiteleys (Map 30)** or the Behemoth that is **Westfield Shopping Centre (Map 33)**.

Haute Et High Street

For flexing that plastic, Bond Street has always been the place to spend but Bruton Street, which branches off the main drag, is setting quite a precedent with **Stella McCartney (Map 9)** in residence. If you want to feel like Alice down the rabbit hole, make a trip to **Dover Street Market (Map 9)**, owned by Rei Kawakubo of Comme Des Garçons—a real experience even if you're not buying. Throwing down the gauntlet when it comes to experiential retail is **LN-CC (Map 86)**. For super-slick, sharp ready-to-wear you can't beat Spanish stores, **Zara (Map 2)** and **Mango (Map 3)** which both do high street with an edge and turnover is pretty quick to ensure their stock remains covetable. New contenders for higher end high-street include **Cos (Map 10)**, and let's not forget our Stateside cousins who have sent ripples of excitement through the fash pack by opening flagship stores of **Anthropologie**, **Banana Republic**, and **Abercrombie & Fitch (Map 10)** all in the big smoke. There are also little shopping oases to be found in the capital. St Christopher's Place is hidden behind the hustle and bustle of Oxford Street and houses cool European brands alongside more familiar fare. Kingly Court (behind Carnaby Street—itself a great shopping spot for trend-led labels) has independent boutiques. The area around Seven Dials in Covent Garden which includes Neal's Yard is eclectic with skatewear at **Slam City Skates (Map 13)** and **Superdry (Map 13)** on Earlham. Edgy fashion abounds out East: head to **Good Hood (Map 84)** to start your shopping crawl.

Back to the Future

'Vintage' seems to be the term for anything over five years old nowadays but London's vintage (and secondhand) scene is thriving. Some of the best-known, best-loved shops include **Rellik (Map 25)** in Portobello, **Annie's (Map 80)** in Islington (a favourite of La Moss), and **Beyond Retro (Map 91)** in Shoreditch (famous hunting ground for stylists). If you want to hear what the young, stylish and clueless get up to head to **Rokit (Maps 13, 71)** and eavesdrop on the staff's mindnumbing conversations. For genuine thrift, the turnover of goods in our charity shops is mind-boggling. **Oxfam Dalston (Map 86)** is renowned for being a good rummage: it's hit and miss but then that's the nature of the thrifting beast. Most hardy shoppers will happily tread the city twice over for good charity shop finds but if you want some certainty of finding designer threads you can't beat the **British Red Cross (Map 5)** where you will discover the likes of Ralph Lauren, Armani and pairs of Manolos amongst the usual flotsam and jetsam. The **Octavia Foundation Charity Shop (Map 35)** is also a reliable source of local celebrities' cast-offs from like, yesterday. For all you true vintage fashion fiends who want to mingle with like-minded souls and find genuine vintage togs (i.e. pre-1980s) the **Frock Me! Vintage Fashion Fair (Map 45)** is unequalled for choice and variety. Wake up and smell the mould.

Keep on Running, Cycling, Skating Etc.

Lillywhite's (Map 10) is the obvious place to go for cheap sportswear—it has earned a bit of a bargain basement tag where once it was prestigious (the Lillywhites were instrumental in the game of cricket during the 19th century) but it doesn't stop the shoppers pouring in, and tourists buying their favourite London football team shirts. A good indie chain is **Runners Need (Map 20)**. If it's sweatshop-made kit you're after head to **Niketown (Map 2)**, which is as scary as the name suggests. Though we're no Amsterdam, the economic shitstorm has inspired many Londoners to don skintight clothes and take to two wheels. If you're after a battered old charmer of a bike, **Recycling (Map 112)** does a fab job at selling secondhand wheels. If you've had your designer bike nicked, head down to Brick Lane at the weekend and buy it off some dodgy geezer. **Slam City Skates (Map 13)** is the only dedicated place for Southbank skaters to get their duds.

Home Sweet Home

John Lewis (Map 2) is a British standard (read: very sensible) and has been the store of choice for middle-class couples' wedding lists for decades. With fantastic staff (who all get a share of the profits) and well-made stuff, their maxim is "never knowingly undersold." **Twentytwentyone (Map 80)** is a designer's wet dream selling originals as well as new items. So impressive is their collection that they often lend out furniture to film companies who want the authentic look of an era on set. **SCP (Maps 30, 84)** is perfect for unnecessary-yet-tasteful knick-knacks. The wonderfully named **Timorous Beasties (Map 6)** make wickedly amusing wallpapers—their most famous being a toile de jouy design for modern days (spot the alcopop-drinking chavs and the Gherkin in the background). **Labour and Wait (Map 91)** does the retro home stuff better than most. If you want personable, "Where can I find one of these?" type of service try **Russell's Hardware & DIY (Map 151)** in Tooting or **KTS The Corner (Map 86)** in Dalston.

Electricity for You and Me

Apple have done a very good job at monopolising our lives and getting everyone to 'Think Different,' so why you'd need to go anywhere other than the **Apple Store (Map 10)** we're not sure. However, traditionally, Tottenham Court Road is the hideout for the anally retentive hi-fi nut and the nerdoid pirate radio enthusiast a-like. The area positively thrums with electricity. In all cases it's best to shop around, play prices against each other and barter until you get the lowest price—often cash payment will get you well below the RRP. **CeX (Map 3)** is the one-stop shop for gaming, DVDs, computing and phones, which—as the name suggests—will part-exchange and knock money off for cash transactions. For audiovisual, **Richer Sounds (Map 106)** is a trusted chain, and if we're talking electronics in the purist sense, **Maplin (Map 3)** is geek central. Whether you'll get anyone who knows what they're talking about is another matter. Photography enthusiasts should check out the **London Camera Exchange (Map 24)** for old-school SLRs and digital cameras and **Red Dot Cameras for Leicas (Map 7)**.

Food for Thought

We like our food in London and the more diverse the better. Whether it's chowing down on burgers from Lucky Chip down **Broadway Market (Map 89)** or fresh scallops and some raclette down Borough Market (Map 106) before moseying on down to **Maltby Street Market (Map 107)** for gelato, we're not afraid to say, "Please Sir, I want some more" (mainly because we're paying for it). **Whitecross Street (Map 7)** also has an impressive selection of foodie stalls. We have New York (and in particular, the Magnolia Bakery) to thank for the invasion of cupcake stores but the original and best is the **Hummingbird Bakery (Maps 29, 45)** which makes Red Velvet cupcakes that taste like little pieces of baked orgasm. Just try and restrain yourself from licking the last morsels of frosting from the paper. Numerous Italian delis can be found around the city selling cured meats, buffalo mozzarella, biscotti and everything else that Mama used to make—**I Camisa & Son (Map 11)** is small but crammed full of delicacies. Organic freaks can bypass the rather average Whole Foods chain and head to local independent places like **The Grocery (Map 91)** or **Mother Earth (Map 75)**. For the cheapest and best coffee-to-go in Soho try the **Algerian Coffee Stores (Map 11)**. Looking for Unicum? Look no further than **Gerry's Spirits Shop (Map 11)** where you can find obscure liquors like Zubrowka Bison Grass Vodka and good quality Cachaça.

Art and Craft Supplies

Crafty types and closet Van Goghs can pick up supplies at **Cass Art's (Map 80)** three-storey flagship store in Islington. There's everything here for aspiring Manga cartoonists and weekend watercolourists alike, and lots of fun bits and pieces for school holiday/rainy day projects in the basement. Much of the high quality stock can be found at cut-price throughout the year—stock up on Moleskine note and sketchbooks which are frequently marked down. **The London Graphic Centre (Map 13)** has more design-led stock as well as fine art material attracting architects and graphic designers. Known for its greeting cards and stationery, **Paperchase (Map 3)** on Tottenham Court Road also has—true to its name—an astonishing array of handmade papers on its top floor—from flocked designs to fibrous papers made with dried flowers. You've got to love **Blade Rubber (Map 4)** just for its name, and for keeping sketches, photos, and memories intact. **Wyvern Bindery (Map 64)** is one of few of its kind to offer book-making services.

Axes, Saxes, Drums, Strums…

Traditionally, Tin Pan Alley (real name: Denmark Street) has always been the hub of musical creativity in the city. Back in the day when rents were affordable, a community grew up around this little side street which went on to see Jimi Hendrix and The Beatles record in the basements, and a young Elton John sitting on the rooftops penning "Your Song". Nowadays you may spot Jack White trying out a Digitech Whammy or Jonny Greenwood looking for some new toy to replace his Marshall Shred Master. If we had to choose one, we'd choose **Wunjos (Map 12)** for friendliness. There are plenty of independent music stores to be found in London's boroughs, and often they are specialists, happy to have a natter about what exactly it is that you're looking for and what the weather's like. Try **Phil Parker (Map 1)** for all you jazz cats needing a hand with your brass. For the medieval troubadour in your life, **Hobgoblin (Map 3)** has its own luthier who makes lutes. Try **Ray Man (Map 71)** in Camden for unusual ethnic instruments and drone boxes. One thing though, will you instrument shop assistants please stop jamming while you're talking to us?

Music Nonstop

The slow, painful death of the CD can be seen in almost every indie music store in London, and it coincides with the financial doom and gloom that has befallen Virgin Records, Zavvi and Sanctuary (thankfully we still have one branch of **Fopp (Map 12)** left). Bizarrely, the death march of the recorded music store has become a moonwalk: more and more boutique record shops are springing up selling new and used wax. The Berwick Street vinyl epicenter may have been drained of late, but other parts of London have become haunts for us of haunched posture and good taste. **Sister Ray (Map 11)** is forever teetering on the edge, but **Reckless Records (Map 11)** seems here to stay. If you find yourself on the Essex Road, have a gander at **Flashback (Maps 53, 83)**. The **Music & Video Exchange (Map 29)** in Notting Hill was way ahead of its time and has been the swapshop of choice for years, it's still the king as far as we're concerned. To guarantee a withering look from a record shop lifer go and discuss the use of naivety in Legowelt's output at **Phonica (Map 10)** in Soho. Many a muso's all-round fave, **Sounds of the Universe (Map 11)** is owned by the **Soul Jazz** label.

Antiques and Bric-A-Brac, Flea Markets and Stalls

There may have been a time, dear reader, when markets sold fleas. And brics and bracs. Perhaps we used to know what these elusive words meant. Frankly, we numbskulls at NFT don't care about etymology unless it's secondhand and collectable. First stop on many shoppers' lists—both serious collectors and weekend browsers—are **Alfie's Antique Market (Map 76)** and **Gray's Antique Market (Map 2)**. Here you'll find art, antiques, jewellery, vintage clothing and rare books all housed under one roof.

Once the centre of the Britpop phenomenon in the '90s and a thriving mini-metropolis for vintage and antique stalls, Camden is now rather anaesthetised, but packs of German and French kids on school trips still rifle through the emo and goth gear that overflows th.

Well-known to scavengers, **Camden Passage (Map 80)** in Angel rather confusingly, is a welcome retreat from the mallrat-filled N1 centre across the road in Islington. The Mall and also Plerrepoint Arcade (tucked away behind the passage) offer a cornucopia of clothing, jewelry, military paraphernalia, homewares, prints, and a host of other bits and bobs. On Saturdays, market stalls set up in the street and surprises like original Givenchy earrings from 1978 (4 quid!) can be salvaged from amongst the knick-knacks. This is another brilliant little vintage bazaar continually threatened by chains and redevelopment. Go protest by buying any old crap.

Brick Lane (Map 91) also opens up on Sunday and in the summer there is a real carnival feel with fruit and veg, plumbing and DIY bits and pieces, electricals, toiletries, furniture (dentist's chair anyone?), clothes, DVDs lining the lane and spilling into Sclater Street. Watch your bags and all the silly haircuts. Brick Lane also has the added advantage of having many a watering hole and curry house where you can stop and people-watch if it all makes you want to go all 'Falling Down' on their asses. If that's not your thing, (Up)Market is held in the **Truman Brewery (Map 91)** every Sunday and showcases new designers as well as housing some vinyl, vintage and gourmet street food. **Spitalfields Market (Map 91)** has been tarted up to be a sanitized precinct of chain stores but there are still some unusual boutiques and independent shops.

The triumvirate of hipster markets consists of **Columbia Road Market (Map 91)**, **Broadway Market (Map 89)**, and Chatsworth Road Market (just north of Map 90). Also in the East is **Roman Road Market (Map 94)**. It's proper gorblimey,

lor' love a duck cockerney territory but you may find yourself soaking up the atmosphere more than finding anything of real interest. If Lady Luck is stroking your inner thigh you get some great bargains Sarf of the river at **Deptford Market (Map 119)**.

Though certainly not as bountiful in treasure as the car boot sales of other parts of the country, London does have some. The best in Zone 2 is definitely the **Battersea Car Boot Sale (Map 141)**, a sprawling mess that kicks off around midday is a godsend to all us alcoholics and narcoleptics.

Map 1 · Marylebone (West)

Maroush Deli	56 Edgware Rd	020 7724 8197	Lebanese food emporium—fresh coffee, ice-creams and best houmous in town.
Phil Parker	14 Gravel Ln	020 7383 5300	Brass-o-rama.
Primark	499 Oxford St	020 7495 0420	Enter the scrum.
Totally Swedish	32 Crawford St	020 7224 9300	Salt liquorice and Plopp bars for scandiphiles.

Map 2 · Marylebone (East)

Browns	39 Brook St	020 7514 0016	Sleep with someone rich, then bring them here.
Content Beauty & Wellbeing	436 Essex Rd	020 3375 1960	Exceptional selection of organic beauty products.
Daunt Books	83 Marylebone High St	020 7224 2295	Almost intimidatingly beautiful book shop.
Fenwick	63 New Bond St	020 7629 9161	A welcome escape from Oxford Street for those in the know.
French Sole	61 Marylebone Ln	020 7486 0021	Spendy but these pumps can withstand London's terrible pavements.
Gray's Antique Market	58 Davies St	020 7629 7034	A world of bygone beauty a skip away from Bond Street.
John Lewis	300 Oxford St	020 7629 7711	Where John Betjeman would have gone if the world exploded.
Niketown	236 Oxford St	020 7660 4453	Like a real town! Owned by Nike! But without sweatshops.
Paul Smith	38 Marylebone High St	020 7935 5384	Kitsch and dolls from the fashion designer. Don't ask why.
Postcard Teas	9 Dering St	020 7629 3654	Taste tea. Send tea. Love tea. Right here.
Selfridges & Co.	400 Oxford St	020 7160 6222	A Mecca for the shopping elite who want everything.
VV Rouleaux	102 Marylebone Ln	020 7224 5179	Trimmings and ribbons like you've never seen.
Zara	215 Oxford St	080 0368 4990	Spiffy suits and cute casualwear from the Balearic brand.

Map 3 · Fitzrovia

CeX	32 Rathbone Pl	084 5345 1664	Good selection of secondhand DVDs, games and gadgets.
Harmony	109 Oxford St	020 7846 4585	Also known as Butt Plugs R Us.
Hobgoblin Music	24 Rathbone Pl	020 7323 9040	Folky paradise; impressive/amusing collection of alternative instruments.
Mango	229 Oxford St	077 7586 1491	Let's go Mango!
Scandinavian Kitchen	61 Great Titchfield St	020 7580 7161	Smorgasbord!
Urban Outfitters	200 Oxford St	020 3514 7175	Heaps of streetwear and crazy things for your house.

Map 4 · Bloomsbury (West)

Blade Rubber Stamps	12 Bury Pl	020 7831 4123	Scrapbooking materials plus traditional and made-to-order rubber stamps.
Gosh!	1 Berwick St	020 7437 0187	A Japanese school boy's wet dream. Comics galore!
James Smith & Sons	53 New Oxford St	020 7836 4731	Umbrella shop—because you might just need one.
London Review Bookshop	14 Bury Pl	020 7269 9030	Big books, big name personal appearances—and cake!

Map 5 · Bloomsbury (East)

Antoni & Alison	43 Rosebery Ave	020 7833 2141	Home of "bonkers" fashion duo.
The Brunswick	Hunter St	020 7833 6066	Brutalist shopping centre pushing the utopian/dystopian envelope.
Folk	53 Lamb's Conduit St	020 8616 4191	Great clothes, even better shoes.
Gay's the Word	66 Marchmont St	020 7278 7654	Britain's only dedicated Gay & Lesbian book store.
International Magic	89 Clerkenwell Rd	020 7405 7324	When you need some tricks up your sleeve.
Magma	117 Clerkenwell Rd	020 7242 9503	Funky book & novelty shop.

Map 6 · Clerkenwell

EC One	41 Exmouth Market	020 7713 6185	Gorgeous sparkly fings.
The Family Business Tattoo Shop	58 Exmouth Market	020 7278 9526	Tatts for all the family.
Gypsy Blood Tattoo	332 Goswell Rd	020 7833 5996	Was on the telly. Caused quite a buzz.
Metro Imaging	32 Great Sutton St	020 7865 0000	Photo processing.
Timorous Beasties	46 Amwell St	020 7833 9867	Outlandish prints for the daringly tasteless home.
Turner & George	399 St. John St	020 7837 1781	So meat-savvy they'll even know the best cut on you.
The Wyvern Bindery	187 Hoxton St	020 7490 7899	Book binding for theses, portfolios and presentations. Repairs and restoration.

Map 7 · Barbican / City Road (South)

Red Dot Cameras	86 Goswell Rd	020 7490 8444	Like yer Leica.
Whitecross Market	Whitecross St		Street food central.

Map 9 · Mayfair / Green Park

Dover Street Market	17 Dover St	020 7518 0680	Serious designer wear for people with serious money.
Stella McCartney	23 Old Bond St	020 7518 3100	Stella's star keeps rising despite initial doubts in Fahionland.

Map 10 · Piccadilly / Soho (West)

Anthropologie	158 Regent St	020 7529 9800	Go check out the innovative window dressing if nothing else.
Apple Store	235 Regent St	020 7153 9000	Get your hardware here so you can buy NFT apps.
Beyond Retro	19 Argyll St	020 7729 9001	Biggest, original, live-bands-on-Saturday vintage.
Burlington Arcade	51 Piccadilly	020 7493 1764	Welcoming shoppers since 1819.
COS	222 Regent St	020 3139 2440	COS you can. See what I did there?
The European Bookshop	123 Gloucester Rd	020 7734 5259	For when you get sick of English.
Fortnum & Mason	181 Piccadilly	020 7734 8040	The world's poshest marmalades.
Hamley's	188 Regent St	020 7479 7398	World's biggest toy store. Terrifying just before Christmas.
Hatchards Bookshop	187 Piccadilly	020 7439 9921	Still musty, floors still creak, despite being owned by The Man.
Lazy Oaf	2 Ganton St	020 7287 2060	Rockin good little design shop with the emphasis on illustration.
Liberty	214 Regent St	020 3893 3062	Splendid wood-panelled department store. Beautiful and obscure scents and perfumes.
Lillywhites	24 Regent St	084 4332 5602	Good if you know exactly what you're looking for.
Muji	41 Carnaby St	020 7287 7323	Japanese chain hits London—simple, minimalist goods but great quality.
Phonica	51 Poland St	020 7025 6070	Cutting edge vinyl/CD shop; alas, no Michael Bolton in stock.
Richard James	29 Savile Row	020 7434 0605	Bespoke contemporary Savile Row tailoring.
Rigby & Peller	22 Conduit St	020 7491 2200	Furnishers of the Queen's basement.

Map 11 • Soho (Central)

Algerian Coffee Store	52 Old Compton St	020 7437 2480	Pick up some Blue Mountain beans and a 95p cappu-to-go.
Gerry's	74 Old Compton St	020 7734 2053	A veritable alcoholic's Utopia.
I. Camisa & Son	61 Old Compton St	020 7437 7610	The best Italian deli outside of Italy.
Reckless Records	30 Berwick St	020 7437 4271	Sickly phoenix risen from the ashes of Reckless Records.
Sister Ray	75 Berwick St	020 7734 3297	Alternative vinyl, CDs and DVDs.
Sounds of the Universe	7 Broadwick St	020 7734 3430	Blow your friends' minds with obscure African vinyl.

Map 12 • Soho (East)

Fopp	1 Earlham St	033 3323 8418	May Fopp never, ever die again. Long live the music bargain!
Forbidden Planet	179 Shaftesbury Ave	020 7420 3666	Cult/film/TV memorabilia shop that will leave Star Wars fans salivating.
Foyles	107 Charing Cross Rd	020 7437 5660	Convivial shop/cafe. Essential for Americana and, uh, jazz!
Magma	29 Short's Gardens	020 7240 7571	Super-cool housewares and knick-knacks from the Magma gods.
Wunjo Guitars	5 Denmark St	020 7379 0737	Mind-bendingly friendly Scot selling lovely vintage gear...

Map 13 • Covent Garden

Artbox	44 Shelton St	020 7240 0097	Hello Kitty overload.
The Astrology Shop	78 Neal St	020 7813 3051	For people who believe that shit—and people who don't.
Ben's Cookies	13 The Piazza	020 7240 6599	Cookie chain good. Chips in dough yum.
Blackout II	51 Endell St	020 7240 5006	Vintage heaven.
Coco de Mer	23 Monmouth St	020 7836 8882	High-class, kinky fun.
Libidex at Liberation	49 Shelton St	020 7836 5894	Caters for all your kinks. Yes, even that one.
London Graphic Centre	16 Shelton St	020 7759 4500	One stop shop for graphics geeks.
Neal's Yard Dairy	17 Shorts Gardens	020 7500 7520	Follow your nose to very fine cheeses.
Pop Boutique	30 Short's Gardens	020 7836 9819	Retrotastic!
Rokit	42 Shelton St	020 7836 6547	Vast array of vintage clothing.
Stanfords	7 Mercer Walk	020 7836 1321	Treasure trove of maps, travel books and accessories.
Tabio	51 Neal St	020 7836 3713	Only the Japanese could create such an array of socks.
Urban Outfitters	42 Earlham St	020 7759 6390	Heaps of streetwear and crazy things for your house.

Map 14 • Holborn / Temple

Konditor & Cook	46 Grays Inn Rd	020 7633 3333	Unusual location to find K&C's famous Magic Cakes.

Map 16 • Square Mile (West)

Church's	90 Cheapside	020 7606 1587	An English shoe institution.

Map 18 • Tower Hill / Aldgate

Petticoat Lane Market	119 Middlesex St	020 7364 1717	No petticoats here love, but look for the FCUK stall.
Precious	98 Columbia Rd	020 7729 2197	One of few independent boutiques left standing.

Map 19 • Belgravia

Daylesford Organic Farmshop and Cafe	44 Pimlico Rd	020 7881 8060	Fresh as you can get ingredients from their Gloucestershire farm.
Mungo & Maud	79 Elizabeth St	020 7467 0823	Real dogs don't wear clothes! Chihuahuas do though...and pugs.

Map 20 • Victoria / Pimlico (West)

Capital Carboot Sale	Lupus St	084 5094 3871	We love a rummage through other people's rubbish.
Grays of Westminster	40 Churton St	020 7828 4925	Charming period shop specializing in Nikon.
Rippon Cheese Stores	26 Upper Tachbrook St	020 7931 0628	A world of cheese.
Runners Need	23 Piccadilly	020 7437 7399	Place for all you joggers "who go round and round."

Map 22 • Westminster

Haelen Centre	41 Broadway	020 8340 1518	All your hippy, wholemeal, organic needs under one roof.

Map 24 • Trafalgar Square / The Strand

London Camera Exchange	98 Strand	020 7379 0200	My lens is longer than yours.
Stanley Gibbons	399 Strand	014 2547 2363	World's leading stamp dealer attracts collectors, investors and the curious.

Map 25 • Kensal Town

Honest Jon's	278 Portobello Rd	020 8969 9822	Obscure and rare Jazz, Funk, Reggae and Hip-Hop.
Rellik	8 Golborne Rd	020 8962 0089	Opposite the Trellik Tower—geddit? Specialises in Queen Viv (Westwood).

Map 28 • Ladbroke Grove / Notting Hill (West)

The Cross	141 Portland Rd	020 7727 6760	The original London boutique, still going.
Jeroboams	96 Holland Park Ave	020 7727 9359	London's largest independent wine merchant.

Map 29 • Notting Hill Gate

Clarke's	124 Kensington Church St	020 7221 9225	All-butter brioche and honey loaves for Harvey Nicks, Selfridges—and you.
The Grocer on Elgin	6 Elgin Crescent	020 7221 3844	Restaurant standard ready-meals for lazy people.
The Hummingbird Bakery	133 Portobello Rd	020 7851 1795	Takeaway cupcakes reminiscent of New York's Magnolia Bakery.
Melt Chocolates	59 Ledbury Rd	020 7727 5030	Posh chocs made before your bulging eyes.
Music & Video Exchange	38 Notting Hill Gate	020 7727 2040	Invented second hand record shops. Best in London.

Portobello Road Market	Portobello Rd	020 7727 7684	The Notting Hill institution.
R. Garcia and Sons	246 Portobello Rd	020 7221 6119	Overwhelming selection of Spanish groceries.
Retro Man	28 Pembridge Rd	020 7727 2040	Vintage fixes for modern men. And men only.
Retro Woman	20 Pembridge Rd	020 7727 2040	Exclusive vintage ware that's worth it.
Rough Trade West	130 Talbot Rd	020 7229 8541	More character and better records than the soulless East Branch.

Map 30 · Bayswater

Planet Organic	42 Westbourne Grove	020 7727 2227	Organic heaven.
Porchester Gate Spa	Queensway & Porchester Rd £25!	020 7792 3980	Proper old school art deco Turkish baths and spa for less than
Whiteleys Shopping Centre	Queensway	020 3019 0636	Slightly more soulful than Smithfields.

Map 32 · Shepherd's Bush (West)

| Damas Gate | 81 Uxbridge Rd | 020 8743 5116 | Incredible range of Middle Eastern food. |
| Nut Case | 352 Uxbridge Rd | 020 8743 0336 | About time nuts got some respect. |

Map 33 · Shepherd's Bush

| Westfield Centre | Ariel Way | 020 3371 2300 | Very likable shopping center. Really. |

Map 34 · West Kensington / Olympia

| Design Museum Shop | 224 Kensington High St | 020 3862 5900 | Stuff you wish you'd thought of. |

Map 35 · Kensington

Ben's Cookies	12 Kensington High St	020 7376 0559	Chunky cookies in wonderous flavours. Hidden in High Street Ken station.
Octavia Foundation Charity Shop	266 Kensington High St	020 7602 6043	There's gold in them thar (clothes) hills.
Trailfinders	194 Kensington High St	020 7938 3939	Personable one-stop shop for travel bookings, advice and services.
Urban Outfitters	36 Kensington High St	020 3985 5573	Heaps of streetwear and crazy things for your house.
Whole Foods Market	63 Kensington High St	020 7368 4500	Overwhelming selection of organic exotica.

Map 36 · South Kensington / Gloucester Rd

| Maitre Choux | 15 Harrington Rd | 020 3583 4561 | Pimp your choux! |
| Partridges | 17 Gloucester Rd | 020 7581 0535 | Family run mega-deli to the queen. |

Map 37 · Knightsbridge

Divertimenti	227 Brompton Rd	020 7581 8065	Go and pretend you need a £500 coffee machine.
Harrods	87 Brompton Rd	020 7730 1234	Arch conspiracy theorist Mr Al-Fayed's still classy department store.
Harvey Nichols	109 Knightsbridge	020 7235 5000	Not sure who really shops here.
Rigby & Peller	2 Hans Rd	020 7225 4760	Sexy lingerie fit for a queen...for THE Queen?
Skandium	14 Bacon St	020 3633 7626	For lottery winners who can't shake their love of Ikea.
Space NK Apothecary	40 Hans Cres	020 7581 2518	Skincare heaven.

Map 38 · Chiswick

Gail's Bread	282 Chiswick High Rd	020 8995 2266	Enough artisan pastries to tempt you for seconds. Busy weekends.
Outsider Tart	83 Chiswick High Rd	020 7096 1609	Two American dudes start a US baked goods revolution—cupcakes!
Oxfam Books	90 Turnham Green Terrace	020 8995 6059	Fantastic fiction selection—the rich read too!
Wheelers Flowers	Turnham Green Terrace	020 8747 9505	Last chance station for forgotten occasions next to Turnham Green tube.

Map 39 · Stamford Brook

Thai Smile	287 King St	020 8846 9960	Heaven for those who love Asian cooking. For the rest it's just intriguing.

Map 40 · Goldhawk Rd / Ravenscourt Park

Bushwacker Wholefoods	132 King St	020 8748 2061	Small and friendly organic and health food shop. Booja Booja ice-cream!
Patisserie Sainte-Anne	204 King St	020 8563 2046	Heavenly Parisian cakes, breads, and pastries.

Map 43 · West Brompton / Fulham Broadway / Earl's Court

Vagabond Wines	18-22 Vanston Pl	020 7381 1717	Try before you buy wine.

Map 44 · Chelsea

The Furniture Cave	533 Kings Rd	020 7352 2046	Swanky. Huge. Quintessentially Kings Road.
Richer Sounds	258 Fulham Rd	033 3900 0027	Chain selling all things electronic, technologic, and so forth.
Worlds End	430 King's Rd	020 7352 6551	Ever changin outlet of Dame Viv.

Map 45 · Chelsea (East)

Ad Hoc	153 King's Rd	020 7376 8829	Gold sequin knickers—what more do you want?
British Red Cross	69 Old Church St	020 7376 7300	Known locally as La Croix Rouge Boutique.
Frock Me! Vintage Fashion Fair	Hornton St	020 7503 9171	Held every couple of months, "pre-war" tearoom refreshes shopping casualties.
The Hummingbird Bakery	47 Old Brompton Rd	020 7851 1795	Notting Hill's big brother with seating to devour Red Velvets and lattes.
Nomad Books	781 Fulham Rd	020 7736 4000	Glorious little place with added coffee shop.
Sweaty Betty	125 King's Rd	020 7349 7597	Clothes for you to stretch in, Gretchen.

Map 46 · Sloane Square

Partridges	2 Duke of York Sq	020 7730 0651	Family run mega-deli to the queen.
Rigby & Peller	13 Kings Rd	020 7824 1844	Sexy lingerie fit for a queen...the queen?
Space NK Apothecary	307 King's Rd	020 7351 7209	The Superdrug for the Sloane Square ladies who lunch.

Map 48 · Fulham

Hurlingham Books	91 Fulham High St	020 7736 4363	More stacked than Arnie was in the 70s.

Map 51 · Highgate

Highgate Butchers	76 Highgate High St	020 8340 9817	Reassuringly expensive meat. Them cows must have lived like kings.
Hops N' Pops	389 Archway Rd	020 8348 0624	Great selection for all budgets.
Mind	329 Archway Rd	020 8341 1188	Great selection for skint book worms.
Oxfam	80 Highgate High St	020 8340 3888	Musty bookstore with some cracking titles.

Map 52 · Archway (North)

Pax Guns	166 Archway Rd	020 8340 3039	Errm..."best" gun shop in the area?

Map 53 · Crouch End

Flashback	26 Topsfield Parade	020 8342 9633	2nd hand vinyl and DVD goldmine.
Soup Dragon	27 Topsfield Parade	020 8348 0224	Paradise for yummy mummies and their tots.
Urban Native Organic & Wholefoods	188 Stroud Green Rd	020 7281 1115	Well-stocked local shop.
Walter Purkis And Sons	17 The Broadway	020 8340 6281	Proof that fish don't need their tasty batter skins.

Map 54 · Hornsey

Mycicle N4	8 Ferme Park Rd	020 8347 9180	Friendly bike repairs and cafe.

Map 55 · Harringay

Beans and Barley	595 Green Lanes		Organic emporium.
Harringay Local Stores	581 Green Lanes	074 4603 0507	Hipsters do their grocery shopping.
Yasar Halim	491 Green Lanes	020 8340 8090	Amazing Turkish grocery store.

Map 56 · Hampstead Village

Happy Returns	36 Rosslyn Hill	020 7435 2431	Boring posh toys...and some cool stuff for normal kids.
Keith Fawkes	1 Flask Walk	020 7435 0614	Books, books, books. A glorious mess of a shop.

Map 57 · Hampstead Heath

Daunt Books	51 S End Rd	020 7794 8206	A right daunty little shop.
Giocobazzi's Delicatessen	150 Fleet Rd	020 7267 7222	The taste of posh Italy.

Map 59 · Tufnell Park

North London Adoption Centre	135 Junction Rd	020 7272 6048	Need a cat? Of course you do! Miaow!

Map 60 · Archway

Second Chance	7 St John's Way	020 7281 5449	Heaps of rubbish and the occasional incredible find.

Map 61 · Holloway (North)

Holloway Car Boot	Opposite Odeon Cinema	019 9271 7198	Scavenge with North London's finest.

Map 62 · Finsbury Park

The Deli at 80	80 Stroud Green Rd	020 7272 6622	Epicurean delights.
The Happening Bagel Bakery	284 Seven Sisters Rd	020 8809 1519	Another Haringey gem, with some delicious pastries too!

Map 63 · Manor House

Sargent & Co.	74 Mountgrove Rd	020 7359 7642	Passionate about bike building and bespoke.
Simply Organique	316 Green Lanes	020 8800 4668	Local organic store.
Sylvanian Families	68 Mountgrove Rd	020 7226 1329	It is indeed a shop that solely sells Sylvanian Families.

Map 64 · Stoke Newington

The Ark	161 Stoke Newington Rd	020 7275 9311	Cute little interiors and gift shop.
Beaucatcher Salon	44 Stoke Newington Church St	020 7923 2522	Hairdressers and community hub.
Belle Epoque Patisserie	37 Newington Green	020 7249 2222	Fancy schmancy, delicious pastries.
Bridgewood & Neitzert	146 Stoke Newington Church St	020 7249 9398	Renowned string section repair, exchange and sales.
Church Street Bookshop	142 Stoke Newington Church St	020 7241 5411	Great shack with out-of-print books and shite records.
Metal Crumble	13 Stoke Newington Church St	020 7249 0487	Affordable, flippin' gorgeous, jewellery made on site.
Of Cabbages & Kings	127 Stoke Newington High St	020 7998 3282	Another of those crafty little shops that keep popping up.
Ribbons and Taylor	157 Stoke Newington Church St	020 7254 4735	Long-standing vintage clothes shop—Stokey original.

S'Graffiti	172 Stoke Newington Church St	020 7254 7961	You've been framed.
Sacred Art Tattoos	148 Albion Rd	020 7254 2223	(Needles + Ink + Skin) x Pain = Art.
The Spence Bakery & Cafe	161 Stoke Newington Church St	020 7249 4927	Bread elevated to an art form.
Stoke Newington Farmers' Market	Stoke Newington High St	020 7502 7588	Overpriced, organic, natural, hea... Zzzzzzzzz

Map 70 • Primrose Hill

Nicolas	67 Regent's Park Rd	020 3962 4121	A wide range of wines, including some cheap ones.
Press	160 Regent's Park Rd	020 7449 0081	Impressive array of brands for a boutique. Good sales.
Primrose Hill Books	134 Regent's Park Rd	020 7586 2022	Fabulously curated selection of new books.
Primrose Hill Pets	132 Regent's Park Rd	020 7483 2023	Everything your handbag mutt could need.
Primrose Newsagent	91 Regent's Park Rd	020 7722 0402	Newsagent, stationers, post office, drycleaners and internet cafe.
Richard Dare	93 Regent's Park Rd	020 7722 9428	Quite lovely kitchen/cooking products.
Shepherd Foods	59 Regent's Park Rd	020 7586 4592	Highly priced but quaint local deli.
Shikasuki	67 Gloucester Ave	020 7722 4442	Affordable vintage and modern design.
Sweet Pea	77 Gloucester Ave	020 7449 9292	Unusual handmade jewelry.
Tann Rokka	123 Regent's Park Rd	020 7722 3999	Wildly expensive "lifestyle store" in old Primrose Hill train station.

Map 71 • Camden Town / Chalk Farm / Kentish Town (West)

AcuMedic	105 Camden High St	020 7388 6704	Chinese medicine centre offering acupuncture AKA polite masochism.
Cyberdog	Stables Market		...t & not displaying PVC, neon, and leather clubbing gear.
Graham and Green	164 Regent's Park Rd	020 7586 2960	Wonderfully dinky yet scarily pricey shop.
Rokit	225 Camden High St	020 7267 3046	Secondhand, sorry, vintage clothing store to the stars.
Three Amigos Skateboard Shop	118 Camden Rd	020 7284 4515	Skater owned, skater run. Best in London.
TRAID	154 Camden High St	020 7485 5253	Characterful recycled clothes. Touch of wank, but still we like.
Whole Foods Market	49 Parkway	020 7428 7575	Organic and wholefood oasis with eat-in possibilities.

Map 72 • Kentish Town

Phoenicia	186 Kentish Town Rd	020 7267 1267	Olives, just-roasted nuts, baclava, ice-cream bar. Meze heaven. Ditch Sainsburys.
Ruby Violet	3 Wharf Rd	020 7609 0444	Housemade ice cream with bold, inventive flavours.

Map 73 • Holloway

Bumblebee Natural Foods	33 Brecknock Rd	020 7284 1314	Hot veggie lunches, lush cakes. Organic fruitopia over the road.

Map 74 • Holloway Road / Arsenal

Vivien of Holloway	294 Holloway Rd	020 7609 8754	Want to dress like Joan from Mad Men?

Map 75 • Highbury

Cabbies Delight Autospares Car Parts	9 Green Lanes	020 7226 1692	21,000 car parts and 21 years experience.
Highbury Vintners	71 Highbury Park	020 7226 1347	Discount when you buy 6 or 12 bottles.
La Fromagerie	30 Highbury Park	020 7359 7440	Blow your inheritance on some Abbaye De Trois Vaux.
Mother Earth	282 St. Paul's Rd	020 7354 9897	Unfortunate New Age name, decent little shop.
Prawn on the Lawn	292 Saint Paul's Rd	020 3302 8668	Ethically and sustainably sourced fish.

Map 76 • Edgware Road / Marylebone (North)

Alfie's Antiques Market	25 Church St	020 7723 6066	Kitsch oddball sanctuary for vintage treats.
Archive Bookstore	83 Bell St	020 7402 8212	Old and unusual books.
London Beatles Store	231 Baker St	020 7935 4464	All you need is love, and no taste.
Lord's Cricket Store	Lisson Grove	020 7616 8570	They won't even ask why you want a cricket bat.

Map 78 • Euston

All Ages Records	27 Pratt St	020 7267 0303	Truly independent punk & hardcore record shop. F*** the system!
Housman's Bookshop	5 Caledonian Rd	020 7837 4473	Bookshop for progressive peaceniks and radical revolutionaries.
Transformation	52 Eversholt St	020 7388 0627	The world's largest shop for transvestites and transexuals. Seriously.

Map 80 • Angel / Upper St

After Noah	121 Upper St	020 7359 4281	Stuff your Nintendo Wiis—these are proper toys, retro-style.
Camden Passage	Camden Passage		Thingamebobs, whatsits and doodahs aplenty.
Cass Art	66 Colebrooke Row	020 7354 2999	Large, neat-as-a-pin, extremely pleasing art supply shop.
Gill Wing Cook Shop	190 Upper St	020 7226 5392	Splendid array of kitchen gadgetry to keep foodies amused.
Monte's Italian Deli	23 Canonbury Ln	020 7354 4335	Tasty, but look elsewhere if you need a hearty meal.
Paul A. Young Fine Chocolates	33 Camden Passage	020 7424 5750	"Everytime you go away..." you take a piece of chocolate.
twentytwentyone	274 Upper St	020 7288 1996	Bauhaus to Boontje and beyond.

Map 81 • Canonbury

Get Stuffed	105 Essex Rd	020 7226 1364	Polar bear for the living room, anyone? Taxidermy emporium.
James Elliott Butchers	96 Essex Rd	020 7226 3658	So much choice they'd probably stock human if they could.
Planet Organic	64 Essex Rd	020 7288 9460	Organic heaven.
Steve Hatt	88 Essex Rd	020 7226 3963	A fishmonger's so good, people queue to get in.

Map 82 • De Beauvoir Town / Kingsland

Mother Earth	101 Newington Green Rd	020 7359 7353	Organic, vegan and raw produce.
North One Garden Centre	25 Englefield Rd	020 7923 3553	Dinky little garden centre catering for dinky little London gardens.

Map 83 • Angel (East) / City Rd (North)

Flashback	50 Essex Rd	020 7354 9356	Don't come in whistling Barbie Girl.

Map 84 • Hoxton

Good Hood	151 Curtain Rd	020 7729 3600	Like American Apparel before it got shit.
Hoxton Street Monster Supplies	159 Hoxton St	020 7729 4159	World's only grocer for monsters, don't forget your fang floss.
SCP	135 Curtain Rd	020 7739 1869	Design-led homeware.
Tord Boontje Shop	Dragonfly Pl	020 7717 5398	Whimsical, magical things.

Arts & Entertainment · **Shopping**

Map 85 · Stoke Newington (East)

Hamdy's	167 Stoke Newington High St	020 7254 0681	Porn-free newsagents run by stubborn maverick.
Rouge	158 Stoke Newington High St	020 7275 0887	Cool Chinese housewares. Via Belgium of course.
Stoke Newington Bookshop	159 Stoke Newington High St	020 7249 2808	Long-standing local stellar indie bookshop.

Map 86 · Dalston / Kingsland

Dalston Mill Fabrics	69 Ridley Rd	020 7249 4129	Veritable treasure trove for budding Vivienne Westwoods and John Gallianos.
Healthy Stuff	168 Dalston Ln	020 7812 9604	Fresh health foods and organic goods in Hackney.
LN-CC	24 Shacklewell Ln	020 4530 5082	Appointment only darling.
Oxfam	514 Kingsland Rd	020 7254 5318	Flagship charity shop. Go find treasures!
Party Party	9 Ridley Rd	020 7254 5168	Fancy dress and party supplies plus an outstanding cake decorating department.
Ridley Road Market	Ridley Rd	020 8356 5300	Giant (live!) snails, Nigerian DVDs, fresh fish, 'taters, "Pound a bowl"
St Vincent's	484 Kingsland Rd	020 7249 3511	Christian charity shop. Jesus galore.
Turkish Food Centre	89 Ridley Rd	020 7254 6754	Olives and feta galore, bakery onsite, plus other fresh groceries.

Map 87 · Hackney Downs / Lower Clapton

Hute Chikinum	181 Lower Clapton Rd	020 8985 7500	Covetable prints.
Palm 2	152 Lower Clapton Rd	020 8985 0121	Ludicrously friendly corner shop beloved of bloggers.
The Pet Shop	40 Amhurst Rd	020 3441 3830	Brilliant local pet shop.
Salvation Army Clapton	122 Lower Clapton Rd	020 8985 3902	Come all ye unfaithful...
Umit & Son	35 Lower Clapton Rd	020 8985 1766	Crazed film buff selling vintage porn, super 8 and crisps?!
Viktor Wynd's Little Shop of Horrors	11 Mare St	020 8533 5297	Macabre and marvellous shop and gallery.

Map 88 · Haggerston / Queensbridge Rd

KTS The Corner	415 Kingsland Rd	020 7249 3199	Helpful DIY store if you can't do it yourself.

Map 89 · London Fields / Hackney Central

Broadway Market	Broadway Market		Yummy mummies and Guardian-reading couples peruse.
Burberry Factory Shop	29 Chatham Pl	020 8328 4287	Ever wondered how Burberry became associated with chavs?
Candle Factory	184 Mare St	020 8986 2240	Well-made, well-priced candles.
E5 Bakehouse	395 Mentmore Terrace	020 8525 2890	Sour dough to make you happy.
L'eau a la Bouche	35 Broadway Market	020 7923 0600	Cute French delicatessen shop.

Map 90 · Homerton / Victoria Park North

Eat 17	64-66 Brooksby's Walk	020 8986 6242	A bit like a farmers' market but you don't have to wait for the weekend.
The Ginger Pig	99 Lauriston Rd	020 3869 7830	Brilliant butcher bequeathing beef to the Borough.
Perlie Rides	137 Well St	020 8525 5694	Need a Dick Van Dyke? (Bike)
Sublime	225 Victoria Park Rd	020 8986 7243	Boudoir-like boutique selling select and independent labels.
Work Shop	77 Lauriston Rd	020 8986 9585	Beautiful handmade pottery for home and kitchen by Caroline Bousfield Gregory.

555

Map 91 · Shoreditch / Brick Lane / Spitalfields

A Portuguese Love Affair	326 Hackney Rd	020 3490 2662	Wonderfully curated collection of beautifully packaged items from Portugal.
Blackman's Shoes	46 Cheshire St	078 5088 3505	Chaotic hole-in-the-wall selling £5 plimsolls.
The Grocery	54 Kingsland Rd	020 7729 6855	Selling the good life to lower Kingsland Road.
Labour And Wait	85 Redchurch St	020 7729 6253	Brilliant wee shop selling old and old-looking goods.
Lily Vanilli	18 Ezra St		Cult bakery.
Luna and Curious	24 Calvert Ave	020 3222 0034	Curiouser and curiouser..lovely local artists' and designers' co-operative.
Peloton & Co	4 Market St	020 3974 2674	Get off your face on coffee before buying some cycling gear.
Rough Trade East	91 Brick Ln	020 7392 7788	East London outpost of the absurdly cool Rough Trade Records.
Sunday (Up)Market	Brick Ln	020 7770 6028	Great Sunday market with lots of food and cool clothes.
Taj Stores	112 Brick Ln	020 7377 0061	Weird and wonderful Eastern food.
Taylor Taylor	137 Commercial St	020 7377 2737	French boudoir-style hairdressers with free cocktail bar. Feel like a princess.

Map 92 · Bethnal Green

AP Fitzpatrick Fine Art Materials	142 Cambridge Heath Rd	020 7790 0884	Art supplies and expert advice.

Map 94 · Bow

Roman Road Market	Roman Rd	020 7364 1717	Big, colourful, cheap as chips—bargain tat hawked by lively east-end traders.

Map 95 · Whitechapel (West) / St Katharine's Dock

Freedom Press	84 Whitechapel High St	075 64 546063	Long running bastion of radical thinking.

Map 97 · Stepney / Shadwell (East)

John Lester Wigs	32 Globe Rd	020 7790 2278	Need a syrup?

Map 101 · Poplar (East) / Canary Wharf (East)

Billingsgate Fish Market	Trafalgar Way	020 7987 1118	Slice of real London in the shadow of Canary Wharf.

Map 104 · South Bank / Waterloo / Lambeth North

Calder Bookshop & Theatre	51 The Cut	020 7620 2900	Enduringly fashionable hub for the unfashionably literate.
Greensmiths	27 Lower Marsh	020 7921 2970	Old skool greengrocer's and fine foods.
Konditor & Cook	22 Cornwall Rd	020 7633 3333	Yummy scrummy choccies and cake.
ScooterCaffe	132 Lower Marsh	020 7620 1421	Scooter shop has superb coffee. Word spreads. Becomes café too.
Southbank Centre Book Market	337 Belvedere Rd	020 3879 9555	Fun little scribe's market in brilliant surroundings.

Map 106 • Bankside (East) / Borough / Newington

Borough Market	8 Southwark St	020 7407 1002	Go on an empty stomach and feast on samples.
Brindisa Shop	Borough Market	020 7407 1036	Chorizo, salchichon, Serrano ham—famed importers Brindisa have it all.
Richer Sounds	100 Tooley St	033 3900 0021	The original store of this small chain offering low prices.

Map 107 • Shad Thames

Fine Foods	218 Long Ln	020 7403 7513	Little, local Italian deli to coo over.
Maltby Street Market	Maltby St		Snapping at the ankles of Borough Market.

Map 108 • Bermondsey

The Kernel Brewery	11 Dockley Road Industrial Estate	020 7231 4516	Open on Saturdays for brewskis.

Map 111 • Rotherhithe (East) Surrey Quays

Decathlon	Surrey Quays Rd	020 7394 2000	The Daddy of sports & outdoors shops.

Map 112 • Kennington / Elephant and Castle

Recycling	110 Elephant Rd	020 7703 7001	They sell'em bikes, they fix'em bikes. Secondhand.

Map 119 • Deptford (East)

Deptford Market	Deptford High St		Cheap, busy, eclectic: Proof that there IS life in Deptford.

Map 120 • Greenwich

Casbah Records	320-322 Creek Rd	020 8858 1964	Greenwich's quirky vinyl-vintage cohabitation.
The Cheeseboard	26 Royal Hill	020 8305 0401	Buy your cheese then head to Theatre of Wine.
The Junkshop	9 Greenwich South St	020 8305 1666	Voodoo masks, Guiness mugs and everything in between.
Mr Humbug	Greenwich Market	020 7871 4944	Infinitissimal old-fashioned sweets to relive your childhood sugar buzzes.
Music & Video Exchange	23 Greenwich Church St	020 8858 8898	Greenwich branch of the second hand empire.

Map 121 • Camberwell (West)

Butterfly Walk	Denmark Hill		The usual attractions.

Map 122 • Camberwell (East)

Architectural Rescue	1-3 Southampton Way	020 7277 0081	Dig through the architectural salvage of South London's past.
Cowling and Wilcox	8-12 Orpheus St	020 7703 1342	Suppliers to the local art school hordes.

Map 123 • Peckham

Persepolis	30 Peckham High St	020 7639 8007	Can a deli change your life? Yes. Yes, it can.
Primark	51 Rye Lane	020 7639 9655	More of a chance of scoring that 'it' item at this branch.

Map 127 · Coldharbour Lane / Herne Hill (West)

Blackbird Bakery	230 Railton Rd	020 7095 8800	London needs more lovely independent bakeries (like this).

Map 128 · Denmark Hill / Herne Hill (East)

Tales on Moon Lane	25 Half Moon Ln	020 7274 5759	Cute children's bookshop (as if there were any other kind!).

Map 130 · Peckham Rye

Flock and Herd	155 Bellenden Rd	020 7635 7733	Posho butchers for Peckhams new residents. Good sausages.

Map 133 · Battersea (East)

London Recumbents	Battersea Park	020 7228 6843	Much more fun in theory than in practice.

Map 134 · South Lambeth

Fetish Freak	76 Bolton Crescent	020 7091 0031	Witness the wall of dildos.
LASSCO	30 Wandsworth Rd	020 7394 2100	Homebase for the unique, antique, or eccentric.
New Covent Garden Market	New Covent Garden Market	020 7720 2211	Known as London's Larder. Nowhere near Covent Garden
The Nine Elms Sunday Market	New Covent Garden		Challenge yourself to think of something this place doesn't sell.

Map 139 · Wandsworth (East)

Cake Boy	2 Kingfisher House	020 7978 5555	Cookery school and cake emporium extraordinaire.

Map 140 · Clapham Junction / Northcote Rd

The Hive Honey Shop	93 Northcote Rd	020 7924 6233	Every kind of honey you could want.
Huttons	29 Northcote Rd	020 7223 5523	Eclectic mix of unusual clothes, furniture and gifts.
Party Superstores	268 Lavender Hill	020 7924 3210	The queues on Halloween will scare you to death.
Space NK Apothecary	46 Northcote Rd	020 7228 7563	Skincare heaven.
Sweaty Betty	66 Northcote Rd	020 7223 9500	Look like a total Betty, like, even when you're sweaty.
TK Maxx	St John's Rd & Barnard Rd	020 7228 8072	The best bargains in town.
TRAID	28 St John's Rd	020 7924 3065	Characterful recycled clothes. Touch of wank, but still we like.
Whole Foods Market	305 Lavender Hill	020 7585 1488	Overwhelming selection of organic exotica.

Map 141 · Battersea (South)

Battersea Boot	401 Battersea Park Rd	079 4138 3588	Yeah! A huge, tumultous boot sale that starts mid afternoon!
Get A Grip Bicycle Workshop	19 Lavender Hill	020 7223 4888	These people know their stuff.

Map 142 · Clapham Old Town

M. Moen & Sons	24 The Pavement	020 7622 1624	Butcher for the bourgeoisie, incredibly good, massively expensive.
Puppet Planet	787 Wandsworth Rd	020 7627 0111	Not great if you're pupaphobic but otherwise rather charming.

Map 143 · Clapham High Street

Apex Cycles	40 Clapham High St	020 7622 1334	Bikes fixed, bikes sold.
Today's Living Health Store	92 Clapham High St	020 7622 1772	Health foods, herbal remedies and other jiggery pokery.

Map 144 · Stockwell / Brixton (West)

Funchal Bakery	141-143 Stockwell Rd	020 7733 3134	Portuguese grocery with good coffee and better pastel de nata.
The Old Post Office Bakery	76 Landor Rd	020 7326 4408	Disued P.O turned artisan baker's. Local loaf? The Brixton Rye

Map 148 · Balham (East)

Moxon's Fishmongers	Westbury Parade	020 8675 2468	Fresh fish for foodies with deep pockets. Knowledgeable staff.

Map 149 · Clapham Park

MacFarlane's	48 Abbeville Rd	020 8673 5373	Gourmet goodness galore.

Map 150 · Brixton

Bookmongers	439 Coldharbour Ln	020 7738 4225	Truly great local bookshop with friendly staff and dog.
Supertone Records	110 Acre Ln	020 7737 7761	Legendary reggae shop.
TRAID	2 Acre Ln	020 7326 4330	Characterful recycled clothes. Touch of wank, but still we like.

Map 151 · Tooting Bec

Crazy Horse Bike Workshop	275 Balham High Rd	020 8767 5614	Bikes and bike repairs.
Russell's Trade & DIY	46 Upper Tooting Rd	020 8672 1576	DIY treasure chest. Friendly, helpful owners.
Wandsworth Oasis HIV/AIDS Charity Shop	40 Trinity Rd	020 8767 7555	Thrift store treasure trove.

Map 152 · Tooting Broadway

Tooting Market	21 Tooting High St	020 8672 4760	Quaint indoor labyrinth worth nosing about.

MapMovies get ACTION

Quickmap makes very special maps for clients around the world.
See our map of London Buses in this London Not for Tourist guide. Quickmap makes MapMovies **MM**s too. Here buses run around their London routes on screen. **MM**s are Information Entertainment. **MM**s get the viewer's attention and change behaviour.

Quickmap has made **MM**s for sport venues such as Wembley National Stadium in the UK, major shopping centres and many new office or commercial developments that show how visitors can travel to that new location.
MMs can show environmentally friendly walking, cycling and transit routes to schools, town centers, airports, national parks and leisure destinations.

MM = more visitors

by animating your existing maps (send sample for costing) or develop new maps as MapMovies **MM** online.
Search for **Quickmap MapMovies** on the web.

Quickmap Limited
The Hat Factory
65-67 Bute Street
Luton
Bedfordshire
LU1 2EY
United Kingdom

44 (0)20 7813 3397
info@quickmap.com
www.quickmap.com

Street Index

Street Index

Street Index

Street Index

Street Index

Street Index

Street Index

Street Index

Street Index

Street Index

Street Index

Street Index

Street Index

Street Index

Street Index

Street Index

Street Index

Street Index

Street Index

Street Index

Street Index

Street Index

Street Index

Street Index

Street Index

Street Index

Street Index

Street Index

Street	Page	Grid
Westbourne Park Road	29	A1/A2
Westbourne Park Villas	30	A1
Westbourne Road	74	B1
	80	A1
Westbourne Street	31	B1
Westbourne Terrace	31	A1/B1
Westbourne Terrace Mews	30	B2
Westbourne Terrace Road	27	B1
	31	A1
Westbridge Road	132	A1
Westbury Street	142	A2
Westcott Road	112	B2
Westcott Square	39	B2
Westdean Close	138	B2
Western Lane	147	A2
Western Mews	25	B2
Western Place	110	A1
Western Road	145	B2
Western Terrace	39	B1
Westferry Circus	100	B1
Westferry Road	100	A1
	102	A1/B1/B2
	103	B1
Westfield Close	44	A2
Westfield Way	93	B2
Westgate Street	89	B2
Westgate Terrace	43	A2
Westgrove Lane	120	B2
Westland Place	83	B2
Westlands Terrace	148	A2
Westminster Bridge	22	A2
Westminster Bridge Road	104	B1/B2
Westminster Gardens	21	A2
Westmoreland Place	20	B1/B2
Westmoreland Road	113	B1/B2
Westmoreland Street	2	A2
Westmoreland Terrace	20	B1/B2
Weston Park	53	B2
	54	A1/A2
Weston Rise	5	A2
Weston Street	106	A2/B2
Weston Walk	89	B2
Westover Road	146	A1
Westport Street	97	B2
Westway	28	A1
	29	A1/A2
	30	A1/A2
	31	A1/A2
Westwick Gardens	33	B1/B2
Wetherby Gardens	43	A2
	44	A1
Wetherby Mews	43	A2
Wetherby Place	44	A1
Wetherell Road	90	B2
Wexford Road	147	B1
Weybridge Court	115	A2
Weyhill Road	95	A1
Weymouth Mews	2	A1
Weymouth Street	2	A1/A2
	3	A1
Weymouth Terrace	88	B1
Whadcote Street	62	B1
Wharf Place	92	A2
Wharf Road	78	B2
	79	B2
	83	B1/B2
Wharfdale Road	79	B1
Wharfedale Street	43	A2
Wharton Street	6	A1
Whateley Road	129	B2
	130	B1
Wheat Sheaf Close	102	B1
Wheatlands Road	151	A1
Wheatley Street	2	A1
Wheatsheaf Lane	47	A1
	134	A1
Wheatsheaf Terrace	48	A2
Wheatstone Road	25	B2
Wheelwright Street	79	A2
	80	A1
Wheler Street	91	A1/B1
Whetstone Park	14	A1/A2
Whewell Road	61	B1
Whidborne Street	5	A1
Whiskin Street	6	B2
Whistler Mews	123	A1
Whistler Street	74	B2
Whistlers Avenue	132	A1
Whiston Road	88	B1/B2
	92	A2
Whitacre Mews	112	A2
Whitby Street	91	A1
Whitchapel Close	125	A2
Whitcher Place	72	B1
Whitchurch Road	28	B1
Whitcomb Street	11	B2
	23	A2
White Bear Place	56	A2
White Church Lane	95	A1
White Church Passage	95	A1
White City Close	32	A2
White City Road	32	A2
	33	A1
White Conduit Street	80	B1
White Hart Street	112	A1
White Hart Yard	106	A2
White Horse Lane	93	B1
	97	A1
White Horse Mews	104	B2
White Horse Road	97	A2/B2
	98	A1
White Horse Street	9	A2/B2
White Horse Yard	16	A2
White Kennett Street	18	A1/A2
White Lion Court	17	A2
White Lion Hill	15	B2
White Lion Street	80	B1
White Post Street	124	A2
White Swan Mews	38	A2
White's Row	18	A2
White's Square	143	B2
Whitechapel High Street	95	A1
Whitechapel Road	95	A1
	96	A1/A2
Whitecross Street	7	A2/B2
Whitefriars Street	15	B1
Whitehall	24	B1
Whitehall Court	24	B1
Whitehall Gardens	24	B1
Whitehall Park	52	B1/B2
Whitehall Place	24	B1
Whitehaven Street	76	B1
Whitehead Close	146	A1
Whitehead's Grove	46	A1
Whites Grounds	107	A1
Whitethorn Street	99	A2
Whitfield Place	3	A1
Whitfield Street	3	A2/B2
Whitgift Street	131	A1
Whitman Road	93	B2
Whitmore Road	82	B2
	84	A2
Whitnell Way	136	B1
Whittaker Street	19	B2
Whittingstall Road	48	A2
Whittlesey Street	104	A2
Whorlton Road	130	B2
Wick Road	90	A1/A2
Wickersley Road	141	A2
Wickford Street	92	B2
Wickham Close	97	A2
Wickham Road	126	B2
Wickham Street	131	B1
Wicklow Street	5	A2
Wickwood Street	121	B1
Widdenham Road	74	A1
Widegate Street	18	A1
Widley Road	27	A1
Wightman Road	55	A1/B1
Wigmore Place	2	B2
Wigmore Street	1	B1/B2
	2	B1/B2
Wigton Place	112	B1
Wilberforce Mews	143	B1
Wilberforce Road	62	B1
	63	B1
Wilbraham Place	19	B1
Wilby Mews	29	B1
Wilcox Road	134	A2
Wilcox Road Market	134	A2
Wild Court	13	B2
Wild Goose Drive	124	A1
Wild Street	13	B2
Wild's Rents	106	B1
	107	A1
Wilde Close	88	A2
Wilde Place	146	A2
Wilderness Mews	142	B1
Wilfred Street	9	B2
	20	B1
Wilkes Street	91	B1
Wilkin Street	71	A2
Wilkin Street Mews	71	A1
Wilkinson Street	135	B1
Wilks Place	84	A2
Willard Street	142	A1
Willes Road	71	A2
Willesden Lane	65	B1
William Close	42	B1
William IV Street	24	A1
William Margrie Close	123	B2
William Mews	19	A1
William Morris Way	50	B1
William Road	77	B1
William Square	111	A2
William Street	10	A1
Williams Buildings	92	B2
Williams Close	53	A1
Williamson Street	73	A2
Willingham Close	72	A1
Willingham Terrace	72	A1
Willington Road	143	B1
	144	B1

Street Index